Hopkinton

New Hampshire

VITAL

RECORDS

— VOLUME II —

Pauline Johnson Oesterlin

HERITAGE BOOKS
2012

HERITAGE BOOKS

AN IMPRINT OF HERITAGE BOOKS, INC.

Books, CDs, and more—Worldwide

For our listing of thousands of titles see our website
at
www.HeritageBooks.com

Published 2012 by
HERITAGE BOOKS, INC.
Publishing Division
100 Railroad Ave. #104
Westminster, Maryland 21157

Other Heritage Books by the author:

Hillsborough County, New Hampshire Court Records, 1772–1799

Hopkinton, New Hampshire Vital Records: Volumes 1 and 2

New Hampshire 1742 Estate List

New Hampshire Marriage Licenses and Intentions, 1709–1961

Rockingham County, New Hampshire Paupers

Surname Guide to Massachusetts Town Histories
Pauline J. Oesterlin and Phyllis O. Longver

International Standard Book Numbers
Paperbound: 978-0-7884-5434-9
Clothbound: 978-0-7884-0974-5

TABLE OF CONTENTS

ACKNOWLEDGEMENTS

I want to thank and acknowledge Thomas Johnson, Jr., the Town Clerk, for allowing me access to the records and also to Sue and Nancy of the Town Office - they were all very cooperative at all times. If it was not for them this book would not have been possible.

A special thanks to Frances Ordway of Contoocook for the many hours that she spent helping me edit the works.

Also I wish to thank the Congregation Church of Hopkinton, NH for their cooperation.

Pauline Johnson Oesterlin

PREFACE

From the time of its settlement in 1737, Hopkinton has undergone many changes. The legal incorporation of the territory known as #5 was passed January 10, 1765. In March of 1765 the first town meeting was held.

Hopkinton Massachusetts derives its name from Edward Hopkins, a prosperous merchant from London, England. The town became New Hopkinton and was originally a part of #5. There was what was called a Bow Controversy which went on for years, and in 1763 the town became part of Hopkinton, New Hampshire.

The original grant was made by Massachusetts Bay Province to citizens of Hopkinton, Massachusetts November 24 1736 and was at that time #5 from the Connecticut River to the Merrimack River, and was to be known as New Hopkinton. In 1738 that was sufficient settlement for a legal meeting of the township. Among the original grantees were the Jones, Kimball, Mellen, Haven, & Morris Families.

Between 1744 and 1763 there were many Indian wars, and a garrison was built at the foot of Putney Hill and on what is now Penacook Road in Contoocook. The Indians took captives from Contoocook (Boscawen) and took them to Canada.

It was in 1766 that the first land was purchased for a town burial. Up until that time there were only private lots.

Hopkinton NH also includes West Hopkinton and Contoocook (which was Boscawen NH and part of #5 in 1732). Contoocook is still a village of Hopkinton.

The section that is called Hopkinton was where the first church was, where the legislatures met, and where the first jail, taverns and hotel were. The Contoocook section was an industrial area, because of the Contoocook River running through it, on which a number of mills were built. It also had a number of taverns and hotels and many notable summer residents. The West Hopkinton section of the town was the site of a mill and still today (1997) there is a paper mill in West Hopkinton. The Congregational Church was one of the first churches in the town (see chapter of vital records) which is home to many other denominations.

Hopkinton, NH was a rapidly growing town early in its development and was very prosperous, receiving a lot of recognition in its home state. The town was in Hillsborough County until 1823, when it became Merrimack County. Most of the county business was carried on in Amherst, but because of the distance to Amherst, the town of Hopkinton also became a place for the Common Pleas and General Court, Superior Court and the General Court sessions. In 1796 a court building was completed, and provision was made for state legislature. It was in June of 1798 that the state legislature held its first meeting in Hopkinton, NH. There were sessions also held in 1801, 1806, and 1807. Four inaugurals were held, being John Taylor Gilman in 1798, and John Langdon in 1806 and 1807. It was not until 1814 that Concord, NH was selected as the permanent state capital. Hopkinton, NH lost out on being the capital by just one vote.

SOURCE INFORMATION

The source records were in a form-type of book, but of course every few years the information on the form would change, and as in Volume 1 the handwriting or the pages had faded, it made it hard to read. You will also find that some of the original volumes contained records for years outside their nominal span, for example, the original book Volume 4, from which our Chapter 1 is taken, nominally spans the years 1858-1879, but actually contains some marriage records from as early as 1851. One or more of the original volumes are divided into two sections, but it is not unusual to find the years out of order.

Source Book	Records Contained in it	Chapter in this book
Volume 4	Marriages 1858-1879	1
	Births 1858-1879	2
	Deaths 1858-1879	3
Volume 5	Marriages 1879-1883	4
	Births 1879-1883	5
	Deaths 1879-1883	6
Volume 6	Deaths 1898-1913	6
	Marriages 1898-1913	7
Volume 7	Marriages 1914-1918	9
	Deaths 1914-1918	10
Volume 8	Marriages 1919-1926	9
	Deaths 1919-1926	10
Volume 9	Marriages 1927-1932	9
	Deaths 1927-1932	10
Volume 10	Marriages 1933-1937	9
	Deaths 1933-1937	10
Annual Town Reports	Births 1902-1937	8

INTRODUCTION

Town of Hopkinton, NH
Vital Records 1858-1937 Volume 2

This book contains records of births, marriages and deaths chiefly in Hopkinton (both before and after its incorporation) in the Province of New Hampshire, and is divided into ten chapters, with three types of records: births, marriages and deaths.

Births

These chapters contain records of births, usually including the child's name, the parents' names, the date and place of the child's birth, the father's occupation and place of birth, and the mother's place of birth, along with a source volume, page and line number. The children of parents living in Hopkinton who were born before their parents moved to Hopkinton and who were not recorded in the places of their birth are recorded in this book. Any children who died before their parents came to Hopkinton will appear, with their births and deaths entered together.

In New Hampshire you are not allowed access to original records unless you are a blood relative, but most of the towns published the births, marriages and deaths each year in the town report. Therefore, the births for the years 1902-1937 have been taken from the town reports and not from the original town records.

Marriages

These chapters contain the accounts of marriages of persons in Hopkinton whether they were married before or after the incorporation of the town. These records often include details of when and by whom the couples were joined in marriage. If only one spouse was from Hopkinton then the records often indicate where the other one was from.

Deaths

These chapters contain the accounts of deaths of people of Hopkinton, usually including when they died, their age at death, and the cause of death if known (or a notation that the cause of death was not known).

Abbreviations used:

b	born
d	died
s/o	son of
d/o	daughter of
**	correction given

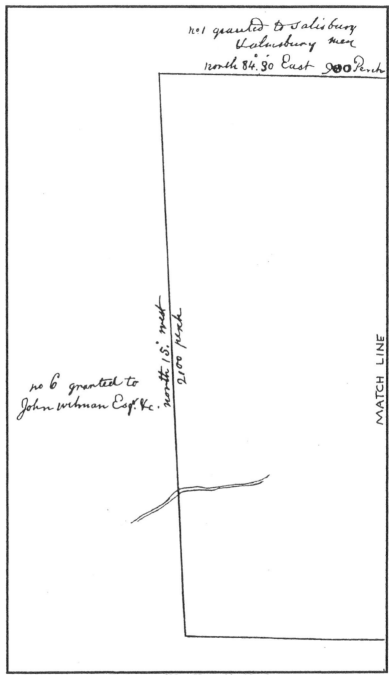

no 1 granted to Salisbury
Salusbury men
north 84.30 East 900 Perch

no 6 granted to
John wilman Esqr &c.

north 15. west
2100 perch

MATCH LINE

Early map of New Hampshire No. 5

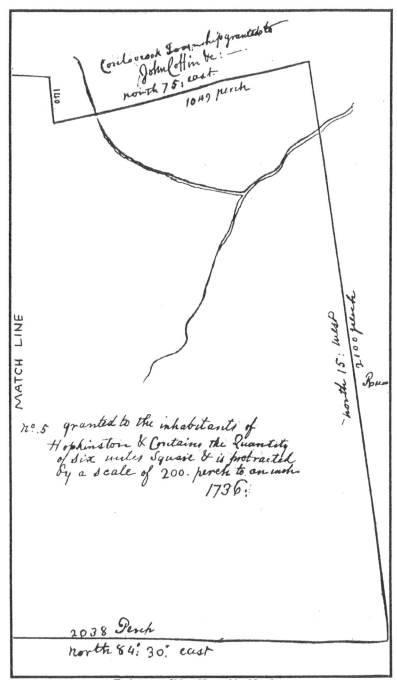

Early map of New Hampshire No. 5

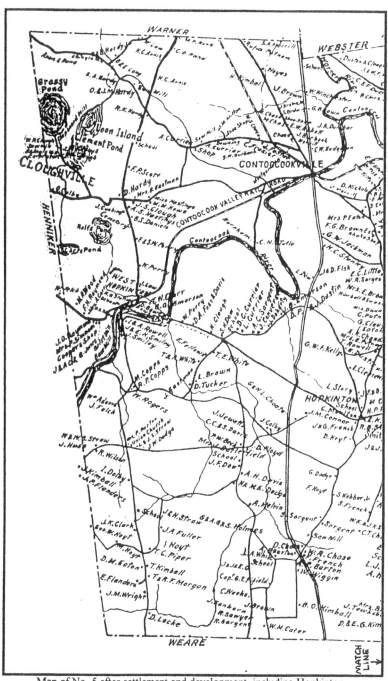

Map of No. 5 after settlement and development, including Hopkinton

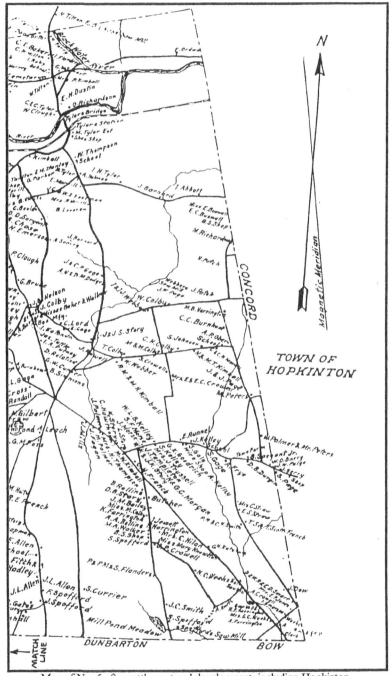

Map of No. 5 after settlement and development, including Hopkinton

Hopkinton, NH Marriages 1858-1879

Note: A few of the marriages in this chapter fall in the years 1851-1857, but the book from which these marriages are taken (Volume 4) is labeled "1858-1879".

HOLLAND John of Swansey & FLANDERS Lydia W of Hopkinton m 1858-06-02 Hopkinton. Groom: age 40, marr 1st time, b Swansey. Bride: age 34, marr 1st time, b Bradford d/o FLANDERS Nathaniel. Vol: 4 Page: 3 Line: 001

BURBANK David of Hopkinton & CHASE Amanda of Warner m 1861-01-01 Hopkinton. Groom: age 32, b Hopkinton s/o BURNBANK Hiriam b Hopkinton & Hannah b Warner. Bride: age 16, b Warner d/o CHASE Jacob b Warner & Elsie b Warner. Vol: 4 Page: 4 Line: 10

DOW Alphonse of Concord & CURRIER Annie A of Concord m 1860-08-19 Hopkinton. Groom: age 24, marr 1st time, b Croyden s/o DOW Zebediah b Derry & Asenath b Derry. Bride: age 17, marr 1st time, b Concord d/o CURRIER Sylvester b Concord & Mary b Hopkinton. Vol: 4 Page: 4 Line: 03

CURRIER John F & PUTNEY Nellie H, m 1861-04-07 Hopkinton. Vol: 4 Page: 5 Line: 01

BARTLETT Charles of Warner & CHASE Melissa of Hopkinton m 1859-07-04 Hopkinton. Vol: 4 Page: 3 Line: 05

CHASE James M of Fisherville & DUNBAR Florence of Hopkinton m 1859-08-28 Hopkinton. Vol: 4 Page: 3 Line: 06

CHASE Moses & HAMBLET Susan, m 1860-04-21 Hopkinton. Vol: 4 Page: 4 Line: 01

ROBY William D of Sutton & HUBBARD Lucy R of Hopkinton m 1861-10-16 Hopkinton. Groom: marr 1st time, b Sutton s/o ROBY Ichabod b NY ?? Hebron & Betsey b NY ?? Hebron. Bride: marr 1st time, b New London d/o HUBBARD Rodney & Sally b Salem. Vol: 4 Page: 3 Line: 08

BURNHAM Edward D of Contoocook & DAVIS Georgia of Contoocook m 1859-10-12 Hopkinton. Groom: age 21, marr 1st time, b Warner s/o BURNHAM John b Hopkinton & Susan b Sutton. Bride: age 24, marr 1st time, b Contoocook d/o EASTMAN Addie b Hopkinton. Vol: 4 Page: 3 Line: 07

STANLEY Horace C of Hopkinton & SAVORY Plumma of Warner m 1859-04-26 Warner. Groom: marr 1st time. Bride: marr 1st time. Vol: 4 Page: 3 Line: 03

SMART Hiriam F of Concord & EVANS Mary J E of Canterbury m 1859-05-22 Hopkinton. Groom: marr 1st time, b Hopkinton s/o SMART Wm N b Hopkinton & Nancy. Bride: marr 1st time, b Lowell Mass d/o EVANS Henry P b Hopkinton & NANCY S b Canterbury. Vol: 4 Page: 3 Line: 04

GOODSPEED Ober of Boston Mass & MORSE Ellen B of Hopkinton m 1859-11-24 Hopkinton. Groom: age 29, marr 1st time, b Sandwich Mass s/o GOODSPEED Joseph b Sandwich Mass & Maria b Sandwich Mass. Bride: age 24, marr 1st time, b Hopkinton d/o MORSE Joshua b Boscawen & LAURA S b New Benton. Vol: 4 Page: 3 Line: 10

ROGERS Alexander of Hopkinton & GOODRICH Sophia of Hopkinton m 1860-01-03 Hopkinton. Groom: age 44, marr 1st time, b Exeter s/o ROGERS Robert b Berwick Me & Margery b Berwick Me. Bride: age 19, marr 1st time, b Boston

Hopkinton, NH Marriages 1858

Mass d/o GOODRICH George b Springfield Vt & FRANCES A b Boston Mass. Vol: 4 Page: 3 Line: 15

FELCH Sylvester of Weare & BROWN Delia E of Weare m 1859-12-31 Hopkinton. Vol: 4 Page: 3 Line: 13

DODGE Moses D of Hopkinton & WEEKS Abbie A of Hopkinton m 1860-01-29 Hopkinton. Groom: age 33, marr 1st time, b Hopkinton s/o DODGE Henry b Hopkinton & Susan b Beverley Mass. Bride: age 21, marr 1st time, b Hopkinton d/o WEEKS Charles b Greenland & Phebe b Bow. Vol: 4 Page: 3 Line: 16

TEWKSBURY Robert of Lawrence Mass & HAWTHORNE Angelia of Hopkinton m 1859-11-23 Hopkinton. Groom: age 26, marr 1st time, b Hopkinton s/o TEWKSBURY Joseph b Hopkinton Mass & Elizabeth b Hopkinton Mass. Bride: age 25, marr 1st time, b Hopkinton d/o Harthorne Calvin b Weare & Rachel b Weare. Vol: 4 Page: 3 Line: 09

HACKETT Warren S & SCRIBNER Nellie S m 1860-03-15 Hopkinton. Vol: 4 Page: 3 Line: 17

STRAW John S of Hopkinton & HOLMES Mary A of Hopkinton m 1860 Sept 16 Hopkinton. Groom: age 22, marr 1st time, b Hopkinton s/o STRAW Levi b Hopkinton & Harriet b Hopkinton. Bride: age 23, marr 1st time, b Hopkinton d/o HOLMES Gardner b Hopkinton & Betsey b Amherst. Vol: 4 Page: 4 Line: 05

SEVERANCE Charles E of Claremont & DOWNING Martha of Hopkinton m 1860-11-21 Hopkinton. Groom: age 24, marr 1st time, b Claremont s/o SEVERANCE Nathan b Claremont. Bride: age 16, marr 1st time, b Boscawen d/o DOWNING Joshua b Boscawen & SARAH J b Hopkinton. Vol: 4 Page: 4 Line: 07

HOYT Thomas of Beverly Mass & PATCH Mary C of Windham Mass m 1858-08-01 Hopkinton. Vol: 4 Page: 2 Line: 02

LOCK John D & HARDY Julia C of Warner m 1859-08-09 Hopkinton. Vol: 4 Page: 2 Line: 03

WHITTIER David & PAGE Juncha[??] Ann of Boscawen m 1859-06-29 Hopkinton. Vol: 4 Page: 2 Line: 04

CUMMINGS A J & PUTNAM Sarah N m 1861-06-29 Hopkinton. Vol: 4 Page: 5 Line: 02

HARDY Samuel A of Hopkinton & PUTNEY Abby A of Hopkinton m 1859-11-11 Hopkinton. Groom: age 29, b Hopkinton s/o HARDY Ozias. Bride: age 16. Vol: 4 Page: 2 Line: 05

ROLLINS Samuel P of Alton & WATSON Susan E of Alton m 1860-09-08 Hopkinton. Groom: marr 1st time, b Alton. Bride: marr 1st time, b Alton. Vol: 4 Page: 4 Line: 04

MERRILL Isaac of Hopkinton & MUNROE Betsey of Henniker m 1855-02-25 Hopkinton. Vol: 4 Page: 8 Line: 01

FULLER Henry H of Hopkinton & GEORGE Jane of Warner m 1860-11-14 Hopkinton. Groom: marr 1st time, b Francestown. Bride: marr 1st time, b Topsham Vt. Vol: 4 Page: 4 Line: 06

DAVIS J B of Fisherville & WARD Adeleline E of Bradford m 1856-01-22 Hopkinton. Vol: 4 Page: 8 Line: 02

Hopkinton, NH Marriages 1858

PUTNAM Rufus of Hopkinton & GOSS Lydia of Henniker m 1860-12-01 Warner. Groom: b Hopkinton s/o PUTNAM Rufus & GOSS Martha. Bride: b Henniker. Vol: 4 Page: 4 Line: 08

GERISH Thomas of Boscawen & COLBY Susan M of Hopkinton m 1856-08-03 Hopkinton. Vol: 4 Page: 8 Line: 03

BUSWELL J F of Bradford & NOYES Sarah E of Hopkinton m 1861-01-18 Hopkinton. Vol: 4 Page: 4 Line: 11

BENNETT A G of Concord & RUNNELLS Marciaett of Boscawen m 1857-01-01 Hopkinton. Vol: 4 Page: 8 Line: 04

BURBANK George M of Hopkinton & SMITH Mary of Loudon m 1861-01-31 Hopkinton. Groom: marr 1st time. Bride: marr 1st time. Vol: 4 Page: 4 Line: 13

MILLS Charles N of Hopkinton & TOWNS Olive N of Weare Center m 1861-02-16 Hopkinton. Groom: age 26, marr 1st time, b Hopkinton s/o MILLS Joseph b Dunbarton & Linda. Bride: age 21, marr 1st time, b Weare d/o TOWNS Luke b Goffstown & CLOUGH Roxy b Dunbarton. Vol: 4 Page: 4 Line: 14

EATON William H of Hopkinton & FULLER Mary J of Hopkinton m 1861-02-24 Hopkinton. Groom: age 21, marr 1st time, b Hopkinton s/o EATON David M b New Brenton & MARY A b Henniker. Bride: age 19, marr 1st time, b Hopkinton d/o FULER John A b Unknown & LUCY J b Warner. Vol: 4 Page: 4 Line: 15

SANBORN Levi W of Gilmanton & ALLEN Martha of Gilmanton m 1861-03-05 Hopkinton. Groom: age 33, marr 2nd time, b Gilmanton s/o SANBORN Isaac b Gilmanton & ROWE Deborah b Gilford. Bride: marr 2nd time, b Gilmanton d/o MORRILL Joseph. Vol: 4 Page: 4 Line: 16

GILE George B of Hopkinton & TILTON Sarah Lizzie of Hopkinton m 1868-05-01 Hopkinton. Groom: age 21, marr 1st time, b Newton s/o GILE L H & SARAH H. Bride: age 18, marr 1st time, b Hopkinton d/o TILTON[??] William W & Sarah. Vol: 4 Page: 14 Line: 03

SEAVEY John of Andover & STEVENS Drusill J of Andover m 1861-03-21 Hopkinton. Groom: age 24, marr 1st time, b Andover s/o SEAVEY Andrew b Andover & ELKINS Lydia b Andover. Bride: age 28, marr 1st time, b Dunbarton d/o STEVENS Benjamin b Dunbarton & ELLIOT A b Dunbarton. Vol: 4 Page: 4 Line: 18

FELCH Henry B of Weare & HOYT Ellen M of Weare m 1861-03-25 Hopkinton. Groom: age 24, marr 1st time, b Sutton s/o FELCH Benjamin b Weare & HOYT Lydia b Hopkinton. Bride: age 19, marr 1st time, b Lowell Mass d/o HOYT Horace b Weare & FELCH Polly b Weare. Vol: 4 Page: 4 Line: 19

FEMINGTON Stephen of Hopkinton & CROSS Hannah B of Hopkinton m 1859-11-29 Hopkinton. Groom: age 76, marr 2nd time, b Sandwich Mass s/o FEMINGTON Samuel b Concord & Muriel?? b Concord. Bride: age 63, marr 2nd time, b Hopkinton d/o BLASDEL David b Peacham Vt & Hannah b Peacham Vt. Vol: 4 Page: 3 Line: 11

HOWE Edward W of Portsmouth & JOHNSON Anna M of Contoocook m 1859-12-25 Hopkinton. Groom: age 29, marr 1st time, b Hopkinton s/o HOWE Winslow b Ringe & Patty b Templeton Mass. Bride: age 28, marr 1st time, b

Hopkinton, NH Marriages 1858

Peachman Vt d/o JOHNSON Joshua b Henniker & CLARA A b Hennkier. Vol: 4 Page: 3 Line: 12

CROWELL Martin T of Hopkinton & TIBBITTS Mary J of Concord m 1860-12-27 Hopkinton. Groom: age 19, b Hopkinton s/o CROWELL Jonathan & Mary. Bride: age 20, b Concord d/o TIBBETTS John & Ann. Vol: 4 Page: 4 Line: 09

KILBORN John Jr of Boscawen & FLANDERS Phinnette of Boscawen m 1860-01-01 Hopkinton. Groom: age 22, marr 1st time, b Boscawen s/o KILBORN John b Boscawen & Mary b Boscawen. Bride: age 22, marr 1st time, b Lowell Mass d/o FLANDERS Phineas b Newbury Mass & Charlotte b Newbury Mass. Vol: 4 Page: 3 Line: 14

CHASE Baruch of Hopkinton & DWINNELLS Lucy S of Hopkinton m 1861-01-23 Hopkinton. Groom: age 53, marr 2nd time, b Hopkinton s/o CHASE Moses b Nothingham & LYDIA R b Warner. Bride: age 51, marr 2nd time, b Weare. Vol: 4 Page: 4 Line: 12

MORGAN Frank W of Hopkinton & BOHONAN Linda of Hopkinton m 1875-04-03 Weare. Groom: age 35, marr 2nd time, b Hopkinton s/o MORGAN Richard F & MARY A. Bride: age 21, marr 2nd time, b Sutton d/o BOHONAN Samuel & Ellen. Vol: 4 Page: 22 Line: 01

PATTERSON Daniel N of Contoocook & BATCHELDER Sarah W of Contoocook m 1875-06-15 Hopkinton. Groom: age 74, marr 2nd time. Bride: age 65, marr 2nd time. Vol: 4 Page: 22 Line: 02

ROWELL John A of Chichester & HOLMES Almira N of Hopkinton m 1875-07-05 Hopkinton. Groom: age 24, marr 1st time, b Chichester s/o ROWELL Asa T & ABIGAIL S. Bride: age 20, marr 1st time, b Hopkinton d/o HOLMES Albert & Johanna. Vol: 4 Page: 22 Line: 03

CURRIER Edgar of Milford Mass & UNDERHILL Ella F of Hopkinton m 1875-09-15 Hopkinton. Groom: age 25, marr 1st time, b Concord s/o CURRIER Herbert & Ester. Bride: age 23, marr 1st time, b Blackstone Mass d/o UNDERHILL Charles W & SUSAN E. Vol: 4 Page: 22 Line: 05

UNDERHILL William Pearl of Hopkinton & CHANDLER Caroline M of Hopkinton m 1875-12-14 Hopkinton. Groom: age 25, marr 1st time, b Blackstone Mass s/o UNDERHILL Charles & Susan. Bride: age 31, marr 1st time, b Hopkinton d/o CHANDLER Isaac M & CAROLINE Eliz. Vol: 4 Page: 22 Line: 06

SEAVEY David of Hopkinton & DOW Nina (Mrs) of Hopkinton m 1861-08-15 Hopkinton. Groom: age 29, marr 1st time, b Concord s/o SEAVEY Andrew b Hopkinton & FISK Betsey b Concord. Bride: age 29, marr 1st time, d/o BRUCE Caleb b Hopkinton & BROWN Neannah b Hopkinton. Vol: 4 Page: 5 Line: 03

PUTNAM Augustus R of Hopkinton & RAND Eliza of Hopkinton m 1861-08-29 Hopkinton. Groom: age 26, marr 1st time, b Hopkinton s/o PUTNAM Herrick b Hopkinton & KEZER R C b Sutton. Bride: age 25, marr 1st time, b Warner d/o RAND Rufus b Hopkinton & CARR A b West Neqbury Mass. Vol: 4 Page: 5 Line: 04

ROBERTS Geo Theodore of Philadelphia Pa & GREEN Sarah C of Hopkinton m 1861-10-03 Hopkinton. Groom: age 23, marr 1st time, b Philadelphia Pa s/o ROBERTS A b Philadelphia Pa & Elizabeth b Philadelphia Pa. Bride: age 23, marr 1st time, b Hopkinton d/o GREEN N N b Concord & Ellen b Norwich Vt. Vol: 4 Page: 5 Line: 05

CLOUGH M Jerry of Hopkinton & BEAN N Orestia of Candia m 1861-10-22 Manchester. Groom: age 23, marr 1st time, b Hopkinton s/o CLOUGH William b Hopkinton & DUSTIN Charlott b Hopkinton. Bride: age 18, marr 1st time, b Hopkinton d/o BEAN Levi b Candia & MERRILL Rachel b Hudson. Vol: 4 Page: 5 Line: 06

TENNEY William of Concord & CARPENTER Estella of Contoocook m 1873-05-01 Hopkinton. Groom: age 22, marr 1st time, b Concord s/o TENNEY Daniel & Judith. Bride: age 19, marr 1st time, d/o CARPENTER Sarah. Vol: 4 Page: 20 Line: 01

CHASE James M of Cambridge Mass & TYLER Sarah A of Hopkinton m 1861-10-31 Hopkinton. Groom: age 31, marr 1st time, b Hopkinton s/o CHASE Moses B b Salisbury & Sarah b Virginia. Bride: age 24, marr 1st time, b Hopkinton d/o TYLER Ernie C b Thereford Vt & TYLER Sarah. Vol: 4 Page: 5 Line: 08

BARRETT Luther H of Brattleborough Vt & BURBANK Martha of Hopkinton m 1861-11-03 Hopkinton. Groom: age 25, marr 1st time, b Vt s/o BARRETT Peardon b Dunneston Vt & Amy b Boston Mass. Bride: age 18, marr 1st time, b Hopkinton d/o BURBANK Thomas b Contoocook & Susan b Contoocook. Vol: 4 Page: 5 Line: 09

HOLMES Daniel G of Hopkinton & CHASE Melinda of Hopkinton m 1861-11-28 Hopkinton. Groom: age 21, marr 1st time, b Hopkinton s/o HOLMES Albert b Hopkinton & MRS Albert Holmes b Hopkinton. Bride: age 21, marr 1st time, b Hopkinton d/o CHASE Enoch J b Hopkinton & Mrs Enoch Chase b Hopkinton. Vol: 4 Page: 5 Line: 11

DWINNELLS Warren Perley of Bow & CHASE Connie Matilda of Hopkinton m 1861-12-15 Hopkinton. Groom: age 22, marr 1st time, b Bow s/o DWINNELLS James b Haverhill Mass & GREENLIE Lena b NH. Bride: age 17, marr 1st time, b Hopkinton d/o CHASE Raborn???? b Hopkinton & RYAN Betsey b Concord. Vol: 4 Page: 5 Line: 12

PRESCOTT John A of Concord & GOODRICH Georgia W of Hopkinton m 1862-01-19 Hopkinton. Groom: age 22, marr 1st time, b Pittsfield s/o PRESCOTT J C b Northfield Vt & HODGDON Mary H b Pittsfield Vt. Bride: age 22, marr 1st time, b Boston Mass d/o GOODRICH George R b Springfield & WHITEMAN Frances b Boston Mass. Vol: 4 Page: 5 Line: 13

BROWN Charles L of Hopkinton & SARGENT Emma C of Hopkinton m 1862-02-20 Hopkinton. Groom: age 19, marr 1st time, b Hopkinton s/o BROWN Franklin G b Hopkinton & DIAMOND Julia b Concord. Bride: marr 1st time, b Hopkinton d/o SARGENT Daniel b Newport & CHASE Mary W b Hopkinton. Vol: 4 Page: 5 Line: 14

BERNARD Hollis G of Plainfield & HOWARD Cora of Hopkinton m 1869-12-06 Hopkinton. Groom: age 24, marr 1st time, s/o BERNARD Samuel & Hulda K. Bride: age 24, marr 1st time, d/o KEZIA Moses & Sarah. Vol: 4 Page: 15 Line: 13

CARPENTER Cyrus F of Henniker & LAW Phebe of Hopkinton m 1862-03-27 Hopkinton. Groom: marr 3rd time, b Deering s/o CARPENTER Jonathan b Deering & HOWE R b Vt. Bride: marr 3rd time, b Hopkinton d/o PERRY

Hopkinton, NH Marriages 1858

Joseph b Chelmsford Mass & DUSTIN Sarah b Newburyport Mass. Vol: 4 Page: 5 Line: 16

RICHARDSON Thomas B of Hopkinton & HARDY Eliza A of Hopkinton m 1861-08-10 Hopkinton. Groom: marr 1st time, b Deering s/o RICHARDSON Thomas & STODDARD Nancy R. Bride: marr 1st time, b Norwood Mich d/o HARDY W H b Warner & MORGAN P b Manchester Mass. Vol: 4 Page: 5 Line: 17

LAKE James F F of Loudon & SAWYER Sarah A of Loudon m 1861-08-31 Hopkinton. Groom: marr 1st time, b Chichester s/o LAKE David b Chichester & SANBORN Julia b Gilmanton. Bride: marr 1st time, b Loudon d/o SAWYER John b Gilmanton & DURRELL Mary A b Gilmanton. Vol: 4 Page: 5 Line: 18

BUXTON Edwin W of Bradford & HARVEY Ellen N of Warner m 1857-04-03 Hopkinton. Vol: 4 Page: 8 Line: 05

WILLIAMS Robert of NH & HARDY Lavina of Hopkinton m 1857-04-24 Hopkinton. Vol: 4 Page: 8 Line: 06

STORY Warren A of Boscawen & SMITH Sarah P of Pitsfield m 1857-08-15 Hopkinton. Vol: 4 Page: 8 Line: 07

DAVIS Charles of Warner & FOSS Sarah B of Warner m 1857-09-24 Warner. Vol: 4 Page: 8 Line: 08

TAYLOR Charles E of Warner & UPTON Clara of Hopkinton m 1858-02-14 Hopkinton. Vol: 4 Page: 8 Line: 09

HOWARD Daniel of Northfield & PATTERSON Susan M of Hopkinton m 1858-08-19 Hopkinton. Vol: 4 Page: 8 Line: 11

COLBY George W of Henniker & GOODNOW Fidelia of West Deering m 1859-05-31 Hopkinton. Vol: 4 Page: 8 Line: 12

SWETT Stephen of Hopkinton & DANFORTH Mary A of Hopkinton m 1851-11-27 Hopkinton. Vol: 4 Page: 7 Line: 01

REYSEN James of Hopkinton & ORDWAY Nancy of Hopkinton m 1851-12-23 Hopkinton. Vol: 4 Page: 7 Line: 02

BURNHAM Abraham of Hopkinton & CROSS Elisabeth of Hopkinton m 1852-04-06 Hopkinton. Vol: 4 Page: 7 Line: 03

CHANDLER Alfred N of Hopkinton & HAMMOND Hellen M of Hopkinton m 1852-03-11 Hopkinton. Vol: 4 Page: 7 Line: 04

SCRIBNER Moses B of Wilton & PERRY Sylvia C of Henniker m 1852-03-30 Hopkinton. Vol: 4 Page: 7 Line: 05

LESLIE Wm of Hopkinton & McALPINE Betsey of Warner m 1862-03-10 Hopkinton. Vol: 4 Page: 7 Line: 06

EVERETT David of New London & FULLER Sarah A of Hopkinton m 1853-04-07 Hopkinton. Vol: 4 Page: 7 Line: 07

HOYT Seth B of Concord & WHITAKER Lydia of Hopkinton m 1853-05-24 Hopkinton. Vol: 4 Page: 7 Line: 08

McALPINE George of Warner & HARDY Betsey L of Warner m 1853-08-25 Hopkinton. Vol: 4 Page: 7 Line: 09

MOULTON William H of Concord & STRAW Susan of Hopkinton m 1853-10-16 Hopkinton. Vol: 4 Page: 7 Line: 10

KIMBALL Charles C of Hopkinton & CARPENTER Martha of Hopkinton m 1854-03-16 Hopkinton. Vol: 4 Page: 7 Line: 11

Hopkinton, NH Marriages 1858

GUILFORD S Taylor of Salisbury & DANIELS Frances of Hopkinton m 1854-05-09 Hopkinton. Vol: 4 Page: 7 Line: 12

CARPENTER Guy of Cambridge Mass & KIMBALL Mary A of Hopkinton m 1854-05-14 Hopkinton. Vol: 4 Page: 7 Line: 13

FRENCH Charles E of Sutton & PUTNAM Julia A of Hopkinton m 1854-06-27 Hopkinton. Vol: 4 Page: 7 Line: 14

REED Ezekiel of Danbury & GILMAN Betsey B of Danbury m 1854-10-30 Hopkinton. Vol: 4 Page: 7 Line: 15

FLANDERS Benjamin of Hopkinton & DOW Melissa I of Henniker m 1854-11-29 Hopkinton. Vol: 4 Page: 7 Line: 16

HARDY Edwin R of Warner & McALPINE Rosinna of Warner m 1854-12-31 Warner. Vol: 4 Page: 7 Line: 17

BREAD James of Warner & McALPINE Eliza of Warner m 1855-10-07 Hopkinton. Vol: 4 Page: 7 Line: 18

SCRIBNER Frank B of Salisbury & STANLEY Hennel C of Hopkinton m 1862-04-30 Hopkinton. Groom: age 27, marr 1st time, b Andover s/o SCRIBNER B F b Andover & BROWN Abigial b Andover. Bride: age 26, marr 1st time, b Hopkinton d/o STANLEY Horace b Hopkinton & KIMBALL ?? b Hopkinton. Vol: 4 Page: 6 Line: 01

AGER Walter C of Hopkinton & CLOUGH C Maria of Hopkinton m 1862-05-22 Hopkinton. Groom: age 23, marr 1st time, b Warner s/o AGER Uniah b N Y & SMITH Margaret b Boston Mass. Bride: age 20, marr 1st time, b Hopkinton d/o CLOUGH William b Hopkinton & DUSTIN Charlotte b Hopkinton. Vol: 4 Page: 6 Line: 02

KEMPTON William H of Hopkinton & BURBANK Jennie of Hopkinton m 1862-08-09 Hopkinton. Groom: age 20, marr 1st time, b Croydon s/o KEMPTON Edward b Newport & Mary b Newport. Bride: age 15, marr 1st time, b Hopkinton d/o BURBANK Thomas b Hopkinton & Susan b Hopkinton. Vol: 4 Page: 6 Line: 03

PATTERSON William A of Hopkinton & ALLEN Clare Amanda of Hopkinton m 1862-08-10 Hopkinton. Groom: age 25, marr 1st time, b Hopkinton s/o PATTERSON David b Henniker & WOODS Maria b Henniker. Bride: age 23, marr 1st time, b Deering d/o ALLEN William b Cornish & STONE Alvira b Grantham. Vol: 4 Page: 6 Line: 04

DANFORTH Charles Henry of Hopkinton & KEMPTON Harriette of Hopkinton m 1862-08-11 Hopkinton. Groom: age 25, marr 1st time, b Weare s/o DANFORTH Gilman b Warner & NOYES Ruth b Hopkinton. Bride: age 18, marr 1st time, b Croydon d/o KEMPTON Edward b Newport & HARRIS Mamie b Newport. Vol: 4 Page: 6 Line: 05

RIPLES James of Henniker & ROLLINS Anna R of Henniker m 1862-08-21 Hopkinton. Groom: age 20, marr 1st time, b Litchfield s/o RIPLES Ningict?? b Londonderry & GREELEY Lydia b Londonderry. Bride: age 21, marr 1st time, b Henniker d/o ROLLINS Samuel b Hopkinton & PALMER Roxanna A b Henniker. Vol: 4 Page: 6 Line: 06

WEBSTER Noah P of Concord & ROWELL Lorinda A of Hopkinton m 1862-10-07 Hopkinton. Groom: age 20, marr 1st time, b Salisbury s/o WEBSTER Joseph b Unity & PEASLES Susan b Sutton. Bride: age 20, marr 1st time, b Henniker d/o ROWELL John b Sutton & TUTTLE Lydia b Weare. Vol: 4 Page: 6 Line: 07

SAWYER John 2nd of Concord & STONE Charlotte A of Webster m 1862-10-08 Hopkinton. Groom: age 41, marr 2nd time, b Hopkinton s/o SAWYER Amos & Martha b Webster. Bride: age 23, marr 2nd time, b Webster d/o STONE Peter & Ruth. Vol: 4 Page: 6 Line: 08

CHANDLER Augustus of Concord & SCALES Herietta O of Concord m 1862-10-31 Hopkinton. Groom: age 30, marr 1st time, b Hopkinton s/o CHANDLER Stephen & Mary. Bride: age 17, marr 1st time, b Hopkinton d/o SCALES John & Mary. Vol: 4 Page: 6 Line: 09

BENTON Reuben C of Norwich Vt & SMILEY Emily of Hopkinton m 1862-11-12 Hopkinton. Vol: 4 Page: 6 Line: 10

CARROLL Clarence of Hopkinton & EMERSON Harrett of Hopkinton m 1862-12-02 Hopkinton. Groom: age 28, marr 1st time, b Chelsa Vt s/o CARROLL John & Rosetta b Ireland. Bride: age 17, marr 1st time, b Hopkinton d/o EMERSON Isaac & Lucretia b Hopkinton. Vol: 4 Page: 6 Line: 11

WATSON John P of Boscawen & WATSON Sarah A of Boscawen m 1863-03-14 Hopkinton. Groom: age 25, b Warner s/o WATSON David b Warner & PETTEY Mary b Salisbury. Bride: age 19, b Warner d/o WATSON Nicholas b Webster & WATKINS Elisa b Mass. Vol: 4 Page: 6 Line: 12

PHILBRICK Nathaniel of Newport & SARGENT Mary of West Hopkinton m 1868-04-04 Hopkinton. Groom: age 41, marr 3rd time, b Newport s/o PHILBRICK John & Dorothy. Bride: age 55, marr 3rd time. Vol: 4 Page: 14 Line: 01

BARNES Leander of Concord & QUIMBY Mary Ann of Hopkinton m 1862-08-21 Hopkinton. Groom: age 22, b Concord s/o BARNES Jefferson b Concord & Harriette b Concord. Bride: age 16, b Concord d/o QUIMBY Enoch b Concord & Elisabeth b Concord. Vol: 4 Page: 9 Line: 02

CLOUGH Charles A of Manchester & RICHARDS Lizzie of Manchester m 1863-07-05 Hopkinton. Groom: age 25, b Bow s/o CLOUGH Enoch b Bow & Jenney b Plaistow. Bride: age 22, b Me d/o BABCOCK Giddeon & NUDDING Mary b Perry Me. Vol: 4 Page: 9 Line: 03

PINKHAM Fred A of Concord & HARVEY Fannie A of Concord m 1863-07-08 Hopkinton. Groom: age 19, marr 1st time, b Lowell Mass s/o PINKHAM Hazen b Alton & ---- ---- b Warner. Bride: age 19, marr 1st time, d/o HARVEY John. Vol: 4 Page: 9 Line: 05

KELLY Aaron of Warner & DODGE Lydia A of Hopkinton m 1863-11-18 Hopkinton. Groom: age 60, b Mt Vernon s/o KELLY Thomas b Mt Vernon & HUBBARD Mary b Eastberry. Bride: age 31, b Hopkinton d/o DODGE Grover b New Boston & FRENCH Lydia b Hopkinton. Vol: 4 Page: 9 Line: 06

MUDGETT William of Hopkinton & STRAW M Anna of Hopkinton m 1863-08-11 Hopkinton. Groom: age 23, marr 1st time, b New Boston s/o MUDGETT Moses b Weare & BOYNTON Arminda b New Boston. Bride: age 20, marr 1st time, b Hopkinton d/o STRAW Asahel b Waterbrury Vt & JEWELL Abbie b Hopkinton. Vol: 4 Page: 9 Line: 05

FAIRBANKS George L of Washington & CHASE Caroline of Washington m 1863-11-24 Hopkinton. Groom: age 23, b Springfield Vt s/o FAIRBANKS Aaron b

Hopkinton, NH Marriages 1858

Springfield Vt & CONANT Nancy b Windsor Vt. Bride: age 23, b Washington d/o CHASE Martin b Unity & WRIGHT Betsey b Washington. Vol: 4 Page: 9 Line: 07

SANBORN Charles H of Concord & STORY Sarah A of Hopkinton m 1865-09-27 Hopkinton. Groom: age 26, marr 1st time, b Concord s/o WEBSTER Herman b Webster & CLARISA B b Loudon. Bride: age 19, marr 1st time, b Hopkinton d/o STORY James H b Hopkinton & Sarah b Hopkinton. Vol: 4 Page: 11 Line: 03

CHOATE Horace C of Hopkinton & HEATH Mary M of Northfield Vt m 1863-12-10 Hopkinton. Groom: age 30, b Henniker s/o CHOATE George b Hopkinton & DAVIS Betsy b Hopkinton. Bride: age 27, b Pittsburg d/o HEATH Christopher b Springfield & CARR Sarah b Lisbon. Vol: 4 Page: 9 Line: 10

GLOVER David B of Warner & ORDWAY Sarah E of Warner m 1863-12-24 Hopkinton. Groom: age 36, b Warner s/o GLOVER James b Hudson & SEAVEY Elisabeth b Warner. Bride: age 15, b Warner d/o ORDWAY Ralph C b Hopkinton & TEWSBURY Hannah b Goshen. Vol: 4 Page: 9 Line: 11

FRAZIER Caleb of Hopkinton & DAVIS Sarah W of Sutton m 1864-01-09 Hopkinton. Groom: age 41, marr 2nd time, b Hopkinton s/o FRAZIER Samuel b Me & BURBANK Phebe b Hopkinton. Bride: age 32, marr 2nd time, b Sutton d/o COLBURN A & Sarah. Vol: 4 Page: 9 Line: 12

MUDGETT John F of Weare & UPTON Mary of Contoocook m 1864-01-10 Hopkinton. Groom: age 21, b Weare s/o MUDGETT Moses & BOYNTON Aurinda b Reading Mass. Bride: age 20, b Contoocook d/o UPTON Joseph b Weare & Clarrisa b Contoocook. Vol: 4 Page: 9 Line: 13

SMART William H of Webster & TUCK Annie M of Hopkinton m 1864-03-09 Hopkinton. Groom: age 36, b Concord s/o SMART Benjamin b New Chester & TANDY Nancy b Deerfield. Bride: age 20, b London England d/o ---- ---- b England & ---- ---- b England. Vol: 4 Page: 9 Line: 14

HOPKINS Harry B of Antrim & PRESBY Charlotte A of Bradford m 1864-03-24 Hopkinton. Groom: age 27, b Antrim s/o HOPKINS Robert P b Antrim & RUGG Caroline b Rindge. Bride: age 21, b Bradford d/o PRESBY Hazen b Bradford & Eunice b Lemster. Vol: 4 Page: 9 Line: 15

KIMBALL Charles H 2nd of Hopkinton & CLARK Ellen F of Hopkinton m 1863-11-29 Hopkinton. Groom: age 27, b Hopkinton s/o KIMBALL Asa b Hopkinton & LITTLE Hannah C b Boscawen. Bride: age 23, b Hopkinton d/o CLARK Jacob b Hopkinton & STRAW Mary b Weare. Vol: 4 Page: 9 Line: 09

GILMAN George of Warner & FLANDERS Almira of Warner m 1862-08-10 Hopkinton. Groom: age 30, marr 1st time, b Hopkinton s/o GILMAN Joseph S b Warner & STRAW Mary b Warner. Bride: age 24, marr 1st time, b Warner d/o FLANDERS Willam G b Warner & WARNER M b Warner. Vol: 4 Page: 9 Line: 01

CHANDLER Samuel of Concord & SWETT Caroline of Hopkinton m 1864-04-03 Hopkinton. Groom: age 41, marr 2nd time, b Concord s/o CHANDLER Daniel b Concord. Bride: age 49, marr 2nd time, b Bradford d/o Jewett. Vol: 4 Page: 10 Line: 01

CUSHMAN Ezekiel of Boston Mass & MORRISON Mary M of Boston Mass m 1864-04-17 Hopkinton. Groom: age 43, marr 2nd time, b Rochester s/o

CUSHMAN Bartlett b Rochester Ny & Sarah b Freetown Mass. Bride: age 33, marr 2nd time, b Hopkinton d/o MORRISON Ebenezer b Dunbbarton & HANSON Melinda b Hopkinton. Vol: 4 Page: 10 Line: 02

JACKMAN Benjamin of Webster & FLANDERS Eliz Jane of Webster m 1864-04-19 Hopkinton. Groom: age 50, marr 2nd time, b Boston Mass s/o JACKMAN Nehimiah b Boscawen & WALKER Sally b Goffstown. Bride: age 28, marr 2nd time, b Northwood d/o KNIGHT Stephen b Northwood & SHAW Lucy b Northwood. Vol: 4 Page: 10 Line: 03

CORSER John of Boscawen & CARLTON Hannah of Hopkinton m 1864-06-08 Hopkinton. Groom: age 54, marr 2nd time, b Boscawen s/o CORSER John b Boscawen & CLARK M b Newburyport Mass. Bride: age 45, marr 2nd time, b Warner d/o FLANDERS Philip b Warner & EASTMAN Emma b Hopkinton. Vol: 4 Page: 10 Line: 04

GIBSON Lewis of Henniker & FERRON Elizabeth B of Hopkinton m 1864-09-25 Hopkinton. Groom: age 20, marr 1st time, b Henniker s/o GIBSON Otis b Henniker & HARRIET D b Boscawen. Bride: age 29, marr 1st time, b Hopkinton d/o CHASE Barach b Hopkinton & MORRISON Lydia b Stoddard. Vol: 4 Page: 10 Line: 05

PATTERSON Samuel F of Hopkinton & HERSEY Susan E of Hopkinton m 1864-09-29 Hopkinton. Groom: age 25, marr 1st time, b Hopkinton s/o PATTERSON Joab b Henniker & LARSEN Mary b Deering. Bride: age 27, marr 1st time, b Grantham d/o HERSEY Jeremiah b Grantham & HERBERT Cynthia. Vol: 4 Page: 10 Line: 06

STEVENS Frank of Fisherville & MILLS Mary of Hopkinton m 1864-10-08 Hopkinton. Groom: age 33, marr 1st time, b Salisbury s/o STEVENS Daniel & Dorothy. Bride: age 18, marr 1st time, b Hopkinton d/o MILLS Joseph & MILLS Lydia. Vol: 4 Page: 10 Line: 07

WHITTIER Horatio of Hopkinton & KEMPTON Arvilla of Hopkinton m 1864-10-16 Hopkinton. Groom: age 19, marr 1st time, b Londonderry s/o DAVIS Lucy b Hopkinton. Bride: age 17, marr 1st time, b Croydon d/o KEMPTON Edward B b Newport & HARRIS Mary b Newport. Vol: 4 Page: 10 Line: 08

BAKER John E of Concord & CLOUGH Eliza J of Hopkinton m 1864-11-23 Hopkinton. Groom: age 24, marr 1st time, b Concord s/o BAKER Samuel b Marshfield Mass & ELIZABETH Ann. Bride: age 22, marr 1st time, b Hopkinton d/o CLOUGH Hazen & Mary. Vol: 4 Page: 10 Line: 09

HEATH John of Hopkinton & SARGENT Frances of London m 1864-11-26 Hopkinton. Groom: age 26, marr 1st time, b Boscawen s/o HEATH Alfred b Boscawen & BROWN Mary G b Boscawen. Bride: age 18, marr 1st time, b London. Vol: 4 Page: 10 Line: 10

DOW Cyrus B of Warner & COUCH Ellen M of Warner m 1864-11-29 Hopkinton. Groom: age 30, marr 1st time, b Warner s/o DOW Isaac b Warner & WATSON Polly b Salisbury. Bride: age 21, marr 1st time, b Warner d/o COUCH Albert J b Warner & SARGENT Ruth M b Warner. Vol: 4 Page: 10 Line: 11

MORGAN Frank W of Hopkinton & JONES Fannie A of Hopkinton m 1865-01-17 Hopkinton. Groom: age 24, marr 1st time, b Hopkinton s/o MORGAN Richard F b Hopkinton & ALLEN Mary Ann b East Providence RI. Bride: age 20, marr

1st time, b Concord d/o JONES Thaoms B b Pittsfield & JONES Amelia b Cornish. Vol: 4 Page: 10 Line: 12

WIGGIN G Henry of Wagner Claton Iowa & KELLEY Addie M of Hopkinton m 1865-02-03 Hopkinton. Groom: age 24, marr 1st time, s/o WIGGIN George W b Warner & HARRIMAN L N ? b Warner. Bride: age 23, marr 1st time, d/o KELLEY Amos b Hampstead & EVANS Sarah E b East Waymouth. Vol: 4 Page: 10 Line: 13

DUNBAR Willard of West Concord & ROBINSON N F of Warner m 1865-02-08 Hopkinton. Groom: age 51, marr 2nd time, b Grantham s/o DUNBAR Azel & HANNAH T b Royalston Mass. Bride: age 35, marr 2nd time, b Henniker. Vol: 4 Page: 10 Line: 14

SWEATT John D of Manchester & JONES Sarah E of Bradford m 1865-03-18 Hopkinton. Groom: age 21, b Eaton Canada s/o SWEATT Moses b Salisbury & MITCHELL Caroline b Campton. Bride: age 22, b Henniker d/o JONES Jacob b Hampton & EVENS Betsey b Salisbury. Vol: 4 Page: 10 Line:.15

WISE Charles W of Farley Vt & CROWELL Mary R of Hopkinton m 1863-11-26 Hopkinton. Groom: age 33, b Groton Mass s/o WISE Jonathan b Herborn & BLANCHARD Anna b Plymouth. Bride: age 23, b Concord d/o CROWELL Nathaniel b Hopkinton & DAY Esther S b Weare. Vol: 4 Page: 9 Line: 08

CLEMENT Charles of Maine & KIMBALL Abbie H of Hopkinton m 1865-07-25 Hopkinton. Groom: age 49, marr 2nd time, b Newport Maine s/o CLEMENT Joseph b Newburyport Mass & FITZ Mary b Haverhill Mass. Bride: age 29, marr 2nd time, b Hopkinton d/o KIMBALL Daniel b Hopkinton & HERRICK Asenath b Hopkinton. Vol: 4 Page: 11 Line: 01

CHILD Jonathan B of Casinovia & ROBINSON Sarah J of Hopkinton m 1865-09-05 Hopkinton. Groom: age 30, marr 1st time, b Fitchburg Mass s/o CHILD David b Templeton Mass & BURRAGE Adeline b Templeton Mass. Bride: age 28, marr 1st time, b Bow d/o BURNHAM Samuel b Bow & SARGENT Sally P b Bow. Vol: 4 Page: 11 Line: 02

GATLEY William A of Concord & GOODRICH Mary G of Hopkinton m 1865-10-17 Hopkinton. Groom: age 21, marr 1st time, b England s/o GATLEY Wm H b England & Anna b England. Bride: age 20, marr 1st time, b NH d/o GOODRICH Geo R b Vermont & FRANCES A b Mass. Vol: 4 Page: 11 Line: 04

SANBORN Thomas L of Alexandria & WILSON Julia E of Hopkinton m 1865-11-23 Hopkinton. Groom: age 29, marr 1st time, b Henniker s/o SANBORN Nathan b Sanbornton & LANCASTER Lena b Sanbornton. Bride: age 24, marr 1st time, b Hopkinton d/o WILSON Robert b Londonderry & HUSE Lencinda b Hopkinton. Vol: 4 Page: 11 Line: 05

WOODBURN Charles of Concord & RUSSELL Rush ? of Concord m 1866-02-22 Hopkinton. Groom: age 28, marr 1st time, b Loudonderry s/o WOOBURN John b Londonderry & Mahittable b Londonderry. Bride: age 22, marr 1st time, b Meredith d/o RUSSELL John & BICKFORD Abigail b Meriden. Vol: 4 Page: 11 Line: 07

KEMPTON Bryon of Hopkinton & HARDY Emma J of Hopkinton m 1866-02-22 Hopkinton. Groom: age 20, marr 1st time, b Cryndon s/o KEMPTON Edward

Hopkinton, NH Marriages 1858

& Mary. Bride: age 18, marr 1st time, b Hopkinton d/o HARDY Wm Morrison. Vol: 4 Page: 11 Line: 08

COLBY John G of Hopkinton & RAND Emma W of Hopkinton m 1866-03-03 Concord. Groom: age 23, marr 1st time, b Hopkinton s/o COLBY James b Hopkinton & EMERSON Hannah b Wilmot. Bride: age 22, marr 1st time, b Hopkinton d/o RAND Charles D & DAVIS Harrott b Warner. Vol: 4 Page: 11 Line: 09

EASTMAN George W of Hopkinton & FLANIGAN Eliza of Hopkinton m 1866-03-18 Hopkinton. Groom: age 29, marr 1st time, b Hopkinton s/o EASTMAN Jonathan b Henniker & ROWELL Elizabeth b Hopkinton. Bride: age 20, marr 1st time, b Ireland d/o FLANIGAN Michael b Ireland & Catherine b Ireland. Vol: 4 Page: 11 Line: 10

WALDRON Robert S of Wilminton & LOUNSBURY Lydia M of New York m 1866-03-18 Hopkinton. Groom: age 30, marr 2nd time, b Rye s/o WALDRON Robert S b Rye & Hannah b Rye. Bride: age 34, marr 2nd time, b Canada d/o KELLEY John G b Vermont & Jane b New York. Vol: 4 Page: 11 Line: 11

PEASLEE Edwin N of Weare & DELANEY Ann of Weare m 1866-04-14 Hopkinton. Groom: age 32, marr 1st time, b Weare s/o PEASLEE Jonathan b Weare & Susan b Bradford. Bride: age 26, marr 1st time, b Ireland d/o DELANEY Timothy R b Ireland & Mary b Ireland. Vol: 4 Page: 11 Line: 12

COLLINS David of Hopkinton & SMITH Susan E of Warner m 1866-10-03 Hopkinton. Groom: age 61, marr 3rd time, b So Hampton s/o COLLINS Timothy b So Hampton & OSGOOD Jane b Seabrook. Bride: age 52, marr 3rd time, b Ipswich Mass d/o SMITH Bernsley b Ipswich Mass & KINSMAN Mary b Ipswich Mass. Vol: 4 Page: 12 Line: 01

COREY Augustus B of Boscawen & SANBORN Hannah of Webster m 1866-11-15 Hopkinton. Groom: age 22, marr 1st time, b Lowell Mass s/o COREY Ephraim b Crafsbury & Mary b Boscawen. Bride: age 22, marr 1st time, b Webster d/o SANBORN John b Boscawen & REBEKAH C b Boscawen. Vol: 4 Page: 12 Line: 02

CRAWFORD William of Chester & CRAWFORD Elisa R of Brooklyn Ny m 1866-09-25 Hopkinton. Groom: age 43, marr 1st time, b Chester s/o CRAWFORD Robert b Chester & Dorothy b Chester. Bride: age 31, marr 1st time, b Portsmouth d/o CRAWFORD Luther & Almirs. Vol: 4 Page: 12 Line: 03

HOWLETT John F of Hopkinton & ROWELL H Etta of Hopkinton m 1866-10-24 Hopkinton. Groom: age 31, marr 1st time, b Bradford s/o HOWLETT John F b Bradford & Susan b Langdon. Bride: age 20, marr 1st time, b Hopkinton d/o ROWELL Isaac b Hopkinton & Harriett b Hennkier. Vol: 4 Page: 12 Line: 04

NOYES Lucius P of Contoocook & DEAN Laura of Contoocook m 1867-04-16 Hopkinton. Groom: age 28, marr 1st time, b Clarkson Ny s/o NOYES Nathaniel b Newburyport Mass & SARAH A b Hopkinton. Bride: age 24, marr 1st time, b Salem Mass d/o DEAN Thomas b Salem Mass & Elizabeth b Hopkinton. Vol: 4 Page: 12 Line: 05

TENNEY Eldad of Fisherville & FOSS Emily P of Hopkinton m 1866-05-01 Hopkinton. Groom: age 66, marr 2nd time, b Hopkinton s/o TENNEY Moses b Bradford Mass. Bride: age 58, marr 2nd time, b Concord d/o WODLEY Nathaniel b Sudbury Mass & Abigail b Exeter. Vol: 4 Page: 12 Line: 06

Hopkinton, NH Marriages 1858

HASTINGS Alfred L of Hopkinton & PERRY Susan E of Hopkinton m 1866-11-13 Hopkinton. Groom: age 37, marr 1st time, s/o HASTINGS Abel b Hopkinton & Allmira b Hopkinton. Bride: age 25, marr 1st time, d/o PERRY William b Henniker & Aseneth b Hennkier. Vol: 4 Page: 12 Line: 07

HEATH Thomas B of Hopkinton & HEATH Emma Jane of Salisbury m 1867-04-28 Hopkinton. Groom: age 22, marr 1st time, b Lowell Mass s/o HEATH Alfred b Webster & Mary b Boscawen. Bride: age 17, marr 1st time, b Webster d/o HEATH J Sullivan b Webster & Mary b Andover. Vol: 4 Page: 13 Line: 01

MARTIN Charles H of Concord & CLARK Lida of Hopkinton m 1867-05-16 Hopkinton. Groom: age 25, marr 1st time, b Grafton s/o MARTIN Asa b Grafton & Amy b Grafton. Bride: age 22, marr 1st time, b Allen Ny d/o CLARK John W b Allen Ny & Mary E b Rochester Ny. Vol: 4 Page: 13 Line: 02

STEVENS Henry C of Contoocookville & MORRILL Mary A of Contoocookville m 1867-07-03 Hopkinton. Groom: age 25, marr 2nd time, b Warner s/o STEVENS Enoch b Warner & Nancy b Charlestown. Bride: age 20, marr 2nd time, b Methuen Mass d/o MORRILL Jonathan b Salisbury Mass & EUNICE P b Salisbury NH. Vol: 4 Page: 13 Line: 03

MILLS John C of Hopkinton & RICHARDS Lizzie of Hopkinton m 1867-09-09 Hopkinton. Groom: age 18, marr 1st time, b Hopkinton s/o MILLS Joseph b Dunbarton & Sylinda b Dunbarton. Bride: age 21, marr 1st time, b Boston Mass d/o RICHARDS Daniel b Boston Mass. Vol: 4 Page: 13 Line: 04

HOWARD Joseph W of Fitchburg Mass & HOWARD Cora E of Contoocookville m 1867-11-03 Hopkinton. Groom: age 23, marr 1st time, b Fitchburg Mass s/o HOWARD Chester b Northfield & Elizabeth b Northfield. Bride: age 21, marr 1st time, b Contoocookville d/o KEEZER Moses. Vol: 4 Page: 13 Line: 05

BARNES Leander of Concord & LEONARD Annie of Boston Mass m 1866-11-03 Hopkinton. Groom: age 26, marr 2nd time, b Concord s/o BARNES Jefferson b Vermont & Harriet E b Concord. Bride: age 22, marr 2nd time, b Boston Mass d/o John b Boston Mass & Mary b Mass. Vol: 4 Page: 13 Line: 06

CHASE Frank of Hopkinton & RUNNELLS Anne A of Concord m 1867-11-13 Hopkinton. Groom: age 22, marr 1st time, b Hopkinton s/o CHASE Ambrose b Hopkinton & Joan b Hopkinton. Bride: age 23, marr 1st time, b Concord d/o RUNNELLS Samuel b Concord & Anne b Concord. Vol: 4 Page: 13 Line: 07

SINCLAIR Noah of Meredith & LAWRENCE Etta of Moultonborough m 1867-11-16 Hopkinton. Groom: age 25, marr 1st time, b Concord s/o SINCLAIR Noah b Meredith & COTTEN Hannah b Meredith. Bride: age 22, marr 1st time, b Meredith d/o LAWRENCE James b Farnsworth & HILL Hannah L b Holland Vt. Vol: 4 Page: 13 Line: 08

BARNES George of Concord & JENNESS Georgianna of Concord m 1867-11-23 Hopkinton. Groom: age 25, marr 1st time, b Concord s/o BARNES Jefferson b Montpelier Vt & Harriett b Concord. Bride: age 19, marr 1st time, b Exeter d/o JENNESS Hiriam & Eliza. Vol: 4 Page: 13 Line: 09

GOODRICH George H of Hopkinton & LORD Lydia of Hopkinton m 1867-12-12 Hopkinton. Groom: age 56, marr 3rd time, b Springfield Vt s/o GOODRICH Samuel b Marblehead Mass & Esther b Winchendon Mass. Bride: age 28, marr 3rd time, b So Berwick Me d/o LORD Charles b So Berwick Me & Sarah b Hopkinton. Vol: 4 Page: 13 Line: 10

Hopkinton, NH Marriages 1858

STORY Frederick D of Hopkinton & PIPER Mary A of Concord m 1867-12-12 Hopkinton. Groom: age 21, marr 1st time, b Sharon s/o STORY Frederick H b Washington & Pamelia b Mason. Bride: age 22, marr 1st time, b Piermont d/o PIPER George b Gilmanton & Hannah D b Hill. Vol: 4 Page: 13 Line: 11

SILVER Daniel of Hopkinton & WALKER Sarah Jane of Weare m 1868-01-15 Hopkinton. Groom: age 29, marr 1st time, b Hopkinton s/o Lottie b Hopkinton. Bride: age 32, marr 1st time, b Dunbarton d/o DOW Edmond b Bow & Sarah. Vol: 4 Page: 13 Line: 13

BROWN Charles W of Henniker & DOW Addie M of Hopkinton m 1868-01-21 Hopkinton. Groom: age 21, marr 1st time, b Henniker s/o BROWN Mark b Hopkinton & Melisia b Hopkinton. Bride: age 23, marr 1st time, b Dunbarton d/o DOW Rufus b Hopkinton & Maria b Hopkinton. Vol: 4 Page: 13 Line: 14

TUTTLE Jacob of Hopkinton & HARDY Sussia?? of Hopkinton m 1868-03-05 Hopkinton. Groom: age 24, marr 1st time, b Lincoln s/o TUTTLE Charles & MARY J. Bride: age 23, marr 1st time, b Contoocookville d/o HARDY George B b Hopkinton & Hannah b Warner. Vol: 4 Page: 13 Line: 15

HOIT Moses of Hopkinton & NICHOLS Elizabeth of Hopkinton m 1868-03-05 Hopkinton. Groom: age 66, marr 2nd time, b Hopkinton s/o HOIT Moses b Hopkinton & Elizabeth b Hopkinton. Bride: age 41, marr 2nd time, b Hopkinton d/o CROSS Moses b Hopkinton & Hannah b Peachman Vt. Vol: 4 Page: 13 Line: 16

BOHONAN Daniel N of Hopkinton & WIGGIN Martha A of Hopkinton m 1870-05-01 Hopkinton. Groom: age 25, marr 1st time, b Sutton s/o BOHONAN David b Boscawen & Berlinda b Boscawen. Bride: age 22, marr 1st time, b Hopkinton d/o WIGGIN William A b Topsfield Mass & Julian b Salem Mass. Vol: 4 Page: 16 Line: 01

BLAISDELL George C of Hopkinton & CURTIS L Arvilla of Hopkinton m 1868-05-14 Hopkinton. Groom: age 24, marr 1st time, b Goffstown s/o BLAISDELL Stephen & Amanda. Bride: age 24, marr 1st time, b Lemester d/o CURTIS Samuel & Lenore. Vol: 4 Page: 14 Line: 02

LANDERS Joseph E of Fisherville & KIMBALL Lucie A of Fisherville m 1868-07-11 Hopkinton. Groom: age 26, marr 1st time, b Westminster Mass s/o LANDERS Amos & Lucy. Bride: age 18, marr 1st time, b Franklin d/o KIMBALL Zilden & Betsey. Vol: 4 Page: 14 Line: 04

RIPLEY Winford of Henniker & HEATH Jennie B of Henniker m 1868-07-23 Hopkinton. Groom: age 24, marr 1st time, b Londonderry s/o RIPLEY Hugh N & GREELEY Lydia L. Bride: age 19, marr 1st time, b Contoocook d/o HEATH Samuel B & CHASE Catharine. Vol: 4 Page: 14 Line: 05

DWINNELLS Warren P of Hopkinton & CHASE Susan E of Henniker m 1868-09-09 Hopkinton. Groom: age 26, marr 2nd time, b Bow s/o DWINNELLS James & Lucy. Bride: age 23, marr 2nd time, b Hillsboro d/o HOWLETT Charles. Vol: 4 Page: 14 Line: 06

LAUGHTON Oscar R of Hopkinton & CAMPBELL Lizzie D of Hopkinton m 1868-09-09 Hopkinton. Groom: age 41, marr 1st time, b Demaston Vt?? s/o LAUGHTON Rodney & Oletta ??. Bride: age 33, marr 1st time, b Hillsboro d/o CAMPBELL Daniel & WILLOUGHBY Elizabet. Vol: 4 Page: 14 Line: 07

14

Hopkinton, NH Marriages 1858

PETERS Henry L of Weare & COLBURN Apphia B of Weare m 1868-11-25 Hopkinton. Groom: age 21, marr 1st time, b Deering s/o PETERS Benj Martin & Sarah. Bride: age 24, marr 1st time, b Newbury d/o COLBURN Abram & WITHINGTON Thirza. Vol: 4 Page: 14 Line: 08

DOWNS John H of Weare & MONTGOMERY Mary C of Hopkinton m 1868-11-26 Hopkinton. Groom: age 23, marr 1st time, b Manchester s/o DOWNS John & Mary. Bride: age 19, marr 1st time, b Hopkinton d/o MONTGOMERY Charles & BURNBANK Adeline. Vol: 4 Page: 14 Line: 09

DOW George of Concord & BARNES Chastina of Concord m 1868-11-28 Hopkinton. Groom: age 20, marr 1st time, b Concord s/o DOW Alfred & Eliza. Bride: age 19, marr 1st time, b Concord d/o Ann. Vol: 4 Page: 14 Line: 10

GILMAN Joseph P of Laconia & ROBINSON Margrietta of Laconia m 1868-12-24 Hopkinton. Groom: age 36, marr 1st time, b Bethelham s/o GILMAN Nehemiah S & MELOON Alice. Bride: age 42, marr 1st time, b Gilford d/o ROBINSON Aaron & WELLS Joanna. Vol: 4 Page: 14 Line: 11

SYMONDS Ephiriam B of Hopkinton & CHASE Mary of Salisbury m 1868-12-27 Hopkinton. Groom: age 21, marr 1st time, b Hillsboro s/o SYMONDS Tilton & CATHARINE B. Bride: age 18, marr 1st time, b Salisbury d/o CHASE Albert G & Clarissa. Vol: 4 Page: 14 Line: 12

RUNNELLS Edward G of Hopkinton & MILLS Jennie of Hopkinton m 1868-12-31 Hopkinton. Groom: age 25, marr 1st time, b Hopkinton s/o RUNNELLS Farnum & Jerusha. Bride: age 20, marr 1st time, b Hopkinton d/o MILLS Charles & Mary. Vol: 4 Page: 14 Line: 13

TERRY Edwin E of Concord & LOVERING Ella F of Tilton m 1875-08-01 Hopkinton. Groom: age 27, marr 1st time, b Warner s/o TERRY Edwin & LYDIA K. Bride: age 16, marr 1st time, b Tilton d/o LOVERING Samuel. Vol: 4 Page: 22 Line: 04

STORY Andrew J of Warner & CHASE Ann J of Warner m 1869-04-15 Hopkinton. Groom: age 22, marr 1st time, b Warner s/o STORY Lowell C & Mary B. Bride: age 20, marr 1st time, b Deering d/o CHASE Nathaniel b Henniker & CHASE Harriet b Warner. Vol: 4 Page: 15 Line: 01

ABBOTT John G of Dunbarton & TILTON Maria J of Hopkinton m 1869-05-02 Hopkinton. Groom: age 20, marr 1st time, b Concord s/o ABBOTT Mills b Concord & Betsey b Concord. Bride: age 17, marr 1st time, b Concord d/o TILTON William b NH & AMES Sara b NH. Vol: 4 Page: 15 Line: 02

McALPINE Gilman E of Hopkinton & TYRILL Josephine of Boscawen m 1869-05-01 Hopkinton. Groom: age 22, marr 1st time, b Hopkinton s/o McALPINE George W b Weare & Hannah J b Weare. Bride: age 23, marr 1st time, b Boscawen. Vol: 4 Page: 15 Line: 03

GUILD Edmund of Hopkinton & STORY Abby M of Hopkinton m 1869-06-13 Hopkinton. Groom: age 30, marr 2nd time, b Hartford Ct s/o GUILD Ezra & Sara. Bride: age 24, marr 2nd time, b Hopkinton d/o STORY Luther b Hopkinton & Mary b Boscawen. Vol: 4 Page: 15 Line: 04

DANFORTH Gilman of Contoocook & FELCH Hatie A of Weare m 1869-06-12 Hopkinton. Groom: age 21, marr 1st time, b Contoocook s/o DANFORTH Gilman & Ruth F. Bride: age 23, marr 1st time, b Weare d/o FELCH Benjamin & Lydia. Vol: 4 Page: 15 Line: 05

Hopkinton, NH Marriages 1858

MILLS George W of Concord & BROWN Eunice of Concord m 1869-06-19 Hopkinton. Groom: age 27, marr 1st time, b Hopkinton s/o MILLS Joseph b Dunbarton & Sylindia b Dunbarton. Bride: age 16, marr 1st time, b Hopkinton. Vol: 4 Page: 15 Line: 06

TILTON William of Hopkinton & GOULD Merin of Goffstown m 1869-06-29 Hopkinton. Groom: age 22, marr 1st time, b Hopkinton s/o TILTON William C & Sara. Bride: age 18, marr 1st time, b Dunbarton d/o GOULD Willliam & Sarah. Vol: 4 Page: 15 Line: 07

FLANDERS Elijah P of Henniker & PLUMER Lucy H of Henniker m 1869-08-19 Hopkinton. Groom: age 42, marr 2nd time, b Weare s/o FLANDERS Jonathan b Weare & Amy b Goffstown. Bride: age 44, marr 2nd time, b Henniker d/o PLUMER David & Mary. Vol: 4 Page: 15 Line: 08

COLBY George O of Derry & CHANDLER Delia G of Hopkinton m 1869-11-08 Hopkinton. Groom: age 25, marr 1st time, b Hopkinton s/o COLBY Isaac & Lucy A. Bride: age 18, marr 1st time, b Hopkinton d/o CHANDLER Horatio & Susan V. Vol: 4 Page: 15 Line: 09

RAND Oscar L of Warner & DOW Frances C of Warner m 1869-11-13 Hopkinton. Groom: age 24, marr 1st time, b Hopkinton s/o RAND Mathew P & Sarah A. Bride: age 22, marr 1st time, b Warner d/o DOW Samuel & Harrit C. Vol: 4 Page: 15 Line: 10

SPOFFORD L Alfred of Hopkinton & PAIGE Abbie Ms of Hopkinton m 1869-12-08 Hopkinton. Groom: age 25, marr 1st time, b Hopkinton s/o SPOFFORD Samuel & Sarah J. Bride: age 24, marr 1st time, b Hopkinton d/o PAIGE John W & Lizzie. Vol: 4 Page: 15 Line: 11

UPTON Barton of Hopkinton & PERRY Sara of Hopkinton m 1869-12-02 Hopkinton. Groom: age 22, marr 1st time, s/o UPTON J L & Clarinda. Bride: age 22, marr 1st time, d/o PERRY William & Aseneth. Vol: 4 Page: 15 Line: 12

CROWELL Joseph of Boscawen & GETCHELL Ruth A of Boscawen m 1869-12-15 Hopkinton. Groom: age 50, marr 2nd time, b Hopkinton s/o CROWELL Joseph & Mary. Bride: age 44, marr 2nd time, b Boscawen d/o GETCHELL Ezra B & Harriet. Vol: 4 Page: 15 Line: 14

UPHAM Sidney of Concord & WHITTIER Ausebia [Auscilia??] of Hopkinton m 1870-01-28 Hopkinton. Groom: age 28, marr 1st time, b Hooksett s/o UPHAM Thomas & Aseneth. Bride: age 24, marr 1st time, b Danville d/o WHITTIER Jacob & Harriett. Vol: 4 Page: 15 Line: 15

HILL Frank B N of Bow & ELIOTT Sarah of Bow m 1870-01-29 Hopkinton. Groom: age 23, marr 1st time, b Bow s/o HILL Nelson & CLOUGH Hannah. Bride: age 24, marr 1st time, b Bow d/o ELIOTT John B & FOLLANSBEE Sally. Vol: 4 Page: 15 Line: 16

DAVIS Paine of Warner & BABCOCK Ester of Perry m 1858-02-17 Warner. Vol: 4 Page: 8 Line: 10

HOLMES Richard of Hopkinton & BURBANK Meriam of Hopkinton m 1861-11-16 Hopkinton. Groom: age 21, marr 1st time, b Hopkinton s/o HOLMES Albert b Hopkinton & Mrs Albert Holmes b Hopkinton. Bride: age 21, marr 1st time, b Hopkinton d/o CHASE Enoch b Hopkinton & Mrs Enoch Chase b Hopkinton. Vol: 4 Page: 5 Line: 10

Hopkinton, NH Marriages 1858

MORRILL Charles A of Hopkinton & KIMBALL Thressa F of Hopkinton m 1866-01-01 Hopkinton. Groom: age 25, marr 1st time, b Hopkinton s/o MORRILL Ebenezer b Salisbury Mass & SWEATT Phebie L b Boscawen. Bride: age 27, marr 1st time, b Derry d/o KIMBALL Iddo b Bradford Ms & RICHARDSON Fannie b Londonderrie. Vol: 4 Page: 11 Line: 06

PUTNAM James of Hopkinton & DAVIS Sarah of Hopkinton m 1861-03-14 Hopkinton. Groom: age 25, marr 1st time, b Hopkinton s/o PUTNAM Martin b Hopkinton & BUTLER Margaret b Hopkinton. Bride: age 26, marr 1st time, b Quincy Mass d/o DAVIS John C b Hopkinton & BUTTERFIELD Sarah b Mass. Vol: 4 Page: 4 Line: 17

SPOFFORD James of Hopkinton & RESTIEUX Ellen Chase of Hopkinton m 1868-01-01 Hopkinton. Groom: age 43, marr 2nd time, b Chester s/o SPOFFORD Sebastain b Danville & Lottie b Danville. Bride: age 24, marr 2nd time, b Concord d/o RESTIEUX William b Boston Mass & Betsey F b Hopkinton. Vol: 4 Page: 13 Line: 12

CHASE Jonathan of Boston & BRUCE Hannah of Hopkinton m 1870-05-23 Hopkinton. Groom: age 60, marr 2nd time, b Sutton s/o CHASE Isaac b Nottingham & Mary b Amesbury. Bride: age 63, marr 2nd time, b Hopkinton d/o BROWN Jonathan. Vol: 4 Page: 16 Line: 02

PEACOCK Charles N of Concord & MEALEY Nellie of Concord m 1870-05-26 Hopkinton. Groom: age 24, marr 1st time, b Concord s/o PEACORK Lorenzo b Milford & Clementin b Glucester Mass. Bride: age 19, marr 1st time, b Bristol. Vol: 4 Page: 16 Line: 03

NILAN George B of Hopkinton & KIMBALL Priscilla A of Hopkinton m 1870-06-01 Hopkinton. Groom: age 25, marr 1st time, b Hopkinton s/o NILAN John B b Uxbridge Mass & Chole. Bride: age 24, marr 1st time, b Hopkinton d/o KIMBALL Moses b Hopkinton & Harriett b Hopkinton. Vol: 4 Page: 16 Line: 04

ELLIOTT Dighton B of Franklin & McALPINE Ella J of Hopkinton m 1870-08-02 Hopkinton. Groom: age 23, marr 1st time, b Webster s/o ELLIOTT Geroger J b Webster & SHATTUCK Mary b Webster. Bride: age 17, marr 1st time, d/o McALPINE George & LULL Hannah. Vol: 4 Page: 16 Line: 05

WIGGIN George W of Warner & KELLEY Mary H of Hopkinton m 1870-08-11 Hopkinton. Groom: age 56, marr 2nd time, b Warner s/o WIGGIN Jonathan b Stratham & WALKER Zipporah b Warner. Bride: age 32, marr 2nd time, b Hopkinton d/o KELLEY Arros b Hopkinton & EVANS Sarah b Weymouth Mass. Vol: 4 Page: 16 Line: 06

WHEELER Christie M of Dunbarton & HOIT Clara B of Dunbarton m 1870-08-30 Hopkinton. Groom: age 21, marr 1st time, b Dunbarton s/o WHEELER Nathanile H b Dunbarton & DURGIN Mary J b Dunbarton. Bride: age 20, marr 1st time, b Dunbarton d/o HOIT Benj b Dunbarton & Lovina b Weare. Vol: 4 Page: 16 Line: 07

TILTON George Frank of Hopkinton & NADEAU Miriam J F of Hopkinton m 1870-10-20 Hopkinton. Groom: age 19, marr 1st time, b Concord s/o TILTON Ransom b Hill & MARY A b Concord. Bride: age 17, marr 1st time, b Canada d/o NADEAU Bruce b Canada & Martha b Concord. Vol: 4 Page: 16 Line: 08

Hopkinton, NH Marriages 1858

CURRIER Loren E of Concord & CHANDLER Mary A of Hopkinton m 1870-11-12 Hopkinton. Groom: age 21, marr 1st time, b Concord s/o Sylvester b Concord & Mary b Concord. Bride: marr 1st time, b Hopkinton d/o ABIAH R b Hopkinton & Philinder b Northfield Vt. Vol: 4 Page: 16 Line: 09

LORD Philander M of Hopkinton & KIMBALL Ellen L of Hopkinton m 1870-12-12 Hopkinton. Groom: age 20, marr 1st time, b Dunbarton s/o LORD Thomas b Boston Mass & Lolinda ?? b Hopkinton. Bride: age 24, marr 1st time, b Hopkinton d/o KIMBALL Moses T b Hopkinton & Harriett b Unity. Vol: 4 Page: 16 Line: 10

PIKE Charles C of Sutton & PIPER Emily E of Hopkinton m 1870-12-25 Hopkinton. Groom: age 26, marr 1st time, b New London s/o PIKE James M b New London & COLBY Sarah b Warner. Bride: age 24, marr 1st time, b Hopkinton d/o PIPER Thomas b Hopkinton & EATON Louisa B b Hopkinton. Vol: 4 Page: 16 Line: 11

DUNBAR Willard C of Warner & RAND Mahala F of Hopkinton m 1871-03-04 Hopkinton. Groom: age 30, marr 1st time, b Springield s/o DUNBAR Marshall b Grantham & Ruth C b Grantham. Bride: age 30, marr 1st time, b Hopkinton d/o RAND Rufus b Hopkinton & Abigail b West Newbury. Vol: 4 Page: 16 Line: 12

FOSS George E of Hopkinton & CLARK Emma A of Hopkinton m 1877-04-04 Hopkinton. Groom: age 25, marr 1st time, b Hopkinton s/o FOSS Jonathan G M & Almira. Bride: age 18, marr 1st time, b Phil Pa d/o CLARK Oliver b Henniker & CLARK Minerva. Vol: 4 Page: 24 Line: 02

ABBOTT Stephen of Hopkinton & FRENCH Mary A of Hopkinton m 1871-02-23 Hopkinton. Groom: age 60, marr 2nd time, b Andover s/o ABBOTT Enos & Sarah. Bride: age 48, marr 2nd time, b Henniker d/o FRENCH Benj & Eliza. Vol: 4 Page: 16 Line: 14

EVANS Lewis D of Hopkinton & TYLER Isabel of Hopkinton m 1870-08-01 Hopkinton. Groom: age 41, marr 1st time, b Merrimack s/o EVANS Nathaniel b Peterboro & WIGGINS Harriet b Concord. Bride: age 38, marr 1st time, d/o TYLER Cyrus C b Charlestown & PUTAUM Sarah b Mass. Vol: 4 Page: 17 Line: 01

HOLMES Lyman W of Gloucester Mass & GIRDLY Mary of Gloucester Mass m 1871-04-24 Hopkinton. Groom: age 50, marr 2nd time, b Hopkinton s/o HOLMES John & MERRILL Joanna. Bride: age 38, marr 2nd time, b Manchester Mass d/o GIRDLY John & STONE Betsey. Vol: 4 Page: 17 Line: 02

STANLEY Edward W of Hopkinton & PILLSBURY Adeline of Webster m 1871-04-30 Hopkinton. Groom: age 22, marr 1st time, b Hopkinton s/o STANLEY Horace C b Hopkinton & Mary A b Hopkinton. Bride: age 19, marr 1st time, b Webster d/o PILLSBURY Paul & Sarah S. Vol: 4 Page: 17 Line: 03

CUSHING Charles of Concord & HALL Hannah of Concord m 1871-05-24 Hopkinton. Groom: age 23, marr 1st time, b Hardwick Vt s/o CUSHING Anthony & Matilda. Bride: age 20, marr 1st time, b Canada. Vol: 4 Page: 17 Line: 04

WILSON Henry of Stoddard & CLOUGH Victoria A of Henniker m 1871-06-11 Hopkinton. Groom: age 19, marr 1st time, b Stoddard s/o WILSON George R

Hopkinton, NH Marriages 1858

& Mehitable. Bride: age 19, marr 1st time, b Hopkinton d/o CLOUGH Phineas & Abbie. Vol: 4 Page: 17 Line: 05

BATTERS Charles H of Concord & HOLT Rassizia Q of Manchester m 1871-06-11 Hopkinton. Groom: age 29, marr 1st time, b Concord s/o BATTERS Charles b Concord & Margaret b Webster. Bride: age 22, marr 1st time, b Manchester d/o HOLT Daniel & Alviria. Vol: 4 Page: 17 Line: 06

DAVIS Adoniram of Sutton & FLINT Caroline A of Sutton m 1871-07-01 Hopkinton. Groom: age 22, marr 1st time, b Sutton s/o DAVIS Elisha b Sutton & COLBURN Sarah b Sutton. Bride: age 18, marr 1st time, b Sutton d/o FLINT Levi b Sutton & BEAN Emily b Sutton. Vol: 4 Page: 17 Line: 07

YOUNG James of Cambridge Mass & FLANDERS Margaret L of Hopkinton m 1871-08-30 Hopkinton. Groom: age 46, marr 2nd time, b Maine s/o YOUNG Joseph & Edna. Bride: age 45, marr 2nd time, b Hopkinton d/o FLANDERS Daniel & Mary Eliza. Vol: 4 Page: 17 Line: 08

WIGHT Edwin Oscar of Keene & CURRIER Abbie L of Contoocook m 1871-09-11 Hopkinton. Groom: age 21, marr 1st time, b Westmoreland s/o WIGHT Albert b Westmoreland. Bride: age 21, marr 1st time, b Contoocook d/o CURRIER Alonzo & Emily. Vol: 4 Page: 17 Line: 09

HOLMES Edward of Hopkinton & ENCOTT Louisa D of Lowell Mass m 1871-11-06 Lowell Mass. Groom: age 22, marr 1st time, b Hopkinton s/o HOLMES Albert & Joanne. Bride: age 22, marr 1st time, b Lowell Mass. Vol: 4 Page: 17 Line: 10

DUSTIN Henry D of Hopkinton & TUCKER Hellen M of Hopkinton m 1871-11-30 Hopkinton. Groom: age 22, marr 1st time, b Hopkinton s/o DUSTIN Daniel P b Hopkinton & Sarah A b Hopkinton. Bride: age 19, marr 1st time, b Hopkinton d/o TUCKER David b Henniker & Sarah E b Hopkinton. Vol: 4 Page: 17 Line: 11

SMITH Leroy P of Franklin & MORSE Emma J of Franklin m 1871-12-28 Hopkinton. Groom: age 19, marr 1st time, b Lebanon s/o SMITH William b Gilmanton & DURGIN Lydia M b Campton. Bride: age 18, marr 1st time, b Franklin d/o MORSE Wilson W b Cabot Vt & CLARKE Anna M b Franklin. Vol: 4 Page: 17 Line: 12

TRASKER George H of Hopkinton & KILBURN Emma B of Hopkinton m 1871-12-28 Hopkinton. Groom: age 21, marr 1st time, b Nashua s/o TASKER Joseph B & Julia. Bride: age 23, marr 1st time, b Bershire Vt d/o KILBURN Rosewell & Lucy. Vol: 4 Page: 17 Line: 13

DEARBORN Fred A of Pembroke & CROWELL Ida M of Hopkinton m 1875-10-24 Hopkinton. Groom: age 29, marr 1st time, b Pembroke s/o DEARBORN John & Ann. Bride: age 18, marr 1st time, b Hopkinton d/o Crowell. Vol: 4 Page: 22 Line: 07

STORY Timothy F of Hopkinton & CHANDLER Mary H of Hopkinton m 1872-01-13 Hopkinton. Groom: age 24, marr 1st time, b Hopkinton s/o STORY Moses & Mehitabel. Bride: age 19, marr 1st time, b Hopkinton d/o CHANDLER Alfred N & Helen b Mass. Vol: 4 Page: 17 Line: 15

BAILEY William P of Contoocook & DOW Annie of Contoocook m 1872-02-12 Hopkinton. Groom: age 28, marr 2nd time, b Albany NY s/o BAILEY E C &

19

Hopkinton, NH Marriages 1858

Susan. Bride: age 19, marr 2nd time, b Webster d/o DOW Lorenzo & Mary Ann. Vol: 4 Page: 17 Line: 16

HOYT James of Hopkinton & CHASE Almira of Weare m 1872-02-15 Hopkinton. Groom: age 61, marr 2nd time, b Henniker s/o HOYT James b Hopkinton & Hannah b Newton. Bride: age 45, marr 2nd time, b Woodbury Vt d/o HUNT Anthony b Tilton & Mary b Deerfield. Vol: 4 Page: 17 Line: 18

MORGAN Frank E of Lynn Mass & KEMPTON Ada E of Hopkinton m 1872-11-04 Hopkinton. Groom: age 21, marr 1st time, b Concord s/o MORGAN Ezra & Eristle(??). Bride: age 21, marr 1st time, b Croydon d/o KEMPTON Edward B & Mary. Vol: 4 Page: 18 Line: 01

BROWN Henry C of Concord & SWEATT Sarah D of Hopkinton m 1872-11-28 Hopkinton. Groom: age 23, marr 1st time, b Hopkinton s/o BROWN George & Rosette C. Bride: age 19, marr 1st time, b Webster d/o SWEATT Wm. M & Lydia. Vol: 4 Page: 18 Line: 02

DANFORTH Enoch J of Okland Cal & FISK Lydia A of Hopkinton m 1873-03-27 Hopkinton. Groom: age 48, marr 2nd time, b Boscawen s/o DANFORTH Edmund b Boscawen & CLOUGH Rhoda b Warner. Bride: age 42, marr 2nd time, b Hopkinton d/o CONNER James b Henniker & KIMBALL Lydia b Hopkinton. Vol: 4 Page: 18 Line: 03

CHASE Baruch of Hopkinton & BROWN Heath Mary of Warner m 1873-05-18 Hopkinton. Groom: age 65, marr 3rd time, b Hopkinton s/o CHASE Moses b Nottingham Mass & KIMBALL Lydia b Warner. Bride: age 66, marr 3rd time, b Boscawen d/o Brown. Vol: 4 Page: 18 Line: 04

FULLER John A of Contoocook & MERRILL Julia F of Contoocook m 1872-04-30 Hopkinton. Groom: age 23, marr 1st time, b NH s/o FULLER A J b Hopkinton & Adoline b Hopkinton. Bride: age 18, marr 1st time, b Contoocook d/o MERRILL Jacob M & Sarah C. Vol: 4 Page: 18 Line: 05

PUTNAM Joseph E of Contoocook & STRAW Margarett of Contoocook m 1873-02-11 Hopkinton. Groom: age 29, marr 1st time, b Contoocook s/o PUTNAM Rufus & Harriet. Bride: age 25, marr 1st time, b Contoocook d/o STRAW Ashel & Abagial. Vol: 4 Page: 18 Line: 06

HARDY Charles W of Hopkinton & GEORGE Mary of Webster m 1872-04-28 Hopkinton. Groom: age 36, marr 1st time, b NH s/o HARDY Digias & SONNA Anna. Bride: age 23, marr 1st time, b Webster d/o GEORGE William & Submitt. Vol: 4 Page: 19 Line: 01

BROCKWAY John of Hopkinton & SARGENT Betsey P of Hopkinton m 1872-06-01 Hopkinton. Groom: age 78, marr 2nd time, b Bradford s/o BROCKWAY Asa b Washington. Bride: age 68, marr 2nd time, b NH d/o EATON Thomas. Vol: 4 Page: 19 Line: 02

FRENCH Charles of Hopkinton & HARDY Sarah A of Hopkinton m 1872-09-15 Hopkinton. Groom: age 30, marr 2nd time, b NH s/o FRENCH Reuben E b Hopkinton & Sarah Chase b Dunbarton. Bride: age 25, marr 2nd time, b Nh d/o HARDY Albert & LANCASTER Lydia. Vol: 4 Page: 19 Line: 03

MERRILL George E of Hopkinton & DUNBAR Mary E of Hopkinton m 1872-06-25 Hopkinton. Groom: age 23, marr 1st time, b Nashua s/o MERRILL Parker b Groton & Betsey A b Hooksett. Bride: age 18, marr 1st time, b Hopkinton d/o

Hopkinton, NH Marriages 1858

DUNBAR Elmer B b Grantham & WEBBER Ann b Hopkinton. Vol: 4 Page: 19 Line: 04

BURNHAM John F of Contoocook & RICHMOND Frances E of W Randolph Vt m 1872-09-15 Randolph Vt. Groom: age 39, marr 2nd time, b NH s/o BURNHAM John b Hopkinton & WADLEIGH Susan b Sutton. Bride: age 34, marr 2nd time, b Derby Vt d/o RICHMOND Lauriston F b Barnard Vt & Deborah b Pompret Vt. Vol: 4 Page: 19 Line: 05

FRENCH George O of Boston Mass & STORY Nellie of Hopkinton m 1872-11-17 Hopkinton. Groom: age 26, marr 1st time, b Boston Mass s/o FRENCH Oliver A & Julia A. Bride: age 24, marr 1st time, b Hopkinton d/o STORY Moses & Mehitable. Vol: 4 Page: 19 Line: 06

MAYNARD John H of Manchester & CLOUGH Jennie S of Henniker m 1872-11-27 Henniker. Groom: age 24, marr 1st time, b Lancaster s/o MAYNARD John & Mary. Bride: age 19, marr 1st time, b Henniker d/o CLOUGH Phineas & Abigail. Vol: 4 Page: 19 Line: 07

DEARBORN Henry H of Hopkinton & SMITH Sarah of Peabody Mass m 1873-01-01 Salem Mass. Groom: age 26, marr 1st time, b Epsom s/o DEARBORN Edwin & Lettice. Bride: age 21, marr 1st time, b London England d/o SMITH Edward & WINCHESTER Sarah. Vol: 4 Page: 19 Line: 08

ANDREWS Henry S of Charlestown Mass & SMITH Annie of Hopkinton m 1873-02-08 Hopkinton. Groom: age 41, marr 1st time, b Charlestown Mas s/o ANDREWS Abraham b Hillsboro & Caroline b Charlestown Mass. Bride: age 36, marr 1st time, b Hopkinton d/o SMITH Richard K & Almira. Vol: 4 Page: 19 Line: 09

SYMONDS Samuel T of Hopkinton & JOHNSON Annie H of Hopkinton m 1873-02-15 Hopkinton. Groom: age 23, marr 1st time, b Hillsborough s/o SYMONDS Tilton & Catharine B. Bride: age 22, marr 1st time, b Weare d/o JOHNSON Judith. Vol: 4 Page: 19 Line: 10

CARNES Willis N of Henniker & PAIGE Elizabeth A of Henniker m 1873-06-11 Hopkinton. Groom: age 20, marr 1st time, b Henniker s/o CARNES George W & Abigail. Bride: age 20, marr 1st time, b Henniker d/o PAIGE Samuel & Mary A. Vol: 4 Page: 20 Line: 02

BURNHAM John F of Hopkinton & PEABORY Satira of Antrim m 1858-05-12 Dearing NH. Groom: age 39, marr 1st time, b Hopkinton s/o BURNHAM John. Bride: age 34, marr 1st time, b Antrim d/o LAURISTON T Richmond. Vol: 4 Page: 2 Line: 01

MecCOY of Weare & EDMUNDS Allice F of Hopkinton m 1873-12-01 Hopkinton. Groom: age 25, marr 2nd time, b Thornton s/o MecCOY Nathan b Goffstown & Mary Ann b Weare. Bride: age 25, marr 2nd time, b Hopkinton d/o EDMUNDS Horace b Weare & Bridgett b Weare. Vol: 4 Page: 20 Line: 04

SMITH Nathan of Salem Mass & CHOATE Lizzie A of Hopkinton m 1873-12-10 Hopkinton. Groom: age 42. Bride: age 33. Vol: 4 Page: 20 Line: 05

WELLMAN H C of Manchester & BROWN Emma L of Contoocook m 1874-02-06 Hopkinton. Groom: age 27, marr 2nd time, b Montwill Me s/o WELLMAN Benj T & Margaret. Bride: age 22, marr 2nd time, d/o BROWN Otis H & Mary. Vol: 4 Page: 20 Line: 06

Hopkinton, NH Marriages 1858

JAMESON Daniel D of Concord & HOYT Olive J of Hopkinton m 1874-03-12 Hopkinton. Groom: age 21, marr 1st time, b Hopkinton s/o JAMESON Jonas H b Dunbarton & Caroline b Goffstown. Bride: age 26, marr 1st time, b Dunbarton d/o HOYT French b Hopkinton & Mahala b Hopkinton. Vol: 4 Page: 20 Line: 07

CROWELL Smith of Hopkinton & STRAW Nyra A of Hopkinton m 1874-03-24 Hopkinton. Groom: age 24, marr 1st time, b Hopkinton s/o CROWELL Albert & Lydia. Bride: age 19, marr 1st time, b Hopkinton d/o STRAW Edmund S & Emeline K. Vol: 4 Page: 20 Line: 08

LEACH Warren P of Dunbarton & COLBY Diantha D of Dunbarton m 1874-04-05 Hopkinton. Groom: age 22, marr 1st time, b Dunbarton s/o LEACH John b Dunbarton & Elmira b Sanbornton. Bride: age 29, marr 1st time, b Londonderry d/o COLBY Abram b Londonderry & Mary Abline b Londonderry. Vol: 4 Page: 21 Line: 01

WEEKS George K of Hopkinton & MUDGETT Annie N of Contoocook m 1874-04-03 Hopkinton. Groom: age 40, marr 2nd time, b Hopkinton s/o WEEKS Charles & Phebe. Bride: age 30, marr 2nd time, b Contoocook d/o STRAW Ashel L & Abbie. Vol: 4 Page: 21 Line: 02

JOHNSON Richard D of Sanbornton & STORY Mary A of Hopkinton m 1874-04-26 Hopkinton. Groom: age 28, marr 1st time, b Sanbornton s/o JOHNSON Simon b Sanbornton & HOIT Nancy b Sanbornton. Bride: age 36, marr 1st time, b Hopkinton d/o HOWE Rufus b Henniker & MILLS Sally b Dunbarton. Vol: 4 Page: 21 Line: 03

DOWNING William H of Contoocook & STORY Mary E of Fisherville m 1874-05-10 Hopkinton. Groom: age 26, marr 2nd time, b Boscawen s/o DOWNING Joshua b Boscawen & BROWN Sarah Jane b Webster. Bride: age 18, marr 2nd time, b Boscawen d/o STORY Joseph & HANSON Clara. Vol: 4 Page: 21 Line: 04

GOVE George P of Hopkinton & ROWELL Mary E of Hopkinton m 1874-06-09 Hopkinton. Groom: age 27, marr 1st time, b Henniker s/o GOVE Wyer & PIPER Mary C. Bride: age 24, marr 1st time, b Hopkinton d/o ROWELL Isaac & ADAMS Harriet. Vol: 4 Page: 21 Line: 05

DOW William H of Contoocook & ELLIOTT Priscilla A of Webster m 1874-08-16 Hopkinton. Groom: age 20, marr 1st time, b Hill s/o DOW Henry E b Fisherville & BOUTWELL Charlott b Contoocook. Bride: age 22, marr 1st time, b Webster d/o ELLIOTT William P b Boscawen & SANBORN Amanda b Warner. Vol: 4 Page: 21 Line: 06

HASKELL Alfred C of Franklin & STEVENS Carrie E of Franklin m 1874-08-24 Hopkinton. Groom: age 24, marr 1st time, b Weare s/o HASKELL George b East Weare & PHILBRICK Fannie b Wilmot. Bride: age 20, marr 1st time, b Andover d/o STEVENS Moses & CALL Emiley b Boscawen. Vol: 4 Page: 21 Line: 07

THURSTON Charles E of Lyme & KNOX Minnie E of Pembroke m 1874-09-27 Hopkinton. Groom: age 27, marr 1st time, b Warren s/o HILL Asa b Haverhill & Eliza. Bride: age 24, marr 1st time, b Pembroke d/o KNOX Crosby b Pembroke. Vol: 4 Page: 21 Line: 08

Hopkinton, NH Marriages 1858

LAWRENCE Elijah B of Milford & AUSTIN N Jennie of Contoocook m 1874-11-05 Hopkinton. Groom: age 21, marr 1st time, b Dracut Mass s/o LAWRENCE Nathaniel & BUXTON Charlotte. Bride: age 19, marr 1st time, b Goffstown d/o AUSTIN Daniel B & CHRISTY Sabiah Jane. Vol: 4 Page: 21 Line: 09

RICHARDS Ai P of Sutton & WEEKS Georgie A of Goshen m 1874-11-08 Hopkinton. Groom: age 27, marr 1st time, b Sutton s/o RICHARDS George W b Warren Vt & PEASLEY Martha B b Sutton. Bride: age 20, marr 1st time, b Goshen d/o WEEKS Carlton & CUTTS Mary b Goshen. Vol: 4 Page: 21 Line: 10

STEVENS Henry of Pembroke & CURRIER Allis of Hopkinton m 1874-11-25 Hopkinton. Groom: age 24, marr 1st time, b Pembroke s/o STEVENS Philip & Eliza. Bride: age 20, marr 1st time, b Hopkinton d/o CURRIER Lazar & Ann. Vol: 4 Page: 21 Line: 11

HOWLETT John F of Hillsboro & EASTMAN Tamson of Hopkinton m 1874-11-24 Hopkinton. Groom: age 29, marr 2nd time, b Bradford s/o HOWLETT John 2nd b Bradford & LANGDON Susan S b Bradford. Bride: age 35, marr 2nd time, b Hopkinton d/o EASTMAN Jonathan b Washington & ROWELL Elisabeth b Hopkinton. Vol: 4 Page: 21 Line: 13

FRENCH Charles E of Hopkinton & JONES Abbie H of Warner m 1874-12-29 Hopkinton. Groom: age 26, marr 1st time, b Hopkinton s/o FRENCH Sullivan W b Hopkinton & Elmira L b Hopkinton. Bride: age 20, marr 1st time, b Webester d/o JONES William & Theodate. Vol: 4 Page: 21 Line: 14

TYRRELL Ezra of Boscawen & PERRY Elizabeth (Mrs) of Hopkinton m 1875-03-11 Hopkinton. Groom: age 53, marr 2nd time, b Handock s/o TYRELL Joseph b Bedford & CRAM Sally b Lyndeboro. Bride: age 48, marr 2nd time, b Hopkinton. Vol: 4 Page: 21 Line: 15

PERKINS Zebina of NH & BURLEIGH Emily A of NH m 1860-07-31 Hopkinton. Groom: age 38, marr 2nd time, b Loudon s/o PERKINS Levi b Wheelock Vt & SANBORN Hannah. Bride: marr 2nd time, b New Hampton. Vol: 4 Page: 4 Line: 02

CLOUGH Charles E of Weare & LEACH Ella F of Weare m 1876-07-26 Hopkinton. Groom: age 21, marr 1st time, b Concord s/o CLOUGH Cyrus & Hannah. Bride: age 19, marr 1st time, b Manchester d/o LEACH H H b Gilmanton. Vol: 4 Page: 23 Line: 07

HOWE Madison M of Hopkinton & FELCH Elmira L of Weare m 1869-02-21 Hopkinton. Groom: age 40, b Hopkinton s/o HOWE Peter & Polly. Bride: age 25, b Boscawen d/o FELCH Benj & Lydia. Vol: 4 Page: 14 Line: 14

RAND Frank P of Concord & DUSTIN Clara of Hopkinton m 1869-02-11 Hopkinton. Groom: age 28, marr 1st time, b Hopkinton s/o RAND Mattthew P b Hopkinton & Sara A b Hopkinton. Bride: age 30, marr 1st time, b Hopkinton d/o DUSTIN Cyrus b Hopkinton & Edna R b Salisbury. Vol: 4 Page: 14 Line: 15

JONES John F of Hopkinton & BARNARD Nana N of Amesbury Mass m 1861-10-23 Hopkinton. Groom: age 26, marr 1st time, b Hopkinton s/o JONES Jonathan b Boscawen & CURRIER Sarah b Hopkinton. Bride: age 26, marr 1st time, b Hopkinton d/o BARNARD James K b Amesbury Mass & FROST Nermiah b NH. Vol: 4 Page: 5 Line: 07

Hopkinton, NH Marriages 1858

HOWLETT John 2nd of Bradford & ROWELL Roxanna of Hopkinton m 1875-12-08 Hopkinton. Groom: age 56, marr 2nd time, b Bradford s/o HOWLETT Thomas & Eunice. Bride: age 52, marr 2nd time, b Hopkinton d/o ROWELL Moses & Tamson. Vol: 4 Page: 22 Line: 08

GOODWIN Charles P of Concord & CROWELL Etta of Hopkinton m 1876-01-29 Hopkinton. Groom: age 27, marr 2nd time, b Concord s/o GOODWIN Alphones & Caroline. Bride: age 17, marr 2nd time, b Hopkinton d/o CROWELL Henry U. Vol: 4 Page: 22 Line: 09

SMART Durrill of Hopkinton & CROWELL Lydia L of Hopkinton m 1876-02-12 Hopkinton. Groom: age 68, marr 2nd time, b Hopkinton s/o SMART Benning (Benjamin) b Newmarket** & Abigail b Weare**. Bride: age 61, marr 2nd time, b Hopkinton d/o KIMBALL Daniel b Hopkinton**. Vol: 4 Page: 22 Line: 10

SPOFFORD Frederich of Hopkinton & PHELPS Julia A of Weare m 1876-03-04 Hopkinton. Groom: age 49, marr 2nd time, b Chester s/o SPOFFORD Lebastin & Sally. Bride: age 48, marr 2nd time, b Weare d/o ESTOW Moses & Mary. Vol: 4 Page: 22 Line: 11

SMART Joseph H of Hopkinton & LONG Nettie B of Hopkinton m 1876-04-01 Hopkinton. Groom: age 25, marr 1st time, b Hopkinton s/o SMART George W b Hopkinton** & HARDY Ester b Warner**. Bride: age 16, marr 1st time, b Hopkinton d/o LONG Benj b Hopkinton & BARTLETT Melindy. Vol: 4 Page: 23 Line: 01

CURTICE Grovenor of Hopkinton & WILSON Augusta of Hopkinton m 1876-04-18 Hopkinton. Groom: age 34, marr 2nd time, b Lempster s/o CURTICE Samuel & Lennore??. Bride: age 27, marr 2nd time, b Hopkinton d/o WILSON Robert & HUSE Lucinda. Vol: 4 Page: 23 Line: 02

FLANDERS Frank of Hopkinton & MONTGOMERY Mariam of Hopkinton m 1876-04-22 Hopkinton. Groom: age 21, marr 1st time, b Hopkinton s/o FLANDERS Benj & Melisa. Bride: age 20, marr 1st time, b Hopkinton d/o MONTGOMERY George & Lydia. Vol: 4 Page: 23 Line: 03

BOHONAN John W of Hopkinton & JEWELL Delia A of Weare m 1876-05-02 Hopkinton. Groom: age 28, marr 1st time, b Sutton s/o BOHANAN David & Belinda B. Bride: age 21, marr 1st time, b Weare d/o JEWELL Otis F & Mary P. Vol: 4 Page: 23 Line: 04

EASTMAN Sidney F of Hopkinton & GREELEY Octavia of Salisbury m 1876-05-10 Hopkinton. Groom: age 28, marr 1st time, b Hopkinton s/o EASTMAN Jonathan & Elizabeth. Bride: age 26, marr 1st time, b Salisbury d/o GREELEY S B & Louisa. Vol: 4 Page: 23 Line: 05

HARDY George B of Contoocook & DAVIS Laura B of Contoocook m 1876-06-28 Hopkinton. Groom: age 66, marr 2nd time, b Hopkinton s/o HARDY Isaac & Hannah. Bride: age 49, marr 2nd time, b Warner d/o BARTLETT Richard. Vol: 4 Page: 23 Line: 06

HARRINGTON Thomas O of Hopkinton & WOODBURY Hattie R of New Boston m 1876-10-01 Hopkinton. Groom: age 25, marr 1st time, b Concord s/o HARRINGTON Moses B & Rebecca C. Bride: age 20, marr 1st time, b Campton Me d/o WOODBURY Benj F & Caroline W. Vol: 4 Page: 23 Line: 08

CHASE Cyrus F of Contoocook & BARTLETT Ella F of Warner m 1876-10-09 Hopkinton. Groom: age 31, marr 1st time, b Hopkinton s/o CHASE Moses &

Louisa. Bride: age 21, marr 1st time, b Warner d/o BARTLETT Jasper N & Lucinda. Vol: 4 Page: 23 Line: 09

HOLMES Charles A of Hopkinton & WEBBER Evangeline of Hopkinton m 1876-11-04 Hopkinton. Groom: age 24, marr 1st time, b Webster s/o HOLMES Ezra M & Mahala E. Bride: age 23, marr 1st time, b Weare d/o WEBBER Josiah & Sarah. Vol: 4 Page: 23 Line: 10

CROWELL Henry N of Hopkinton & BURROUGHS Melinda J of Bow m 1876-11-15 Hopkinton. Groom: age 42, marr 2nd time, b Hopkinton s/o CROWELL Albert & Lydia. Bride: age 25, marr 2nd time, b Weare d/o BURROUGHS Alfred & Maria. Vol: 4 Page: 23 Line: 11

ELLIOTT Edson E of Hopkinton & COLBY Nettie L of Henniker m 1876-11-30 Hopkinton. Groom: age 20, marr 1st time, b Webster s/o ELLIOTT Joseph R & Angelina b Danville Mass. Bride: age 16, marr 1st time, b Deering d/o COLBY George & Fidelia. Vol: 4 Page: 23 Line: 12

CHAPMAN Charles H of Hopkinton & WHITNEY Carrie E of Pittsfield m 1876-11-29 Hopkinton. Groom: age 28, marr 2nd time, b Weare s/o CHAPMAN Charles & Merriam M. Bride: age 19, marr 2nd time, b Pittsfield d/o WHITNEY Israel C & Caroline. Vol: 4 Page: 23 Line: 13

GILCHRIST John J of Henniker & COLBY Mary A of Hopkinton m 1876-11-30 Hopkinton. Groom: age 26, marr 1st time, b Goffstown s/o GILCHRIST John & Sarah Jane. Bride: age 25, marr 1st time, b Hopkinton d/o COLBY Samuel H & Louisa. Vol: 4 Page: 23 Line: 14

CARPENTER Edwin Sibley of Hopkinton & MUDGE Hattie F of Mills Maine m 1876-12-20 Hopkinton. Groom: age 20, marr 1st time, b Hopkinton s/o CARPENTER Guy & Mary A Kimball. Bride: age 22, marr 1st time, b Rochester d/o MUDGE Orrin & AUSTIN Harriet N. Vol: 4 Page: 23 Line: 15

BROWN Charles H of Hopkinton & HILL Addie F of Hopkinton m 1877-01-19 Hopkinton. Groom: age 23, marr 1st time, b Hopkinton s/o BROWN Jonathan b Concord & Mary. Bride: age 17, marr 1st time, b Concord d/o HILL Howard & MAKEPEACE Nancy. Vol: 4 Page: 23 Line: 16

THOMPSON Orvis D of Contoocook & KETCHUM Jessie A of Contoocook m 1877-02-14 Hopkinton. Groom: age 25, marr 1st time, b Goshen s/o THOMPSON Nathan & Adaline. Bride: age 19, marr 1st time, b Hopkinton d/o KETCHUM George H & Almira. Vol: 4 Page: 23 Line: 17

SPOFFORD Luther F of Hopkinton & STORY Clara J of Hopkinton m 1871-03-05 Hopkinton. Groom: age 22, marr 1st time, b Hopkinton s/o SPOFFORD Samuel b Chester & FELCH Sarah Jane b Hopkinton. Bride: age 18, marr 1st time, b Hopkinton d/o STORY J S b Hopkinton & SMART Sophronia b Hopkinton. Vol: 4 Page: 16 Line: 13

WATKINS George N of Hopkinton & STORY Helen J of Hopkinton m 1877-04-17 Hopkinton. Groom: age 34, marr 2nd time, b Warner s/o WATKINS Jason A & SEAVEY Nancy. Bride: marr 2nd time, b Hopkinton d/o STORY Jeremiah & SMART Sophronia. Vol: 4 Page: 24 Line: 03

HALL Frank E of Hopkinton & PALMER Ann of Hopkinton m 1877-04-22 Hopkinton. Groom: age 25, marr 1st time, b Boscawen. Bride: age 36, marr 1st time, b Hopkinton d/o PALMER William & CHASE Annie E. Vol: 4 Page: 24 Line: 05

Hopkinton, NH Marriages 1858

PRESCOTT William L of Franklin & CUNNINGHAM Genie N of Contoocook m 1871-12-24 Hopkinton. Groom: age 21, marr 1st time, b Franklin s/o PRESCOTT Bradbury N b Franklin & BATCHELDER Annette b Chichester. Bride: age 16, marr 1st time, b Canaan d/o CUNNINGHAM John B & Frances. Vol: 4 Page: 17 Line: 14

CARR Chas M of Concord & MORRILL Ellen A of Concord m 1878-09-07 Hopkinton. Groom: age 24, marr 1st time, b Concord s/o CARR Wm F & Julia. Bride: age 24, marr 1st time, b Concord d/o MORRILL James. Vol: 4 Page: 25 Line: 05

PALMER Willie O of Hopkinton & CLARK Cora J of Hopkinton m 1877-10-07 Hopkinton. Groom: age 23, marr 1st time, b Hopkinton s/o PALMER William & CHASE Ann E. Bride: age 20, marr 1st time, b Antrim d/o CLARK Oliver & AYERS Minerva. Vol: 4 Page: 24 Line: 08

CLARK Jeremiah G of Franklin & FRENCH Ellen L of Hopkinton m 1877-11-29 Hopkinton. Groom: age 42, marr 2nd time, b Franklin s/o CLARK David & PILBRICK Abigail. Bride: age 37, marr 2nd time, b Hopkinton d/o FRENCH Jonathan & HUNTOON Mary. Vol: 4 Page: 24 Line: 09

SMITH Joseph P of Stoneham Mass & CURRIER Harriett of Hopkinton m 1878-01-01 Hopkinton. Groom: age 54, marr 2nd time, b Wendell s/o SMITH Nathan & PILLSBURY Sally. Bride: age 51, marr 2nd time, b Concord d/o SMITH Richard & CHASE Almira. Vol: 4 Page: 24 Line: 10

CHANDLER Frank W of Hopkinton & ROGERS Margie S of Hopkinton m 1878-04-25 Hopkinton. Groom: age 24, marr 1st time, b Hopkinton s/o CHANDLER Isaac H & SHAW Caroline E. Bride: age 17, marr 1st time, b Hopkinton d/o ROGERS Alexander & GOODRICH Sophie W. Vol: 4 Page: 25 Line: 01

LOCK George H of Hopkinton & WRIGHT Mary A of Hopkinton m 1878-05-11 Weare. Groom: age 34, marr 1st time, b Hopkinton s/o LOCK Daniel & Elizabeth. Bride: age 35, marr 1st time, b Hopkinton d/o WRIGHT James M & Mary. Vol: 4 Page: 25 Line: 02

GOODRICH Lurman R of Hopkinton & POWELL Jennie V of Loudon m 1878-05-19 Hopkinton. Groom: age 20, marr 1st time, b Hopkinton s/o GOODRICH George K & WHITMAN Adaline. Bride: age 19, marr 1st time, b Loudon d/o POWELL William B & BAILEY Elizabeth. Vol: 4 Page: 25 Line: 03

FULLER Orrin F of Hopkinton & CAMPBELL Lillie E of Hopkinton m 1878-07-29 Hopkinton. Groom: age 23, marr 1st time, b Hopkinton s/o FULLER Abraham & FELLOWS Adaline. Bride: age 18, marr 1st time, b Hopkinton d/o CAMPBELL Francis & COURSER Caroline. Vol: 4 Page: 25 Line: 04

CHASE Oscar N of Hopkinton & LONG Etta M of Hopkinton m 1878-09-29 Hopkinton. Groom: age 22, marr 1st time, b Hopkinton s/o CHASE Nathaniel C & CURRIER Nancy L. Bride: age 19, marr 1st time, b Hopkinton d/o LONG Benj. Vol: 4 Page: 25 Line: 06

JEWELL Philip B of Hopkinton & SPOFFORD Ellen F of Hopkinton m 1878-12-13 Hopkinton. Groom: age 60, marr 3rd time, b Hopkinton s/o JEWELL Ezra & BICKFORD Abagail. Bride: age 35, marr 3rd time, d/o RESTIEAUX W & CHASE Betsey. Vol: 4 Page: 25 Line: 07

BOHONAN David N of Hopkinton & FISK Jeannie M of Hopkinton m 1878-11-13 Hopkinton. Groom: age 33, marr 2nd time, b Sutton s/o BOHONAN Daniel &

BEAN Belinda. Bride: age 20, marr 2nd time, b Hopkinton d/o FISK Daniel & COURSER Lydia O. Vol: 4 Page: 25 Line: 08

BARSTOW Amos of Hopkinton & BEASEL Jadidok ?? of Concord m 1878 Dec ?? Hopkinton. Groom: age 77, marr 3rd time, b Pittsfield s/o BASTOW Josiah & Mehitable. Bride: age 61, marr 3rd time, b Fairfield Me d/o Jones & BLACKWELL Misha. Vol: 4 Page: 25 Line: 09

DOW Charles of Hopkinton & CURRIER Ida A of Hopkinton m 1878-12-23 Hopkinton. Groom: age 21, marr 1st time. Bride: age 16, marr 1st time, b Hopkinton. Vol: 4 Page: 25 Line: 10

KIMBALL John Stevens of Hopkinton & FRENCH Claire of Hopkinton m 1878-12-31 Hopkinton. Groom: age 33, marr 1st time, b Boston Mass s/o KIMBALL John S & STEVENS Mary E. Bride: age 30, marr 1st time, b Hopkinton d/o FRENCH Ruben E & CHASE Sarah. Vol: 4 Page: 25 Line: 11

HOYT Walter F of Hopkinton & PHELPS Sarah O of Tilton m 1879-01-01 Tilton. Groom: age 24, marr 1st time, b Hopkinton s/o HOYT Moses F & FLANDERS Mahala. Bride: age 24, marr 1st time, b Danvers Mass d/o PHELPS Francis & BROWELL Elizabeth. Vol: 4 Page: 25 Line: 12

BROWN Charles of Hopkinton & BARNES Ida M of Henniker m 1879-02-03 Hopkinton. Groom: age 25, marr 2nd time, b Hopkinton s/o BROWN Jonathana & DUNBAR Mary. Bride: age 17, marr 2nd time, b Henniker d/o BARNES George E. Vol: 4 Page: 25 Line: 13

DOW Samuel of Hopkinton & WALKER Jennie M of Henniker m 1879-02-28 Hennkier. Groom: age 52, marr 2nd time, b Concord s/o DOW Samuel & HARVEY Sarah. Bride: age 44, marr 2nd time. Vol: 4 Page: 25 Line: 14

HOWARD Lewis of Hopkinton & CLEMENT Ferona of Springfield m 1879-03-25 Newport. Groom: age 76, marr 2nd time, b W Bridgewater M s/o HOWARD Abial & BARTLETT Keziah. Bride: age 59, marr 2nd time, b Springfield d/o JOHNSON Abner & QUIMBY Mary. Vol: 4 Page: 25 Line: 15

HASELTON Barnes of Contoocook & BOYCE Ruth L of Andover m 1877-02-02 Franklin. Groom: age 76, marr 3rd time, b Concord s/o HAZELTON Timoty & BRICKET Lydia. Bride: age 73, marr 3rd time, b Salisbury d/o ADAMS Joseph. Vol: 4 Page: 24 Line: 01

STANLEY Edward W of Hopkinton & CLOUGH Mary E of Hopkinton m 1877-04-16 Hopkinton. Groom: age 28, marr 2nd time, b Hopkinton s/o STANLEY Horace C & Mary. Bride: age 19, marr 2nd time, b Hopkinton d/o CLOUGH Charles F & Mary L. Vol: 4 Page: 24 Line: 04

MORRILL Frank J of Hopkinton & STEVENS Hattie F of Haverhill m 1877-08-01 Haverhill. Groom: age 26, marr 1st time, b Hopkinton s/o MORRILL George W & Laura A. Bride: age 25, marr 1st time, b Haverhill d/o STEVENS Govl?? & Lydia. Vol: 4 Page: 24 Line: 06

GREENE Herman W of Hopkinton & CLARK Austis of Hopkinton m 1877-09-08 Hopkinton. Groom: age 41, marr 2nd time, b Cannaan s/o GREENE Herman H & LITTLE Ellen C. Bride: age 37, marr 2nd time, b Canaan d/o CAHRAN Rhuhamac. Vol: 4 Page: 24 Line: 07

STEVENS Edgar W of Hopkinton & PUTNAM George of Hopkinton m 1873-09-30 Hopkinton. Groom: age 22, marr 1st time, b Manchester s/o STEVENS Gilman G b Manchester & Louisa b Hopkinton. Bride: age 21, marr 1st time, b

Hopkinton, NH Marriages 1858

Bradford Mass d/o PUTNAM George b Bradford Mass & BLACKSTONE Betsey. Vol: 4 Page: 20 Line: 03

PENNIMAN James E of New Boston & EDWARDS E Abbie of New Boston m 1858-09-01 Hopkinton. Groom: age 24, marr 1st time, b Boston Mass. Bride: age 24, marr 1st time, b Boston Mass. Vol: 4 Page: 3 Line: 02

PUTNAM Charles of Hopkinton & EASTMAN Almira of Hopkinton m 1862-03-19 Hopkinton. Groom: marr 1st time, b Hopkinton s/o PUTNAM Martin b Hopkinton & BUTLER Margaret b Henniker. Bride: marr time, b Hopkinton d/o EASTMAN J G b Hopkinton & KIMBALL Charlotte b Hopkinton. Vol: 4 Page: 5 Line: 15

GLAWSON Charles N of Hillsboro & PEASLEE Ida E of Weare m 1874-11-25 Hopkinton. Groom: age 20, marr 1st time, b Deering s/o CLAWSON Francis b Nova Scotia & BLANCHARD Angeline b Richmond. Bride: age 19, marr 1st time, b Weare d/o PEASLEE Nathaniel b Weare & GOVE Jennett b Weare. Vol: 4 Page: 21 Line: 12

Hopkinton, NH Births 1858-1879

ABBOTT Alice Gill b Hopkinton 1860-05-24 child of ABBOTT Jeremiah shoemaker b Vt & Hannah b Concord Vol: 4 Page: 53 Line: 007.

ABBOTT Andrew Peter b Hopkinton 1862-07-28 child of ABBOTT Jeremiah farmer b Pomfret Vt & Hannah b Concord Vol: 4 Page: 55 Line: 006.

ABBOTT Not Named b Hopkinton 1864-03-06 child of ABBOTT Jeremiah farmer b Pomfret Vt & Hannah b Concord Vol: 4 Page: 56 Line: 043.

ABBOTT Not Named b Hopkinton 1867-07-15 child of ABBOTT Jeremiah farmer b Pomfret Vt & Hannah b Concord Vol: 4 Page: 59 Line: 027.

ADAMS Claud Delna b Hopkinton 1869-05-26 child of ADAMS Joseph Henry mechanic b Sutton & Judith b Warner Vol: 4 Page: 61 Line: 019.

ADAMS Lila Jona b Hopkinton 1863-07-27 child of ADAMS Joseph H farmer b Sutton & Judith b Warner Vol: 4 Page: 56 Line: 013.

ADAMS Lola H b Hopkinton 1865-09-20 child of ADAMS Joseph H laborer b Sutton & Judith b Warner Vol: 4 Page: 59 Line: 022.

AGER Clara S b Hopkinton 1872-08-13 child of AGER Walter C farmer b Warner & Mari b Hopkinton Vol: 4 Page: 65 Line: 007.

AGER Lizzie H b Hopkinton 1867-01-14 child of AGER Walter farmer b Warner & MARIA C b Hopkinton Vol: 4 Page: 59 Line: 014.

AGER Mary Charlotte b Hopkinton 1868 child of AGER Walter C farmer b Franklin & CHAROLETT M b Hopkinton Vol: 4 Page: 61 Line: 002.

AGER Not Named b Hopkinton 1863-08-30 child of AGER Walter C farmer b Warner & Nana b Hopkinton Vol: 4 Page: 56 Line: 017.

ATKINS Lizzie b Hopkinton 1869-01-13 child of ATKINS Melvin painter b Hopkinton & HANNAH E b Hopkinton Vol: 4 Page: 61 Line: 018.

ATWATER Theadore b Hopkinton 1870-08-17 child of ATWATER Howell mechanic b New Haven Conn & Harriett b Phil Pa Vol: 4 Page: 63 Line: 008.

BACON Annie Laurie b Hopkinton 1875-03-20 child of BACON Henry mason b Contoocook & ANN P b Vol: 4 Page: 67 Line: 026.

BACON J A b Hopkinton 1859-06-05 child of BACON John N mason b Hopkinton & PLUMA Ann B b Hopkinton Vol: 4 Page: 52 Line: 007.

BAILEY Edson C b Hopkinton 1870-06-24 child of BAILEY Wm farmer b Hopkinton & Hattie b Vol: 4 Page: 63 Line: 004.

BAILEY William b Hopkinton 1878-07-25 child of BAILEY William farmer b Boston Mass & Annie b Vol: 4 Page: 71 Line: 005.

BAILEY Not Named b Hopkinton 1873-09-13 child of BAILEY W P b Boston Mass & Annie b Hopkinton Vol: 4 Page: 66 Line: 010.

BAKER Adella F b Hopkinton 1859-01-24 child of BAKER Charles E b Concord & MARY F b Concord Vol: 4 Page: 51 Line: 38.

BALCH Edward D b Hopkinton 1858-10-03 child of BALCH Theodore carpenter b Lyme & ELLEN N b Boscawen Vol: 4 Page: 51 Line: 021.

Hopkinton, NH Births 1858

BALCH Margie? b Hopkinton 1864-10-26 child of BALCH Theodore E carpenter b Lyme & ELLEN R b Boscawen Vol: 4 Page: 57 Line: 020.

BARBER Nora b Hopkinton 1858-08-06 child of BARBER Lewis laborer b St Albans Vt & MARIA W b Hopkinton Vol: 4 Page: 51 Line: 012.

BARNARD J Henry b Hopkinton 1860-10-25 child of BARNARD Joseph 2nd lumber dealer b Hopkinton & N G b Boscawen Vol: 4 Page: 53 Line: 028.

BARNARD Mary E b Hopkinton 1859-01-11 child of BARNARD Joseph Jr lumberman b Hopkinton & GERRISH Maria b Boscawen ** Vol: 4 Page: 51 Line: 36 Note: xx corrected birth certi Correction: ** Canterbury.

BARNARD Rhoda F b Hopkinton 1867-06-28 child of BARNARD Joseph Jr lumberman b Hopkinton & MARIA ** b Boscawen Vol: 4 Page: 60 Line: 022 Note: ** Maria Gerrish.

BARNARD Not Named b Hopkinton 1870-03-24 child of BARNARD Joseph lumberman b Hopkinton & Maria b Canterbury Vol: 4 Page: 62 Line: 013.

BARTON Not Named b Hopkinton 1866-05-25 child of BARTON Charles O farmer b Hopkinton & Philanda b Goshen Vol: 4 Page: 59 Line: 003.

BEAN Not Named b Hopkinton 1869-03-29 child of BEAN Darius K farmer b Meridith & Isabella b Hooksett Vol: 4 Page: 61 Line: 011.

BEAN Not Named b Hopkinton 1874-12-23 child of BEAN Gary b & Rapsey b Andover Vol: 4 Page: 67 Line: 022.

BISBIE Not Named b Loudon 1862 FEB 00 child of NO Farther ** farmer b & BISBIE Elisa b Hopkinton Vol: 4 Page: 55 Line: 017 Note: ** as record states.

BLAKE Albert H b Hopkinton 1871-11-24 child of BLAKE Charles H farmer b Hopkinton & ELLA F b Warner Vol: 4 Page: 64 Line: 014.

BLAKE Not Named b Hopkinton 1867-01-29 child of BLAKE John farmer b Canada East & Hannah b Loudon Vol: 4 Page: 59 Line: 025.

BOHONAN Barasia (Burnice) b Hopkinton 1877-03-15 child of BOHONAN John W farmer b Sutton & JEWELL Delia b Weare Vol: 4 Page: 69 Line: 018 Correction: vtr - Burnice - went by Bernice.

BOUTWELL Henry E b Berlin 1862-08-28 child of BOUTWELL Eli A shoemaker b Willimstown Vt & Harriett b Hopkinton Vol: 4 Page: 55 Line: 009.

BOUTWELL Not Named b Hopkinton 1867 child of BOUTWELL Eli A shoemaker b Berry Vt & Harriet b Hopkinton Vol: 4 Page: 59 Line: 028.

BOUTWELL Not Named b Hopkinton 1871-06-19 child of BOUTWELL Eli A farmer b Barre Vt & Harriett b Hopkinton Vol: 4 Page: 64 Line: 004.

BROCKWAY Etta A b Hopkinton 1861-10-10 child of BROCKWAY John G farmer b Wilmot & Amanada b Crydon Vol: 4 Page: 54 Line: 021.

BROCKWAY Not Named b Sutton 1860-02-24 child of BROCKWAY John G farmer b Wilton & Amanada b Croydon Vol: 4 Page: 52 Line: 033.

BROWN Charles b Hopkinton 1863-11-29 child of BROWN James P farmer b Boscawen & Mary b Hopkinton Vol: 4 Page: 56 Line: 028.

BROWN Charles N b Hopkinton 1864-05-28 child of BROWN Langdon farmer b Hopkinton & Catherine b Sutton Vol: 4 Page: 57 Line: 010.

BROWN Cora b Hopkinton 1859-05-20 child of BROWN Jonathan farmer b Hopkinton & Mary b Grantham Vol: 4 Page: 52 Line: 004.

Hopkinton, NH Births 1858

BROWN Elisa A b Hopkinton 1862-01-01 child of BROWN James P farmer b Boscawen & Mary b Hopkinton Vol: 4 Page: 54 Line: 030.

BROWN Frank O b Hopkinton 1858-12-19 child of BROWN James P farmer b Boscawen & Mary b Hopkinton Vol: 4 Page: 51 Line: 032.

BROWN Mary C b Hopkinton 1865-05-04 child of BROWN George farmer b Hopkinton & ROSETTA C b Hopkinton Vol: 4 Page: 58 Line: 003.

BROWN Not Named b Hopkinton 1874-10-07 child of Brown machinist b & LAFRONIA B b Vol: 4 Page: 67 Line: 017.

BURBANK Albert H b Hopkinton 1863-09-14 child of BURBANK Moses W shoemaker b Hopkinton & MARY F b Hopkinton Vol: 4 Page: 56 Line: 020.

BURBANK Francis A b Hopkinton 1861-03-09 child of BURBANK Moses W shoemaker b Hopkinton & Mary b Hopkinton Vol: 4 Page: 53 Line: 041.

BURBANK Lizzie E b Hopkinton 1860-06-05 child of BURBANK Wm P laborer b Hopkinton & Laura b Maine Vol: 4 Page: 53 Line: 010.

BURBANK Mary b Hopkinton 1864-09-01 child of BURBANK Matthew N laborer b Hopkinton & Eliza b Orange Vol: 4 Page: 57 Line: 015.

BURBANK Nella May b Hopkinton 1865-02-01 child of BURBANK Alonzo laorer b Hopkinton & Laura b Loudon Vol: 4 Page: 59 Line: 021.

BURBANK Rosina b Hopkinton 1862-01-24 child of BURBANK Matthew N farmer b Hopkinton & ELIZA N b Orange Vol: 4 Page: 54 Line: 031.

BURBANK Not Named b Hopkinton 1866-10-13 child of BURBANK Moses W laborer b Hopkinton & MARY F b Hopkinton Vol: 4 Page: 59 Line: 007.

BURKE Not Named b Hopkinton 1876-06-21 child of BURKE Will Vol: 4 Page: 69 Line: 009 Note: no other information.

BURNHAM Not Named b Hopkinton 1867-10-02 child of BURNHAM James lumberman b Hopkinton & Emma b Deerfield Vol: 4 Page: 60 Line: 23 Note: xx

BURNHAM Addie Lenoa b Hopkinton 1863-12-19 child of BURNHAM John F farmer b Hopkinton & SALIRA ?? b New Boston Vol: 4 Page: 56 Line: 034.

BURNHAM Almon?? b Hopkinton 1868-04-01 child of BURNHAM Christie clergyman b Bow & Frances b New Sharon Me Vol: 4 Page: 61 Line: 017.

BURNHAM Charles D b Hopkinton 1875-07-17 child of BURNHAM Edward D lumberman b Hopkinton & Georgia b Warner Vol: 4 Page: 68 Line: 003.

BURNHAM Grace L b Hopkinton 1859-12-02 child of BURNHAM Edward D farmer b Hopkinton & GEORGIA B b Warner Vol: 4 Page: 52 Line: 026.

BURNHAM Herbert B b Hopkinton 1859-04-07 child of BURNHAM John F farmer b Hopkinton & LATIRA W ?? b Antrim Vol: 4 Page: 52 Line: 027.

BURNHAM Samuel B b Hopkinton 1865-01-02 child of BURNHAM Christe W minister b Bow Vol: 4 Page: 57 Line: 025.

BURNHAM Walter M b Hopkinton 1861-10-23 child of BURNHAM James N farmer b Wilmot & EMMA F b Deeryfield Vol: 4 Page: 54 Line: 022.

BURNHAM Not Named b Hopkinton 1864 APR 00 child of BURNHAM Edward D miller b Hopkinton & Georgia b Warner Vol: 4 Page: 57 Line: 003.

BURNHAM Not Named b Hopkinton 1869 child of BURNHAM Edward D miller b Hopkinton & Georgia b Warner Vol: 4 Page: 61 Line: 006.

Hopkinton, NH Births 1858

BURTON Elroy C b Hopkinton 1862-01-01 child of BURTON Charles C farmer b Hopkinton & Claranna?? b Goshen Vol: 4 Page: 54 Line: 029.

BURTON Warren B b Hopkinton 1858-07-15 child of BURTON Charles C farmer b Hopkinton & Philinda b Goshen Vol: 4 Page: 51 Line: 010.

BUSWELL Not Named b Hopkinton 1867-03-17 child of BUSWELL Edward farmer b Hopkinton & Sarah b Canada Vol: 4 Page: 59 Line: 024.

BUSWELL Not Named b Hopkinton 1870-10-13 child of BUSWELL Smith farmer b Hopkinton & b Vol: 4 Page: 63 Line: 015.

BUTTERFIELD Arthur b Hopkinton 1860-10-28 child of BUTTERFIELD J C lumber dealer b Goffstown & ANNIE E b Warner Vol: 4 Page: 53 Line: 027.

CAMPBELL George b Hopkinton 1864-08-28 child of CAMPBELL Francis Jones farmer b Henniker & CAROLINE E b Hopkinton Vol: 4 Page: 57 Line: 014.

CAMPBELL Not Named b Hopkinton 1874-03-23 child of CAMPBELL Harry register b Hopkinton & Adeline b Hopkinton Vol: 4 Page: 66 Line: 022.

CARPENTER Susan b Hopkinton 1858-10-21 child of CARPENTER Guy farmer b Derby Vt & Mary b Hopkinton Vol: 4 Page: 51 Line: 023.

CARR Anna C b Hopkinton 1872-02-28 child of CARR Frank H mechanic b Hopkinton & MARY A b Hopkinton Vol: 4 Page: 64 Line: 019.

CARR John F b Hopkinton 1878-09-26 child of CARR Frank H lumberman b Hopkinton & MARY Ann b Henniker Vol: 4 Page: 71 Line: 020.

CARR Lucy Clara b Hopkinton 1876-09-05 child of CARR Frank H lumberman b Hopkinton & MARY Ann b Henniker Vol: 4 Page: 69 Line: 021.

CARR Thomas William b Hopkinton 1873-09-08 child of CARR Frank H lumber-man b Hopkinton & MARY Ann b Henniker Vol: 4 Page: 66 Line: 025 Correction: see line 12 also.

CARR William Thomas b Hopkinton 1873-10-08 child of CARR Frank H mechanic b Hopkinton & MARY A b Hopkinton Vol: 4 Page: 66 Line: 012 Correction: see line 25 also.

CARTER Jessie E b Hopkinton 1877-08-29 child of CARTER William C F farmer b Concord & Josephine b Bath Ny Vol: 4 Page: 70 Line: 007.

CARTER Martha E b Hopkinton 1861-03-03 child of CARTER Augustine farmer b Concord & SARAH E b Concord Vol: 4 Page: 53 Line: 040.

CAVENNO (#) b Hopkinton 1860-04-06 child of CAVENNO Arthur farmer b Ireland & Bridgett b Ireland Vol: 4 Page: 53 Line: 003.

CAVENNO Julette b Hopkinton 1860-04-06 child of CAVENNO Arthur farmer b Ireland & Bridgett b Ireland Vol: 4 Page: 53 Line: 002.

CHAMBERLAIN Not Named b Hopkinton 1871-02-12 child of CHAMBERLAIN James butcher b Maine & b Hopkinton Vol: 4 Page: 63 Line: 032.

CHANDLER Annie M b Hopkinton 1871-11-01 child of CHANDLER Henry brakeman b Boston Mass & Eliza b Wales Vol: 4 Page: 64 Line: 011.

CHANDLER Delta E b Hopkinton 1864-09-15 child of CHANDLER Horatio J farmer b Hopkinton & SUSAN V b Hopkinton Vol: 4 Page: 57 Line: 016.

CHANDLER Dolly Etta b Hopkinton 1867-06-04 child of CHANDLER Horatio farmer b Hopkinton & Susan b Hopkinton Vol: 4 Page: 60 Line: 014.

CHANDLER Henry Clarence b Hopkinton 1870-09-17 child of CHANDLER Horatio laborer b Hopkinton & Susan b Hopkinton Vol: 4 Page: 63 Line: 013.

Hopkinton, NH Births 1858

CHANDLER Isaac S b Hopkinton 1860-06-07 child of CHANDLER Isaac N gentleman b Mass & Caroline b Winthrop Me Vol: 4 Page: 53 Line: 011.

CHANDLER Orin N b Hopkinton 1858-05-30 child of CHANDLER Horatio J shoemaker b Hopkinton & SUSAN V b Hopkinton Vol: 4 Page: 51 Line: 003.

CHANDLER Susie M b Hopkinton 1860-06-26 child of CHANDLER Horatio shoemaker b Hopkinton & SUSAN C b Hopkinton Vol: 4 Page: 53 Line: 015.

CHANDLER Not Named b Hopkinton 1873-02-02 child of CHANDLER Horatio J farmer b Hopkinton & SUSAN V b Hopkinton Vol: 4 Page: 65 Line: 020.

CHASE Alden M b Hopkinton 1870-09-22 child of CHASE David farmer b Hopkinton & Clara b Hopkinton Vol: 4 Page: 63 Line: 022.

CHASE Alden N b Hopkinton 1871-09-08 child of CHASE David N laborer b Hopkinton & CLARA A b Hopkinton Vol: 4 Page: 64 Line: 010.

CHASE Fred b Hopkinton 1870-11-06 child of CHASE Orrin farmer b Hopkinton & Hattie b Warner Vol: 4 Page: 63 Line: 020.

CHASE Fred Harvey b Hopkinton 1868 child of CHASE Harvey farmer b Hopkinton & MARTHA Jane b Concord Vol: 4 Page: 61 Line: 001.

CHASE Harry A b Hopkinton 1871-11-19 child of CHASE Orrin A farmer b Hopkinton & Hattie b Warner Vol: 4 Page: 64 Line: 013.

CHASE Hattie b Hopkinton 00 SEP 1860 child of CHASE Edward laborer b Hopkinton & MARY A b Hopkinton Vol: 4 Page: 53 Line: 023.

CHASE Ida Frances b Hopkinton 1875-06-13 child of CHASE Lucuis E farmer b Hopkinton & Lucy?? b Antrim Vol: 4 Page: 68 Line: 002.

CHASE Joseph S b Hopkinton 1860-03-12 child of CHASE Reginald lawyer b Hopkinton & Susan b Hopkinton Vol: 4 Page: 52 Line: 022.

CHASE Lucinda F b Hopkinton 1877-12-13 child of CHASE Cyrus F laborer b Hopkinton & ELLA F b Warner Vol: 4 Page: 70 Line: 016.

CHASE Martha b Hopkinton 1870-12-06 child of CHASE Harvey farmer b Hopkinton & Martha b Concord Vol: 4 Page: 63 Line: 026.

CHASE Samuel A b Hopkinton 1872-02-01 child of CHASE Frank B ferrier b Hopkinton & Annie b Hopkinton Vol: 4 Page: 64 Line: 018.

CHASE Not Named b Hopkinton 1859-03-30 child of CHASE Horace J b Hopkinton & MARY A b Beverley Mass Vol: 4 Page: 51 Line: 43.

CHASE Not Named b Hopkinton 1874-08-31 child of CHASE Orrin laborer b Contoocook & Hattie b Warner Vol: 4 Page: 67 Line: 011.

CLARK Allaton b Hopkinton 1862-05-16 child of CLARK Jonathan G farmer b Hopkinton & Caroline b Hopkinton Vol: 4 Page: 55 Line: 003.

CLARK Fred b Hopkinton 1860-05-29 child of CLARK Benjamin N laborer b Warner & MARY J b Hopkinton Mass Vol: 4 Page: 53 Line: 009.

CLARK Henry b Hopkinton 1859-09-04 child of CLARK Jonathan G laborer b Warner & Caroline b Hopkinton Vol: 4 Page: 52 Line: 028.

CLARK Lilla b Hopkinton 1864-07-30 child of CLARK Benjamin laborer b Warner & MARY Jane b Vol: 4 Page: 57 Line: 012.

CLEMONS Charlott C b Hopkinton 1862-02-09 child of CLEMONS Henry W shoemaker b Salem Mass & BETSEY S b Hopkinton Vol: 4 Page: 54 Line: 032.

Hopkinton, NH Births 1858

CLEMONS Sarah P b Hopkinton 1859-03-17 child of CLEMONS Henry b Salem Mass & BETSY D b Hopkinton Vol: 4 Page: 51 Line: 42.

CLOUGH Alice Marie b Hopkinton 1875 child of CLOUGH Willie E farmer b Hopkinton & CLARA A b Essex Mass Vol: 4 Page: 68 Line: 013.

CLOUGH Charles Edgar b Hopkinton 1863-08-07 child of CLOUGH Charles mechanic b Hopkinton & MARY J b Warner Vol: 4 Page: 56 Line: 015.

CLOUGH Ellen O b Hopkinton 1878 child of CLOUGH Moses farmer b Hopkinton & MARY O b Candia Vol: 4 Page: 70 Line: 022.

CLOUGH Flora b Hopkinton 1861-06-23 child of CLOUGH Charles F farmer b Hopkinton & MARY J b Warner Vol: 4 Page: 54 Line: 007.

CLOUGH Josephine E b Hopkinton 1870-10-12 child of CLOUGH Charles farmer b Hopkinton & Mary b Warner Vol: 4 Page: 63 Line: 014.

CLOUGH Levi W b Hopkinton 1863-07-17 child of CLOUGH Moses farmer b Hopkinton & Mary b Candia Vol: 4 Page: 56 Line: 012.

CLOUGH Mary E b Hopkinton 1858-12-10 child of CLOUGH Charles F joiner b Hopkinton & MARY M b Hopkinton Vol: 4 Page: 51 Line: 030.

CLOUGH Mary R b Hopkinton 1872-06-24 child of CLOUGH Moses farmer b Hopkinton & Mary b Candia Vol: 4 Page: 65 Line: 004.

CLOUGH Rachel Maria b Hopkinton 1865-11-01 child of CLOUGH Charles F carpenter b Hopkinton & MARY J b Warner Vol: 4 Page: 58 Line: 013.

CLOUGH Not Named b Hopkinton 1868-12-15 child of CLOUGH Moses farmer b Hopkinton & MARY O b Candia Vol: 4 Page: 61 Line: 004.

CLOUGH Not Named b Hopkinton 1873-06-01 child of CLOUGH Willey carpenter b Hopkinton & CLARA A b Manchester Vol: 4 Page: 66 Line: 009.

COLBY Fred Henry b Hopkinton 1865-07-11 child of COLBY Melvin painter b Hopkinton & Hannah b Hopkinton Vol: 4 Page: 58 Line: 008.

COLBY Herman P b Hopkinton 1863-04-30 child of COLBY Melvin painter b Hopkinton & Hannah b Hopkinton Vol: 4 Page: 56 Line: 005.

COLBY Melvin Crawford b Hopkinton 1860-11-24 child of COLBY Melvin farmer b Hopkinton & HANNAH P b Hopkinton Vol: 4 Page: 53 Line: 032.

COLBY Melvin F b Hopkinton 1871-09-12 child of COLBY Melvin painter b Hopkinton & Hannah b Warner Vol: 4 Page: 64 Line: 009.

COLBY Nettie L b Hopkinton 1865-11-13 child of COLBY Samuel H laborer b Hopkinton & LOUISA F b Concord Vol: 4 Page: 58 Line: 015.

COLBY Richard F b Hopkinton 1858-09-07 child of COLBY Samuel W laborer b Hopkinton & Lucinda b Hopkinton Vol: 4 Page: 51 Line: 016.

COLBY Not Named b Hopkinton 1858-12-07 child of COLBY Melvin painter b Hopkinton & Hannah b Hopkinton Vol: 4 Page: 51 Line: 029.

COLBY Not Named b Hopkinton 1867-03-04 child of COLBY Melvin farmer b Hopkinton & Hannah b Hopkinton Vol: 4 Page: 59 Line: 031.

COLLINS George Augustus b Hopkinton 1863-12-14 child of COLLINS Proctor solidier b Bradford & LUCY Ann b Warner Vol: 4 Page: 56 Line: 032.

CONNER Charles N b Hopkinton 1872-09-24 child of CONNER James farmer b Henniker & JUDITH W b Hopkinton Vol: 4 Page: 65 Line: 010.

CONNER Grace E b Hopkinton 1874-08-30 child of CONNER James farmer b Warner & Judith b Hopkinton Vol: 4 Page: 67 Line: 010.

Hopkinton, NH Births 1858

CONNER Laura b Hopkinton 1859-06-02 child of CONNER Harlow carpenter b Hopkinton & Oleomin b Warner Vol: 4 Page: 52 Line: 024.

CONNER Maria Putney b Hopkinton 1862-09-20 child of CONNER James N farmer b Henniker & Judith b Hopkinton Vol: 4 Page: 55 Line: 011.

CONNOR Not Named b Hopkinton 1866-03-15 child of CONNOR James N farmer b Henniker & Judith b Hopkinton Vol: 4 Page: 58 Line: 022.

COOPER Eugene b Hopkinton 1877-02-05 child of COOPER Joseph farmer b Sunapee & Augusta b Concord Vol: 4 Page: 70 Line: 002.

COOPER Joseph ** b Hopkinton 1877-02-05 child of COOPER Joseph farmer b Sunapee & Augusta b Concord Vol: 4 Page: 69 Line: 014 Correction: see page 70 line 2.

CORLIS Charles N b Hopkinton 1860-10-04 child of CORLIS Elbridge G farmer b Boscawen & Amanda b Hopkinton Vol: 4 Page: 53 Line: 024.

CORLIS Freddie Elmer b Hopkinton 1863-09-04 child of CORLIS Elbridge G mechanic b Boscawen & MARY Jane b Methuen Mass Vol: 4 Page: 56 Line: 018.

CORLIS Mary F b Hopkinton 1858-12-03 child of CORLIS Elbridge G farmer b Boscawen & AMANDA M b Hopkinton Vol: 4 Page: 51 Line: 027.

CROWELL Albert R b Hopkinton 1873-04-09 child of CROWELL Samuel E laborer b Hopkinton & LUCY A b Hopkinton Vol: 4 Page: 66 Line: 003.

CROWELL George Henry b Hopkinton 1861-12-05 child of CROWELL Henry N laborer b Hopkinton & Lucinda b Concord Vol: 4 Page: 54 Line: 025.

CROWELL Lewis Albert b Hopkinton 1870-10-26 child of CROWELL Henry farmer b Hopkinton & Lucinda b Concord Vol: 4 Page: 63 Line: 017.

CROWELL Lillian L b Hopkinton 1877-08-30 child of CROWELL Henry H farmer b Hopkinton & Melinda b Bow Vol: 4 Page: 70 Line: 008.

CROWELL Margarette b Hopkinton 1859-07-24 child of CROWELL Henry farmer b Hopkinton & Lucinda b Concord Vol: 4 Page: 52 Line: 014.

CROWELL Oliver W b Hopkinton 1858-06-30 child of CROWELL Albert farmer b Hopkinton & Lydia b Hopkinton Vol: 4 Page: 51 Line: 006.

CROWELL Not Named b Hopkinton 1862-03-24 child of CROWELL Joseph laborer b Hopkinton & Nancy b Plainfield Vol: 4 Page: 54 Line: 037 Note: ?? twins.

CROWELL Not Named b Hopkinton 1862-03-24 child of CROWELL Joseph laborer b Hopkinton & Nancy b Plainfield Vol: 4 Page: 54 Line: 036.

CROWELL Not Named b Hopkinton 1864-03-16 child of CROWELL Joseph farmer b Hopkinton & MARY B b Plainfield Vol: 4 Page: 57 Line: 031.

CROWELL Not Named b Hopkinton 1873-10-30 child of CROWELL Henry H farmer b Hopkinton & Lucinda b Concord Vol: 4 Page: 66 Line: 013.

CURRENETT Mary N b Hopkinton 1870-11-29 child of CURRENETT?? George farmer b & Helen b Hopkinton Vol: 4 Page: 63 Line: 021.

CURRIER Charles C b Hopkinton 1865-07-08 child of CURRIER John F farmer b Hopkinton & ELLEN N b Hopkinton Vol: 4 Page: 58 Line: 006.

CURRIER Ester Elizabeth b Hopkinton 1859-09-17 child of CURRIER George W farmer b Hopkinton & HANNAH F b Hopkinton Vol: 4 Page: 52 Line: 009.

Hopkinton, NH Births 1858

CURRIER George A b Hopkinton 1874-10-02 child of CURRIER Loren stage driver b Concord & MARY A b Hopkinton Vol: 4 Page: 67 Line: 015.

CURRIER John Jr b Hopkinton 1867-09-27 child of CURRIER John F farmer b Hopkinton & Ellen b Hopkinton Vol: 4 Page: 60 Line: 024.

CURRIER John Jr b Hopkinton 1868-09-27 child of CURRIER John F farmer b Hopkinton & Ellen b Hopkinton Vol: 4 Page: 60 Line: 015.

CURRIER Linnie B b Hopkinton 1871-08-25 child of CURRIER Loren stage driver b Concord & MARY Ann b Hopkinton Vol: 4 Page: 64 Line: 007.

CURRIER Mary E b Hopkinton 1867-07-15 child of CURRIER Lozaro farmer b Hopkinton & Annie b Ireland Vol: 4 Page: 60 Line: 011.

CURRIER Mary Morgan b Hopkinton 1861-12-24 child of CURRIER John F farmer b Hopkinton & NETTA N b Hopkinton Vol: 4 Page: 54 Line: 027.

CURRIER True P b Hopkinton 1872-04-06 child of CURRIER John F farmer b Hopkinton & NELLIE N b Hopkinton Vol: 4 Page: 65 Line: 001.

CURRIER Willie A b Hopkinton 1860-12-05 child of CURRIER Lozaro farmer b Hopkinton & ANNIE C b Europe-sweden Vol: 4 Page: 53 Line: 035.

CURRIER Not Named b Hopkinton 1877-03-14 child of CURRIER Loren farmer b & MARY A b Hopkinton Vol: 4 Page: 69 Line: 017.

CURTIS Delbert b Hopkinton 1864-10-06 child of CURTIS Isaiah B laborer b Lyneborough & MARY Jane b Lyndborough Vol: 4 Page: 57 Line: 018.

CURTIS Vada Ann b Lyneborough 1863-06-20 child of CURTIS Isaiah B farmer b Lyndeborough & MARY Jane b Lyndeborough Vol: 4 Page: 56 Line: 010.

DANFORTH Charles B b Hopkinton 1861-05-04 child of farmer b Dunbarton & DANFORTH Sara b Hopkinton Vol: 4 Page: 54 Line: 003.

DANFORTH Edmund G b Hopkinton 1874-03-23 child of DANFORTH Enoch farmer b Webster & Lydia b Henniker Vol: 4 Page: 66 Line: 021.

DANFORTH Edward b Hopkinton 1863-04-03 child of DANFORD Erastrus blacksmith b Weare & MARY S b Hopkinton Vol: 4 Page: 56 Line: 001.

DANFORTH Estella F b Hopkinton 1866-09-25 child of DANFORTH Henry C mechanic b Hopkinton & Marietta b Crydon Vol: 4 Page: 59 Line: 020.

DANFORTH Fred V b Hopkinton 1878-12-21 child of DANFORTH Fred farmer b Hopkinton & b Canada Vol: 4 Page: 71 Line: 013.

DANFORTH George N b Hopkinton 1858-07-08 child of DANFORTH John blacksmith b Weare & J A b Corinth Vt Vol: 4 Page: 51 Line: 008.

DANFORTH Herbert b Hopkinton 1864-11-02 child of DANFORD John solider b Henniker & ELLEN M b Canada Vol: 4 Page: 57 Line: 021.

DANFORTH Mary Lilian b Hopkinton 1861-05-04 child of farmer b Dunbarton & DANFORTH Sara b Hopkinton Vol: 4 Page: 54 Line: 003 Note: twin.

DANIELS Mary Bell b Hopkinton 1860-04-17 child of DANIELS George S farmer b Brookiline & SARAH J b Hopkinton Vol: 4 Page: 53 Line: 005.

DANIELS Nettie M b Hopkinton 1858-06-15 child of DANIELS George S farmer b Brooklyne & SARAH C b Hopkinton Vol: 4 Page: 51 Line: 004.

DAVIS Charles b Hopkinton 1874-10-14 child of DAVIS Walter L paper hana fac b Warner & DOLLY J b Warner Vol: 4 Page: 67 Line: 019.

DAVIS Charles C b Hopkinton 1860-04-13 child of DAVIS Amos farmer b Hopkinton & BETSEY A b Bradford Vol: 4 Page: 53 Line: 004.

Hopkinton, NH Births 1858

DAVIS George C b Hopkinton 1858-08-25 child of DAVIS George W shoemaker b Meridith & ROSETTA M b Orange Vol: 4 Page: 51 Line: 013.

DAVIS Henry B b Hopkinton 1858-09-14 child of DAVIS Amos farmer b Hopkinton & Betsey b Hopkinton Vol: 4 Page: 51 Line: 017.

DAY George H b Hopkinton 1868-01-13 child of DAY Henry C farmer b Weare & Lucy b Merrimack Vol: 4 Page: 59 Line: 006.

DEARBORN Alfred N b Hopkinton 1876-02-17 child of DEARBORN Lewis N farmer b Epsom & ELVIRA C b Weare Vol: 4 Page: 68 Line: 009.

DEARBORN Bertha b Hopkinton 1872-05-18 child of DEARBORN Lewis N farmer b Epsom & ELOUISE E b Weare Vol: 4 Page: 65 Line: 003.

DERRY Not Named b Hopkinton 1879-01-31 child of DERRY Joseph blacksmith b & Julia b Ireland Vol: 4 Page: 71 Line: 015.

DIAMOND Fred A b Hopkinton 1859-01-20 child of DIAMOND Asa jack of all trades b Concord & LUCY N b Hopkinton Vol: 4 Page: 52 Line: 030 Note: date xx.

DODGE Emma F b Hopkinton 1860-12-26 child of DODGE Jonathan farmer b Hopkinton & Jerusha b Meridith Vol: 4 Page: 53 Line: 036.

DODGE Grover W b Hopkinton 1871-06-04 child of DODGE William farmer b Hopkinton & Martha b Meridith Vol: 4 Page: 64 Line: 003.

DODGE Helen b Hopkinton 1863-05-20 child of DODGE Addison farmer b Maine & MARY E b Maine Vol: 4 Page: 56 Line: 009.

DODGE Henry b Hopkinton 1863-01-02 child of DODGE Moses E farmer b Hopkinton & ABBIE A b Hopkinton Vol: 4 Page: 55 Line: 016.

DODGE Lewis E b Hopkinton 1863-10-25 child of DODGE William farmer b Hopkinton & Martha b New Hampton Vol: 4 Page: 56 Line: 024.

DOW Josephine b Hopkinton 1859-12-14 child of DOW George L farmer b Hopkinton & Henretta b Concord Vol: 4 Page: 52 Line: 008.

DOW Samuel Oscar b Hopkinton 1862-06-30 child of DOW Samuel H farmer b Concord & Sarah b Hopkinton Vol: 4 Page: 55 Line: 005.

DOW Sarah Jane b Hopkinton 1860-08-31 child of DOW Joseph P farmer b Henniker & Eliza b Weare Vol: 4 Page: 53 Line: 021.

DOWNING Henry N b Hopkinton 1859-03-31 child of DOWNING Josiah farmer b Ellsworth & Georgianna b Hopkinton Vol: 4 Page: 52 Line: 015.

DOWNS Charles M b Hopkinton 1871-08-17 child of DOWNES John mechanic b Manchester & Mary b Hopkinton Vol: 4 Page: 64 Line: 006.

DREW Carrie E b Hopkinton 1876-10-18 child of DREW George A laborer b Allenstown & O J b Pembroke Vol: 4 Page: 69 Line: 011.

DUNBAR Carrie Bailey b Hopkinton 1861-12-28 child of DUNBAR Elmer B joiner b Grantham & ANN J b Hopkinton Vol: 4 Page: 54 Line: 028.

DUNBAR Elmer E b Hopkinton 1864-05-18 child of DUNBAR Elmer B carpenter b Grantham & Ann b Hopkinton Vol: 4 Page: 57 Line: 009.

DUNBAR Flora b Hopkinton 1861-01-06 child of DUNBAR Justis A farmer b Hopkinton & MARY N b Orange Vol: 4 Page: 53 Line: 037.

DUNBAR George E b Hopkinton 1867-10-04 child of DUNBAR Elmer B mechanic b Grantham & Ann b Hopkinton Vol: 4 Page: 60 Line: 004.

Hopkinton, NH Births 1858

DUNBAR Grace Wanda b Hopkinton 1874-08-20 child of DUNBAR Elmer carpenter b Granthamn & ANN L b Hopkinton Vol: 4 Page: 67 Line: 005.

DUNBAR Henry F b Hopkinton 1858-04-26 child of DUNBAR Elmer B farmer b & ANN J b Hopkinton Vol: 4 Page: 51 Line: 002.

DUNBAR Ida E b Hopkinton 1870-12-11 child of DUNBAR Elmer B insurance agt b Hopkinton & ANN T b Perry City Ny Vol: 4 Page: 63 Line: 035.

DWINELLS Georgiannie b Hopkinton 1858-08-30 child of DWINELLS John G farmer b Dunbarton & NOT Given b Henniker Vol: 4 Page: 51 Line: 014.

DWINELLS Rosilla b Hopkinton 1863-03-15 child of DWINELLS Warren P laborer b Dunbarton & CAROLINE N b Hopkinton Vol: 4 Page: 55 Line: 018.

DWINELLS Not Named b Hopkinton 1868-03-14 child of DWINELLS John G laborer b Dunbarton & Matilda b Hopkinton Vol: 4 Page: 60 Line: 017.

DWINNELLS Arthur B b Hopkinton 1876-06-12 child of DWINELLS John G laborer b Hopkinton & CARRIE M b Vol: 4 Page: 69 Line: 004.

DWINNELLS Charles W b Hopkinton 1861-08-22 child of DWINELLS John G laborer b Dunbarton & SARAH A b Henniker Vol: 4 Page: 54 Line: 012.

DWINNELLS Emma Frances b Hopkinton 1864-04-29 child of DWINNELLS John laborer b Dunbarton & Sarah b Henniker Vol: 4 Page: 57 Line: 006.

DWINNELLS Frank Orlando* b Hopkinton 1871-05-25 child of DWINNELLS John G laborer b Bow & CARRIE M b Hopkinton Vol: 4 Page: 64 Line: 002 Correction: ** changed to Frank Pierce.

DWINNELLS Not Named b Hopkinton 1860-03-27 child of DWINELLS John S laborer b Dunbarton & Sarah b Henniker Vol: 4 Page: 52 Line: 021.

DWINNELLS Not Named b Hopkinton 1866-01-24 child of DWINNELLS John b Hopkinton & CLARA Matilda b Hopkinton Vol: 4 Page: 58 Line: 017.

DWINNELLS Not Named b Hopkinton 1873-09-02 child of DWINNELLS John laborer b Henniker & Matilda b Hopkinton Vol: 4 Page: 66 Line: 019.

DWINNELLS Not Named b Hopkinton 1878-09-09 child of DWINNELLS John laborer b Hopkinton & Matilda b Hopkinton Vol: 4 Page: 71 Line: 009.

EASTMAN Henry b Hopkinton 1864-03-20 child of EASTMAN Walter C farmer b Hopkinton & Helen b Hopkinton Vol: 4 Page: 57 Line: 032.

EATON Irvin H b Hopkinton 1864-09-30 child of EATON William clergman b Hopkinton & MARY J b Hopkinton Vol: 4 Page: 58 Line: 001.

EATON Nellie Nina b Hopkinton 1862-08-14 child of EATON William H rancher b Hopkinton & MARY J b Hopkinton Vol: 4 Page: 55 Line: 008.

EDMUNDS Harry b Hopkinton 1871-02-01 child of EDMUNDS Harry farmer b Hopkinton & Marrion b Hopkinton Vol: 4 Page: 63 Line: 031.

ELLIOT Lennie J b Hopkinton 1866-08-20 child of ELLIOT Joseph R farmer b Boscawen & ANEGELINE P b Bow Vol: 4 Page: 59 Line: 004.

ELLIOT Not Named b Hopkinton 1869-01-16 child of ELLIOT Joseph R farmer b Concord & Angeline b Danville Vol: 4 Page: 61 Line: 014.

ELLIOTT Ernest E b Hopkinton 1877-09-17 child of ELLIOT Edson E farmer b Boscawen & ANNETTE C b Deering Vol: 4 Page: 70 Line: 011.

ELLIOTT Marcia b Hopkinton 1872-12-03 child of ELLIOTT George W farmer b Grafton & Ellen b Dunbarton Vol: 4 Page: 65 Line: 013.

Hopkinton, NH Births 1858

ELLIOTT Not Named b Hopkinton 1874-08-27 child of ELLIOTT Joseph R farmer b Boscawen & Angeline b Bow Vol: 4 Page: 67 Line: 009.

EMERSON Annie Maude b Hopkinton 1874-10-14 child of EMERSON Hanson D laborer b Hopkinton & Mary b Hopkinton Vol: 4 Page: 67 Line: 018.

EMERSON Bertie F b Hopkinton 1873-02-04 child of EMERSON Stephen D farmer b Deerfield & CLARA C b Concord Vol: 4 Page: 65 Line: 016.

EMERSON Blanche Mabel b Hopkinton 1877-09-04 child of EMERSON Hanson D laborer b Hopkinton & MARY M b Hopkinton Vol: 4 Page: 70 Line: 009.

EMERSON George Arthur b Hopkinton 1872-02-18 child of EMERSON Hanson D farmer b Hopkinton & M F b Hopkinton Vol: 4 Page: 64 Line: 020.

EMERSON Not Named b Hopkinton 1871-09-10 child of EMERSON Hanson laborer b Hopkinton & Mary b Hopkinton Vol: 4 Page: 63 Line: 012.

EVANS Henry C b Hopkinton 1866-11-02 child of EVANS Simeon A physican b Fryburg Me & Louisia b Fryburg Me Vol: 4 Page: 59 Line: 010.

FAGAN Christopher b Hopkinton 1860-08-18 child of FAGAN John laborer b Ireland & Margarett b Ireland Vol: 4 Page: 53 Line: 019.

FAGAN Eliza J b Hopkinton 1859-01-07 child of FAGAN John farmer b Ireland & FAGAN M b   Vol: 4 Page: 51 Line: 34.

FAGAN John b Hopkinton 1861-11-02 child of FAGAN John laborer b Ireland & Margarette b   Vol: 4 Page: 54 Line: 024.

FELLOWS Frank William b Hopkinton 1872-01-06 child of FELLOWS Charles clerk b Hopkinton & Maria b Bath Vol: 4 Page: 64 Line: 017.

FELLOWS Hellen b Hopkinton 1860-05-05 child of FELLOWS James merchant b Salisbury & Jane b Salisbury Vol: 4 Page: 52 Line: 023.

FELLOWS John Henry b Hopkinton 1861-07-08 child of FELLOWS James trader b Salisbury & Jenie b Sutton Vol: 4 Page: 54 Line: 009.

FERRIN Clara b Hopkinton 1859-01-20 child of FERRIN Freeman   b Concord & Harriet b Warner Vol: 4 Page: 51 Line: 037.

FERRIN Wilis C?? b Sutton 1863-04-24 child of FERRIN Caleb B farmer b Hopkinton & SARAH W b Canterbury Vol: 4 Page: 56 Line: 004

FISK Ida b Hopkinton 1861-01-26 child of FISK Daniel farmer b Hopkinton & LYDIA A b Meridith Vol: 4 Page: 53 Line: 039.

FLANDERS Albert b Hopkinton 1876-08-21 child of FLANDERS Ashael laborer b Hopkinton & Ellen b Salisbury Vol: 4 Page: 69 Line: 007.

FLANDERS Cora M b Hopkinton 1858-12-22 child of FLANDERS Sullivan farmer b Hopkintin & FLANDERS N M b Henniker Vol: 4 Page: 51 Line: 033.

FLANDERS Edith E b Hopkinton 1877-03-09 child of FLANDERS Frank N farmer b Hopkinton & Maria b Hopkinton Vol: 4 Page: 69 Line: 016.

FLANDERS Lewis C b Hopkinton 1858-09-04 child of FLANDERS Charles C laborer b Boscawen & ADALINE F b Concord Vol: 4 Page: 51 Line: 015.

FLANDERS Parker b Hopkinton 1862-08-03 child of FLANDERS Parker M farmer b Hopkinton & ANNA C b Henniker Vol: 4 Page: 55 Line: 007.

FLANDERS Rhoda b Hopkinton 1862-03-25 child of FLANDERS Charles C laborer b Boscawen & Adaline b Concord Vol: 4 Page: 54 Line: 039.

FLANDERS Walter H b Hopkinton 1864-04-03 child of FLANDERS Benjamin farmer b Hopkinton & Melissa b Henniker Vol: 4 Page: 56 Line: 002 Note: xx date // 63/64.

FLANDERS Willie A b Hopkinton 1858-09-16 child of FLANDERS Andrew J shoemaker b Warner & Hannah b Concord Vol: 4 Page: 51 Line: 018.

FLANDERS Not Named b Hopkinton 1862-03-25 child of FLANDERS Charles C laborer b Boscawen & Adaline b Concord Vol: 4 Page: 53 Line: 038.

FOGGS Frank Emunmond b Hopkinton 1859-08-11 child of FOGGS Sherburn farmer/carpen b Meridith & Miriam b Hopkinton Vol: 4 Page: 52 Line: 034.

FOSS Angie Grace b Hopkinton 1858-07-15 child of FOSS Charles W shoemaker b Strafford & ANGELINE D b Orange Vol: 4 Page: 51 Line: 009.

FOSS Lucy Elvira b Hopkinton 1877-09-17 child of FOSS George E farmer b Hopkinton & EMMA A b Phil Pa Vol: 4 Page: 70 Line: 010.

FRENCH Adams Clark b Hopkinton 1861-06-21 child of FRENCH Thomas Scott faarmer b Hopknton & MARY Elizabet b Franklin Vol: 4 Page: 54 Line: 006 Note: twin.

FRENCH Abbie Aususta b Hopkinton 1859-12-03 child of FRENCH Thomas Scott farmer b Hopkinton & SARAH E b Franklin Vol: 4 Page: 52 Line: 011.

FRENCH Alice C b Hopkinton 1858-12-01 child of FRENCH Oliver N farmer b Henniker & JULIA A b Bedford Vol: 4 Page: 51 Line: 026.

FRENCH Anna L b Hopkinton 1863-11-12 child of FRENCH Sulivan farmer b Hopkinton & ALMIRA S b Chichester Vol: 4 Page: 56 Line: 025.

FRENCH Augustin b Hopkinton 1861-03-23 child of FRENCH George W farmer b Hopkinton & Hellen b Boscawen Vol: 4 Page: 53 Line: 0042.

FRENCH Charles E L b Hopkinton 1860-06-26 child of FRENCH Edward D butcher b Hopkinton & Jennie b Hopkinton Vol: 4 Page: 53 Line: 016.

FRENCH Clara M b Hopkinton 1877-11-28 child of FRENCH Edward D butcher b Hopkinton & Jennie b So Boston Mass Vol: 4 Page: 70 Line: 015.

FRENCH Clarence b Hopkinton 1867-11-11 child of FRENCH Edward D butcher b Hopkinton & Jane b Boston Mass Vol: 4 Page: 60 Line: 008.

FRENCH Edward Chase b Hopkinton 1870-03-08 child of FRENCH Edward D butcher b Hopkinton & Jennie b Boston Mass Vol: 4 Page: 62 Line: 011.

FRENCH Edwin Jeremiah b Hopkinton 1861-06-21 child of FRENCH Thomas Scott farmer b Hopkinton & MARY Elizabet b Franklin Vol: 4 Page: 54 Line: 005.

FRENCH Emma G b Hopkinton 1859-01-11 child of FRENCH Edward D b Hopkinton & JENNIE L b Boston Mass Vol: 4 Page: 51 Line: 35.

FRENCH George B b Hopkinton 1863-07-31 child of FRENCH Charles farmer b Hopkinton & Sarah b Concord Vol: 4 Page: 56 Line: 014.

FRENCH Grace A b Hopkinton 1858-06-20 child of FRENCH T S farmer b Hopkinton & SARAH E b Franklin Vol: 4 Page: 51 Line: 005.

FRENCH Henry B b Hopkinton 1863-07-31 child of FRENCH Charles farmer b Hopkinton & Sarah b Concord Vol: 4 Page: 56 Line: 014.

FRENCH Herbert b Hopkinton 1873-04-23 child of FRENCH Edward D butcher b Hopkinton & Janice b Boston Mass Vol: 4 Page: 66 Line: 024.

FRENCH Kate Pearl b Hopkinton 1867-05-23 child of FRENCH Oliver N farmer b Henniker & Julia b Bedford Vol: 4 Page: 59 Line: 030.

FRENCH Sarah Jane b Hopkinton 1862-11-11 child of FRENCH Oliver N farmer b Henniker & JULIA Ann b Bedford Vol: 4 Page: 55 Line: 013.

FRENCH Not Named b Hopkinton 1868 child of FRENCH C C farmer b & Fedora b Hopkinton Vol: 4 Page: 61 Line: 007.

FROST Abbie b Hopkinton 1863-09-19 child of FROST Franklin butcher b Glover Vt & Martha b Hopkinton Vol: 4 Page: 56 Line: 021.

FULLER Cora G b Hopkinton 1864-04-03 child of FULLER Henry M trader b Francestown & Jennie b Topsham Vt Vol: 4 Page: 57 Line: 002.

FULLER Della J b Hopkinton 1872-08-10 child of FULLER George L farmer b Nashua & Jennie b Wilmot Vol: 4 Page: 65 Line: 006.

FULLER Willie Francis** b Hopkinton 1875-07-25 child of FULLER John A mechanic b Bridgewater & Julia b Hopkinton Vol: 4 Page: 68 Line: 004 Note: **changed to William F Correction: per court order.

GAGE Edith N b Hopkinton 1867-12-24 child of GAGE David L merchant b Hopkinton & Emily b Hillsboro Vol: 4 Page: 60 Line: 005.

GAGE Edward b Hopkinton 1864-02-27 child of GAGE David L farmer b Hopkinton & Emily b Hillsborough Vol: 4 Page: 56 Line: 039.

GAGE Eliza Morgan b Hopkinton 1870-08-15 child of GAGE Harlan P laborer b Hopkinton & Nayette b Hopkinton Vol: 4 Page: 62 Line: 018.

GAGE Guy Harlan b Hopkinton 1871-08-15 child of GAGE Harlan P laborer b Hopkinton & Nayette b Hopkinton Vol: 4 Page: 63 Line: 038.

GAGE Hugh b Boston Mass 1873-05-20 child of GAGE Harlan P laborer b Hopkinton & Nayette b Hopkinton Vol: 4 Page: 65 Line: 023.

GAGE James Prescott b Hopkinton 1874-09-14 child of GAGE Alfred P teacher b Hopkinton & MARY P b Vol: 4 Page: 67 Line: 012.

GAGE Kate S b Hopkinton 1872-10-02 child of GAGE David L merchant b Hopkinton & Emily b Hillsborough Vol: 4 Page: 65 Line: 011.

GAGE Mary E b Hopkinton 1860-12-11 child of GAGE John F farmer b Hopkinton & SARAH E b Hopkinton Vol: 4 Page: 53 Line: 033.

GAGE Myra Margette b Hopkinton 1875-09-22 child of GAGE Harlan P laborer b Hopkinton & Margrette b Hopkinton Vol: 4 Page: 67 Line: 027.

GAGE Timothy Colby b Penfield Ny 1867-09-29 child of GAGE Harlan P laborer b Hopkinton & N Margette b Hopkinton Vol: 4 Page: 59 Line: 033.

GALE Georgia B b Hopkinton 1869-03-07 child of GALE George B farmer b Hopkinton & LIZZIE S b Vol: 4 Page: 61 Line: 016.

GEORGE Not Named b Hopkinton 1864-11-04 child of GEORGE?? W b Hopkinton & ?? b Hopkinton Vol: 4 Page: 57 Line: 023.

GILE Frederick b Hopkinton 1870-04-28 child of GILE Edwarrd farmer b Bradford & Abbie b Hopkinton Vol: 4 Page: 63 Line: 002.

GOODRICH Charles S b Hopkinton 1872-09-09 child of GOODRICH George N farmer b Springfield Vt & Lydia b Maine Vol: 4 Page: 65 Line: 008.

GOODRICH Erving b Hopkinton 1878-09-18 child of GOODRICH Larzo farmer b Vermont & Lydia b Maine Vol: 4 Page: 71 Line: 010.

GOODRICH Florance A b Hopkinton 1869-04-01 child of GOODRICH Geo K farmer b Springfield Vt & Lydia b Berwick Me Vol: 4 Page: 61 Line: 015.

GOODRICH Henry Willie b Hopkinton 1876-01-07 child of GOODRICH George K farmer b Springfield Vt & Lydia b Maine Vol: 4 Page: 68 Line: 007.

GOODSPEED J Arthur b Hopkinton 1860-08-08 child of GOODSPEED Obed clerk b Sandwich Mass & HELLEN B b Hopkinton Vol: 4 Page: 53 Line: 001.

GOODWIN Walter E b Hopkinton 1876-11-15 child of GOODWIN Charles F stone cutter b Concord & Etta b Hopkinton Vol: 4 Page: 69 Line: 012.

GOODWIN Not Named b Hopkinton 1878-08-18 child of GOODWIN Charles R farmer b Concord & Etta b Hopkinton Vol: 4 Page: 71 Line: 007.

GOULD Herbert J * b Hopkinton 1870-02-26 child of GOULD Charles farmer b Hopkinton & Ruth b Hopkinton Vol: 4 Page: 62 Line: 010 Note: ** records is democrat.

GOULD Lida May b Hopkinton 1873-03-14 child of GOULD Charels F laborer b Greenfield & Cordelia b Hopkinton Vol: 4 Page: 65 Line: 019..

GOULD Robert S b Hopkinton 1861-05-21 child of GOULD Charles farmer b Hopkinton & Ruth b Hopkinton Vol: 4 Page: 54 Line: 004.

GREENE Harriet b Hopkinton 1861-04-07 child of GREEN Newman laborer b Chichester & Sarah b Sutton Vol: 4 Page: 54 Line: 002.

GREENE Not Named b Hopkinton 1863-11-20 child of GREENE Lurman mechanic b Chichester & Sarah b Sutton Vol: 4 Page: 56 Line: 026.

GRIFFIN Charles H b Hopkinton 1862-05-12 child of GRIFFIN Joshua S laborer b Chichester & Susan b Bradford Vol: 4 Page: 55 Line: 002.

HACKETT Not Named b Hopkinton 1867-01-09 child of HACKETT Warren F mechanic b Henniker & Nellie b Springfield Vol: 4 Page: 59 Line: 019.

HADLEY Bertha b Hopkinton 1871-01-27 child of HADLEY Augusuts farmer b Not Given & Catherine b Not Given Vol: 4 Page: 63 Line: 030.

HADLEY Edward b Hopkinton 1867-05-16 child of HADLEY Augustus farmer b Henniker & Catherine b Ireland Vol: 4 Page: 60 Line: 002.

HADLEY Ellen E b Hopkinton 1865-01-04 child of HADLEY Augustus Vol: 4 Page: 57 Line: 027.

HADLEY Mary Ann b Hopkinton 1863-05-04 child of HADLEY Augustus farmer b Hopkinton & Catherine b Ireland Vol: 4 Page: 56 Line: 006.

HADLEY Not Named b Hopkinton 1865-01-04 child of HADLEY Augustus Vol: 4 Page: 57 Line: 028 Note: twin- stillborn.

HARDY Catharine b N Y City 1861-03-11 child of HARDY Augustus laborer b Hopkinton & Catharine b Ireland Vol: 4 Page: 54 Line: 001.

HARDY Clara b Hopkinton 1870-12-16 child of HARDY Woodbury farmer b Grantham & Ellen b Hopkinton Vol: 4 Page: 63 Line: 036.

HARDY Ella May b Hopkinton 1874-03-29 child of HARDY Carlos F farmer b Hopkinton & Olivia b Manchester Vol: 4 Page: 66 Line: 002.

HARDY Ella May * b Hopkinton 1875-03-23 child of HARDY Carlos F farmer b Hopkinton & OBID J b Manchester Vol: 4 Page: 67 Line: 025.

HARDY Isabell b Hopkinton 1861-09-23 child of HARDY Samuel A A farmer b Hopkinton & ABBY A b Hopkinton Vol: 4 Page: 54 Line: 019.

HARDY Jane b Hopkinton 1859-06-06 child of HARDY Samuel farmer b Hopkinton & ABBIE Ann b Hopkinton Vol: 4 Page: 52 Line: 001.

HARDY Jane b Hopkinton 1866-12-15 child of HARDY Carlos F farmer b Hopkinton & OLIVIA J b Manchester Vol: 4 Page: 59 Line: 012.

HARDY Josephine b Hopkinton 1865-11-17 child of HARDY Samuel A b Hopkinton & ABBY A b Hopkinton Vol: 4 Page: 59 Line: 013.

HARDY Lewis B b Hopkinton 1878 child of HARDY Samuel A farmer b Hopkinton & ABBY A b Hokinton Vol: 4 Page: 70 Line: 023.

HARDY Maria L b Hopkinton 1858-09-29 child of HARDY Augustus farmer b Hopkinton & Catharine b Ireland Vol: 4 Page: 51 Line: 019.

HARDY Stilman A b Hopkinton 1873-02-12 child of HARDY Samuel A farmer b Hopkinton & Abbie b Hopkinton Vol: 4 Page: 65 Line: 017.

HARDY Not Named b Hopkinton 1860-07-23 child of HARDY Samuel A farmer b Hopkinton & ABBY A b Hopkinton Vol: 4 Page: 53 Line: 017.

HARDY Not Named b Hopkinton 1863-09-28 child of HARDY Samuel A farmer b Hopkinton & Abby b Hopkinton Vol: 4 Page: 56 Line: 022.

HARDY Not Named b Hopkinton 1868-02-09 child of HARDY Samuel A farmer b Hopkinton & Abby b Hopkinton Vol: 4 Page: 60 Line: 021.

HARRIAM Warren W b Hopkinton 1878-11-30 child of HARRIAM Charles W physician b Goffstown & Servilla b Vol: 4 Page: 71 Line: 012.

HARRINGTON Benjamin** b Hopkinton 1877-07-22 child of HARRINGTON Thomas farmer b Concord & HATTIE R b Vol: 4 Page: 70 Line: 005 Correction: **Moses Bailey Harrington.

HASTINGS Della b Hopkinton 1869-04-15 child of HASTINGS Alfred farmer b Newbury & Susan b Goffstown Vol: 4 Page: 62 Line: 001.

HASTINGS George b Hopkinton 1868-01-30 child of HASTINGS Alfred S farmer b Hopkinton & Susan b Hopkinton Vol: 4 Page: 60 Line: 018.

HASTINGS Gertrude Ethel b Hopkinton 1871-09-02 child of HASTINGS Alfred S farmer b Hopkinton & Susan b Hopkinton Vol: 4 Page: 64 Line: 008.

HASTINGS Padie Bell b Hopkinton 1878-07-11 child of HASTINGS Alfred S farmer b Hopkinton & Susan b Hopkinton Vol: 4 Page: 71 Line: 003.

HAZELTON Not Named b Hopkinton 1872-03-22 child of HAZELTON Rufus rule maker b Hebron & Ida b Meredith Vol: 4 Page: 64 Line: 022.

HEATH ?? b Hopkinton 1861 child of HEATH James A machinist b Salisbury & HARRIET G b Warner Vol: 4 Page: 54 Line: 017.

HEATH Not Named b Hopkinton 1874-05-17 child of HEATH Charles laborer b Not Given & b Not Given Vol: 4 Page: 67 Line: 004.

HENRY Albert b Hopkinton 1879-02-10 child of ?? Charles V farmer b Hopkinton & Sarah b Hopkinton Vol: 4 Page: 71 Line: 016.

HILAN John H b Hopkinton 1873-11-11 child of HILAN George farmer b Hopkinton & Priscilla b Hopkinton Vol: 4 Page: 66 Line: 014.

HILAN Minnie Gertrude b Hopkinton 1878-01-02 child of HILAN George R farmer b Hopkinton & PRISCILLA D b Hopkinton Vol: 4 Page: 70 Line: 018.

HODGEDON N M b Hopkinton 1860-06-26 child of HODGEDON Charles carpenter b Concord & NEMI ?? b Hopkinton Vol: 4 Page: 53 Line: 014.

Hopkinton, NH Births 1858

HODGEDON H M b Hopkinton 1860-06-26 child of HODGEDON Charles N carpenter b Concord & Harriett b Hopkinton Vol: 4 Page: 52 Line: 035.

HOFFMAN Gracia N b Hopkinton 1867-01-02 child of HOFFMAN Wendall laborer b Hopkinton & MARY C b Hopkinton Vol: 4 Page: 59 Line: 006.

HOLMES Benjamin b Hopkinton 1875-11-14 child of HOLMES Walter farmer b Hopkinton & NOT Given b Johnson Vt Vol: 4 Page: 68 Line: 006.

HOLMES Emma b Hopkinton 1870-08-09 child of HOLMES Willard farmer b Hopkinton & Mary b Hopkinton Vol: 4 Page: 63 Line: 007.

HOLMES Grace D b Hopkinton 1863-01-19 child of HOLMES Daniel G farmer b Hopkinton & Melinda b Concord Vol: 4 Page: 55 Line: 020.

HOLMES Grace D b Hopkinton 1863-01-19 child of HOLMES Daniel G farmer b Hopkinton & Melinda b Concord Vol: 4 Page: 57 Line: 033.

HOLMES Henry P b Manchester 1865-08-28 child of HOLMES Willard laborer b Boscawen & MARY E b Plymouth Vol: 4 Page: 58 Line: 010.

HOLMES Nellie Mary b Long Island Ny 1863-05-17 child of HOLMES Richmond A mechanic b Hopkinton & Minvira b Hopkinton Vol: 4 Page: 56 Line: 008.

HOLMES No Name b Hopkinton 1867-10-21 child of HOLMES Daniel G farmer b Hopkinton & Melinda b Hopkinton Vol: 4 Page: 60 Line: 020.

HOLMES Wallace b Hopkinton 1865-11-10 child of HOLMES Aquilla D farmer b Hopkinton & Abby b Johnson Vt Vol: 4 Page: 58 Line: 014.

HOOK Clara B b Hopkinton 1868-03-25 child of HOOK James farmer b Concord & Mary b Hopkinton Vol: 4 Page: 60 Line: 016.

HOOK Edward M b Lowell Mass 1877-01-24 child of HOOK James M & Mary Vol: 4 Page: 69 Line: 020.

HOOK Emma J b Hopkinton 1875-07-28 child of HOOK James M farmer & MARY A Vol: 4 Page: 68 Line: 014.

HOOK Grace A b Hopkinton 1871-11-30 child of HOOD James M farmer b Concord & HOOK Mary A b Hopkinton Vol: 4 Page: 64 Line: 015.

HOOK Gusta J b Hopkinton 1877-09-18 child of HOOK James M farmer & MAY A Vol: 4 Page: 70 Line: 024.

HOOK Lizzie Charlott b Hopkinton 1865-05-16 child of HOOK James farmer b Concord & Mary b Hopkinton Vol: 4 Page: 58 Line: 004.

HOOK Nathan J b Hopkinton 1866-06-15 child of HOOK James farmer b Concord & Mary b Hopkinton Vol: 4 Page: 59 Line: 011.

HOOK Sarah E b Hopkinton 1870-02-26 child of HOOK James farmer b Concord & Mary b Hopkinton Vol: 4 Page: 62 Line: 008.

HOUSE Not Named b Hopkinton 1874-10-02 child of HOUSE Charles b & Clara b Hopkinton Vol: 4 Page: 67 Line: 014.

HOW Everet b Hopkinton 1860-10-28 child of HOW Madison pedler b Hopkinton & ELIZ J b Henniker Vol: 4 Page: 53 Line: 026.

HOW Juliette b Hopkinton 1858-08-06 child of HOW Madirdon laborer b Hopkinton & JANE C b Hopkinton Vol: 4 Page: 51 Line: 011.

HOW Sulivan b Hopkinton 1863-12-19 child of HOW Madison M farmer b Hopkinton & Elizabeth b Henniker Vol: 4 Page: 56 Line: 033.

HOWARD Ralph R b Hopkinton 1860-06-09 child of HOWARD Alonzo D laborer b Springfield & AUGUSTA N b Hollis Vol: 4 Page: 53 Line: 012.

Hopkinton, NH Births 1858

HOWARD Willis P b Hopkinton 1865-04-30 child of HOWARD Daniel E mechanic b Grantham & Susan b Hopkinton Vol: 4 Page: 58 Line: 002.

HOWE Lilla J b Hopkinton 1870-12-22 child of HOWE Madison farmer b Hopkinton & Elmira b Weare Vol: 4 Page: 63 Line: 027.

HOWE Minnie b Hopkinton 1866-08-20 child of HOWE William farmer b Hopkinton & SARAH C b Bow Vol: 4 Page: 59 Line: 005.

HOWE William b Hopkinton 1859-05-08 child of HOWE William farmer b Hopkinton & Sarah b Bow Vol: 4 Page: 52 Line: 003.

HOWLETT Erwin Elmore b Hopkinton 1868-04-23 child of HOWLETT John farmer b Hopkinton & HARRIET E b Hopkinton Vol: 4 Page: 61 Line: 012.

HOWLETT Not Named b Hopkinton 1870-05-26 child of HOWLETT Frank farmer b Hopkinton & Helen b Vol: 4 Page: 63 Line: 003.

HOYT Not Named b Hopkinton 1873-03-09 child of HOYT John C millwright b Weare & Lena b Warner Vol: 4 Page: 65 Line: 018.

HUGHES James b Hopkinton 1867-07-27 child of HUGHES Thomas farmer b Ireland & Catharine b Ireland Vol: 4 Page: 60 Line: 012.

HUGHES Not Named b Hopkinton 1860-12-25 child of HUGHES Thomas farmer b Ireland & Catherine b Ireland Vol: 4 Page: 53 Line: 034

HUNTOON Albert D b Hopkinton 1858-10-12 child of HUNTOON S D farmer b & Martha b Francestown Vol: 4 Page: 51 Line: 022.

HUNTOON Charles N b Hopkinton 1860-11-18 child of HUNTOON John F farmer b Andover & NOT Given b Hopkinton Vol: 4 Page: 53 Line: 031.

HUTCHINSON Homer b Hopkinton 1863-04-13 child of HUTCHINSON Sulivan merchant b Albany Me & Eliza b Whitefield Vol: 4 Page: 56 Line: 003.

JEFFERS Martin b Hopkinton 1872-09-09 child of JEFFERS Dighten mechanic b & Althea b So Weare Vol: 4 Page: 65 Line: 022.

JONES Charles Currier b Hopkinton 1871-03-22 child of JONES John F farrier b Hillsboro & Maria b Salisbury Vol: 4 Page: 63 Line: 034.

JONES John Arthur b Hopkinton 1864-04-03 child of JONES John F trader b Hopkinton & Maria b Ny Vol: 4 Page: 57 Line: 001.

JONES Nellie b Hopkinton 1874-12-05 child of JONES Thomas Jr caprenter b Concord & LUCY A b Georgetown Mass Vol: 4 Page: 67 Line: 020.

KELLEY Agnes M b Hopkinton 1863-06-28 child of KELLEY Henry L B wire maker b Delhi N Y & PHEBE M b Bernard Vt Vol: 4 Page: 56 Line: 011.

KELLEY Arthur Jones b Hopkinton 00 JAN 1874 child of KELLEY A J farmer b Andover & Roxanna b Mass Vol: 4 Page: 66 Line: 016.

KELLEY Cyntha H b Hopkinton 1866-03-10 child of KELLEY Francis C pedder b Hopkinton & Judith b Hopkinton Vol: 4 Page: 58 Line: 020.

KELLEY Edith Stella b Hopkinton 1860-02-11 child of KELLEY Frederick b & Neannett b Vol: 4 Page: 52 Line: .

KELLEY Harriet E b Hopkinton 1858-10-30 child of KELLEY Francis C farmer b Hopkinton & Julia b Hopkinton Vol: 4 Page: 51 Line: 024.

KELLEY Leowen H b Hopkinton 1875-07-24 child of KELLEY Fred U tin peddler b Hopkinton & Harriet b Hopkinton Vol: 4 Page: 68 Line: 005.

KELLEY Mabel Naisissa b Hopkinton 1861-09-15 child of KELLEY Henry L B ??? b ?? & PHEBE M b ?? Vol: 4 Page: 54 Line: 018.

Hopkinton, NH Births 1858

KELLEY Robert L b Hopkinton 1858-12-14 child of KELLEY N L B farmer b Stockbridge & Phebe b Hopkinton Vol: 4 Page: 51 Line: 031.

KELLEY Not Named b Hopkinton 1862-03-06 child of KELLY Frederick C mill worker b Hopkinton & Mary b Barry Vt Vol: 4 Page: 54 Line: 036.

KEMPTON Eva May b Hopkinton 1866-07-20 child of KEMPTON Byron mechanic b Croydon & Emma b Hopkinton Vol: 4 Page: 59 Line: 923.

KEMPTON Isabella b Hopkinton 1863-12-14 child of KEMPTON Warren M mechanic b Charlestown & Orintha b Grantham Vol: 4 Page: 56 Line: 031.

KEMPTON Lewis E b Hopkinton 1860-06-07 child of KEMPTON Warren N kitt mfg b Charlestown & EMMA C b Springfield Vol: 4 Page: 53 Line: 013.

KEZER Nettie Martel b Hopkinton 1870-08-27 child of KEZER James farmer b Hopkinton & Nancy b Hopkinton Vol: 4 Page: 63 Line: 009.

KIMBALL E G b Hopkinton 1870-03-18 child of KIMBALL E G farmer b Hopkinton & Mary b Essex Mass Vol: 4 Page: 62 Line: 012.

KIMBALL Emma B b Hopkinton 1859-03-14 child of KIMBALL Elbridge G b Hopkinton & Mary b Essex Mass Vol: 4 Page: 51 Line: 41.

KIMBALL Frederick E A b Hopkinton 1863-10-22 child of KIMBALL Stephen S farmer b Hopkinton & W Kimball b Concord Vol: 4 Page: 56 Line: 023.

KIMBALL Gilbert b Hopkinton 1860-08-24 child of KIMBALL George carpenter b Hopkinton & Lucy b Henniker Vol: 4 Page: 53 Line: 020.

KIMBALL Hattie M b Hopkinton 1869-07-26 child of KIMBALL Stephen farmer b Bradford & Laura b Hopkinton Vol: 4 Page: 62 Line: 002.

KIMBALL Henry Harvey b Hopkinton 1862-02-13 child of KIMBALL Elbridge G farmer b Hopkinton & MARY S b Essex Mass Vol: 4 Page: 54 Line: 033.

KIMBALL Moses Herbert b Hopkinton 1862-12-02 child of KIMBALL Moses S farmer b New London & Mary b Hopkinton Vol: 4 Page: 55 Line: 015.

KIMBALL Nelson D b Hopkinton 1864-07-16 child of KIMBALL Elbridge G farmer b Hopkinton & Mary b Essex Mass Vol: 4 Page: 57 Line: 011.

KIMBALL Richard F b Hopkinton 1859-03-11 child of KIMBALL Matthew N b Chelsea Vt & Mary b Hopkinton Vol: 4 Page: 51 Line: 40.

KIMBALL Stephen S b Hopkinton 1861-07-08 child of KIMBALL Stephen S farmer b Hopkinton & Janette b Concord Vol: 4 Page: 054 Line: 010.

KIMBALL Not Named b Hopkinton 1873-03-15 child of KIMBALL Chas K farmer b Hopkinton & Ellen b Hopkinton Vol: 4 Page: 66 Line: 001.

KNAPP Geo Dennis b Hopkinton 1871-04-30 child of KNAPP Geo W clergyman b New York & Carrie b New York Vol: 4 Page: 65 Line: 021.

LANG Not Named b Hopkinton 1870-04-11 child of LANG George carpenter b & Elizabeth b Hopkinton Vol: 4 Page: 63 Line: 037.

LEWIS Harry D b Hopkinton 1875-12-30 child of LEWIS Cyrus A cabinet maker b E Vassalboro Me & Ellen b Lawrence Mass Vol: 4 Page: 68 Line: 011 Correction: see 1950 records.

LIBBEY Not Named b Hopkinton 1874-03-23 child of LIBBEY George caprenter b Webster & b Webster Vol: 4 Page: 66 Line: 023.

LIBBY Edna H b Contoocook 1877-04-16 child of LIBBY George D carpenter b Webster & ESTELLA A b Andover Vol: 4 Page: 70 Line: 003.

LIBBY Not Named b Hopkinton 1874-02-20 child of LIBBY Fillmor carpenter b Webster & Sarah b Andover Vol: 4 Page: 66 Line: 018.

LOCKE Anne E b Hopkinton 1878-08-05 child of LOCKE George H farmer b Hopkinton & WRIGHT Mary b Hopkinton Vol: 4 Page: 71 Line: 006.

LOCKE Arthur S b Hopkinton 1862-03-06 child of LOCKE Warren L farmer b Warner & HARRIETT J b Hopkinton Vol: 4 Page: 54 Line: 035.

LOCKE Daniel b Hopkinton 1860-07-24 child of LOCKE Warren farmer b Warner & ISABELLA D b Hopkinton Vol: 4 Page: 53 Line: 018.

LOCKE John Alston b Weare 1859-10-11 child of LOCKE John D farmer b Weare & JULIA A b Hopkinton Vol: 4 Page: 52 Line: 032.

LOCKE Warren D b Hopkinton 1858-11-08 child of LOCKE Warren T farmer b Warner & Isabella b Hopkinton Vol: 4 Page: 51 Line: 025.

LONG Ben Antionette b Hopkinton 1862-09-10 child of LONG Benjamin S farmer b Amesbury Mass & Belinda b Warner Vol: 4 Page: 55 Line: 010.

LONG Etta May b Hopkinton 1861-09-02 child of LONG Benjamin farmer b Amesbury Mass & b Warner Vol: 4 Page: 54 Line: 016.

LOVEJOY Claudia D b Hopkinton 1871-06-28 child of LOVEJOY John G mechanic b Amherst & Anna b Woodstock Vt Vol: 4 Page: 64 Line: 005.

LOVEJOY Maud b Hopkinton 1872-09-18 child of LOVEJOY John G mechanic b Amherst & Annie b Rockport Ny Vol: 4 Page: 65 Line: 009.

MCALPINE Abba b Weare 1859-05-11 child of MCALPINE Newton G farmer b Hopkinton & SARAH J b Lowell Mass Vol: 4 Page: 52 Line: 005.

MCALPINE Etta b Hopkinton 1870-08-04 child of MCALPINE Gilman farmer b Hopkinton & Josephine b Hill Vol: 4 Page: 63 Line: 006.

MCALPPINE Ednah Alvira b Hopkinton 1859-12-21 child of MCALPINE George W farmer b Not Know & Hannah b Hopkinton Vol: 4 Page: 52 Line: 031.

MCCOY Olive Cornelia b Hopkinton 1875-04-24 child of MCCOY James M clerk b Thornton & Alice b Hopkinton Vol: 4 Page: 68 Line: 001.

MCCOY Philip J b Hopkinton 1879-03-19 child of MCCOY James roofer b Weare & Alice b Hopkinton Vol: 4 Page: 71 Line: 019.

MCKENZIE Laura b Hopkinton 1861-02-21 child of MCKENZIE George painter b Scotland & Bedilla b Ireland Vol: 4 Page: 53 Line: 043.

MERRILL Anna B b Hopkinton 1874-01-16 child of MERRILL George E farmer b Nashua & MARY E b Hopkinton Vol: 4 Page: 66 Line: 017.

MERRILL Etta M b Hopkinton 1860-05-20 child of MERRILL Stephen A farmer b Groton & MARTHA W b Hopkinton Vol: 4 Page: 53 Line: 006.

MERRILL Frank E b Hopkinton 1867-04-17 child of MERRILL Samuel farmer b Hopkinton & LORA A b Warner Vol: 4 Page: 60 Line: 007.

MERRILL Franklin b Hopkinton 1869-12-17 child of MERRILL Samuel W farmer b Hopkinton & Laura b Warner Vol: 4 Page: 62 Line: 007.

MERRILL Parker Elmer b Hopkinton 1876-07-16 child of MERRILL George E farmer b & MARY E b Hopkinton Vol: 4 Page: 69 Line: 006.

MILLS Charles A b Hopkinton 1866-02-10 child of MILLS Charles H farmer b Hopkinton & OLIVE H b Weare Vol: 4 Page: 59 Line: 032.

Hopkinton, NH Births 1858

MILLS Fannie b Hopkinton 1875-02-22 child of MILLS Charles H farmer b Hopkinton & Olive b Weare Vol: 4 Page: 67 Line: 024.

MILLS Fanny W b Hopkinton 1864-11-12 child of MILLS Charles N b Hopkinton & OLIVE H b Weare Vol: 4 Page: 57 Line: 024.

MILLS Fred H b Hopkinton 1874-03-03 child of MILLS George W farmer b Hopkinton & Eunice b Concord Vol: 4 Page: 67 Line: 001.

MILLS George C b Hopkinton 1876-06-20 child of MILLS George W laborer b Hopkinton & Eunice b Concord Vol: 4 Page: 69 Line: 005.

MILLS James b Hopkinton 1870-06-26 child of MILLS John C laborer b Hopkinton & Lizzie b Vol: 4 Page: 63 Line: 005.

MILLS Lerman b Hopkinton 1870-02-08 child of MILLS Charles H farmer b Hopkinton & OLIVE H b Weare Vol: 4 Page: 62 Line: 014.

MILTON Willy b Hopkinton 1861-08-27 child of MILTON George W farmer b Concord & MARY A b Londonderry Vol: 4 Page: 54 Line: 015.

MILTON Not Named b Hopkinton 1864-01-30 child of MILTON George M farmmer b Concord & MARY Ann b Nova Scotia Vol: 4 Page: 56 Line: 037 Note: xx wilton or milton.

MITCHELL Not Named b Hopkinton 1874-03-10 child of MITCHELL Joseth wood choppker b Canada & b Canada Vol: 4 Page: 66 Line: 020.

MONTGOMERY Alice b Hopkinton 1861-10-27 child of MONTGOMERY George farmer b Salem Ny & Elizabeth b Aigsle N Y Vol: 4 Page: 54 Line: 023.

MONTGOMERY Martha b Hopkinton 1863-09-09 child of MONTGOMERY George mechanic b Salem & Elizabeth b Ny Vol: 4 Page: 56 Line: 019.

MONTGOMERY Not Named b Hopkinton 1869-11-19 child of MONTGOMERY William carpenter b New York & Lucy b Warner Vol: 4 Page: 62 Line: 005.

MONTOGOMERY Levi b Hopkinton 1864-01-01 child of MONTGOMERY William soldier b Salem Ny & Lucy b Warner Vol: 4 Page: 56 Line: 035.

MONTOGOMERY Sarah A b Hopkinton 1860-10-30 child of MONTGOMERY Charles joiner b Sutton?? & MONTGOMERY A b Warner Vol: 4 Page: 53 Line: 030.

MORAN Eliza b Hopkinton 1864-03-02 child of MORAN James laborer b Ireland & Mary b Ireland Vol: 4 Page: 56 Line: 041.

MORAN Fanny b Hopkinton 1867 JUL 00 child of MORAN Thomas farmer b Ireland & Margerett b Ireland Vol: 4 Page: 60 Line: 010.

MORAN Lizzie b Hopkinton 1870-12-02 child of MORAN Thomas farmer b Ireland & Mary b England Vol: 4 Page: 63 Line: 025.

MORAN Margarete b Hopkinton 1869-05-02 child of MORAN Thomas farmer b Ireland & Margarete b Ireland Vol: 4 Page: 62 Line: 016.

MORAN Mary b Hopkinton 1866-05-09 child of MORAN Patrick farmer b Ireland & Ann b Ireland Vol: 4 Page: 59 Line: 009.

MORGAN Alden O b Hopkinton 1865-07-19 child of MORGAN Gilman C farmer b Hartford Vt & EVELINE L b Hopkinton Vol: 4 Page: 58 Line: 009.

MORGAN Arthur B b Hopkinton 1867-03-15 child of MORGAN Francis W farmer b Hopkinton & FRANCES A b Cornish Vol: 4 Page: 59 Line: 008.

Hopkinton, NH Births 1858

MORGAN Edwin N b Hopkinton 1860-05-27 child of MORGAN Gilman C farmer b Hartford Vt & Eveline b Hopkinton Vol: 4 Page: 53 Line: 008.

MORGAN Gilman b Hopkinton 1870-09-21 child of MORGAN Gilman farmer b Hopkinton & b Hopkinton Vol: 4 Page: 63 Line: 019.

MORGAN Warren Francis b Hopkinton 1877-12-13 child of MORGAN Frank W farmer b Hopkinton & BELINDA M b Sutton Vol: 4 Page: 70 Line: 017.

MORGAN Not Named b Hopkinton 1876-03-03 child of MORGAN Frank W farmer b Hopkinton & Linda b Sutton Vol: 4 Page: 68 Line: 010.

MORRILL Bertha F b Hopkinton 1866-10-17 child of MORRILL Charles A farmer b Hopkinton & Theresa b Derry Vol: 4 Page: 59 Line: 016.

MORRILL Fanny Gertrude b Hopkinton 1868-04-12 child of MORRILL Charles A farmer b Hopkinton & Theresa b Derry Vol: 4 Page: 61 Line: 003.

MORRILL Lizzie Mary b Hopkinton 1870-11-04 child of MORRILL Charles A farmer b Hopkinton & Theresa b Sutton Vol: 4 Page: 63 Line: 024.

MORSE Harris b Hopkinton 1865-01-03 child of MORSE Ezekiel Vol: 4 Page: 57 Line: 026.

MUDGETT Annie S b Hopkinton 1864-05-09 child of MUDGETT William S musician b New Boston & Annie b Hopkinton Vol: 4 Page: 57 Line: 007.

MUDGETT Clara L b Hopkinton 1867-05-05 child of MUDGETT Frank J blacksmith b Weare & Mary b Hopkinton Vol: 4 Page: 60 Line: 019.

MUDGETT Nellie May b Bristol 1877-10-22 child of MUDGETT William E farmer b Northfield & SALOMI P b Sutton Vol: 4 Page: 70 Line: 013.

NEALY Mary b Hopkinton 1860-02-25 child of NEALY John F farmer b Northwood & MARGARETT C b Springfield Mass Vol: 4 Page: 52 Line: 13.

NICHOLS Fanny A b Hopkinton 1861-08-25 child of NICHOLS Hiram farmer b W Amesbury Mass & Elizabeth b Hopkinton Vol: 4 Page: 54 Line: 014.

NOYES Charles Story b Hopkinton 1874-08-25 child of NOYES David farmer b Hopkinton & ABBY P b Vol: 4 Page: 67 Line: 008.

NOYSE Alice Frances b Hopkinton 1879-03-09 child of NOYES Daniel farmer b & Abbie b Hooksett Vol: 4 Page: 71 Line: 018.

ORDWAY Frederick Eugene b Hopkinton 1859-10-31 child of ORDWAY Eben Jr farmer b Hopkinton & Ann b Alton Vol: 4 Page: 52 Line: 006.

PAGE Elizabeth b Hopkinton 1859-06-10 child of PAGE Samuel S farmer b Dunbarton & Ellen b Weston Mass Vol: 4 Page: 52 Line: 010.

PALMER Effa W b Hopkinton 1865-01-13 child of Unknown Vol: 4 Page: 57 Line: 029.

PATTERSON Sarah A b Hopkinton 1871-01-24 child of PATTERSON William farmer b Hopkinton & Olive b Deering Vol: 4 Page: 63 Line: 029.

PERRY Emma b Hopkinton 1869-08-20 child of PERRY Sylvester farmer b Hopkinton & BERTHAN L b Maine Vol: 4 Page: 62 Line: 003.

PERRY Willie b Hopkinton 1861-09-26 child of PERRY William P farmer b Henniker & Elizabeth b Hopkinton Vol: 4 Page: 54 Line: 020.

PERRY Not Named b Hopkinton 1868 child of PERRY Sylvester W farmer b Hopkinton & BERTHA S b Not Given Vol: 4 Page: 61 Line: 005.

PIERCE Ellen N b Hopkinton 1864-08-05 child of PIERCE George W farmer b Warner & Mira b Hopkinton Vol: 4 Page: 57 Line: 013.

Hopkinton, NH Births 1858

PIERCE Not Named b Hopkinton 1859-01-24 child of PIERCE George W b Warner & MARIA F b Hopkinton Vol: 4 Page: 51 Line: 39.

POLAND Evangie b Hopkinton 1874-05-08 child of POLAND Ezra E b & CORA E b Contoocookville Vol: 4 Page: 67 Line: 003.

POWELL?? Charles E b Hopkinton 1870-10-29 child of POWELL Lewett?? farmer b Hopkinton & Sarah b Warner Vol: 4 Page: 63 Line: 018.

PUTNAM Charles b Hopkinton 1863-12-08 child of PUTNAM Rufus farmer b Hopkinton & Lydia b Hopkinton Vol: 4 Page: 56 Line: 029.

PUTNAM Clara A b Hopkinton 1865-07-20 child of PUTNAM James laborer b Hopkinton & Sarah b Maine Vol: 4 Page: 58 Line: 007.

PUTNAM George Augustus b Hopkinton 1862-05-28 child of PUTNAM Augustus R trader b Hopkinton & Eliza b Warner Vol: 4 Page: 55 Line: 004 Correction: cert correction- Eliza Rand.

PUTNAM Gorge N b Hopkinton 1864-01-18 child of PUTNAM Charles farmer b Hopkinton & Almira b Hopkinton Vol: 4 Page: 56 Line: 036.

PUTNAM Grace Emma b Hopkinton 1868-10-13 child of PUTNAM Charles farmer b Hopkinton & Elmira b Hopkinton Vol: 4 Page: 61 Line: 010.

PUTNAM Helen Bickford b Contoocook 1877-10-12 child of PUTNAM Joseph carpenter b Hopkinton & MARGARET A b Hopkinton Vol: 4 Page: 70 Line: 012.

PUTNEY Ira b Hopkinton 1878-07-21 child of PUTNEY True J farmer b Hopkinton & Ellen b Manchester Mass Vol: 4 Page: 71 Line: 004.

RAND Not Named b Hopkinton 1877-02-12 child of RAND Warren S mechanic b & CARRIE M b Vol: 4 Page: 69 Line: 015.

RAYMOND Nannie E b Hopkinton 1873-05-07 child of RAYMOND W H mechanic b Hopkinton & ELIZA J b Henniker Vol: 4 Page: 66 Line: 004.

REED Not Named b Hopkinton 1878-08-25 child of REED Harry A broker b New Haven Conn & Nettie b Vol: 4 Page: 71 Line: 008.

RELATION George b Hopkinton 1858-12-06 child of RELATION Dennis laborer b Canada & Lucy b Canada Vol: 4 Page: 51 Line: 028.

RICHARDS Lena Maud b Contoocook 1877-08-15 child of RICHARDS J Bert clerk b Sutton & Nellie b Hopkinton Vol: 4 Page: 70 Line: 006.

RICHARDS Nettie May b Hopkinton 1865-07-05 child of RICHARDS Thomas B teacher b Deering & ELIZA A b Michigan Vol: 4 Page: 58 Line: 005.

RICHARDSON Julia Edna b Hopkinton 1863-12-14 child of RICHARDSON Thomas B farmer b Dearing & ELIZABETH A b Michigan Vol: 4 Page: 56 Line: 030.

RION Frances E b Hopkinton 1864-04-23 child of RION Samuel laborer b Canterbury & Cynthia b Hopkinton Vol: 4 Page: 57 Line: 004.

RION Noah N b Hopkinton 1864 APR child of RION Samuel T laborer b Canterbury & Cynthia b Hopkinton Vol: 4 Page: 057 Line: 005.

RIPLEY George Henry b Hopkinton 1874-08-15 child of RIPLEY James b & Julia b Vol: 4 Page: 67 Line: 007.

ROACH Agnes R b Hopkinton 1874-12-29 child of ROACH John farmer b Ireland & Ann b Ireland Vol: 4 Page: 67 Line: 023.

Hopkinton, NH Births 1858

ROACH Mary A b Hopkinton 1870-03-08 child of ROACH John farmer b Ireland & Ann b Ireland Vol: 4 Page: 62 Line: 015.

ROACH William b Hopkinton 1871-04-26 child of ROACH John farmer b Ireland & Ann b Ireland Vol: 4 Page: 64 Line: 001.

ROBY Not Named b Hopkinton 1870-11-20 child of ROBY Lyman farmer b Warner & b New York Vol: 4 Page: 63 Line: 023.

ROGERS Georgia b Hopkinton 1864-05-18 child of ROGERS Alexander physcian b Exeter & SOPHIA W b Boston Mass Vol: 4 Page: 57 Line: 008.

ROGERS Margery S b Hopkinton 1861-06-28 child of ROGERS Alexander physician b Exeter & Sophia b Boston Mass Vol: 4 Page: 54 Line: 008.

ROGERS Not Named b Hopkinton 1870-03-24 child of ROGERS John & Clara b Hopkinton Vol: 4 Page: 63 Line: 036.

ROLLINS George G b Hopkinton 1862-12-04 child of ROLLINS Alfred farmer b Antrim & MARY E b Hopkinton Vol: 4 Page: 55 Line: 014.

ROLLINS William N b Hopkinton 1860-09-26 child of ROLLINS Alfred A farmer ?? b Antrim & MARY E b Hopkinton Vol: 4 Page: 53 Line: 025.

ROWELL Franklin b Henniker 1861-08-23 child of ROWELL Alonzo laborer b Hopkinton & Abigial b Weare Vol: 4 Page: 54 Line: 013.

RUNNELLS Albert Farnum b Hopkinton 1874-10-03 child of RUNNELLS Edward P farmer b Boscawen & Jennie b Concord Vol: 4 Page: 67 Line: 016.

RUNNELLS Edward # b Hopkinton 1873-06-04 child of RUNNELLS Harry J farmer b Boscawen & b Concord Vol: 4 Page: 66 Line: 005.

RUSSELL Not Named b Hopkinton 1874-04-06 child of RUSSELL Smith farmer b Nh & Deborah b Maine Vol: 4 Page: 67 Line: 002.

SANBORN Bertha b Hopkinton 1866-10-15 child of SANBORN Thomas L collector internal revenue b Henniker & E b Hopkinton Vol: 4 Page: 59 Line: 002.

SANBORN Margarett b Hopkinton 1864-03-04 child of SANBORN Richard farmer b Ireland & Mary b Ireland Vol: 4 Page: 56 Line: 042.

SARGENT Coral T b Hopkinton 1867-05-15 child of SARGENT John B farmer b Loudon & Harriet b Barnstead Vol: 4 Page: 60 Line: 003.

SAVORY Annie M b Hopkinton 1866-09-15 child of SAVORY William T farmer b Hopkinton & HANNAH G b Henniker Vol: 4 Page: 59 Line: 018.

SCHWARTZ Mary Louise b Hopkinton 1870-04-01 child of SCHWARTS Frederick farmer b Hopkinton & Cordelia b Vol: 4 Page: 63 Line: 001.

SCOTT Herbert D N b Hopkinton 1863-11-23 child of SCOTT Frederick farmer b Stoddard & LUCINDA M b Hopkinton Vol: 4 Page: 56 Line: 027.

SCOTT Wallace b Hopkinton 1859-11-14 child of SCOTT Fredick farmer b Stoddard & Lensetta?? b Hopkinton Vol: 4 Page: 52 Line: 002.

SEAVEY Henrietta b Hopkinton 1864-09-29 child of SEAVEY David farmer b Concord & Maria b Hopkinton Vol: 4 Page: 57 Line: 017.

SHEPARD Geo Scott** b Hopkinton 1871-10-09 child of SHEPPARD Scott farmer b Canterbury & Lizzie b Cornish Vol: 4 Page: 63 Line: 039 Correction: **.

SHURTLIFF Grace E b Hopkinton 1876-05-07 child of SHURTLIFF Samuel E carpenter b Stannard Vt & MILTON Mary b Claremont Vol: 4 Page: 69 Line: 019.

SHUTE Henry R b Contoocook 1878-01-04 child of SHUTE John J machinist b Laconia & FANNIE D b Bradford Vol: 4 Page: 70 Line: 019.

SHUTE Not Named b Hopkinton 1879-01-12 child of SHUTE John machinist b Laconia & Fannie b Vol: 4 Page: 71 Line: 014.

SIMONDS Andrew b Hopkinton 1858-04-05 child of SIMONDS Biran laboror b Ireland & Ann b Ireland Vol: 4 Page: 51 Line: 001.

SIMONDS Thomas b Hopkinton 1859-12-19 child of SIMONDS Brian laborer b Ireland & Anne b Ireland Vol: 4 Page: 52 Line: 018.

SKILLEN Henry A b Hopkinton 1866-02-08 child of SKILLEN William W blacksmith b Not Known & LAURA J b Hopkinton Vol: 4 Page: 58 Line: 019.

SMART Calvin b Hopkinton 1863-05-17 child of SMART George laborer b Hopkinton & Ester b Warner Vol: 4 Page: 56 Line: 007.

SMART Edward Hamilton b Hopkinton 1862-11-03 child of SMART Edwin D farmer b Hopkinton & Sophia b Northwood Vol: 4 Page: 55 Line: 012.

SMART Joseph B b Hopkinton 1877-04-02 child of SMART Joseph farmer b Warner & NETTIE B b Hopkinton Vol: 4 Page: 70 Line: 001.

SMART Malinda b Hopkinton 1868-10-01 child of SMART George W laborer b Hopkinton & Esther b Warner Vol: 4 Page: 51 Line: 020.

SMART Mary Ann b Hopkinton 1864-11-04 child of SMART William b Hopkinton & Ann b Hopkinton Vol: 4 Page: 57 Line: 022.

SMILEY Ann b Hopkinton 1867-08-28 child of SMILEY John S farmer b Dover & Mary b Milford Vol: 4 Page: 60 Line: 013.

SMILEY Charles G b Hopkinton 1865-10-02 child of SMILEY John S miller b Dover & Mary b Milford Vol: 4 Page: 58 Line: 011.

SMITH Fanny W b Hopkinton 1864-10-13 child of SMITH Josiah G farmer b Hopkinton & SUSAN W b Hopkinton Vol: 4 Page: 57 Line: 019.

SMITH George G b Hopkinton 1859-11-30 child of SMITH Josiah G farmer b Hopkinton & SUSAN W b Hopkinton Vol: 4 Page: 52 Line: 016.

SMITH John Currier b Hopkinton 1862-05-02 child of SMITH Charles H farmer b Concord & Nancy b Rumford Vol: 4 Page: 55 Line: 001.

SMITH Nellie R b Hopkinton 1867-10-07 child of SMITH Josiah G farmer b Hopkinton & Susan b Hopkinton Vol: 4 Page: 59 Line: 029.

SON Ann E b Hopkinton 1874-12-10 child of SON Willian laborer b Montreal Canda & Rosa b Ireland Vol: 4 Page: 67 Line: 021.

SON Henry b Hopkinton 1872-04-12 child of SON Wm farmer b Canada & Rosa b Ireland Vol: 4 Page: 65 Line: 002.

SON William b Hopkinton 1869-08-27 child of SON William farmer b Canada & Rosa b Ireland Vol: 4 Page: 62 Line: 017.

SPOFFORD Arthur F b Hopkinton 1870-12-29 child of SPOFFORD L Alfred farmer b Hopkinton & Abby b Hopkinton Vol: 4 Page: 63 Line: 028.

SPOFFORD Frederick E b Hopkinton 1860-10-29 child of SPOFFORD Frederick farmer b Antrim & SARAH A b Londonderry Vol: 4 Page: 53 Line: 029.

Hopkinton, NH Births 1858

SPOFFORD George b Hopkinton 1873-01-11 child of SPOFFORD S Alfred farmer b Hopkinton & Abbie b Hopkinton Vol: 4 Page: 65 Line: 014.

SPOFFORD Not Named b Hopkinton 1868-12-27 child of SPOFFORD James shoemaker b Chester & ELLEN C b Concord Vol: 4 Page: 61 Line: 009.

SPOFFORD Not Named b Hopkinton 1873-01-18 child of SPOFFORD Luther F farmer b Hopkinton & NYRA C b Hopkinton Vol: 4 Page: 65 Line: 015.

STANLEY Clinton John?? b Hopkinton 1878-03-22 child of STANLEY Edward farmer b Hopkinton & MARY E b Hopkinton Vol: 4 Page: 71 Line: 001.

STEVENS Blanche May b Hopkinton 1877-11-16 child of STEVENS Nathan P farmer b Barnard Vt & HARRIETTE A b Concord Vol: 4 Page: 70 Line: 014.

STEVENS George E b Hopkinton 1876-05-19 child of STEVENS Henry C b Warner & MARY A b Methuen Mass Vol: 4 Page: 69 Line: 003.

STEVENS Jonathan M b Hopkinton 1871-12-14 child of STEVENS Henry painter b Warner & MARY C b Methuen Mass Vol: 4 Page: 64 Line: 016.

STEVENS Linnie ?? b Hopkinton 1876-10-10 child of STEVENS Edgar merchant b Manchester & Georgia b Bradford Mass Vol: 4 Page: 69 Line: 010.

STORY Ada B b Hopkinton 1860-10-02 child of STORY David butcher b Hopkinton & Sara b Salem Vol: 4 Page: 52 Line: 019.

STORY Benjamin French b Hopkinton 1869-01-05 child of STORY David B hotel keeper b Hopkinton & SARAH J b Salem Mass Vol: 4 Page: 61 Line: 008.

STORY Charles F b Hopkinton 1865-10-10 child of STORY David B hotel keeper b Hopkinton & SARAH J b Salem Mass Vol: 4 Page: 58 Line: 012.

STORY Fred William b Hopkinton 1861-12-09 child of STORY David B butcher b Hopkinton & SARAH J b Salem Mass Vol: 4 Page: 54 Line: 026.

STORY Hattie M b Hopkinton 1866-10-03 child of STORY Warren laborer b Washington & Pamelia b Mason Vol: 4 Page: 59 Line: 017.

STORY Timothy F b Hopkinton 1878-05-22 child of STORY Hilan farmer b Hopkinton & Mary b Hopkinton Vol: 4 Page: 71 Line: 002.

STORY Not Named b Hopkinton 1866-01-27 child of STORY Moses farmer b Hopkinton & Sarah b Hopkinton Vol: 4 Page: 58 Line: 018.

STRAW Andrew L F b Hopkinton 1865-01-29 child of STRAW Horace Vol: 4 Page: 57 Line: 030.

STRAW Charles Herbert b Hopkinton 1859-01-22 child of STRAW William S farmer b Hopkinton & MARY Ann b Hopkinton Vol: 4 Page: 52 Line: 025.

STRAW Charles N b Hopkinton 1860-09-07 child of GILMAN Gilman J section hand b Hopkinton & Weltha b Bradford Vol: 4 Page: 53 Line: 022.

STRAW Della L b Hopkinton 1862-02-23 child of STRAW John farmer b Hopkinton & Mary b Hopkinton Vol: 4 Page: 54 Line: 034.

STRAW Frank b Hopkinton 1864-02-25 child of STRAW Gilman J mechanic b Hopkinton & Weltha b Henniker Vol: 4 Page: 56 Line: 038.

STRAW Minnie B b Hopkinton 1866-04-19 child of STRAW Gilman J laborer b Hopkinton & WELTHA A b Henniker Vol: 4 Page: 59 Line: 014.

STRAW True J b Hopkinton 1871-11-15 child of STRAW Gilman J railroad laborer b Hopkinton & Weltha b Henniker Vol: 4 Page: 64 Line: 012.

STRAW Not Named b Hopkinton 1864-02-29 child of STRAW John farmer b Hopkinton & MARY A b Hopkinton Vol: 4 Page: 56 Line: 040.

Hopkinton, NH Births 1858

STRAW Not Named b Hopkinton 1869-12-25 child of STRAW John farmer b Hopkinton & MARY Ann b Hopkinton Vol: 4 Page: 62 Line: 006.

SYMONDS Albert Tilton b Hopkinton 1871-03-22 child of SYMONDS Ephraim ferrier b Hillsboro & MARY A b Salisbury Vol: 4 Page: 63 Line: 033.

SYMONDS Byran Kinght b Hopkinton 1876-04-12 child of SYMONDS Samuel farmer b Hillsboro & ANN M b Weare Vol: 4 Page: 69 Line: 001.

SYMONDS Edna Ann b Hopkinton 1878-03-02 child of SYMONDS Samuel T farmer b Hillsboro & ANNIE M b Weare Vol: 4 Page: 70 Line: 20.

SYMONDS Ellen Fannie b Hopkinton 1873-12-22 child of SYMONDS Samuel clerk b Hillsoboro & ANN H b Weare Vol: 4 Page: 66 Line: 015.

SYMONDS Helen B b Hopkinton 1876-09-14 child of SYMONDS George farmer b Concord & Lucy b Verron Conn Vol: 4 Page: 69 Line: 008.

SYMONDS Not Named b Hopkinton 1873-05-19 child of SYMONDS Ephraim farmer b Hillsboro & MARY A b Salisbury Vol: 4 Page: 66 Line: 008.

TAYLOR Martha May b Hopkinton 1876-05-18 child of TAYLOR Charles E hotel l keeper b Hancock & CARRIE E b Warner Vol: 4 Page: 69 Line: 002.

TILTON Helen A b Hopkinton 1863-08-07 child of TILTON Wm W farmer b Hill & SARAH A b Amesbury Mass Vol: 4 Page: 56 Line: 016.

TUCKER Charles H b Hopkinton 1870-10-18 child of TUCKER Durrell C farmer b Henniker & CARRIE E b Hopkinton Vol: 4 Page: 63 Line: 016.

TUCKER Florence b Hopkinton 1870-09-01 child of WEBBER Benjamin farmer b West Concord & Mary b Concord Vol: 4 Page: 63 Line: 010.

TUCKER Harry L b Hopkinton 1874-06-23 child of TUCKER David C farmer b Hopkinton & CARRIE E b Contoocook Vol: 4 Page: 67 Line: 006.

TUCKER Helen E b Hopkinton 1858-07-08 child of TUCKER George farmer b Grafton & Lucinda b Grafton Vol: 4 Page: 51 Line: 007.

TUCKER Mary Emma b Hopkinton 1878-11-29 child of TUCKER William L clergyman b Plmouth England & Emma b Goffstown Vol: 4 Page: 71 Line: 011.

TUCKER Not Named b Hopkinton 1869-02-08 child of TUCKER David C farmer b Henniker & CARRIE E b Hopkinton Vol: 4 Page: 61 Line: 013.

TUCKER Not Named b Hopkinton 1872-03-18 child of TUCKER Samuel farmer b Henniker & Nancy b Derby Vt Vol: 4 Page: 64 Line: 021.

TYLER Not Named b Hopkinton 1867-05-15 child of TYLER Lucius farmer b Hopkinton & Sarah b Canada East Vol: 4 Page: 59 Line: 026.

UPTON Alice Azenith b Hopkinton 1873-09-16 child of UPTON Barton carpenter b Hopkinton & BARLOW Sarah b Hopkinton Vol: 4 Page: 66 Line: 011.

UPTON Willie b Contoocook 1878-03-22 child of UPTON Barton mechanic b Contoocook & SARAH P b Hopkinton Vol: 4 Page: 70 Line: 021.

WALKER Mary J b Hopkinton 1859-04-28 child of WALKER Moses A farmer b Croydon & ELIZABETH Ann b Northwood Vol: 4 Page: 52 Line: 017.

WATKINS Francis S b Hopkinton 1867-10-21 child of WATKINS George N farmer b Warner & Nancy b Hopkinton Vol: 4 Page: 60 Line: 009.

WATTS Louisa b Hopkinton 1872-12-06 child of WATTS William b Bennington Vt & Sarah b Warner Vol: 4 Page: 65 Line: 012.

Hopkinton, NH Births 1858

WEBBER (Hubbard ??) Not Named b Hopkinton 1859-12-29 child of WEBBER William C laborer b Windham & SARA A b Bradford Vol: 4 Page: 52 Line: 029 Note: Hubbard??.

WEBBER Gilbert D b Hopkinton 1865-11-19 child of WEBBER Cyril laborer b Webster & Jenett b Croydon Vol: 4 Page: 58 Line: 016.

WEBBER Horace b Hopkinton 1871-09-05 child of WEBBER Cyril laborer b Webster & Jeanette b Croydon Vol: 4 Page: 63 Line: 011.

WEBSTER Della M ** b Hopkinton 1877-01-22 child of WEBSTER Frank D blacksmith b Sandwich & Nettie b Concord Vol: 4 Page: 69 Line: 013 Correction: page 61 in 1950 birth record.

WEBSTER Edward Eugene b Hopkinton 1875 child of WEBSTER Charles F farmer b Maine & LYDIA A b Claremont Vol: 4 Page: 68 Line: 012.

WEBSTER Not Named b Hopkinton 1879-02-22 child of WEBSTER Frank blacksmith b & Nettie b Vol: 4 Page: 71 Line: 017.

WEEKS George W b Hopkinton 1872-07-02 child of WEEKS Jacob farmer b Hopkinton & Mary b Charlestown Mass Vol: 4 Page: 65 Line: 005.

WEEKS Not Named b Hopkinton 1866-03-12 child of WEEKS N Cogswell farmer b Hopkinton & Jane b Hopkinton Vol: 4 Page: 58 Line: 021.

WEEKS Not Named b Hopkinton 1867-08-19 child of WEEKS N Cogswell mechanic b Hopkinton & Hannah b Boscawen Vol: 4 Page: 60 Line: 001.

WELLS Not Named b Hopkinton 1870-02-26 child of WELLS William farmer b Hill & Mary b Hopkinton Vol: 4 Page: 62 Line: 009.

WEST Josie Pauline b Hopkinton 1876-01-24 child of WEST Thomas F carpenter b Rhode Island & Emma b Boston Mass Vol: 4 Page: 68 Line: 008.

WHEELER Mary F b Hopkinton 1874-09-20 child of WHEELER Henry E kitt mfg b Bradford & Lavina b Hillsborough Vol: 4 Page: 67 Line: 013.

WHITE Sarah C b Hopkinton 1861-08-09 child of WHITE Anson farmer b Hopkinton & Roxanna b Hopkinton Vol: 4 Page: 54 Line: 011.

WHITTEMORE Mary A b Henniker 1859-10-15 child of WHITTEMORE William farmer b Concord & NANCY S b Piermont Vol: 4 Page: 52 Line: 020 Note:

WHITTEMORE Nellie M b Hopkinton 1866-08-28 child of WHITTEMORE William B farmer b Concord & S b Bradford Vol: 4 Page: 59 Line: 001.

WHITTEMORE Not Named b Hopkinton 1863-03-30 child of WHITTEMORE William B farmer b Concord & NANCY S b Bradford Vol: 4 Page: 55 Line: 019.

WIGHT Clarence Alonso b Hopkinton 1873-08-19 child of WRIGHT Oscar carpenter b Westmorland & Abbie b Hopkinton Vol: 4 Page: 66 Line: 007.

WILLEY John b Hopkinton 1861-01-15 child of WILLEY John J farmer b Greenborough Vt & Nancy b Warner Vol: 4 Page: 53 Line: 038.

WILLIAMS Belle M b Hopkinton 1869-11-05 child of WILLIAMS David farmer b Albany Ny & Sarah b Concord Vol: 4 Page: 62 Line: 004.

WOODS Not Named b Hopkinton 1873-07-18 child of WOODS Perkins farmer b Not Given & Ida b Henniker Vol: 4 Page: 66 Line: 006.

WRIGHT Liza F b Contoocook 1877-04-21 child of WRIGHT Oscar Wright farmer b West Milan & Abba b Contoocook Vol: 4 Page: 70 Line: 004.

Hopkinton, NH Deaths 1858-1879

GILBERT Lydia d Hopkinton 1858 b Meridith child of Shattuck Vol: 4 Page: 100 Line: 009

CURRIER Dolly d Hopkinton 1858 ?? b Hopkinton child of CURRIER Sargent & Sarah Vol: 4 Page: 100 Line: 008

DURGIN Mary A d Hopkinton 1858 Jun age 29yrs b Tilton child of DURGIN David B & Elizabeth Vol: 4 Page: 100 Line: 001

MORRILL Joseph d Hopkinton 1858-05-18 age 86yrs b Salisbury Vol: 4 Page: 100 Line: 024

GILL Francis d Hopkinton 1858-08-16 age 15yrs b Hopkinton child of GILL Norman & Sara of Concord Vol: 4 Page: 100 Line: 002

CONNER James d Hopkinton 1858-10-11 age 56yrs b Henniker child of CONNER James Vol: 4 Page: 100 Line: 005

CROSS Moses d Hopkinton 1858-10-13 age 63yrs b Newbury child of CROSS Moses Vol: 4 Page: 100 Line: 006

CLOUGH Martha d Hopkinton 1859 Apr 00 age 5yrs b Hopkinton child of CLOUGH Phineas of Hopkinton & Abigial of Weare Vol: 4 Page: 101 Line: 024

DANFORTH George S d Hopkinton 1859-01-06 age 6yrs b Hopkinton child of DANFORTH John & Jemmia of Weare Vol: 4 Page: 100 Line: 010

JEWETT Joseph d Hopkinton 1859-01-08 b Hopkinton child of JEWETT Samuel of Mass & Jemmia of Epping Vol: 4 Page: 100 Line: 011

RELATION George d Hopkinton 1859-01-18 age 1yrs b Hopkinton child of Lucy of Canada Vol: 4 Page: 100 Line: 012

FROST Grace C d Hopkinton 1859-01-26 age 1yrs 8mos b Hopkinton child of FROST Franklin of Glover Vt & Martha L of Hopkinton Vol: 4 Page: 101 Line: 029

DOW Alice C d Hopkinton 1859-01-28 age 12yrs b Hopkinton child of DOW Joseph & Maria of New Boston Vol: 4 Page: 100 Line: 013

HUBBARD ---- d Hopkinton 1859-02-10 age 1mos 12dys b Hopkinton child of HUBBARD William of Windham & Sarah of Bradford Vol: 4 Page: 101 Line: 025

GATES Betsey d Bow 1859-02-22 age 73??yrs b Hopkinton child of TEWKSBURY John & Sarah Vol: 4 Page: 100 Line: 014

STORY Frank P d Hopkinton 1859-03-09 age 4yrs b Hopkinton child of STORY F Warren & Peinella of Hopkinton Vol: 4 Page: 100 Line: 023

HUNTOON Ida P M d Hopkinton 1859-03-20 b Andover child of HUNTOON S D & Martha Vol: 4 Page: 100 Line: 015

STORY Judith d Hopkinton 1859-03-21 age 74yrs b Concord child of FARNUM Stephen & Martha Vol: 4 Page: 100 Line: 017

JEWETT Josiah d Hopkinton 1859-03-21 age 13yrs b Hopkinton child of JEWETT Samuel of Mass & Jemmia Vol: 4 Page: 100 Line: 018

Hopkinton, NH Deaths 1858

CLOUGH Martha W d Hopkinton 1859-03-25 age 4yrs b Hopkinton child of CLOUGH Phinehas & Abigail of Weare Vol: 4 Page: 100 Line: 016

HOYT Mary d Hopkinton 1859-03-28 age 66yrs b Hamilton Mass child of ROBERTS Francis of Mass & Sally Vol: 4 Page: 100 Line: 019

FERRINGTON Mary H d Hopkinton 1859-03-29 age 77yrs b Manchester Mass child of HERRICK Asa of Manchester Mass & Anna of Manchester Mass Vol: 4 Page: 101 Line: 003

STRAW Ange d Hopkinton 1859-04-19 age 2yrs 9mos 17dys b Hopkinton child of STRAW Horace of Hopkinton & Amanda of Dunbarton Vol: 4 Page: 101 Line: 018

TUTTLE James d Hopkinton 1859-04-23 age 18yrs 5mos 13dys b Hopkinton child of TUTTLE Jedidiah of Hamilton Mass & Lucy of Lempster Vol: 4 Page: 101 Line: 013

STORY Jeremiah d Hopkinton 1859-05-13 age 84yrs 1mos 17dys b Hopkinton child of STORY Jeremiah of Essex Mass & Polly of Essex Mass Vol: 4 Page: 101 Line: 001

SPOFFORD Ella Jane d Hopkinton 1859-06-13 age 2yrs 11mos 19dys b Hopkinton child of SPOFFORD Samuel of Chester & Sarah of Hopkinton Vol: 4 Page: 101 Line: 006

FROST Frederick J d Hopkinton 1859-06-13 age 4yrs b Hopkinton child of FROST Franklin D of Blover Vt & Martha L of Hopkinton Vol: 4 Page: 101 Line: 008

DUNBAR Freddie Howard d Hopkinton 1859-07-22 age 2yrs 10mos b Hopkinton child of DUNBAR Elmer of Grantham & Anna of Hopkinton Vol: 4 Page: 101 Line: 009

KELLEY Amos d Hopkinton 1859-08-02 age 63yrs b Hampstead Mass child of KELLEY Richard of Amesbury Mass & Eunice of Amesbury Mass Vol: 4 Page: 101 Line: 005

CLOUGH Abigail B d Hopkinton 1859-08-26 age 33yrs 8mos b Weare child of BECK Clement of Concord & Abigial of Loudon Vol: 4 Page: 101 Line: 023

CURRIER Abram S d Hopkinton 1859-08-29 age 31yrs b Concord child of CURRIER James & Elizabeth of Bow Vol: 4 Page: 100 Line: 021

PATCH Lydia D d Hopkinton 1859-09-09 age 20yrs b Hopkinton child of PATCH John of Salem Mass & Betsey M of Hopkinton Vol: 4 Page: 101 Line: 002

STANWOOD Joseph d Hopkinton 1859-10-11 age 53yrs b W Newbury Mass child of STANWOOD William of W Newbury Mass & Susan of W Newbury Mass Vol: 4 Page: 101 Line: 028

CHANDLER Lucy d Hopkinton 1859-10-13 age 71yrs b Roxbury Mass child of WITHINGTON Phineas of Dorchester Mass & HANNAH W of Dorchester Mass Vol: 4 Page: 101 Line: 007

RESTIEAUX Robert d Hopkinton 1859-10-25 age 17yrs b Concord child of RESTIEAUX Willam & Betsey of Hopkinton Vol: 4 Page: 100 Line: 022

SARGENT Benjamin Jr d Hopkinton 1859-11-04 age 42yrs b Warner child of SARGENT Benjamin of Warner & Eunice of Warner Vol: 4 Page: 101 Line: 004

KIMBALL Anna C d Hopkinton 1859-12-01 age 85yrs b Newbury Mass child of CARR Samuel of Newbury Mass & Eunice of Newbury Mass Vol: 4 Page: 101 Line: 010

Hopkinton, NH Deaths 1858

DUSTIN Sarah d Hopkinton 1859-12-06 age 73yrs 8mos 21dys b Warner child of PIERCE Daniel of Hudson & Hannah Vol: 4 Page: 101 Line: 022

HOYT Nathan G d Hopkinton 1859-12-19 age 50yrs 8mos 1dys b Henniker child of HOYT James of Hopkinton & Hannah of Newton Vol: 4 Page: 101 Line: 012

CHADWICK Hiram d Hopkinton 1859-12-24 age 59yrs 20dys b Hopkinton child of CHADWICH John of Bradford Mass & Abigial of W Newbury Mass Vol: 4 Page: 101 Line: 015

JACKMAN Nancy d Hopkinton 1859-12-28 age 66yrs 6mos b Hopkinton child of JACKMAN Noah of Palistow & Pauline of Plaistow Vol: 4 Page: 101 Line: 011

CAVENO ---- d Hopkinton 1860 age 1dys b Hopkinton child of CAVENO Arthur of Hollis & Bridget of Ireland Vol: 4 Page: 102 Line: 001

MERRILL Asa d Hopkinton 1860-01-12 age 83yrs 9mos 25dys b Manchester Mss child of MERRILL Jonathan of Manchester Mass & Rachel of Manchester Mass Vol: 4 Page: 101 Line: 026

JACKMAN William C d Hopkinton 1860-01-26 age 32yrs 21dys b Manchester Mass child of JACKMAN Ezra of Boscawen & Mary N of Hopkinton Vol: 4 Page: 101 Line: 019

SERGENT Hannah C d Hopkinton 1860-02-06 age 65yrs 8mos 2dys b Hopkinton child of ORDWAY John of Salem Mass & Hannah Vol: 4 Page: 101 Line: 021

DOW Simeon d Hopkinton 1860-02-12 age 98yrs 8mos 8dys b Amesbury Mass child of DOW Simeon & Phebe Vol: 4 Page: 101 Line: 020

HARVEY Jacob d Hopkinton 1860-02-23 age 41yrs 1mos 9dys b Dracut Mass child of HARVEY John of Dracut Mass & Mary of Hopkinton Vol: 4 Page: 101 Line: 027

SARGENT Hannah d Hopkinton 1860-03-11 age 83yrs 28dys b Chester child of DEARBORN D Vol: 4 Page: 101 Line: 016

CURRIER Charles d Hopkinton 1860-03-16 age 55yrs 1mos 23dys b Hopkinton child of CURRIER Amos of Hopkinton & Mary of Hopkinton Vol: 4 Page: 101 Line: 017

BAILEY Moses S d Hopkinton 1860-03-22 age 61yrs 5mos 8dys b Dunbarton child of BAILEY Isaac of Newbury Mass & Abigial of Hopkinton Vol: 4 Page: 101 Line: 014

HOWARD Nellie F d Hopkinton 1860-05-21 age 21yrs 21dys b Hopkinton child of HOWARD Alonzo of Hollis & A H of Hollis Vol: 4 Page: 102 Line: 002

DANFORTH Jon d Hopkinton 1860-06-22 age 30yrs b Hopkinton Vol: 4 Page: 102 Line: 003

THOMPSON Louisa P d Hopkinton 1860-08-23 age 13yrs 17mos 7dys b Hopkinton child of THOMPSON William of Mass ?? & Susan E of W Newbury Vol: 4 Page: 102 Line: 004

NEALY John d Hopkinton 1860-09-01 age 72yrs 1mos b Hopkinton Vol: 4 Page: 102 Line: 005

HUNTOON Sylvester P d Hopkinton 1860-09-09 age 37yrs b Hopkinton child of HUNTOON William of NH & Lydia Vol: 4 Page: 102 Line: 006

CORLIS Amanda d Hopkinton 1860-10-22 age 37yrs b Hopkinton child of GAGE John & Sally Vol: 4 Page: 102 Line: 007

HARDY ---- d Hopkinton 1860-10-23 age 3dys b Hopkinton child of HARDY Samuel of NH & Abbie Vol: 4 Page: 102 Line: 008

Hopkinton, NH Deaths 1858

CARLTON Sumner?? d Hopkinton 1860-11-13 age 51yrs 7mos 3dys b Warner child of ---- ---- of NH Vol: 4 Page: 102 Line: 009

WAY Sarah d Hopkinton 1860-11-15 age 19yrs 1mos 17dys b Hopkinton Vol: 4 Page: 102 Line: 010

PATTERSON George N d Hopkinton 1860-12-13 age 24yrs b Hopkinton child of PATTERSON Jacob of Me & Mary S of Deering Vol: 4 Page: 102 Line: 011

JEWETT Patty d Hopkinton 1860-12-26 age 89yrs b Manchester Mass Vol: 4 Page: 102 Line: 012

MONTGOMERY Alice d Hopkinton 1860-12-28 age 7yrs b Salem NY child of MONTGOMERY George of NY & E H of NY Vol: 4 Page: 102 Line: 013

KIMBALL Sarah d Hopkinton 1861-01-04 age 56yrs 3mos b Cambridge Vt child of TIRRILL Jonathan of Vt & Elizabeth of Cambridge Vt Vol: 4 Page: 102 Line: 014

RAND Sally d Hopkinton 1861-01-14 age 40yrs 2mos b Hopkinton child of HOLMES William & Sally of Hopkinton Vol: 4 Page: 102 Line: 0.16

CLOUGH William d Hopkinton 1861-01-22 age 63yrs b Pittsfield child of CLOUGH William & Sarah of Bennington Vol: 4 Page: 102 Line: 016

MORRILL Mary D d Hopkinton 1861-03-14 age 45yrs b Warner child of MOR-RILL John of NH & Hannah N Vol: 4 Page: 102 Line: 017

MCKENZIE Laura d Hopkinton 1861-03-24 age 1mos b Hopkinton child of McKENZIE George of Scotland & Bedilla of Scotland Vol: 4 Page: 102 Line: 018

DESMOND Alvira d Hopkinton 1861-03-29 age 46yrs 4mos b Warner child of CLARK Stephen of NH & Susan G of Canan Vol: 4 Page: 102 Line: 019

BLANCHARD Mary d Hopkinton 1861-03-30 age 52yrs b Hopkinton child of CURRIER Stephen & Lucy Vol: 4 Page: 102 Line: 020

HOYT Moses d Hopkinton 1861-04-22 age 64yrs 9mos b Hopkinton child of HOYT Benjamin of Weare & Jane of Kingston Vol: 4 Page: 103 Line: 001

BROWN Jonathan d Hopkinton 1861-04-30 age 78yrs 7dys b Bradford child of BROWN John B of Newbury Mass Vol: 4 Page: 103 Line: 002

HUNTOON Horace d Hopkinton 1861-06-22 age 66yrs 10mos 27dys b Unity Vol: 4 Page: 102 Line: 021

PERRY George W d Hopkinton 1861-07-20 age 32yrs 2mos 16dys b Hopkinton child of PERRY William of Henniker & Asenak of Hopkinton Vol: 4 Page: 103 Line: 003

SEAVEY Mary d Hopkinton 1861-07-26 age 84yrs 2mos 27dys b Andover Mass Vol: 4 Page: 103 Line: 004

CHANDLER Timothy d Hopkinton 1861-08-13 b Hopkinton child of CHANDLER Isaac & M Vol: 4 Page: 103 Line: 005

STANLEY Hannah d Hopkinton 1861-08-24 age 89yrs Vol: 4 Page: 103 Line: 007

CARR Abigail d Hopkinton 1861-08-25 age 85yrs 8mos b W Newbury Mass child of WILLIAMS Thomas & Elizabeth Vol: 4 Page: 103 Line: 006

CHASE Sarah d Hopkinton 1861-08-31 age 82yrs 7mos b Warner child of FERRIN Francis & Betsey Vol: 4 Page: 103 Line: 009

CHANDLER Isaac d Hopkinton 1861-08-31 age 83yrs b Hopkinton child of CHANDLER Isaac & CHANDLER M Vol: 4 Page: 103 Line: 008

Hopkinton, NH Deaths 1858

MORRILL Elisabeth d Hopkinton 1861-09-04 age 37yrs 4mos b Hopkinton child of BROWN Abram of Hopkinton & Eunice of Plainfield Vol: 4 Page: 103 Line: 010

LONG Isaac d Hopkinton 1861-09-18 b Hopkinton child of LONG Enoch & Mary of Hopkinton Vol: 4 Page: 103 Line: 011

PIERCE David d Hopkinton 1861-09-28 age 72yrs 4mos b Hudson child of PIERCE Daniel of Hudson & Hannah of Hudson Vol: 4 Page: 103 Line: 012

KIMBALL Ellen C d Hopkinton 1861-10-01 age 27yrs 2mos 4dys b Hopkinton child of KIMBALL Daniel of Hopkinton & Asenath of Hopkinton Vol: 4 Page: 103 Line: 013

MORRILL Rhoda d Hopkinton 1861-10-03 age 87yrs 9mos 12dys b Hopkinton child of BARNARD Joseph of Bath & Rhoda of Ireland Vol: 4 Page: 103 Line: 014

CAVENO Elisabeth d Hopkinton 1861-10-09 age 9yrs 5mos 25dys b Hopkinton child of CAVENO Arthur of Bath & Bridget of Ireland Vol: 4 Page: 103 Line: 015

GOULD Hannah d Hopkinton 1861-11-08 age 77??yrs 8mos b Warner child of CURRIER Nathan of Amesbury Mass & Abigail of Amesbury Mass Vol: 4 Page: 103 Line: 016

DERRICK Harriett d Hopkinton 1861-11-25 age 25yrs 2mos b Lyme child of DERRICK Wilson of Lyme & Eise of Oxford Vol: 4 Page: 103 Line: 017

PETERS William d Hopkinton 1861-12-25 age 50yrs b England child of PETERS Cornelia of England & Deborah of Vol: 4 Page: 103 Line: 018

HUTCHINS William d Hopkinton 1861-12-30 age 83yrs b child of of & of Vol: 4 Page: 103 Line: 019

WHITTIER Charles d Hopkinton 1861-12-30 age 19yrs 2mos 20dys b Londonderry child of WHITTIER Ebenezer of Londonerry & Lucy of Hopkinton Vol: 4 Page: 103 Line: 020

PUTNAM Herrick d Hopkinton 1862 age 58yrs b Hopkinton child of PUTNAM Rufus of Danvers Mass & ---- ---- of Danvers Vol: 4 Page: 103 Line: 028

KIMBALL Abel d Hopkinton 1862-01-08 age 84yrs b Hopkinton child of KIMBALL Aaron of Hopkinton & Abigial Vol: 4 Page: 103 Line: 021

GREENE Herman N d Hopkinton 1862-01-08 age 59yrs 8mos 9dys b Concord child of GREENE Samuel & Lucretia Vol: 4 Page: 103 Line: 022

ORDWAY Rebecca d Hopkinton 1862-02-08 age 80yrs b Hopkinton child of ORDWAY Peter Vol: 4 Page: 103 Line: 021

MERRILL Enos d Hopkinton 1862-02-09 age 80yrs b Hopkinton child of MERRILL Parker of Hopkinton & Rebecca Vol: 4 Page: 103 Line: 024

LITTLE William d Hopkinton 1862-02-23 age 83yrs 23dys b Atkinson Vol: 4 Page: 103 Line: 024

CURRIER Stephen d Hopkinton 1862-03-23 age 89yrs 9mos 12dys b Hopkinton child of CURRIER John of Sometown?? Mass & Lucy Vol: 4 Page: 103 Line: 026

STANLEY Moses d Hopkinton 1862-03-27 b Hopkinton child of STANLEY John & Sarah Vol: 4 Page: 103 Line: 027

GOODRICH Francis Adalie d Hopkinton 1862-05-05 age 46yrs b Boston Mass child of WHITMAN Thomas of NH?? & Sophia of Hopkinton Vol: 4 Page: 104 Line: 002

Hopkinton, NH Deaths 1858

LONG Benjamin d At Sea 1862-05-27 age 26yrs b Amesbury Mass child of LONG Nathan of Mass?? & Sally of Warner Vol: 4 Page: 104 Line: 003

FELLOWS Sarah d Hopkinton 1862-08-26 age 86yrs b Haverhill Mass child of --------- of Haverhill & EMERSON Sarah of Haverhill Vol: 4 Page: 104 Line: 006

PERRY Wm P d Hopkinton 1862-09-01 age 42yrs b Henniker child of PERRY William of Henniker & Asenath of Hopkinton Vol: 4 Page: 104 Line: 007

BROWN Eunice d Hopkinton 1862-10-04 age 79yrs b Plainfield child of KIMBALL Joseph of Plainfield Conn & Eleanor Vol: 4 Page: 104 Line: 008

NELSON Joseph d Hopkinton 1862-10-08 age 54yrs 6mos b Sutton child of ---- ---- of Sutton & ---- ---- of Hopkinton Vol: 4 Page: 104 Line: 010

JONES Horace F d Fitchbury Mass 1862-10-27 age 29yrs b Hopkinton child of JONES Jonathan of Boscawen & Sarah of Hopkinton Vol: 4 Page: 104 Line: 009

BUTTERFIELD Anna E d Hopkinton 1862-11-10 age 25yrs b Warner child of BARNARD Winthrop of Warner & Lucinda of Warner Vol: 4 Page: 104 Line: 011

ROGERS Obediah d Hopkinton 1862-11-27 age 85yrs b Newbury Mass child of ROGERS Simeon of Newbury Mass & Nancy Vol: 4 Page: 104 Line: 012

HARRINGTON Moses A d Hopkinton 1862-11-28 age 26yrs b Salisbury Mass child of HARRINGTON Moses B of Cornish & Betsey of Deerfield Vol: 4 Page: 104 Line: 013

FLANDERS George d Hopkinton 1862-12-05 age 30yrs 7mos 17dys b Bradford child of FLANDERS Nathaniel of Hopkinton & Betsey of Sutton Vol: 4 Page: 104 Line: 014

ASH Charles E d New Orleans Ga 1863 Jan 00 age 19yrs b Hopkinton child of ASH James of Salisbury & Matilda of Boscawen Vol: 4 Page: 104 Line: 016

WALKER Richard d Monroe?? 1863-01-08 age 21yrs b Hopkinton child of WALKER Moses A of NH & Ellisa A of Northwood Vol: 4 Page: 104 Line: 004 Note: battle at Williamsbaurg

SWEET Moses d Hopkinton 1863-01-11 age 58yrs b Andover child of SWEET William of Hopkinton & Abigial of Sutton Vol: 4 Page: 104 Line: 015

STORY Charles L d Hopkinton 1863-01-18 age 2yrs 11mos 26dys b Hopkinton child of STORY Frederick of Washington & STORY P of Washington Vol: 4 Page: 105 Line: 036

COLBY Susannah d Hopkinton 1863-01-26 age 91yrs 4mos 6dys b Hopkinton child of STORY?? Thomas of Essex Mass & Hannah Vol: 4 Page: 104 Line: 017

HARRINGTON David d Poolsville Md 1863-02-23 age 20yrs b Manchester child of HARRINGTON Moses B of Cornish & Betsey of Deerfield Vol: 4 Page: 104 Line: 018

-ifford??? Mary d Hopkinton 1863-03-17 age 82yrs 5mos 2dys b Hopkinton child of BAILEY Isaac of Newbury Mass & Mary of Newbury Mass Vol: 4 Page: 104 Line: 019

ABBOTT Sarah C d Hopkinton 1863-03-21 age 7yrs 2mos b Hopkinton child of ABBOTT Jeremiah of Pomfort Vt & Hannah of Concord Vol: 4 Page: 104 Line: 020

DEMMICK Elisa d Hopkinton 1863-03-23 age 56yrs b Oxford child of ROBERTS Elmador & Sarah Vol: 4 Page: 104 Line: 021

Hopkinton, NH Deaths 1858

COPPS Moses d Hopkinton 1863-03-30 age 85yrs 4mos 24dys b Plaistown child of COPPS John of Plaistow & Sarah of Plaistow Vol: 4 Page: 104 Line: 023

COLBY Nathaniel K d Hopkinton 1863-03-30 age 54yrs b Hopkinton child of COLBY Richard & Lois Vol: 4 Page: 104 Line: 022

FISK Daniel d Hopkinton 1863-03-30 age 35yrs b Hopkinton child of FISK Joseph of Concord & Lucy of Essex Mass Vol: 4 Page: 104 Line: 024

KIMBALL Mary J d Hopkinton 1863-04-01 age 14yrs b Derry child of KIMBALL Iddo R of Bradford Mass & Fannie of Londonderry Vol: 4 Page: 105 Line: 001

WILLIAMS Eunice d Hopkinton 1863-04-04 age 88yrs 9mos b Ipswich Mass child of WADE William of Ipswich Mass & Eunice of Ipswich Mass Vol: 4 Page: 105 Line: 002

NELSON Ester d Hopkinton 1863-04-04 age 52yrs 6mos b Weare child of HUBBARD John of Mass?? & Ruth of Weare Vol: 4 Page: 104 Line: 001

KIMBALL Charles d Hopkinton 1863-04-11 age 17yrs 3mos 7dys b Derry child of KIMBALL Iddo of Bradford Mass & Fanney of Londonderry Vol: 4 Page: 105 Line: 004

MUDGETT Ebenezer d Hopkinton 1863-04-22 age 62yrs 6mos 7dys b Weare child of MUDGETT Ebenezer of Weare & Sarah of Weare Vol: 4 Page: 105 Line: 005

FOSTER William N d Hopkinton 1863-04-23 age 23yrs 10mos 13dys b Hopkinton child of FOSTER John of Reading Mass & Belinda of Hopkinton Vol: 4 Page: 105 Line: 003

BALCH Edwin R d Hopkinton 1863-04-27 age 4yrs 6mos 4dys b Hopkinton child of BALCH Theodore of Lime(lyme) & Ellen of Boscawen Vol: 4 Page: 105 Line: 007

FOSS John d Hopkinton 1863-04-30 age 82yrs 8mos 2dys b Bennington child of FOSS George of Bennington & Elisabeth of Bennington Vol: 4 Page: 105 Line: 008

DUSTIN Eben N d Baton Rogue La 1863-05-06 age 50yrs 5mos 23dys b Hopkinton child of DUSTIN Ebenezer of Hopkinton & Sarah of Nashua Vol: 4 Page: 105 Line: 009

PATCH Nathaniel d Hopkinton 1863-05-14 age 84yrs 2mos 4dys b Hamilton Mass child of PATCH John of Hamilton Mass & Lucy of Hamilton Mass Vol: 4 Page: 105 Line: 011

MOULTON Henry d New Orleans La 1863-05-14 age 21yrs 6mos 11dys b Hopkinton child of MOULTON Caleb of Hampton Falls & Mary of Chichester Vol: 4 Page: 105 Line: 010

THOMPSON Sarah E d New York City 1863-06-04 age 35yrs 2mos 1dys b Gilmanton child of THOMPSON Levi of Gilmanton & Mehitable of Barnstead Vol: 4 Page: 105 Line: 012

HEATH Elizia F d Hopkinton 1863-06-08 age 37yrs 10mos b Henniker child of PERRY David & Hannah Vol: 4 Page: 105 Line: 013

JOHNSON Anna d Hopkinton 1863-06-26 age 93yrs 1mos 6dys b Hopkinton child of COLBY Anothy of Newbury Mass & Elizabeth of Salisbury Mass Vol: 4 Page: 104 Line: 005

KIMBALL Warren C d Charlestown Sc 1863-07-18 age 23yrs 4mos b Derry child of KIMBALL Iddo of Bradford Mass & Fanney of Londonderry Vol: 4 Page: 105 Line: 015

Hopkinton, NH Deaths 1858

DUSTIN Gilbert F d Fort Wagner Sc 1863-07-18 age 28yrs 5mos 7dys b Hopkinton child of DUSTIN Cyrus of Hopkinton & Edna of Wilmot Vol: 4 Page: 105 Line: 014

WEEKS Sarah d Hopkinton 1863-07-20 age 91yrs 9mos 21dys b Greenfield child of WEEKS Ichabod of Greenfield & Comfort Vol: 4 Page: 105 Line: 016

ADAMS Lilla Jona d Hopkinton 1863-08-15 age 21dys b Hopkinton child of ADAMS Joseph N of Sutton & Judith of Warner Vol: 4 Page: 105 Line: 017

DOW George L d Hopkinton 1863-08-18 age 42yrs 5mos 27dys b Hopkinton child of DOW Joseph of Hopkinton & Hannah of Litchfield Vol: 4 Page: 105 Line: 019

WHITTIER Jacob d Hopkinton 1863-08-18 age 42yrs 11mos 18dys b Danville child of WHITTIER James of Haverhill & WHITTIER N of Hampstead Vol: 4 Page: 105 Line: 018

AGER ---- d Hopkinton 1863-08-30 b Hopkinton child of AGER Walter C of Warner & ---- ---- of Hopkinton Vol: 4 Page: 105 Line: 020

GOODRICH Arthur d Hopkinton 1863-09-08 age 19yrs 6mos 13dys b Boston Mass child of GOODRICH George R of Springfield Vt & Frances of Boston Mass Vol: 4 Page: 105 Line: 021

EATON Moses d Hopkinton 1863-09-20 age 17yrs 8mos b Hopkinton child of EATON Ichabod of Haverhill Mass & Lousa of Cannan Vol: 4 Page: 105 Line: 022

FLANDERS Jonathan d Hopkinton 1863-09-27 age 39yrs 11mos b Hopkinton child of FLANDERS Philip of So Hampton & Sarah of Hopkinton Vol: 4 Page: 105 Line: 023

BARNARD Joseph N d Hopkinton 1863-10-20 age 3yrs b Hopkinton child of BARNARD Joseph Jr of Hopkinton & Nana G of Canterbury Vol: 4 Page: 105 Line: 025

BUSWELL Aaron W d Hopkinton 1863-10-20 age 71yrs 38dys b Boxford Mass child of BUSWELL James of Brunswick Me & Jane of Boxford Mass Vol: 4 Page: 105 Line: 024

LAW Etta L d Hopkinton 1863-11-05 age 5yrs 8mos 3dys b Henniker child of LAW Joseph P of Vt & Belinda of Haverhill Vol: 4 Page: 105 Line: 026

ORDWAY Eben d Hopkinton 1863-11-09 age 77yrs 5mos 14dys b Hopkinton child of ORDWAY Eben & Sarah N Vol: 4 Page: 105 Line: 027

GREEN ---- d Hopkinton 1863-11-25 age 4dys b Hopkinton child of GREEN Newman L of Chichester & Sarah of Sutton Vol: 4 Page: 105 Line: 028

FOGG George N d Hopkinton 1863-12-07 age 19yrs 2mos 18dys b Manchester child of FOGG Sherburn of Merdith & Merriam of Hopkinton Vol: 4 Page: 105 Line: 029

DOW Martain U B d Hopkinton 1863-12-09 age 27yrs 7mos 8dys b Hopkinton child of DOW Thomas of Concord & Rhoda of Hopkinton Vol: 4 Page: 105 Line: 030

HARDY Phebe d Hopkinton 1863-12-11 age 81yrs 11mos 9dys b Nottingham child of HARDY Isaac of Bradford Mass & Lydia of Hopkinton Vol: 4 Page: 105 Line: 032

WEEKS Charles d Hopkinton 1863-12-14 age 72yrs 2mos 5dys b Hopkinton child of ---- ---- of Greenland & ---- ---- of Greenland Vol: 4 Page: 105 Line: 031

Hopkinton, NH Deaths 1858

BARNARD Augustus d Hopkinton 1863-12-16 age 30yrs 9mos 13dys b Amesbury Mass Vol: 4 Page: 105 Line: 033

DANFORTH Augustus d Hopkinton 1863-12-23 age 36yrs b Weare Vol: 4 Page: 111 Line: 026

BURNHAM ---- d Hopkinton 1864 b Hopkinton child of BURNHAM Edward D of Hopkinton & Georgie of Warner Vol: 4 Page: 106 Line: 004

CURRIER George A d Hopkinton 1864 Mar 00 age 19yrs 3mos 15dys b Hopkinton child of CURRIER Erastus E of Hopkinton & Lucy of Hopkinton Vol: 4 Page: 105 Line: 039

MOULTON Charles A d New Orleans La 1864 Spe 24 age 25yrs 6mos 12dys b Loudon child of MOULTON Caleb of Hampton Falls & Mary of Chichester Vol: 4 Page: 106 Line: 014

JONES Augustia J d Hopkinton 1864-01-05 age 23yrs 5mos 5dys b Charlestown Mass child of FLANDERS Collins of Warner & Mehitable of Boscawen Vol: 4 Page: 105 Line: 034

NICHOLS Hirren d Washinton Dc 1864-01-09 age 41yrs 11mos 24dys b W Amesbury Mass child of NICHOLS Moses of W Amesbury Mass & Nancy of W Amesbury Mass Vol: 4 Page: 105 Line: 035

STINSON Ruth d Hopkinton 1864-03-06 age 90yrs 6mos 6dys b Hopkinton child of STINSON Daniel of Ipswich Mass & Ruth of Ipswich Mass Vol: 4 Page: 105 Line: 037

KENT Thomas d Hopkinton 1864-03-22 age 87yrs 22dys b Boston Mass child of KENT Philip G of Boston Mass & Sally of Haverhill Vol: 4 Page: 105 Line: 038

QUIMBY John d Hopkinton 1864-05-01 age 73yrs 8mos 13dys b Hopkinton child of QUIMBY Jonathan of So Hampton & Mary of So Hampton Vol: 4 Page: 106 Line: 001

RAYMOND Geo J d Spotsylvania Va 1864-05-14 age 24yrs 6mos 15dys b Hopkinton child of RAYMOND Joshua of Hopkinton & Margaret of Hopkinton Vol: 4 Page: 106 Line: 002

CLARK J Oscar d Hopkinton 1864-05-21 age 7yrs 3mos b Franklinn child of CLARK Jonathan of Warner & Caroline of Hopkinton Vol: 4 Page: 106 Line: 003

BRUCE Henry d Hopkinton 1864-06-26 age 21yrs 4mos 12dys b Boston Mass child of BRUCE Goerge W & Isabelle Vol: 4 Page: 106 Line: 005

HEATH Origin d Hopkinton 1864-07-12 age 2yrs 10mos b Hopkinton child of HEATH James of Salisbury & Harriet of Warner Vol: 4 Page: 106 Line: 006

HEATH James d Hopkinton 1864-07-13 age 4yrs 10mos 22dys b Hopkinton child of HEATH James of Salisbury & Harriet of Warner Vol: 4 Page: 106 Line: 007

BROWN Cora d Hopkinton 1864-07-19 age 5yrs 11mos 29dys b Hopkinton child of BROWN Jonathan of Hopkinton & Mary of Hopkinton Vol: 4 Page: 106 Line: 008

BARRETT Luther N d Hopkinton 1864-08-09 age 28yrs 9mos b Brattleboro Vt child of BARRETT John & Dolly Vol: 4 Page: 106 Line: 009

DWINNELLS Emma d Hopkinton 1864-08-15 age 3mos 23dys b Hopkinton child of DWINNELLS John of Dunbarton & Sarah A of Henniker Vol: 4 Page: 106 Line: 010

Hopkinton, NH Deaths 1858

RION Frances E d Hopkinton 1864-08-21 age 3mos b Hopkinton child of RION Samuel of Canterbury & Cynthia of Hopkinton Vol: 4 Page: 106 Line: 011

COLLINS Achsah A d Amesbury Mass 1864-09-07 age 48yrs 5mos 21dys b Derrfield child of MOOERS John of Derrfield & Hannah of Derrfield Vol: 4 Page: 106 Line: 012

HOLMES Elijah d Hopkinton 1864-10-02 age 76yrs b Hopkinton Vol: 4 Page: 106 Line: 016

HARDY Lucinda d Hopkinton 1864-10-24 age 64yrs b Stoddard Vol: 4 Page: 106 Line: 015

CURRIER David C d Hopkinton 1864-10-24 age 67yrs 5mos 8dys b Hopkinton child of CURRIER Edmund & Betsey Vol: 4 Page: 106 Line: 014

FARNSWORTH Mary d Hopkinton 1864-11-13 age 89yrs 3mos b Hopkinton Vol: 4 Page: 106 Line: 017

CARPENTER Hiram d Hopkinton 1864-12-13 age 38yrs 11mos 15dys b Canada child of CARPENTER Joseph of Canada & Martha of Canada Vol: 4 Page: 106 Line: 018

DUNBAR Flora A d Hopkinton 1864-12-15 age 3yrs 10mos 24dys b Hopkinton child of DUNBAR Justice of Hopkinton & Mary P of Orange Vol: 4 Page: 106 Line: 019

COLBY Melvin Crawford d Hopkinton 1864-12-24 age 4yrs 1mos b Hopkinton child of COLBY Melvin of Hopkinton & Hannah of Hopkinton Vol: 4 Page: 106 Line: 020

JONES Charles G d Hopkinton 1864-12-28 age 37yrs b Hopkinton child of JONES Jonathan of Boscawen & Sarah of Hopkinton Vol: 4 Page: 106 Line: 021

HENSE?? James d Hopkinton 1865-01-11 age 78yrs 5mos 1dys b Hampstead Vol: 4 Page: 106 Line: 023

FRENCH Maria L d Hopkinton 1865-01-18 age 12yrs 1mos 20dys b Hopkinton child of FRENCH Reuben E of Hopkinton & Sarah of Dunbarton Vol: 4 Page: 106 Line: 023

FRENCH Annie L d Hopkinton 1865-01-19 age 1yrs 2mos 7dys b Hopkinton child of FRENCH Sullivan of Hopkinton & Almira of Chichester Vol: 4 Page: 106 Line: 024

DUNBAR Mary A d Hopkinton 1865-01-21 age 9yrs 9mos 6dys b Hopkinton child of DUNBAR Justice A of Hopkinton & Mary P of Orange Vol: 4 Page: 106 Line: 025

CLOUGH Mary P d Hopkinton 1865-01-25 age 82yrs 8mos 17dys b Boscawen child of CLOUGH William of Hampstead & Mary P of Hampstead Vol: 4 Page: 106 Line: 026

RAYMOND Neannah N d Hopkinton 1865-02-02 age 44yrs 9mos b Manchester Vol: 4 Page: 106 Line: 027

TILTON Neelen A d Hopkinton 1865-02-02 age 1yrs 5mos 26dys b Hopkinton child of TILTON William W of Hill & Sarah A of Amesbury Mass Vol: 4 Page: 106 Line: 028

RAYMOND Josiah d Hopkinton 1865-02-04 age 17yrs 37mos 26dys b Lynn Mass child of RAYMOND Nathaniel of Salem & Hannah of Beverly Mass Vol: 4 Page: 107 Line: 001

Hopkinton, NH Deaths 1858

COLBY Lydia N d Hopkinton 1865-03-11 age 87yrs 6mos 15dys b Manchester child of HERRICK Asa & Anna Vol: 4 Page: 107 Line: 023

PLUMMER Lydia d Hopkinton 1865-04-10 age 71yrs 17dys b Henniker Vol: 4 Page: 107 Line: 002

ROWELL Abram d Hopkinton 1865-05-01 age 54yrs 4mos 26dys b Hopkinton child of ROWELL Moses of Hopkinton & Tamson of Hopkinton Vol: 4 Page: 107 Line: 003

HARVEY Mary d Hopkinton 1865-05-12 age 79yrs 2mos 16dys b Hopkinton child of STRAW Jacob of Hopkinton & Betsey of Hopkinton Vol: 4 Page: 107 Line: 004

CLEMONS Lottie C d Hopkinton 1865-05-23 age 3yrs 3mos 15dys b Hopkinton child of CLEMONS Henry W & Betsey of Hopkinton Vol: 4 Page: 107 Line: 005

TYLER Cyrel C d Hopkinton 1865-05-27 age 52yrs 4mos b Theford Vt child of TYLER Jeremiah & Irene Vol: 4 Page: 107 Line: 006

HARVEY John d Hopkinton 1865-06-07 age 82yrs 9mos 1dys b Dracut Mass child of HARVEY William of Dracut Mass & Mary of Methuen Mass Vol: 4 Page: 107 Line: 007

CAMPBELL Carrie E d Hopkinton 1865-08-03 age 25yrs 3mos b Henniker child of CONNOR James of Henniker & Lydia of Hopkinton Vol: 4 Page: 107 Line: 008

LOCKE Dexter W d Hopkinton 1865-08-07 age 6yrs 9mos b Hopkinton child of LOCKE Warren F of Warner & Harriet T of Hopkinton Vol: 4 Page: 107 Line: 009

RAYMOND Francis d Hopkinton 1865-08-31 age 42yrs 2mos 22dys b Salem Mass child of RAYMOND Joshua & Hannah of Salem Mass Vol: 4 Page: 107 Line: 010

EMERSON Hazen d Hopkinton 1865-09-04 age 78yrs 1mos b Hopkinton child of -- -- ---- of Hopkinton Vol: 4 Page: 107 Line: 011

SMART Elizebet E d Hopkinton 1865-10-14 age 26yrs 3mos 14dys b Hopkinton child of SMART Durrill of Hopkinton & Arian Vol: 4 Page: 107 Line: 012

MILTON Judith d Hopkinton 1865-10-16 age 73yrs 9mos b Hopkinton child of ---- ---- of Henniker & ---- ---- of Hopkinton Vol: 4 Page: 107 Line: 014

EMERSON Clara Ann d Hopkinton 1865-10-16 age 14yrs b Hopkinton child of EMERSON Isaac & Luentia Vol: 4 Page: 107 Line: 013

WAY William d Hopkinton 1865-10-18 age 71yrs 6mos 23dys b Salem Mass child of Samuel H of Salem Mass & Mary of Hopkinton Vol: 4 Page: 107 Line: 015

DODGE Henry d Hopkinton 1865-11-02 age 79yrs 1mos b Beverly Mass child of DODGE Jonathan & Hannah of Beverly Mass Vol: 4 Page: 107 Line: 016

CARPENTER Martha d Hopkinton 1865-11-03 age 67yrs b Lime(lyme) child of BURR Salvanns & Sarah Vol: 4 Page: 107 Line: 017

FLANDERS Israel d Hopkinton 1865-11-20 age 85yrs 20dys b Boscawen child of FLANDERS Ezekiel of Boscawen & Rusha of Concord Vol: 4 Page: 107 Line: 018

EMERSON Isaac d Hopkinton 1865-12-27 age 49yrs b Bow child of ---- ---- of Bow Vol: 4 Page: 107 Line: 019

CROWELL Ester S d Hopkinton 1866-01-08 age 62yrs 5mos b Weare Vol: 4 Page: 107 Line: 020

Hopkinton, NH Deaths 1858

CLOUGH Willard d Hopkinton 1866-01-23 age 54yrs 3mos b Hopkinton child of CLOUGH Phineas of Hopkinton & Judith of Warner Vol: 4 Page: 107 Line: 021

PALMER Sarah T d Hopkinton 1866-03-11 age 81yrs 9mos 1dys b Hopkinton child of TRUSSELL John of Mass & Mary of Mass Vol: 4 Page: 107 Line: 022

WRIGHT Willie N d Hopkinton 1866-03-18 age 16yrs 26dys b Warner child of WRIGHT Mary Ann of Cambridge Mass Vol: 4 Page: 107 Line: 024

RAND Elizabeth d Hopkinton 1866-04-14 age 94yrs b Warner child of DAVIS Zebulon of Warner & Hannah Vol: 4 Page: 108 Line: 014

EVERETT David d Hopkinton 1866-04-25 age 82yrs 8mos b Mass Vol: 4 Page: 108 Line: 018

CLEMENT Miriam d Hopkinton 1866-06-07 age 91yrs 1mos 20dys b Salisbury Mass child of MORRILL Mark & JEWELL Anna Vol: 4 Page: 108 Line: 003

SARGENT Stephen d Wilmington Mass 1866-06-09 age 48yrs 10mos b Hopkinton child of SARGENT Moses & Hannah of Chester Vol: 4 Page: 108 Line: 008

SPOFFORD Elisa A d Hopkinton 1866-06-13 age 39yrs 6mos 15dys b Hopkinton child of HOWTHORN Calvin & Rachael Vol: 4 Page: 108 Line: 011

FRENCH George E d Hopkinton 1866-07-02 age 15yrs 6mos b Hopkinton child of FRENCH Charles E of Concord & Mary of Hopkinton Vol: 4 Page: 108 Line: 004

CLOUGH Phineas d Hopkinton 1866-07-12 age 82yrs 11mos b Hopkinton Vol: 4 Page: 108 Line: 022

COLBY Timothy d Hopkinton 1866-07-15 age 84yrs 4dys b Hopkinton child of COLBY William of Hopkinton & STRAW Sallia of Hopkinton Vol: 4 Page: 108 Line: 002

WHITE Susan d Hopkinton 1866-08-08 age 83yrs b Cannan child of SPRINGER John & Hannah Vol: 4 Page: 108 Line: 007

DAVIS Betsey A d Hopkinton 1866-08-09 age 43yrs 7mos b Bradford child of CRESSEY Robert of Bradford & Abigial of Bradford Vol: 4 Page: 108 Line: 009

KNOWLTON Isreal P?? d Hopkinton 1866-09-02 age 71yrs 6mos b Hopkinton child of KNOWLTON Daniel of Gloucester Mass & Mary of Newburyport Mass Vol: 4 Page: 108 Line: 005

TYLER Nancy d Hopkinton 1866-09-09 age 92yrs 8mos b Pembroke Vol: 4 Page: 108 Line: 021

TYLER Henry?? d Hopkinton 1866-10-18 age 25yrs 9mos b Hopkinton child of ---- ---- of Concord & ---- ---- of Hopkinton Vol: 4 Page: 108 Line: 016 Note: xx ck original

HOYT Nancy C d Hopkinton 1866-11-04 age 58yrs 3mos b Bow child of PALMER Joseph & Rebecca Vol: 4 Page: 108 Line: 012

TEWKSBURY Joseph d Hopkinton 1866-11-12 age 69yrs 6mos 8dys b Hopkinton child of TEWKSBURY John of Manchester Mass & Sarah of Manchester Mass Vol: 4 Page: 108 Line: 010

CLARK Joseph d Hopkinton 1866-11-15 age 86yrs 11mos b Hopkinton child of ---- ---- of Hopkinton Vol: 4 Page: 108 Line: 015

MORGAN Mary d Hopkinton 1866-11-22 age 74yrs 4mos 11dys b Hopkinton child of HOYT Benjamin of Hopkinton & Jane of East Kingston Vol: 4 Page: 108 Line: 006

DWINNELLS Frank d Hopkinton 1866-12-03 age 12yrs 11mos b Dungarton child of ---- ---- of Haverhill & ---- ---- of Weare Vol: 4 Page: 108 Line: 019

BOUTILL Charlotte F d Hopkinton 1866-12-30 age 61yrs b Concord child of ---- ---- ---- of Concord Vol: 4 Page: 108 Line: 020

EATON Ichabod d Hopkinton 1867-01-02 age 63yrs b Haverhill Mass Vol: 4 Page: 108 Line: 013

MORRILL Bertha d Hopkinton 1867-03-05 age 4mos 16dys b Hopkinton child of MORRILL Charles of Hopkinton & Theresia of Derry Vol: 4 Page: 108 Line: 017

MERRILL Rebald d Hopkinton 1867-03-16 age 93yrs 11mos 5dys b Hopkinton child of KIMBALL Samuel of Hopkinton & Susan Vol: 4 Page: 108 Line: 001

SMART Sophronia E d Hopkinton 1867-06-22 age 20yrs b Hopkinton child of SMART Durilll of Hopkinton & Margarett of Kensingston Vol: 4 Page: 109 Line: 013

HUGHES James d Hopkinton 1867-08-02 age 6dys b Hopkinton child of HUGHES Thomas of Ireland & Catherin E of Ireland Vol: 4 Page: 109 Line: 001

STRAW Mary Ann d Hopkinton 1867-08-16 age 45yrs b Hopkinton child of STRAW Jacob of Hopkinton & ---- ---- of Hopkinton Vol: 4 Page: 109 Line: 003

LOCKE Elizabeth C d Hopkinton 1867-08-20 age 71yrs b Hopkinton child of CHASE Samuel of Hopkinton & Heoleley?? of Hopkinton Vol: 4 Page: 109 Line: 002

STORY William K d Hopkinton 1867-09-16 age 84yrs 8mos b Hopkinton child of STORY Nathan of Mass & Hannah of Mass Vol: 4 Page: 109 Line: 015

TUTTLE Lucy S d Hopkinton 1867-10-14 age 54yrs b Hopkinton child of TUTTLE James of Hopkinton Mass & Elizabeth of Hopkinton Mass Vol: 4 Page: 109 Line: 004

CHASE Georgia O d Hopkinton 1867-10-18 age 10yrs 4mos 7dys b Concord child of CHASE Harvey of Hopkinton & Martha Vol: 4 Page: 109 Line: 005

MERRILL Frank E d Hopkinton 1867-11-16 age 6dys b Hopkinton child of MERRILL S W of Hopkinton & Laura of Warner Vol: 4 Page: 109 Line: 014

HOWE Eliza J d Hopkinton 1867-12-08 b Hopkinton child of CHASE Daniel & ---- ---- of Henniker Vol: 4 Page: 109 Line: 009

KIMBALL Judith d Hopkinton 1867-12-16 age 49yrs 10mos 3dys b Alton child of KIMBALL Ezekiel of Alton & Abigail of Gilmanton Vol: 4 Page: 109 Line: 012

BURBANK Jonathan d Hopkinton 1867-12-21 age 76yrs 11mos 6dys b Hopkinton child of BURBANK Ebenezer of Hopkinton & Lydia of Hopkinton Vol: 4 Page: 109 Line: 006

HARDY Sarah d Hopkinton 1868 Dec 00 age 68yrs b Hopkinton child of KELLEY Carlos & ---- ---- of Hopkinton Vol: 4 Page: 110 Line: 008

DAVIS Cornelia d Hopkinton 1868 Oct 00 age 23yrs b Warner child of DAVIS Dudley B of Warner & ---- ---- of Warner Vol: 4 Page: 110 Line: 016

DROWN Mary C d Hopkinton 1868-01-07 age 66yrs 3mos 13dys b Rehoboth Mass child of DROWN Isreal of Rehoboth Mass & Christine of Seekonk Mass Vol: 4 Page: 109 Line: 010

MUDGETT William S d Hopkinton 1868-01-28 age 28yrs 1mos 29dys b New Boston child of MUDGETT Moses & Lucindia Vol: 4 Page: 109 Line: 007

Hopkinton, NH Deaths 1858

HARDY ---- d Hopkinton 1868-02-19 age 10dys b Hopkinton child of HARDY Samuel A of Hopkinton & Abby A of Hopkinton Vol: 4 Page: 109 Line: 011

DANFORD Gilman d Hopkinton 1868-03-09 age 60yrs 10mos 7dys b Warner child of DANFORTH Sarah Vol: 4 Page: 109 Line: 008

WHITE Thomas d Hopkinton 1868-03-17 age 82yrs 10mos 28dys b Gilsum child of WHITE Henry & Sarah Vol: 4 Page: 111 Line: 022

HASTINGS Hannah d Hopkinton 1868-06-05 age 78yrs 6mos 15dys b Hopkinton child of HASTINGS Joseph of Hopkinton & Rebecca of Bath Vol: 4 Page: 110 Line: 005

HARVEY Augusta E d Hopkinton 1868-06-09 age 21yrs 1mos b Manchester child of HARVEY John W of Meuthen Mass & Mary of Salem Mass Vol: 4 Page: 110 Line: 001

CHASE Abner d Hopkinton 1868-06-10 age 61yrs b Hopkinton child of CHASE Enoch & Mary Vol: 4 Page: 110 Line: 002

TYLER Nancy d Hopkinton 1868-06-30 age 21yrs 9dys b Hopkinton child of TYLER Calvin of Hopkinton & Zilpha of Hopkinton Vol: 4 Page: 110 Line: 006

TILTON Mary W d Hopkinton 1868-08-25 age 83yrs 6mos 10dys b Hopkinton child of FOWLER Jonathan of Hopkinton & Hannah of Hopkinton Vol: 4 Page: 110 Line: 004

CLOUGH Judith d Hopkinton 1868-09-03 age 80yrs b Hopkinton child of CURRIER Daniel Vol: 4 Page: 110 Line: 007

HASTINGS Albert d Hopkinton 1868-12-05 age 42yrs 3mos 3dys b Hopkinton child of HASTINGS Ard of Hopkinton & Elkemena of Hopkinton Vol: 4 Page: 110 Line: 003

FRENCH Thomas S d Hopkinton 1869 age 74yrs 3mos b Hopkinton child of FRENCH Jonathan of Hopkinton & Lydia of Hopkinton Vol: 4 Page: 110 Line: 020

HOLMES John d Hopkinton 1869 Jul 00 age 77yrs b Hopkinton child of HOLMES John of Hopkinton & ---- ---- of Hopkinton Vol: 4 Page: 111 Line: 002

DANFORTH Eddie d Hopkinton 1869 Mar 4?? age 6yrs b Hopkinton child of DANFORTH Erastur of Hopkinton & Mary S of Hopkinton Vol: 4 Page: 110 Line: 018

CURRIER Amos d Hopkinton 1869 Nov 00 age 79yrs b Hopkinton child of CURRIER Edmund of Hopkinton Vol: 4 Page: 111 Line: 012

MILTON ?? Daniel d Hopkinton 1869-01-11 age 83yrs Vol: 4 Page: 110 Line: 012

FRENCH Benjamin d Hopkinton 1869-02-01 age 74yrs b Lichfield child of FRENCH Asa Vol: 4 Page: 110 Line: 019

KELLEY Sarah E d Hopkinton 1869-02-05 b Hopkinton Vol: 4 Page: 110 Line: 014

HOLMES Walter d Hopkinton 1869-02-21 age 5mos b Hopkinton child of HOLMES Aquilla of Hopkinton Vol: 4 Page: 110 Line: 013

DOWN Christina d Hopkinton 1869-02-26 age 70yrs Vol: 4 Page: 110 Line: 010

KELLEY Cynthia d Hopkinton 1869-03-14 age 3yrs b Hopkinton child of KELLEY Carlos Vol: 4 Page: 110 Line: 009

GOODHUE Dora d Hopkinton 1869-03-18 age 9yrs b Chichester child of GOODHUE Edw H Vol: 4 Page: 110 Line: 011

SAVORY Jemmi? d Hopkinton 1869-03-20 age 7yrs b Hopkinton child of SAVORY William of Hopkinton & ---- ---- of Henniker Vol: 4 Page: 110 Line: 015

FRENCH Sarah E d Hopkinton 1869-03-24 age 31yrs 20dys b Concord Vol: 4 Page: 110 Line: 017

WHITE Oliver?? d Hopkinton 1869-04-01 age 76yrs b Boxford Mass Vol: 4 Page: 111 Line: 027

POLFREY L d Hopkinton 1869-04-18 age 84yrs b Hopkinton Vol: 4 Page: 111 Line: 024

CHASE Martha F d Hopkinton 1869-05-31 age 21yrs 6mos b Hopkinton child of CHASE Ambrose of Hopkinton & Joanna of Hopkinton Vol: 4 Page: 111 Line: 001

SMITH Hannah d Hopkinton 1869-06-01 b Hopkinton child of BAILEY Thomas of Hopkinton Vol: 4 Page: 111 Line: 028

CURTICE A?? d Hopkinton 1869-07-04 age 28yrs b Lowell Mass Vol: 4 Page: 111 Line: 030

FULLER John A d Hopkinton 1869-07-19 age 82yrs b Vermont child of ---- ---- of Hopkinton Vol: 4 Page: 111 Line: 003

GALE George B d Hopkinton 1869-07-29 age 21yrs 3mos 25dys b Newton child of GALE ---- B of Hopkinton & Sarah S of Hopkinton Vol: 4 Page: 110 Line: 021

LAROS Lydia d Hopkinton 1869-08-03 age 65yrs b Hopkinton Vol: 4 Page: 111 Line: 031

BRUCE Caleb d Hopkinton 1869-08-27 age 74yrs b Hopkinton Vol: 4 Page: 111 Line: 032

STEVENS Willie d Hopkinton 1869-08-28 age 19yrs b Warner child of STEVENS James of Sutton & Mary J of Warner Vol: 4 Page: 111 Line: 004

JONES Polly or Dolly?? d Hopkinton 1869-09-01 b Hopkinton Vol: 4 Page: 111 Line: 033

BARNARD Mirram d Hopkinton 1869-09-16 age 69yrs b Concord Vol: 4 Page: 111 Line: 034

FRYE Laura A d Hopkinton 1869-09-20 age 42yrs b Concord child of FRYE Aaroz of Andover Mass & Laura of Hopkinton Vol: 4 Page: 111 Line: 005

CHASE Mary J d Hopkinton 1869-09-25 age 14yrs 5mos b Hopkinton child of CHASE Harvey of Hopkinton & Martha of Freedom Vol: 4 Page: 111 Line: 006

LERNED Catharine d Hopkinton 1869-09-30 age 84yrs b Middleton Mass child of PERKINS Timothy of Salem Mass & TROWBRIDGE Hannah of Groton Mass Vol: 4 Page: 111 Line: 023

WOOD Moses R d Hopkinton 1869-10-04 age 44yrs b Warner Vol: 4 Page: 111 Line: 007

HARDY Hannah C D d Hopkinton 1869-10-09 age 59yrs 3mos 18dys b Warner child of DAVIS Stephen of Warner & Deborah of Warner Vol: 4 Page: 111 Line: 008

FISK Joseph d Hopkinton 1869-10-18 age 67yrs b Concord child of FISK Ephraim of Concord & ---- ---- of Concord Vol: 4 Page: 111 Line: 009

STRAW Jacob d Hopkinton 1869-10-20 age 74yrs b Hopkinton Vol: 4 Page: 111 Line: 010

Hopkinton, NH Deaths 1858

EMERSON Jennie d Hopkinton 1869-10-30 age 5yrs 2mos b Hopkinton child of EMERSON Stephen of Derrfield & Clara of Concord Vol: 4 Page: 111 Line: 011

GREEN Emma d Hopkinton 1869-10-30 age 10yrs 9mos b Hopkinton child of GREEN Newman of Chichester & Sarah J of Sutton Vol: 4 Page: 111 Line: 029

FARRINGTON Stephen d Hopkinton 1869-11-11 age 89yrs b Hopkinton Vol: 4 Page: 111 Line: 035

RICHARDSON Jessie d Hopkinton 1869-11-11 age 20yrs 1mos 11dys b Hopkinton child of RICHARDSON Daniel of Hopkinton & Sarah of Hopkinton Vol: 4 Page: 111 Line: 013

EMERSON Susie d Hopkinton 1869-11-18 age 7yrs 5mos b Hopkinton child of EMERSON Stephen of Derrfield & Clara of Concord Vol: 4 Page: 111 Line: 014

BURNHAM Satirra d Hopkinton 1869-11-22 age 34yrs 4mos b Antrim child of PEABODY John of New Boston & Mary of New Boston Vol: 4 Page: 111 Line: 015

DANFORD Ruth d Hopkinton 1869-11-22 age 63yrs child of NOYES Parker Vol: 4 Page: 111 Line: 016

KIMBALL Nathaniel d Hopkinton 1869-11-27 age 83yrs 4mos b Hopkinton child of KIMBALL Nathaniel & Lydia Vol: 4 Page: 111 Line: 036

MILLS Mary B d Hopkinton 1869-12-02 age 78yrs 3mos b Rye child of BROWN Joseph & Sarah Vol: 4 Page: 111 Line: 037

TUCKER ?? d Hopkinton 1869-12-21 age 64yrs b Hopkinton Vol: 4 Page: 111 Line: 038

PERRY William d Hopkinton 1870 Mar 00 age 74yrs b Henniker Vol: 4 Page: 111 Line: 019

CLARK Abigail C d Hopkinton 1870 Mar 00 age 86yrs b Mount Vernon child of WOODBURY Ebenezer & Abigail Vol: 4 Page: 111 Line: 018

CROWELL Abert d Hopkinton 1870-01-10 age 61yrs 5mos b Hopkinton child of CROWELL Joseph of Medford Mass Vol: 4 Page: 112 Line: 011

SANBORN Dyer d Hopkinton 1870-01-10 age 71yrs b Gilmanton child of SANBORN David of Gilmanton Vol: 4 Page: 112 Line: 022

STEVENS Walter d Hopkinton 1870-01-20 b Warner child of ---- ---- of Warner & ---- ---- of Henniker Vol: 4 Page: 112 Line: 033 Note: age ??

AUSTIN James d Hopkinton 1870-01-24 b Hopkinton Vol: 4 Page: 112 Line: 032 Note: age`??

STRAW William d Hopkinton 1870-03-12 age 89yrs b Hopkinton Vol: 4 Page: 111 Line: 017

BARNARD Joseph d Hopkinton 1870-03-15 age 75yrs b Hopkinton Vol: 4 Page: 111 Line: 025

FISK Margrate d Hopkinton 1870-03-27 age 67yrs b Concord child of DOW Moody of Concord & ---- ---- of Concord Vol: 4 Page: 111 Line: 021

CLEMENT Nancy d Hopkinton 1870-05-19 age 68yrs b Hopkinton child of CELMENT John of Hopkinton & Merriam of Hopkinton Vol: 4 Page: 112 Line: 026

HALL Obadiah d Hopkinton 1870-05-25 age 85yrs 2mos 2dys b Northfield child of HALL Obadiah of Concord & Mary of Concord Vol: 4 Page: 112 Line: 021

Hopkinton, NH Deaths 1858

MOORE Geo R d Hopkinton 1870-06-13 age 49yrs 10mos b Hopkinton child of MOORE Jason & Sukey Vol: 4 Page: 112 Line: 027

MONTGOMERY Clara A d Hopkinton 1870-07-12 age 6dys b Hopkinton child of MONTGOMERY William of Salem & Lucy of Warner Vol: 4 Page: 112 Line: 017

CRESSEY Abagial d Hopkinton 1870-08-08 age 76yrs 12dys b Bradford child of BAILEY Ebenezer of Bradford & Sarah of Vol: 4 Page: 112 Line: 007

HOYT Betsey d Hopkinton 1870-08-09 age 71yrs 3mos 9dys b Dunbarton child of PALMER Simeon of Dunbarton Vol: 4 Page: 112 Line: 005

HOYT Elizabeth d Hopkinton 1870-08-30 age 68yrs b Hopkinton child of HOYT Moses of Hopkinton & Elizabeth Vol: 4 Page: 112 Line: 028

DOW Walter d Hopkinton 1870-09-08 Vol: 4 Page: 112 Line: 029

MORSE Fred D d Hopkinton 1870-10-11 age 10yrs 10mos child of MORSE Nelson D of Franklin & Ann W Vol: 4 Page: 112 Line: 012

ROACH Mary Ann d Hopkinton 1870-10-13 age 7mos b Hopkinton child of ROACH John of Ireland & Ann of Ireland Vol: 4 Page: 112 Line: 009

DAVIS Seth d Hopkinton 1870-10-27 age 51yrs b Hopkinton child of ---- ---- of Hopkinton & ---- ---- of Hopkinton Vol: 4 Page: 112 Line: 030

CHADWICK Mary d Hopkinton 1870-11-05 b Hopkinton Vol: 4 Page: 112 Line: 031

CLOUGH Mary G d Hopkinton 1870-11-05 age 50yrs b Warner child of HARDY Josepheph of Warner & Eliza Vol: 4 Page: 112 Line: 025

BROCKWAY Nancy d Hopkinton 1870-11-24 age 74yrs 5mos 20dys b Hopkinton child of EATON Joshua Vol: 4 Page: 112 Line: 010

HOYT Clerrinda J d Hopkinton 1870-12-13 age 55yrs 2mos 9dys b Hopkinton child of SIBLEY Arros of Hopkinton & Abagial of Bradford Vol: 4 Page: 112 Line: 006

HARRINGTON Rebecca d Hopkinton 1870-12-16 b Hopkinton child of HASTINGS Moses Vol: 4 Page: 112 Line: 001 Note: xx age

CROSS Doheriel d Hopkinton 1870-12-24 age 79yrs 6mos 24dys b Newbury Vol: 4 Page: 112 Line: 015

LOCKE Ann d Hopkinton 1870/71 age 33yrs b Epsom child of LOCKE David of Epsom Vol: 4 Page: 112 Line: 004

NOYES George d Hopkinton 1871 age 23yrs b Hopkinton child of NOYES Lucius of Hopkinton & Charlotte of Hopkinton Vol: 4 Page: 113 Line: 031

BACON John d Hopkinton 1871 Oct age 73yrs 6dys b Medford Mass child of BACON John & Hannah Vol: 4 Page: 113 Line: 030

NOYES Lucius ?? d Hopkinton 1871-01-05 b Hopkinton Vol: 4 Page: 112 Line: 019

MORRILL Abbie d Hopkinton 1871-01-05 age 22yrs 8mos 3dys b Hopkinton child of MORRILL Jacob of Hopkinton & Sarah C Vol: 4 Page: 112 Line: 014

COPPS Mary d Hopkinton 1871-01-14 age 83yrs 9mos b Haverhill Mass child of GEORGE Amos Vol: 4 Page: 112 Line: 003

FRENCH Hannah B d Hopkinton 1871-02-02 age 60yrs 7mos 6dys b Hopkinton child of WEEKS William of Greenland & Sarah Vol: 4 Page: 112 Line: 008

Hopkinton, NH Deaths 1858

KIBBALL Asa d Hopkinton 1871-02-04 age 76yrs 3mos b Hopkinton child of KIMBALL John of Manchester & Lydia of Hopkinton Vol: 4 Page: 112 Line: 024

HERRICK Susan d Hopkinton 1871-02-04 age 85yrs 11mos b Hopkinton child of EVERETTE Jonathan of New London Vol: 4 Page: 112 Line: 015

SAWYER William H d Hopkinton 1871-02-26 b Henniker child of SAWYER Rufus Vol: 4 Page: 113 Line: 027

GREENOUGH Joseph d Hopkinton 1871-03-03 age 68yrs 9mos b Newburyport Mass Vol: 4 Page: 112 Line: 002

STEVENS Minnie d Hopkinton 1871-03-31 age 5dys b Hopkinton child of STEVENS Henry H of Warner & Mary of Methuen Mass Vol: 4 Page: 112 Line: 018

GAGE Nancy H d Hopkinton 1871-04-14 age 71yrs 6mos b Hopkinton child of LONG Isaac of Mass & Susanna Vol: 4 Page: 113 Line: 001

PATTERSON Sarah A d Hopkinton 1871-04-20 age 3mos b Hopkinton child of PATTERSON William of Hopkinton & Olive A of Deering Vol: 4 Page: 113 Line: 002

PALMER Moses T d Hopkinton 1871-04-25 b Bow Vol: 4 Page: 113 Line: 024

STORY Luther d Hopkinton 1871-05-06 age 70yrs b Hopkinton Vol: 4 Page: 113 Line: 025

KNOWLTON Roxana d Hopkinton 1871-05-15 age 78yrs b Newprot child of Wilcox Vol: 4 Page: 113 Line: 003

GILBERT Walter J d Hopkinton 1871-05-30 age 47yrs b Bridgewater Mass child of GILBERT Nathaniel of Easton Mass & Betsey of Bridgewater Mass Vol: 4 Page: 113 Line: 022

RAYMOND Nellie E d Hopkinton 1871-05-31 age 25yrs 3mos b Danvers Mass child of RAYMOND Nathaniel of Salem Mass & Hannah of Beverly Mass Vol: 4 Page: 113 Line: 005

BLANCHARD Hiraim d Hopkinton 1871-07-14 age 68yrs 8mos b Hopkinton child of BLANCHARD Stephen of Cambrige Mass Vol: 4 Page: 113 Line: 004

RUNNELLS Charlie d Hopkinton 1871-08-15 b Lawrence Mass child of RUNNELLS Osborn Vol: 4 Page: 113 Line: 026

DAVIS Delia d Hopkinton 1871-08-28 age 17yrs b Warner child of ---- ---- of Warner & ---- ---- of Warner Vol: 4 Page: 113 Line: 029

CHASE Reuben d Hopkinton 1871-09-04 age 70yrs 11mos 29dys b Hopkinton child of CHASE Moses & Lydia Vol: 4 Page: 113 Line: 006

EVANS Hattie R d Hopkinton 1871-09-09 age 22yrs b Concord child of EVANS Nathaniel of Concord & Harriett of Pitsfield Vol: 4 Page: 113 Line: 023

RANDALL Henry P d Hopkinton 1871-09-20 age 51yrs 16dys b New Bedford Mass child of RANDALL James & Abagail Vol: 4 Page: 113 Line: 007

CLARKE Betsey d Hopkinton 1871-09-25 age 87yrs 1mos 27dys b Hopkinton child of HUSE Thomas & Sarah Vol: 4 Page: 113 Line: 008

PALMER Matilda N d Hopkinton 1871-10-13 age 36yrs 11mos 6dys b Hopkinton child of PALMER William of Bradford Mass & Ann E of W Amesbury Mass Vol: 4 Page: 113 Line: 009

GOODHUE E N d Hopkinton 1871-10-21 age 50yrs b Corinth Me Vol: 4 Page: 112 Line: 020

Hopkinton, NH Deaths 1858

HOLMES Gorden d Hopkinton 1871-10-30 age 71yrs 4mos 20dys b Hopkinton child of HOLMES Eliphalet & Nancy Vol: 4 Page: 113 Line: 010

MORGAN Timothy d Hopkinton 1871-11-08 age 81yrs 8mos 8dys b Hopkinton child of MORGAN Nathaniel of Pembroke & Mary of Hopkinton Vol: 4 Page: 113 Line: 011

KIMBALL Lydia d Hopkinton 1871-11-11 age 98yrs 8mos b Hopkinton Vol: 4 Page: 112 Line: 023

EDMUNDS Harry d Hopkinton 1871-11-16 age 9mos 16dys b Hopkinton child of EDMMUNDS H E of Hopkinton & Mirriam of Hopkinton Vol: 4 Page: 113 Line: 013

HARDY Joseph d Hopkinton 1871-11-16 age 82yrs 7mos 5dys b Bradford Mass child of HARDY Stephen of Bradford Mass & Mary J of Cap Ann Mass Vol: 4 Page: 113 Line: 012

DUSTIN George A d Hopkinton 1871-11-20 age 26yrs b Hopkinton child of DUSTIN Ebenezer of Hopkinton & Harriet Vol: 4 Page: 112 Line: 016

BURBANK Harriett N d Hopkinton 1871-11-29 age 52yrs b Hopkinton child of ORDWAY Nathaniel of Canada & Lydia Vol: 4 Page: 113 Line: 014

HOLMES Arbella d Hopkinton 1871-12-02 age 76yrs 5mos b Taunton Mass child of WHITE John of Mansfield Mass & Martha of RI Vol: 4 Page: 113 Line: 032

FIFIELD Luel?? d Hopkinton 1871-12-04 age 75yrs 8mos 5dys b Salsbury child of FIFIELD Jonathan & Dorcas Vol: 4 Page: 113 Line: 028

DANFORTH Etta d Hopkinton 1872 age 4yrs b Carroll child of DANFORTH Henry of Hopkinton & Mary Etta of Grantham Vol: 4 Page: 114 Line: 027

ROACH William H d Hopkinton 1872 Oct 00 age 1yrs 2mos b Hopkinton child of ROACH John of Ireland & Ann R of Ireland Vol: 4 Page: 114 Line: 015

HEATH William N d Hopkinton 1872-01-07 age 18mos 3dys b Hopkinton child of HEATH James C of Salaisbury & Harriett of Warner Vol: 4 Page: 114 Line: 005

DUSTIN Ebenezer d Hopkinton 1872-01-14 age 90yrs 10mos 26dys b Warner child of Eunice of Hopkinton Vol: 4 Page: 113 Line: 015

GORDEN Epha d Hopkinton 1872-01-23 age 76yrs 4mos 17dys b Henniker child of GORDEN Samuel of Henniker & Sarah of Henniker Vol: 4 Page: 114 Line: 006

WYMAN Mary d Hopkinton 1872-01-30 age 74yrs 4mos 4dys b Amherst child of Stearns Vol: 4 Page: 114 Line: 007

FITCH Luther J d Hopkinton 1872-02-05 age 79yrs 4mos 27dys b Jaffrey child of FITCH Paul & Mary Vol: 4 Page: 113 Line: 016

FLANDERS Philip d Hopkinton 1872-03-13 age 86yrs 2mos 14dys b So Hampton child of FLANDERS Richard C of So Hampton & Rachel of So Hampton Vol: 4 Page: 114 Line: 017

PATCH Rebecca R d Hopkinton 1872-03-14 age 83yrs 3mos b Hopkinton child of ROWELL Job Vol: 4 Page: 113 Line: 033

MERRILL Jonanah d Hopkinton 1872-03-17 age 77yrs 2dys b Manchester Mass child of ALLEN Stephen of Mass Vol: 4 Page: 113 Line: 017

DOW Sarah E d Hopkinton 1872-03-22 age 48yrs 1mos 25dys b Hopkinton child of HOYT Moses & Betsey Vol: 4 Page: 113 Line: 018

RONAN Hannah d Hopkinton 1872-03-24 age 42yrs 1mos 25dys b Ireland Vol: 4 Page: 113 Line: 019

Hopkinton, NH Deaths 1858

EMERSON George A d Hopkinton 1872-03-31 age 1mos 12dys b Weare child of EMERSON Hanson of Hopkinton & M F of Hopkinton Vol: 4 Page: 113 Line: 020

RANDALL Georgie W d Hopkinton 1872-04-03 age 27yrs 4mos 27dys b Hopkinton child of RANDALL Humphrey L of New Bedford Mass & Mary of Hopkinton Vol: 4 Page: 113 Line: 021

LITTLE Elizabeth d Hopkinton 1872-04-20 age 93yrs 10mos b Hamilton Mass child of LITTLE Charles Vol: 4 Page: 114 Line: 001

MORGAN Nathaniel d Hopkinton 1872-05-04 age 79yrs 29dys b Hopkinton Vol: 4 Page: 114 Line: 002

MOULTON William H d Hopkinton 1872-05-07 age 49yrs 11mos b ?? child of MOULTON James of Hopkinton & Patience of   Vol: 4 Page: 114 Line: 003

MORRILL Eunice d Hopkinton 1872-05-26 age 57yrs b Salisbury child of SCRIBNER Iddo of Hopkinton & Huldah of Rowley Mass Vol: 4 Page: 114 Line: 004

PATCH E Everett d Hopkinton 1872-07-01 age 30yrs b Hopkinton child of PATCH John of Salem Mass & Betsey of Hopkinton Vol: 4 Page: 114 Line: 008

MERRILL Abagial d Hopkinton 1872-07-20 age 63yrs b Newburyport Mass child of Hale of Newbury Mass & Nancy of Marblehead Mass Vol: 4 Page: 114 Line: 009

ANDREWS Mary A d Hopkinton 1872-08-10 age 40yrs 1mos 10dys b Warner child of NOYES Leonard of Haverhill & Julia S of Hopkinton Vol: 4 Page: 114 Line: 010

WOODBURY Laura J d Hopkinton 1872-08-24 age 28yrs 4mos b Lowell Mass child of GRAY Alanson of Wilton & Martha of Concord Vol: 4 Page: 114 Line: 011

BARNES Emma G d Hopkinton 1872-08-24 age 11yrs b Henniker child of BARNES George A of Weare & Hannah J of Hopkinton Vol: 4 Page: 114 Line: 012

CROWELL Lewis Albert d Hopkinton 1872-09-06 age 1yrs 10mos b Hopkinton child of CROWELL Henry of Hopkinton & Lucinda of Concord Vol: 4 Page: 114 Line: 014

CURRIER Lucy d Hopkinton 1872-09-06 age 87yrs b Hopkinton child of STORY Thomas Vol: 4 Page: 114 Line: 013

HOLMES Leola Mae d Hopkinton 1872-11-09 age 4dys b Hopkinton child of HOLMES Aquilla of Hopkinton & Abbie of Johnson Vt Vol: 4 Page: 114 Line: 016

ROGERS Hannah d Hopkinton 1872-11-17 age 91yrs 27dys b Hopkinton child of FLANDERS Jeremiah of So Hampton & Maria of So Hampton Vol: 4 Page: 114 Line: 018

PACKARD Mrs d Hopkinton 1873 age 70yrs Vol: 4 Page: 114 Line: 029

BLODGETT John d Hopkinton 1873 age 37yrs b Sunapee Vol: 4 Page: 114 Line: 028

FRYE Nancy d Hopkinton 1873-01-20 age 78yrs 10mos b Merrimack child of BUSWELL James of Hopkinton & Mary of Bow Vol: 4 Page: 114 Line: 019

STRAW Daniel d Hopkinton 1873-01-28 age 74yrs b Hopkinton child of JAMES Straw of Hopkinton & Buswell?? of Kingston Vol: 4 Page: 114 Line: 020

GOULD Jonny A?? d Hopkinton 1873-02-16 age 2yrs 8mos b Hopkinton child of GOULD Charles L of Greenfield & Cornelia of Hopkinton Vol: 4 Page: 114 Line: 021

AUSTIN Elizabeth A d Hopkinton 1873-02-26 age 52yrs child of Haskell Vol: 4 Page: 114 Line: 022

GREENE Frances d Hopkinton 1873-03-02 age 38yrs 28dys b Boston Mass child of WILLARD Henry of Boston Mass & Frances of Boston Mass Vol: 4 Page: 114 Line: 026

CHASE Elisa A d Hopkinton 1873-03-19 age 19yrs 8mos b Hopkinton child of CHASE Baruch of Hopkinton & Lydia of Stoddard Vol: 4 Page: 114 Line: 023

STRAW Harriett C d Hopkinton 1873-03-24 age 76yrs 4mos b Hopkinton child of CARLTON David of So Hampton & Sarah of So Hampton Vol: 4 Page: 114 Line: 024

BOHONAN Josephine d Hopkinton 1873-04-03 age 21yrs 5mos b Sutton child of BOHONAN David of Washington Vt & Belinda of Sutton Vol: 4 Page: 114 Line: 025

PHILLIPS ---- d Hopkinton 1873-04-04 b West Concord child of PHILLIPS Ira C of Henniker & Angie of Hopkinton Vol: 4 Page: 115 Line: 001 Note: twins were born

PATTERSON Maria W d Hopkinton 1873-05-09 age 65yrs 9mos b Henniker child of WOODS William D & Betsey D Vol: 4 Page: 115 Line: 006

BURNBANK Hannah d Hopkinton 1873-05-12 age 72yrs b Meridith Vol: 4 Page: 115 Line: 003

FOGG Sherburn d Hopkinton 1873-06-04 age 53yrs 10mos b Meredith child of FOGG Seth & Betsey Vol: 4 Page: 115 Line: 004

FRENCH Nellie d Hopkinton 1873-06-13 age 27yrs 9mos 7dys b Hopkinton child of STORY Moses of Hopkinton & Mehitable Vol: 4 Page: 115 Line: 005

HOWLETT Ella H d Hopkinton 1873-06-23 age 27yrs 6mos b Hopkinton child of ROWELL Isaac of Hopkinton & Harriett of Henniker Vol: 4 Page: 115 Line: 007

TERRILL Warren d Hopkinton 1873-07-07 age 22yrs b Contoocookville child of Abbie of Hopkinton Vol: 4 Page: 115 Line: 008

FOSTER Belind d Hopkinton 1873-07-09 age 60yrs b Hopkinton child of BURBANK Eben of Hopkinton & Mehitable of Hopkinton Vol: 4 Page: 115 Line: 010

MASON Elizabeth d Hopkinton 1873-07-11 age 94yrs 5mos b Lexington Mass child of REED Moses of Mass & Sarah of Mass Vol: 4 Page: 115 Line: 009

GOODSPEED Henry B d Hopkinton 1873-08-05 age 21dys b Boston Mass child of GOODSPEED Obed of Hopkinton & Helen B of Hopkinton Vol: 4 Page: 115 Line: 011

HILLS Fannie W d Hopkinton 1873-08-14 age 8yrs 9mos 2dys b Hopkinton child of HILLS Charles H of Hopkinton & Olive of Weare Vol: 4 Page: 115 Line: 012

HARRINGTON Clara A d Hopkinton 1873-09-14 age 19yrs b New York child of HARRINGTON Moses of Cornish & Rebecca of Manchester Vol: 4 Page: 115 Line: 013

WRIGHT James H d Hopkinton 1873-09-22 age 54yrs b Weare child of WRIGHT John of Weare & Sarah of Amesbury Mass Vol: 4 Page: 115 Line: 014

Hopkinton, NH Deaths 1858

ABBOTT Luther d Hopkinton 1873-10-08 age 80yrs 5mos 5dys b Concord child of ABBOTT Moses Vol: 4 Page: 115 Line: 015

BATCHELDER Moses d Hopkinton 1873-10-12 age 73yrs b Hopkinton child of BATCHELDER David & Dorothea Vol: 4 Page: 115 Line: 016

PHELPS Betsey B d Hopkinton 1873-11-06 age 75yrs 4mos 11dys b Hopkinton child of GILMAN Trueworthy & Betsey Vol: 4 Page: 115 Line: 017

TUCKER Hannah d Hopkinton 1873-11-13 age 93yrs b Beverly Mass child of HARDY Stepehn & Hannah Vol: 4 Page: 115 Line: 018

WOOD Alanson d Hopkinton 1873-11-18 age 60yrs b Topsham Vt Vol: 4 Page: 115 Line: 019

FLANDERS Betsey P d Hopkinton 1873-12-22 age 62yrs 7mos 10dys b Topsham Vt child of FLANDERS James of Warner & Mary of Weare Vol: 4 Page: 115 Line: 020

CLARK Mary d Hopkinton 1873-12-27 age 63yrs 9mos 20dys b Weare child of STRAW Samuel & Betsey Vol: 4 Page: 115 Line: 021

SMITH Henry W d Hopkinton 1874 Par 6 b Hopkinton Vol: 4 Page: 116 Line: 002

MESSER Betsey d Hopkinton 1874-01-14 age 84yrs 9mos 23dys b Bow child of ------- ---- of Bow & ---- ---- of Bow Vol: 4 Page: 115 Line: 022

PHILBRICK John H d Hopkinton 1874-01-16 age 18yrs b Hillsboro child of PHILBRICK Nat'l of Sutton & N B of Hillsboro Vol: 4 Page: 115 Line: 023

CROWELL Frank C d Hopkinton 1874-02-11 age 4mos 11dys b Hopkinton child of CROWELL H H of Hopkinton & Lucindia of Concord Vol: 4 Page: 115 Line: 024

BROWN Sophronia d Hopkinton 1874-03-11 age 61yrs child of ATWOOD Joseph & Rachel Vol: 4 Page: 115 Line: 025

HOLMES Betsey d Hopkinton 1874-03-15 age 76yrs 2mos b Amherst child of MELVIN David & Mary Vol: 4 Page: 115 Line: 026

BLAKE Nellie d Hopkinton 1874-04-07 age 8yrs 11mos b Hopkinton child of BLAKE John of Stanstead C East & MANSFIELD Hannah of Loudon Vol: 4 Page: 116 Line: 003

CROWELL Lucinda N d Hopkinton 1874-04-08 age 36yrs 11mos b Concord child of CURRIER Benjamin of Concord & Martha of Cavendish Vt Vol: 4 Page: 116 Line: 001

KIMBALL Moses L d Hopkinton 1874-04-14 age 56yrs 11mos b New London child of KIMBALL Nathaniel of Hopkinton & Silcone of Hopkinton Vol: 4 Page: 116 Line: 004

KELLEY Almira F d Hopkinton 1874-05-13 age 34yrs 7mos 13dys b Nashua child of RIPLEY William of Londonderry & Elisa of Londonderry Vol: 4 Page: 116 Line: 005

PHILBRICK Hatch d Hopkinton 1874-05-17 b Hopkinton child of Philbrick Vol: 4 Page: 116 Line: 006

TEWSKSBURY Elizabeth B d Hopkinton 1874-06-12 age 76yrs 6mos b Essex Mass child of BUTLER John & Lufkin Vol: 4 Page: 116 Line: 007

STRAW Dernard d Hopkinton 1874-07-09 age 1yrs 6mos b Hopkinton child of SPOFFORD Lawier F of Hopkinton & STRAW Myra of Hopkinton Vol: 4 Page: 116 Line: 008

Hopkinton, NH Deaths 1858

EASTMAN Jonathan d Hopkinton 1874-07-28 age 73yrs Vol: 4 Page: 116 Line: 009

ADAMS Mary E d Hopkinton 1874-07-30 age 74yrs 10mos Vol: 4 Page: 116 Line: 010

KAST Abigail C d Hopkinton 1874-08-01 age 77yrs 9mos 10dys b Rowley Mass child of SMITH Isaac of Rowley Mass & COGSWELL Abigail of Rowley Mass Vol: 4 Page: 116 Line: 011

RUSSELL Jennie d Hopkinton 1874-08-09 age 9yrs b Hopkinton child of RUSSELL Smith of N H & Debra of Maine Vol: 4 Page: 116 Line: 012

CORLISS Ruth d Hopkinton 1874-08-15 age 73yrs child of LORD Peter & Rhoda Vol: 4 Page: 116 Line: 013

ELLIOT ---- d Hopkinton 1874-08-31 age 4dys b Hopkinton child of ELLIOTT Joseph R & Angeline P Vol: 4 Page: 116 Line: 014

CORLISS T E d Hopkinton 1874-09-30 age 7yrs child of CORLISS E G & Mary J Vol: 4 Page: 116 Line: 016

DORR John d Hopkinton 1874-10-08 age 74yrs 5mos b Boston Mass child of DORR John of Boston Mass & Esther of Boston Mass Vol: 4 Page: 116 Line: 017

QUIMBY Enos G d Hopkinton 1874-10-11 age 45yrs 11mos 4dys b Hopkinton child of QUIMBY John of Hopkinton & BLANCHARD Hannah L of Hopkinton Vol: 4 Page: 116 Line: 018

DOWNS Charles d Hopkinton 1874-10-19 age 6dys b Contoocookville child of DOWNS Walter L & Dolly of Warner Vol: 4 Page: 116 Line: 019

TUCKER Elizabeth d Hopkinton 1874-10-20 age 35yrs 1mos 20dys b Henniker child of TUCKER Cyrus of Henniker & Betsey G of Henniker Vol: 4 Page: 116 Line: 020

TUCKER Betsey d Hopkinton 1874-10-26 age 64yrs 2mos 26dys b Henniker child of Gordon of Henniker & Conner of Henniker Vol: 4 Page: 116 Line: 021

HOYT George C d Hopkinton 1874-11-03 age 45yrs 6mos b Dunbarton child of HOYT Kilborn of Weare & A of Dunbarton Vol: 4 Page: 116 Line: 022

SMITH Richard R d Hopkinton 1874-11-05 age 81yrs 4mos b Sanbornton child of SMITH Solomon & Hannah R Vol: 4 Page: 116 Line: 023

LEARNARD Elizabeth S d Hopkinton 1874-11-24 age 47yrs b Hopkinton child of LEARNARD Ebenezer of Medford Mass & PERKINS Catharine of Middleton Mass Vol: 4 Page: 116 Line: 024

KNOWLTON Josiah S d Hopkinton 1874-12-04 age 78yrs 8mos b New London child of KNOWLTON Robert of Hopkinton & SMITH Jemima of Hopkinton Vol: 4 Page: 116 Line: 025

HARDY Lucy Ella d Hopkinton 1874-12-11 age 24yrs 10mos 10dys b Boston Mass child of McCLENNER Robert & Marianna Vol: 4 Page: 116 Line: 026

KNOWLTON Abigail L d Hopkinton 1874-12-12 age 76yrs b Manchester Mass child of LEE Edward of Winham Mass & DODGE Mercy Vol: 4 Page: 116 Line: 027

BROCKWAY John d Hopkinton 1874-12-27 age 81yrs b Bradford Vol: 4 Page: 116 Line: 029

HOYT Emily d Hopkinton 1874-12-27 age 70yrs 8mos 8dys b Concord child of SCALES John & ALLEN Sarah Vol: 4 Page: 116 Line: 028

Hopkinton, NH Deaths 1858

CHATMAN Benjamin F d Hopkinton 1874-12-27 age 61yrs 2mos 2dys b Meridith child of CHATMAN Joseph of Newmarket & Olive D of Chester Vol: 4 Page: 116 Line: 030

FRENCH Edward C d Hopkinton 1875-01-05 age 4yrs 7mos b Hopkinton child of FRENCH Edward D of Hopkinton & STEARNS Jane E of S. Boston Mass Vol: 4 Page: 116 Line: 031

MESSER Betsey d Hopkinton 1875-01-14 age 84yrs b Bow child of WALKER Williama of Bow & ORDWAY Phebe Vol: 4 Page: 116 Line: 032

GERRISH Thomas d Hopkinton 1875-02-13 age 88yrs 5mos 7dys b Boscawen child of GERRISH Henry of Boscawen & CLOUGH Martha of Canterbury Vol: 4 Page: 116 Line: 033

COLBY Sarah Bella d Hopkinton 1875-02-15 age 18yrs 10mos b Hopkinton child of COLBY Melvin of Hopkinton & EDMUNDS Hannah P Vol: 4 Page: 116 Line: 034

COURSER Luke d Hopkinton 1875-02-16 b Hopkinton Vol: 4 Page: 117 Line: 011

WEEKS Abigail Rogers d Hopkinton 1875-02-20 age 87yrs 7mos b Hopkinton child of WEEKS William of Greenland & COTTON Sarah of Greenland Vol: 4 Page: 116 Line: 035

TUTTLE Susan J d Hopkinton 1875-02-20 age 31yrs b Contoocook child of HARDY George B of Contoocook & Hannah of Warner Vol: 4 Page: 116 Line: 036

MILLS Francis d Hopkinton 1875-02-24 age 2dys b Hopkinton child of MILLS Charles of Hopkinton & Olive of Weare Vol: 4 Page: 116 Line: 037

CHASE Horace d Hopkinton 1875-03-01 age 86yrs 214mos 4dys b Hopkinton child of CHASE Samuel of Hopkinton & Molly of Hopkinton Vol: 4 Page: 116 Line: 038

TYLER Sarah d Hopkinton 1875-04-01 age 53yrs Vol: 4 Page: 116 Line: 039

ELLIOTT Barton J d Hopkinton 1875-04-01 age 16yrs 8mos 8dys b Boscawen child of ELLIOT Joseph P of Boscawen & Angeline of Bow Vol: 4 Page: 116 Line: 040

HUSE Betsey d Hopkinton 1875-04-11 b Hopkinton child of ---- ---- of Manchester Mass & ---- ---- of New Boston Vol: 4 Page: 117 Line: 001

PATCH John d Hopkinton 1875-04-16 age 71yrs 3mos 22dys b Salem Mass child of PATCH Josiah of Hamilton Mass & Betsey of New Boston Vol: 4 Page: 117 Line: 002

ELLIOTT Mary d Hopkinton 1875-04-26 b Hopkinton child of ELLIOTT Joseph Vol: 4 Page: 117 Line: 003

BOHONAN Lizzie M d Hopkinton 1875-05-23 age 7mos 20dys b Weare child of BOHONAN David N of Sutton & Martha of Hopkinton Vol: 4 Page: 117 Line: 004

BURBANK Stephen d Hopkinton 1875-07-10 age 65yrs b Hopkinton child of BURBANK Eben & Lydia Vol: 4 Page: 117 Line: 005

FRYE Carrie Bell d Hopkinton 1875-07-12 age 18yrs b Concord child of FRYE Drew & Susan Vol: 4 Page: 117 Line: 006

ROWELL Manley A d Hopkinton 1875-07-20 age 68yrs 2mos 22dys b Hopkinton child of ROWELL Moses of So Hampton & Mary of Newbury Mass Vol: 4 Page: 117 Line: 007

Hopkinton, NH Deaths 1858

SPOFFORD Sarah A d Hopkinton 1875-07-26 b Hopkinton Vol: 4 Page: 117 Line: 008

WALKER Jane d Hopkinton 1875-08-03 b Hopkinton Vol: 4 Page: 117 Line: 009

PHILLIPS Emma R d Hopkinton 1875-08-07 age 72yrs 7mos 10dys b W Newbury Mass child of CARR John & Abigail Vol: 4 Page: 117 Line: 010

BROWN John d Hopkinton 1875-09-21 b Hopkinton Vol: 4 Page: 117 Line: 012

BRUCE Nellie M d Hopkinton 1875-11-02 age 70yrs 7mos 29dys b W Newbury Mass child of CARR John & Abigail Vol: 4 Page: 117 Line: 013

NOYES Leonard d Hopkinton 1875-12-02 age 77yrs 10mos 24dys b Haverhill Mass Vol: 4 Page: 117 Line: 014

HARRINGTON Moses B d Hopkinton 1875-12-13 age 73yrs 10mos 15dys b Cornish child of HARRINGTON Moses of N Braintree Mass & OBER Abigail of W Newbury Mass Vol: 4 Page: 117 Line: 015

HOYT James d Hopkinton 1876 May 00 age 66yrs b Henniker child of HOYT James Vol: 4 Page: 118 Line: 005

THOMPSON Hannah d Hopkinton 1876-01-16 age 84yrs 8mos 11dys b Hopkinton child of COBLY Nathan & Hannah Vol: 4 Page: 117 Line: 016

COLBY Moses d Hopkinton 1876-01-28 age 79yrs 28dys b New London child of COLBY James & STORY Susan Vol: 4 Page: 117 Line: 017

TEWKSBURY Betsey d Hopkinton 1876-02-02 age 89yrs b Manchester Mass child of TEWKSBURY Thomas & Annie Vol: 4 Page: 117 Line: 019

EDMUNDS Bridget W d Hopkinton 1876-02-16 age 70yrs b Weare child of CILLEY Philip & Susan Vol: 4 Page: 117 Line: 018

GAGE Sarah E d Hopkinton 1876-02-18 age 49yrs 11mos 1dys b Hopkinton child of SMITH Josiah of Hopkinton & Mary of Hopkinton Vol: 4 Page: 117 Line: 020

CROWELL Charles d Hopkinton 1876-02-21 age 19yrs b Hopkinton child of CROWELL Joseph of Hopkinton & Nancy of Hopkinton Vol: 4 Page: 117 Line: 021

FAGAN Edward d Hopkinton 1876-03-10 age 19yrs 2mos 10dys b Hopkinton child of FAGAN John of Ireland & Margarett of Ireland Vol: 4 Page: 117 Line: 024

BAILEY Sophie W d Hopkinton 1876-03-31 age 72yrs b Hopkinton child of BAILEY Isacc of Hopkinton & Abigail Vol: 4 Page: 117 Line: 022

WIGGIN Elizabeth d Hopkinton 1876-03-31 age 25yrs 6mos 20dys b Hopkinton child of WIGGINS William C of Salem Mass & Julia A of Topsfield Mass Vol: 4 Page: 117 Line: 023

MORAN Patrick d Hopkinton 1876-04-23 age 52yrs b Ireland child of MORAN Christopher of Ireland & Elizabeth of Ireland Vol: 4 Page: 118 Line: 001

KIMBALL Emma d Hopkinton 1876-04-27 age 17yrs 1mos 17dys b Hopkinton child of KIMBALL Elbridge G & Mary Vol: 4 Page: 118 Line: 002

JONES Peter d Hopkinton 1876-05-19 age 74yrs b Cambridge Mass child of JONES Samuel & Lydia Vol: 4 Page: 118 Line: 003

EVANS Nathaniel d Hopkinton 1876-05-23 age 80yrs 5mos b Peterboro Vol: 4 Page: 118 Line: 004

BURNHAM Emma L d Hopkinton 1876-05-23 age 20yrs b Hopkinton child of BURNHAM Charles of Antrim & Elziabeth of Canterbury Vol: 4 Page: 118 Line: 006

81

Hopkinton, NH Deaths 1858

MORRILL Eben O d Hopkinton 1876-05-30 b Hopkinton Vol: 4 Page: 118 Line: 007

SMART Anna d Hopkinton 1876-06-10 b Hopkinton Vol: 4 Page: 118 Line: 008

DOW William H d Hopkinton 1876-07-18 age 22yrs 19dys b Hopkinton child of DOW Henry E of Concord & Charlott of Hopkinton Vol: 4 Page: 118 Line: 009

CROWELL Lucy A d Hopkinton 1876-08-01 age 22yrs b Hopkinton child of CILLEY Albert R & Lucy Vol: 4 Page: 118 Line: 011

CROWELL Albert R d Hopkinton 1876-08-01 age 3yrs b Hopkinton child of CROWELL Samuel of Concord & Lucy of Hopkinton Vol: 4 Page: 118 Line: 010

GREENLEAF Elvira d Hopkinton 1876-08-09 age 56yrs 6mos b Henniker child of GREENLEAF William Vol: 4 Page: 118 Line: 012

ROGERS Mertie Bell d Hopkinton 1876-08-28 age 6mos b Manchester child of ROGERS George & Sarah Vol: 4 Page: 118 Line: 014

HILTER Goerge N ?? d Manchester 1876-09-01 age 2yrs 10mos 14dys b Newport child of HILTER John B of England & Annie of Sutton Vol: 4 Page: 117 Line: 025

CHASE Henry L d Hopkinton 1876-09-02 age 25yrs 3mos 22dys b Hopkinton child of SEVERENCE Holland & Margaret Vol: 4 Page: 118 Line: 016

RICHARDSON Joseph d Hopkinton 1876-09-02 age 66yrs 10mos b Hopkinton child of RICHARDSON Joseph & Joanna Vol: 4 Page: 118 Line: 015

STORY Jeremiah L d Hopkinton 1876-10-10 b Hopkinton child of STORY Jeremiah Vol: 4 Page: 118 Line: 017

TEWKSBURY Anna d Hopkinton 1876-10-20 age 93yrs 3mos b Manchester Mass Vol: 4 Page: 118 Line: 018

CURRIER Dollie d Hopkinton 1876-11-03 b Hopkinton Vol: 4 Page: 118 Line: 019

TILTON John R d Hopkinton 1876-11-10 age 89yrs 20dys b Epping Vol: 4 Page: 118 Line: 020

CARR Caroline d Hopkinton 1876-11-15 b Hopkinton Vol: 4 Page: 118 Line: 021

ROWAN?? Mary Ann d Hopkinton 1876-11-20 age 21yrs b Sutton child of ROWAN?? Michael of Ireland & Hannah of Ireland Vol: 4 Page: 118 Line: 022

KIMBALL Perkins d Hopkinton 1876-12-16 age 66yrs 9mos b Pembroke child of KIMBALL David of Pembroke & Abby of Pembroke Vol: 4 Page: 118 Line: 023

STRAW Joannah G d Hopkinton 1876-12-31 age 83yrs b Hopkinton Vol: 4 Page: 118 Line: 024

HOWARD Sally d Hopkinton 1877 age 73yrs b Grantham child of STONE Daniel of Bridgewater Mass & Susannah R of Upton Mass Vol: 4 Page: 119 Line: 025

STEVENS Eugene d Hopkinton 1877 age 19yrs 11mos child of STEVENS N P & Harriet Vol: 4 Page: 118 Line: 031

HOLMES Anna d Hopkinton 1877 age 77yrs 2mos 7dys b Bradford Vol: 4 Page: 118 Line: 032

COLBY Louisa A d Hopkinton 1877 age 46yrs b Concord child of FLANDERS Richard & Abigail Vol: 4 Page: 118 Line: 030

KIMBALL ---- d Hopkinton 1877 b Hopkinton child of KIMBALL John & Lydia Vol: 4 Page: 119 Line: 001

SYMONDS Daniel d Hopkinton 1877-01-11 age 73yrs b Hillsboro child of SYMONDS Eliphet & ---- ---- of Hopkinton Vol: 4 Page: 118 Line: 026

Hopkinton, NH Deaths 1858

STANWOOD Fred W d Hopkinton 1877-01-24 age 40yrs b Hopkinton child of STANWOOD Joseph of W Newbury & Louisa A P of Hopkinton Vol: 4 Page: 118 Line: 027

JONES Martha d Hopkinton 1877-02-20 age 85yrs 4mos 11dys b Boscawen child of JONES Jonathan of Amesbury Mass & Judith Vol: 4 Page: 118 Line: 028

STEVENS Lina?? d Hopkinton 1877-02-24 age 4mos b Hopkinton child of STEVENS Edgar W of Manchester & Georgie L of Bradford Mass Vol: 4 Page: 118 Line: 029

KIMBALL Hazen d Hopkinton 1877-03-28 age 74yrs 7mos b Hopkinton child of KIMBALL John & Lydia Vol: 4 Page: 118 Line: 033

CONNOR Judith M d Hopkinton 1877-05-09 age 39yrs b Hopkinton child of PUTNEY Ira of Hopkinton & Hannah of Bristol Vol: 4 Page: 119 Line: 002

STRAW Mirriam d Hopkinton 1877-05-20 age 80yrs b Hopkinton child of FLANDERS Jeremiah & Mirriam Vol: 4 Page: 119 Line: 003

FRAZER Maggie d Hopkinton 1877-06-24 age 29yrs b Nova Scotia child of ---- ---- of Germany?? Vol: 4 Page: 119 Line: 004

FRENCH Henry C d Hopkinton 1877-06-27 age 14yrs b Hopkinton child of FRENCH Charles of Hopkinton & PAGE Sarah Vol: 4 Page: 119 Line: 007

FLANDERS Alice d Hopkinton 1877-07-04 age 94yrs 6mos b Concord child of CONWAY Samuel & Alice Vol: 4 Page: 118 Line: 025

CAMPBELL Mrs d Hopkinton 1877-07-15 b Hopkinton child of Jones Vol: 4 Page: 119 Line: 005

DOW Joseph d Hopkinton 1877-07-24 age 89yrs Vol: 4 Page: 119 Line: 006

MAKEPEACE ---- d Hopkinton 1877-08-08 age 10yrs b Concord child of MAKEPEACE Henry & Nancie Vol: 4 Page: 119 Line: 008

STEVENS Lena d Hopkinton 1877-09-10 age 71yrs 2mos 15dys b Henniker child of TEMPLE Jasper & CUTTS Rhoda of Rindge Vol: 4 Page: 119 Line: 009

DOWNING Ada d Hopkinton 1877-09-13 Vol: 4 Page: 119 Line: 010

FLANDERS Maria A d Hopkinton 1877-09-14 age 53yrs b Henniker child of ADAMS James of Henniker & Lydia Vol: 4 Page: 119 Line: 011

PAGE Rachal D d Hopkinton 1877-10-17 b Hopkinton Vol: 4 Page: 119 Line: 012

FULLER Mary d Hopkinton 1877-11-02 age 94yrs b Haverhill Mass child of GEORGE Austin of Haverhill Mass Vol: 4 Page: 119 Line: 013

KIMBALL Mary A d Hopkinton 1877-11-05 Vol: 4 Page: 119 Line: 014

WYMAN Hannah d Hopkinton 1877-11-13 age 60yrs b Hopkinton child of FLANDERS Philip Vol: 4 Page: 119 Line: 015

WRIGHT Sarah d Hopkinton 1877-11-27 Vol: 4 Page: 119 Line: 016

CHASE Frank D d Hopkinton 1877-12-06 age 5yrs 10mos b Hopkinton child of CHASE Frank B of Hopkinton & Annie A of Concord Vol: 4 Page: 119 Line: 017

CLOUGH Hattie O d Hopkinton 1878 age 1dys b Hopkinton child of CLOUGH Moses L of Hopkinton & BEAU Mary O Vol: 4 Page: 120 Line: 020

BURNHAM Grace d Hopkinton 1878 age 17yrs b Hopkinton child of BURNHAM Edward of Hopkinton & Georgia of Warner Vol: 4 Page: 120 Line: 003

MERRILL Charles d Hopkinton 1878 age 70yrs b Hopkinton child of MERRILL Parker of Hopkinton & Rebecca of Hopkinton Vol: 4 Page: 120 Line: 006

Hopkinton, NH Deaths 1858

SLEEPER Mariah d Hopkinton 1878 age 77yrs b Hopkinton child of HILDREATH Levi of Dracut Mass & DARLING Sarah of Hopkinton Vol: 4 Page: 120 Line: 002

CHASE Moses d Hopkinton 1878 age 73yrs b Cannan child of CHASE Moses & KIMBALL Lydia Vol: 4 Page: 120 Line: 004

CHASE Susan E d Hopkinton 1878 age 27yrs b Antrim child of THAYER Charles of Rochester Mass & Rebecca Vol: 4 Page: 120 Line: 005

HASTINGS Sarah d Hopkinton 1878 b Warner Vol: 4 Page: 120 Line: 001

CHASE Charles d Hopkinton 1878 Jul age 27yrs b Hopkinton child of CHASE Baruch of West Moreland & MORRISON Lydia of Warner Vol: 4 Page: 120 Line: 008

BURBANK Hiram d Hopkinton 1878-01-12 age 76yrs b Hopkinton child of BURBANK Eben & Lidia Vol: 4 Page: 119 Line: 019

WEEKS Jaez ? d Hopkinton 1878-01-15 age 81yrs b Hopkinton child of WEEKS William of Greeland & Sarah C of Greeland Vol: 4 Page: 119 Line: 020

CHASE Joanna L d Hopkinton 1878-01-18 age 68yrs b Hopkinton child of GOULD Moses of Hopkinton & Hannah of Warner Vol: 4 Page: 119 Line: 021

CURTICE William d Hopkinton 1878-01-20 Vol: 4 Page: 119 Line: 018

WEBBER Hannah D d Hopkinton 1878-02-06 age 85yrs 10mos b W Newbury Mass child of Davis of W Newbury Mass Vol: 4 Page: 119 Line: 022

DANIELS George d Hopkinton 1878-02-12 b Henniker child of DANIELS Joseph of Canada & Andrea ?? of Canada Vol: 4 Page: 119 Line: 023

FELCH Leonard d Hopkinton 1878-02-17 age 76yrs b Weare child of FELCH Jonathan of Weare & Abagial Vol: 4 Page: 119 Line: 024

STORY Stephen F d Hopkinton 1878-02-22 age 74yrs b Hopkinton child of STORY Jeremiah of Hopkinton & Judith of Concord Vol: 4 Page: 017 Line:

BARTON Mary d Hopkinton 1878-07-19 age 77yrs b Concord child of ABBOTT Arron & SARGENT Mary Vol: 4 Page: 120 Line: 009

EATON David M d Hopkinton 1878-10-06 age 63yrs 7mos b Hopkinton child of EATON Moses & MERRILL Judith of Hopkinton Vol: 4 Page: 120 Line: 011

EATON Judith Herrick d Hopkinton 1878-10-23 age 87yrs child of MERRILL Daniel of Meuthen Mass Vol: 4 Page: 120 Line: 012

ASH James d Hopkinton 1878-11-13 age 80yrs b Salisbury Mass child of ASH Nathaniel of Mass & Nancy of Salisbury Mass Vol: 4 Page: 120 Line: 013

WEBBER Martha d Hopkinton 1878-12-03 age 37yrs b Hopkinton child of WEBBER ???? of Hopkinton & Lottie of Henniker Vol: 4 Page: 120 Line: 014

ALLEN Mary d Hopkinton 1878-12-22 age 72yrs b Hooksett child of ALLEN Daniel of Hooksett & Polly of Hooksett Vol: 4 Page: 120 Line: 015

DERRY Julia A d Hopkinton 1879-01-31 age 36yrs b Ireland child of FAGAN James of Ireland & Elizabeth of Ireland Vol: 4 Page: 120 Line: 016

STORY Stephen d Hopkinton 1879-02-22 age 74yrs 7mos 18dys b Hopkinton child of STORY Jeremiah of Hopkinton & FERRIN Judith of Concord Vol: 4 Page: 120 Line: 017

BURKES Elvira?? d Hopkinton 1879-03-15 age 24yrs child of LIBBY Wiliam Vol: 4 Page: 120 Line: 018

PATTERSON Joab d Hopkinton 1879-03-28 age 83yrs b Hopkinton Vol: 4 Page: 120 Line: 019

Hopkinton, NH Deaths 1858

TRUSSELL Jemmia d Hopkinton 1859-03-28 age 83yrs b Hopkinton child of COLBY Anthony & Sarah Vol: 4 Page: 100 Line: 020

CURRIER Martha d Hopkinton 1970-03-24 age 79yrs b Brownsville Vt Vol: 4 Page: 111 Line: 020

CHASE Willard d Hopkinton ?? Nov 10 age 3yrs 7mos 10dys b Hopkinton child of CHASE Horace J of Hopkinton & Mary of Beverly Mass Vol: 4 Page: 104 Line: 025

DWINNELLS Sasan d Hopkinton Jun 1878 age 27yrs b Hopkinton child of CHASE Baruch of Hopkinton & MORRISON Lydia of Antrim Vol: 4 Page: 120 Line: 007

BUSEWELLL Sarah G d Hopkinton Oct 00 1858 age 56?yrs b Hopkinton child of TYLER Moses & Betsey Vol: 4 Page: 100 Line: 007

KNOWLTON Mary d Hopkinton Sep b Manchester child of KNOWLTON Ezekiel & Elizabeth Vol: 4 Page: 100 Line: 003

THOMPSON William L d Hopkinton Sep 1878 age 70yrs b Maine child of THOPMSON Robert & Hannah Vol: 4 Page: 120 Line: 010

SMITH Eliza d Hopkinton September age 23yrs b Hopkinton child of SHERBURN Andrew & Elizabeth Vol: 4 Page: 100 Line: 004

Hopkinton, NH Marriages 1880-1897
Note: This chapter contains a few 1879 marriages, but the book from which these marriages were taken (Volume 5) was labeled "1880-1897".

UPTON Edson of Contoocook & FRENCH Emma of Contoocook m May 3, 1879 Contoocook. Groom: age 44 b Warner s/o UPTON Joseph b Contoocook & MERRILL Clarida. Bride: age 22 b Hopkinton d/o FRENCH Sullivan b Hopkinton & Smith. Vol: 5 Page: 001 Line: 001 Section: 1st

ELLIOTT Alonzo W of Fisherville & KETCHUM Susie A of Fisherville m Jun 5, 1879 Contoocook. Groom: age 25 b Fisherville s/o ELLIOTT Hall b Fisherville. Bride: age 22 b New York d/o KETCHUM George H & Lottie H. Vol: 5 Page: 001 Line: 002 Section: 1st

HARVEY George J of Warner & DWINNELLS Mary F of Hopkinton m Oct 2, 1879 Contoocook. Groom: age 17 b Bow s/o HARVEY James R b Bow & LOWYD-LOUYD? Maria b RI. Bride: age 16 b Fishervile d/o DWINNELLS James b Hopkinton & HEATH Susan. Vol: 5 Page: 001 Line: 010 Section: 1st

SANBORN Edwin N of Concord & SHAW Helen J of Manchester m Sep 2, 1879 Contoocook. Groom: age 19 b Concord s/o SANBORN Edwin b Dorchester & Charlotte G b Boscawen. Bride: age 17 b Pittsfield d/o SHAW James b Pittsfield. Vol: 5 Page: 001 Line: 009 Section: 1st

FOSS John M of Hopkinton & HOLMES Ida F of Bradford m Nov 10, 1879 Hopkinton. Groom: age 31 b Hopkinton s/o FOSS Jonathan b Strafford & CONNOR Alvira b Henniker. Bride: age 26 b Bedford d/o HOLMES Willard b Webster & KIMBALL Eliza b Hopkinton. Vol: 5 Page: 001 Line: 011 Section: 1st

MONTGOMERY Jerome of Hopkinton & DUNBAR Eliza J of Warner m Jul 3, 1879 Contoocook. Groom: age 24 b Hopkinton s/o MONTGOMERY William b Salem Ny & SAVORY Lucy b Warner. Bride: age 22 b Warner d/o DUNBAR Jonathan b & BRUCE Mary Jane b Warner. Vol: 5 Page: 001 Line: 004 Section: 1st

DOWNING Frank E of Hopkinton & KNOWLTON Nettie M of Fisherville m Jun 5, 1879 Warner. Groom: age 23 b Fisherville s/o DOWNING Daniel b Webster & BOWMAN Elizabeth b Henniker. Bride: age 28 b Sutton d/o KNOWLTON Josiah & ANNIS Eliza Ann. Vol: 5 Page: 001 Line: 005 Section: 1st

ALLEN Walton P of Contoocook & MONTGOMERY Mattie of Contoocook m Aug 13, 1881 Hopkinton. Groom: age 32 b Chelsia Mass s/o ALLEN Willard b Cornish & STONE Alvira?? b Grantham. Bride: age 18 b Hopkinton d/o MONTGOMERY George b Salem Ny & SNYDER Elisabeth b Salem Ny. Vol: 5 Page: 009 Line: 002 Section: 1st

BURNS Benjamin A of Hopkinton & PAIGE Lucy A of Hopkinton m Mar 7, 1890 Hopkinton. Groom: age 69 b Bingham Me s/o BURNS James b Madison Me & ANNIS Dorcas. Bride: age 52 b Richmond Vt. Vol: 5 Page: 015 Line: 001 Section: 2nd

DUSTIN Cyrus F of Hopkinton & SPAULDING S Nellie of Hopkinton m Jan 13, 1891 Hopkinton. Groom: age 37 b Hopkinton s/o DUSTIN Daniel b Hopkinton

Hopkinton, NH Marriages 1880

& BARNARD Sarah A b Hopkinton. Bride: age 31 b Manchester d/o SPAULDING Dustin A b Hudson & PUTNEY Sanamatha b Webster. Vol: 5 Page: 017 Line: 001 Section: 2nd

CARTER Enos of Henniker & BURTT Ella N of Contoocook m Dec 1, 1879 Henniker. Groom: age 33 b Hillsboro s/o CARTER Samuel b Hillsboro & RAY Mary b Henniker. Bride: age 18 b Hopkinton d/o BURTT Herman b Hillsboro & FOSTER Nancy T b Hopkinton. Vol: 5 Page: 001 Line: 012 Section: 1st

FLANDERS Fred of Contoocook & WHITTIER Nettie of Contoocook m Nov 27, 1879 Hopkinton. Groom: age 21 b Hopkinton s/o FLANDERS Rufus & GALE Mary C. Bride: age 18 b Hopkinton d/o WHITTIER Amos H & DANFORD Sarah. Vol: 5 Page: 001 Line: 013 Section: 1st

COLBY George W J of Hopkinton & MONTGOMERY Mary E of Hopkinton m Jul 18, 1879 Contoocook. Groom: age 25 b Manchester s/o COLBY Samuel b Hopkinton & FLANDERS Louisa A b Concord. Bride: age 21 b Ny d/o MONTGOMERY George b New York & SNYDER Elizabeth H b New York. Vol: 5 Page: 001 Line: 006 Section: 1st

WHITE Eugene Frank of Hopkinton & DOW Ada of Henniker m Jul 22, 1879 Hopkinton. Groom: age 27 b Hopkinton s/o WHITE Thomas b Hopkinton & ROGERS Lois b Hopkinton. Bride: age 20 b Henniker d/o DOW Wallace b Bradford & SAWYER Emily b Manchester. Vol: 5 Page: 001 Line: 007 Section: 1st

PERRY James M of Hopkinton & KELLEY Edithene E of Hopkinton m Aug 24, 1879 Hopkinton. Groom: age 24 b Hopkinton s/o PERRY William b Hopkinton & MORGAN Elizabeth. Bride: age 19 b Hopkinton d/o KELLEY Frederick b Hopkinton & HOLLAND Harriet b Wilmot. Vol: 5 Page: 001 Line: 008 Section: 1st

BARNES Darrel of Hopkinton & PHILBRICK Louia B of Hopkinton m Mar 25, 1880 Contoocook. Groom: age 20 b Henniker s/o BARNES George b Henniker. Bride: age 17 b Hillsboro d/o PHILBRICK Nathaniel b Sutton & SAWYER Mary b Henniker. Vol: 5 Page: 003 Line: 005 Section: 1st

GREEN Willard L of Hopkinton & BAILEY Etta C of Hopkinton m Jan 1, 1881 Concord. Groom: age 23 b Hopkinton s/o GREENE Herman b Hopkinton & Frances b Boston Mass. Bride: age 16 b Boston Mass d/o BAILEY George & Henrrietta. Vol: 5 Page: 003 Line: 003 Section: 1st

KIMBALL Charlie of Hopkinton & WEBBER Martha Ella of Concord m Apr 17, 1880 Hopkinton. Groom: age 24 b Webster s/o KIMBALL Charles b Hopkinton & CARPENTER Martha b Derby Vt. Bride: age 19 b Webster d/o WEBBER Horatio b & BURBANK Amanda b Webster. Vol: 5 Page: 005 Line: 001 Section: 1st

BROWN Valorous W of Contoocook & LIBBY Sarah G of Contoocook m Apr 21, 1880 Hopkinton. Groom: age 28 b Hopkinton s/o BROWN Gould b Hopkinton & Almira b Hopkinton. Bride: age 18 b Hopkinton d/o LIBBY William T b Pembroke & Etna b Pittsfield. Vol: 5 Page: 005 Line: 002 Section: 1st

HILL John B of Pittsfield & MOORE Ruth E of Pittsfield m Nov 25, 1880 Hopkinton. Groom: age 62. Bride: age 34 b Contoocook. Vol: 5 Page: 005 Line: 010 Section: 1st

Hopkinton, NH Marriages 1880

MORGAN Charles N of Hopkinton & FLANDERS H Violee of Burlington Iowa m Dec 24, 1879 Hopkinton. Groom: age 23 b Hopkinton s/o MORGAN Gilman & MERRILL Elsa L b Hopkinton. Bride: age 22 b Burlington Iowa d/o FLANDERS Samuel & EMERSON Emiley. Vol: 5 Page: 001 Line: 014 Section: 1st

SANBORN Tristan of Webester & FLANDERS Emma J of Hopkinton m Jan 8, 1880 Contoocook. Groom: age 35 b Boscawen s/o SANBORN Jessa D b Boscawen & BATCHELDER Arvillee b Loudon. Bride: age 20 b Hopkinton d/o FLANDERS Benjamin & DOW Jennie. Vol: 5 Page: 003 Line: 001 Section: 1st

LEET Charles N of Contoocook & COPELAND Edna L of Unity m Jan 1, 1881 Charlestown. Groom: age 26 b Claremont s/o LEET George H b Claremont & CHASE Sarah F b Unity. Bride: age 32 b Unity d/o COPELAND Joseph b Acworth & FINLEY Hannah b Rockingham Vt. Vol: 5 Page: 003 Line: 002 Section: 1st

COLBY Watler H of Hopkinton & DOW Lizzie D m Mar 2, 1880 Contoocook. Groom: age 31 b Hopkinton s/o COLBY Samuel b Hopkinton & FLANDERS Louisa b Concord. Bride: age 21 b Concord d/o DOW Henry E b Concord & BOUTWELL Charlotte. Vol: 5 Page: 003 Line: 004 Section: 1st

DUSTIN Herbert C of Hopkinton & RICHARDSON Sarah A of Hopkinton m Jun 15, 1880 Concord. Groom: age 25 b Hopkinton s/o DUSTIN Cyrus b Hopkinton & FISK Edna b Salisbury. Bride: age 24 b Hopkinton d/o RICHARDSON David & DODGE Sarah. Vol: 5 Page: 005 Line: 003 Section: 1st

KELLEY George B of Merrimack Mass & SMITH Clara of Hopkinton m Oct 2, 1880 Hopkinton. Groom: age 24 b Amesbury Mass s/o KELLEY B Atkinson & Anna E. Bride: age 24 b Hopkinton d/o SMITH Charles & Nancy. Vol: 5 Page: 005 Line: 004 Section: 1st

KIMBALL Richard M of Hopkinton & ROGERS Luella F of Hopkinton m Oct 7, 1880 Hopkinton. Groom: age 88 b Hopkinton s/o KIMBALL Jacob b Hopkinton. Bride: age 51 b Canada East d/o COPP Alvaro b Moulttonboro & CLIFFORD Susan b Brookfield Vt. Vol: 5 Page: 005 Line: 005 Section: 1st

FELLOWS Frank Perley of Concord & CURRIER Helen M of Hopkinton m Oct 16, 1880 Hopkinton. Groom: age 27 b Concord s/o FELLOWS Albert & Alma. Bride: age 19 b Concord d/o CURRIER Slyvanus b Sutton & MARY B b Hopkinton. Vol: 5 Page: 005 Line: 006 Section: 1st

NELSON John H of Hopkinton & SEAVEY Nettie M of Hopkinton m Nov 3, 1880 Hopkinton. Groom: age 29 b Hopkinton s/o NELSON Joseph b Concord & Ester U. Bride: age 17 b Hopkinton d/o SEAVEY David b Hopkinton & Sarah M b Hopkinton. Vol: 5 Page: 005 Line: 007 Section: 1st

HAZELTON Herman R of Hopkinton & DWINNELLS Nellie of Hopkinton m Nov 15, 1880 Hopkinton. Groom: age 24 b Groton s/o HAZELTON Rufus & Martha N. Bride: age 15 b Warner d/o DWINNELLS Monroe & Susan. Vol: 5 Page: 005 Line: 008 Section: 1st

LIVINGSTON Isaiak L of Hopkinton & FRENCH N Ella of Hopkinton m Nov 18, 1880 Hopkinton. Groom: age 44 b Hopkinton s/o LIVINGSTON James & Marinda. Bride: age 25 b Hopkinton d/o FRENCH Sullivan & Almira E. Vol: 5 Page: 005 Line: 009 Section: 1st

Hopkinton, NH Marriages 1880

FOSS Ruben C of Manchester & RICHARDSON Ella F of Hopkinton m Dec 18, 1881 Hopkinton. Groom: age 33 b Dorchester s/o FOSS Ezekiel. Bride: age 27 b Hopkinton d/o RICHARDSON Daniel. Vol: 5 Page: 009 Line: 007 Section: 1st

HADLEY Augustus of Hopkinton & REILY Elisabeth of Halifax N S m Jan 26, 1884 Hopkinton. Groom: age 55 b Uxbridge Mass s/o HADLEY Stephen & MILAND Chloe. Bride: age 35 b Halifax N S d/o HENDERSON John b Halifax & Margret b Halifax. Vol: 5 Page: 003 Line: 001 Section: 2nd

FLANDERS Walter of Hopkinton & ROBY Etta of Webster m Apr 3, 1884 Webster. Groom: age 20 s/o FLANDERS Benjamin & Dow. Bride: age 18 d/o ROBY Hiriam. Vol: 5 Page: 003 Line: 002 Section: 2nd

RANDALL George W of Hopkinton & GOODWIN Mary C of Hopkinton m Apr 16, 1884 Hopkinton. Groom: age 36 b Plymouth s/o RANDALL Thomas & FRENCH Mahala. Bride: age 21 b Boston Mass d/o GOODWIN George & Margaret. Vol: 5 Page: 003 Line: 003 Section: 2nd

CROWELL Oliva Wellman of Hopkinton & COLBY Hannah P of Hopkinton m Apr 30, 1884 Hopkinton. Groom: age 25 b Hopkinton s/o CROWELL Albert & Lydia S. Bride: age 20 b Hopkinton d/o COLBY Melvin & Hannah P. Vol: 5 Page: 003 Line: 004 Section: 2nd

STRAW Andrew S of Hopkinton & CHANDLER Dolly V of Hopkinton m Jun 4, 1884 Hopkinton. Groom: b Hopkinton s/o STRAW Horace b Hopkinton & WEEKS Amanda b Hopkinton. Bride: b Hopkinton d/o CHANDLER Horatio J & CURRIER Susan b Hopkinton. Vol: 5 Page: 003 Line: 005 Section: 2nd

CHASE N Lucius of Hopkinton & SPAULDING Lillian F of Hopkinton m Dec 22, 1880 Hopkinton. Groom: age 23 b Hopkinton s/o CHASE Horace b Hopkinton & Mary Ann b Hopkinton. Bride: age 19 b Manchester d/o SPAULDING Dustin b Hopkinton & Susan b Webster. Vol: 5 Page: 005 Line: 011 Section: 1st

STRAW James O of Hopkinton & WHITTEMORE Ada M of Hopkinton m Jan 8, 1881 Hopkinton. Groom: age 27 b Hopkinton s/o STRAW William b Hopkinton & FLANDERS Mary A b Weare. Bride: age 21 b Henniker d/o WHITTEMORE Willia & RANDALL Mary L b Bradford Vt. Vol: 5 Page: 005 Line: 012 Section: 1st

COLBY Fred U of Warner & POTTER Eva L of Warner m Jan 25, 1881 Hopkinton. Groom: age 24 b Warner s/o COLBY Charles Jr b Warner & HANNAH C b Warner. Bride: age 23 b Henniker d/o POTTER William G b Henniker & CLARISA N b Deering. Vol: 5 Page: 005 Line: 013 Section: 1st

PRIEST Allan A of Randolph Vt & BURNHAM Susie W of Hopkinton m Jan 26, 1881 Hopkinton. Groom: age 27 b Shrewsbury Vt s/o PRIEST Charles R b Shrewsbury Vt & Mary b Shrewsbury Vt. Bride: age 19 b Hopkinton d/o BURNHAM John J b Hopkinton & SABRINA N b New Boston. Vol: 5 Page: 005 Line: 014 Section: 1st

CHASE George of Hopkinton & BOHONAN Jennie M of Hopkinton m May 31, 1881 Hopkinton. Groom: age 39 b Hopkinton s/o CHASE Ambrose b Hopkinton & Joanna b Hopkinton. Bride: age 23 b Hopkinton d/o FISH Daniel b Hopkinton & CONNOR Lydia b Hopkinton. Vol: 5 Page: 009 Line: 001 Section: 1st

Hopkinton, NH Marriages 1880

BROWN Waldren of Hopkinton & OSIR?? Ada of Hopkinton m Aug 25, 1897 Hopkinton. Groom: age 22 s/o ---- ---- b Jay Maine & ---- ---- b Camden Me. Bride: age 17 d/o WELCH William b Concord & HEATH Sarah b Concord. Vol: 5 Page: 029 Line: 004 Section: 2nd

DOW Warren H of Hopkinton & KEYES Emma F of Milford m Aug 21, 1881 Contoocook. Groom: age 26 b Hopkinton s/o DOW Samuel b Concord & HOYT Sarah E b Hopkinton. Bride: age 19 b Milford d/o KEYES Horace N b Hancock & Sophia. Vol: 5 Page: 009 Line: 003 Section: 1st

CONNOR James M of Hopkinton & WATSON Catherine S of Hopkinton m Sep 6, 1881 Concord. Groom: age 53 b Henniker s/o CONNOR James b Hopkinton & KIMBALL Lydia b Hopkinton. Bride: age 45 b Newport d/o HOYT Joseph G b Newport & PARNELL Catherine C b Newport. Vol: 5 Page: 009 Line: 004 Section: 1st

BROWN Irvin F of Hopkinton & GREENE Hattie A of Hopkinton m Sep 18, 1881 Concord. Groom: age 26 b Manchester s/o BROWN Francis b Greensboro Vt & Mary L b Newmarket. Bride: age 21 b Hopkinton d/o GREEN Newman & Sarah H. Vol: 5 Page: 009 Line: 005 Section: 1st

POWERS George H of Hopkinton & STERNS Hattie A of Lebanon m Nov 17, 1881 Lebanon. Groom: age 29 b Groton s/o POWERS George b Groton & STEARNS Elsie b Cannan. Bride: age 24 b Lebanon d/o STERNS Nathan b Mansfield Ct & CHAPIN Justina b Newport. Vol: 5 Page: 009 Line: 006 Section: 1st

KEMPTON Lewis E of Contoocook & MONTGOMERY Carrie of Contoocook m Dec 18, 1881 Contoocook. Groom: age 21 b Contoocook s/o KEMPTON Warren M b Croydon & HOWARD Emma b Grantham. Bride: age 22 d/o MONTGOMERY Chas b Salem Ny & BURBANK Adalin b Warner. Vol: 5 Page: 009 Line: 008 Section: 1st

SARGENT John H of Hopkinton & DOW Carrie J of Hopkinton m Dec 20, 1881 Contoocook. Groom: age 27 b Hopkinton s/o SARGENT Abner b Hopkinton & RODERS Emaline b Concord. Bride: age 20 b Libbertyville Ill d/o BLACKSTONE Billy W b Me & DOW Derriel b Hopkinton. Vol: 5 Page: 009 Line: 009 Section: 1st

WHITE Lewis of Hopkinton & CHASE Laura F of Hopkinton m Nov 13, 1897 Hopkinton. Groom: age 32 b Canada. Bride: age 19 b Hopkinton d/o CHASE Cyrus F b Hopkinton & BARTLETT Ella F b Warner. Vol: 5 Page: 029 Line: 006 Section: 2nd

PUTNEY Milton K of Bow & COLBY Nellie S of Bow m Dec 29, 1881 Bow. Groom: age 29 b Bow s/o PUTNEY David b Dunbarton & May b Bow. Bride: age 21 b Bow d/o COLBY Geo N b Bow & Eunice. Vol: 5 Page: 009 Line: 011 Section: 1st

SARGENT Charles of Hopkinton & CURRIER Hester E of Hopkinton m Jan 14, 1882 Hopkinton. Groom: age 24 b Springfield s/o SARGENT Charles D b Concord & Keziah b Springfield. Bride: age 21 b Hopkinton d/o CURRIER George b Hopkinton & Hannah. Vol: 5 Page: 009 Line: 012 Section: 1st

MORRILL Charles of Concord & CURRIER Mary of Concord m Jan 23, 1882 Hopkinton. Groom: age 23 b Concord s/o MORRILL James b Amesbury Mass & Sarah E b Warner. Bride: age 22 b Concord d/o CURRIER Hanson b

Hopkinton, NH Marriages 1880

Concord & KENISTON Miranda b Granthan. Vol: 5 Page: 009 Line: 013 Section: 1st

ANNIS Franklin of Hopkinton & CHILDS Hattie M of Henniker m Mar 7, 1881 Hillsboro. Groom: age 24 b Hopkinton s/o ANNIS Herrick C b Hopkinton & HARDY Cynthia L b Hopkinton. Bride: age 18 b Warner d/o CHILDS Lewis b Manchester & BROWN Livona b Bradford Mass. Vol: 5 Page: 007 Line: 001 Section: 1st

FRAZIER Mills C of Hopkinton & CHASE Frances of Warner m Mar 15, 1881 Warner. Groom: age 21 b Hopkinton. Bride: age 25 b Lawrences Mass. Vol: 5 Page: 007 Line: 002 Section: 1st

FISK Daniel F of Hopkinton & CHANDLER Dell E of Hopkinton m Apr 8, 1882 Hopkinton. Groom: age 22 b Hopkinton s/o FISK Daniel b Hopkinton & CONNOR Lydia A b Hopkinton. Bride: age 17 b Hopkinton d/o CHANDLER Horatio b Hopkinton & CURRIER Susan b Hopkinton. Vol: 5 Page: 013 Line: 001 Section: 1st

ROLLINS Benjamin of Hopkinton & SANDERS Clara A of Pittsfield m Apr 20, 1882 Pittsfield. Groom: age 27 b Hopkinton. Bride: age 27 b Hopkinton. Vol: 5 Page: 013 Line: 002 Section: 1st

HUTCHINSON James R W of Manchester & CRESSEY Sarah E of Manchester m May 25, 1882 Hopkinton. Groom: age 40 b Merrimack s/o HUTCHINSON Hubbard & Phebe. Bride: age 29 b Bradford d/o CRESSEY Azariaiala & Dorothea. Vol: 5 Page: 013 Line: 003 Section: 1st

STEVENS Frank E of Concord & BARBER Louisa H of Concord m May 30, 1882 Hopkinton. Groom: age 23 b Concord s/o STEVENS Abial b Concord. Bride: age 22 b Canada d/o LECLAIR Arthur b Canada. Vol: 5 Page: 013 Line: 004 Section: 1st

CURRIER Willie A of Hopkinton & DOW Jennie S of Hopkinton m May 31, 1882 Hopkinton. Groom: age 21 b Hopkinton s/o CURRIER L b Hopkinton & ANDERSON Annie b Sweden. Bride: age 17 b Concord d/o DOW Henry E b Hopkinton & BOUTELLE Charlotte b Hopkinton. Vol: 5 Page: 013 Line: 005 Section: 1st

EMERSON Fred N of Hopkinton & KIMBALL Nellie F of Hopkinton m May 27, 1882 Warner. Groom: age 22 b Hopkinton. Bride: age 21. Vol: 5 Page: 013 Line: 006 Section: 1st

GREER Frank A of Goffstown & CURRIER Lizzie D of Hopkinton m Jun 4, 1882 Hopkinton. Groom: age 26 b Goffstown s/o GREER Benjamin b Goffstown & Sarah N. Bride: age 25 b Hopkinton d/o CURRIER Lazaio b Hopkinton & ANDERSON Annie b Sweden. Vol: 5 Page: 013 Line: 007 Section: 1st

DWINELLS Warren P of Hopkinton & LIBBIE Ida A of Hopkinton m Jun 14, 1882 Hopkinton. Groom: age 38 b Concord s/o DWINELLS James b Haverhill Mass & Lucy S b Brattlebor Vt. Bride: age 21 b Hopkinton d/o LIBBIE William T & Sarah. Vol: 5 Page: 013 Line: 008 Section: 1st

GORMAN Thomas of Concord & REED Jennie of Hopkinton m Jun 21, 1882 Hopkinton. Groom: age 33 b Henniker s/o GORMAN Michal b Ireland & Mary b Ireland. Bride: age 30 b Hopkinton d/o REED David b Scotland & Jass b Scotland. Vol: 5 Page: 013 Line: 009 Section: 1st

Hopkinton, NH Marriages 1880

DANIELS Charles of Hopkinton & BILL Lina M of Woodbury Vt m Jul 7, 1882 Hopkinton. Groom: age 20 b Bradley Vt s/o DANIEL Samuel b Woodbury Vt & DOWNS Ada. Bride: age 18 b Bradley Vt d/o BILL Gilman & Rosanna. Vol: 5 Page: 013 Line: 010 Section: 1st

WITHEY Louis C of Hopkinton & JOHNSON Mary L of Sutton m Jul 12, 1882 Hopkinton. Groom: age 32 b Sutton s/o WITHEY Asa & Lucreta. Bride: age 26 b Sutton d/o JOHNSON Daniel & Mary. Vol: 5 Page: 013 Line: 011 Section: 1st

ROBBINS Alphonso D of Hopkinton & ROBERTS Jennie S of So Parsonfield Me m Jul 23, 1882 Parsonfield Me. Groom: age 23 b Woodstock Me s/o ROBBINS Samuel S b Greenwood Me & Dorcas. Bride: age 16 b S. Parsonfield Me d/o ROBERTS Joseph. Vol: 5 Page: 013 Line: 012 Section: 1st

BRYANT Eben G of Boston Mass & MORSE Sarah E of Boston Mass m Aug 15, 1882 Hopkinton. Groom: age 38 b Boothbay Me s/o BRYANT Charles b Boothby Me & MADOX Etta b Me. Bride: age 39 b Boston Mass d/o MORSE John b Boston Mass & Sarah b England. Vol: 5 Page: 013 Line: 013 Section: 1st

MORRILL Stephen E of Hopkinton & DEARBORN Mary I of Candia m Oct 5, 1882 Candia. Groom: age 27 b Hopkinton s/o MORRILL Eben b Hopkinton & SWEATT Phebe b Webster. Bride: age 22 b Candia d/o DEARBORN Thomas & BEAN Hannah. Vol: 5 Page: 013 Line: 014 Section: 1st

HEATH Charles J of Grafton & BROWN Etta F of Contoocook m Mar 4, 1882 Hopkinton. Groom: age 21 b Springfield s/o HEATH Charles b Grafton & Melissa A b Springfield. Bride: age 16 b Hopkinton d/o BROWN Ralph & Abby. Vol: 5 Page: 011 Line: 001 Section: 1st

SPOFFORD Samuel of Hopkinton & FOSTER Rose P of Manchester m Mar 28, 1882 Manchester. Groom: age 62 b Hopkinton. Bride: age 43 b Saxton Vt. Vol: 5 Page: 011 Line: 002 Section: 1st

SARGENT Abner Jr of Warner & ANNIS Evaline of Warner m Oct 17, 1882 Hopkinton. Groom: age 65 b Warner s/o SARGENT William b Amesbury Mass & Polly b Amesbury Mass. Bride: age 45 b Warner d/o BARTLETT Haven b Warner. Vol: 5 Page: 015 Line: 001 Section: 1st

HUNT George W of Warner & CHASE Ella of Hopkinton m Nov 13, 1882 Hopkinton. Groom: age 45 b Sutton s/o HUNT Joseph & DAVIS Triphene. Bride: age 21 b Webster d/o CHASE Joseph b & Alice. Vol: 5 Page: 015 Line: 003 Section: 1st

ANNIS Charles S of Warner & HOOK Lizzie C of Hopkinton m Nov 29, 1882 Hopkinton. Groom: age 24 b Warner s/o ANNIS Wm W b Warner & SARGENT Evaline b Warner. Bride: age 17 b Hopkinton d/o HOOK James M b Hopkinton & Mary A b Hopkinton. Vol: 5 Page: 015 Line: 004 Section: 1st

STEVENS Gilman of Hopkinton & COOPER Mary A of Concord m Dec 21, 1882 Concord. Groom: age 56 b Goffstown s/o STEVENS John b Manchester & TARBOX Susan b Hudson. Bride: age 46 b Tamworth d/o PERKINS True b Tamworth & CHAPMAN Mary A b Parsonfield Me. Vol: 5 Page: 015 Line: 005 Section: 1st

PIERCE George of Hopkinton & STRAW Luella E of Hopkinton m Dec 30, 1882 Hopkinton. Groom: age 24 b Hopkinton s/o PIERCE George b Hopkinton &

Hopkinton, NH Marriages 1880

COPPS Fannie b Hopkinton. Bride: age 36 b Hopkinton d/o STRAW William S b Hopkinton & FLANDERS Mary A b Hopkinton. Vol: 5 Page: 015 Line: 006 Section: 1st

BARTLETT Henry of Hopkinton & HARDY Isabella M of Hopkinton m Jul 2, 1882 Henniker. Groom: age 26 b Warner s/o BARTLETT Zenas. Bride: age 20 b Hopkinton d/o HARDY Samuel. Vol: 5 Page: 015 Line: 009 Section: 1st

CHASE Westley J of Hopkinton & ELA Lottie of Hopkinton m Jan 8, 1883 Hopkinton. Groom: age 30 b Hopkinton s/o CHASE Timothy b Hopkinton & SEVERANCE Lucinda J b Hillsboro. Bride: age 22 b Quincy Mass d/o ELA Elijah G C b Quincy Mass & DAVIS Lucy b Quincy Mass. Vol: 5 Page: 015 Line: 007 Section: 1st

SPOFFORD Luther F of Hopkinton & CHANDLER Dora S of Hopkinton m Feb 1, 1883 Hopkinton. Groom: age 34 b Hopkinton s/o SPOFFORD Samuel b Auburn & FITCH Sarah J b Hopkinton. Bride: age 22 b Hopkinton d/o CHANDLER Horatio J b Hopkinton & CURRIER Susan b Hopkinton. Vol: 5 Page: 015 Line: 008 Section: 1st

TURCOTT William H of Concord & SALTMARSH Emma S of Concord m Feb 12, 1883 Hopkinton. Groom: age 25 b Canada Pq s/o TURCOTT Joseph b Canada Pq & Apoline b Canada Pq. Bride: age 23 b Concord d/o SALTMARSH Andrew b Concord & Sarah b Concord. Vol: 5 Page: 015 Line: 010 Section: 1st

DANFORTH George W of Warner & SANBORN Cordelia A of Concord m Oct 10, 1883 Contoocook. Groom: age 28 b Warner s/o DANFORTH W C b Danbury & Martha b Henniker. Bride: age 36 b Springfield d/o SANBORN George W b Springfield & Jane G b Derring. Vol: 5 Page: 017 Line: 001 Section: 1st

COLBY Samuel H of Hopkinton & WEBBER Annie J of Hopkinton m Jun 12, 1883 Concord. Groom: age 58 b Hopkinton s/o COLBY Samuel b Hopkinton & STRAW Mary. Bride: age 34 b Hopkinton d/o WEBBER Jewett & ADAMS Sally. Vol: 5 Page: 017 Line: 002 Section: 1st

ROWELL Alonzo of Hopkinton & ROWELL Marcia of Concord m Oct 15, 1883 Concord. Groom: age 50 b Hopkinton s/o ROWELL John b Hopkinton & TUTTLE Lydia E b Weare. Bride: age 28 b Saco Me. Vol: 5 Page: 017 Line: 003 Section: 1st

TYLER Lucious H of Hopkinton & EATON Frances A of Warner m Jun 26, 1883 Warner. Groom: age 60 b Hopkinton s/o TYLER Symon b Henniker & ROWELL Hannah b Hopkinton. Bride: age 47 b Warner d/o EATON Elijah b Warner & SAWYER Fannie b Warner. Vol: 5 Page: 017 Line: 004 Section: 1st

CHOATE Horace S of Hopkinton & COMBS Frances E of Boston Mass m Dec 10, 1883 Hopkinton. Groom: age 50 b Henniker s/o CHOATE George b Hopkinton & Betsey b Hopkinton. Bride: age 42 b Munroe Me d/o FORD Cyrus K b Munroe Me & Hannah N b Munroe Me. Vol: 5 Page: 017 Line: 005 Section: 1st

LIBBY Joseph G of Contoocook & BARTLETT Clara of Warner m Jan 1, 1884 Contoocook. Groom: age 29 b Hopkinton s/o LIBBY Wm T b Epsom & Elinor b Deerfield. Bride: age 17 b Warner d/o BARTLETT Zenas & Caroline. Vol: 5 Page: 017 Line: 006 Section: 1st

HOYT James F of Hopkinton & DOW Lilla M Or Lydia?? of Bradford m Aug 22, 1883 Hopkinton. Groom: age 24 b Wareham Mass s/o HOYT Benj b Hopkinton & REED Sarah C b Milleborough Ma. Bride: age 19 b Bradford d/o DOW

Horace b Bradford & MURDER Eliz b Bradford. Vol: 5 Page: 017 Line: 007 Section: 1st

CHASE Nelson A of Hopkinton & CLARK Annie J of Warner m Oct 25, 1883 Hopkinton. Groom: age 33 b Hopkinton s/o CHASE Moses M & Louisa b Hopkinton. Bride: age 21 b Warner d/o CLARK Alvah b Warner & Harriett b Bradford. Vol: 5 Page: 017 Line: 008 Section: 1st

KIMBALL Francis R of Hopkinton & CONNOR Maria P of Hopkinton m Nov 6, 1883 Hopkinton. Groom: age 24 b Hopkinton s/o KIMBALL Matheu b Hopkinton & GOODRICH Maria. Bride: age 21 b Hopkinton d/o CONNOR James M b Hopkinton & PUTNEY Judith b Hopkinton. Vol: 5 Page: 017 Line: 009 Section: 1st

CORLISS Fred E of Hopkinton & MUZZEY Isabella M of Concord m Oct 5, 1883 Concord. Groom: age 20 b Hopkinton s/o CORLISS Elbridge & Mary J. Bride: age 18 d/o HALL Ednah. Vol: 5 Page: 017 Line: 010 Section: 1st

DODGE Henry of Hopkinton & HOYT Jessie A of Hopkinton. m Jul 5, 1883 Hopkinton. Groom: age 20 b Hopkinton s/o DODGE Moses E b Hopkinton & Abbie b Hopkinton. Bride: age 20 b Wareham Mass d/o HOYT Benj b Hopkinton & S C b Middleboro Mass. Vol: 5 Page: 017 Line: 011 Section: 1st

HOOK Asa E of Hopkinton & DWINELLS Minnie B of Hopkinton m Jul 2, 1884 Concord. Groom: age 23 b Concord s/o HOOK Asa J & Harriet N b Canterbury. Bride: age 15 b Hopkinton d/o DWINELLS John G b Dunbarton & CHASE Matitda b Hopkinton. Vol: 5 Page: 003 Line: 006 Section: 2ND Note:

ROWE Calvin J of Hopkinton & WEEKS Mary B of Hopkinton m Aug 9, 1884 Concord. Groom: age 45 b Boscawen s/o ROWE Calvin b England & PHELPS Lucinda b Wilmot. Bride: age 46. Vol: 5 Page: 003 Line: 007 Section: 2nd

CORLISS Charles H of Hopkinton & PAIGE Etta M of Warner m Oct 4, 1884 Hopkinton. Groom: age 24 s/o CORLISS Elbridge G & Stevens. Bride: age 21 d/o PAIGE James O & PAGE Samantha. Vol: 5 Page: 003 Line: 008 Section: 2nd

STRAW Charles A of Hopkinton & MONTGOMERY Lida S of Hopkinton m Dec 31, 1884 Hopkinton. Groom: age 24 b Hopkinton s/o STRAW Gilman J & HOYT Wealthy b Henniker. Bride: age 24 b Hopkinton d/o MONTGOMERY Charles & BURBANK Adaline. Vol: 5 Page: 003 Line: 009 Section: 2nd

CARTER Dana M of Concord & STRAW Idella of Hopkinton m Feb 25, 1885 Hopkinton. Groom: age 29 b New Boston s/o CARTER David S b Concord & SHEPHERD Mary A b New Boston. Bride: age 22 b Hopkinton d/o STRAW John b Hopkinton & HOLMES Mary A. Vol: 5 Page: 005 Line: 001 Section: 2nd

DOW Oscar F of Hopkinton & YOUNG Augusta A of Henniker m Jun 30, 1879 Concotoook. Groom: age 18 b Hopkinton s/o DOW Samuel & HOYT Sarah. Bride: age 22 b Manchester d/o YOUNG Robert & DOW Jennie. Vol: 5 Page: 001 Line: 003 Section: 1st

DUNBAR Henry P of Hopkinton & GAGE Mary E of Hopkinton m Nov 4, 1882 Hopkinton. Groom: age 24 b Hopkinton s/o DUNBAR Elmer B & WEBBER Amy G. Bride: age 21 b Hopkinton d/o GAGE Frederick G. Vol: 5 Page: 015 Line: 002 Section: 1st

Hopkinton, NH Marriages 1880

CLARK Henry N of Tilton & FRENCH Agusta J of Hopkinton m Dec 24, 1881 Hopkinton. Groom: age 26 b Sanborton s/o CLARK Washington H b Sanborton & PIKE Mary b Franklin. Bride: age 20 b Hopkinton d/o FRENCH Geo W b Hopkinton & Helen b Hopkinton. Vol: 5 Page: 009 Line: 010 Section: 1st Note: VITAL RECORDS GIVES -'CLAK'

DAVIS Charles C of Hopkinton & DANFORTH M Lizzie of Hopkinton m 1885 Concord. Groom: age 25 b Hopkinton s/o DAVIS Arron. Bride: age 27 d/o DANFORTH Albert. Vol: 5 Page: 005 Line: 002 Section: 2nd

DOWNING Frank E of Hopkinton & SAWTELLE Emma W of Lancaster Mass m Aug 12, 1885 Henniker. Groom: age 29 b Hopkinton s/o DOWNING Daniel & Elizabeth. Bride: age 29 b Lancaster Mass d/o SAWTELLE Nathaniel. Vol: 5 Page: 005 Line: 003 Section: 2nd

MORAN Christopher of Hopkinton & MAHON Mary B of Concord m Aug 9, 1885 Concord. Groom: age 26 b Concord s/o MORAN Patrick b Ireland & Ann b Ireland. Bride: age 20 b Ireland d/o MAHON James b Ireland & Margrette b Ireland. Vol: 5 Page: 005 Line: 004 Section: 2nd

BORDEN Arthur of Denver Col & PAIGE Lucy E of Hopkinton m Sep 2, 1885 Hopkinton. Groom: age 29 b Fall River Mass s/o BORDEN Samuel & Margrette. Bride: age 26 b Hopkinton d/o PAIGE S Smith & Maria. Vol: 5 Page: 005 Line: 005 Section: 2nd

WEBSTER Charles F of Hopkinton & WALACE Bessie of Hopkinton m Sep 12, 1885 Warner. Groom: age 39 b New Sharon Me. Bride: age 34 b Strong Me. Vol: 5 Page: 005 Line: 006 Section: 2nd

BARTON Robert W of Hopkinton & THOMPSON Mabel of Hopkinton m Oct 11, 1885 Hopkinton. Groom: age 21 b Hopkinton s/o BARTON Charles O & CUTTS Lindia. Bride: age 18 b Springfield d/o KIMBALL Susan. Vol: 5 Page: 005 Line: 007 Section: 2nd

PAIGE Thomas W of Hopkinton & STRAW Minnie B of Hopkinton m Nov 1, 1885 Hopkinton. Groom: age 31 b Lowell Mass s/o PAIGE Thomas E & BLACK Sally F. Bride: age 20 b Hopkinton d/o STRAW Gilman J & HOYT Wealty. Vol: 5 Page: 005 Line: 008 Section: 2nd

JONES Thomas B of Hopkinton & TRUE Hattie M of Pittsfield m Nov 5, 1885 Hopkinton. Groom: age 71 b Pittsfield s/o JONES Jacob & ROLLINS Nancy b Northwood. Bride: age 72 b Epping d/o CHASE James b Freemont & SMITH Harriet b Amesbury Mass. Vol: 5 Page: 005 Line: 009 Section: 2nd

HOLMES Charles A of Salisbury & LOW Helen N of Hopkinton m Dec 23, 1885 Concord. Groom: age 35 b Salisbury s/o HOLMES William b Hopkinton & JOHNSON Jane b Sutton. Bride: age 31 b Hopkinton d/o LOW Seth b Dunbarton & EASTMAN Flora b Hopkinton. Vol: 5 Page: 005 Line: 010 Section: 2nd

BOUTELLE Henry B A of Hopkinton & MONTGOMERY Alice of Hopkinton m Dec 31, 1885 Hopkinton. Groom: age 23 b New Berlin Ill s/o BOUTELLE Eli A b Barre Vt & WEEKS Harriett W b Hopkinton. Bride: age 24 b Hopkinton d/o MONTGOMERY George & Elizabeth H. Vol: 5 Page: 005 Line: 011 Section: 2nd

HOWE Jason C of Hopkinton & HEMPHILL Jennie of Warner m Mar 20, 1886 Bradford. Groom: age 35 b Bradford s/o HOWE Lyman & Sophrona. Bride:

Hopkinton, NH Marriages 1880

age 32 b Warner d/o HEMPHILL Mathew & MORGAN Rhoda B. Vol: 5 Page: 007 Line: 001 Section: 2nd

DAVIS Henry B of Hopkinton & COOK Eliza J of Middleton Mass m May 5, 1886 Middleton Mass. Groom: age 30 b Hopkinton s/o DAVIS Amos N b Hopkinton & CRESSEY Betsey A b Hopkinton. Bride: age 22 b Peabody Mass d/o COOK Hugh & Mary A. Vol: 5 Page: 007 Line: 003 Section: 2nd

WEBBER Lerman S of Hopkinton & RILEY Margrett of Hillboro Br m Jun 8, 1886 Hillsborough. Groom: age 22 b Hopkinton s/o WEBBER Cyrel T b Webster & JEFFUS Jennette b Croydon. Bride: age 25 b Conway Mass d/o RILEY Patrick b Ireland & STANTON Margett b Ireland. Vol: 5 Page: 007 Line: 004 Section: 2nd

BAKER William A of Hopkinton & PALMER Effie V of Hopkinton m Sep 5, 1886 Hopkinton. Groom: age 20 b Hopkinton s/o BAKER John b Concord & PUTNAM Eliza b Hopkinton. Bride: age 21 b Hopkinton. Vol: 5 Page: 007 Line: 004 Section: 2nd

KIMBALL Herbert M of Hopkinton & COLBY N Abbie of Dunbarton m Oct 6, 1886 Hopkinton. Groom: age 23 b Hopkinton s/o KIMBALL Moses St b Hopkinton & SMITH Mary F b Hopkinton. Bride: age 26 b Hopkinton d/o COLBY Frank b Bow. Vol: 5 Page: 007 Line: 005 Section: 2nd

DAVIS Horace J of Hopkinton & CARROLL Jennie B of Hopkinton m Dec 14, 1886 Hopkinton. Groom: age 24 b Warner s/o DAVIS Walter b Warner & JONES Dolly b Warner. Bride: age 24 b Sutton d/o CARROLL Lyander H & LOVERING Adaline b Sutton. Vol: 5 Page: 007 Line: 006 Section: 2nd

FLANDERS Anson B of Hopkinton & PAGE Carrie S of Lancaster m Jan 15, 1887 Lancaster. Groom: age 23 b Wilmot s/o FLANDERS H C & Lauri. Bride: age 21 b Dunbarton d/o PAGE L S. Vol: 5 Page: 009 Line: 001 Section: 2nd

JONES J Arthur of Hopkinton & BAILEY Mabel N of Hopkinton m Jan 19, 1887 Hopkinton. Groom: age 22 b Hopkinton s/o JONES J F b Hopkinton & BARNARD Maria b NY. Bride: age 19 b Newbury d/o BAILEY George P b Newbury & Addie b Newbury. Vol: 5 Page: 009 Line: 002 Section: 2nd

MILTON Charles A of Hopkinton & JEFFERSON Lillia of Brookline Mass m Mar 21, 1887 Brookline Mass. Groom: age 23 b Nova Scotia s/o MILTON George & Mary A. Bride: age 19 b Nova Scotia d/o JEFFERSON Charles & Lizzie. Vol: 5 Page: 009 Line: 003 Section: 2nd

DERRY Joseph of Hopkinton & MORAN Mary E of Hopkinton m Apr 25, 1887 Concord. Groom: age 48 b Canada s/o DERRY Louis & Adalade. Bride: age 21 b Hopkinton d/o MORAN Patrick & Ann. Vol: 5 Page: 009 Line: 004 Section: 2nd

BURBANK Ivan D of Hopkinton & CLARK Agusta J of Hopkinton m May 21, 1887 Hopkinton. Groom: age 26 b Hopkinton s/o BURBANK Moses W b Hopkinton & PALMER Mary F b Hopkinton. Bride: age 26 b Hopkinton d/o FRENCH George W b Hopkinton & RUNNELLS Helen C b Hopkinton. Vol: 5 Page: 009 Line: 005 Section: 2nd

BARTON Elroy C of Hopkinton & CURRIER Mary E of Hopkinton m Jul 2, 1887 Hopkinton. Groom: age 25 b Hopkinton s/o BARTON Charles O b Hopkinton & Philandie b Hopkinton. Bride: age 20 b Hopkinton d/o CURRIER Lozaro b Hopkinton & Anna. Vol: 5 Page: 009 Line: 006 Section: 2nd

Hopkinton, NH Marriages 1880

LAMPREY Geo of Concord & ABBOTT Orrilla of Hopkinton m Aug 9, 1887 Hopkinton. Groom: age 20 b Concord s/o LAMPREY Morris. Bride: age 17 b Concord d/o ABBOTT William & Sarah. Vol: 5 Page: 009 Line: 007 Section: 2nd

WOLCOTT Robert O of Hopkinton & WALTON Alice M of Exeter m Aug 17, 1887 Exeter. Groom: age 29 b Leicester Mass s/o WOLCOTT Loren & WOOD Mary A B. Bride: age 29 b New Portland Me d/o WALTON Joseph D & BATES Betty B. Vol: 5 Page: 009 Line: 008 Section: 2nd

WALKER Milton J of Dunbarton & ELLIOTT Alice M of Hopkinton m Aug 21, 1887 Hopkinton. Groom: age 21 b Dunbarton s/o WALKER David P & Lydia A. Bride: age 20 b Hopkinton d/o ELLIOTT Joseph R. Vol: 5 Page: 009 Line: 009 Section: 2nd

KEMPTON Charles H of Griggsville Ill & GOODHUE Eliza H of Hopkinton m Sep 21, 1887 Concord. Groom: age 29 b Hopkinton s/o KEMPTON Warren M b Charleston & HOWARD E Orgiretta b Springfield. Bride: age 26 b Epsom d/o GOODHUE Edward F b Epsom & HAM Mary H b Epsom. Vol: 5 Page: 009 Line: 010 Section: 2nd

MUDGETT Calvin H of Hopkinton & LAMPREY Clara of Hopkinton m Oct 29, 1887 Hopkinton. Groom: age 64 b Bristol s/o MUDGETT William & HUCHINS Eunice. Bride: age 63 b Northfield Vt d/o FISHER John E & NOYES Hannah. Vol: 5 Page: 009 Line: 011 Section: 2nd

HEATH Albert H of Hopkinton & SCRIBNER Ida N of Hillsborough m Nov 23, 1887 Hillsborough. Groom: age 25 b Grafton s/o HEATH Ora M & Marcy A. Bride: age 23 b Hillsborough d/o SCRIBNER Francis B & Fannie M. Vol: 5 Page: 009 Line: 012 Section: 2nd

WHITTIER Leon D of Hopkinton & STORY Hattie N of Hopkinton m Dec 24, 1887 Hopkinton. Groom: age 30 b Hopkinton s/o WHITTIER Jacob & Harriet S. Bride: age 20 b Hopkinton d/o STORY Moses & Harriet D. Vol: 5 Page: 009 Line: 013 Section: 2nd

BURBANK Alberto H of Hopkinton & TUCKER Eliza J of Hopkinton m Dec 24, 1887 Hopkinton. Groom: age 24 b Hopkinton s/o BURBANK Moses & Mary F. Bride: age 16 b Henniker d/o TUCKER Samuel & Nancy. Vol: 5 Page: 009 Line: 014 Section: 2nd

BACON John N of Hopkinton & ADAMS Leola H of Hopkinton m Mar 22, 1888 Hopkinton. Groom: age 28 b Hopkinton s/o BACON John H b Hopkinton & Ann P b Hopkinton. Bride: age 21 b Hopkinton d/o ADAMS Joseph H b Sutton & Judith b Warner. Vol: 5 Page: 011 Line: 001 Section: 2nd

DANFORTH Frank C of Hopkinton & BURNHAM Ella M of Hopkinton m Jun 30, 1888 Hopkinton. Groom: age 22 b Hopkinton s/o DANFORTH Erastrus b Hopkinton & NICHOL Mary S b Hopkinton. Bride: age 21 b Hopkinton d/o BURNHAM John F b Hopkinton & SITARH ?? W b Anrtim. Vol: 5 Page: 011 Line: 002 Section: 2nd

DUNBAR Elmer E of Hopkinton & PAIGE Mary E of Hopkinton m Jul 3, 1888 Hopkinton. Groom: age 24 b Hopkinton s/o DUNBAR Elmer & Ann T. Bride: age 23 b Dunbarton d/o PAIGE George W & Martha H. Vol: 5 Page: 011 Line: 003 Section: 2nd

Hopkinton, NH Marriages 1880

THAYER Herbert Edgar of Hopkinton & BARNEY Mary Eliza of S. Hadley Falls Ma m Aug 2, 1888 Hopkinton. Groom: age 27 b Farmingdale Me s/o THAYER George A b Foxboro Mass & Louisa b Foxboro Mass. Bride: age 25 b Wilmington Vt d/o BARNEY Gilis W b S Hadley Mass & Frances S b S. Hadley Mass. Vol: 5 Page: 011 Line: 004 Section: 2nd

KIMBALL John Stevens of Hopkinton & FRENCH Margarette A of Hopkinton m Nov 7, 1888 Hopkinton. Groom: age 43 b Boston Mass s/o KIMBALL John S b Pembroke & STEVENS Mary E b Goffstown. Bride: age 42 b Hopkinton d/o FRENCH Rueben E b Hopkinton & CHASE Sarah b Dunbarton. Vol: 5 Page: 011 Line: 006 Section: 2nd

HARTHORN Arthur of Concord & DARLING Sarah D of Hopkinton m Aug 11, 1888 Hopkinton. Groom: age 48 b Me s/o HATHRON Chas & Margaret. Bride: age 42 b Hopkinton d/o EMERSON James K & DIAMOND Julia. Vol: 5 Page: 011 Line: 007 Section: 2nd Note: ON RECORD CROSSED OUT ??

CARD Thomas B of Kingston Ns & EMERSON Blanche of Hopkinton m Sep 15, 1888 Hopkinton. Groom: age 24 b Nova Scotia s/o CARD Chas & ROBINSON Mary. Bride: age 19 b Hopkinton. Vol: 5 Page: 011 Line: 008 Section: 2nd Note: ENTERY HAS BEEN CROSSED OUT SEE PAGE 29

EASTMAN Henry C of Hopkinton & MUDGETT Ellen F of Hopkinton m Jan 26, 1889 Hopkinton. Groom: age 24 b Hopkinton s/o EASTMAN Wlater S & CHASE Helen N. Bride: age 23 b Bristol d/o MUDGETT Calvin H & FISHER Julio. Vol: 5 Page: 013 Line: 001 Section: 2nd

CURRIER John of Hopkinton & WHITTEMORE Mabel of Hopkinton m Feb 14, 1889 Hopkinton. Groom: age 21 b Hopkinton s/o CURRIER John F b Hopkinton & CURRIER Nellie H b Hopkinton. Bride: age 22 b Hopkinton d/o WHITTEMORE William B b Hopkinton & Nancy b Hopkinton. Vol: 5 Page: 013 Line: 002 Section: 2nd

FLANDERS Walter H of Hopkinton & ORDWAY Lilla of Loudon m Jun 15, 1889 Hopkinton. Groom: age 26 b Hopkinton s/o FLANDERS Benjamin & DOW Lizzie J. Bride: age 20 b Loudon d/o ORDWAY Willard & HALL Sarah. Vol: 5 Page: 013 Line: 003 Section: 2nd

MILLS Frank C of Hopkinton & HOWARD Mamie A of Hopkinton m Nov 9, 1889 Weare. Groom: age 37 b Hopkinton s/o MILLS Joseph & MILL Celinda. Bride: age 17 b Newport d/o HOWARD Charles & GREEN Alvira A. Vol: 5 Page: 013 Line: 005 Section: 2nd

GETCHILL Ezekiel Y of Hopkinton & SMART Sarah E of Warner m Nov 21, 1889 Bradford. Groom: age 38 b Boscawen. Bride: age 41. Vol: 5 Page: 013 Line: 006 Section: 2nd

BARNARD George E of Hopkinton & TYLER Bertha S of Hopkinton m Nov 23, 1889 Hopkinton. Groom: age 25 b Hopkinton s/o BARNARD Joseph b Hopkinton & GERRISH Maria b Canterbury. Bride: age 23 b Hopkinton d/o TYLER Lucius H b Hopkinton & HALL Sarah b Candia. Vol: 5 Page: 013 Line: 007 Section: 2nd

STEVENS Ernest S of Hopkinton & RICHARDSON Nettie M of Hopkinton m Nov 27, 1889 Hopkinton. Groom: age 21 b Manchester s/o STEVENS Horace S b Manchester & YOUNG Roxanna D b Manchester. Bride: age 24 b Hopkinton

Hopkinton, NH Marriages 1880

d/o RICHARDSON Thomas b Deering & HARDY Eliza A b Howard Mich. Vol: 5 Page: 013 Line: 008 Section: 2nd

PUTNAM Charles R of Hopkinton & CLOUGH Nancy of Hopkinton m Nov 21, 1891 Concord. Groom: age 27 b Hopkinton s/o PUTNAM Rufus & Lydia. Bride: age 23 b Hopkinton d/o CLOUGH Charles & HARDY Mary J. Vol: 5 Page: 017 Line: 009 Section: 2nd

BROWN Henry F of Penacook & MORRILL S Maria of Hopkinton m Apr 8, 1890 Hopkinton. Groom: age 53 b Attleboro Mass s/o BROWN Henry H b Seekonk Mass & DAGGETT Mary A b Surry. Bride: age 43 b Hopkinton d/o MORRILL Jacob M b Hopkinton & ABBOTT Sarah C b Hopkinton. Vol: 5 Page: 015 Line: 003 Section: 2nd

BUSWELL Loren W of Hopkinton & CARPENTER Mary S of Hopkinton m May 14, 1890 Hopkinton. Groom: age 35 b Concord s/o BUSWELL Smith b Hopkinton & Deborah b E. Machia Me. Bride: age 18 b Hopkinton d/o CARPENTER Guy b Hopkinton & Mary b Hopkinton. Vol: 5 Page: 015 Line: 004 Section: 2nd

TYLER Frank A of Hopkinton & CARTLAND Jane S of Lee m Jul 2, 1890 Lee. Groom: age 36 b Lawrence Mass s/o TYLER Daniel. Bride: age 31 b Weare d/o CARTLAND Moses A. Vol: 5 Page: 015 Line: 005 Section: 2nd

DUSTON Arthur M of Hopkinton & CLOUGH Josephine of Hopkinton m Sep 1, 1890 Salem Mass. Groom: age 27 b Hopkinton s/o DUSTON Mark G & SANBORN Eliza. Bride: age 20 b Hopkinton d/o CLOUGH Charles F & HARDY Mary J. Vol: 5 Page: 015 Line: 006 Section: 2nd

DROWN Jasper E of Hopkinton & NICHOLS Sarah E** of Hopkinton m Oct 22, 1890 Hopkinton. Groom: age 23 b Thornton s/o BROWN Daniel & Laura. Bride: age 20 b So Boston Mass d/o NICHOLS George H & Lucy E. Vol: 5 Page: 015 Line: 007 Section: 2nd Note: Correction on record(Lilla)

GOODHUE Frank B of Salem & CHOATE Carrie J of Hopkinton m 1890 Hopkinton. Groom: age 31 b Salem s/o GOODHUE Frederick & STEVENS Almira W. Bride: age 23. Vol: 5 Page: 015 Line: 008 Section: 2nd

SMITH John C of Hopkinton & TAYLER Sarah A of No Hampton m Nov 5, 1890 Concord. Groom: age 28 b Hopkinton s/o SMITH Charles H b Tayler Richard & DELINO Nancy J b Sarah. Bride: age 30 b No Hampton. Vol: 5 Page: 015 Line: 009 Section: 2nd

CURRIER Willie A of Hopkinton & WEBSTER Gertie J of Hopkinton m Nov 23, 1890 Concord. Groom: age 29 b Hopkinton s/o CURRIER Lozario & Anna C. Bride: age 16 b Hopkinton. Vol: 5 Page: 015 Line: 010 Section: 2nd

SHURTLEFF John of Hopkinton & ELWOOD Fannie of Hopkinton m 1890 Hopkinton. Groom: age 21 b Lebanon N s/o SHURTLEFF Samuel & MILTON Mary E. Bride: age 26 b Manchester d/o ELWOOD John B & ALCOCK Lenora. Vol: 5 Page: 015 Line: 011 Section: 2nd

CONNOR Alvah L of Hopkinton & MORGAN Jennie A of Hopkinton m Jan 19, 1891 Hillsborough. Groom: age 24 b Concord s/o CONNOR Frederick W & Sophia. Bride: age 20 b Hopkinton d/o MORGAN Frank W & JONES Fannie. Vol: 5 Page: 017 Line: 002 Section: 2nd

Hopkinton, NH Marriages 1880

MILTON John N of Hopkinton & DOW Eliza A of Hopkinton m Jan 23, 1891 Hopkinton. Groom: age 76 b Hopkinton s/o MILTON Daniel & PRESSEY Judith. Bride: age 69 b Henniker. Vol: 5 Page: 017 Line: 003 Section: 2nd

BROWN George A of Hopkinton & FLANDERS Anzonetta J of Gilmanton m Mar 24, 1891 Hopkinton. Groom: age 57 b Concord s/o BROWN Cotton S b Hopkinton & COLCORD Betsey A b New Market. Bride: age 38 b Gilmanton d/o FLANDERS Rufus L b Gilmanton & HACKETT Mary J b New Hampton. Vol: 5 Page: 017 Line: 004 Section: 2nd

FOWLER Jonathan of So Sioux City Neb & BARNARD Mary E of Hopkinton m Mar 24, 1891 Hopkinton. Groom: age 40 b Mission Ill s/o FOWLER Jonathan & PHILLIPS Sarah b Henniker. Bride: age 32 b Hopkinton d/o BARNARD Joseph b Hopkinton & Maria b Canterbury. Vol: 5 Page: 017 Line: 005 Section: 2nd

CHASE Charles T of Hopkinton & WEBBER Florence of Hopkinton m Jun 2, 1891 Newport. Groom: age 30 b Charlestown Mass s/o THOMPSON Justin & ROGERS Sarah E. Bride: age 20 b Hopkinton d/o WEBBER Cyril T & JEFFERS Jennette. Vol: 5 Page: 017 Line: 006 Section: 2nd

HOYT Wallie F of Hopkinton & BROWN Alice M of Hopkinton m Jun 27, 1891 Hopkinton. Groom: age 35 b Hopkinton s/o HOYT Moses & FLANDERS Mahala. Bride: age 33 b Hopkinton d/o BROWN Otis M & Mary E. Vol: 5 Page: 017 Line: 007 Section: 2nd

KIMBALL Nelson D of Hopkinton & PATCH Adelaide M of Hopkinton m Oct 29, 1891 Hopkinton. Groom: age 27 b Hopkinton s/o KIMBALL Elbridge & BUTLER Mary L. Bride: age 20 b Newfield Me d/o PATCH D E & STONE Melvina. Vol: 5 Page: 017 Line: 008 Section: 2nd

LAMPREY Daniel of Hopkinton & CALKIN Ollie of Hopkinton m Dec 22, 1891 Concord. Groom: age 60 b Concord. Bride: age 48 b Weare d/o WILLARD Cyrus. Vol: 5 Page: 017 Line: 010 Section: 2nd

DOW Harvey M of Hopkinton & WEBSTER Della of Hopkinton m Feb 22, 1892 Hopkinton. Groom: age 30 b Hopkinton s/o DOW Samuel & HOYT Sarah. Bride: age 16 b Hopkinton d/o WEBSTER Frank D & DOW Nettie. Vol: 5 Page: 019 Line: 001 Section: 2nd

PAIGE John W of Hopkinton & ADAMS Sophronia of Springfield m Feb 28, 1892 Concord. Groom: age 70 b Hopkinton s/o PAIGE John & DRAKE Rachel. Bride: age 63 b Claremont d/o PIERCE June ?? & JOSLIN Sally. Vol: 5 Page: 019 Line: 003 Section: 2nd

BARNES George D of Hopkinton & GLINES Nettie J of Hopkinton m Apr 9, 1892 Hopkinton. Groom: age 27 b Henniker s/o BARNES George D & CHASE Sarah. Bride: age 18 b Salisbury d/o GILNES Anson W & Lucy A. Vol: 5 Page: 019 Line: 003 Section: 2nd

KILLAM John of Littleton & LOCK Sarah A of Hopkinton m Apr 23, 1892 Hopkinton. Groom: age 48 b N B s/o KILLAM Merk?? & PIPER Mercy. Bride: age 42 b Canterbury d/o LOCKE Olive & SHAW Harriet. Vol: 5 Page: 019 Line: 004 Section: 2nd

HOLMES Henry P of Webster & WHITE Lucy A of Hopkinton m Apr 26, 1892 Hopkinton. Groom: age 26 b Manchester s/o HOLMES Willard M &

Hopkinton, NH Marriages 1880

SANBORN Mary E. Bride: age 31 b Hopkinton d/o WHITE Jacob A & WARD Maria. Vol: 5 Page: 019 Line: 005 Section: 2nd

ROWE James C of Hopkinton & SILVER Sarah J of Orange Mass m May 7, 1892 Concord. Groom: age 51 b Boscawen s/o ROWE Calvin & PHELPS Lucinda. Bride: age 52 b St Ablbans Vt d/o CRAWFORD Frank & BICKFORD Julia. Vol: 5 Page: 019 Line: 006 Section: 2nd

RUSSELL Arthur C of No Woodstock & FISK Mabel B of Hopkinton m Jun 5, 1892 Concord. Groom: age 23 b Lincoln s/o RUSSELL Stephen & Eunice. Bride: age 23 b New London. Vol: 5 Page: 019 Line: 007 Section: 2nd

MUDGETT Calvin N of Hopkinton & DOW Mary of Hopkinton m Sep 7, 1892 Hopkinton. Groom: age 69 b Bristol s/o MUDGETT William & HUTCHINS Eunice. Bride: age 67 b New Boston d/o PERRY Farnum & FRENCH Dorothy. Vol: 5 Page: 019 Line: 008 Section: 2nd

RUSS William C of Hopkinton & COLBY Nora M of Nashua m Oct 19, 1892 Hopkinton. Groom: age 38 b Nashua s/o RUSS Nathan & BARRETT Clarisa D. Bride: age 33 d/o COLBY Abram. Vol: 5 Page: 019 Line: 009 Section: 2nd

DUNBAR George E of Hopkinton & ELLSWORTH Mattie B of Hopkinton m Nov 1, 1892 Gilmanton. Groom: age 26 b Hopkinton s/o DUNBAR Elmer B & WEBBER Ann T. Bride: age 25 b Gilmanton d/o FLANDERS Rufus & HACKETT Mary J. Vol: 5 Page: 019 Line: 010 Section: 2nd

HAZELTON John of Concord & DAVIS Martha J of Hopkinton m Nov 2, 1892 Hopkinton. Groom: age 58 b Concord s/o HAZELTON Joseph & WHIT-MARSH Abagial b Lyndeborough. Bride: age 38 b Lowell Mass d/o HODGDON Charles W & HOLMES Margaret. Vol: 5 Page: 019 Line: 011 Section: 2nd

GOODWIN Wm Knapp of Hopkinton & JOHNSON Hattie J of Lowell Mass m Nov 24, 1892 Lowell Mass. Groom: age 26 b New Brunswick s/o GOODWIN Wm C & HUDDLESTON Mary. Bride: age 25 b Nova Scota d/o JOHNSON Mathew & MCALMIRA Abagial. Vol: 5 Page: 019 Line: 012 Section: 2nd

CLOUGH Charles E of Hopkinton & HASTINGS Gertrude E of Hopkinton m Dec 10, 1892 Hopkinton. Groom: age 29 b Hopkinton s/o CLOUGH Charles F & HARDY Mary J. Bride: age 21 b Hopkinton d/o HASTINGS Alfred S & PERRY Susan. Vol: 5 Page: 019 Line: 013 Section: 2nd

PAIGE Orrill M of Hopkinton & ABBOTT Isabella of Hopkinton m Dec 20, 1892 Hopkinton. Groom: age 19 b Henniker s/o PAIGE Horace & HURD Lucy A. Bride: age 15 b Keene d/o ABBOTT John P & SCOTT Ella J. Vol: 5 Page: 019 Line: 014 Section: 2nd

MILTON Willie N of Hopkinton & MOORE Carrie A of Weare m Jan 22, 1893 Hopkinton. Groom: age 32 b Hopkinton s/o MILTON George b Hopkinton & CUMMINGS Mary A b Nova Scotia. Bride: age 30 d/o MOORE Charles b Amherst & BLANDING Eliza. Vol: 5 Page: 021 Line: 001 Section: 2nd

FIFIELD Frank A of Hopkinton & BACON Annie L of Hopkinton m Mar 22, 1893 Hopkinton. Groom: age 26 b Alstead s/o FIFIELD Abram & COLBY Lydia J b Hopkinton. Bride: age 18 b Hopkinton d/o BACON John H b Hopkinton & BURBANK Ann P b Hopkinton. Vol: 5 Page: 021 Line: 002 Section: 2nd

CHASE Oscar N of Hopkinton & THORNTON Marguriete of Hopkinton m Apr 12, 1893 Hopkinton. Groom: age 36 b Hopkinton s/o CHASE Nathaniel C b

Hopkinton, NH Marriages 1880

Hopkinton & CURRIER Nancy T b Concord. Bride: age 22 b England d/o THORNTON Henry b England & LEHAY Elizabeth b England. Vol: 5 Page: 021 Line: 003 Section: 2nd

BOUTWELL Wallace E of Hopkinton & WARD Lilie A of Hopkinton m Jun 16, 1893 Hopkinton. Groom: age 19 b Pelham s/o BOUTWELL Elmer b Vt & WOODBURY Julia b Pelham. Bride: age 18 b Cambridge Mass d/o WARD Samuel Jr b E Cambridge Mass & HANES Lillie B b Boston Mass. Vol: 5 Page: 021 Line: 004 Section: 2nd

HOWE Edwin B of Hopkinton & WYMAN Etta of Hopkinton m Jun 21, 1893 Hopkinton. Groom: age 39 b Warner s/o HOWE Job M b Henniker & WOODS Elizabeth B b Bradford. Bride: age 28 b Bradford d/o WYMAN Charles b Bradford & CHENEY Jennette. Vol: 5 Page: 021 Line: 005 Section: 2nd

DUNBAR Henry P of Hopkinton & DANFORTH Emma L of Hopkinton m Jul 8, 1893 Boscawen. Groom: age 35 b Hopkinton s/o DUNBAR Elmer B b Crydon & WEBBER Ann T b Hopkinton. Bride: age 32 b Webster d/o DANFORTH Albert b Boscawen & CAPEN Rosanna b Stewartstown. Vol: 5 Page: 021 Line: 006 Section: 2nd

ELLIOTT Charles E of Hopkinton & HOWE A Gertrude of Hopkinton m Sep 7, 1893 Concord. Groom: age 32 b Hopkinton s/o ELLIOTT Joseph R b Hopkinton & Angeline P b Webster. Bride: age 26 b Boston Mass d/o HOWE Edward W b Templeton Ma & HOWE Anna N b Deering. Vol: 5 Page: 021 Line: 007 Section: 2nd

CURRIER Charles C of Hopkinton & KILBORN Mary J of Webster m Sep 30, 1893 Webster. Groom: age 28 b Hopkinton s/o CURRIER John F b Hopkinton & Nellie N b Hopkinton. Bride: age 28 b Webster d/o KILBORN John b Webster & Nettie. Vol: 5 Page: 021 Line: 008 Section: 2nd

DOW Charlie J of Henniker & CUTTER Clara E of Hopkinton m Nov 19, 1893 Hopkinton. Groom: age 21 b Henniker s/o DOW Jackson P & HOYT Hannah. Bride: age 18 b Hudson d/o CUTTER James & STEWART Carolin. Vol: 5 Page: 021 Line: 009 Section: 2nd

MONTGOMERY William of Hopkinton & SAVORY Helen of Warner m Nov 30, 1893 Manchester. Groom: age 70 b New York s/o MONTGOMERY John W & BURBANK Mary. Bride: age 62 b Warner d/o HARRIMAN Benj. Vol: 5 Page: 021 Line: 010 Section: 2nd

SMITH Robert of Hopkinton & WESCOTT Gertrude of Hopkinton m Jan 8, 1894 Warner. Groom: age 21 b Webster s/o SMITH Charles W b Canterbury & Livonia L b Warner. Bride: age 16 b Shirley Mass d/o WESCOTT Charles H b Andover & Mary R b Loudon. Vol: 5 Page: 023 Line: 001 Section: 2nd

MORRILL Stephen E of Hopkinton & PERRY Emma L of Hopkinton m Jan 22, 1894 Hopkinton. Groom: age 38 b Hopkinton s/o MORRILL Eben b Salisbury Mass & SWEATT Phebe L b Webster. Bride: age 24 b Hopkinton d/o PERRY Sylvester W b Hopkinton & FLINT Bertha S b Damariscotta Me. Vol: 5 Page: 023 Line: 002 Section: 2nd

CALL Edward J of Hopkinton & JARDINE Bessie of Hopkinton m Feb 7, 1894 Hopkinton. Groom: age 27 b Warner s/o CALL Luke b Webster & COUCH Rachal b Warner. Bride: age 16 b Lowell Mass d/o JARDINE Alexander & MARA Shiro b Lowell Mass. Vol: 5 Page: 023 Line: 003 Section: 2nd

Hopkinton, NH Marriages 1880

MURPHY James J of Hopkinton & SON Annie E of Hopkinton m May 22, 1894 Concord. Groom: age 27 b Andover Mass s/o MURPHY Patrick b Ireland & CASSEY Ellen b Ireland. Bride: age 19 b Hopkinton d/o SON William b Canada & Rosa. Vol: 5 Page: 023 Line: 004 Section: 2nd

DUNBAR Charles S of Peterborough & KEMP Jennie S of Hopkinton m May 26, 1894 Hopkinton. Groom: age 38 b Sharon s/o DUNBAR James & HOLDEN Irene. Bride: age 43 b Stoneham Mass d/o EASTMAN George S & Mary J. Vol: 5 Page: 023 Line: 005 Section: 2nd

ADAMS William H N of Hopkinton & MELCHER Laura A of Hopkinton m May 30, 1894 Concord. Groom: age 31 b Concord s/o ADAMS Dennis H & CLOUGH Betsey A. Bride: age 31 b Thorntonn d/o BROWN Daniel & ELKINS Laura. Vol: 5 Page: 023 Line: 006 Section: 2nd

DOWNES Charles of Hopkinton & SCRIBNER Mary F of Raymond m Sep 5, 1894 Cape Eliz Me. Groom: age 23 b Hopkinton s/o DOWNES John H b Manchester & MONTGOMERY Mary M b Hopkinton. Bride: age 23 b Raymond d/o SCRIBNER Mark b Raymond & Helen K. Vol: 5 Page: 023 Line: 007 Section: 2nd

JEPSON James of Hopkinton & TAYLOR Mattie M of Hopkinton m Oct 9, 1894 Hopkinton. Groom: age 24 b Warner s/o JEPSON James H b Bennington Vt & SARGENT Normia B b Warner. Bride: age 18 b Hopkinton d/o TAYLER Charles b Hancock & UPTON Clara E b Warner. Vol: 5 Page: 023 Line: 008 Section: 2

CLOUGH George A of Hopkinton & ROWE Sara B of Campbridge Mass m Oct 24, 1894 Hopkinton. Groom: age 25 b Hopkinton s/o CLOUGH Moses T b Hopkinton & Mary O b Candia. Bride: age 33 b Boston Mass d/o ROWE Joseph F b Candia & Mary B b Brighton England. Vol: 5 Page: 023 Line: 009 Section: 2nd

FLANDERS Frank L of Hopkinton & MUNROE Marrillo of Boston Mass m Oct 25, 1894 Cambridge Mass. Groom: age 40 b Hopkinton s/o FLANDES Dnaiel b Hopkinton & LERNED Mary E b Hopkinton. Bride: age 34 b Boston Mass d/o ELLIS John J b Boston Mass & BALDWIN Catherine b Devonshire Eng. Vol: 5 Page: 023 Line: 010 Section: 2nd

FOLLANSBEE Henry O of Henniker & SYMONDS Nellie F of Hopkinton m Nov 3, 1894 Warren. Groom: age 29 b Dorchester s/o FOLLANSBEE John b Danbury & MUZZY Selana b Henniker. Bride: age 20 b Hopkinton d/o SYMONDS Samuel T b Hillsborough & Annie W b Weare. Vol: 5 Page: 023 Line: 011 Section: 2nd

MILLS Leman H of Hopkinton & POTHOFF Annie J of Boston Mass m Nov 12, 1894 Hopkinton. Groom: age 24 b Hopkinton s/o MILLS Charles b Hopkinton & TOWNS Olive b Dunbarton. Bride: age 19 b Belgiam d/o POTHOFF John C b Netherlands & Sangeline b Netherlands. Vol: 5 Page: 023 Line: 012 Section: 2ND

BOUTWELL Frank E of Hopkinton & RUSSELL Fannie F of Hopkinton m Jan 1, 1895 Hopkinton. Groom: age 26 b Pelham s/o BOUTWELL Elmer W & WOODBURY Julia A. Bride: age 23 b Wareham Mass. Vol: 5 Page: 025 Line: 001 Section: 2nd

Hopkinton, NH Marriages 1880

CONANT Dwight E of Hopkinton & KEMP Blanche S of Hopkinton m Jan 26, 1895 Hopkinton. Groom: age 23 b Willamantic Conn s/o CONANT Hiram E b Marshfield Conn & SHATTLE Lena. Bride: age 19 b Warner d/o KEMP Frank P & EASTMAN Jennie S. Vol: 5 Page: 025 Line: 002 Section: 2nd

HARDY James F of Hopkinton & AGER C Lilian of Hopkinton m Jan 28, 1895 Hopkinton. Groom: age 28 b Hopkinton s/o HARDY Charles b Hopkinton & JOHNSON Olivia b Manchester. Bride: age 22 b Hopkinton d/o AGER Walter C b Warner & CLOUGH Maria C b Hopkinton. Vol: 5 Page: 025 Line: 003 Section: 2nd

GOULD Robert T of Hopkinton & CURRIER Mary M of Hopkinton m Apr 3, 1895 Hopkinton. Groom: age 33 b Hopkinton s/o GOULD Charles b Hopkinton & HILL Ruth b Hopkinton. Bride: age 33 b Hopkinton d/o CURRIER John F b Hopkinton & PUTNEY Ellen H b Hopkinton. Vol: 5 Page: 025 Line: 004 Section: 2nd

CHASE Harry A of Hopkinton & HOOK Emma J of Hopkinton m May 1, 1895 Hopkinton. Groom: age 23 b Hopkinton s/o CHASE Orrin b Hopkinton & BADGER Hattie M b Warner. Bride: age 19 b Hopkinton d/o HOOK James & DOYING Mary A. Vol: 5 Page: 025 Line: 005 Section: 2nd

HUNTOON Arthur C of Hopkinton & EASTMAN Ethelyn A of Hopkinton m Jun 5, 1895 Henniker. Groom: age 22 b Unity s/o HUNTOON Ora M b Unity & CURTICE M Velona b Windsor. Bride: age 24 b Warner d/o EASTMAN Timothy B b Warner & MERRILL Christinia b New London. Vol: 5 Page: 025 Line: 006 Section: 2nd

LOTHROP Herbert D of No Raynham Mass & MORRILL Lizzie M of Hopkinton m Jun 5, 1895 Hopkinton. Groom: age 32 b No Raynham Mass s/o LOTHROP James b No Raynham Mass & DEAN Sophia b Berkley Mass. Bride: age 24 b Hopkinton d/o MORRILL Charles A b Hopkinton & KIMBALL Theresa F b Derry. Vol: 5 Page: 025 Line: 007 Section: 2nd

CHASE Joseph S of Hopkinton & DOLE Augusta A of Cambridge Mass m Jul 31, 1895 Dunbaarton. Groom: age 35 b Hopkinton s/o CHASE Reginald H b Salisbury & STANWOOD Susan b Hopkinton. Bride: age 19 b Cambridge Mass d/o DOLE Cyrus. Vol: 5 Page: 025 Line: OO8 Section: 2nd

FOOTE William N of Hopkinton & WATTS Helen M of Hopkinton m Sep 10, 1895 Hopkinton. Groom: age 29 b Farmington Me s/o FOOTE Enoch W & TAYLOR Fannie M. Bride: age 19 b Hopkinton d/o WATTS Charles & RYON Mary I. Vol: 5 Page: 025 Line: 009 Section: 2nd

KENNEY Frank B of Hopkinton & PRESCOTT Jessie of Hopkinton m Nov 28, 1895 Concord. Groom: age 39 b Brintree Vt s/o KENNEY Andrew J & REID Sarah E. Bride: b Pembroke d/o ADAMS Nathaniel & FRENCH Ella B. Vol: 5 Page: 025 Line: 010 Section: 2nd

BROWN Valorous of Hopkinton & SLOCOMB Georgiana of Hopkinton m May 17, 1896 Hopkinton. Groom: age 45 b Hopkinton s/o BROWN Gould b Hopkinton & BURBANK Almira b Hopkinton. Bride: age 38 b Hopkinton d/o DWINELLS John G b Dunbarton & GOODWIN Sarah A b Henniker. Vol: 5 Page: 027 Line: 001 Section: 2nd

HARTHORN Arthur of Concord & DARLING Sarah K of Hopkinton m Aug 11, 1896 Hopkinton. Groom: age 48 b Palmer Mass s/o HATHORN Charles &

Hopkinton, NH Marriages 1880

MUSTARD Margaret. Bride: age 42 b Hopkinton d/o EMERSON James & DIAMOND Julia A. Vol: 5 Page: 027 Line: 002 Section: 2nd

CILLEY William H of Hopkinton & SMALL Ellen S of Goffstown m Feb 16, 1897 Hopkinton. Groom: age 39 b Andover s/o CILLEY Philip & COLE Sarah. Bride: age 42 b Me ??. Vol: 5 Page: 029 Line: 001 Section: 2nd

CARD Thomas of Kingsford N S & EMERSON Blanche M of Hopkinton m Sep 15, 1896 Hopkinton. Groom: age 24 b Nova Scotia s/o CARD Charles & ROBINSON Mary. Bride: age 19 b Hopkinton d/o EMERSON Harrison D & MILLS Mary. Vol: 5 Page: 027 Line: 003 Section: 2nd

GREGG John G of Hopkinton & WOODMAN Emma F of Hopkinton m Oct 28, 1896 Hopkinton. Groom: age 44 b Weare s/o GREGG Joseph H b Derry & LORD Emma L b Francestown. Bride: age 47 b Concord d/o WILLARD Persin?? & PROCTOR Alice b Francestown. Vol: 5 Page: 027 Line: 004 Section: 2nd

SEAVEY David of Hopkinton & GETCHEL Charlotte of Hopkinton m Dec 8, 1896 Hopkinton. Groom: age 64 b Concord s/o SEAVEY Andrew & FISH Betsey. Bride: age 50 b Northfield d/o COLLINS Levi & ALLEN Charlotte. Vol: 5 Page: 027 Line: 005 Section: 2nd

GOODSPEED Arthur W of Hopkinton & BAILEY Annie N of Hyde Park Mass m Jun 24, 1896 Hyde Park Mass. Groom: age 36 b Hopkinton s/o GOODSPEED Obed & Helen B. Bride: age 30 b New Castle N B d/o BAILEY Joseph & Mary. Vol: 5 Page: 027 Line: 006 Section: 2nd

CHASE Fred H of Hopkinton & JACKMAN Lillian J of Concord m Mar 10, 1897 Concord. Groom: age 28 b Hopkinton s/o CHASE Harry b Hopkinton & BENNETTE Martha b Freedom. Bride: age 25 b Hopkinton d/o JACKMAN Enoch b Boscawen & HARDY Mary E b Concord. Vol: 5 Page: 029 Line: 002 Section: 2nd

RICE James G of Hopkinton & BOHONAN Bernice M of Hopkinton m Apr 29, 1897 Manchester. Groom: age 38 b Henniker s/o RICE Geo W b Henniker & COLBY Abbie b Henniker. Bride: age 20 b Hopkinton d/o BOHONAN John W b Hopkinton & JEWELL Delia A b Weare. Vol: 5 Page: 029 Line: 003 Section: 2nd

CHANDLER Arthur S of Hopkinton & CORBIT Ida of Weare Mass m Aug 27, 1897 Goffstown. Groom: age 17 b Henniker s/o CHANDLER Chas b Nashua & MCALPINE Mary J b Warner. Bride: age 23 b Me d/o CORBIT Thomas b Weare Mass & BRIDGMAN Marrin b Weare Mass. Vol: 5 Page: 029 Line: 005 Section: 2nd

COLBY Arthur P of Hopkinton & WHIPPLE Lida J of Hopkinton m Oct 7, 1888 Henniker. Groom: age 21 b Hopkinton s/o COLBY Melvin b Hopkinton & EDMUNDS Hannah b Hopkinton. Bride: age 20 b Manchester d/o WHIPPLE Joheph b Hebron & EATON Hannah b Weare. Vol: 5 Page: 011 Line: 005 Section: 2nd

CROWELL Dixi H of Hopkinton & CLARK Lillian B of Hopkinton m Jul 7, 1889 Concord. Groom: age 33 b Hopkinton s/o CROWELL Samuel & HALL May P. Bride: age 22 b Concord d/o CLARK Charles E & BADGE Mary A. Vol: 5 Page: 013 Line: 004 Section: 2nd

106

LORD George E of Hopkinton & HODGDON Hattie M of Hopkinton m Mar 31, 1890 Hopkinton. Groom: age 37 b New Market s/o LORD Charles b So Berwick Me & HUBBARD Sally b Hopkinton. Bride: age 29 b Hopkinton d/o HODGDON Charles J V b Hopkinton & HOLMES Harriett b Hopkinton. Vol: 5 Page: 015 Line: 002 Section: 2nd

Hopkinton, NH Births 1880-1901
Note: This chapter includes some births from the years 1833-1851 and a number of births from 1879.

GREENE Sarah R b Hopkinton Feb 23, 1884 child of GREEN Willard T farmer b Hopkinton & Etta C b Chelsea Mass Vol: 5 Page: 033 Line: 001 Section: 2nd.

FOSS Minnie B b Hopkinton Apr 11, 1879 child of FOSS George E farmer b Hopkinton & SYMONDS Emma b Philadelphia Pa Vol: 5 Page: 019 Line: 001 Section: 1st.

SHURTLEFF Charles A b Hopkinton May 23, 1879 child of SHURTLEFF Samuel S carpenter b Walden Vt & MILTON Mary E b Claremont Vol: 5 Page: 019 Line: 002 Section: 1st.

DOW Grace Emily** b Hopkinton Jul 9, 1879 child of DOW Charles farmer b Concord & CURRIER Annette b Hopkinton Vol: 5 Page: 019 Line: 007 Section: 1st.

FULLER G Irving b Hopkinton Jun 25, 1879 child of FULLER Orrin farmer b Hopkinton & CAMPBELL Lillie b Hopkinton Vol: 5 Page: 019 Line: 005 Section: 1st.

DEARBORN Anna Maria b Hopkinton Jun 27, 1879 child of DEARBORN Ezra farmer b Vermont & WEEKS Mary b Hopkinton Vol: 5 Page: 019 Line: 006 Section: 1st.

PRINCE ---- b Hopkinton Jun 27, 1898 child of PRINCE Hebrie & LIBBY Stella G A b Hopkinton Vol: 6 Page: 002.

UPTON Annie B b Hopkinton Jul 16, 1879 child of UPTON Edson carpenter & FRENCH Eunice b Hopkinton Vol: 5 Page: 019 Line: 008 Section: 1st.

WATTS Etta E b Hopkinton Sep 5, 1898 child of WATTS Chas F laborer b Warner & RION Mary A b Warner Vol: 6 Page: 003.

GOODRICH Frances W b Hopkinton Aug 1, 1879 child of GOODRICK Lurman R farmer b Hopkinton & POWELLL Jennie V b Loudon Vol: 5 Page: 019 Line: 010 Section: 1st.

HOYT Bessie Ethyline b Hopkinton Aug 23, 1879 child of HOYT Walter F farmer b Hopkinton & PHELPS Lottie A b Danvers Mass Vol: 5 Page: 019 Line: 012 Section: 1st.

MARSH ---- b Hopkinton Dec 22, 1898 child of MARSH Frank P pedler b Weare & DUSTIN Mary Etta b Antrim Vol: 6 Page: 004.

SYMONDS Jennie D b Hopkinton Sep 14, 1879 child of SYMONDS Benjamin farmer b Hillsboro & PORTER Emma J b Hartford Vt Vol: 5 Page: 019 Line: 014 Section: 1st.

DENSMORE Hattie May b Hopkinton Aug 24, 1881 child of DENSMORE James M farmer & LIBBIE Ellen Vol: 5 Page: 023 Line: 007 Section: 1st.

HOPKINS ---- b Hopkinton Aug 11, 1881 child of HOPKINS Adorinen J clergyman b Jefferson Me & May C b Springfield Vt Vol: 5 Page: 023 Line: 008 Section: 1st.

HOOK Charles F b Hopkinton Sep 1, 1881 child of HOOK James M farmer b Concord & ---- ---- b Candia Vol: 5 Page: 023 Line: 010 Section: 1st.

Hopkinton, NH Births 1880

HOOK Gusta Jane b Hopkinton Sep 18, 1879 child of HOOK James farmer b Concord & DOYING Mary A b Dasivile Canada Vol: 5 Page: 019 Line: 015 Section: 1st.

CHASE Ruth Ellen b Hopkinton Apr 25, 1899 child of CHASE Marl D laborer b Warner & HARDY Clara M b Hopkinton Vol: 6 Page: 006.

BLAKE Arthur F b Hopkinton Sep 29, 1879 child of BLAKE Charles H farmer & Foster b Weare Vol: 5 Page: 019 Line: 017 Section: 1st.

HOWE Helen b Hopkinton Nov 13, 1899 child of HOWE Edwin B farmer b Warner & WYMAN Etta M b Bradford Vol: 6 Page: 009.

KIMBALL John Prescott b Hopkinton Nov 17, 1879 child of KIMBALL John Stevens merchant b Boston Mass & FRENCH Clara b Hopkinton Vol: 5 Page: 019 Line: 019 Section: 1st.

DOW ---- b Hopkinton Feb 13, 1880 child of DOW Warren blacksmith b Hopkinton & YOUNG Jennie b Manchester Vol: 5 Page: 019 Line: 024 Section: 1st.

FELCH ---- b Hopkinton Jan 23, 1880 child of FELCH S S laborer b Webster Vol: 5 Page: 019 Line: 022 Section: 1st.

LIBLEY Mrytie b Hopkinton Feb 8, 1880 child of LIBBEY George Vol: 5 Page: 019 Line: 023 Section: 1st.

GOULD ---- b Hopkinton Dec 7, 1899 child of GOULD Robert farmer b Hopkinton & CURRIER Mary b Hopkinton Vol: 6 Page: 009.

LIBLEY Rogilla b Hopkinton Mar 4, 1880 child of ---- ---- b Hopkinton & LIBLEY Idee Vol: 5 Page: 019 Line: 025 Section: 1st.

AGER Flora b Hopkinton Mar 25, 1880 child of AGER Walter C farmer b Hopkinton & CLOUGH Maria b Warner Vol: 5 Page: 019 Line: 026 Section: 1st.

FERRIN ---- b Hopkinton Dec 4, 1879 child of FERRIN Walter F kit maker b Hopkinton & FERRIN Mrs b Warner Vol: 5 Page: 019 Line: 029 Section: 1st.

MORGAN Ellen G b Hopkinton Apr 26, 1880 child of MORGAN Frank farmer b Hopkinton & BOHONAN Linda M b Sutton Vol: 5 Page: 021 Line: 002 Section: 1st.

BROWN ---- b Hopkinton Mar 7, 1900 child of BROWN William farmer & CLARK Sarah M b Lisbon Vol: 6 Page: 010.

DUCHARME Mary A b Hopkinton Apr 27, 1880 child of DUCHARME C farmer b Canada Vol: 5 Page: 021 Line: 003 Section: 1st.

SHEFFIELD ---- b Hopkinton May 2, 1880 child of SHEFFIELD Will C aporthacary b Canada Vol: 5 Page: 021 Line: 004 Section: 1st.

HEATH ---- b Hopkinton May 7, 1880 child of HEATH Frank R R worker Vol: 5 Page: 021 Line: 005 Section: 1st.

HARRINGTON Benjamin F** b Hopkinton May 29, 1880 child of HARRINGTON Thomas farmer b Hopkinton & WOODBURY Hattie b Hampton Vol: 5 Page: 021 Line: 006 Section: 1st.

WAYNE Dorris b Hopkinton Mar 28, 1900 child of WAYNE Henry & BARTLETT Cora b Hopkinton Vol: 6 Page: 010.

POWERS Florence A b Hopkinton Jul 20, 1880 child of POWERS George farmer b Greenfield & ROWELL Emma A b Hopkinton Vol: 5 Page: 021 Line: 010 Section: 1st.

Hopkinton, NH Births 1880

MOTTS Fred Henry b Hopkinton Jun 18, 1880 child of MOTTS Charles F laborer b Warner & Me b Hopkinton Vol: 5 Page: 021 Line: 008 Section: 1st Note: `xx.

WEBSTER Edith W b Hopkinton Jul 3, 1880 child of WEBSTER Charles laborer b Me & SEVERENCE Lydia b Claremont Vol: 5 Page: 021 Line: 009 Section: 1st.

CLARK Julia b Hopkinton Jul 27, 1880 child of CLARK Laruia Vol: 5 Page: 021 Line: 011 Section: 1st.

HAMMOND L Mabel b Hopkinton Oct 1, 1880 child of HAMMOND George farmer b Dunbarton & FADESO?? Dora R?? b Webster Vol: 5 Page: 021 Line: 012 Section: 1st.

KIMBALL Arthur C b Hopkinton Oct 2, 1880 child of KIMBALL Charles farmer b Webster & WEBBER Martha E b Webster Vol: 5 Page: 021 Line: 013 Section: 1st.

AYER Flora M b Hopkinton Nov 25, 1880 child of AYER Walter farmer b Warner & MARIA C b Hopkinton Vol: 5 Page: 021 Line: 014 Section: 1st.

HEATH Alvira Gertrude b Hopkinton Jul 7, 1884 child of HEATH Arthur N butcher b Hopkinton & Maggie Vol: 5 Page: 033 Line: 004 Section: 2nd.

GREENE Laurie E b Hopkinton Jan 6, 1881 child of GREEN Willard farmer b Hopkinton & BAILEY Etta C b Chelsea Mass Vol: 5 Page: 021 Line: 016 Section: 1st.

MARSH Winfield S b Hopkinton Apr 28, 1881 child of MARSH Winfield farmer b Canterbury & ---- ---- b Canterbury Vol: 5 Page: 023 Line: 001 Section: 1st.

CLINTON ---- b Hopkinton Jan 15, 1881 child of Clinton & Sarah Vol: 5 Page: 021 Line: 017 Section: 1st.

PUTNEY Fred Silver b Hopkinton Nov 10, 1881 child of PUTNEY True J farmer b Hopkinton & AYERS Ellen W b Mass Vol: 5 Page: 023 Line: 018 Section: 1st.

EMERSON ---- b Hopkinton Jan 31, 1881 child of EMERSON Hanson D laborer b Hopkinton & MILLS Mary Vol: 5 Page: 021 Line: 020 Section: 1st.

ROLLINS Mary Alice b Hopkinton Feb 18, 1881 child of ROLLINS John farmer b Hopkinton & SARGENT Nettie b Hopkinton Vol: 5 Page: 021 Line: 021 Section: 1st.

HEMPHILL ---- b Hopkinton Feb 18, 1881 child of HEMPHILL Loren kit maker b Hopkinton Vol: 5 Page: 021 Line: 022 Section: 1st.

BARTON ---- b Hopkinton Mar 2, 1881 child of BARTON Charles farmer b Hopkinton & Philinda b Goshen Vol: 5 Page: 021 Line: 023 Section: 1st.

HOYT Mabel F b Hopkinton May 11, 1881 child of HOYT Walter F farmer b Hopkinton & SADIE E b Dunbarton Vol: 5 Page: 023 Line: 002 Section: 1st.

SOUTHWICK ---- b Hopkinton May 28, 1881 child of SOUTHWICK William farmer & COLBY Louisa Vol: 5 Page: 023 Line: 003 Section: 1st.

HUNTOON Frank W S b Hopkinton Jul 4, 1881 child of HUNTOON Warren farmer b Salisbury & MORRILL Nellie b Andover Vol: 5 Page: 023 Line: 004 Section: 1st.

LOCKE James W b Hopkinton Jul 12, 1881 child of LOCKE George N farmer b Hopkinton & WRIGHT Mary Ann b Hopkinton Vol: 5 Page: 023 Line: 005 Section: 1st.

BARNES Flora E b Hopkinton Jul 21, 1881 child of BARNES George D farmer b Henniker & PHILBRICK Louisa b Hillsboro Vol: 5 Page: 023 Line: 006 Section: 1st.

Hopkinton, NH Births 1880

BOHONAN Etta S b Hopkinton Jun 18, 1884 child of BOHONAN John W telegrath operator b Manchester & JEWELL Delia A b R I Vol: 5 Page: 033 Line: 003 Section: 2nd.

FULLER Eva S b Hopkinton Sep 12, 1884 child of FULLER Orren F farmer & CAMPBELL Lillian b Webster Vol: 5 Page: 033 Line: 010 Section: 2nd.

DUSTIN Gilbert b Hopkinton Sep 16, 1881 child of DUSTIN Herbert farmer b Hopkinton & RICHARDSON Ada b Hopkinton Vol: 5 Page: 023 Line: 011 Section: 1st.

SYMONDS Arthur b Hopkinton Oct 4, 1881 child of SYMONDS Samuel farmer & JOHNSON Ann b Weare Vol: 5 Page: 023 Line: 013 Section: 1st.

STRAW Percy W b Hopkinton Oct 5, 1881 child of STRAW James O farmer b Hopkinton & WHITTIMORE Ada Vol: 5 Page: 023 Line: 014 Section: 1st.

GRIFFIN Jessannie M b Hopkinton Oct 5, 1881 child of GRIFFIN Alfren farmer & MORRILL Hellen J Vol: 5 Page: 023 Line: 015 Section: 1st.

PERRY James Earl b Hopkinton Oct 6, 1881 child of PERRY James M farmer b Hopkinton & Edithine Vol: 5 Page: 023 Line: 016 Section: 1st.

HARVEY George Henry b Hopkinton Oct 10, 1881 child of HARVEY Geo J farmer & DWINELLS Mary P Vol: 5 Page: 023 Line: 017 Section: 1st.

FELCH ---- b Hopkinton Jul 17, 1882 child of FELCH Ira J butcher b Weare & CURRIER Addie b Hopkinton Vol: 5 Page: 025 Line: 006 Section: 1st.

NELSON David Homer b Hopkinton Nov 15, 1881 child of NELSON John H farmer b Hopkinton & SEAVEY Nettie Vol: 5 Page: 023 Line: 021 Section: 1st.

CLARK Ernest Jewell b Hopkinton Dec 5, 1881 child of CLARK Frank J peddler & JEWELL Emma Vol: 5 Page: 023 Line: 022 Section: 1st.

STEVENS Lucy b Hopkinton Dec 21, 1881 child of STEVENS Henry C painter & MORRILL Mary Vol: 5 Page: 023 Line: 023 Section: 1st.

COLBY Mary b Hopkinton Feb 6, 1882 child of COLBY Edward N b NH & SANBORN Maggie F Vol: 5 Page: 023 Line: 024 Section: 1st.

WOOD Elmer G b Hopkinton Feb 10, 1882 child of WOOD Andrew J farmer b Hopkinton & Sarah b Deering Vol: 5 Page: 023 Line: 025 Section: 1st.

FULLER Carrie A b Hopkinton Feb 14, 1882 child of FULLER Oren F wheelright b Bristol & CAMPBELL Lillie b Hopkinton Vol: 5 Page: 023 Line: 026 Section: 1st.

GLEASON ---- b Hopkinton Sep 21, 1884 child of Gleason farmer b Webster & Waldron b Webster Vol: 5 Page: 033 Line: 011 Section: 2nd.

LIBBIE Walton Allen b Hopkinton Aug 3, 1882 child of LIBBIE George A farmer Vol: 5 Page: 025 Line: 001 Section: 1st.

ALLEN ---- b Hopkinton Apr 25, 1882 child of ALLEN Walton P kit maker b Chelsea Mass & MONTGOMERY Mattie b Hopkinton Vol: 5 Page: 025 Line: 002 Section: 1st.

MUDGETT Willie Chase b Hopkinton May 8, 1882 child of MUDGETT William E farmer b Franklin & CHASE Salome P b Warner Vol: 5 Page: 025 Line: 003 Section: 1st.

CURRIER J Blanchard b Hopkinton Jun 19, 1882 child of CURRIER Willie A farmer b Hopkinton & DOW Jennie E b Concord Vol: 5 Page: 025 Line: 005 Section: 1st.

Hopkinton, NH Births 1880

LADD Althea b Hopkinton Sep 17, 1900 child of LADD Dexter tinsmith b Epping & DAVIS Maud Athea b Raymond Vol: 6 Page: 011.

POWERS Harry Millis b Hopkinton Aug 22, 1882 child of POWERS George N farmer b Greenfield & ROWELL Emma A b Hopkinton Vol: 5 Page: 025 Line: 008 Section: 1st.

KIMBALL ---- b Hopkinton Aug 25, 1882 child of KIMBALL Charlie farmer b Webster & WEBBER Mattie Ella b Webster Vol: 5 Page: 025 Line: 009 Section: 1st.

CHASE Forest Everett b Hopkinton Sep 2, 1882 child of CHASE Edward E farmer b Hopkinton & MOULTON Etta E b Concord Vol: 5 Page: 025 Line: 010 Section: 1st.

PHILBRICK George E b Hopkinton Sep 8, 1882 child of PHILBRICK George E mill operator b Manchester & ELLIOTT Eva b Hopkinton Vol: 5 Page: 025 Line: 011 Section: 1st.

DWINNELLS Edith Mand b Hopkinton Oct 2, 1882 child of DWINELLS John G laborer b Dunbarton & CHASE Matitia b Hopkinton Vol: 5 Page: 025 Line: 012 Section: 1st.

GUILE Grace Edna b Hopkinton Oct 19, 1882 child of GUILE Edmund R farmer b Shetford Vt & STORY Abbie M b Hopkinton Vol: 5 Page: 025 Line: 013 Section: 1st.

MILLS Arthur Pearl b Hopkinton Nov 4, 1882 child of MILLS Charles farmer b Hopkinton & TOWNS Olive N b Weare Center Vol: 5 Page: 025 Line: 014 Section: 1st.

CHASE Florence Netie b Hopkinton Nov 28, 1882 child of CHASE Horace printer b Manchester & SPAULDING Littie b Manchester Vol: 5 Page: 025 Line: 015 Section: 1st.

STRAW Ernest G ** b Hopkinton Dec 16, 1882 child of STRAW Gilman J rail road b Hopkinton & HOYT Wealtha b Bradford Vol: 5 Page: 025 Line: 016 Section: 1st Correction: see Dec 1945 for name corr.

COURSER Stella Maybelle b Hopkinton Jan 12, 1883 child of COURSER Hamlet carpenter b Webster & HOLMES M Bella b Webster Vol: 5 Page: 025 Line: 018 Section: 1st.

MARSH Walter F b Hopkinton Feb 7, 1883 child of MARSH Winfred farmer b Canterbury & GLINES Lizzie b Canterbury Vol: 5 Page: 025 Line: 019 Section: 1st.

CHANDLER ---- b Hopkinton Mar 16, 1883 child of CHANDLER Frank N farmer b Hopkinton & ROGERS Margie S b Hopkinton Vol: 5 Page: 025 Line: 020 Section: 1st.

ANNIS Cornelia Maj b Hopkinton Mar 24, 1883 child of ANNIS Charles C farmer b Hopkinton & FLANDERS Eva b Hillsboro Vol: 5 Page: 025 Line: 021 Section: 1st.

DONELL ---- b Hopkinton 1883 child of DONELL Warren P laborer b Concord & LIBLEY Ida A b Webster Vol: 5 Page: 025 Line: 022 Section: 1st.

PERRY Bertha M b Hopkinton Oct 28, 1883 child of PERRY James farmer b Hopkinton & KELLEY Edithene b Hopkinton Vol: 5 Page: 027 Line: 004 Section: 1st.

Hopkinton, NH Births 1880

POOR Grace E b Hopkinton Sep 17, 1883 child of POOR Eri stone man b Hooksett & BROWN Alice b Hopkinton Vol: 5 Page: 027 Line: 009 Section: 1st.

FARRILL Edgar Powers** b Hopkinton Jul 8, 1883 child of FARRILL Edgar S clegryman b Providence RI & FENNER M Alice b Providence RI Vol: 5 Page: 027 Line: 003 Section: 1st.

GRIFFIN Clement Alfred b Hopkinton Apr 30, 1883 child of GRIFFIN Alfred farmer & MORRILL Hellen Vol: 5 Page: 027 Line: 005 Section: 1st.

MORRILL Clinton E b Hopkinton Jul 13, 1883 child of MORRILL Stephen E mechanic b Hopkinton & DEARBORN May Vol: 5 Page: 027 Line: 008 Section: 1st.

BOYCE Harley A b Hopkinton Aug 1888 child of BOYCE Melzer D b Concord & Nellie b Concord Vol: 5 Page: 043 Line: 010 Section: 2nd.

HEATH Elroy b Hopkinton Dec 29, 1883 child of HEATH Charles farmer b Springfield & BROWN Etta b Sunapee Vol: 5 Page: 027 Line: 012 Section: 1st.

DWINNELLS Lottie May b Hopkinton Oct 26, 1883 child of DWINELLS Warren laborer b Hopkinton & LIBBY Ida b Webster Vol: 5 Page: 027 Line: 011 Section: 1st.

COLBY Jessie b Hopkinton May 20, 1883 child of COLBY George W J mechanic b Hopkinton & MONTGOMERY Mary b Hopkinton Vol: 5 Page: 027 Line: 013 Section: 1st.

COBURN Phillip b Hopkinton May 14, 1883 child of COBURN Henry H mechanic b Worcester Mass & ROBERTIE F b Concord Vol: 5 Page: 027 Line: 014 Section: 1st.

SOUTHWICK Harland b Hopkinton Aug 9, 1883 child of SOUTHWICK William R farmer b Corinth Vt & COLBY Louisa b Dunbarton Vol: 5 Page: 027 Line: 015 Section: 1st.

FLANDERS Ethel R b Hopkinton Aug 24, 1883 child of FLANDERS William R laborer b Webster & FRENCH Lizzie b Newbury Vol: 5 Page: 027 Line: 016 Section: 1st.

EMERSON ---- b Hopkinton Sep 21, 1883 child of EMERSON Hanson farmer b Hopkinton & MILLS Mary F b Hopkinton Vol: 5 Page: 027 Line: 017 Section: 1st.

CLARK Goerge Henry b Hopkinton Aug 6, 1883 child of CLARK Henry N farmer b Sanbornton & FRENCH Augusta J b Hopkinton Vol: 5 Page: 027 Line: 019 Section: 1st.

LOCKE ---- b Hopkinton Aug 28, 1883 child of LOCKE George N farmer b Hopkinton & WRIGHT Mary Ann b Hopkinton Vol: 5 Page: 027 Line: 020 Section: 1st.

HOOK William J b Hopkinton Aug 28, 1883 child of HOOK James M farmer & Mary Vol: 5 Page: 027 Line: 022 Section: 1st.

CARR John Alfred b Hopkinton May 30, 1835 child of CARR John?? farmer Vol: 5 Page: 028 Line: 002 Section: 1st.

CARR George Thomas b Hopkinton Jun 18, 1837 child of CARR John?? farmer Vol: 5 Page: 028 Line: 003 Section: 1st.

CARR Thomas Tyler b Hopkinton Apr 2, 1839 child of CARR John?? farmer Vol: 5 Page: 028 Line: 004 Section: 1st.

Hopkinton, NH Births 1880

CARR Frank Henry b Hopkinton Feb 8, 1841 child of CARR John?? farmer Vol: 5 Page: 028 Line: 005 Section: 1st.

AUSTIN ---- (black) b Hopkinton Aug 13, 1890 child of AUSTIN Olive b New Boston & Bertha b Pittsfield Vol: 5 Page: 047 Line: 007 Section: 2nd.

CARR Helen Bruce b Hopkinton Jun 4, 1851 child of CARR John?? farmer Vol: 5 Page: 028 Line: 008 Section: 1st.

CHASE Walter B ** b Hopkinton Dec 19, 1880 child of CHASE Orrin farmer b Hopkinton & BADGER Hattie b Warner Vol: 5 Page: 021 Line: 015 Section: 1st Correction: ** in 1938.

TERRILL ---- b Hopkinton Sep 3, 1881 child of TERRILL Henry J farmer b Goffstown & COLLEY Mary J b Dunbarton Vol: 5 Page: 023 Line: 027 Section: 1st.

GREGG Arthur E b Hopkinton Jun 18, 1882 child of GREGG Frank farmer b Manchester & HOOK Hattie b Concord Vol: 5 Page: 025 Line: 004 Section: 1st.

MILLS Frank B b Hopkinton Jul 7, 1884 child of MILLS George W farmer b Hopkinton & BROWN Eunice b Hopkinton Vol: 5 Page: 033 Line: 005 Section: 2nd.

SPOFFORD Herman F b Hopkinton Jul 21, 1884 child of SPOFFORD Luther F farmer b Wareham Mass & DORA S b Bradford Vol: 5 Page: 033 Line: 006 Section: 2nd.

HOYT Harry L b Hopkinton Aug 9, 1884 child of HOYT James Frank student b Hopkinton & LYDIA Maria b Wareham Mass Vol: 5 Page: 033 Line: 007 Section: 2nd.

DODGE Clarence Blenden b Hopkinton Aug 30, 1884 child of DODGE Henry kit maker b Chelsea Mass & Josephine b Hopkinton Vol: 5 Page: 033 Line: 008 Section: 2nd.

PATCH Robert Ray b Hopkinton Feb 17, 1898 child of PATCH Masten laborer b Weare & GILBERT Lizzie b St Louis Me Vol: 6 Page: 001.

CALL Elfleda May b Hopkinton Mar 22, 1898 child of CALL Arthur C merchant b Webster & McEWEN Nettie M b Cotton NY Vol: 6 Page: 001.

CORSER Marian Louise b Hopkinton Mar 28, 1898 child of CORSER Hamblet farmer b Webster & HOLMES M Belle b Webster Vol: 6 Page: 001.

DASTINGS Edna May b Hopkinton Apr 23, 1898 child of HASTINGS Delmer W farmer b Hopkinton & CHASE Lena M b Hopkinton Vol: 6 Page: 001.

ALLEN Ethel Alvira ** b Hopkinton Sep 6, 1884 child of ALLEN Walton P farmer b New Hampton & MONTGOMERY Mattie b Hopkinton Vol: 5 Page: 033 Line: 009 Section: 2nd Correction: correction in 1943 **.

COURSER Idella F b Hopkinton Oct 29, 1884 child of COURSER Hamlet farmer b Hopkinton & HOLMES Isebel b Webster Vol: 5 Page: 033 Line: 012 Section: 2nd.

FLANDERS ---- b Hopkinton Nov 14, 1884 child of FLANDERS Walter N farmer b Henniker & ROBY Etta b Webster Vol: 5 Page: 033 Line: 013 Section: 2nd.

COLE Walter Herbert** b Hopkinton Jan 1, 1885 child of COLE Charles farmer b Stoneham Me & SMALL Nina b Stonemam Me Vol: 5 Page: 035 Line: 001 Section: 2nd Correction: correction in 1941**.

SARGENT Lena N b Hopkinton Jan 3, 1885 child of SARGENT John H farmer b Hopkinton & DOW Carrie J b Libertville Ill Vol: 5 Page: 035 Line: 002 Section: 2nd.

STRAW Clayton B b Hopkinton Apr 20, 1885 child of STRAW James O farmer b Hopkinton & WHITTIMORE Ada b Hopkinton Vol: 5 Page: 035 Line: 003 Section: 2nd.

FARRILL Ethel Aline ** b Hopkinton Apr 28, 1885 child of FARRILL Edgar T clergeyman b Providence RI & M Alice b Providence RI Vol: 5 Page: 035 Line: 004 Section: 2nd Correction: correction in 1942 **.

STRAW Earnest Gale b Hopkinton May 20, 1885 child of STRAW Andrew S farmer b Hopkinton & CHANDLER Dollie b Hopkinton Vol: 5 Page: 035 Line: 005 Section: 2nd.

DUTTON ---- b Hopkinton Jun 19, 1885 child of DUTTON George W farmer b Hudson & MARY E b Acworth Vol: 5 Page: 035 Line: 006 Section: 2nd.

MAXFIELD Geo Henry b Hopkinton Jul 2, 1885 child of MAXFIELD George F farmer b East Concord & Sarah E b Bow Vol: 5 Page: 035 Line: 007 Section: 2nd.

WATERBURY Etta Grace b Hopkinton Jul 8, 1885 child of WATERBURY Willard E clergeyman b Hastings NY & NELLIE G b Rochester NY Vol: 5 Page: 035 Line: 008 Section: 2nd.

BAILY William b Hopkinton Jul 9, 1885 child of BAILY Eugene farmer & Bell b Hopkinton Vol: 5 Page: 035 Line: 009 Section: 2nd.

REYNO Frank I b Hopkinton Jul 15, 1885 child of REYNO Thomas laborer b Canada & LIBBIE Augusta L b Hopkinton Vol: 5 Page: 035 Line: 010 Section: 2nd.

LITTLE William B b Hopkinton Jul 27, 1885 child of LITTLE Charles farmer b Webster & KIMBALL Mattie B b Webster Vol: 5 Page: 035 Line: 011 Section: 2nd.

BROWN Benj Franklin b Hopkinton Aug 1, 1885 child of BROWN Valorous W laborer b Hopkinton & SARAH T b Webster Vol: 5 Page: 035 Line: 012 Section: 2nd.

GETCHEL Joseph S b Hopkinton Aug 8, 1885 child of GETCHEL Charles farmer b Boscawen & COLLINS Charlotte b Northfield Vol: 5 Page: 035 Line: 013 Section: 2nd.

GRIFFIN Ethel Helen ** b Hopkinton Sep 1, 1885 child of GRIFFIN Alfred farmer b Hopkinton & Helen b Hopkinton Vol: 5 Page: 035 Line: 014 Section: 2nd Correction: see page 49 for correction.

DUSTIN Daniel H b Hopkinton Sep 13, 1885 child of DUSTIN Herbert C farmer b Hopkinton & RICHARDSON Sara A b Hopkinton Vol: 5 Page: 035 Line: 015 Section: 2nd.

ROLLINS Edith Farill b Hopkinton Sep 15, 1885 child of ROLLINS John farmer b Berlin Vt & SARGENT Ellen H b Hopkinton Vol: 5 Page: 035 Line: 016 Section: 2nd.

HOLMES Clarence J b Hopkinton Sep 17, 1885 child of HOLMES Curtice D currier b Salisbury & HOLMES Mary E b Enfield Vol: 5 Page: 035 Line: 017 Section: 2nd.

Hopkinton, NH Births 1880

DWINNELLS Fred W b Hopkinton Sep 21, 1885 child of DWINNELLS Warren laborer b Hopkinton & LIBBIE Ida b Webster Vol: 5 Page: 035 Line: 018 Section: 2nd.

PRAY ---- b Hopkinton Oct 9, 1885 child of PRAY Thomas Jr editor b Conn & FLORENCE M b Somersville Mass Vol: 5 Page: 035 Line: 019 Section: 2nd.

FISKE Mabel Dell b Hopkinton Dec 9, 1885 child of FISKE D Frank lumberman b Hopkinton & DELL E b Hopkinton Vol: 5 Page: 035 Line: 020 Section: 2nd.

GEORGE ---- b Hopkinton Dec 14, 1885 child of GEORGE C S farmer b Warner & Christiana b Newbury Vol: 5 Page: 035 Line: 021 Section: 2nd.

HOOK Alice M b Hopkinton Jul 27, 1885 child of HOOK James M farmer & Mary A Vol: 5 Page: 035 Line: 022 Section: 2nd.

CHASE Gertrude M b Hopkinton Jan 5, 1886 child of CHASE Nelson A rail road employee b Hopkinton & CLARK Anna J b Warner Vol: 5 Page: 037 Line: 001 Section: 2nd.

WARD George S b Hopkinton Jan 25, 1886 child of WARD Charles S cabinet maker b Lebanon & LILLA May b Hopkinton Vol: 5 Page: 037 Line: 002 Section: 2nd.

MONTGOMERY ---- b Hopkinton Jan 29, 1886 child of MONTGOMERY Guy farmer b Hopkinton & MARTIN Nellie E b Brooklin NY Vol: 5 Page: 037 Line: 003 Section: 2nd.

SUMMER ---- b Hopkinton Feb 2, 1886 child of SUMMER George hostler b Hopkinton & ABBOTT Aurilla b Hopkinton Vol: 5 Page: 037 Line: 004 Section: 2nd.

BARTON Forest C b Hopkinton Mar 22, 1886 child of BARTON Robert W farmer b Hopkinton & THOMPSON Mabel b Springfield Vol: 5 Page: 037 Line: 005 Section: 2nd.

SARGENT Daniel D b Hopkinton Apr 18, 1886 child of SARGENT John N miller b Hopkinton & DOW Carrie J Vol: 5 Page: 037 Line: 006 Section: 2nd.

LOVEJOY ---- b Hopkinton May 5, 1886 child of LOVEJOY O T clergyman & Marcia Vol: 5 Page: 037 Line: 007 Section: 2nd.

CHANDLER Carrie b Hopkinton May 19, 1886 child of CHANDLER Frank W rail road man b Hopkinton & ROGERS Margery S b Hopkinton Vol: 5 Page: 037 Line: 008 Section: 2nd.

KEMPTON Lida M b Hopkinton May 19, 1886 child of KEMPTON Lewis E r r brakeman & MONTGOMERY Carrie M b Hopkinton Vol: 5 Page: 037 Line: 009 Section: 2nd.

MARSH Elisabeth Betsey b Hopkinton May 23, 1886 child of MARSH Winfield S farmer b Canterbury & Lizzie b Canterbury Vol: 5 Page: 037 Line: 010 Section: 2nd.

MORAN Margret Ann b Hopkinton Jun 8, 1886 child of MORAN Christopher farmer b Concord & MAHON Mary b Ireland Vol: 5 Page: 037 Line: 011 Section: 2nd.

CORSER Helen J b Hopkinton Jun 9, 1886 child of CORSER Hamlet farmer b Webster & HOLMES M Belle b Webster Vol: 5 Page: 037 Line: 012 Section: 2nd.

REYNO Susie J b Hopkinton Jun 15, 1886 child of REYNO Israel laborer b Vt & LIBBY Augusta b Webster Vol: 5 Page: 037 Line: 013 Section: 2nd.

Hopkinton, NH Births 1880

NILE ---- b Hopkinton Jun 28, 1886 child of NILE Thomas Jefferson farmer b Weare & ELSIE Ann b Antrim Vol: 5 Page: 037 Line: 014 Section: 2nd.

PUTNEY ---- b Hopkinton Jul 2, 1886 child of PUTNEY True J farmer b Hopkinton & ELLEN W b Manchester Vol: 5 Page: 037 Line: 015 Section: 2nd.

BORDEN Marguertie ** b Hopkinton Aug 29, 1886 child of BORDEN Arthur clerk b Fall River Mass & PAGE(PAIGE) Lucie b Hopkinton Vol: 5 Page: 037 Line: 017 Section: 2nd Correction: correction in 1919.

BULLARD ---- b Hopkinton Oct 5, 1886 child of BULLARD Almond C farmer b Bennington & Kate b Boston Mass Vol: 5 Page: 037 Line: 018 Section: 2nd.

LIBBY Alice Ward b Hopkinton Oct 20, 1886 child of LIBBY George A farmer b Webster & Estella Vol: 5 Page: 037 Line: 019 Section: 2nd.

FLANDERS ---- b Hopkinton Oct 31, 1886 child of FLANDERS Walter H butcher b Hopkinton & ETTA F b Webster Vol: 5 Page: 037 Line: 020 Section: 2nd.

EMERSON ---- b Hopkinton Nov 28, 1886 child of EMERSON Hanson D farmer b Hopkinton & MILLS May b Hopkinton Vol: 5 Page: 037 Line: 022 Section: 2nd.

ABBOTT Susie Jane b Hopkinton Dec 10, 1886 child of ABBOTT William C farmer b Bow & HATTIE A b East Concord Vol: 5 Page: 037 Line: 023 Section: 2nd.

STACKPOLE Daniel Eugene b Hopkinton Dec 25, 1886 child of STACKPOLE Daniel E clerk b Lowell Mass & IDA Ellis b Boston Mass Vol: 5 Page: 037 Line: 024 Section: 2nd.

STEARNS Anna N b Hopkinton Feb 7, 1887 child of STEARNS John laborer b Lyneborough & SHERMAN Anna E Vol: 5 Page: 039 Line: 008 Section: 2nd.

HACKETT Edwin J b Hopkinton Jan 8, 1887 child of HACKETT Walter C farmer b Sanbornton & NELLIE M b Hopkinton Vol: 5 Page: 039 Line: 002 Section: 2nd.

DWINNELLS Harry W b Hopkinton Jan 9, 1887 child of DWINNELLS Warren P laborer b Concord & LIBBY Ida b Webster Vol: 5 Page: 039 Line: 023 Section: 2nd.

HOLMES Alvah P b Hopkinton Jan 8, 1887 child of HOLMES Charles A farmer b Webster & EVA D b Hopkinton Vol: 5 Page: 039 Line: 004 Section: 2nd.

HARRINGTON Flora Belle b Hopkinton Jan 14, 1887 child of HARRINGTON Thomas O farmer b Concord & WOODBURY Hattie R ** b Minnesota ** Vol: 5 Page: 039 Line: 005 Section: 2nd Correction: correction 1938.

WATTS Ida May b Hopkinton Jan 24, 1887 child of WATTS Charles F farmer b Warner & Mary A b Hopkinton Vol: 5 Page: 039 Line: 006 Section: 2nd.

DUTTON ---- b Hopkinton Jan 30, 1887 child of DUTTON George W farmer b Hudson & Mary E b Acworth Vol: 5 Page: 039 Line: 007 Section: 2nd.

WEST Delia b Hopkinton Feb 13, 1887 child of WEST Frank sawyer b St Johns Canada & Delia b Hemysville Canada Vol: 5 Page: 039 Line: 009 Section: 2nd.

SPOFFORD ---- b Hopkinton Feb 14, 1887 child of SPOFFORD S A farmer b Hopkinton & PAIGE Abbie A b Hopkinton Vol: 5 Page: 039 Line: 010 Section: 2nd.

FULLER John F b Hopkinton Feb 25, 1887 child of FULLER Orin F farmer b Hopkinton & CAMPBELL Lilla b Hopkinton Vol: 5 Page: 039 Line: 011 Section: 2nd.

Hopkinton, NH Births 1880

WATERBURY Mabel Gladys b Hopkinton Mar 8, 1887 child of WATERBURY Willard E clergyman b Hastings NY & Nellie b Rochester NY Vol: 5 Page: 039 Line: 012 Section: 2nd.

PERRY Edna Holland b Hopkinton Apr 6, 1887 child of PERRY James M farmer b Hopkinton & EDITHEEN E b Hopkinton Vol: 5 Page: 039 Line: 013 Section: 2nd.

DAVIS Thomas Edward b Hopkinton Apr 30, 1887 child of DAVIS Henry B farmer b Hopkinton & Eliza J b Middleton Mass Vol: 5 Page: 039 Line: 014 Section: 2nd.

GLEASON ---- b Hopkinton May 15, 1887 child of GLEASON John F farmer b Groton Mass & Eveline A b Boscawen Vol: 5 Page: 039 Line: 015 Section: 2nd.

SPOFFORD Fred Luther b Hopkinton May 27, 1887 child of SPOFFORD Luther F farmer b Hopkinton & Dora b Hopkinton Vol: 5 Page: 039 Line: 016 Section: 2nd Note: a twin.

SPOFFORD Della Etta b Hopkinton May 27, 1887 child of SPOFFORD Luther F farmer b Hopkinton & Dora b Hopkinton Vol: 5 Page: 039 Line: 017 Section: 2nd Note: a twin.

HAZELTON Homer Harding b Hopkinton Jun 3, 1887 child of HAZELTON Herman R rule maker b Groton Mass & Nellie b Webester Vol: 5 Page: 039 Line: 018 Section: 2nd.

TUCKER Leon Carlton b Hopkinton Jun 14, 1887 child of TUCKER D Carlton farmer b Hopkinton & Eva C (Perry) b Hopkinton Vol: 5 Page: 039 Line: 019 Section: 2nd.

FRENCH Laura Ella b Hopkinton Jul 12, 1887 child of FRENCH Charles butcher b Hopkinton & Sarah A H b Hopkinton Vol: 5 Page: 039 Line: 020 Section: 2nd.

COLBY Blanche b Hopkinton Dec 9, 1887 child of COLBY Forrest farmer b Litchfield & Abbie b Dunbarton Vol: 5 Page: 041 Line: 002 Section: 2nd.

GREEN George Gardner b Hopkinton Sep 7, 1887 child of GREENE Willard T livery stable keeper b Hopkinton & BAILY Etta C b Chelsea Mass Vol: 5 Page: 039 Line: 022 Section: 2nd.

RENO Cora M ?? b Hopkinton Sep 10, 1887 child of RENO Isreal farmer & LIBBY Augusta b Webster Vol: 5 Page: 039 Line: 023 Section: 2nd.

SYMONDS Mildred G b Hopkinton Sep 10, 1887 child of SYMONDS Samuel farmer & Ann b Weare Vol: 5 Page: 039 Line: 024 Section: 2nd.

GRIFFIN Harold R b Hopkinton Sep 11, 1887 child of GRIFFIN Alfred E farmer b Bow & Helen b Lowell Mass Vol: 5 Page: 039 Line: 025 Section: 2nd.

WATTERSON George Hanson b Hopkinton Nov 24, 1887 child of WATTERSON Nathaniel W farmer b Philadelphia & Minnie J b Weare Vol: 5 Page: 039 Line: 026 Section: 2nd.

BURBANK Helen A b Hopkinton Dec 3, 1887 child of BURBANK Irving D farmer b Hopkinton & AUGUSTA J b Hopkinton Vol: 5 Page: 039 Line: 027 Section: 2nd.

WALKER Ethel Beatrice b Hopkinton Dec 12, 1887 child of WALKER Milton J farmer b Hopkinton & ELLIOTT Alice Vol: 5 Page: 039 Line: 028 Section: 2nd.

CLOUGH Francis b Hopkinton Aug 18, 1887 child of CLOUGH Moses T farmer b Hopkinton & BEAN Mary Oresta** Vol: 5 Page: 039 Line: 021 Section: 2nd Correction: correction 1942.

Hopkinton, NH Births 1880

SMART Maud F b Hopkinton Dec 3, 1887 child of SMART Hamilton E farmer b Hopkinton & Nellie b Nashville Tenn Vol: 5 Page: 041 Line: 001 Section: 2nd.

BAILEY Fred Arthur b Hopkinton May 13, 1888 child of PAGE Joseph farmer b Warner & PALMER Nelly b Sutton Vol: 5 Page: 043 Line: 005 Section: 2nd.

CHASE Luella W b Hopkinton Feb 4, 1888 child of CHASE George farmer b Hopkinton & HOLMES Jennie b Hopkinton Vol: 5 Page: 043 Line: 002 Section: 2nd.

MORAN Mary K b Hopkinton Mar 31, 1888 child of MORAN Christopher laborer b Concord & Mary b Ireland Vol: 5 Page: 043 Line: 003 Section: 2nd.

HUNT Arthur Wallace b Hopkinton May 3, 1888 child of HUNT Charles mechanic b Warner & Ella A b Nova Scotia Vol: 5 Page: 043 Line: 004 Section: 2nd.

MILLS Fred E b Hopkinton May 23, 1888 child of MILLS Fred W W laborer b Boscawen & BROWN Bell M b Hopkinton Vol: 5 Page: 043 Line: 006 Section: 2nd.

ANNIS Grover Cleveland b Hopkinton May 25, 1888 child of ANNIS Frank P farmer b Hopkinton & CHILDS Hattie b Warner Vol: 5 Page: 043 Line: 007 Section: 2nd.

CHASE Susie May b Hopkinton Jun 23, 1888 child of CHASE Edward E laborer b Hopkinton & MOULTON Emma E b Concord Vol: 5 Page: 043 Line: 008 Section: 2nd.

MORAN Patrick James b Hopkinton Oct 20, 1889 child of MORAN Christopher farmer b Concord & Mary b Ireland Vol: 5 Page: 045 Line: 018 Section: 2nd.

BAKER Mildred F b Hopkinton Aug 26, 1888 child of BAKER William A clerk b Concord & PALMER Effie V b Hopkinton Vol: 5 Page: 043 Line: 011 Section: 2nd.

ABBOTT ---- b Hopkinton Sep 25, 1888 child of ABBOTT William C laborer b Concord Vol: 5 Page: 043 Line: 012 Section: 2nd.

FISH Lida N b Hopkinton Oct 23, 1888 child of FISH Dnaiel F lumberman b Hopkinton & CHANDLER Delle b Hopkinton Vol: 5 Page: 043 Line: 013 Section: 2nd.

COLLER Ethel C b Hopkinton Oct 31, 1888 child of COLLER Edwin S clergyman b Northfield Mass & Hattie B b Keene Vol: 5 Page: 043 Line: 014 Section: 2nd.

BROWN Minnie Ether ** b Hopkinton Nov 10, 1888 child of BROWN Ivan F farmer b Manchester & GREENE Hattie b Hopkinton Vol: 5 Page: 043 Line: 015 Section: 2nd Correction: ** correction in 1954.

LAMPREY James Alfred** b Hopkinton Nov 12, 1888 child of LAMPREY George farmer b Concord & ABBOTT Aurelia S b Concord Vol: 5 Page: 043 Line: 016 Section: 2nd Correction: ** correction made 1952.

PERRY Ernest S b Hopkinton Nov 14, 1888 child of PERRY James M farmer b Hopkinton & Editheen E b Hopkinton Vol: 5 Page: 043 Line: 017 Section: 2nd.

CHANDLER Bertha b Hopkinton Feb 18, 1889 child of CHANDLER Frank W farmer b Hopkinton & ROGERS Margery S b Hopkinton Vol: 5 Page: 045 Line: 001 Section: 2nd.

SANBORN ---- b Hopkinton Feb 22, 1889 child of SANBORN Edith b Hopkinton Vol: 5 Page: 045 Line: 002 Section: 2nd.

LIBBY Jessie b Hopkinton Mar 1, 1889 child of LIBBY George A laborer b Webster & Estella b Franklin Vol: 5 Page: 045 Line: 003 Section: 2nd.

Hopkinton, NH Births 1880

CHASE Lida H b Hopkinton Mar 25, 1889 child of CHASE Nelson A r r section b Hopkinton & CLARKE Anna J b Warner Vol: 5 Page: 045 Line: 004 Section: 2nd.

REYNO Cora May b Hopkinton Apr 1, 1889 child of REYNO Thomas laborer & LIBBY Augusta b Webster Vol: 5 Page: 045 Line: 005 Section: 2nd.

DENSMORE John Edward b Hopkinton Aug 27, 1889 child of DENSMORE James A laborer b Northfield & LIBBY Ellen J b Webster Vol: 5 Page: 045 Line: 006 Section: 2nd Correction: triples-all living.

DENSMORE Wm Ernest b Hopkinton Aug 27, 1889 child of DENSMORE James A laborer b Northfield & LIBBY Ellen J b Webster Vol: 5 Page: 045 Line: 007 Section: 2nd Correction: triples-all living.

DENSMORE Harlon Wills b Hopkinton Aug 27, 1889 child of DENSMORE James A laborer b Northfield & LIBBY Ellen J b Webster Vol: 5 Page: 045 Line: 008 Section: 2nd Correction: triples-all living.

ORDWAY Clarence C b Hopkinton May 6, 1889 child of ORDWAY George L farmer b Concord & DURGIN Ella J b Wilmot Vol: 5 Page: 045 Line: 009 Section: 2nd.

LOVERING Leon N b Hopkinton Aug 4, 1889 child of LOVERING William laborer & BROWN Belle b Warner Vol: 5 Page: 045 Line: 010 Section: 2nd.

DAVIS Amos H b Hopkinton Aug 8, 1889 child of DAVIS Henry B farmer b Hopkinton & COOK Eliza b Peabody Mass Vol: 5 Page: 045 Line: 011 Section: 2nd.

MIGNAULT Lena N b Hopkinton Sep 7, 1889 child of MIGNAULT Albert M laborer b Canada & STEVENS Emma L b Hopkinton Vol: 5 Page: 045 Line: 012 Section: 2nd.

BARTLETT Leason Roy b Hopkinton Aug 29, 1889 child of BARTLETT Henry farmer b Warner & HARDY Isabella M b Hopkinton Vol: 5 Page: 045 Line: 013 Section: 2nd.

KEMP Harold C b Hopkinton Sep 11, 1889 child of KEMP Frank P drummer b Hooksett & EASTMAN Jennie b Stoneham Mass Vol: 5 Page: 045 Line: 014 Section: 2nd.

LAPORRITON ---- b Hopkinton Sep 14, 1889 child of LAPORRITON David A woodchopper b Canada & Addie P b Canada Vol: 5 Page: 045 Line: 015 Section: 2nd.

FULLER Irvan M b Hopkinton Sep 14, 1889 child of FULLER Orrin Y mechanic b New Hampton & CAMPBELL Lilla E b Hopkinton Vol: 5 Page: 045 Line: 016 Section: 2nd.

ANNIS James H b Hopkinton Sep 20, 1889 child of ANNIS Charles farmer b Hopkinton & FLANDERS Eva Vol: 5 Page: 045 Line: 017 Section: 2nd.

DUNBAR Alvin Paige b Hopkinton Oct 16, 1889 child of DUNBAR Eugene carpenter b Hopkinton & PAIGE Mary E b Dunbarton Vol: 5 Page: 045 Line: 019 Section: 2nd.

DOWNING ---- b Hopkinton Dec 8, 1889 child of DOWNING Frank E laborer b Hopkinton & Emma b Shirley Mass Vol: 5 Page: 045 Line: 021 Section: 2nd.

BUZZELL ---- b Hopkinton Dec 30, 1889 child of BUZZELL Wills farmer & May b Warren Vt Vol: 5 Page: 045 Line: 022 Section: 2nd.

Hopkinton, NH Births 1880

THAYER Frances Louse b Hopkinton Dec 26, 1889 child of THAYER Herbert E clergyman b Farmingdale Me & BARREY Mary b Wilington Vt Vol: 5 Page: 045 Line: 023 Section: 2nd.

CLAISOL?? ---- b Hopkinton Dec 14, 1883 child of CLAISOLIS?? Rodrice b Nova Scotia Nb & GOULD Ella Vol: 5 Page: 027 Line: 021 Section: 1st.

BARTLETT Carlos W b Hopkinton Jan 24, 1890 child of BARTLETT Woodbury farmer b Warner & DAVIS Clarindo b Hartland Vt Vol: 5 Page: 047 Line: 002 Section: 2nd.

BURBANK Irvin Walter b Hopkinton Feb 3, 1890 child of BURBANK Irvin D farmer b Hopkinton & Augusta J b Hopkinton Vol: 5 Page: 047 Line: 003 Section: 2nd.

LITTLE Emma J b Hopkinton Jul 12, 1890 child of LITTLE Charles E farmer b Webster & KIMBALL Mattie B b Webster Vol: 5 Page: 047 Line: 004 Section: 2nd.

ROLLINS Wm Long b Hopkinton Jul 5, 1890 child of ROLLINS Wm H farmer b Hopkinton & ROBINSON Margaret P b North Caroline Vol: 5 Page: 047 Line: 005 Section: 2nd.

KIMBALL Harold Chase b Hopkinton Aug 12, 1890 child of KIMBALL John Stevens gentleman b Boston Mass & FRENCH Margarette A b Hopkinton Vol: 5 Page: 047 Line: 006 Section: 2nd.

SYMONDS Benjamin P b Hopkinton Aug 18, 1890 child of SYMONDS Benjamin D farmer b Hillsborough & PORTER Emma J b Hartford Vt Vol: 5 Page: 047 Line: 008 Section: 2nd.

HOLMES Annie B b Hopkinton Aug 23, 1890 child of HOLMES Charles A farmer b Webster & Eva D b Hopkinton Vol: 5 Page: 047 Line: 009 Section: 2nd.

ORDWAY Eva N b Hopkinton Sep 10, 1890 child of ORDWAY George L farmer b Concord & Ella J b Wilmot Vol: 5 Page: 047 Line: 011 Section: 2nd.

HEATH Pauline ** b Hopkinton Sep 28, 1890 child of HEATH Elbridge G farmer b Salisbury & Marrietta F b Hudson Vol: 5 Page: 047 Line: 012 Section: 2nd Correction: ** correction 1938.

HOWE Sadie C b Hopkinton Oct 5, 1890 child of HOWE Jason C fireman r r b Sutton & HANNAH J b Warner Vol: 5 Page: 047 Line: 013 Section: 2nd.

REYNO Flora (twin) b Hopkinton Oct 6, 1890 child of REYNO Isreal r r shop b Vermont & LIBBY Augusta b Webster Vol: 5 Page: 047 Line: 014 Section: 2nd.

REYNO Dora (twin) b Hopkinton Oct 6, 1890 child of REYNO Isreal r r shop b Vermont & LIBBY Augusta b Webster Vol: 5 Page: 047 Line: 015 Section: 2nd.

LUFKIN Bertha M b Hopkinton Oct 17, 1890 child of LUFKIN Parmeter H farmer b Weare & SMITH Nellie A b Lyndeboro Vol: 5 Page: 047 Line: 016 Section: 2nd.

FAGAN ---- b Hopkinton Dec 9, 1890 child of FAGAN Christopher blacksmith b Hopkinton & Mary b Ireland Vol: 5 Page: 047 Line: 017 Section: 2nd.

SMART Alice M b Hopkinton Jul 14, 1890 child of SMART Edward H farmer b Hopkinton & FISKE Nellie C b Nashville Tenn Vol: 5 Page: 047 Line: 018 Section: 2nd.

MILLS Jessie May b Hopkinton Jan 10, 1891 child of MILLS Frank C carpenter b Hopkinton & HOWARD Mammie A b Newport Vol: 5 Page: 049 Line: 001 Section: 2nd.

Hopkinton, NH Births 1880

BARNARD Raymond Joseph b Hopkinton Jan 28, 1891 child of BARNARD George E lumberman b Hopkinton & TYLER Bertha b Hopkinton Vol: 5 Page: 049 Line: 002 Section: 2nd.

DUNBAR Mary E G b Hopkinton Feb 2, 1891 child of DUNBAR Henry P farmer b Hopkinton & GAGE Mary E b Hopkinton Vol: 5 Page: 049 Line: 003 Section: 2nd.

RAND William H b Hopkinton Feb 21, 1891 child of RAND True W farmer b Warner & WOODMAN Maria b Lexington Ohio Vol: 5 Page: 049 Line: 004 Section: 2nd.

ALLEN Earnest b Hopkinton Feb 28, 1891 child of BOUTWELL Henry B farmer b Hopkinton & MONTGOMERY Alice b Hopkinton Vol: 5 Page: 049 Line: 005 Section: 2nd.

GRIFFIN Daniel A b Hopkinton Mar 19, 1891 child of GRIFFIN Alfred E farmer b Bow & MORRILL Helen J b Lowell Mass Vol: 5 Page: 049 Line: 007 Section: 2nd.

SANBORN Carlton E b Hopkinton Mar 20, 1891 child of SANBORN George F farmer b Bangor Me & Mary b Stoddard Vol: 5 Page: 049 Line: 008 Section: 2nd.

DOUSE ---- b Hopkinton Apr 3, 1891 child of DOUSE John teamster b Epsom & Ella b Loudon Vol: 5 Page: 049 Line: 009 Section: 2nd.

LIBBY Edna Agnes b Hopkinton Apr 5, 1891 child of LIBBY Joseph G laborer b Webster & BARTLETT Clara b Warner Vol: 5 Page: 049 Line: 010 Section: 2nd.

COLBY Ira N b Hopkinton Apr 7, 1891 child of COLBY Frank T farmer b Salisbury & Clara b Haverhill Vol: 5 Page: 049 Line: 011 Section: 2nd.

TYLER Phebe Austin C b Hopkinton Apr 10, 1891 child of TYLER Frank A clergyman b Lawrence Mass & CARLTON Jane Smith b No Weare Vol: 5 Page: 049 Line: 012 Section: 2nd.

BOYCE Loren I b Hopkinton Apr 13, 1891 child of BOYCE Mezher teamester b Concord & Clarinda b Concord Vol: 5 Page: 049 Line: 013 Section: 2nd.

LORD Mabel Estella b Hopkinton Apr 19, 1891 child of LORD George E farmer b Hopkinton & HODGDON Hattie M b Hopkinton Vol: 5 Page: 049 Line: 014 Section: 2nd.

HOWE George M b Hopkinton Apr 1, 1894 child of HOWE Edwin B farmer b Warner & WYMAN Etta M b Bradford Vol: 5 Page: 053 Line: 007 Section: 2nd.

BROWN Ida May b Hopkinton Jun 12, 1891 child of BROWN Valorous laborer b Hopkinton & LIBBY Sarah b Webster Vol: 5 Page: 049 Line: 016 Section: 2nd.

DAVIS Arthur Bradstreet b Hopkinton Jul 4, 1891 child of DAVIS Henry B farmer b Hopkinton & DAVIS Eliza J b Middleton Ass Vol: 5 Page: 049 Line: 017 Section: 2nd Correction: correction in 1932.

CONNER Arthur Clinton b Hopkinton Jul 10, 1891 child of CONNER Alvah farmer & MORGAN Jennie A b Hopkinton Vol: 5 Page: 049 Line: 018 Section: 2nd.

HAZELTON Pearl V b Hopkinton Aug 13, 1891 child of HAZELTON Herman rule maker b Alexander & DWINELLS Nellie b Boscawen Vol: 5 Page: 049 Line: 020 Section: 2nd.

Hopkinton, NH Births 1880

ALLEN Olive Amanda b Hopkinton Nov 25, 1891 child of ALLEN Walton P r r employee b Chelsea Mass & MONTGOMERY Martha S b Hopkinton Vol: 5 Page: 049 Line: 021 Section: 2nd.

LINCOLN Howard Walter b Hopkinton Dec 14, 1891 child of LINCOLN Walter F wheelwright b Cohassett Mass & BARTON Caroline M b Brooklyn NY Vol: 5 Page: 049 Line: 022 Section: 2nd.

RANDALL Mabel b Hopkinton Dec 20, 1891 child of RANDALL George W laborer b Plymouth & Mary E b Boston Mass Vol: 5 Page: 049 Line: 023 Section: 2nd.

DUNBAR Mildred F b Hopkinton Dec 20, 1891 child of DUNBAR Eugene carpenter b Hopkinton & PAGE May E Vol: 5 Page: 049 Line: 024 Section: 2nd.

CURRIER Helen b Hopkinton Jan 13, 1892 child of CURRIER Willie A farmer b Hopkinton & WEBSTER Gertie J b Concord Vol: 5 Page: 051 Line: 001 Section: 2nd.

MORRILL Delia I b Hopkinton Feb 22, 1892 child of MORRILL Stephen E mechanic b Hopkinton & DEARBORN Mary b Candia Vol: 5 Page: 051 Line: 003 Section: 2nd.

BURBANK Ernest C ** b Hopkinton Apr 1, 1892 child of BURBANK Alberto H laborer b Hopkinton & TUCKER Eliza J b Hopkinton Vol: 5 Page: 051 Line: 005 Section: 2nd Correction: ** correction in 1966.

BUSWELL Lorene D b Hopkinton Apr 3, 1892 child of BUSWELL Loren W lumberman b Concord & CARPENTER Mary E b Warner Vol: 5 Page: 051 Line: 006 Section: 2nd.

DOWNING Ernest Eugene** b Hopkinton Apr 7, 1892 child of DOWNING Frank E laborer b Hopkinton & SARTELLE Emily M b Shirley Mass Vol: 5 Page: 051 Line: 007 Section: 2nd Correction: correction in 1932.

HODGMAN ---- b Hopkinton Apr 8, 1892 child of HODGMAN Henry L quaryman b Campton & GUNN Mary E b Penacook Vol: 5 Page: 051 Line: 008 Section: 2nd.

KIMBALL Edgar H b Hopkinton Mar 28, 1892 child of KIMBALL Herbert M farmer b Hopkinton & COLBY Mary A b Bow Vol: 5 Page: 051 Line: 009 Section: 2nd.

PERKINS Frank H b Hopkinton Apr 13, 1892 child of PERKINS Philip H laborer b Philadelphia & BATCHELDER Ida A b New London Vol: 5 Page: 051 Line: 010 Section: 2nd.

HOLMES Myron W b Hopkinton Mar 8, 1892 child of HOLMES Charles A farmer b Webster & EVANGLINE D b Hopkinton Vol: 5 Page: 051 Line: 011 Section: 2nd.

PERRY Charles N b Hopkinton May 3, 1892 child of PERRY James M laborer b Hopkinton & KELLEY Therria b Hopkinton Vol: 5 Page: 051 Line: 012 Section: 2nd.

DUSTIN ---- b Hopkinton May 20, 1892 child of DUSTIN Cyrus F farmer b Hopkinton & SPAULDING Nellie Vol: 5 Page: 051 Line: 013 Section: 2nd.

LORD Cora May b Hopkinton May 22, 1892 child of LORD George E farmer b New Market & HODGDON Hattie M b Hopkinton Vol: 5 Page: 051 Line: 014 Section: 2nd.

Hopkinton, NH Births 1880

COLBY Elsie J b Hopkinton May 30, 1892 child of COLBY Arthur mechanic b Hopkinton & WHIPPLE Lida b Manchester Vol: 5 Page: 051 Line: 015 Section: 2nd.

DUSTON Freeman C ** b Hopkinton Jun 5, 1892 child of DUSTON Arthur W blacksmith b Boscawen & CLOUGH Josephine E b Hopkinton Vol: 5 Page: 051 Line: 016 Section: 2nd Correction: correction 1929 **.

RUTHERFORD ---- b Hopkinton Aug 12, 1892 child of RUTHERFORD George R laborer b Scotland & Mattie b Vermont Vol: 5 Page: 051 Line: 017 Section: 2nd.

LIBBY Lillian D b Hopkinton Aug 13, 1892 child of LIBBY George A laborer b Webster & Estella b Andover Vol: 5 Page: 051 Line: 018 Section: 2nd.

EASTMAN Richard Scott b Hopkinton Aug 22, 1892 child of EASTMAN Clarence M mechanic b Warner & Mary b Newark NJ Vol: 5 Page: 051 Line: 020 Section: 2nd.

DANIELS Ida N b Hopkinton Aug 16, 1892 child of DANIELS Mark farmer b Woodbury Vt & MERRILL Annie b Hopkinton Vol: 5 Page: 051 Line: 021 Section: 2nd.

CLARK Ruben E b Hopkinton Aug 23, 1892 child of CLARK Ruben E brakeman b Hartford Vt & BAILEY Sadie b St Johnsbury Vt Vol: 5 Page: 051 Line: 022 Section: 2nd.

KIMBALL Ruth N b Hopkinton Aug 28, 1892 child of KIMBALL Nelson D farmer b Hopkinton & PATCH Adelaid b Newfield Me Vol: 5 Page: 051 Line: 023 Section: 2nd.

LITTLE Robert B b Hopkinton Sep 30, 1892 child of LITTLE Charles E farmer b Webster & KIMBALL Mattie B b Webster Vol: 5 Page: 051 Line: 024 Section: 2nd.

CHASE Carroll Thompson b Hopkinton Oct 27, 1892 child of CHASE Charles S miller b Charlestown Mass & Florence b Hopkinton Vol: 5 Page: 051 Line: 025 Section: 2nd.

KING Harold Edward b Hopkinton Mar 4, 1893 child of KING Joseph E B farmer b Canada & Kate b St John N B Vol: 5 Page: 053 Line: 010 Section: 2nd.

MORAN John T b Hopkinton Jun 26, 1892 child of MORAN Christopher farmer Vol: 5 Page: 051 Line: 028 Section: 2nd.

CHANDLER Arthur Ray b Hopkinton Aug 13, 1892 child of CHANDLER Frank W hostler-(stable boy) b Hopkinton & ROGERS Margery b Hopkinton Vol: 5 Page: 051 Line: 019 Section: 2nd.

WILLIAMS Arthur P b Hopkinton Jan 15, 1893 child of WILLIAMS Clarence W clergyman b Geensvoro Vt & STRETTER Lilla A b Littleton Vol: 5 Page: 053 Line: 001 Section: 2nd.

ROLLINS George b Hopkinton Jan 13, 1893 child of ROLLINS William N farmer b Hopkinton & Margaret b N C Vol: 5 Page: 053 Line: 002 Section: 2nd.

WATTS Fannie Bell (t) b Hopkinton Feb 3, 1893 child of WATTS Charles F currier b Hopkinton & Mary A b Hopkinton Vol: 5 Page: 053 Line: 003 Section: 2nd.

WATTS John Arthur (t) b Hopkinton Feb 3, 1893 child of WATTS Charles F currier b Hopkinton & Mary A b Hopkinton Vol: 5 Page: 053 Line: 004 Section: 2nd.

Hopkinton, NH Births 1880

MONTGOMERY Lucy Savory b Hopkinton Feb 4, 1893 child of MONTGOMERY Guy farmer b Hopkinton & Nellie N b New York Vol: 5 Page: 053 Line: 005 Section: 2nd.

BULLOCK George Frances b Hopkinton Mar 16, 1893 child of BULLOCK Emery mason b New York State & Annie E b Chichester Vol: 5 Page: 053 Line: 006 Section: 2nd.

NELSON John Leland b Hopkinton Apr 10, 1893 child of NELSON John H machinist b Hopkinton & SEAVEY Nettie N b Hopkinton Vol: 5 Page: 053 Line: 007 Section: 2nd.

BROWN E Ida b Hopkinton Mar 27, 1893 child of BROWN Valorous laborer b Hopkinton & LIBBY Sarah G b Webster Vol: 5 Page: 053 Line: 008 Section: 2nd.

MERRILL Donald Allen b Hopkinton May 3, 1893 child of MERRILL Frank I mechanic b Hopkinton & STEVENS Nettie b Piermont Vol: 5 Page: 053 Line: 009 Section: 2nd.

BURBANK Carl H b Hopkinton Apr 27, 1893 child of BURBANK Irvan D farmer b Hopkinton & FRENCH Augusta b Hopkinton Vol: 5 Page: 053 Line: 011 Section: 2nd.

WHYTOCK Jennie Victoria b Hopkinton Jun 1, 1893 child of WHYTOCK David butcher b Madoc Canada & Bella b Huntington Canada Vol: 5 Page: 053 Line: 012 Section: 2nd.

BARNARD Perley D b Hopkinton Jun 6, 1893 child of BARNARD George E farmer b Hopkinton & TYLER Bertha b Hopkinton Vol: 5 Page: 053 Line: 014 Section: 2nd.

ABBOTT Ana Alice b Hopkinton Jun 16, 1893 child of ABBOTT E C millwright & ADDIE E b Troy Vt Vol: 5 Page: 053 Line: 015 Section: 2nd.

CURRIER Florence Grace b Hopkinton Jul 15, 1893 child of CURRIER Willie A farmer b Hopkinton & WEBSTER Gertie b Hopkinton Vol: 5 Page: 053 Line: 016 Section: 2nd.

DOWNING Victor Harold** b Hopkinton Jul 26, 1893 child of DOWNING Frank E laborer b Hopkinton & SARTELLE Emily M b Shirley Mass Vol: 5 Page: 053 Line: 017 Section: 2nd Correction: correction 1932.

LIBBY Josephine Alma b Hopkinton Aug 16, 1893 child of LIBBY Joseph G laborer b Salisbury & BARTLETT Clara b Warner Vol: 5 Page: 053 Line: 018 Section: 2nd.

HOYT Pearl Lowell b Hopkinton Sep 4, 1893 child of HOYT William C sewing machine agt b Weare & STURTEVANT Effie A b Buffalo NY Vol: 5 Page: 053 Line: 019 Section: 2nd.

BOUTWELL Helen M b Hopkinton Sep 13, 1893 child of BOUTWELL Henry B A farmer b Berlin Ill & MONTGOMERY Alice b Hopkinton Vol: 5 Page: 053 Line: 020 Section: 2nd.

CHASE Leon Webber b Hopkinton Sep 18, 1893 child of CHASE Charles T carpenter b Charlestown Mass & WEBBER Florence b Hopkinton Vol: 5 Page: 053 Line: 021 Section: 2nd.

RUSSELL ---- b Hopkinton Sep 21, 1893 child of RUSSELL Arthur farmer b Woodstock & TUTTLE Mabel b New London Vol: 5 Page: 053 Line: 022 Section: 2nd.

Hopkinton, NH Births 1880

TOBYNE Emory J b Hopkinton Nov 24, 1893 child of TOBYNE Rodney H farmer b Ashland & BROWN Mary F b Woodstock Vol: 5 Page: 053 Line: 023 Section: 2nd.

SIMON ---- b Hopkinton Jun 12, 1893 child of SIMON Will laborer b Canada & PAIGE Leora b Canada Vol: 5 Page: 053 Line: 024 Section: 2nd.

DANIELS Ralph C b Hopkinton Aug 28, 1893 child of DANIELS Mark farmer b Woodbury Vt & MERRILL Annie B b Hopkinton Vol: 5 Page: 053 Line: 025 Section: 2nd.

KIMBALL Edith G b Hopkinton Nov 22, 1893 child of KIMBALL Nelson D farmer b Hopkinton & ADDIE M b Newfield Me Vol: 5 Page: 053 Line: 026 Section: 2nd.

GOODWIN William Crane b Hopkinton Dec 7, 1893 child of GOODWIN William K laborer b New Brunswick & JOHNSON Hattie b Nova Scotia Vol: 5 Page: 053 Line: 027 Section: 2nd.

THAYER Ruth Harriett b Hopkinton May 18, 1891 child of THAYER Herbert E clergyman & BARNERY Mary Vol: 5 Page: 049 Line: 015 Section: 2nd.

BOUTWELL Earle Fitts b Hopkinton Jan 15, 1894 child of BOUTWELL Arthur J lumberman b Hopkinton & FITTS Carrie J b Dunbarton Vol: 5 Page: 055 Line: 001 Section: 2nd.

SANBORN Donald E b Hopkinton Jan 17, 1894 child of SANBORN Elihu Q miller b Webster & HARDY Lizzie b Hebron Vol: 5 Page: 055 Line: 002 Section: 2nd.

LINCOLN Fanny Esther b Hopkinton Feb 13, 1894 child of LINCOLN Walter F wheelwright b Cohassett Mass & BARTON Caroline M b Brooklyn NY Vol: 5 Page: 055 Line: 003 Section: 2nd.

DUSTIN Sarah A b Hopkinton Feb 14, 1894 child of DUSTIN Cyrus farmer b Hopkinton & SPAULDING Nellie S b Manchester Vol: 5 Page: 055 Line: 004 Section: 2nd.

LORD Eugene H b Hopkinton Mar 20, 1894 child of LORD George E farmer b Newmarket & HODGDON Hattie b Hopkinton Vol: 5 Page: 055 Line: 005 Section: 2nd.

DUNBAR Edward C b Hopkinton Mar 30, 1894 child of DUNBAR Henry P butcher b Hopkinton & DANFORTH Emma L b Webster Vol: 5 Page: 055 Line: 006 Section: 2nd.

ALLEN Chassie E b Hopkinton Apr 9, 1894 child of ALLEN Walton P farmer b Chelsea Mass & MONTGOMERY Martha S b Hopkinton Vol: 5 Page: 055 Line: 008 Section: 2nd.

MONTGOMERY Earl Roger b Hopkinton Apr 21, 1894 child of MONTGOMERY Jerome farmer b Hopkinton & DUNBAR Eliza J b Warner Vol: 5 Page: 055 Line: 009 Section: 2nd.

DAVIS Alice Marion b Hopkinton May 13, 1894 child of DAVIS Henry B farmer b Hopkinton & Eliza J b Peabody Mass Vol: 5 Page: 055 Line: 010 Section: 2nd.

ABBOTT ---- b Hopkinton May 11, 1894 child of ABBOTT Elden laborer b Underhill Vt & POWERS Addie E b Troy Vt Vol: 5 Page: 055 Line: 011 Section: 2nd.

CLOUGH Wendell Alfred b Hopkinton May 19, 1894 child of CLOUGH Charles E farmer b Hopkinton & HASTINGS Gertrude b Hopkinton Vol: 5 Page: 055 Line: 012 Section: 2nd.

Hopkinton, NH Births 1880

WELCH William b Hopkinton Jun 8, 1894 child of WELCH Wm laborer b Concord & Sadie b Boscawen Vol: 5 Page: 055 Line: 013 Section: 2nd.

BOUTWELL Pearl Abbie b Hopkinton Jun 24, 1894 child of BOUTWELL Wallace E farmer b Methuen Mass & WARD Lillie A b Cambridgeport Mass Vol: 5 Page: 055 Line: 014 Section: 2nd.

ELLIOTT Flossie O b Hopkinton Jul 12, 1894 child of ELLIOTT Edson E farmer b Webster & COLBY Nettie b Deering Vol: 5 Page: 055 Line: 015 Section: 2nd.

DUSTON Arthur S b Hopkinton Jul 16, 1894 child of DUSTON Arthur M blacksmith b Boscawen & CLOUGH Josephine E b Hopkinton Vol: 5 Page: 055 Line: 016 Section: 2nd.

ELLIOTT Gertrude Howe b Hopkinton Jul 28, 1894 child of ELLIOTT Charles E farmer b Hopkinton & HOWE Anna Gertrude b Jamaca Plains Mass Vol: 5 Page: 055 Line: 017 Section: 2nd.

CURRIER John b Hopkinton Jul 28, 1894 child of CURRIER Charles C clothier b Hopkinton & KILBORN Mary I b Webster Vol: 5 Page: 055 Line: 018 Section: 2nd.

ARMSTRONG George Oliver b Hopkinton Sep 3, 1894 child of ARMSTRONG Oliver laborer b Brooklyn NY & Cora S b Hopkinton Vol: 5 Page: 055 Line: 020 Section: 2nd.

BOYCE Lanson b Hopkinton Oct 21, 1894 child of BOYCE Melzer laborer b Concord & Alice C b Concord Vol: 5 Page: 055 Line: 021 Section: 2nd.

STRAW Roger b Hopkinton Oct 28, 1894 child of STRAW James O farmer b Hopkinton & WHITTEMORE Ada M b Henniker Vol: 5 Page: 055 Line: 022 Section: 2nd.

SANBORN Roy Ernest b Hopkinton Oct 29, 1894 child of SANBORN Simeon F carpenter b Boscawen & Blanche H b Haverhill Vol: 5 Page: 055 Line: 023 Section: 2nd.

ROLLINS Agnes May b Hopkinton Nov 2, 1894 child of ROLLINS William H farmer b Hopkinton & Margaret P b Beaufort NC Vol: 5 Page: 055 Line: 024 Section: 2nd.

BALL Perla Cecil b Hopkinton Nov 2, 1894 child of BALL Albert F painter b Vermont & GILMAN Melvina L b Canada Vol: 5 Page: 055 Line: 025 Section: 2nd.

DUNBAR Arthur Eugene b Hopkinton Nov 15, 1894 child of DUNBAR Eugene E carpenter b Hopkinton & DUNBAR Mary E b Dunbarton Vol: 5 Page: 055 Line: 026 Section: 2nd.

GOODWIN Mary Margurite b Hopkinton Nov 19, 1894 child of GOODWIN Wm Knapp r r section b New Brunswick & JOHNSON Hattie J b Nova Scotia Vol: 5 Page: 055 Line: 027 Section: 2nd.

WHYTOCK ---- b Hopkinton Nov 19, 1894 child of WHYTOCK David butcher b Madoc Canada & Bella b Huntington Canada Vol: 5 Page: 055 Line: 028 Section: 2nd.

STANLEY Frederick W b Hopkinton Nov 25, 1894 child of STANLEY John N brakeman b Grafton & HUNTOON Minnie B b Andover Vol: 5 Page: 057 Line: 001 Section: 2nd.

SIMON ---- b Hopkinton Dec 7, 1894 child of SIMON True laborer b Canada & PAIGE Leora b Canada Vol: 5 Page: 057 Line: 002 Section: 2nd.

Hopkinton, NH Births 1880

MORAN ---- b Hopkinton Aug 31, 1895 child of MORAN Christopher fireman b Concord & Mary b Ireland Vol: 5 Page: 059 Line: 026 Section: 2nd.

WATTS Mildred E b Hopkinton Dec 14, 1894 child of WATTS Charles F currier b Hopkinton & Mary A b Hopkinton Vol: 5 Page: 057 Line: 003 Section: 2nd.

HACKETT Jennnie May** b Hopkinton Dec 13, 1894 child of HACKETT Walter farmer b Sanbornton & CROWELL Nellie b Hopkinton Vol: 5 Page: 057 Line: 004 Section: 2nd Correction: correction in 1962.

CHANDLER ---- b Hopkinton Jan 2, 1895 child of CHANDLER Frank W freeman b Hopkinton & ROGERS Margery S b Hopkinton Vol: 5 Page: 059 Line: 001 Section: 2nd.

FIFIELD Alice Leola b Hopkinton Jan 3, 1895 child of FIFIELD Frank A mechanic b Alstead & BACON Annie L b Hopkinton Vol: 5 Page: 059 Line: 002 Section: 2nd.

JEPSON Clara Belle b Hopkinton Feb 11, 1895 child of JEPSON James carpenter b Warner & TAYLOR Mattie M b Hopkinton Vol: 5 Page: 059 Line: 003 Section: 2nd.

KIMBALL ---- b Hopkinton Mar 7, 1895 child of KIMBALL Nelson D farmer b Hopkinton & PATCH Adalade M b Newfield Me Vol: 5 Page: 059 Line: 004 Section: 2nd.

BERRY Samuel Quimby** b Hopkinton Mar 25, 1895 child of BERRY Fred L farmer b Holderness & FIELD Nellie b Portland Me Vol: 5 Page: 059 Line: 005 Section: 2nd.

KIMBALL Grace Paulina b Hopkinton Mar 12, 1895 child of KIMBALL Herbert M farmer b Hopkinton & COLBY Abbie b Bow Vol: 5 Page: 059 Line: 006 Section: 2nd.

ADAMS Howard Daniel b Hopkinton Apr 10, 1895 child of ADAMS William H H tinsmith b Concord & BROWN Laura b Thornton Vol: 5 Page: 059 Line: 007 Section: 2nd.

EASTMAN Timothy Stedman b Hopkinton Apr 30, 1895 child of EASTMAN Clarence M salesman b Warner & SCOTT Mary J b Newwark N J Vol: 5 Page: 059 Line: 008 Section: 2nd.

MILTON Olive b Hopkinton Jun 10, 1895 child of MILTON Willie A farmer b Hopkinton & MOORE Carrie b Otis Mass Vol: 5 Page: 059 Line: 059 Section: 2nd.

ANDREWS Walter Shirley b Hopkinton Jun 12, 1895 child of ANDREWS C Y W machinst b Limerick & MILLER Hannah J b Nova Scotia Vol: 5 Page: 059 Line: 010 Section: 2nd.

RUSS Viola Marguerite b Hopkinton Jul 3, 1895 child of RUSS William C merchant b Nashua & COLBY Nora M b Mass Vol: 5 Page: 059 Line: 011 Section: 2nd.

ORDWAY Ardenna Villa b Hopkinton Jul 19, 1895 child of ORDWAY George L farmer b Concord & DURGIN Ella J b Wilmot Vol: 5 Page: 059 Line: 012 Section: 2nd.

CALL Florence Lela b Hopkinton Jul 22, 1895 child of CALL Edward laborer b Warner & JARDINE Bessie b Boston Mass Vol: 5 Page: 059 Line: 013 Section: 2nd.

Hopkinton, NH Births 1880

CHASE Leon Thornton b Hopkinton Aug 1, 1895 child of CHASE Oscar N farmer b Hopkinton & THORNTON Maragaret b Manchester England Vol: 5 Page: 059 Line: 014 Section: 2nd.

CARTE Russell Weley b Hopkinton Aug 7, 1895 child of CARTER Wm T clergyman b Calaire Me & GRIFFORD Ann E b W Falmouth Mass Vol: 5 Page: 059 Line: 015 Section: 2nd.

CONANT Hiram Eugene b Hopkinton Aug 12, 1895 child of CONANT Dwight E silk mfg b Willimantic Conn & KEMP Blanche L b Concord Vol: 5 Page: 059 Line: 016 Section: 2nd.

DOW Ernest Clyde b Hopkinton Aug 26, 1895 child of DOW Samuel Oscar farmer b Hopkinton & WOOD Grace M b Pepperell Mass Vol: 5 Page: 059 Line: 017 Section: 2nd.

BOHONAN Josephine A b Hopkinton Jul 12, 1895 child of BOHONAN John W farmer b Hopkinton & JEWELL Delia A b Weare Vol: 5 Page: 059 Line: 018 Section: 2nd Correction: see correction in 1946.

CLOUGH Richard Rowe b Hopkinton Sep 1, 1895 child of CLOUGH George A clerk b Hopkinton & ROWE Sara B b Boston Mass Vol: 5 Page: 059 Line: 019 Section: 2nd.

FOOTE Mabel Helen b Hopkinton Sep 24, 1895 child of FOOTE William N painter b Farmington Me & WATTS Helen M b Hopkinton Vol: 5 Page: 059 Line: 020 Section: 2nd.

CURRIER Mary Della b Hopkinton Sep 26, 1895 child of CURRIER Willie A farmer b Hopkinton & WEBSTER Gertie J b Concord Vol: 5 Page: 059 Line: 021 Section: 2nd.

TANDY James Everett b Hopkinton Oct 16, 1895 child of TANDY John G farmer b Concord & HALLIDAY Minnie M b New Boston Vol: 5 Page: 059 Line: 022 Section: 2nd.

BOYCE Weley Adson ** b Hopkinton Nov 3, 1895 child of BOYCE Melzer D laborer b Concord & ORDWAY Alice C b Concord Vol: 5 Page: 059 Line: 023 Section: 2nd.

WELCH ---- ** b Hopkinton Nov 17, 1895 child of WELCH William laborer b Concord & HEATH Sadie b Boscawen Vol: 5 Page: 059 Line: 024 Section: 2nd Correction: correction in 1947 **.

FLANDERS Elmer Howard b Hopkinton Oct 29, 1895 child of FLANDERS Samuel farmer b Concord & PERKINS Nellie B b Epsom Vol: 5 Page: 059 Line: 025 Section: 2nd.

GOODWIN Grace Darling b Hopkinton Jan 5, 1896 child of GOODWIN Wm Knapp farmer b New Brunswick & JOHNSON Hattie b Nova Scotia Vol: 5 Page: 061 Line: 001 Section: 2nd.

DUSTIN ---- b Jan 11, 1896 child of DUSTIN Cyrus F farmer b Hopkinton & SPAULDING Nellie S b Manchester Vol: 5 Page: 061 Line: 002 Section: 2nd.

PHALEN Francis Elmer b Hopkinton Feb 13, 1896 child of PHALEN James H & WIGHT Florence b Hopkinton Vol: 5 Page: 061 Line: 002 Section: 2nd.

DUNBAR Charles Morton b Hopkinton Feb 23, 1896 child of DUNBAR Henry P farmer b Hopkinton & DANFORTH Emma L b Webster Vol: 5 Page: 061 Line: 004 Section: 2nd.

Hopkinton, NH Births 1880

KIMBALL Edwin Nelson b Hopkinton Apr 19, 1896 child of KIMBALL Nelson D b Hopkinton & ADELAID M b Newfield Me Vol: 5 Page: 061 Line: 005 Section: 2nd.

CARNES Herbert Clifton b Hopkinton Apr 26, 1896 child of CARNES Herbert shoe mfg b Henniker & KEMP Clara May b West Concord Vol: 5 Page: 061 Line: 006 Section: 2nd.

ELLIOTT Eddie Elmer b Hopkinton May 3, 1896 child of ELLIOTT Edson E farmer b Webster & COLBY Nettie b Deering Vol: 5 Page: 061 Line: 007 Section: 2nd.

BOUTWELL Leroy A ** b Hopkinton Mar 25, 1896 child of BOUTWELL Arthur J lumberman b Hopkinton & FITTS Carrie J b Dunbarton Vol: 5 Page: 061 Line: 008 Section: 2nd Correction: correction in 1942.

DUNBAR Grace Mand b Hopkinton May 12, 1896 child of DUNBAR Elmer Eugene carpenter b Hopkinton & PAIGE Mary E b Dunbarton Vol: 5 Page: 061 Line: 009 Section: 2nd.

STEVENS Ernest Lee b Hopkinton May 21, 1896 child of STEVENS Ernest L merchant b Manchester & RICHARDSON Nettie M b Hopkinton Vol: 5 Page: 061 Line: 010 Section: 2nd.

LIBBY Geo Keniston b Hopkinton Jun 16, 1896 child of LIBBY George A carpenter b Webster & KENISTIN Stella b Andover Vol: 5 Page: 061 Line: 011 Section: 2nd.

CURTIS Faith Helen b Hopkinton May 15, 1896 child of CURTIS John S clergyman b Presque Isle Me & LORD Fannie A b Lebanon Me Vol: 5 Page: 061 Line: 012 Section: 2nd.

EMERSON Fred Harold b Hopkinton Jul 16, 1896 child of EMERSON Fred H farmer b Hopkinton & KIMBALL Nellie F b Maine Vol: 5 Page: 061 Line: 013 Section: 2nd.

CHANDLER Ella Kimball b Hopkinton Aug 8, 1896 child of CHANDLER Frank hostler b Hopkinton & ROGERS Margery b Hopkinton Vol: 5 Page: 061 Line: 014 Section: 2nd.

CONANT Dwight Lucien b Hopkinton Aug 25, 1896 child of CONANT Eugene Dwight silk mfg b Willmantic Con & KEMP Blanche L b Concord Vol: 5 Page: 061 Line: 015 Section: 2nd.

SCRIBNER Clair B ** b Hopkinton Sep 11, 1896 child of SCRIBNER Gilman farmer b Bucksport Me & BENNETT Mary b Milo Vt Vol: 5 Page: 061 Line: 016 Section: 2nd Correction: ** correction 1942 records.

CONANT Paul Winfield b Hopkinton Sep 15, 1896 child of CONANT Frank E silk mfg b Mansfield Conn & BURNS Alice S b Mystic Conn Vol: 5 Page: 061 Line: 017 Section: 2nd.

MILLS Elmer Frank b Hopkinton Aug 31, 1896 child of MILLS Frank C carpenter b Hopkinton & HOWARD Mary b Newport Vol: 5 Page: 061 Line: 018 Section: 2nd.

SANBORN Sadie Wand b Hopkinton Oct 6, 1896 child of SANBORN Herman farmer b Webster & FRENCH Lizzie b Northfield Vol: 5 Page: 061 Line: 019 Section: 2nd.

Hopkinton, NH Births 1880

FOOTE ---- b Hopkinton Oct 18, 1896 child of FOOTE William H painter b Farmington Me & WATTS Helen b Hopkinton Vol: 5 Page: 061 Line: 020 Section: 2nd.

DUSTIN Harrison Rufus b Hopkinton Sep 24, 1896 child of DUSTIN Arthur M blacksmith b Boscawen & CLOUGH Josie E b Hopkinton Vol: 5 Page: 061 Line: 021 Section: 2nd.

FISK ---- b Hopkinton Jan 6, 1897 child of FISK Daniel lumberman b Hopkinton & CHANDLER Delle b Hopkinton Vol: 5 Page: 063 Line: 001 Section: 2nd.

GREENLAND Frank Henry b Hopkinton Jan 11, 1897 child of GREENLAND Delmer farmer b Deer Island Me & SANBORN Lizzie b Webster Vol: 5 Page: 063 Line: 002 Section: 2nd.

WHYTOCK Vada Isabell b Hopkinton Feb 2, 1897 child of WHYTOCK David W butcher b Madoc Canada & FLEMING Isabella b Huntington Canada Vol: 5 Page: 063 Line: 003 Section: 2nd.

RUSS Clarence K b Hopkinton Feb 3, 1897 child of RUSS William C clerk b Nashua & COLBY Nora M b Mass Vol: 5 Page: 063 Line: 004 Section: 2nd.

SANBORN Carl Roscoe b Hopkinton Feb 19, 1897 child of SANBORN Simeon carpenter b Webster & WHITTIER Hattie B b Haverhill Vol: 5 Page: 063 Line: 005 Section: 2nd.

DWINNELLS Florence A b Hopkinton Mar 14, 1897 child of DWINNELLS Frank P farmer b Hopkinton & LIBBY Emma H b Hopkinton Vol: 5 Page: 063 Line: 006 Section: 2nd.

SMART Florence May b Hopkinton Mar 22, 1897 child of SMART Benjamin r r section b Hopkinton & BARTLETT Stella G b Warner Vol: 5 Page: 063 Line: 007 Section: 2nd.

SIMEON ---- b Hopkinton Mar 25, 1897 child of SIMEON True laborer b Canada & PAIGE Lenora b Canada Vol: 5 Page: 063 Line: 008 Section: 2nd.

WALKER Bertha Lorraine b Hopkinton Apr 27, 1897 child of WALKER Robert E farmer b Manchester & HUTCHINSON Bella E b Roxbury Vt Vol: 5 Page: 063 Line: 009 Section: 2nd.

THOMPSON Ruth M b Hopkinton Jun 5, 1897 child of THOMPSON William clergyman b Magherafelt Ireland & BERRY Alice Mabel b Newington Vol: 5 Page: 063 Line: 010 Section: 2nd.

BROWN Hazel Bell May b Hopkinton Jun 27, 1897 child of BROWN Willis domestic b Hopkinton & McINTIRE Dora b Sweden Vol: 5 Page: 063 Line: 011 Section: 2nd.

MILTON Dorothy Mae b Hopkinton Jul 3, 1897 child of MILTON Will H farmer b Hopkinton & MOORE Carrie b Otis Mass Vol: 5 Page: 063 Line: 013 Section: 2nd.

GOODWIN Hattie H b Hopkinton Aug 9, 1897 child of GOODWIN Wm K farmer b Nova Scotia & JOHNSON Hattie b New Brunswick Vol: 5 Page: 063 Line: 014 Section: 2nd.

CLOUGH Gladys Mary b Hopkinton Aug 11, 1897 child of CLOUGH Charles E farmer b Hopkinton & HASTINGS Gertrude b Hopkinton Vol: 5 Page: 063 Line: 015 Section: 2nd.

HOWE Bernice May b Hopkinton Aug 20, 1897 child of HOWE Edward farmer b Warner & WYMAN Etta b Bradford Vol: 5 Page: 063 Line: 016 Section: 2nd.

HUNTOON Ora Morse b Hopkinton Aug 21, 1897 child of HUNTOON Arthur C clerk b Unity & EASTMAN Ethlyn A b Warner Vol: 5 Page: 063 Line: 017 Section: 2nd.

BOUTWELL Harley ** b Hopkinton Aug 11, 1897 child of BOUTWELL Arthur J lumberman b Hopkinton & FITTS Carrie J b Dunbarton Vol: 5 Page: 063 Line: 018 Section: 2nd Correction: correction- 1949 records.

WELCH Ethel b Hopkinton Sep 30, 1897 child of WELCH William stone work b Concord & HEATH Sadie b Boscawen Vol: 5 Page: 063 Line: 019 Section: 2nd.

CURRIER Sadie Frances b Hopkinton Oct 7, 1897 child of CURRIER Willie farmer b Hopkinton & WEBSTER Gertie b Hopkinton Vol: 5 Page: 063 Line: 020 Section: 2nd.

CHASE Mirriam b Hopkinton Nov 14, 1897 child of CHASE Charles T laborer b Charleston Mass & WEBBER Florence b Hopkinton Vol: 5 Page: 063 Line: 021 Section: 2nd.

SANDERSON Arthur Garvin b Hopkinton Sep 4, 1897 child of SANDERSON Elisha clergyman b Vt & GARVIN Clara W b Rollinsford Vol: 5 Page: 063 Line: 022 Section: 2nd.

MAKEPEACE ---- b Hopkinton Dec 29, 1897 child of MAKEPEACE George A b Concord & POLAND Mammie E b Hopkinton Vol: 5 Page: 063 Line: 023 Section: 2nd.

BOUTWELL Helen R b Hopkinton Sep 26, 1897 child of BOUTWELL Wallace E farmer b Methuen Mass & WARD Lily A b Cambridgeport Mass Vol: 5 Page: 063 Line: 024 Section: 2nd.

MERRILL Jennie b Hopkinton May 26, 1879 child of MERRILL Frank farmer b Hopkinton & FLANDERS Ida b Webster Vol: 5 Page: 019 Line: 003 Section: 1st.

GILE Frank E b Hopkinton Jun 4, 1879 child of GILE Edwin R farmer b Thetford Vt & STORY Abby M b Hopkinton Vol: 5 Page: 019 Line: 004 Section: 1st.

MILLS Walter B b Hopkinton Jul 24, 1879 child of MILLS George W laborer b Hopkinton & BROWN Eunice b Concord Vol: 5 Page: 019 Line: 009 Section: 1st.

MUDGETT Lillie J b Hopkinton Aug 30, 1879 child of MUDGETT Will E farmer b Bristol & CHASE Dona?? b Warner Vol: 5 Page: 019 Line: 013 Section: 1st.

BOHONAN Elsie Dianna b Hopkinton Sep 26, 1879 child of BOHONAN John farmer b Sutton & JEWELL Delia A b Weare Vol: 5 Page: 019 Line: 016 Section: 1st.

EVANS ---- b Hopkinton Oct 11, 1879 child of EVANS Hanson D farmer b Hopkinton & MILLS Mary b Dunbarton Vol: 5 Page: 019 Line: 018 Section: 1st.

GOVE ---- b Hopkinton Nov 28, 1879 child of GOVE George P farmer b Henniker & ROWELL Mary Etta b Hopkinton Vol: 5 Page: 019 Line: 020 Section: 1st.

BOHONAN Ida Mary b Hopkinton Dec 15, 1879 child of BOHONAN David N farmer b Sutton & FISK Jennie b Hopkinton Vol: 5 Page: 019 Line: 021 Section: 1st.

McCOY Philp Jarvis b Hopkinton Mar 19, 1880 child of McCOY James N roofer b Thornton & Alice F b Hopkinton Vol: 5 Page: 019 Line: 027 Section: 1st.

Hopkinton, NH Births 1880

GOVE ---- b Hopkinton Nov 28, 1879 child of GOVE George farmer b Henniker & ROWELL Mary Etta b Hopkinton Vol: 5 Page: 019 Line: 028 Section: 1st.

DUNN ---- b Hopkinton Jun 12, 1880 child of DUNN Albert b Manchester & FOOTE Florence b Concord Vol: 5 Page: 021 Line: 007 Section: 1st.

UPTON Freddie E b Hopkinton Jan 22, 1881 child of UPTON Edson wheelwright b Concord & Eunice b Hopkinton Vol: 5 Page: 021 Line: 018 Section: 1st.

MILLS Bertie E b Hopkinton Jan 29, 1881 child of MILLS Charles laborer b Hopkinton & TOWNE Olive U b Weare Vol: 5 Page: 021 Line: 019 Section: 1st.

PALMER Albert O b Hopkinton Nov 12, 1881 child of PALMER Willie O clerk b Hopkinton & CLARK Cora J b Antrim Vol: 5 Page: 023 Line: 019 Section: 1st.

MORGAN Richard F b Hopkinton Aug 1, 1882 child of MORGAN Frank N farmer b Hopkinton & BOHONAN Linda b Sutton Vol: 5 Page: 025 Line: 023 Section: 1st.

COLBY Myron Hillard b Hopkinton Apr 5, 1883 child of COLBY Forest farmer b Litchfield & Abbie N b Dunbarton Vol: 5 Page: 027 Line: 001 Section: 1st.

CHASE Bertha Mand b Hopkinton May 24, 1883 child of CHASE George farmer b Hopkinton & FISK Jennie b Hopkinton Vol: 5 Page: 027 Line: 006 Section: 1st.

BROWN Nellie A b Hopkinton Jun 9, 1883 child of BROWN Valorous laborer b Hopkinton & LIBBEY Sarah b Webster Vol: 5 Page: 027 Line: 007 Section: 1st.

CARR Caroline Elizabeth b Hopkinton Jan 27, 1849 child of CARR John?? farmer Vol: 5 Page: 028 Line: 007 Section: 1st Note: check vital records xx.

CHANDLER Arthur Charles b Hopkinton Apr 27, 1898 child of CHANDLER Arthur farmer b Henniker & CORBETT Ida b North Coventy Conn Vol: 6 Page: 001.

CONANT Lena Mable b Hopkinton May 2, 1898 child of CONANT Dwight E silk mfg b Williamintic Conn & KEMP Blanche L b Concord Vol: 6 Page: 001.

BROWN Clifford Marden b Hopkinton May 16, 1898 child of BROWN Charles L farmer b England & BROWNE Hattie Roberts b England Vol: 6 Page: 002.

DWINNELLS Edna Maude b Hopkinton May 20, 1898 child of DWINNELLS George A laborer b Hopkinton & HOWLEY Mary b Portland Me Vol: 6 Page: 002.

GUIMOND Laura b Hopkinton May 15, 1898 child of GUIMOND Zoel laborer b Canada & PAGE Leora b Canada Vol: 6 Page: 002 Correction: correction 8/12/59.

HOOPER ---- b Hopkinton Jul 9, 1898 child of HOOPER Thomas W farmer b Mass & BARTLETT Minnie M b Manchester Vol: 6 Page: 002.

KIMBALL Nelson Lewis Butler b Hopkinton Jul 16, 1898 child of KIMBALL Nelson D farmer b Hopkinton & PATCH Adelaide?? b Newfield Vol: 6 Page: 002.

FRAZIER Pearl Leeola b Hopkinton Aug 14, 1898 child of FRAZIER E E teamster b East Burke Vt & ALDRICH Maggie S b East Haven Vt Vol: 6 Page: 003.

BROWN Preston K b Hopkinton Sep 11, 1898 child of BROWN William L lumberman b Ossipee & SMITH Alice L M b New London Vol: 6 Page: 003.

ELLIOTT Carrie F b Hopkinton Sep 23, 1898 child of ELLIOTT Edson E farmer b Hopkinton & COLBY Nettie L b Deering Vol: 6 Page: 003.

BOUTWELL Llewellyn b Hopkinton Sep 27, 1898 child of BOUTWELL Arthur J lumber dealer b Hopkinton & FITTS Carrie J b Dunbarton Vol: 6 Page: 003.

Hopkinton, NH Births 1880

SANBORN Marion L b Hopkinton Nov 22, 1898 child of SANBORN Simeon F carpenter b Webster & WHITCHER Hattie B b Haverhill Vol: 6 Page: 003.

RICE Carl Jewell b Hopkinton Dec 5, 1898 child of RICE James G farmer b Henniker & BOHONAN Bernice M b Hopkinton Vol: 6 Page: 004.

SPOFFORD Ralph William b Hopkinton Dec 27, 1898 child of SPOFFORD Arthur F farmer b Hopkinton & DODGE Maud E b Hopkinton Vol: 6 Page: 004.

SPOFFORD Ethel May b Hopkinton Mar 21, 1898 child of SPOFFORD Eugene F farmer b Hopkinton & MILLS Nellie E b Hopkinton Vol: 6 Page: 004.

KIMBALL Harry Gilman b Hopkinton Dec 13, 1898 child of KIMBALL Herbert M farmer b Hopkinton & COLBY Mabbie b Bow Vol: 6 Page: 004.

CLOUGH Williard b Hopkinton Jan 26, 1899 child of CLOUGH George A clerk b Hopkinton & ROWE Sara B b Boston Mass Vol: 6 Page: 005.

CURRIER Nettie K b Hopkinton Feb 9, 1899 child of CURRIER Willie A farmer b Hopkinton & WEBSTER Gertie b Hopkinton Vol: 6 Page: 005.

LILLIFORD Samuel Fuller b Hopkinton Feb 26, 1899 child of LILLIEFORD Manford clergyman b Kolshult Sweden & FACKENTHAL Katherine b Burham Penn Vol: 6 Page: 005 Correction: correction in 1941.

DERRY Hazel Julia Page b Hopkinton Mar 18, 1899 child of DERRY Joseph E blacksmith b Hopkinton & PAGE Elvira C b Dunbarton Vol: 6 Page: 005.

BUCLAIR Marie b Hopkinton Mar 24, 1899 child of BUCLAIR Mathias laborer b St Flora Canada Pq & MARTELL Rosa b Manchester Vol: 6 Page: 005.

CHASE Martha Elizabeth b Hopkinton Mar 26, 1899 child of CHASE Fredric H lumberman b Hopkinton & JACKMMAN Lillian I b Concord Vol: 6 Page: 005.

ELLIOTT Marion Kate b Hopkinton Apr 2, 1899 child of ELLIOTT Charles E farmer b Hopkinton & HOWE Gertrude H b Jamacia Plains Mass Vol: 6 Page: 006.

PAGE ---- b Hopkinton Apr 7, 1899 child of PAGE William M teamster b Henniker & DWINNELLS Jennie E b Hopkinton Vol: 6 Page: 006.

WALKER Bessie Lorreine* b Hopkinton Apr 12, 1899 child of WALKER Robert E farmer b Manchester & HUTCHINSON Bell E b Hopkinton Vol: 6 Page: 006 Correction: * correction 1953.

CLARK Louise Eldora* b Hopkinton Apr 10, 1899 child of CLARK Henry G farmer b Manchester & WINCH Bertha M C b Boston Mass Vol: 6 Page: 006 Correction: * correction in 1962.

CHANDLER Eva May b Hopkinton May 13, 1899 child of CHANDLER Arthur farmer b Henniker & CORBETT Ida b North Coventry Conn Vol: 6 Page: 006.

DWINNELLS Franklin b Hopkinton Jun 15, 1899 child of DWINNELLS Franklin P section hand b Hopkinton & LIBBY Emily Helen b Hopkinton Vol: 6 Page: 007.

DUNBAR Howard Class b Hopkinton May 25, 1899 child of DUNBAR Henry B carpenter b Hopkinton & DANFORTH Emma Vol: 6 Page: 007.

HARDY Dorathy Eliz b Hopkinton Jul 6, 1899 child of HARDY Stillman A farmer b Hopkinton & BAGLEY Pauline b Melbourne Australia Vol: 6 Page: 007.

REDINGTON Ira Bernice b Hopkinton Jul 24, 1899 child of REDINGTON Clarence M farmer b Claremont & PIERCE Martha E b Warner Vol: 6 Page: 007.

BOUTWELL Harriet b Hopkinton Aug 8, 1899 child of BOUTWELL Henry B A commission b Berlin Ill & MONTGOMERY Alice b Hopkinton Vol: 6 Page: 007.

Hopkinton, NH Births 1880

MARSH ---- b Hopkinton Aug 29, 1899 child of MARSH Frank P merchant b Dunbarton & GREENEY Marrietta b Antrim Vol: 6 Page: 007.

LIBBY Roger William b Hopkinton Aug 11, 1899 child of LIBBY Joseph G laborer b Salisbury & BARTLETT Clara b Warner Vol: 6 Page: 008.

CHASE Fred Nelson b Hopkinton Aug 21, 1899 child of CHASE Nelson A section man b Hopkinton & CLARK Anna J b Warner Vol: 6 Page: 008.

DEARBORN Karl Bert b Hopkinton Jul 21, 1899 child of DEARBORN William C stage driver b Chester & MOULTON Bell b Strafford Vt Vol: 6 Page: 008.

HARRINGTON Carl Edward b Hopkinton Aug 27, 1899 child of HARRINGTON Moses B blacksmith b Hopkinton & BARKER Lillian b Lebanon Vol: 6 Page: 008.

SPOFFORD Ernest John b Hopkinton Aug 28, 1899 child of SPOFFORD Eugene F farmer b Hopkinton & MILLS Nellie E b Hopkinton Vol: 6 Page: 008.

RUSS Alice Emerson b Hopkinton Sep 25, 1899 child of RUSS William C mechanic b Nashua & COLBY Nora M b So Seekonk Mass Vol: 6 Page: 008.

COOPER Marion Viola b Hopkinton Oct 14, 1899 child of COOPER Herbert D laborer b Concord & BURGESS Gertrude V b Caribou Me Vol: 6 Page: 009.

FLANDERS Lucy Carter b Hopkinton Dec 28, 1899 child of FLANDERS Walter N farmer b Warner & THOMPSON Lizzie S b Concord Vol: 6 Page: 009.

BOND ---- * b Hopkinton Dec 29, 1899 child of BOND Walter P farmer b Manchester & FULLER Abbie M b Bow Vol: 6 Page: 009 Correction: * correction see 1950.

FOOTE Wm Nelson * b Hopkinton Dec 12, 1899 child of FOOTE William N hostler b Maine & WATTS Helen b Webster Vol: 6 Page: 009 Correction: correction 1949.

ADAMS Irving Nelson b Hopkinton Jan 6, 1900 child of ADAMS Claud D painter b Hopkinton & GETCHELL Cora B b Hopkinton Vol: 6 Page: 010.

HARDY Mildred Pearl b Hopkinton Mar 1, 1900 child of HARDY Lewis B r r section b Hopkinton & HAZELTON Grace M b Hopkinton Vol: 6 Page: 010.

HARDY Marion Grace b Hopkinton Mar 1, 1900 child of HARDY Lewis B r r section b Hopkinton & HAZELTON Grace M b Hopkinton Vol: 6 Page: 010.

HEMPHILL Edwin Earl* b Hopkinton Apr 23, 1900 child of KENNETT Chas Edgar shoe maker & HEMPHILL Laura May b Henniker Vol: 6 Page: 010 Correction: *correction 1945.

MORRILL Robert L b Hopkinton May 18, 1900 child of MORRILL Stephen E farmer b Hopkinton & PERRY Emma L b Hopkinton Vol: 6 Page: 011.

BARTLETT Ira C b Hopkinton May 22, 1900 child of BARTLETT Ira C laborer b Laconia & THERRON Rose b St Pa Canada Vol: 6 Page: 011.

CHANDLER William H b Hopkinton Aug 8, 1900 child of CHANDLER George W farmer b Hopkinton & DURNIN Sarah b Scotland Vol: 6 Page: 011.

SYMONDS Mabel * b Hopkinton Sep 4, 1900 child of SYMONDS Wm W farmer b Concord & BURNHAM Alice M b Hillsboro Vol: 6 Page: 011 Correction: correction 1944.

RICHARDSON Dorris b Hopkinton Sep 10, 1900 child of RICHARDSON Fred E laborer b Goffstown & RAND Bessie M b Goffstown Vol: 6 Page: 011.

CONANT George E b Hopkinton Dec 19, 1900 child of CONANT Dwight E silk mfg b Willimantic Conn & KEMP Blanche L b Concord Vol: 6 Page: 012.

Hopkinton, NH Births 1880

HASTINGS Floyd Delmer b Hopkinton Jan 5, 1901 child of HASTINGS Delmer W farmer b Hopkinton & CHASE Lena M b Hopkinton Vol: 6 Page: 013.

GRAY Harriet M J b Hopkinton Mar 13, 1901 child of GRAY Charles E laborer b Lebanon & HUCHINS Florence E b Thetford Vt Vol: 6 Page: 013.

CHASE Emily Alphia b Hopkinton Apr 14, 1901 child of CHASE Fred J farmer b Hopkinton & HARDY Emma A b Warner Vol: 6 Page: 013.

LaCLAIR Class b Hopkinton Apr 15, 1901 child of LaCLAIR Charles laborer b Wells River Canada & AMELLE Matilda b St Jais Canada Vol: 6 Page: 013.

BROWN Marguerite U b Hopkinton May 22, 1901 child of BROWN Lanson O painter b Thornton & FLEMING Melissa b Ontario Vol: 6 Page: 014.

SWEATT Marion Julia b Hopkinton Apr 25, 1901 child of SWEATT Edward C r r sec foreman b Hopkinton & HOLMES Hattie B b Andover Vol: 6 Page: 014.

HARDY Regnold S b Hopkinton May 8, 1901 child of HARDY Stillman A farmer b Hopkinton & BAGLEY Pauline b Melbourne Australia Vol: 6 Page: 014.

SPOFFORD Clarence A b Hopkinton May 12, 1901 child of SPOFFORD Arthur F farmer b Hopkinton & DODGE Maud E b Hopkinton Vol: 6 Page: 014.

MATHESON Alice Eliza b Hopkinton Jun 15, 1901 child of MATHESON Frank silversmith b Concord & HOYT Mabel D b Hopkinton Vol: 6 Page: 014.

GAUTHIER Blance Pearl b Hopkinton Jun 20, 1901 child of GAUTHIER Napoleon cigar mfg b Canada & CHAMPAIN Alice M b Raymond Vol: 6 Page: 015.

CARNES Thomas Dorion b Hopkinton Jul 4, 1901 child of CARNES James G clergyman b Portland Me & DORION Laurie b St Andrews P Q Vol: 6 Page: 015.

HOWE Belle b Hopkinton Jul 30, 1901 child of HOWE Edwin B farmer b Warner & WYMAN Etta M b Bradford Vol: 6 Page: 015.

HILAND Minnie Beatrice b Hopkinton Aug 4, 1901 child of HILAND John M farmer b Hopkinton & LAMPSON?? Susie M b Dunbarton Vol: 6 Page: 015.

KIMBALL ---- b Hopkinton Sep 7, 1901 child of KIMBALL Nelson D farmer b Hopkinton & PATCH Adelaide b Newfield Me Vol: 6 Page: 016 Note: xx name and date.

DWINNELLS John Arthur b Hopkinton Aug 26, 1901 child of DWINNELLS George A farmer b Hopkinton & HOWLEY Mary b Portland Me Vol: 6 Page: 016.

DODGE Catherine Eliza b Hopkinton Sep 26, 1901 child of DODGE Frank E lumberman b Webster & McFEELERS Annie b Sheldon Vt Vol: 6 Page: 016.

WELCH ---- b Hopkinton Oct 6, 1901 child of WELCH Samuel A saw mill hand b York Me & PINNEY Sarah b New Haven Conn Vol: 6 Page: 017.

BAILEY ---- b Hopkinton Mar 11, 1884 child of BAILEY Eugene B farmer b Sutton & BROWN Bell M b Weare Vol: 5 Page: 033 Line: 002 Section: 2nd.

FLANDERS Albert Elliot b Hopkinton Oct 19, 1901 child of FLANDERS Walter N farmer b Warner & THOMPSON S Lizzie b Concord Vol: 6 Page: 017.

HODGMAN ---- b Hopkinton Oct 17, 1901 child of HODGMAN Henry laborer b Concord & BOYNTON Ella b Dunbarton Vol: 6 Page: 017.

HANANAFORD Theadore M b Hopkinton Nov 1, 1901 child of HANNAFORD Edward N laborer b Peterboro & HUTCHINSOSN Lucy E b Kennebuckport Me Vol: 6 Page: 017.

Hopkinton, NH Births 1880

WHYLOCK Mary Edna b Hopkinton Dec 16, 1901 child of WHYLOCK David W butcher b Madoe Canada & FLEMMING Isabell b Huntington Canada Vol: 6 Page: 018.

WALKER ---- b Hopkinton Dec 15, 1901 child of WALKER Abraham painter b Barnston P Q & BRADBURY Mabel b Washington Vt Vol: 6 Page: 018.

FOOTE Charles Ralph b Hopkinton Sep 18, 1901 child of FOOTE William laborer b Maine & WATTS Helen Vol: 6 Page: 018.

BOUTWELL Helen R * b Hopkinton Sep 26, 1897 child of BOUTWELL Wallace Elmer fireman on r r b Hopkinton & WOOD Lillie A b Cambridge Mass Vol: 6 Page: 018 Correction: correction 1913.

BROWN Alfred Gordon b Hopkinton Oct 15, 1900 child of BROWN Charles L farmer b Yorkshire England & ROBERTS Nettie b St Austen England Vol: 6 Page: 012.

WELCH Richard George* b Hopkinton Nov 28, 1900 child of WELCH William M day laborer b Concord & STORY Sadie b Boscawen Vol: 6 Page: 012 Correction: correction in 1996.

CHANDLER Frances Ann b Hopkinton Dec 10, 1901 child of CHANDLER George W farmer b Hopkinton & DURNIN Sarah b Scotland Vol: 6 Page: 018.

RICE Neal James b Hopkinton Oct 25, 1900 child of RICE James G farmer b Henniker & BOHANAN Bernice M b Hopkinton Vol: 6 Page: 012.

CHANDLER Ruth I b Hopkinton Nov 18, 1900 child of CHANDLER Henry C farmer b Hopkinton & McCULLIS Hattie M b Suncook Vol: 6 Page: 012.

MARSH Thalma Leola b Hopkinton Dec 11, 1900 child of MARSH Frank P fish dealer b Weare & DUSTIN Etta R b Antrim Vol: 6 Page: 012.

PAIGE Marion b Hopkinton Feb 1, 1901 child of PAIGE Thomas W farmer b Lowell Mass & STRAW Minnie B b Hopkinton Vol: 6 Page: 013.

MORRILL Bertha b Hopkinton Apr 27, 1901 child of MORRILL Stephen E farmer b Hopkinton & PERRY Emma L b Hopkinton Vol: 6 Page: 013.

FULLER Una Sarah b Hopkinton Apr 28, 1901 child of FULLER William F printer b Hopkinton & ELKINS Eva B b Thornton Vol: 6 Page: 014.

CLARK James A b Hopkinton Jul 8, 1901 child of CLARK Henry G farmer b Manchester & WINCH Bertha C b Boston Mass Vol: 6 Page: 015.

SMITH Leroy C b Hopkinton Aug 2, 1901 child of SMITH Robert teamester b Boscawen & BOYCE Ardella L b Concord Vol: 6 Page: 015.

PERRY Ralph b Hopkinton Aug 30, 1901 child of PERRY James M laborer b Hopkinton & KELLEY Thenie E b Hopkinton Vol: 6 Page: 016.

DUSTON John Stanley b Hopkinton Sep 17, 1901 child of DUSTON Arthur M farmer b Boscawen & CLOUGH Josie E b Hopkinton Vol: 6 Page: 016.

HARDY Elwin b Hopkinton Oct 14, 1901 child of HARDY Lewis B r r section b Hopkinton & HAZELTON Grace M b Hopkinton Vol: 6 Page: 017.

MILLS Charles Addison b Hopkinton Nov 4, 1901 child of MILLS Charles A carpenter b Hopkinton & CLARK Effie M b Weare Vol: 6 Page: 017.

WRIGHT Frank A b Hopkinton Aug 19, 1879 child of WRIGHT Oscar harness maker b Hopkinton & CURRIER Alba Vol: 5 Page: 019 Line: 011 Section: 1st.

GOUL ---- b Hopkinton Aug 19, 1881 child of GOUL Geor P farmer b Henniker & ROWELL Mary E b Hopkinton Vol: 5 Page: 023 Line: 009 Section: 1st.

Hopkinton, NH Births 1880

COURSER Blaanchard b Hopkinton Apr 3, 1880 child of COURSER Hamblet barber b Webster & HOLMES Belle Vol: 5 Page: 021 Line: 001 Section: 1st.

HEZELTON Gracie May b Hopkinton Sep 19, 1881 child of HAZELTON Herman R rule maker & DWINELLS Ellen Vol: 5 Page: 023 Line: 012 Section: 1st.

FOSS Everett A b Hopkinton Nov 13, 1881 child of FOSS John M farmer b Hopkinton & HOLMES Ida F b Bedford Vol: 5 Page: 023 Line: 020 Section: 1st.

BOHONAN Lester J b Hopkinton Feb 26, 1882 child of BOHANON John W farmer b Sutton & JEWELL Delia b Weare Vol: 5 Page: 023 Line: 028 Section: 1st.

GORMAN ---- b Hopkinton Nov 30, 1884 child of GORMAN Thomas farmer b Henniker & REID Jass b Hopkinton Vol: 5 Page: 033 Line: 014 Section: 2nd.

BARNES Fred D b Hopkinton Jul 18, 1882 child of BARNES George Dana farmer b Hennker & PHILBRICK Louisa Vol: 5 Page: 025 Line: 007 Section: 1st.

WATTS Arthur J b Hopkinton Dec 21, 1882 child of WATTS Charles F farmer b Warner & RION Mary b Hopkinton Vol: 5 Page: 025 Line: 017 Section: 1st.

MAXFIELD ---- b Hopkinton Jun 26, 1883 child of MAXFILED George farmer b Concord & BURROWS Sarah b Bow Vol: 5 Page: 027 Line: 002 Section: 1st.

HOYT Frank L b Hopkinton Oct 2, 1883 child of HOYT Walter F farmer b Hopkinton & PHELPS Sarah b Tilton Vol: 5 Page: 027 Line: 010 Section: 1st.

CARR Phillip Augustus b Hopkinton Jul 15, 1833 child of CARR John?? farmer Vol: 5 Page: 028 Line: 001 Section: 1st.

GOVE Ira Mary b Hopkinton Oct 28, 1883 child of GOVE George farmer b Hopkinton & ROWELL Mary b Hopkinton Vol: 5 Page: 027 Line: 018 Section: 1st.

BROWN Burt b Hopkinton Jan 13, 1890 child of BROWN Valorous laborer b Hopkinton & LIBBY Sarah b Webster Vol: 5 Page: 047 Line: 001 Section: 2nd.

CARR Charles Clinton b Hopkinton Jul 10, 1845 child of CARR John?? farmer Vol: 5 Page: 028 Line: 006 Section: 1st.

GORMAN ---- b Hopkinton Aug 15, 1886 child of GORMAN Thomas farmer b Henniker & REID Jean b Hopkinton Vol: 5 Page: 037 Line: 016 Section: 2nd.

BOHONAN Edna Francis b Hopkinton Nov 26, 1886 child of BOHONAN John W farmer b Sutton & DELIA A b Weare Vol: 5 Page: 037 Line: 021 Section: 2nd.

PERO Edwidge b Hopkinton Dec 26, 1886 child of PERO Louis woodchoper b Windsor Canada & Edwidge b Canada Vol: 5 Page: 037 Line: 025 Section: 2nd.

SANBORN Clara May b Hopkinton Jan 5, 1887 child of SANBORN Herman farmer b Webster & Lizzie b Northfield Vol: 5 Page: 039 Line: 001 Section: 2nd.

STRAW Blanche M b Hopkinton Dec 30, 1887 child of STRAW Andrew L F farmer b Hopkinton & Dolly b Hopkinton Vol: 5 Page: 041 Line: 003 Section: 2nd.

HOLMES Etta May b Hopkinton Jan 27, 1888 child of HOLMES Curtis D laborer b Salisbury & Mary E b Enfield Vol: 5 Page: 043 Line: 001 Section: 2nd.

PAIGE Bernice P b Hopkinton Aug 11, 1888 child of PAIGE Van R mechanic b Henniker & DOW Ella M b Henniker Vol: 5 Page: 043 Line: 009 Section: 2nd.

BOHONAN J Harry b Hopkinton Oct 29, 1889 child of BOHONAN John W farmer b Sutton & JEWELL Delia A b Weare Vol: 5 Page: 045 Line: 020 Section: 2nd.

Hopkinton, NH Births 1880

SYMONDS Charles D b Hopkinton Aug 25, 1890 child of SYMONDS George farmer b Concord & LUCY A b Vernon Conn Vol: 5 Page: 047 Line: 010 Section: 2nd.

SMITH Ernest Thomas b Hopkinton Mar 11, 1891 child of SMITH W George laborer b Ireland & Maria b England Vol: 5 Page: 049 Line: 006 Section: 2nd.

MIGNAULT Emily L b Hopkinton Jul 28, 1891 child of MIGNAULT Albert M laborer b Canada & STEVENS Emma L Vol: 5 Page: 049 Line: 019 Section: 2nd.

ORDWAY Ernest J b Hopkinton Jan 27, 1892 child of ORDWAY George L farmer b Concord & DURGIN Ella b Wilmot Vol: 5 Page: 051 Line: 002 Section: 2nd.

DAVIS ---- b Hopkinton Feb 26, 1892 child of DAVIS Horace J manufacture b Warner & JENNIE B b Sutoon Vol: 5 Page: 051 Line: 004 Section: 2nd.

JONES Ruth B b Hopkinton Nov 1, 1892 child of JONES J Arthur farmer b Hopkinton & BAILEY Mabel b Newbury Vol: 5 Page: 051 Line: 026 Section: 2nd.

BOHONAN Percy R b Hopkinton Sep 23, 1892 child of BOHONAN John W farmer b Sutton & JEWELL Delia b Weare Vol: 5 Page: 051 Line: 027 Section: 2nd.

DERRY Angus b Hopkinton May 26, 1893 child of DERRY Joseph blacksmith b Canada & MORAN Mary b Hopkinton Vol: 5 Page: 053 Line: 013 Section: 2nd.

EMERSON Frank D b Hopkinton Aug 2, 1894 child of EMERSON Fred H farmer b Hopkinton & KIMBALL Nellie b Me Vol: 5 Page: 055 Line: 019 Section: 2nd.

PLUMMER Helen b Hopkinton Jul 29, 1897 child of PLUMMER Oscar mason b Hebron & MUDGE Gertrude E b Bedford Vol: 5 Page: 063 Line: 012 Section: 2nd.

Hopkinton, NH Deaths 1880-1913

Note: This chapter includes a number 1879 death records.

TIRRELL Elizabeth M d Hopkinton 1898-01-20 age 71yrs 7mos b Hopkinton child of MORGAN Nathan & STANLEY Torida Vol: 6 Page: 001.

WIGHT Frank A d Enfield 1898-02-07 age 18yrs 5mos 16dys b Hopkinton Vol: 6 Page: 001.

CORLISS Mary J d Hopkinton 1898-02-11 age 60yrs b Hopkinton Vol: 6 Page: 001.

MORRILL Clement d Hopkinton 1879-04-03 age 78yrs b Hopkinton child of CLEMENT John & MORRILL Miriam Vol: 5 Page: 029 Line: 001 Section: 1st

PARKER Georgia Ann d Hopkinton 1879-05-31 b Hopkinton Vol: 5 Page: 029 Line: 005 Section: 1st

WEBSTER (Mrs) d Hopkinton 1879-05-31 b Hopkinton Vol: 5 Page: 029 Line: 006 Section: 1st

KIMBALL Maria d Hopkinton 1879-06-11 age 50yrs b Chester Vt child of GOODRICH Eliphalet & KIMBALL Judith Vol: 5 Page: 029 Line: 007 Section: 1st

PIERCE George W d Hopkinton 1879-06-16 age 43yrs b Hopkinton Vol: 5 Page: 029 Line: 008 Section: 1st

HUSE Adaline L d Hopkinton 1880-04-10 age 49yrs b Weare child of EATON Moses & Mary Vol: 5 Page: 033 Line: 002 Section: 1st

LYNCH Julia d Hopkinton Apr 1879 b Ireland Vol: 5 Page: 029 Line: 002 Section: 1st

HOLMES Albert d Hopkinton 1879-06-06 age 70yrs b Hopkinton child of HOLMES Eliphalet & FLANDERS Nancy Vol: 5 Page: 029 Line: 003 Section: 1st

CAMPBELL Jonah d Hopkinton 1879-06-06 age 83yrs child of CAMPBELL Phineas & Susanna Vol: 5 Page: 029 Line: 004 Section: 1st

DODGE John Henry d Hopkinton 1884-01-07 age 59yrs 4mos 10dys b Hopkinton child of DODGE Henry & EATON Susan Vol: 5 Page: 067 Line: 002 Section: 2nd

GUNNERSON Robert d Hopkinton 1884-02-02 age 59yrs 11mos 27dys b Sunapee child of WHITE Aaron & CRAM Loisa Vol: 5 Page: 067 Line: 003 Section: 2nd

HADLEY Stephen A d Hopkinton 1884-02-06 age 56yrs 5mos b Hopkinton child of HADLEY Sephen & WHITE Cloa Vol: 5 Page: 067 Line: 004 Section: 2nd

TYLER Calvin d Hopkinton 1884-03-31 age 87yrs 21mos Vol: 5 Page: 067 Line: 005 Section: 2nd

PAIGE Georgie D d Hopkinton 1879-06-26 age 30yrs b Hopkinton child of PAIGE John W & E J Vol: 5 Page: 029 Line: 009 Section: 1st

COUUGH Daniel d Hopkinton 1879-06-30 age 87yrs b Hopkinton Vol: 5 Page: 029 Line: 010 Section: 1st

HOLT Henry d Hopkinton 1879-07-04 age 63yrs b Andover Mass child of HOLT Joseph & Lydia Vol: 5 Page: 029 Line: 011 Section: 1st

FISK Ida d Hopkinton 1879-07-08 age 18yrs b Lowell Mass?? child of FISK Daniel & Currier Vol: 5 Page: 029 Line: 012 Section: 1st

McALPINE (Mrs) Newton d Hopkinton 1879-07-09 b Henniker child of HERSEY Amos & DICKEY Sarah Vol: 5 Page: 029 Line: 013 Section: 1st

DUSTIN John G d Hopkinton 1879-07-22 age 77yrs b Hopkinton child of DUSTIN Yadorh & GOULD Elizabeth Vol: 5 Page: 029 Line: 014 Section: 1st

LITTLE Seth d Hopkinton 1879-07-29 age 65yrs b Hopkinton child of LITTLE James & Elizabeth Vol: 5 Page: 029 Line: 015 Section: 1st

COLBY Charles Carroll d Hopkinton 1879-08-05 age 20yrs b Hopkinton child of COLBY Melvin & Hannah Vol: 5 Page: 029 Line: 016 Section: 1st

COLLINS (Mrs) Darice d Hopkinton 1879-09-27 Vol: 5 Page: 029 Line: 017 Section: 1st

KIMBALL Azeneth d Hopkinton 1879-11-12 age 82yrs b Hopkinton child of HERRICK Asa & BLAKE Mary Vol: 5 Page: 029 Line: 019 Section: 1st

KIMBALL Joanna Merrill d Hopkinton 1879-11-16 age 84yrs b child of MERRILL Parker & KIMBALL Rebecca Vol: 5 Page: 029 Line: 020 Section: 1st

KIMBALL Clara F d Hopkinton 1879-11-19 age 31yrs child of FRENCH Ruben E & CHASE Sarah Vol: 5 Page: 029 Line: 021 Section: 1st

PARKER Obediah d Hopkinton 1879-11-20 age 76yrs Vol: 5 Page: 031 Line: 004 Section: 1st

WATKINS George N d Hopkinton 1880-01-13 Vol: 5 Page: 029 Line: 023 Section: 1st

BOHONAN David N d Hopkinton 1880-01-31 age 35yrs b Sutton child of BOHONAN Darill & BEAN Belinda Vol: 5 Page: 029 Line: 024 Section: 1st

CHOATE Betsey Davis d Hopkinton 1880-02-08 age 71yrs 11mos b Hopkinton child of DAVIS Abram & Priscilla Vol: 5 Page: 029 Line: 025 Section: 1st

MILLS Celinda d Hopkinton 1880-02-08 age 66yrs 10mos 5dys b Weare child of CLOUGH Daniel & Mary Vol: 5 Page: 029 Line: 026 Section: 1st

FLANDERS Rufus P d Hopkinton 1880-02-22 age 67yrs Vol: 5 Page: 029 Line: 027 Section: 1st

VINTON?? ---- d Hopkinton 1880-03-02 child of VINTON John D Vol: 5 Page: 029 Line: 028 Section: 1st

HAWTHORN Rachel d Hopkinton 1880-03-07 age 84yrs child of JACKMAN Noel & PENEFENURE ?? Vol: 5 Page: 031 Line: 001 Section: 1st

SEAVEY (Mrs) Andrew d Hopkinton 1880-03-06 age 81yrs b Hopkinton child of FISK Ebenezer & Sarah Vol: 5 Page: 031 Line: 002 Section: 1st

GOODWIN Lewis A d Hopkinton 1880-03-18 age 6mos b Hopkinton child of GOODWIN Charles & CROWELL Etta Vol: 5 Page: 031 Line: 003 Section: 1st

COLBY Lizzie D d Hopkinton 1881-04-13 age 21yrs 6mos b Concord child of DOW Henry & BOUTELLE Charolette Vol: 5 Page: 035 Line: 001 Section: 1st

SPOFFORD Sally d Hopkinton 1880-03-27 b Hopkinton Vol: 5 Page: 031 Line: 005 Section: 1st

CONNER Lydia d Hopkinton 1880-03-21 age 76yrs 6mos b Hopkinton child of KIMBALL John & Lydia Vol: 5 Page: 031 Line: 006 Section: 1st

GOVE ---- d Hopkinton 1879-12-04 age 6dys b Hopkinton child of GOVE George & GOVE Mary E Vol: 5 Page: 031 Line: 007 Section: 1st

Hopkinton, NH Deaths 1880

FRENCH Mary A H d Hopkinton 1880-04-13 age 77yrs b Salisbury child of HUNTOON Samuel & TUCKER Martha Vol: 5 Page: 033 Line: 001 Section: 1st

TYLER Sarah P d Hopkinton 1880-04-14 age 81yrs child of PUTNAM Arron Vol: 5 Page: 033 Line: 003 Section: 1st

GAGE Joseph d Hopkinton 1880-04-29 age 93yrs Vol: 5 Page: 033 Line: 004 Section: 1st

DUSTIN Daniel P d Hopkinton 1880 Apr 31 age 70yrs b Hopkinton child of DUSTIN Ebenezer & Sarah Vol: 5 Page: 033 Line: 005 Section: 1st

BECK Catherine d Hopkinton 1880-05-06 age 62yrs child of GARRABAUDT Jacob Vol: 5 Page: 033 Line: 006 Section: 1st

JOHNSON Marrien d Hopkinton 1880 age 94yrs b Danville child of HUNT Moses Vol: 5 Page: 033 Line: 007 Section: 1st

MORGAN Richard F d Hopkinton 1880-05-30 age 65yrs b Hopkinton child of MORGAN Timothy & Mary Vol: 5 Page: 033 Line: 008 Section: 1st

MERRILL Laura A d Hopkinton 1880-06-19 age 35yrs child of TERRY Edwin & DAVIS Lydia Vol: 5 Page: 033 Line: 009 Section: 1st

HARVEY John M d Hopkinton 1880-07-12 age 66yrs b Hopkinton Vol: 5 Page: 033 Line: 010 Section: 1st

BURBANK Thomas J d Hopkinton 1880-07-26 age 76yrs b Hopkinton Vol: 5 Page: 033 Line: 011 Section: 1st

KELLEY ---- d Hopkinton 1880-08-02 age 4yrs 10mos 13dys b Hillsboro child of KELLEY Andrew & JONES Roxanna E Vol: 5 Page: 033 Line: 012 Section: 1st

DODGE Grover d Hopkinton 1880-08-12 age 88yrs b New London?? child of DODGE Nehemiah & SAFFORD Lydia Vol: 5 Page: 033 Line: 013 Section: 1st

DOW Rhoda d Hopkinton 1880-10-22 age 85yrs b Hopkinton child of MORRILL Ezra & BARNARD Rhoda Vol: 5 Page: 033 Line: 014 Section: 1st

PUTNEY Joseph d Hopkinton 1880-10-11 age 86yrs b Hopkinton child of PUTNEY Joseph & PRESCOTT Mary Vol: 5 Page: 033 Line: 015 Section: 1st

COLLEY Rachel C d Hopkinton 1880-11-08 age 73yrs child of CLOUGH William & COUCH ---- Vol: 5 Page: 033 Line: 016 Section: 1st

PHILLIPS Alice d Hopkinton 1880-11-17 age 7yrs b Concord child of PHILLIP Ira C & HARDY Angie Vol: 5 Page: 033 Line: 017 Section: 1st

FOOT Albert D d Hopkinton 1880-11-28 age 5mos b Hopkinton child of DAVIS Albert O & FOOT Florence Vol: 5 Page: 033 Line: 018 Section: 1st

SPOFFORD Sarah J d Hopkinton 1880-12-05 age 57yrs b Jaffrey child of FITCH Luther & HOYT Jane Vol: 5 Page: 033 Line: 019 Section: 1st

FRYE Amas d Hopkinton 1880-12-24 age 83yrs child of FRYE Amos & CHANDLER Fannie Vol: 5 Page: 033 Line: 021 Section: 1st

FRAZIER Sarah W d Hopkinton 1880-12-28 age 49yrs Vol: 5 Page: 033 Line: 022 Section: 1st

SYMONDS Jennie D d Hopkinton 1881-02-24 age 1yrs 5mos b Hopkinton child of SYMONDS Benj & PORTER Emma J Vol: 5 Page: 033 Line: 023 Section: 1st

BALDWIN Sylvia A d Hopkinton 1881-02-28 age 75yrs child of KIMBALL Sarah Vol: 5 Page: 033 Line: 024 Section: 1st

RUSSELLS Grabia d Hopkinton 1881-03-18 age 79yrs 7mos 5dys child of RUSSELL John & COLBY Jenima Vol: 5 Page: 033 Line: 025 Section: 1st

Hopkinton, NH Deaths 1880

DOW Hannah d Hopkinton 1881-03-08 age 85yrs b Weare child of DUSTIN Andrew Vol: 5 Page: 033 Line: 026 Section: 1st

KNOWLTON Sarah L d Hopkinton 1881-03-04 age 84yrs b Hopkinton child of KNOWLTON Daniel & Mary Vol: 5 Page: 033 Line: 027 Section: 1st

CHATMAN Charles d Hopkinton 1881-03-26 age 62yrs child of CHATMAN Joseph Vol: 5 Page: 033 Line: 028 Section: 1st

GOVE ---- d Hopkinton 1880-12-04 age 7dys b Hopkinton child of GOVE George & ROWELL Mary Etta Vol: 5 Page: 033 Line: 029 Section: 1st

HASTINGS Alfred S d Hopkinton 1881-04-13 age 53yrs b Hopkinton Vol: 5 Page: 035 Line: 002 Section: 1st

CLARK Cyrus d Hopkinton 1888-10-15 age 85yrs 10mos Vol: 5 Page: 085 Line: 001 Section: 2nd

CLEMENT Mary d Hopkinton 1881-05-14 age 71yrs 7mos 18dys b Hopkinton child of CLEMENT John & MORRILL Mariam Vol: 5 Page: 035 Line: 004 Section: 1st

REID Jass d Hopkinton 1881-05-14 age 65yrs 10mos b Scotland child of McCANTISH Thomas Vol: 5 Page: 035 Line: 005 Section: 1st

NICHOLS E G d Hopkinton 1881-05-31 Vol: 5 Page: 035 Line: 006 Section: 1st

JONES Aurelia S d Hopkinton 1881-06-06 age 72yrs b Concord child of HARRINGTON Moses & CHASE Abagil Vol: 5 Page: 035 Line: 007 Section: 1st

DOW Hanah F d Hopkinton 1881-07-15 age 92yrs child of FRENCH Asa Vol: 5 Page: 035 Line: 008 Section: 1st

STEVENS Louisa (Mrs) d Hopkinton 1881-07-21 age 55yrs b Contoocook child of CLARK John & PUTNEY Lydia Vol: 5 Page: 035 Line: 009 Section: 1st

STORY Timothy d Hopkinton 1881-07-27 age 35yrs b Hopkinton child of STORY Moses & Mehetible Vol: 5 Page: 035 Line: 010 Section: 1st

MELVIN (Mrs) d Hopkinton 1881-07-30 age 80yrs 9mos b Hopkinton child of STRAW Benj Vol: 5 Page: 035 Line: 011 Section: 1st

GOVE ---- d Hopkinton 1881-08-19 age 1dy b W Hopkinton child of GOVE Geo P & ROWELL May Vol: 5 Page: 035 Line: 012 Section: 1st

WEBBER Isiah d Hopkinton 1881-08-24 age 91yrs 11mos b Hopkinton child of WEBBER Richard & JEWETT Elizabeth Vol: 5 Page: 035 Line: 013 Section: 1st

COLBY William d Hopkinton 1881-09-04 age 71yrs 9mos 4dys b Hopkinton child of COLBY William & HILDRETH May Vol: 5 Page: 035 Line: 014 Section: 1st

SEAVEY Andrew d Hopkinton 1881-09-23 age 83yrs child of SEAVEY David ?? & May Vol: 5 Page: 035 Line: 015 Section: 1st

PUTNEY Eliza F d Hopkinton 1881-10-01 age 89yrs 11mos 7dys b Plainfield child of TRUE Benjamin Vol: 5 Page: 035 Line: 016 Section: 1st

STANWOOD Henry P d San Franciso Calif 1888-07-16 age 56yrs Vol: 5 Page: 085 Line: 002 Section: 2nd

ALLEN Alvira d Hopkinton 1881-10-17 age 64yrs 4mos b Gratham child of STONE David & RAWSON Susannah Vol: 5 Page: 035 Line: 018 Section: 1st

HARDY Lydia d Hopkinton 1881-10-14 age 71yrs 6mos b Henniker child of PUTNEY Lydia Vol: 5 Page: 035 Line: 019 Section: 1st

Hopkinton, NH Deaths 1880

SMITH Almira d Hopkinton 1881-10-20 age 81yrs 2mos b Northfield child of
CHASE Thomas & Lizzie Vol: 5 Page: 035 Line: 020 Section: 1st

SLEEPER Nehemiah D d Hopkinton 1881-10-29 age 88yrs 3mos b Andover Vol: 5
Page: 035 Line: 021 Section: 1st

LOVEREN Benjamin (Mrs) d Hopkinton 1881-10-29 age 76yrs Vol: 5 Page: 035
Line: 022 Section: 1st

BURNHAM Adaline D d Hopkinton 1881-11-30 age 73yrs b Hopkinton child of
EASTMAN Ezra & EATON Polly Vol: 5 Page: 035 Line: 023 Section: 1st

ROLLINS Benjamin d Hopkinton 1881-12-02 age 97yrs 8mos Vol: 5 Page: 035
Line: 024 Section: 1st

DOWNING Sally d Hopkinton 1881-12-18 age 47yrs b Orange child of MORRILL
Ebenezer & JACKMAN Mary Vol: 5 Page: 035 Line: 025 Section: 1st

HALL M Ann d Hopkinton 1881-12-26 age 40yrs b NH child of PALMER William
Vol: 5 Page: 035 Line: 026 Section: 1st

COLBY Sargent (Mrs) d Hopkinton 1881-12-29 age 79yrs 3mos b Dunbarton child
of COLBY Enoch & SENTER Sarah Vol: 5 Page: 035 Line: 027 Section: 1st
Note: (Ruth)

MOULTON Caleb d Hopkinton 1882-06-22 age 77yrs 4mos 11dys b Hampton Falls
child of MOULTON Jacob & TILTON Nancy Vol: 5 Page: 039 Line: 010
Section: 1st

KIMBALL Hannah (Mrs) d Hopkinton 1882-01-14 Vol: 5 Page: 037 Line: 002
Section: 1st

DENSMORE Hattie May d Hopkinton 1882-01-22 b Hopkinton Vol: 5 Page: 037
Line: 003 Section: 1st

SWEATT Lizzie d Hopkinton 1882-01-22 age 9yrs child of SWEATT George W &
FRAZIER Frances Vol: 5 Page: 037 Line: 004 Section: 1st

STRAW Levi (dea) d Hopkinton 1882-01-27 age 86yrs 10mos child of STRAW
Levi Vol: 5 Page: 037 Line: 005 Section: 1st

SWEATT Mary d Hopkinton 1882-02-03 age 10yrs b Hopkinton child of SWEATT
George & FRAZIER Frances Vol: 5 Page: 037 Line: 006 Section: 1st

HASTINGS Har?? d Hopkinton 1882-02-04 age 78yrs child of HASTINGS John
Vol: 5 Page: 037 Line: 007 Section: 1st

BARTON Amos P (Mrs) d Hopkinton 1882-02-12 age 63yrs Vol: 5 Page: 037 Line:
008 Section: 1st

HOYT M French d Hopkinton 1882-02-22 age 62yrs 8mos 21dys child of HOYT
Moses & Betsy Vol: 5 Page: 037 Line: 009 Section: 1st

PERRY Aseneth d Hopkinton 1882-03-02 Vol: 5 Page: 037 Line: 010 Section: 1st

ELLIOTT Annie M d Michigian 1882 age 1yrs 5mos b Oscola On child of
ELLIOTT Edson & COLLEY Nettie Vol: 5 Page: 037 Line: 010 Section: 1st

WELLS Lucinda d Hopkinton 1882-03-15 age 76yrs b Sutton child of WELLS
Thomas G & LYMAN Lucindia Vol: 5 Page: 037 Line: 012 Section: 1st

WELLS Ruth d Hopkinton 1882-03-18 age 66yrs b Hopkinton child of WELLS
Thomas G & LYMAN Lucindia Vol: 5 Page: 037 Line: 013 Section: 1st

WELLS Edwin R d Hopkinton 1882-03-18 age 68yrs b Hopkinton child of WELLS
Thomas G & LYMAN Lucindia Vol: 5 Page: 037 Line: 013 Section: 1st

DUSTIN Pheobe E d Hopkinton 1882-04-14 age 29yrs b Hopkinton Vol: 5 Page:
039 Line: 001 Section: 1st

Hopkinton, NH Deaths 1880

FOSS Everet Warren d Hopkinton 1882-05-07 age 6mos b Hopkinton child of FOSS John M & HOLMES Ida Vol: 5 Page: 039 Line: 002 Section: 1st

DOW Cyntha d Hopkinton 1888-12-08 age 79yrs b Henniker child of PAIGE Nathaniel Vol: 5 Page: 085 Line: 004 Section: 2nd

COLBY James d Hopkinton 1882-05-15 age 75yrs 4mos 19dys b Hopkinton child of COLBY James B & STORY Susannah Vol: 5 Page: 039 Line: 004 Section: 1st

UNDERHILL Charles N d Hopkinton 1882-05-26 age 68yrs Vol: 5 Page: 039 Line: 005 Section: 1st

QUIMBY ---- d Hopkinton 1882-05-28 age 81yrs 3mos 13dys child of BLAN-CHARD Jonis & WHITE Selma Vol: 5 Page: 039 Line: 006 Section: 1st

MILLS Fred E d Hopkinton 1888-12-15 age 6mos 22dys b Hopkinton child of MILLS Fred W W & BROWN Belle M Vol: 5 Page: 085 Line: 005 Section: 2nd

ALLEN Willard d Hopkinton 1882-06-02 age 70yrs 9mos 18dys b Cornish child of ALLEN John Vol: 5 Page: 039 Line: 008 Section: 1st

HARDY David d Hopkinton 1882-06-18 age 88yrs 3mos Vol: 5 Page: 039 Line: 009 Section: 1st

KIMBALL ---- d Hopkinton 1882-09-04 age 9dys b Hopkinton child of KIMBALL Charlie & WEBBER Mattie Ella Vol: 5 Page: 039 Line: 019 Section: 1st

FELCH ---- d Hopkinton 1882-07-17 age 1dy b Hopkinton child of FELCH Ira J & CURRIER Addie Vol: 5 Page: 039 Line: 012 Section: 1st

FOSS J G M d Hopkinton 1882-07-23 age 63yrs b Strafford child of FOSS John & HAYES Lucy Vol: 5 Page: 039 Line: 013 Section: 1st

FOSS Alvira C d Hopkinton 1882-08-09 age 66yrs b Henniker child of CONNOR Abel & WHITNEY Mary Vol: 5 Page: 039 Line: 014 Section: 1st

PAIGE Sarah d Hopkinton 1882-08-11 age 65yrs b Hopkinton child of CLARK Jacob & HUSE Betty Vol: 5 Page: 039 Line: 015 Section: 1st

WIGGIN William C d Hopkinton 1882-08-14 age 75yrs 7mos b Salem child of WIGGIN Chase & HAWTHORNE Elizabeth Vol: 5 Page: 039 Line: 016 Section: 1st

HARVEY May d Hopkinton 1882-08-22 b Hopkinton child of DWINELLS Munroe & HEATH Susan Vol: 5 Page: 039 Line: 017 Section: 1st

KEMP Leroy B d Hopkinton 1882-09-02 age 25dys b Warner child of KEMPT Frank P & EASTMAN Jennie Vol: 5 Page: 039 Line: 018 Section: 1st

PHILBRICK Geo d Hopkinton 1882-09-08 age 1dy b Hopkinton child of PHIL-BRICK George & ELLIOTT Eva Vol: 5 Page: 039 Line: 020 Section: 1st

PUTNEY Hannah M d Hopkinton 1882-09-20 age 77yrs 7mos 11dys b Boscawen child of MUSY Joseph & BARTLETT Jane Vol: 5 Page: 039 Line: 021 Section: 1st

COLBY May d Hopkinton 1882-08-29 age 6mos 23dys b Hopkinton child of COLBY Edward H & SANBORN Maggie Vol: 5 Page: 039 Line: 022 Section: 1st

HOYT Sarah A d Hopkinton 1889-01-07 age 34yrs 2mos 10dys b Danvers Mass child of PHELPS Frances & ELIZABETH C Vol: 5 Page: 087 Line: 001 Section: 2nd

HARDY William H d Hopkinton 1882-10-05 age 62yrs b Warner child of HARDY Joseph & CHASE Eliza Vol: 5 Page: 039 Line: 024 Section: 1st

JEWETT Charlotte d Hopkinton 1882-10-17 age 93yrs 3mos b Hopkinton child of CLOUGH Hannah Vol: 5 Page: 039 Line: 026 Section: 1st

HAZELTON Barnes d Hopkinton 1882-10-22 age 80yrs Vol: 5 Page: 039 Line: 027 Section: 1st

ELLIOTT Annie S d Hopkinton 1882-10-28 age 91yrs b Concord child of FISKE Ephrriam & ANNIE S Vol: 5 Page: 039 Line: 028 Section: 1st

UPTON Joseph d Hopkinton 1882-10-30 age 76yrs b Reading Mass Vol: 5 Page: 041 Line: 001 Section: 1st

CHOATE May M d Hopkinton 1882-11-01 age 47yrs 10mos b Pittsburg child of HEATH Christopher & CARR Sarah Vol: 5 Page: 041 Line: 002 Section: 1st

WEEKS Hannah C d Hopkinton 1882-11-02 age 81yrs 1mos b Rowley Mass Vol: 5 Page: 041 Line: 003 Section: 1st

FRENCH Almira S d Hopkinton 1889-01-07 age 65yrs 3mos b Chester child of SMITH Richard K & CHASE Almira Vol: 5 Page: 087 Line: 002 Section: 2nd

WILSON Elizabeth G d Hopkinton 1882-11-08 age 62yrs 2mos 3dys b Boscawen child of GERRISH Thomas & Betsey Vol: 5 Page: 041 Line: 006 Section: 1st

CLARK Jonathan d Hopkinton 1882-11-09 age 76yrs b Hopkinton child of CLARK Joseph & BAILY Eunice Vol: 5 Page: 041 Line: 007 Section: 1st

COLBY Eliza A d Hopkinton 1882-12-03 age 86yrs 8mos b W. Concord child of ABBOTT Moses & BATCHELDER May Vol: 5 Page: 041 Line: 008 Section: 1st

ABBOTT Stephen d Hopkinton 1882-12-05 age 79yrs 7mos b Rumford Vol: 5 Page: 041 Line: 009 Section: 1st

STORY Lydia d Hopkinton 1883-01-03 age 92yrs 8mos 3dys b Hopkinton child of STORY Nathan & BURNHAM Sarah Vol: 5 Page: 041 Line: 010 Section: 1st

WOOD Elmer G d Hopkinton 1883-01-07 age 10mos 28dys b Hopkinton child of WOOD Andrew J & BURNHAM Sarah Vol: 5 Page: 041 Line: 011 Section: 1st

NICHOLS Mary d Hopkinton 1883-01-25 age 75yrs 7mos 8dys b Hopkinton child of STORY Moses & CHANDLER Sarah Vol: 5 Page: 041 Line: 013 Section: 1st

FRENCH Viola S d Hopkinton 1883-02-08 age 37yrs 11mos 8dys b Unity child of CURRIER Daniel & CUTTS Sarah Vol: 5 Page: 041 Line: 014 Section: 1st

PALMER Joseph d Hopkinton 1883-02-11 age 70yrs Vol: 5 Page: 041 Line: 015 Section: 1st

DUNBAR Ida E d Hopkinton 1883-02-14 age 12yrs b Hopkinton child of DUNBAR Elma B & WEBER Ann T Vol: 5 Page: 041 Line: 016 Section: 1st

COLBY Timothy d Hopkinton 1883-03-09 age 64yrs 11mos b Hopkinton child of COLBY Timothy & HERICK Lydia Vol: 5 Page: 041 Line: 017 Section: 1st

FLANDERS Sarah d Hopkinton 1883-03-19 age 96yrs 20dys b Hopkinton child of SMITH Moody & QUIMBY Hannah Vol: 5 Page: 041 Line: 018 Section: 1st

DOWNER Ann d Hopkinton 1883-05-25 age 71yrs 3mos 10dys child of DOWNER Samuel & MOODY Barah Vol: 5 Page: 041 Line: 020 Section: 1st

FAGAN Thomas d Hopkinton 1882-09-21 age 80yrs b Ireland Vol: 5 Page: 041 Line: 021 Section: 1st

FELLOWS Emma S d Hopkinton 1882-12-01 age 25yrs b Hopkinton child of FELLOWS Ignatious & COPPS Sarah J Vol: 5 Page: 041 Line: 022 Section: 1st

Hopkinton, NH Deaths 1880

WELLS Gustavus d Hopkinton 1883-06-18 age 40yrs Vol: 5 Page: 043 Line: 001 Section: 1st

ANNIS Cythia d Hopkinton 1883-06-13 age 62yrs 10mos child of HARDY Cythia Vol: 5 Page: 043 Line: 002 Section: 1st

JOHNSON Addie d Hopkinton 1883-09-01 age 36yrs 11mos b Hopkinton child of JOHNSON Samuel Vol: 5 Page: 043 Line: 003 Section: 1st

MERRILL Isaac d Hopkinton 1883-09-08 age 99yrs 6mos 23dys Vol: 5 Page: 043 Line: 004 Section: 1st

WEST Charles E d Hopkinton 1883-10-29 age 60yrs Vol: 5 Page: 043 Line: 005 Section: 1st

CONNOR (Mrs) d Hopkinton 1883-11-12 age 66yrs Vol: 5 Page: 043 Line: 006 Section: 1st

BLAISDELL Isaac d Hopkinton 1883-11-14 age 49yrs b Salisbury Vol: 5 Page: 043 Line: 007 Section: 1st

KIMBALL Richard M d Hopkinton 1883-04-22 age 91yrs 4mos 14dys b Hopkinton child of KIMBALL Job Vol: 5 Page: 043 Line: 008 Section: 1st

LANCASTER Alice G d Hopkinton 1883-05-08 age 83yrs b Epsom child of SANDERS John & CHATMAN Lydia Vol: 5 Page: 043 Line: 009 Section: 1st

CONNOR Mahala T d Hopkinton 1883-06-07 age 69yrs 8mos b Canterbury child of INGALLS Jesse & CHASE Hannah Vol: 5 Page: 043 Line: 010 Section: 1st

WATTS Arthur James d Hopkinton 1883-08-12 age 8mos 12dys b Hopkinton child of WATTS Charles F & ANIS May Vol: 5 Page: 043 Line: 011 Section: 1st

FRENCH Nancy d Hopkinton 1883-10-22 age 60yrs 1mos 11dys b Northfield child of BUSWELL James & CLOUGH May Vol: 5 Page: 043 Line: 012 Section: 1st

CLARK Harriett B d Hopkinton 1883-10-31 age 83yrs 2mos 2dys b Quincy Mass child of HAYDEN John P & Delia Vol: 5 Page: 043 Line: 013 Section: 1st

CLOUGH Irene Eva d Hopkinton 1883-11-26 age 19yrs b Hopkinton child of CLOUGH Moses T & BEAN Besty Vol: 5 Page: 043 Line: 014 Section: 1st

JONES Annie E d Hopkinton 1883-04-30 age 78yrs 3mos b Cambridge Mass child of LOCKE Samuel & Learnerd Vol: 5 Page: 043 Line: 015 Section: 1st

NUTTER David R d Hopkinton 1883-05-26 age 43yrs b N. Barnstead child of NUTTER William & DANE Eliza Vol: 5 Page: 043 Line: 016 Section: 1st

KIMBALL Daniel d Hopkinton 1883-06-23 age 86yrs 6mos 28dys b Hopkinton child of KIMBALL Aaron Vol: 5 Page: 043 Line: 017 Section: 1st

FRENCH Jonathan d Hopkinton 1883-06-24 age 76yrs 4mos 12dys child of FRENCH Jonathan & STICKNEY Sarah Vol: 5 Page: 043 Line: 018 Section: 1st

BAILEY George H d Hopkinton 1883-08-01 age 54yrs 18dys b Hopkinton child of BAILY John M & KNOWLTON Lucy Vol: 5 Page: 043 Line: 019 Section: 1st

MORSE Joshua d Hopkinton 1883-12-26 age 79yrs 5mos 21dys b Boscawen child of MORSE Joshua & FARNUM Phebe Vol: 5 Page: 043 Line: 020 Section: 1st

BROCKWAY Betsey d Nashua 1883-09-27 age 80yrs child of EATON Benjamin Vol: 5 Page: 043 Line: 021 Section: 1st

MORGAN Arthur W d Hopkinton 1883-08-18 age 18yrs 1mos child of MORGAN Gilman & MERRILL Eva Vol: 5 Page: 043 Line: 022 Section: 1st

MORGAN Edwin N d Hopkinton 1883-06-07 age 23yrs 11dys child of MORGAN Gilman & MERRILL Eva Vol: 5 Page: 043 Line: 023 Section: 1st

BROWN Jonathan d Hopkinton 1883-10-21 age 66yrs 2mos 29dys b Hopkinton child of BROWN Jonathan & HOLMES Jane Vol: 5 Page: 043 Line: 024 Section: 1st

LOCKE David d Hopkinton 1883-07-15 age 87yrs 5mos 26dys Vol: 5 Page: 043 Line: 025 Section: 1st

GOVE Mary P d Hopkinton 1883-04-28 age 64yrs 5mos 23dys b Hopkinton child of PIPER Benjaman & CURRIER Sally Vol: 5 Page: 043 Line: 026 Section: 1st

DUNBAR Caroline M d Hopkinton 1898-02-23 age 70yrs 11mos 6dys b Lyme child of DEMICK J Wilson Vol: 6 Page: 001

STORY Polly d Hopkinton 1884-04-02 age 79yrs b Mass child of CROWELL John Vol: 5 Page: 067 Line: 006 Section: 2nd

LORD Charles d Hopkinton 1884-04-14 age 71yrs 4mos b So Berwick Me child of LORD Humphrey & LEAVETT Lydia Vol: 5 Page: 067 Line: 007 Section: 2nd

NOYES David S d Hopkinton 1884-04-16 age 56yrs 9mos child of NOYES Lenard & STORY Julia Vol: 5 Page: 067 Line: 008 Section: 2nd

BARTON Amos Prescott d Hopkinton 1884-04-26 age 81yrs 7mos b Pittsfield child of BARTON Josiah & JONES Mehitable Vol: 5 Page: 067 Line: 009 Section: 2nd

WHITE Lois Ann d Hopkinton 1884-05-04 age 64yrs 11mos b Henniker child of ROGERS Obediah & FLANDERS Hannah Vol: 5 Page: 067 Line: 010 Section: 2nd

DODGE Susan E d Hopkinton 1884-07-25 age 92yrs 5mos 5dys b Hopkinton child of EATON Nathaniel & BOWAN Elizabeth Vol: 5 Page: 067 Line: 017 Section: 2nd

CURRIER Lucy Holt d Hopkinton 1884-06-03 age 66yrs 11mos b Hopkinton child of MORRILL Joseph & MARTIN Termelia Vol: 5 Page: 067 Line: 013 Section: 2nd

CURRIER Mary M d Hopkinton 1884-06-18 age 81yrs 4mos 16dys b child of MORGAN Nathan & EMMERSON Mary Vol: 5 Page: 067 Line: 014 Section: 2nd

DOW Joseph F d Hopkinton 1884-07-07 age 67yrs 3mos 27dys b Hopkinton child of DOW Joseph & FRENCH Hannah Vol: 5 Page: 067 Line: 015 Section: 2nd

GREELEY Urana d Hopkinton 1884-07-19 age 82yrs 14dys child of GREELEY Nathan & BAILEY Mary Vol: 5 Page: 067 Line: 016 Section: 2nd

FRENCH Sarah d Hopkinton 1884-08-02 child of FRENCH George & BUSWELL Nancy Vol: 5 Page: 067 Line: 018 Section: 2nd

BAILEY Hellen Young d Ishpenning Mich 1884-08-11 age 52yrs 4mos 20dys b New Albin NY child of YOUNG Horace C & WALKER Lauria Vol: 5 Page: 067 Line: 067 Section: 2nd

ROLLINS Grace G d Boston Mass 1884-08-22 age 1yrs 3mos 12dys b East Boston child of ROLLINS Charles & FRAZIER Bell Vol: 5 Page: 067 Line: 020 Section: 2nd

LIBBIE Mary T d Hopkinton 1884-09-10 age 1yrs b Winchester Mass child of LIBBIE Andrew & McNEIL Susan Vol: 5 Page: 067 Line: 021 Section: 2nd

CHASE Louisa P d Hopkinton 1884-09-10 age 77yrs 9mos b Concord child of Wells & Louisa Vol: 5 Page: 067 Line: 022 Section: 2nd

BAKER Eliza J d Hopkinton 1884-09-10 age 42yrs 1mos 21dys b Hopkinton child of PUTNAM Martin & BUTLER Margaret Vol: 5 Page: 067 Line: 023 Section: 2nd

LAMPREY Ellenor d Hopkinton 1884-09-19 age 91yrs 7mos 13dys b Hopkinton child of BUSWELL Benjamin & CARTER Joanna Vol: 5 Page: 067 Line: 024 Section: 2nd

HOOK Asa E d Boston Mass 1884-09-26 age 23yrs child of HOOK Asa J & HARRIET N Vol: 5 Page: 067 Line: 025 Section: 2nd

CHASE Timothy W d Hopkinton 1884-10-05 age 65yrs 5mos 15dys b Hopkinton child of CHASE Moses & KIMBALL Lydia Vol: 5 Page: 067 Line: 026 Section: 2nd

SWEATT Lydia M d Hopkinton 1884-10-11 age 74yrs 4mos b So Andover child of ABBOTT Holton P & Polly Vol: 5 Page: 067 Line: 027 Section: 2nd

CROWELL Samuel d Hopkinton 1884-10-08 age 79yrs 4mos child of CROWELL Joseph Vol: 5 Page: 067 Line: 028 Section: 2nd

ROWELL Harriett d Hopkinton 1884-11-23 age 66yrs 4mos 20dys b Henniker child of ADAMS James & JOHNSON Lidia Vol: 5 Page: 069 Line: 002 Section: 2nd

DODGE Sarah d Hopkinton 1884-12-15 age 86yrs 10mos 15dys b Londonderry child of HILAND John B & BURNET Sarah Vol: 5 Page: 069 Line: 003 Section: 2nd

SHURTLEFF Mary E d Concord 1884-11-09 age 46yrs Vol: 5 Page: 069 Line: 004 Section: 2nd

FRENCH Sarah d Hopkinton 1884-08-03 age 23yrs 8mos b NH child of FRENCH Geo & Nancy Vol: 5 Page: 069 Line: 005 Section: 2nd

FRENCH Nancy d Hopkinton 1883-10-22 age 60yrs 1mos 11dys b Northfield child of BUSWELL James & CLOUGH May Vol: 5 Page: 069 Line: 006 Section: 2nd

FRENCH Geo d Hopkinton 1884 Jun age 70yrs b NH Vol: 5 Page: 069 Line: 007 Section: 2nd

CLARK Charles E d Hopkinton 1885-01-03 age 69yrs 3mos 2dys b Concord child of CLARK Samuel & BETSEY Ali Vol: 5 Page: 071 Line: 001 Section: 2nd

CALL Charlotte M d Hopkinton 1885-01-13 age 52yrs 4mos b New London child of COLBY James & EMERSON Hannah Vol: 5 Page: 071 Line: 002 Section: 2nd

ROWELL John G d Boston Mass 1885-01-03 age 43yrs Vol: 5 Page: 071 Line: 003 Section: 2nd

CHASE Reginald d Philadelphia Pa 1885-01-11 age 53yrs Vol: 5 Page: 071 Line: 004 Section: 2nd

HOLDEN Aaron d Concord 1885-02-04 age 64yrs 8mos 3dys Vol: 5 Page: 071 Line: 005 Section: 2nd

CLARK Henry N d Hopkinton 1885-02-07 age 30yrs 8mos 23dys b Sanbornton child of CLARK Washington & PIKE Mary Vol: 5 Page: 071 Line: 006 Section: 2nd

NORTON Charles H d Hopkinton 1885-02-22 age 72yrs 2mos b Northwood child of NORTON Mason & ROLLINS Lydia Vol: 5 Page: 071 Line: 007 Section: 2nd

JONES Sarah d Hopkinton 1885-02-27 age 87yrs 6mos 25dys b Hopkinton child of CURRIER Amos & SARGENT Mary Vol: 5 Page: 071 Line: 008 Section: 2nd

EASTMAN Charlotte d Hopkinton 1885-02-28 age 85yrs 3mos 13dys b Hopkinton child of KIMBALL John & CLOUGH Lydia Vol: 5 Page: 071 Line: 009 Section: 2nd

SANBORN Ann d Hopkinton 1885-03-04 age 93yrs 10mos b Ireland child of FAGAN William & QUINN Mary Vol: 5 Page: 071 Line: 011 Section: 2nd

RIPLEY Eliza Ann d Hopkinton 1885-03-22 age 62yrs 1mos 11dys b Londonderry child of GREELY Moody Vol: 5 Page: 071 Line: 012 Section: 2nd

GITCHEL Mary E d Hopkinton 1885-03-31 age 27yrs 5mos 5dys b Canterbury child of WHITNEY Isreal C & SEWELL Sarah A Vol: 5 Page: 071 Line: 014 Section: 2nd

FRAZIER Caleb B d Warner 1885-03-27 age 62yrs 7mos 24dys Vol: 5 Page: 071 Line: 015 Section: 2nd

BROWN Gould d Hopkinton 1885-04-05 age 71yrs 7mos b Hopkinton child of BROWN Jonathan & HOLMES Jane H Vol: 5 Page: 071 Line: 016 Section: 2nd

EASTMAN Jonathan d Hopkinton 1885-04-08 age 79yrs 8mos 29dys b Washington child of EASTMAN Jonathan & DOLE M Vol: 5 Page: 071 Line: 017 Section: 2nd

MORSE Lauria d Hopkinton 1885-04-07 age 81yrs 7mos 26dys b Hopkinton child of LONG Isaac & KIMBALL Susanna Vol: 5 Page: 071 Line: 018 Section: 2nd

JONES Mary C d Lawrence Mass 1885-02-02 age 51yrs Vol: 5 Page: 071 Line: 019 Section: 2nd

CLOUGH Henry S d Salisbury 1885-04-26 Vol: 5 Page: 071 Line: 020 Section: 2nd

SONS Henry d Hopkinton 1885-04-24 age 7dys b Hopkinton child of SONS William & SANBORN Rose Vol: 5 Page: 071 Line: 021 Section: 2nd

KENDALL Sarah d Dublin NH 1885-02-14 age 52yrs Vol: 5 Page: 071 Line: 022 Section: 2nd

BURT Clara d Warner 1885 Vol: 5 Page: 071 Line: 023 Section: 2nd

DODGE Mary E d Middleton Mass 1885-05-09 age 63yrs 1mos 15dys Vol: 5 Page: 071 Line: 025 Section: 2nd

GREENE Newman S d Hopkinton 1885-05-10 age 75yrs 9mos b New Hampshire?? Vol: 5 Page: 071 Line: 026 Section: 2nd

BAILEY George G d Hopkinton 1885-05-11 b New York City child of BAILEY Moses & GREENE Ruth Vol: 5 Page: 071 Line: 027 Section: 2nd

LOVERING Benjamin d Hopkinton 1885-05-14 age 79yrs 8mos 3dys b Deering child of LOVERING Ebenezer & HADLOCK Eunice Vol: 5 Page: 071 Line: 018 Section: 2nd

SYMONDS Catherine B d Hopkinton 1885-05-20 age 45yrs 9mos b Hillsboro child of DUSTIN Jeremiah & BAKER Betsey Vol: 5 Page: 073 Line: 001 Section: 2nd

CLARK Lillian d Hopkinton 1885-06-22 age 20yrs 10mos b Hopkinton child of CLARK Benj & KEIZER Mary Jane Vol: 5 Page: 073 Line: 002 Section: 2nd

CLARK George Henry d Hopkinton 1885-06-25 age 1yrs 10mos 19dys b Hopkinton child of CLARK Henry N & FRENCH Augusta J Vol: 5 Page: 073 Line: 003 Section: 2nd

CROWELL Lewis Carrol d Hopkinton 1886-07-26 age 3mos 14dys b Concord child of CROWELL O Willaim & COLBY Hannah Vol: 5 Page: 073 Line: 004 Section: 2nd

Hopkinton, NH Deaths 1880

JEFFERS Catherine d Hopkinton 1885-08-22 age 63yrs 2mos 2dys b Croydon child of KEMPTON Edward & BISHOP Ruth Vol: 5 Page: 073 Line: 005 Section: 2nd

MERRILL Emiley d Hopkinton 1885-09-04 age 75yrs b Unity Vol: 5 Page: 073 Line: 007 Section: 2nd

CHANDLER Philinda d Hopkinton 1885-09-02 age 60yrs 7mos b Northfield Vt child of BURNHAM Elijah & SYMONDS Alice Vol: 5 Page: 073 Line: 006 Section: 2nd

TUCKER Warren B d Hopkinton 1885-09-13 age 1yrs 7dys b Goffstown child of TUCKER Franklin R & WILLARD Jennie N Vol: 5 Page: 073 Line: 008 Section: 2nd

WEBSTER Frank D d Quechee Vt 1889-01-10 age 39yrs 10mos 17dys Vol: 5 Page: 087 Line: 003 Section: 2nd

CHASE Charlotte d Hopkinton 1885-11-15 age 24yrs 10mos 7dys b Quincy Mass child of ELA E T C & DAVIS Lucy Vol: 5 Page: 073 Line: 011 Section: 2nd

HARDY Jasper M d Hopkinton 1885-11-21 age 66yrs 10mos b Hopkinton child of HARDY Oliver & ANNIS Phebe Vol: 5 Page: 073 Line: 013 Section: 2nd

FULLER Abram G d Hopkinton 1885-12-05 age 71yrs 4mos 8dys b Hopkinton child of FULLER John A & DAVIS Mary Vol: 5 Page: 073 Line: 014 Section: 2nd

CHASE Barach d Hopkinton 1885-12-16 age 77yrs 8mos 15dys b Hopkinton child of CHASE Moses & KIMBALL Lydia Vol: 5 Page: 073 Line: 015 Section: 2nd

BARTLETT Don E d Hopkinton 1885-12-16 age 29yrs 1mos b Warner child of BARTLETT Jasper H & CLARK Lucinda Vol: 5 Page: 073 Line: 016 Section: 2nd

COUCH Ellen M d Hopkinton 1885-12-28 age 49yrs 7mos b Salisbury child of COUCH Samuel & HOWLETT Eunice Vol: 5 Page: 073 Line: 017 Section: 2nd

BARNARD Ellen M d Hopkinton 1886-01-06 age 30yrs 10mos b Hopkinton child of BARNARD Joseph & GERISH Mariah Vol: 5 Page: 075 Line: 001 Section: 2nd

ROWELL Lydia G d Hopkinton 1886-01-10 age 76yrs 6mos b Hopkinton child of ROWELL Moses & PETTINGILL May Vol: 5 Page: 075 Line: 002 Section: 2nd

BAILEY John M d Hopkinton 1886-01-18 age 80yrs 9mos 1dys b Hopkinton child of BAILEY Thomas & SARGENT Hannah Vol: 5 Page: 075 Line: 003 Section: 2nd

RESTIEAUX William d Concord 1886-01-28 age 83yrs 7mos 18dys b Boston Mass child of RESTIEAUX Robert & Catherine Vol: 5 Page: 075 Line: 007 Section: 2nd

SYLVESTER Abi Adams d Hopkinton 1886-02-02 age 92yrs b Henniker Vol: 5 Page: 075 Line: 006 Section: 2nd

ROLLINS George T d Hopkinton 1886-02-13 age 23yrs 2mos 10dys b Hopkinton child of ROLLINS Alfred A & COBLY Mary C Vol: 5 Page: 075 Line: 009 Section: 2nd

FLANDERS Daniel d Hopkinton 1886-08-10 age 86yrs 10mos 15dys b Hopkinton child of FLANDERS Timothy & HOYT Martha Vol: 5 Page: 077 Line: 002 Section: 2nd

HOWARD Alonzo D d Newport 1886-03-03 age 54yrs 14dys Vol: 5 Page: 075 Line: 010 Section: 2nd

PALMER Ann Eliza d Hopkinton 1886-03-06 age 76yrs 11mos b Newbury child of CHASE Jacob & BARKER Hannah Vol: 5 Page: 075 Line: 011 Section: 2nd

REYNO John F d Webster 1886-03-21 age 7yrs 1mos 21dys b Webster child of REYNO Isreal & LIBBY Augusta Vol: 5 Page: 075 Line: 012 Section: 2nd

WADSWORTH Augustus B d Hopkinton 1886-03-24 age 52yrs b Henniker child of WADSWORTH Brittion Vol: 5 Page: 075 Line: 013 Section: 2nd

WYMAN Betsey d Henniker 1886-03-28 age 84yrs 10mos 22dys Vol: 5 Page: 075 Line: 014 Section: 2nd

BROWN Ralph N d Hopkinton Apr 5, 1886** age 53yrs b Charlestown child of BROWN Nathaniel Vol: 5 Page: 075 Line: 015 Section: 2nd

BROWN Mira Burbank d Hopkinton 1886-04-10 age 71yrs 9mos b Hopkinton child of BURBANK Eben & ORDWAY Lidia Vol: 5 Page: 075 Line: 016 Section: 2nd

HARDY Abba A d Hopkinton 1886-04-17 age 44yrs b Hopkinton child of PUTNEY James & BARDER Lucindia Vol: 5 Page: 075 Line: 017 Section: 2nd

HOYT Edmund S d Hopkinton 1869-05-09 b Hopkinton Vol: 5 Page: 075 Line: 018 Section: 2nd Note: removed to Portland

LOVEJOY ---- d Hopkinton 1886-05-05 b Hopkinton child of LOVEJOY O T & LOVEJOY Marcia Vol: 5 Page: 075 Line: 019 Section: 2nd

WEST Betsey B d Manchester 1886-05-13 age 73yrs 1mos 27dys Vol: 5 Page: 075 Line: 020 Section: 2nd

MONTGOMERY Lida K d Hopkinton 1886-05-20 b Hopkinton child of KEMPTON Lewis E & Carrie E Vol: 5 Page: 075 Line: 021 Section: 2nd

KEMPTON Carrie M d Hopkinton 1886-05-25 age 30yrs b Hopkinton child of MONTGOMERY Charles Vol: 5 Page: 075 Line: 022 Section: 2nd

NILES ---- d Hopkinton 1886-06-28 b Hopkinton child of NILES Thomas J & RAYMOND Elsie Ann Vol: 5 Page: 075 Line: 023 Section: 2nd

PUTNEY ---- d Hopkinton 1886-07-02 child of PUTNEY True & AYERS Ellen M Vol: 5 Page: 075 Line: 024 Section: 2nd

HARDY Benjamin d Hopkinton 1886-07-02 age 83yrs 1mos 22dys b Hopkinton child of HARDY Benjamin & SARAH C Vol: 5 Page: 075 Line: 025 Section: 2nd

SANBORN Lucindia C d Hopkinton 1886-07-03 age 85yrs b Danville child of COLLINS Joseph Vol: 5 Page: 075 Line: 026 Section: 2nd

CURRIER John d Hopkinton 1886-07-06 age 83yrs 11mos b Hopkinton child of CURRIER Amos Vol: 5 Page: 075 Line: 027 Section: 2nd

CROWELL Mary B d Hopkinton 1886-07-21 age 92yrs 8mos b Henniker Vol: 5 Page: 075 Line: 028 Section: 2nd

REYNO Ida R d Hopkinton 1886-08-11 age 3yrs 6mos b Webster child of REYNO Israel & LIBBY Augusta Vol: 5 Page: 077 Line: 001 Section: 2nd

LAW Mary Ella d Hopkinton 1886-08-15 age 1yrs 1mos b Sunapee child of LAW John W & KELLEY Cyntha C Vol: 5 Page: 077 Line: 003 Section: 2nd

NILES Elsie d Hopkinton 1886-08-10 age 32yrs 9mos b Antrim child of RAYMOND George & POLLARD Eleanor Vol: 5 Page: 077 Line: 004 Section: 2nd

Hopkinton, NH Deaths 1880

REYNO Eddy Harry d Hopkinton 1886-08-20 age 2mos child of REYNO Isreal & LIBBY Augusta Vol: 5 Page: 077 Line: 005 Section: 2nd

CROWELL Mary P d Hopkinton 1886-09-09 age 73yrs 3mos b Northield child of HALL Obediah & Forest Vol: 5 Page: 077 Line: 006 Section: 2nd

GETCHELL Joseph S d Hopkinton 1886-09-06 age 1yrs 1mos b Hopkinton child of GETCHELL Chas P & COLLINS Charlotte Vol: 5 Page: 077 Line: 007 Section: 2nd

FLANDERS ---- d Hopkinton 1886-10-31 b Hopkinton child of FLANDERS Walter & ROBY Etta Vol: 5 Page: 077 Line: 009 Section: 2nd

DODGE Sally d Hopkinton 1886-10-31 age 90yrs 6mos 17dys b Warner Vol: 5 Page: 077 Line: 010 Section: 2nd

LONG William H d Boston Mass 1886-11-05 age 73yrs 1mos 27dys b Hopkinton child of LONG Isaac & KIMBALL Susanna Vol: 5 Page: 077 Line: 011 Section: 2nd

PERRY Jennie M d Hopkinton 1886-11-07 age ??yrs b Hopkinton child of PERRY Sylvester W & FLINT Bertha S Vol: 5 Page: 077 Line: 012 Section: 2nd

SARGENT Harriet M d Hopkinton 1886-11-18 age 49yrs 1mos 5dys b Barnstead child of NUTTER William & DAME Eliza Vol: 5 Page: 077 Line: 013 Section: 2nd

MORGAN Irvan A d Hopkinton 1886-11-22 age 16yrs 2mos b Hopkinton child of MORGAN Gilman C & Eva Vol: 5 Page: 077 Line: 014 Section: 2nd

GOODHUE Mary d Hopkinton 1886-12-02 age 63yrs 1dys child of HAM William & HOPKINSON Nancy Vol: 5 Page: 077 Line: 015 Section: 2nd

SPOFFORD S Alfred d Hopkinton 1886-12-13 age 42yrs 10mos child of SPOF-FORD Samuel & FITCH Sarah Vol: 5 Page: 077 Line: 016 Section: 2nd

CHASE Frank S d New Haven Conn 1886-12-16 age 36yrs b Hopkinton child of CHASE Horace J & Mary A Vol: 5 Page: 077 Line: 017 Section: 2nd

MILLS Olive N d Hopkinton 1886-12-20 age 47yrs 4mos 12dys b Weare child of TOWNS S & CLOUGH Roxana Vol: 5 Page: 077 Line: 018 Section: 2nd

ROMAN Michael d Hopkinton 1887-01-05 age 73yrs b Ireland Vol: 5 Page: 079 Line: 001 Section: 2nd

STRAW George H d Concord 1887-01-05 age 41yrs 10mos 24dys child of STRAW Asahel Vol: 5 Page: 079 Line: 002 Section: 2nd

WEST Tom Eugene d Hopkinton 1887-01-10 age 6mos 23dys b Sturbridge Mass child of WEST Tom & STONE Maggie Vol: 5 Page: 079 Line: 003 Section: 2nd

PUTNEY Ira A d Hopkinton 1887-02-07 age 82yrs 5mos 26dys b Hopkinton child of PUTNEY Enoch & POWELL Martha Vol: 5 Page: 079 Line: 004 Section: 2nd

TUCKER Elisabeth J d Hopkinton 1887-02-16 age 81yrs 3mos 15dys b Beverly Mass child of WEBBER Seth & THORNDIKE Marg Vol: 5 Page: 079 Line: 006 Section: 2nd

SPOFFORD ---- d Hopkinton 1887-02-14 b Hopkinton child of SPOFFORD S A & PAIGE Abbie A Vol: 5 Page: 079 Line: 007 Section: 2nd

BURNHAM Edward D d Hopkinton 1887-04-01 age 51yrs 7mos 23dys b Hopkinton child of BURNHAM John & WADLEY Susan E Vol: 5 Page: 079 Line: 010 Section: 2nd

FRENCH Helen C d Hopkinton 1887-07-04 age 48yrs 1mos 16dys b Boscawen child of RUNNELLS Farnum & WEBBER Jerusha Vol: 5 Page: 079 Line: 023 Section: 2nd

DWINELLS Fred d Hopkinton 1887-04-04 age 1yrs 8mos b Hopkinton child of DWINNELLS Warren P & LIBBY Ida A Vol: 5 Page: 079 Line: 011 Section: 2nd

DWINELLS Harry W d Hopkinton 1887-04-09 age 3mos b Hopkinton child of DWINELLS Warren P & LIBBY Ida A Vol: 5 Page: 079 Line: 012 Section: 2nd

MILLS Mand A d Hopkinton 1887-04-11 age 1yrs 9mos b Hopkinton child of MILLS Fred W W & BROWN Belle M Vol: 5 Page: 079 Line: 013 Section: 2nd

DWINELLS Ida A d Hopkinton 1887-04-13 age 22yrs 8mos b Webster child of LIBBY William T & Smart Vol: 5 Page: 079 Line: 014 Section: 2nd

ROWELL Isaac d Hopkinton 1887-04-15 age 73yrs 11mos 26dys b Hopkinton child of ROWELL Moses & EASTMAN Tamson Vol: 5 Page: 079 Line: 015 Section: 2nd

WEBBER Margaret d Hillsboro 1887-04-27 age 24yrs b Conway Mass Vol: 5 Page: 079 Line: 016 Section: 2nd

WELLS Mary d Hopkinton 1887-05-03 age 54yrs 8mos 20dys b Orange child of MORRILL Even O & JACKMAN Mary Vol: 5 Page: 079 Line: 017 Section: 2nd

CHANDLER Robert R d Hopkinton 1887 b Hopkinton Vol: 5 Page: 079 Section: 2nd

DANFORTH Marrietta d Philadelphia Pa 1887 age 45yrs Vol: 5 Page: 079 Line: 019 Section: 2nd

FRENCH Hannah B d Hopkinton 1887-06-14 age 90yrs 7mos b Andover child of BROWN Jonathan & Huntoon Vol: 5 Page: 079 Line: 020 Section: 2nd

BOUTELLE Sarah d Hopkinton 1887-06-16 age 79yrs 6mos child of BUTTER-FIELD Simeon & SILLEY Sarah Vol: 5 Page: 079 Line: 021 Section: 2nd

STEVENS Mary J d Haverhill Mass 1887 age 67yrs 9mos 12dys Vol: 5 Page: 079 Line: 022 Section: 2nd

CHASE Sarah J d Hopkinton 1887-07-06 age 58yrs b Boscawen child of ASH James S & EASTMAN Matilda Vol: 5 Page: 079 Line: 024 Section: 2nd

LOCKE Charles A d Hopkinton 1887-07-24 age 3mos 3dys b Lowell Mass child of LOCKE Arthur S & MERRILL Etta Vol: 5 Page: 079 Line: 026 Section: 2nd

FRENCH Laura E d Hopkinton 1887-07-25 age 13dys b Hopkinton child of FRENCH Charles & HARDY Sarah Vol: 5 Page: 079 Line: 028 Section: 2nd

WILSON Lucinda d Hopkinton 1887-08-24 age 72yrs 11mos 14dys b Hopkinton child of HUSE James Vol: 5 Page: 081 Line: 001 Section: 2nd

STRAW Annie G d Hopkinton 1887-09-03 age 83yrs 6mos 3dys b Newton child of GALE Samuel Vol: 5 Page: 081 Line: 002 Section: 2nd

PUTNEY Sarah D S d Haverhill Mass 1887-09-14 age 77yrs 4mos 10dys Vol: 5 Page: 081 Line: 003 Section: 2nd

SPOFFORD Samuel d Gorham 1887-09-22 age 68yrs 24dys b Chester child of SPOFFORD Sebastian & HOOK Sallie Vol: 5 Page: 081 Line: 004 Section: 2nd

CLOUGH Mary P d Hopkinton 1887-10-10 age 82yrs child of PUTNAM Rufus & FELTON Polly Vol: 5 Page: 081 Line: 005 Section: 2nd

MORGAN Sarah d Hopkinton 1887-10-15 age 55yrs b Bradford child of HOYT James & Belinda Vol: 5 Page: 081 Line: 006 Section: 2nd

FULLER George E d Concord 1887-10-25 age 36yrs Vol: 5 Page: 081 Line: 007 Section: 2nd

MILAN Chloe B d Hopkinton 1887-11-13 age 81yrs 1mos b Uxbridge Mass Vol: 5 Page: 081 Line: 008 Section: 2nd

JOHNSON Samuel d Hopkinton 1887-11-14 age 76yrs 9mos 13dys b Hopkinton Vol: 5 Page: 081 Line: 009 Section: 2nd

ELKINS George A d Hopkinton 1887-11-16 age 37yrs 6mos b Franklin child of ELKINS Jonathan & Clara Vol: 5 Page: 081 Line: 010 Section: 2nd

HOLMES Joanna R d Hopkinton 1887-11-21 age 74yrs b Hopkinton Vol: 5 Page: 081 Line: 011 Section: 2nd

MORGAN Mary A d North Weare 1887-11-27 age 67yrs 6mos Vol: 5 Page: 081 Line: 012 Section: 2nd

STARK Susan Maria d Hopkinton 1887-12-05 age 61yrs b New York child of WINIAS?? William & WEBB Winais Vol: 5 Page: 081 Line: 013 Section: 2nd

KEMPTON Olive J d Hopkinton 1887-12-07 age 41yrs b Hopkinton child of BURBANK T J & CROWELL Susan Vol: 5 Page: 081 Line: 014 Section: 2nd

GAGE M Narzette d Boston Mass 1887-12-10 age 42yrs 5mos 1dys b Hopkinton child of COLBY Timothy & ROLLINS Margarett B Vol: 5 Page: 081 Line: 015 Section: 2nd

GAGE Eliza d Hopkinton 1888-01-03 age 74yrs 6mos 20dys b Marblehead Mass child of MORGAN Samuel & Pricilla Vol: 5 Page: 083 Line: 001 Section: 2nd

HARDY Josie L d Hopkinton 1888-01-05 age 22yrs 1mos 19dys b Hopkinton child of HARDY Samuel A & PUTNEY Abbie A Vol: 5 Page: 083 Line: 002 Section: 2nd

GREENE Liscretia F d Boston Mass 1888-01-18 age 83yrs 4mos 8dys Vol: 5 Page: 083 Line: 003 Section: 2nd

SEAVEY Maria d Hopkinton 1888-01-21 age 60yrs 4mos b Hopkinton child of BRUCE Caleb & BROWN Hannah Vol: 5 Page: 083 Line: 004 Section: 2nd

GETCHEL Judith d Hopkinton 1888-01-27 age 81yrs 6mos b Boscawen child of BURBANK Jonathan & Judith Vol: 5 Page: 083 Line: 005 Section: 2nd

MILTON Mary d Hopkinton 1888-03-04 age 69yrs 11mos b Washington child of SEVERANCE Benj Vol: 5 Page: 083 Line: 006 Section: 2nd

PIPER Lauria d Hopkinton 1888-03-05 age 67yrs 2mos 6dys b Hopkinton child of EATON Thomas & ANNA B Vol: 5 Page: 083 Line: 007 Section: 2nd

STANLEY Horace C d Hopkinton 1888-03-18 age 81yrs 8mos 18dys b Hopkinton child of STANLEY Jonathan & CLARK Rebecca Vol: 5 Page: 083 Line: 008 Section: 2nd

BOHONAN David d Hopkinton 1888-03-22 age 87yrs 11dys b Washington child of BOHONAN Jonathan & WELLS Dolla Vol: 5 Page: 083 Line: 009 Section: 2nd

GAGE Laura B H d Hopkinton 1888-03-28 age 72yrs 11dys b Hopkinton child of GAGE John & BICKFORD Sarah Vol: 5 Page: 083 Line: 010 Section: 2nd

FRENCH Ruben E d Hopkinton 1888-04-01 age 79yrs 11mos 25dys b Hopkinton Vol: 5 Page: 083 Line: 011 Section: 2nd

ROLLINS Edna F d Boston Mass 1888-04-05 age 10mos 5dys b Boston Mass Vol: 5 Page: 083 Line: 012 Section: 2nd

CHASE James M d Germantown Pa 1888-03-14 age 58yrs Vol: 5 Page: 083 Line: 013 Section: 2nd

ROY Hannah E d Hopkinton 1888-04-11 age 32yrs 6mos 12dys b So Natick Mass child of MAHONEY Michael & Mary Vol: 5 Page: 083 Line: 0014 Section: 2nd

DOLLOFF Caroline T d Hopkinton 1888-06-03 age 72yrs 8mos b Hopkinton child of WEBBER Seth & THORNDIKE Mary Vol: 5 Page: 083 Line: 015 Section: 2nd

NICHOLS Nancy d Hillsborough 1888-05-16 age 30yrs 6mos Vol: 5 Page: 083 Line: 016 Section: 2nd

ABBOTT Catharine A d Hopkinton 1888-06-11 age 73yrs 17dys Vol: 5 Page: 083 Line: 017 Section: 2nd

STRAW Asahel S d Hopkinton 1888-07-21 age 79yrs 1mos 22dys b Waterbury Vt child of STRAW Valentine & TAYLOR Eunice Vol: 5 Page: 083 Line: 019 Section: 2nd

GAGE John F d Hopkinton 1888-07-27 age 66yrs 2mos b Hopkinton Vol: 5 Page: 083 Line: 020 Section: 2nd

SANBORN Frederick G d Hopkinton 1888-07-29 age 52yrs 6mos 7dys b Sanbornton child of SANBORN Dyer H & NEWMAN Abigail Vol: 5 Page: 083 Line: 021 Section: 2nd

SYMONDS Delia C d Hopkinton 1888-07-31 age 28yrs 9mos b Ireland child of CONNOR Hugh Vol: 5 Page: 083 Line: 022 Section: 2nd

WHITE Anna M d Hopkinton 1888-08-04 age 63yrs 3mos 18dys Vol: 5 Page: 083 Line: 023 Section: 2nd

SAWYER Daniel d Hopkinton 1888-08-24 age 91yrs 5mos 9dys b Warner child of SAWYER Edward & Mehitalbe Vol: 5 Page: 083 Line: 024 Section: 2nd

LONG Martha M d Boston Mass 1888-09-03 age 76yrs 9mos Vol: 5 Page: 083 Line: 025 Section: 2nd

TRUEHART Catherine d Hopkinton 1888-09-09 age 19yrs 5mos b   child of TRUEHART Peter & Phlinda Vol: 5 Page: 083 Line: 026 Section: 2nd

HOYT Moses d Hopkinton 1888-09-13 age 87yrs 5mos b Hopkinton child of HOYT Moses & Elizabeth Vol: 5 Page: 083 Line: 027 Section: 2nd

CHOATE Geeorge d Hopkinton 1888-09-13 age 89yrs 8mos 8dys b Hopkinton child of CHOATE John T & PEARASON Hannah Vol: 5 Page: 083 Line: 028 Section: 2nd

COLBY Margaret (Mrs) d Hopkinton 1881-04-20 age 62yrs 10mos 12dys b Antrim child of ROLLINS Benjamin & NEVINS Martha Vol: 5 Page: 035 Line: 003 Section: 1st

BUSSELL Elizabeth d Hopkinton 1881-10-05 age 84yrs 6mos b Hopkinton child of BUSSELL Benjamin R & CARTER Joanna Vol: 5 Page: 035 Line: 017 Section: 1st

ELLIOTT Grace A d Manchester 1881-12-31 age 18yrs b Hopkinton child of ELLIOTT Joseph R & SANBORN Angline R Vol: 5 Page: 037 Line: 001 Section: 1st

HEMPHILL George N d Hopkinton 1882-05-08 age 1yrs b Hillsboro child of NICHOLS George A & HEMPHILL Nancy A Vol: 5 Page: 039 Line: 003 Section: 1st

Hopkinton, NH Deaths 1880

RICHARDSON Edna J d Hopkinton 1882-05-28 age 18yrs 5mos 14dys b Hopkinton child of RICHARDSON Thomas & HARDY Eliza A Vol: 5 Page: 039 Line: 007 Section: 1st

BUSSWELL Elizabeth d Hopkinton 1882-10-04 age 84yrs 7mos b Hopkinton child of BUSWELL Benjamin & CARTER Johanna Vol: 5 Page: 039 Line: 023 Section: 1st

POWERS Harry Willis d Hopkinton 1882-11-02 age 2mos 11dys b Hopkinton child of POWERS George M & ROWELL Emma A Vol: 5 Page: 041 Line: 004 Section: 1st

MERRILL Samuel W d Hopkinton 1885-10-01 age 49yrs 10mos 22dys b Hopkinton child of MERRILL Charles & EMERSON Emily E Vol: 5 Page: 073 Line: 009 Section: 2nd

BOHONAN Samuel B d Hopkinton 1889-01-13 age 61yrs 8mos child of BOHONAN David Vol: 5 Page: 087 Line: 004 Section: 2nd

CHASE Mary G d Hopkinton 1889-01-29 age 83yrs 26dys b Webster child of BROWN Thomas & DANFORTH Susan Vol: 5 Page: 087 Line: 005 Section: 2nd

PALMER William d Hopkinton 1889-01-30 age 81yrs 4mos 13dys b Bradford Mass Vol: 5 Page: 087 Line: 006 Section: 2nd

CARR Thomas W d Hopkinton 1889-02-02 age 79yrs 8mos 2dys b child of CARR John & WILLIAMS Abagial Vol: 5 Page: 087 Line: 007 Section: 2nd

CLOUGH Gilman d Hopkinton 1889-02-23 age 87yrs Vol: 5 Page: 087 Line: 008 Section: 2nd

COLBY Hannah B d Hopkinton 1889-03-06 age 82yrs 27dys b Sutton Vol: 5 Page: 087 Line: 009 Section: 2nd

WOODBURY Carrie E d Boston Mass 1889-03-13 age 19yrs 6mos 3dys Vol: 5 Page: 087 Line: 010 Section: 2nd

ROSS Nellie M d Hopkinton 1889-03-27 age 26yrs 7mos 27dys b child of ROSS Ruben R & HUBBARD Sarah L Vol: 5 Page: 087 Line: 011 Section: 2nd

WIGHT Abbie S d Hopkinton 1889-04-01 age 38yrs 9mos b Hopkinton child of CURRIER Alonzo & MERRILL Emily Vol: 5 Page: 087 Line: 012 Section: 2nd

DWINELLS Henry d Hopkinton 1889-04-11 age 7yrs 5mos b Hopkinton child of HARVEY George & DWINELLS Mary F Vol: 5 Page: 087 Line: 013 Section: 2nd

ASH Matilda d Hopkinton 1906-05-06 age 85yrs 1mos 1dys b child of EASTMAN John & HUNT Dolly Vol: 5 Page: 087 Line: 015 Section: 2nd

FELCH Sarah d Hopkinton 1889-05-09 age 79yrs b Warner child of DANFORTH Phineas Vol: 5 Page: 087 Line: 017 Section: 2nd

EASTMAN Henry C d Hopkinton 1889-05-11 age 25yrs 11mos b Hopkinton child of EASTMAN Walter & Hellen Vol: 5 Page: 087 Line: 018 Section: 2nd

GOULD ---- d Hopkinton 1899-12-07 b Hopkinton child of GOULD Robert T & CURRIER Mary Vol: 6 Page: 013

PARKER Hariet S d Hudson 1889-06-05 age 78yrs 6mos Vol: 5 Page: 087 Line: 020 Section: 2nd

CLOUGH Amanda A d Brookline Mass 1889-06-15 age 54yrs Vol: 5 Page: 087 Line: 021 Section: 2nd

KIMBALL Carrie E d Hopkinton 1889-06-19 age 31yrs 7mos b Sutton child of KIMBALL Ido K & RICHARDSON Fannie T Vol: 5 Page: 087 Line: 022 Section: 2nd

BROWN Clarissa d Hopkinton 1889-06-25 age 83yrs Vol: 5 Page: 087 Line: 023 Section: 2nd

RANDALL ---- d Boscawen 1889-07-10 age 4yrs Vol: 5 Page: 087 Line: 024 Section: 2nd

DWINELLS Charles W d Prov Of Qubec 1889-07-11 age 21yrs 1mos 2dys Vol: 5 Page: 087 Line: 025 Section: 2nd

ROWE Mary C d Hopkinton 1889-07-18 age 50yrs b Hopkinton Vol: 5 Page: 087 Line: 026 Section: 2nd

BROUGHTON Cora d Boston Mass 1889-07-19 age 41yrs Vol: 5 Page: 087 Line: 027 Section: 2nd

WYMAN Ebenezer d Henniker 1889-08-01 age 83yrs 6mos 20dys Vol: 5 Page: 087 Line: 028 Section: 2nd

DAVIS Amos H d Hopkinton 1889-08-08 age 74yrs b Hopkinton child of DAVIS Abram & CURRIER Priscilla Vol: 5 Page: 089 Line: 001 Section: 2nd

HARDY Almira C d Hopkinton 1889-08-10 age 78yrs 3mos 10dys b Newbury Mass child of CARR John & Abigal Vol: 5 Page: 089 Line: 002 Section: 2nd

THOMPSON Nathan D d Hopkinton 1889-08-31 age 76yrs 5mos 11dys b Goshen child of THOMPSON John Vol: 5 Page: 089 Line: 004 Section: 2nd

TYLER Charles R d Hopkinton 1889-09-03 age 52yrs 5mos 2dys b Hopkinton child of TYLER Calvin & HASTINGS Zilpha Vol: 5 Page: 089 Line: 005 Section: 2nd

WIGHT Clarence A d Cranston RI 1889-09-12 age 16yrs 23dys Vol: 5 Page: 089 Line: 006 Section: 2nd

HARDY Albert d Hopkinton 1889-09-14 age 98yrs 7mos 11dys b Dunbarton child of HARDY Cyrus Vol: 5 Page: 089 Line: 007 Section: 2nd

BURBANK Catherine d Hopkinton 1889-09-19 age 90yrs 11mos b Hopkinton child of CHASE Moses & KIMBALL Lydia Vol: 5 Page: 089 Line: 008 Section: 2nd

KEZER Moses d Hopkinton 1889-10-06 age 83yrs 6mos Vol: 5 Page: 089 Line: 009 Section: 2nd

WIGGINS William A d Hopkinton 1889-10-15 age 43yrs 11mos 15dys b Hopkinton child of WIGGINS William C & WHITE Julia A Vol: 5 Page: 089 Line: 010 Section: 2nd

CLEMENT Malaha d Hopkinton 1889-10-19 age 81yrs 11mos b Gilford child of WEEKS Thomas Vol: 5 Page: 089 Line: 011 Section: 2nd

SMART Edwin D d Hopkinton 1889-10-23 age 60yrs 4mos 23dys b Hopkinton child of SMART Durrell & BROWN Arianne S Vol: 5 Page: 089 Line: 012 Section: 2nd

BURNS Laura d Hopkinton 1889-10-24 age 75yrs 4mos 20dys Vol: 5 Page: 089 Line: 013 Section: 2nd

STEVENS James d Haverhill 1889-11-19 age 71yrs 1mos 6dys Vol: 5 Page: 089 Line: 014 Section: 2nd

RAND Mathew P d Hopkinton 1889-11-24 age 82yrs 7mos b Hopkinton child of RAND Jonathan & DAVIS Elizabeth Vol: 5 Page: 089 Line: 015 Section: 2nd

Hopkinton, NH Deaths 1880

EMERSON Julia A d Hopkinton 1889-12-01 age 72yrs 10mos 25dys DIAMOND Julia A Vol: 5 Page: 089 Line: 016 Section: 2nd

DOWNING ---- d Hopkinton 1889-12-08 b Hopkinton child of DOWNING Frank E & DOWNING Emma Vol: 5 Page: 089 Line: 017 Section: 2nd

PAIGE Alphonso H d Hopkinton 1889-12-16 age 36yrs b Bow child of PAIGE John Vol: 5 Page: 089 Line: 019 Section: 2nd

DODGE Moses E d Hopkinton 1889-12-16 age 63yrs 2mos 17dys b Hopkinton child of DODGE Henry & EATON Susan Vol: 5 Page: 089 Line: 020 Section: 2nd

CHASE Ann W d Hopkinton 1889-12-21 age 83yrs Vol: 5 Page: 089 Line: 022 Section: 2nd

JAMESON Amelia B d Hopkinton 1890-01-01 age 31yrs child of COULTERS Josiah & Ann Vol: 5 Page: 091 Line: 001 Section: 2nd

COOPER Minnie E d Hopkinton 1890-01-19 age 23yrs 10mos 2dys b Concord child of COOPER John & PERKINS Mary A Vol: 5 Page: 091 Line: 002 Section: 2nd

GAGE Sewell d Hopkinton 1890-01-20 age 80yrs 10mos 7dys b Hopkinton child of GAGE John & SAWYER Mary Vol: 5 Page: 091 Line: 002 Section: 2nd

UPTON Clarinda d Hopkinton 1890-01-22 age 79yrs 11mos 5dys b   child of MERRILL Gove & WYMAN Mary Vol: 5 Page: 091 Line: 004 Section: 2nd

MERRILL Stephen A d Hopkinton 1890-01-25 age 67yrs 10mos 25dys b Groton child of MERRILL Enos & ALLEN Joanna Vol: 5 Page: 091 Line: 005 Section: 2nd

BECK Perley W d Hopkinton 1890-01-25 age 65yrs 10mos child of BECK Clement & SARGENT Susan Vol: 5 Page: 091 Line: 006 Section: 2nd

BROWN Mary J d Hopkinton 1890-01-30 age 50yrs 4mos 4dys b Greenland child of BUTTON Reuben & Nancy Vol: 5 Page: 091 Line: 007 Section: 2nd

PAIGE Elizabeth J d Hopkinton 1890-02-02 age 67yrs 5mos 12dys b Barnstead child of BERRY Joshua & DRAKE Abagial Vol: 5 Page: 091 Line: 010 Section: 2nd

SPOFFORD Frederick d Hopkinton 1890-08-17 age 64yrs 1dys b Chester child of SPOFFORD Sebastian & HOOK Sally Vol: 5 Page: 091 Line: 027 Section: 2nd

FLANDERS Nathaniel d Hopkinton 1890-02-14 age 96yrs 25dys b Hopkinton child of FLANDERS Jeremiah & GEORGE Mariann Vol: 5 Page: 091 Line: 011 Section: 2nd

HUBBARD Hannah d Boston Mass 1890-03-08 age 73yrs 3mos 10dys Vol: 5 Page: 091 Line: 012 Section: 2nd

CROWELL George H d Francestown 1890-04-12 age 28yrs 4mos 6dys Vol: 5 Page: 091 Line: 014 Section: 2nd

MERRILL Parker d Hopkinton 1890-04-14 age 70yrs 2mos 9dys b Groton child of MERRILL Enos & ALLEN Joanna Vol: 5 Page: 091 Line: 015 Section: 2nd

TUTTLE Hannah H d Hopkinton 1890-04-21 age 75yrs 11mos 3dys b Ellsworth child of ELKINS Jasper & PERKINS Sarah Vol: 5 Page: 091 Line: 016 Section: 2nd

STANWOOD Louisa A P d Hopkinton 1890-04-29 age 82yrs b Hopkinton child of PERKINS Binsley & LADD Susan Vol: 5 Page: 091 Line: 082 Section: 2nd

KEIZER James S d Hopkinton 1890-05-12 age 72yrs 5mos b Dorchester child of KEIZER Nathaniel & Elliott Vol: 5 Page: 091 Line: 018 Section: 2nd

PATTERSON Sarah N d Hopkinton 1890-06-14 age 79yrs 8mos b Andover child of PHILBRICK Samuel & GOVE Mary Vol: 5 Page: 091 Line: 019 Section: 2nd

SAUNDERS Ellen J d Haverhill Mass 1890-06-16 age 40yrs 8mos Vol: 5 Page: 091 Line: 020 Section: 2nd

BROWN Hattie A d Hopkinton 1890-07-12 age 29yrs 3mos 4dys b Chichester child of GREENE Newman Vol: 5 Page: 091 Line: 021 Section: 2nd

BOUTELLE Calvin d Hopkinton 1890-07-15 age 92yrs 11mos 5dys b Amherst child of BOUTELLE Joseph Vol: 5 Page: 091 Line: 022 Section: 2nd

WEEKS Jennie E d Hopkinton 1890-07-15 age 43yrs b Hopkinton child of KEIZER Moses & ORDWAY Zilpha Vol: 5 Page: 091 Line: 023 Section: 2nd

BROWN Ellen S d Somerville Mass 1890-07-20 age 43yrs 5mos 10dys Vol: 5 Page: 091 Line: 024 Section: 2nd

SHURTLIFF Eva M d Manchester 1890-07-31 age 16yrs Vol: 5 Page: 091 Line: 025 Section: 2nd

CHOATE Frances E d Hopkinton 1890-08-13 age 48yrs 8mos 1dys b Monroe Me child of LORD Cyrus & RAND Hannah H Vol: 5 Page: 091 Line: 026 Section: 2nd

ELLIOTT Frank P d Hopkinton 1890-08-24 age 37yrs 9mos 13dys b Boscawen child of ELLIOTT Joseph R & SANBORN Angeline P Vol: 5 Page: 091 Line: 028 Section: 2nd

GINN William E d Hopkinton 1890-08-26 age 31yrs b Ohio child of GINN Robert & JONES Jane Vol: 5 Page: 091 Line: 029 Section: 2nd

PUTNEY Lucy E d Hopkinton 1890-08-30 age 76yrs 1mos 26dys b   child of PUTNEY Stephen Vol: 5 Page: 093 Line: 001 Section: 2nd

HOLMES Ausel d Hopkinton 1890-09-16 age 61yrs 8mos 8dys b Boscawen child of HOLMES Gardner & MELVIN Betsey Vol: 5 Page: 093 Line: 002 Section: 2nd

GAGE Harlan P d Boston Mass 1890-09-20 age 47yrs 7mos 17dys Vol: 5 Page: 093 Line: 004 Section: 2nd

DUSTON Mark G d Hopkinton 1890-10-11 age 59yrs 21dys b Henniker child of DUSTON John G & PAIGE Phebe Vol: 5 Page: 093 Line: 005 Section: 2nd

THOMPSON Adaline d Hopkinton 1890-10-15 age 73yrs 7mos 7dys b Lempster child of POLLARD Luther & PUFFER Polly Vol: 5 Page: 093 Line: 006 Section: 2nd

DAVIS Sabrina d Hopkinton 1890-11-01 age 77yrs 7mos 3dys b Hopkinton child of DAVIS Abram & CURRIER Priscilla Vol: 5 Page: 093 Line: 007 Section: 2nd

WAY Betsey d Henniker 1890-11-04 Vol: 5 Page: 093 Line: 008 Section: 2nd

BROWN Abbie A d Hillsborough 1890-11-04 age 54yrs 9mos 6dys Vol: 5 Page: 093 Line: 009 Section: 2nd

FULLER Henry M d Concord 1890-11-14 age 73yrs 2mos 15dys Vol: 5 Page: 093 Line: 010 Section: 2nd

RAYMOND Margaret A d Hopkinton 1890-11-15 age 74yrs 7mos 16dys b Hopkinton child of SIMMONS John & STICKLAND Priscilla Vol: 5 Page: 093 Line: 011 Section: 2nd

MOULTON Mary M d Hopkinton 1890-11-16 age 82yrs 3mos 15dys b Chichester child of MARDEN John & Rachal Vol: 5 Page: 093 Line: 012 Section: 2nd

Hopkinton, NH Deaths 1880

FLANDERS Mary E d Hopkinton 1890-11-27 age 83yrs 8mos 18dys b Hopkinton child of LERNED Ebenezer & HALL Mary Vol: 5 Page: 093 Line: 013 Section: 2nd

WALDRON Ezra Hopkinton 1890-12-07 age 68yrs 6mos 18dys b Concord child of WALDRON Jacob Vol: 5 Page: 093 Line: 014 Section: 2nd

FAGAN ---- d Hopkinton 1890-12-09 b Hopkinton child of FAGAN Christopher & Mary Vol: 5 Page: 093 Line: 015 Section: 2nd

FLANDERS Mary C N d Hopkinton 1890-12-10 age 79yrs 1mos 11dys Vol: 5 Page: 093 Line: 016 Section: 2nd

HOLMES Annie C d Hopkinton 1890-12-23 age 4mos b Hopkinton child of HOLMES Charles A & Eva D Vol: 5 Page: 093 Line: 017 Section: 2nd

THOMPSON Rosleth d Ashland 1891-01-02 age 45yrs 2mos 8dys Vol: 5 Page: 095 Line: 001 Section: 2nd

GAGE Stilman B d Hopkinton 1891-01-02 age 72yrs 1mos 8dys b Hopkinton child of GAGE John & Sarah Vol: 5 Page: 095 Line: 002 Section: 2nd

LITTLE Charles B d Hopkinton 1891-01-18 age 68yrs b Boscawen child of LITTLE Joseph & SEAVEY Sarh B Vol: 5 Page: 095 Line: 003 Section: 2nd

DUNBAR Mary E d Hopkinton 1891-01-19 age 30yrs 2mos b Hopkinton child of GAGE John F & Elizabeth Vol: 5 Page: 095 Line: 005 Section: 2nd

CHASE Ambrose d Hopkinton 1891-02-11 age 80yrs 11mos 15dys b Hopkinton child of CHASE Enoch & MORSE Mary Vol: 5 Page: 095 Line: 005 Section: 2nd

STORY Isaac d Hopkinton 1891-02-18 age 82yrs 2mos 10dys b Hopkinton child of Judith Vol: 5 Page: 095 Line: 006 Section: 2nd

MILLS Jessie Mary d Hopkinton 1891-02-25 age 1mos 15dys b Hopkinton child of MILLS Frank C & HOWARD Mamie Vol: 5 Page: 095 Line: 007 Section: 2nd

HARDY Priscilla N d Concord 1891-03-01 age 74yrs 3mos 19dys Vol: 5 Page: 095 Line: 008 Section: 2nd

FITTS Sarah F d Hopkinton 1891-03-03 age 87yrs 7mos 17dys b Hopkinton child of WEEKS William & Sarah Vol: 5 Page: 095 Line: 009 Section: 2nd

SYMONDS Nancy d Hopkinton 1891-03-04 age 84yrs 6mos 8dys b Concord Vol: 5 Page: 095 Line: 010 Section: 2nd

CLOUGH Phineas d Hopkinton 1891-03-07 age 80yrs 17dys b Hopkinton child of CLOUGH William & COUCH Mary Vol: 5 Page: 095 Line: 011 Section: 2nd

BOUTWELL Carrie E d Hopkinton 1891-03-07 age 4mos 10dys b Hopkinton child of BOUTWELL Arthur & CARRIE J Vol: 5 Page: 095 Line: 012 Section: 2nd

HOLMES Mittie d Hopkinton 1891-03-20 age 70yrs 2mos 20dys b Hopkinton child of OSGOOD Levi & BARNARD Marion Vol: 5 Page: 095 Line: 013 Section: 2nd

CARPENTER Guy d Hopkinton 1891-03-20 age 62yrs 11mos 22dys b Hopkinton child of CARPENTER Joseph & BARR Martha Vol: 5 Page: 095 Line: 014 Section: 2nd

STEVENS Ruth H d Hopkinton 1891-04-05 age 69yrs 10mos 19dys b Hopkinton child of YOUNG John & SANDERS Edna Vol: 5 Page: 095 Line: 015 Section: 2nd

COLBY ---- (infant) d Hopkinton 1891-04-10 age 4dys b Hopkinton child of COLBY Frank T & TYLER Sarah L Vol: 5 Page: 095 Line: 016 Section: 2nd

Hopkinton, NH Deaths 1880

FRAZIER Evelyn S d Hopkinton 1891-04-16 age 22yrs Vol: 5 Page: 095 Line: 017 Section: 2nd

DUKE Judith d Hopkinton 1891-04-28 age 74yrs Vol: 5 Page: 095 Line: 018 Section: 2nd

SARGENT Abner C d Hopkinton 1891-04-28 age 74yrs 3mos 15dys b Henniker child of Thomas & Betsey Vol: 5 Page: 095 Line: 019 Section: 2nd

CURRIER Anna C d Hopkinton 1891-05-10 age 58yrs 11mos 15dys b Sweden child of ANDERSON Andrew Vol: 5 Page: 095 Line: 020 Section: 2nd

HOYT Martha P d Hopkinton 1891-05-08 age 73yrs 11mos 16dys b Henniker child of PAIGE Nathaniel & Susanna Vol: 5 Page: 095 Line: 021 Section: 2nd

STRAW Samuel d Hopkinton 1891-06-10 age 71yrs b Hopkinton child of STRAW Joseph A Vol: 5 Page: 095 Line: 022 Section: 2nd

RUNNELLS Farnum d Hopkinton 1891-06-19 age 96yrs 4mos 25dys b Concord child of RUNNELLS Joseph & FARNUM Joanna Vol: 5 Page: 095 Line: 023 Section: 2nd

HARDY Ellen M d Hopkinton 1891-06-22 age 56yrs 3mos 9dys b Peabody Mass child of PRICE William & Eliza Vol: 5 Page: 095 Line: 024 Section: 2nd

RANDALL Arthur d Boscawen 1891-06-23 age 3yrs 9mos Vol: 5 Page: 095 Line: 025 Section: 2nd

ELLIOTT Joseph R d Hopkinton 1891-06-26 age 67yrs 1mos 10dys b Webster child of ELLIOTT Thomas Vol: 5 Page: 095 Line: 026 Section: 2nd

SARGENT John B d Hopkinton 1891-07-06 age 64yrs 5mos b Pittsfield Vol: 5 Page: 095 Line: 027 Section: 2nd

PERKINS Charlotte d Concord 1891-07-08 age 78yrs Vol: 5 Page: 095 Line: 028 Section: 2nd

BARTON Fannie H d Hopkinton 1891-07-19 age 29yrs 8dys b Brooklyn NY child of BARTON Edwin & BROWN Lucy J Vol: 5 Page: 097 Line: 001 Section: 2nd

TAGGART Adeline W d Hopkinton 1891-08-31 age 53yrs b Sutton child of LOVEREA Timothy & WADLEIGH Julia Vol: 5 Page: 097 Line: 002 Section: 2nd

MUDGETT Clara d Hopkinton 1891-09-12 age 67yrs 2mos b Canada child of FISHER J Ella & NOYES Hannah Vol: 5 Page: 097 Line: 003 Section: 2nd

REYNO Dora Ella d Hopkinton 1891-10-05 age 1yrs b Hopkinton child of RENO Isreal & LIBBY Augusta Vol: 5 Page: 097 Line: 005 Section: 2nd

PERRY Dorathy d Hopkinton 1891-10-21 age 92yrs 11mos 17dys b Litchfield child of FRENCH Asa & LOVEJOY Mary Vol: 5 Page: 097 Line: 006 Section: 2nd

FISK Ephriam d Lowell Mass 1891-10-31 age 93yrs 6mos 14dys Vol: 5 Page: 097 Line: 008 Section: 2nd

KEMPTON Lewis E d Concord 1891-10-30 age 30yrs 3mos child of KEMPTON Warren E & HOWARD Emma D Vol: 5 Page: 097 Line: 009 Section: 2nd

JOHNSON Mary A d Hopkinton 1891-11-03 age 53yrs 10mos child of HOWE Rufus & Vol: 5 Page: 097 Line: 010 Section: 2nd

KEIZER Charles N d Hopkinton 1891-11-07 age 49yrs 8mos 29dys b Hopkinton child of KEIZER Moses & ORDWAY Zilpha Vol: 5 Page: 097 Line: 011 Section: 2nd

BAILEY Lucy P d Hopkinton 1891-11-17 age 83yrs 7mos 7dys b Hopkinton child of KNOWLTON Daniel & Mary Vol: 5 Page: 097 Line: 012 Section: 2nd

Hopkinton, NH Deaths 1880

HOLBROOK Lydia W d Hopkinton 1891-12-03 age 66yrs 7mos 13dys b Bradford child of FLANDERS Nathaniel & WRIGHT Betsey Vol: 5 Page: 097 Line: 013 Section: 2nd

WATERSON Ann N d Concord 1891-11-04 age 4mos Vol: 5 Page: 097 Line: 014 Section: 2nd

CLARK Reuben E d Hopkinton 1891-12-17 age 25yrs 9mos 14dys b No Hartland Vt child of CLARK C N & BODY Susan Vol: 5 Page: 097 Line: 015 Section: 2nd

HOWARD Charles C d Concord 1891-12-22 age 73yrs Vol: 5 Page: 097 Line: 016 Section: 2nd

FLANDERS Jennie M d Holyoke Mass 1891-12-29 age 58yrs Vol: 5 Page: 097 Line: 017 Section: 2nd

SLATH Patrick d Bedford 1891-12-29 age 73yrs Vol: 5 Page: 097 Line: 018 Section: 2nd

WELCH Etta M d Hopkinton 1892-01-01 age 6mos b Concord child of WELCH William & STORY Sadie Vol: 5 Page: 099 Line: 001 Section: 2nd

DUSTIN Harriet P d Lowell Mass 1892-01-01 age 79yrs Vol: 5 Page: 099 Line: 002 Section: 2nd

KIMBALL Benjamin O d Hopkinton 1892-01-03 age 83yrs 3mos 20dys b Hopkinton child of KIMBALL Jacob & Anna Vol: 5 Page: 099 Line: 004 Section: 2nd

STEVENS Mary A d Hopkinton 1892-01-07 age 45yrs b Methunen Mass child of MORRILL Jonathan M & SCRIBNER Eunice Vol: 5 Page: 099 Line: 005 Section: 2nd

CONNOR Arthur C d Hopkinton 1892-01-09 age 6mos 9dys b Hopkinton child of CONNOR Alvah & MORGAN Jennie A Vol: 5 Page: 099 Line: 006 Section: 2nd

GILMAN Julia P d Hopkinton 1892-01-22 age 87yrs 14dys b Kensington child of PRESCOTT Timothy & Anna Vol: 5 Page: 099 Line: 007 Section: 2nd

ADAMS Samuel R d Hopkinton 1892-01-22 age 82yrs Vol: 5 Page: 099 Line: 008 Section: 2nd

MORRILL Jonathan M d Hopkinton 1892-01-25 age 7yrs 8mos 12dys b Salisbury Mass child of MORRILL Joseph & MARTIN Parmelia Vol: 5 Page: 099 Line: 010 Section: 2nd

MAKEPEACE William N d Concord 1892-01-27 age 60yrs 7mos 15dys Vol: 5 Page: 099 Line: 010 Section: 2nd

WEEKS Thomas J d Hopkinton 1892-02-01 age 90yrs 9mos 1dys b Hopkinton child of WEEKS William & SARAH C Vol: 5 Page: 099 Line: 011 Section: 2nd

ROGERS William d Hopkinton 1892-02-03 age 90yrs b Henniker child of ROGERS Obidiah & Flanders Vol: 5 Page: 099 Line: 012 Section: 2nd

REYNO Flora Etta d Hopkinton 1892-02-05 age 1yrs 3mos b Hopkinton child of REYNO Thomas & LIBBY Augusta Vol: 5 Page: 099 Line: 013 Section: 2nd

BALLARD Elizabeth M d Brunswick Me 1892-02-06 age 87yrs Vol: 5 Page: 099 Line: 014 Section: 2nd

BURNHAM Lizzie P d Hopkinton 1892-02-08 age 76yrs 2mos 28dys b Canterbury child of HAM Joseph & SARGENT Susan Vol: 5 Page: 099 Line: 015 Section: 2nd

BARTON Harry d Concord 1892-02-21 age 23dys Vol: 5 Page: 099 Line: 016 Section: 2nd

CURRIER Abigal d Laconia 1892-03-09 age 88yrs Vol: 5 Page: 099 Line: 017 Section: 2nd

MILLS Mary E d Concord 1892-03-18 age 1yrs 3mos Vol: 5 Page: 099 Line: 018 Section: 2nd

SAWYER Nancy J d Hopkinton 1892-03-23 age 90yrs 2mos 23dys b Hillsboro Vol: 5 Page: 099 Line: 019 Section: 2nd

PATTERSON David N d Hopkinton 1892-03-28 age 91yrs 9mos 28dys b Henniker child of PATTERSON Alexander & NELSON Mary Vol: 5 Page: 099 Line: 020 Section: 2nd

ROLLINS Mary E d Hopkinton 1892-03-31 age 68yrs 9mos b Hopkinton child of COLBY Moses & Elsie Vol: 5 Page: 099 Line: 021 Section: 2nd

SMART George d Hopkinton 1892-04-03 age 29yrs 10mos b Hopkinton child of SMART George & HARDY Esther Vol: 5 Page: 099 Line: 022 Section: 2nd

COUCH Elbridge d Hopkinton 1892-04-11 age 69yrs 3mos 17dys b Salisbury child of COUCH Samuel & HOWARD Eunice Vol: 5 Page: 099 Line: 024 Section: 2nd

MORRILL Ebenezer d Hopkinton 1892-04-13 age 85yrs 9mos b Salisbury Mass child of MORRILL Joseph & MARTIN Pamelia Vol: 5 Page: 099 Line: 025 Section: 2nd

BUSWELL Samuel d Hopkinton 1892-04-12 age 88yrs 1mos 10dys b Gilmanton child of BUSWELL Nicholas & Hannah Vol: 5 Page: 099 Line: 026 Section: 2nd

TUCKER Mahala d Hopkinton 1892-04-13 age 81yrs 8mos 13dys b Henniker child of TUCKER Ezra & HARDY Hannah Vol: 5 Page: 099 Line: 027 Section: 2nd

CORLISS Eben d Hopkinton 1892-04-21 age 92yrs 7dys b Alexander child of CORLISS George & LADD Ruth Vol: 5 Page: 099 Line: 028 Section: 2nd

WELLS William S d Hopkinton 1892-04-23 age 78yrs 1mos 9dys b Hill child of WELLS Moses & ROWELL Sarah Vol: 5 Page: 101 Line: 001 Section: 2nd

CONNOR Asa d Hopkinton 1892-04-29 age 80yrs 3mos b Henniker child of CONNER Samuel & TRUMBALL Sally Vol: 5 Page: 101 Line: 002 Section: 2nd

MASON Annette d Marboro 1892 Feb Vol: 5 Page: 101 Line: 003 Section: 2nd

FLANDERS Melissa J d Hopkinton 1892-05-01 age 60yrs b Henniker child of DOW Squire & PAIGE Cyntha Vol: 5 Page: 101 Line: 004 Section: 2nd

PUTNAM Charles d Hopkinton 1892-05-02 age 52yrs 1mos 24dys b Hopkinton child of PUTNAM Martin & BAKER Margaret Vol: 5 Page: 101 Line: 005 Section: 2nd

RIMMER Thomas d Hopkinton 1898-02-18 age 79yrs 3mos 21dys b Boston Mass child of RINMER Thomas Vol: 6 Page: 001

DUSTIN ---- d Hopkinton 1892-05-19 b Hopkinton child of DUSTIN Cyrus & SPAULDING Nellie S Vol: 5 Page: 101 Line: 007 Section: 2nd

CONNOR Joel d Hopkinton 1892-06-07 age 76yrs 1mos 19dys b Henniker child of CONNOR Samuel & TRUMBALL Sally Vol: 5 Page: 101 Line: 008 Section: 2nd

HOWE William d Goshen 1892-06-17 age 65yrs Vol: 5 Page: 101 Line: 009 Section: 2nd

Hopkinton, NH Deaths 1880

DOW Henry E d Hopkinton 1892-07-07 age 63yrs 2mos 2dys b Concord child of DOW William & AUSTIN Hannah Vol: 5 Page: 101 Line: 010 Section: 2nd

COOMBS Stephen B d Hopkinton 1892-07-12 age 59yrs 6mos 8dys b Springfield child of COOMBS Stephen & SHAW Lucretia Vol: 5 Page: 101 Line: 011 Section: 2nd

RICHARDSON Eliza d Hopkinton 1892-07-14 age 80yrs 11mos 12dys b Canterbury Vol: 5 Page: 101 Line: 012 Section: 2nd

BEAN Amos d Warner 1892-07-15 age 62yrs 1mos b Fremont Vol: 5 Page: 101 Line: 013 Section: 2nd

MILTON John M d Hopkinton 1892-07-16 age 78yrs 9mos b Henniker child of MILTON Daniel & PRESSEY Judith Vol: 5 Page: 101 Line: 014 Section: 2nd

MORRILL Mary I d Hopkinton 1892-07-25 age 32yrs b Candia child of DEARBORN T B & BEAN N J Vol: 5 Page: 101 Line: 015 Section: 2nd

PHILBRICK Mary S d Hopkinton 1892-07-27 age 82yrs b Henniker child of SAWYER Rufus & HOWE Polly Vol: 5 Page: 101 Line: 016 Section: 2nd

TILTON Minnie J F d Hopkinton 1892-08-14 age 39yrs 4mos 25dys b Canada child of NADEAU Rennie & FRY Martha F Vol: 5 Page: 101 Line: 018 Section: 2nd

WOODBURY Hiriam W d Hopkinton 1892-08-30 age 83yrs 11mos 14dys b Dunbarton child of WOODBURY Ebenezer & KITTRIDGE Mary Vol: 5 Page: 101 Line: 019 Section: 2nd

COLBY Eliza B d Hopkinton 1892-09-18 age 76yrs 2mos b Windham child of BARRETT Elmer & Alice Vol: 5 Page: 101 Line: 021 Section: 2nd

SCOTT Lucitta d Concord 1892-09-20 age 64yrs 8mos 3dys Vol: 5 Page: 101 Line: 022 Section: 2nd

PUTNAM Rachael d Lowell Mass 1892-09-26 age 88yrs 9mos 21dys Vol: 5 Page: 101 Line: 023 Section: 2nd

HOWE Kate A d Hopkinton 1892-10-08 age 28yrs child of HOWE Edward & JOHNSON Ann M Vol: 5 Page: 101 Line: 028 Section: 2nd

WALKER Mary H d Hopkinton 1892-11-09 age 55yrs b Ireland Vol: 5 Page: 101 Line: 025 Section: 2nd

HOYT Isiah d Hopkinton 1892-11-11 age 79yrs 7mos b Hopkinton Vol: 5 Page: 101 Line: 026 Section: 2nd

ROWELL Sarah A d Hopkinton 1892-11-22 age 50yrs 9mos 5dys b Hudson child of DUTTON John & HADLEY Josie Vol: 5 Page: 101 Line: 027 Section: 2nd

CHASE Ida d Hopkinton 1892-11-22 age 17yrs child of CHASE George & THAYER Susie E Vol: 5 Page: 101 Line: 028 Section: 2nd

DANIEL Myra I d Hopkinton 1892-11-26 age 3mos 10dys b Hopkinton child of DANIELS Mark H & MERRILL Annie Vol: 5 Page: 103 Line: 001 Section: 2nd

STANWOOD Caroline N d Malden Mass 1892-12-17 age 64yrs Vol: 5 Page: 103 Line: 003 Section: 2nd

FELLOWS Sarah J d Hopkinton 1892-12-15 age 83yrs 2mos b Plaistow child of COPS Moses & GEORGE Mary Vol: 5 Page: 103 Line: 004 Section: 2nd

MONTGOMERY Lucy d Hopkinton 1892-12-25 age 62yrs b Warner child of SEAVEY Daniel & SNOW Mary Vol: 5 Page: 103 Line: 005 Section: 2nd

LERNERD Catherine C P d Hopkinton 1892-12-26 age 75yrs 5mos 5dys b Hopkinton child of LERNERD Ebenezer & PERKINS Catherine Vol: 5 Page: 103 Line: 006 Section: 2nd

BARTON Phebe d Hopkinton 1892-12-07 age 86yrs 6mos b Hopkinton child of STRAW Joseph & GARDNER Betsey Vol: 5 Page: 103 Line: 002 Section: 2nd

BALDWIN Frederick C d Hopkinton 1893-10-05 age 6mos 18dys b Chelsea Mass child of BALDWIN H F & PARTRIDGE L M Vol: 5 Page: 107 Line: 001 Section: 2nd

SMART Charles H d Webster 1893-01-17 age 54yrs Vol: 5 Page: 105 Line: 003 Section: 2nd

WIGGIN Julia A d Hopkinton 1893-01-20 age 76yrs 2mos 10dys b Topsfield Mass child of WHITE Olive G & BROWN Rebecca Vol: 5 Page: 105 Line: 004 Section: 2nd

DOW Clara J d Salisbury 1893-02-11 age 36yrs 1mos 21dys Vol: 5 Page: 105 Line: 005 Section: 2nd

CARPENTER Hattie F d Newmarket 1893-02-11 age 39yrs 1mos Vol: 5 Page: 105 Line: 006 Section: 2nd

WRIGHT Frank L d Hopkinton 1893-02-17 age 16yrs 10mos 21dys child of WRIGHT Henry P & HOLMES Sarah S Vol: 5 Page: 105 Line: 007 Section: 2nd

MERRILL Julia A d Hopkinton 1893-03-16 age 49yrs 3mos 25dys b Hopkinton child of FOLSMON Sophia Vol: 5 Page: 105 Line: 008 Section: 2nd

WATTERSON Alice Mary d Penacook 1893-03-16 age 1yrs 7mos 19dys Vol: 5 Page: 105 Line: 009 Section: 2nd

LOW Flora d Hopkinton 1893-03-26 age 81yrs 8mos child of EASTMAN Ezra & EATON Polly Vol: 5 Page: 105 Line: 010 Section: 2nd

CLARK Mary A d Hopkinton 1893-04-07 age 75yrs 10mos 22dys b Goffstown child of STICKNEY Isaac & QUIMBY Betsy Vol: 5 Page: 105 Line: 011 Section: 2nd

WILSON Pamelia d Hopkinton 1893-04-16 age 78yrs 10mos 13dys b Canterbury child of INGALLS Jesse & CHASE Hannah Vol: 5 Page: 105 Line: 012 Section: 2nd

TILTON Timothy d Hopkinton 1893-05-02 age 74yrs 7mos 29dys b Hopkinton child of TILTON John R & FOWLER Mary Vol: 5 Page: 105 Line: 013 Section: 2nd

STRAW Emiline K d Hopkinton 1893-05-08 age 66yrs 7mos 27dys b Merrimack Mass child of KELLY Stephen & BARTLETT Hannah Vol: 5 Page: 105 Line: 014 Section: 2nd

STORY Lydia P d Hopkinton 1893-07-02 age 84yrs 6mos 14dys b Hopkinton child of KIMBALL Moses & MOORE Jane M Vol: 5 Page: 105 Line: 015 Section: 2nd

DODGE Sarah S d Hopkinton 1893-07-06 age 63yrs b New Boston child of DODGE Samuel & CHANDLER Sophia Vol: 5 Page: 105 Line: 016 Section: 2nd

BROWN Elesa Ida d Hopkinton 1893-05-13 age 3mos 15dys b Hopkinton child of BROWN Valorous & LIBBY Sarah Vol: 5 Page: 105 Line: 017 Section: 2nd

KNOWLTON John H d Hopkinton 1893-06-19 age 49yrs Vol: 5 Page: 105 Line: 018 Section: 2nd

CLARK Jacob K d Hopkinton 1893-07-22 age 81yrs 3mos 18dys b Hopkinton child of CLARK Jacob & HUSE Betsey Vol: 5 Page: 105 Line: 019 Section: 2nd

CONANT Hiriam E d Hopkinton 1893-08-04 age 53yrs 11mos b Mansfield Conn child of CONANT Lucus & EATON Marcella Vol: 5 Page: 105 Line: 020 Section: 2nd

JENKINS George W d Hopkinton 1893-08-22 age 53yrs Vol: 5 Page: 105 Line: 021 Section: 2nd

ANLDER John d Hopkinton 1893-08-26 age 30yrs b England Vol: 5 Page: 105 Line: 022 Section: 2nd

BURBANK Ruth L d Concord 1893-09-03 age 2mos 14dys Vol: 5 Page: 105 Line: 023 Section: 2nd

CHASE Lucretia Straw d Warner 1893-08-28 age 67yrs Vol: 5 Page: 105 Line: 024 Section: 2nd

KEAZER Zilpha d Henniker 1893-09-12 age 69yrs 11mos Vol: 5 Page: 105 Line: 025 Section: 2nd

BROWN Sarah G d Hopkinton 1893-09-21 age 28yrs 3mos b Webster child of LIBBIE Wm T & SMART Ellen Vol: 5 Page: 105 Line: 026 Section: 2nd

RUSSELL ---- d Hopkinton 1893-09-21 b Hopkinton child of RUSSELL Arthur & TUTTLE Mabel Vol: 5 Page: 105 Line: 027 Section: 2nd

ANNIS Herrick C d Hopkinton 1893-09-30 age 73yrs 4mos 10dys b Hopkinton child of ANNIS Wm & BARNARD Betsey Vol: 5 Page: 105 Line: 028 Section: 2nd

CORLISS Etta N d Hopkinton 1893-09-30 age 30yrs 1mos 23dys b Warner child of PAIGE Dustin & MANSFIELD Samantha Vol: 5 Page: 105 Line: 029 Section: 2nd

HOWARD Lewis d Springfield 1893-10-06 age 90yrs 10mos 2dys Vol: 5 Page: 107 Line: 002 Section: 2nd

NOYES Julia d Hopkinton 1893-10-26 age 86yrs 7mos 19dys b Henniker child of STORY David & CURRIER Mahitable Vol: 5 Page: 107 Line: 004 Section: 2nd

BURBANK Susan d Hopkinton 1893-11-02 age 86yrs 6mos 7dys b Hopkinton child of CROWELL John W & HOLMES Susan Vol: 5 Page: 107 Line: 005 Section: 2nd

CROWELL Martin T d Hopkinton 1893-11-30 age 58yrs b Hopkinton child of CROWELL Proctor & CONNER Mary Vol: 5 Page: 107 Line: 006 Section: 2nd

NYE Nicholas d Hopkinton 1893-12-18 age 57yrs 7mos 3dys b Buffalo NY child of NYE Peter Vol: 5 Page: 107 Line: 007 Section: 2nd

HILAND George B d Hopkinton 1893-12-25 age 49yrs 5mos 15dys b Hopkinton child of HILAND John B & WHITE Chole B Vol: 5 Page: 107 Line: 008 Section: 2nd

HOLMES Alvah P d Hopkinton 1893-12-28 age 7mos b Hopkinton Vol: 5 Page: 107 Line: 009 Section: 2nd

TILTON Ranson S d Hopkinton 1893 age 79yrs 4mos 11dys b Hopkinton Vol: 5 Page: 107 Line: 010 Section: 2nd

BOHONAN Belinda B d Hopkinton 1894-01-07 age 85yrs 3mos 16dys b Sutton Vol: 5 Page: 109 Line: 001 Section: 2nd

WHITTIER Amos H d Hopkinton 1894-01-10 age 68yrs 10mos 10dys b Boscawen child of WHITTIER Enoch & DOW Lucinda Vol: 5 Page: 109 Line: 003 Section: 2nd

BRUCE Robert A d Boston Mass 1894-01-10 age 29yrs 2mos 6dys Vol: 5 Page: 109 Line: 004 Section: 2nd

STRAW Abigail d Hopkinton 1894-01-22 age 82yrs 11mos 28dys b Hopkinton child of JEWELL Ezra & BICKFORD Abigail Vol: 5 Page: 109 Line: 006 Section: 2nd

KELLEY Stephen d Hopkinton 1894-01-27 age 90yrs 8mos 11dys b West Newbury Ma child of KELLEY Nathan & BROWN Elizabeth Vol: 5 Page: 109 Line: 007 Section: 2nd

CONNOR Anna A d Hopkinton 1894-01-31 age 80yrs 8mos 26dys b Concord child of AELIN George & CHANDLER Sarah Vol: 5 Page: 109 Line: 008 Section: 2nd

GILMORE Delia A d Hopkinton 1894-03-26 age 17yrs 8mos 21dys b Newport Vt child of GILMORE Lucius N & BURNHAM Lavina R Vol: 5 Page: 109 Line: 010 Section: 2nd

CROWELL Wm d Boscawen 1894-04-06 age 81yrs Vol: 5 Page: 109 Line: 011 Section: 2nd

MORIN Phebe d Hopkinton 1894-04-07 age 1mos 19dys b New Boston child of MORIN George & BOSLIN? Celestas Vol: 5 Page: 109 Line: 012 Section: 2nd

DWINELLS Carrie N d Manchester 1894-04-16 age 47yrs 8mos 2dys Vol: 5 Page: 109 Line: 013 Section: 2nd

BOUTWELL Elmer N d Hopkinton 1894-04-29 age 49yrs 6mos b Williamstown Vt child of BOUTWELL Samuel & ALLEN Lydia Vol: 5 Page: 109 Line: 015 Section: 2nd

BACON Ann P d Hopkinton 1894-05-04 age 55yrs 7mos 14dys b Hopkinton child of BURBANK Hiram & ORDWAY Hannah Vol: 5 Page: 109 Line: 016 Section: 2nd

HAGER Joseph d Hopkinton 1894-05-15 age 76yrs 7mos b Hartland Vt Vol: 5 Page: 109 Line: 017 Section: 2nd

CLOUGH Parney B?? d Hopkinton 1894-06-01 age 78yrs 9mos 11dys child of ELLIOTT Benjamin & COLBY Judith Vol: 5 Page: 109 Line: 018 Section: 2nd

ABBOTT ---- d Hopkinton 1894-06-08 age 30dys b Hopkinton child of ABBOTT Elden & POWERS Addie E Vol: 5 Page: 109 Line: 019 Section: 2nd

SMITH Aaron d Hopkinton 1894-06-16 age 66yrs 10mos child of SMITH Aaron & SHUBURNE Eliza A Vol: 5 Page: 109 Line: 020 Section: 2nd

RAYNO Augusta d Hopkinton 1894-07-02 age 32yrs b Webster child of LIBBY William T & CARTER Joanna Vol: 5 Page: 109 Line: 021 Section: 2nd

PHELPS George d Warner age 64yrs Vol: 5 Page: 109 Line: 022 Section: 2nd

DUNBAR Mary J d Hopkinton 1894-07-26 age 71yrs 14mos b Hopkinton child of BRUCE Caleb & BROWN Hannah Vol: 5 Page: 109 Line: 024 Section: 2nd

CHASE Thomas d Hopkinton 1894-08-14 age 89yrs 3mos 2dys b Hopkinton child of CHASE Enoch & MORSE Mary Vol: 5 Page: 109 Line: 026 Section: 2nd

OBER Ariel P d Hopkinton 1894-08-23 age 93yrs 9mos b Hopkinton child of OBER Benjamin & WOODBURY Elizabeth Vol: 5 Page: 109 Line: 027 Section: 2nd

WEST Robert S d Hopkinton 1894-08-26 age 40yrs 5mos 21dys b Concord child of WEST George W & SEAVEY Mary A Vol: 5 Page: 111 Line: 001 Section: 2nd

ROBINSON Benjamin F d Hopkinton 1894-08-26 age 65yrs b Kingston Vol: 5 Page: 111 Line: 002 Section: 2nd

Hopkinton, NH Deaths 1880

RAYMOND Joshua d Hopkinton 1894-09-01 age 82yrs b Salem Mass child of RAYMOND Joshua & Hannah Vol: 5 Page: 111 Line: 003 Section: 2nd

BURNHAM Charles C d Hopkinton 1894-09-14 age 79yrs 7mos b Antrim child of BURNHAM Epps & CAVENDER Sarah Vol: 5 Page: 111 Line: 004 Section: 2nd

BURBANK Ruth d Hopkinton 1894-09-19 age 76yrs 1mos Vol: 5 Page: 111 Line: 006 Section: 2nd

ABBOTT Mary Ann d Hopkinton 1898-02-23 age 73yrs 4mos 4dys b Henniker child of FRENCH Benjamin Vol: 6 Page: 001

BROCKWAY Etta B d Hopkinton 1894-09-24 age 32yrs 11mos 14dys b Hopkinton child of BROCKWAY John G & CARROLL Amanda M Vol: 5 Page: 111 Line: 008 Section: 2nd

MORRILL Donald A d Hopkinton 1894-09-29 age 1yrs 4mos 26dys b Hopkinton child of MORRILL Frank I & STEVENS Hattie S Vol: 5 Page: 111 Line: 009 Section: 2nd

BOUTWELL Helen M d Hopkinton 1894-10-03 age 1yrs 19dys b Hopkinton child of BOUTWELL Henry B A & MONTGOMERY Alice Vol: 5 Page: 111 Line: 010 Section: 2nd

DUNBAR Irene d Hopkinton 1894-10-05 age 3mos 15dys b Jaffrey child of DUNBAR Charles S & EASTMAN Jennie S Vol: 5 Page: 111 Line: 011 Section: 2nd

CURTICE Lenora d Hopkinton 1894-10-10 age 78yrs 4mos 15dys b Windsor child of SWEATT John & PRESTON Mary Vol: 5 Page: 111 Line: 012 Section: 2nd

EDMUNDS Horace d Hopkinton 1894-10-17 age 90yrs 7mos 18dys b Weare child of EDMUNDS Ezra & PAIGE Hannah Vol: 5 Page: 111 Line: 013 Section: 2nd

STRAW Roger d Hopkinton 1894-10-29 age 1dys b Hopkinton child of STRAW James & WHITTIMORE Ada M Vol: 5 Page: 111 Line: 014 Section: 2nd

ERICSON Carl L d Hopkinton 1894-11-05 age 40yrs b Sweden Vol: 5 Page: 111 Line: 015 Section: 2nd

BARTON Mary E d Hopkinton 1894-11-05 age 27yrs 3mos 21dys child of CURRIER Lozaro & ANDERSON Anna Vol: 5 Page: 111 Line: 016 Section: 2nd

DANFORTH Enoch d Hopkinton 1894-11-11 age 70yrs 5mos 17dys b Boscawen child of DANFORTH Edmund & CLOUGH Rhoda Vol: 5 Page: 111 Line: 017 Section: 2nd

WHYTUCK ---- d Hopkinton 1894-11-21 age 2dys b Hopkinton child of WHY-TUCK David & Bella Vol: 5 Page: 111 Line: 018 Section: 2nd

DODGE Clarence B d Hopkinton 1894-11-23 age 10yrs 2mos 24dys Vol: 5 Page: 111 Line: 020 Section: 2nd

GAGE Charles P d Hopkinton 1894-11-26 age 83yrs 7mos 21dys b Hopkinton Vol: 5 Page: 111 Line: 021 Section: 2nd

HOYT Benjamin d Concord 1894-12-30 age 81yrs 10mos 19dys child of HOYT James & Harriet Vol: 5 Page: 111 Line: 022 Section: 2nd

TASKER Joseph P d Hopkinton 1895-01-02 age 76yrs 1mos 10dys b Loudon Vol: 5 Page: 113 Line: 002 Section: 2nd

DUSTON Phebe d Hopkinton 1895-01-07 age 91yrs 11mos 15dys b Warner child of PAIGE Nathaniel & MUZZEY Susan Vol: 5 Page: 113 Line: 003 Section: 2nd

DOW Anna P d Hopkinton 1895-01-11 age 77yrs 4mos 6dys b Weare child of PEASLEE James & Mary Vol: 5 Page: 113 Line: 004 Section: 2nd

KIMBALL ---- d Hopkinton 1895-03-07 age 1dys b Hopkinton child of KIMBALL Nelson D & PATCH Adelade M Vol: 5 Page: 113 Line: 010 Section: 2nd

BURNES Fred d Hopkinton 1898-03-16 age 11yrs 9mos child of COPP George & FAIRFIELD Lizzie Vol: 6 Page: 002

KIMBALL Mary S d Washington DC 1895-02-28 age 62yrs 6mos 19dys Vol: 5 Page: 113 Line: 008 Section: 2nd

FLANDERS Daniel d Hopkinton 1895-03-02 age 74yrs 8mos b Concord child of FLANDERS John & ABBOTT Rachel Vol: 5 Page: 113 Line: 009 Section: 2nd

SANBORN Michael d Hopkinton 1895-03-21 age 60yrs b Ireland Vol: 5 Page: 113 Line: 011 Section: 2nd

LERNED Hannah Brooks d Hopkinton 1895-03-30 age 73yrs 11mos 20dys b Hopkinton child of LERNED Ebenezer & HOPKINS Catherine Vol: 5 Page: 113 Line: 012 Section: 2nd

WRIGHT Henry P d Hopkinton 1895-04-05 age 54yrs 2mos 18dys b Bradford child of WRIGHT Joshua Vol: 5 Page: 113 Line: 013 Section: 2nd

STRAW Lucinda d Hopkinton 1895-04-25 age 71yrs 20dys b Hopkinton child of STRAW Jacob & FLANDERS Miriam Vol: 5 Page: 113 Line: 014 Section: 2nd

GIENTY Harriet E d Concord 1895-01-23 age 36yrs 2mos 23dys Vol: 5 Page: 113 Line: 015 Section: 2nd

SCRIBNER Frank B d Concord 1895-04-04 age 60yrs 10mos 21dys Vol: 5 Page: 113 Line: 016 Section: 2nd

WHITE Roxanna d Weare 1895-05-07 age 59yrs 2mos 20dys Vol: 5 Page: 113 Line: 017 Section: 2nd

HOLT Mary A d Hopkinton 1895-05-27 age 75yrs 11mos b New Boston child of COCHRAN Joseph & NELSON Annie Vol: 5 Page: 113 Line: 018 Section: 2nd

NOYES Edna d National City Calif 1895-05-20 age 22yrs Vol: 5 Page: 113 Line: 019 Section: 2nd

---- ---- d Concord 1895-06-08 age 1/4dys Vol: 5 Page: 113 Line: 020 Section: 2nd

RICE Minnie A d Hopkinton 1895-06-15 age 33yrs 2mos 16dys b Hopkinton child of WHITTIMORE William & RANDALL Nancy S Vol: 5 Page: 113 Line: 022 Section: 2nd

DARLING Welcome B d Hopkinton 1895-06-27 age 62yrs 8mos b Providence RI child of DARLING W B Vol: 5 Page: 113 Line: 023 Section: 2nd

PUTNAM Rufus d Hopkinton 1895-07-24 age 81yrs 9mos 24dys b Hopkinton child of PUTNAM Rufus & FELTON Polly Vol: 5 Page: 113 Line: 024 Section: 2nd

PHILBRICK Nathaniel E d Manchester 1895-08-08 age 74yrs 2mos 17dys Vol: 5 Page: 113 Line: 025 Section: 2nd

SMART Durrell d Hopkinton 1895-08-17 age 87yrs 11mos 2dys b Hopkinton child of SMART Benning & HUTCHINS Abigal Vol: 5 Page: 113 Line: 026 Section: 2nd

SMITH Dexter d Hopkinton 1895-08-26 age 71yrs b Francestown Vol: 5 Page: 113 Line: 027 Section: 2nd

MINER Gladys Mabelle d Webster 1895-09-04 Vol: 5 Page: 113 Line: 028 Section: 2nd

Hopkinton, NH Deaths 1880

HILAND Minnie d Hopkinton 1895-09-12 age 17yrs 8mos 10dys b Hopkinton child of HILAND George B & KIMBALL Priscilla Vol: 5 Page: 115 Line: 001 Section: 2nd

RION Cyntha d Warner 1895-09-16 age 63yrs Vol: 5 Page: 115 Line: 002 Section: 2nd

BARTLETT Lucinda d Hopkinton 1895-10-10 age 79yrs 4mos b Warner child of CLARK Amos & Betsey Vol: 5 Page: 115 Line: 004 Section: 2nd

CURRIER Hannah d Hopkinton 1895-10-24 age 77yrs 8mos child of FLANDERS Philip & SMITH Sarah Vol: 5 Page: 115 Line: 005 Section: 2nd

DUSTIN Cyrus d Hopkinton 1895-11-06 age 87yrs 11mos 7dys b Warner child of DUSTIN Ebenezer & PRICE Sarah Vol: 5 Page: 115 Line: 006 Section: 2nd

WHITTIER Harriet d Hopkinton 1895-12-06 age 72yrs 3mos 21dys b Davisville child of SANBORN Peter & COLLINS Lucinda Vol: 5 Page: 115 Line: 007 Section: 2nd

FLETCHER Elvira d Hopkinton 1896-01-07 age 62yrs 9mos 2dys b Bradford child of CRAM Benjamin & WOODS Lucinda Vol: 5 Page: 117 Line: 001 Section: 2nd

DUSTIN ---- d Hopkinton 1896-01-11 b Hopkinton child of DUSTIN Cyrus F & SPAULDING Nelli Vol: 5 Page: 117 Line: 002 Section: 2nd

MORAN Celista d Hopkinton 1896-02-09 age 35yrs 9mos 12dys b Canada Vol: 5 Page: 117 Line: 003 Section: 2nd

OSBORNE Abner d Hopkinton 1896-02-10 age 73yrs b Springfield child of OSBORNE William & HOGG Elizabeth Vol: 5 Page: 117 Line: 004 Section: 2nd

CURRIER Emily M d Hopkinton 1896-02-15 age 72yrs 3dys b Hillsborough child of MERRILL Isaac & WYMAN Mary Vol: 5 Page: 117 Line: 005 Section: 2nd

HERSEY Cyntha F d Concord 1896-02-26 age 84yrs 3mos 9dys Vol: 5 Page: 117 Line: 006 Section: 2nd

GREENE Herman W d Hopkinton 1896-03-01 age 59yrs 10mos 19dys b Hopkinton child of GREENE Herman H & LITTLE Ellen Chase Vol: 5 Page: 117 Line: 007 Section: 2nd

WATTERSON Adelbert N d Concord 1896-03-03 age 7mos 22dys Vol: 5 Page: 117 Line: 008 Section: 2nd

FOLSOM Sophronia d Hopkinton 1896-03-12 age 84yrs 1mos 8dys b Henniker child of TUCKER Ezra & HARDY Hannan Vol: 5 Page: 117 Line: 009 Section: 2nd

RAYMOND Mary J d Concord 1896-03-14 age 55yrs Vol: 5 Page: 117 Line: 010 Section: 2nd

CURTICE Samuel d Hopkinton 1896-03-30 age 83yrs b Windsor child of CURTICE John & GIBSON Mildred Vol: 5 Page: 117 Line: 011 Section: 2nd

BURNHAM John F d Randolph Vt 1896-04-11 age 63yrs Vol: 5 Page: 117 Line: 012 Section: 2nd

HARDY Tyler B d Hopkinton 1896-04-12 age 88yrs 6mos b Warner child of HARDY Isaac & BODWELL Hannah Vol: 5 Page: 117 Line: 013 Section: 2nd

WILSON Jeremiah d Hopkinton 1896-04-30 age 80yrs 3mos 18dys b Franklin child of WILSON Job & FARNUM Nancy Vol: 5 Page: 117 Line: 014 Section: 2nd

HEATH Carrie W N d Concord 1896-01-29 age 2yrs 5mos 10dys Vol: 5 Page: 117 Line: 015 Section: 2nd

UPTON Sara E d Limirick Me 1896-05-14 age 51yrs 7mos 8dys Vol: 5 Page: 117 Line: 016 Section: 2nd

SWEATT Sallie L d Hopkinton 1896-05-18 age 78yrs 3mos b Boscawen child of SWEATT Stephen & LITTLE Judith Vol: 5 Page: 117 Line: 017 Section: 2nd

GOODRICH Florence A d Hopkinton 1896-05-23 age 28yrs 1mos 22dys b Hopkinton child of GOODRICH George K & LORD Lydia Vol: 5 Page: 117 Line: 018 Section: 2nd

HODGDON Charles W d Hopkinton 1896-05-31 age 69yrs 2mos b Concord child of HODGDON C H & MERRILL Betsey Vol: 5 Page: 117 Line: 019 Section: 2nd

ORDWAY Julia Ann d Concord 1896-06-08 age 59yrs 1dys b Sutton Vol: 5 Page: 117 Line: 020 Section: 2nd

BEAN Levi d Hopkinton 1896-06-20 age 77yrs 4mos b Candia child of BEAN Joseph & ROWE Mary Vol: 5 Page: 117 Line: 021 Section: 2nd

COLBY Abbie H d Hopkinton 1896-06-21 age 45yrs 2mos 9dys b Dunbarton child of BARNARD Tristan & CARR Olive Vol: 5 Page: 117 Line: 022 Section: 2nd

WEBBER Seth d Hopkinton 1896-06-24 age 86yrs 5mos 2dys b Beverly Mass child of WEBBER Seth & THORNDIKE Mary Vol: 5 Page: 117 Line: 023 Section: 2nd

CHASE Emma J d Hopkinton 1896-07-03 age 21yrs b Kensey Falls P Q child of HOOK James M & DOYING Mary A Vol: 5 Page: 117 Line: 024 Section: 2nd

JOHNSON Charlotte G d Hopkinton 1896-07-02 age 83yrs 1mos 4dys b Hopkinton child of HOLMES E & FLANDERS Nancy Vol: 5 Page: 117 Line: 025 Section: 2nd

MONTGOMERY Helen d Hopkinton 1896-08-13 age 65yrs 3mos 13dys b Warner child of HARRIMAN Benj & Flanders Vol: 5 Page: 117 Line: 027 Section: 2nd

FLANDERS Fred W d Hopkinton 1896-09-04 age 2yrs 8mos 7dys b Henniker child of FLANDERS Frank W & GRAY Nellie Vol: 5 Page: 117 Line: 028 Section: 2nd

TUTTLE John W E d Hopkinton 1896-09-10 age 79yrs 9mos 12dys b Francestown child of TUTTLE Simeon & SARGENT Sally L Vol: 5 Page: 119 Line: 001 Section: 2nd

SCRIBNER Mary B d Hopkinton 1896-09-11 age 37yrs b Milo child of BENNET James & BARRETT Sarah Vol: 5 Page: 119 Line: 002 Section: 2nd

MAYNARD Aphia P d Manchester 1896-10-12 age 82yrs Vol: 5 Page: 119 Line: 004 Section: 2nd

MORRILL Phebe L d Hopkinton 1896-10-11 age 81yrs 6mos b Boscawen child of SWEATT Stephen & LITTLE Judith Vol: 5 Page: 119 Line: 005 Section: 2nd

BENNETT Olive E d Hopkinton 1896-11-13 age 80yrs 8mos b Baldwin Me child of CROCKETT Andrew & FOSS Catherine Vol: 5 Page: 119 Line: 010 Section: 2nd

PAIGE Samuel Smith d Hopkinton 1896-10-22 age 74yrs b Dunbarton child of PAIGE Peter Vol: 5 Page: 119 Line: 008 Section: 2nd

LIBBY Elinor N d Hopkinton 1896-11-12 age 77yrs 10mos 4dys b Deerfield child of SMART Benjamin & TANDY Nancy Vol: 5 Page: 119 Line: 009 Section: 2nd

BROWN Georgianna S d Hopkinton 1896-11-15 age 38yrs 2mos 15dys b Hopkinton child of DWINNELLS John G & GOODWIN Sarah Vol: 5 Page: 119 Line: 011 Section: 2nd

WEBSTER James d Hopkinton 1896-11-26 age 69yrs b Tolland Conn child of WEBSTER Milton & EDDY Sarah Vol: 5 Page: 119 Line: 012 Section: 2nd

COLBY S Harvey d Hopkinton 1896-12-08 age 71yrs b Hopkinton child of COLBY Samuel Vol: 5 Page: 119 Line: 013 Section: 2nd

SMART Johnie d Hopkinton 1896-12-14 age 14yrs 1mos 7dys Vol: 5 Page: 119 Line: 014 Section: 2nd

EVANS Lewis D d Hopkinton 1896-12-16 age 68yrs 7dys b Sullivan child of EVANS Nathaniel & WIGGIN Harriet Vol: 5 Page: 119 Line: 015 Section: 2nd

FISH ---- d Hopkinton 1897-01-06 b Hopkinton child of FISH Daniel & CHANDLER Dell E Vol: 5 Page: 121 Line: 002 Section: 2nd

LONG Lucia A d Boston Mass 1897-01-24 age 81yrs Vol: 5 Page: 121 Line: 003 Section: 2nd

HOLBROOK John d Hopkinton 1897-02-08 age 78yrs 6mos 17dys b Swanzey child of HOLBROOK John & HILL Mercy Vol: 5 Page: 121 Line: 004 Section: 2nd

MUDGETT Salone d Hopkinton 1897-02-11 age 41yrs 1mos 6dys b Warner child of CHASE Thomas & PIERSON Mary L Vol: 5 Page: 121 Line: 005 Section: 2nd

GREENWOOD Lucy S d Hyde Park Mass 1897-02-17 age 51yrs Vol: 5 Page: 121 Line: 006 Section: 2nd

TYLER Zilpha N d Hopkinton 1897-02-19 age 89yrs 11mos 19dys b Hopkinton child of HASTINGS H H & CONNOR Sally Vol: 5 Page: 121 Line: 007 Section: 2nd

PAIGE Sarah E d Hopkinton 1897-02-22 age 66yrs 2mos 2dys b Hopkinton child of TYLER Calvin & HASTINGS Zilpha Vol: 5 Page: 121 Line: 008 Section: 2nd

CURRIER Lozoro d Hopkinton 1897-03-07 age 77yrs 1mos b Hopkinton child of CURRIER David C & CAMPBELL Dolly Vol: 5 Page: 121 Line: 009 Section: 2nd

CURRIER John F d Mt Dora Fla 1897-03-02 age 56yrs b Hopkinton Vol: 5 Page: 121 Line: 010 Section: 2nd

STORY Moses d Hopkinton 1897-03-10 age 82yrs 2mos 4dys b Hopkinton child of STORY Moses & CHANDLER Sarah Vol: 5 Page: 121 Line: 011 Section: 2nd

SMART Lydia L d Hopkinton 1897-03-26 age 82yrs 2mos 11dys b Hopkinton child of KIMBALL Daniel & Sarah H Vol: 5 Page: 121 Line: 012 Section: 2nd

MONTGOMERY Nellie E d Brooklyn Ny 1897-03-26 age 40yrs 2mos 1dys Vol: 5 Page: 121 Line: 013 Section: 2nd

CHANDLER Isaac H d Concord 1896-12-23 age 76yrs 2mos 11dys b Hopkinton Vol: 5 Page: 121 Line: 014 Section: 2nd

HEATH Elroy J d Danbury 1897-04-17 age 3yrs 3mos 18dys Vol: 5 Page: 121 Line: 015 Section: 2nd

BURNHAM Loella M d Hopkinton 1897-04-27 age 54yrs 6mos 1dys b Deering child of WYMAN Daniel & MOORE Louise Vol: 5 Page: 121 Line: 016 Section: 2nd

GORDON Leonard H d Hopkinton 1897-05-05 age 18yrs 11mos b Concord child of GORDON Leonard & TYLER Addie Vol: 5 Page: 121 Line: 017 Section: 2nd

NICHOLS Lucy d Hopkinton 1897-06-26 age 59yrs 8mos 26dys b Quincy Mass child of DAVIS John C & BUTTERFIELD Sarah Vol: 5 Page: 121 Line: 020 Section: 2nd

TUCKER Sally Neal d Hopkinton 1897-08-01 age 87yrs 11mos 11dys b Northwood child of COFFIN Benjamin & AVERY Alice Vol: 5 Page: 121 Line: 023 Section: 2nd

HUNTOON Aphia K d Hopkinton 1897-07-11 age 77yrs 10mos 27dys b Hopkinton child of PUTNEY Josiah & TRUE Eliza Vol: 5 Page: 121 Line: 021 Section: 2nd

SWEATT Ira C d Hopkinton 1897-07-27 age 75yrs 1mos 8dys b Webster child of SWEATT Stephen & LITTLE Judith Vol: 5 Page: 121 Line: 022 Section: 2nd

KIMBALL Mary E S d Hopkinton 1897-08-10 age 79yrs 6mos 24dys b Goffstown child of STEVENS John & JAMESON Mary Vol: 5 Page: 121 Line: 024 Section: 2nd

SARGENT Clara F d Hopkinton 1897-09-09 age 60yrs 4mos 20dys b Haverhill Mass child of SARGENT Rufus & BUSWELL Abigail Vol: 5 Page: 121 Line: 025 Section: 2nd

BARTON Charles d Hopkinton 1897-09-10 age 83yrs 6mos 10dys b Pittsfield child of BARTON Charles & MARSTON Sarah Vol: 5 Page: 121 Line: 026 Section: 2nd

STORY James K d Hopkinton 1897-09-21 age 83yrs 1mos 4dys b Hopkinton child of STORY William K & KNOWLTON Lydia Vol: 5 Page: 121 Line: 027 Section: 2nd

BROWN Edward d Boston Mass 1897-09-19 age 29yrs Vol: 5 Page: 121 Line: 028 Section: 2nd

BRADBURY Samuel G d Hopkinton 1897-09-27 age 79yrs 3mos 9dys b Hopkinton child of BRADBURY Winthrop & GOODWIN Hannah Vol: 5 Page: 123 Line: 001 Section: 2nd

SMART Jane d Concord 1897-09-28 age 86yrs Vol: 5 Page: 123 Line: 002 Section: 2nd

FLANDERS Almer H d Hopkinton 1897-10-12 age 1yrs 11mos 13dys b Hopkinton child of FLANDERS Samuel B & PERKINS Nellie B Vol: 5 Page: 123 Line: 003 Section: 2nd

CHASE Leon W d Hopkinton 1897-10-27 age 4yrs 1mos 9dys b Hopkinton child of CHASE Charles T & WEBBER Florence Vol: 5 Page: 123 Line: 004 Section: 2nd

WOLFSON Mabel d Popkinton 1897-11-08 age 23yrs b Canana child of WOLFSON Symonds & CLARK Elsia Vol: 5 Page: 123 Line: 005 Section: 2nd

HOYT Mary d Hopkinton 1897-11-17 age 90yrs Vol: 5 Page: 123 Line: 006 Section: 2nd

LOW Seth d Salisbury 1897-11-19 age 57yrs 10mos 27dys Vol: 5 Page: 123 Line: 007 Section: 2nd

HARDY Hannah B d Warner 1897-11-19 age 84yrs 9mos Vol: 5 Page: 123 Line: 008 Section: 2nd

STRAW Mary A d Hopkinton 1898-03-14 age 61yrs 5mos 1dys b Hopkinton child of HOLMES Gardner & MELVIN Betsey Vol: 6 Page: 002

BOUTWELL Samuel E d Hopkinton 1897-12-12 age 57yrs 5mos b Sherburne Vt Vol: 5 Page: 123 Line: 010 Section: 2nd

Hopkinton, NH Deaths 1880

WHITE Thomas E d Hopkinton 1897-12-31 age 80yrs 6mos 16dys b Hopkinton child of WHITE Thomas E & EATON Sarah Vol: 5 Page: 123 Line: 011 Section: 2nd

BOUTWELL Edson d Hopkinton 1897-12-12 age 57yrs 5mos b Barry Vt child of BOUTWELL Samuel & Lydia Vol: 5 Page: 123 Line: 012 Section: 2nd

McALPINE Hannah J d Concord 1889-05-07 age 65yrs 2mos 13dys Vol: 5 Page: 087 Line: 016 Section: 2nd

WEBBER Lerman d Hopkinton 1892-01-02 age 27yrs 7mos 28dys b Hopkinton child of WEBBER Cyrel T & JEFFERS Jennette Vol: 5 Page: 099 Line: 003 Section: 2nd

BOHONAN Ida May d Hopkinton 1892-05-09 age 12yrs 4mos 16dys b Hopkinton child of BOHONAN David V & FISK Jennie M Vol: 5 Page: 101 Line: 006 Section: 2nd

ALLEN Chassie E d Hopkinton 1894-09-23 age 5mos 14dys b Hopkinton child of ALLEN Walton P & MONTGOMERY Martha S Vol: 5 Page: 111 Line: 007 Section: 2nd

MONTGOMERY Elizabeth H d Hopkinton 1895-02-23 age 68yrs 1mos 6dys b Salem NY child of SNYDER G W & SAFFORD Elizabeth Vol: 5 Page: 113 Line: 007 Section: 2nd

JOHNSON Clara A d Hopkinton 1897-11-24 age 88yrs 7mos 17dys b Henniker child of PATTERSON Alexande & WILSON Mary ?? Vol: 5 Page: 123 Line: 009 Section: 2nd Note: xx- nelson??

EATON Mary A d Weare 1898-03-21 age 81yrs 6mos 5dys b Henniker child of ADAMS Stephen & ALEXANDER Abi Vol: 6 Page: 002

FRENCH Eliza d Weare 1898-04-06 age 80yrs 10mos 14dys Vol: 6 Page: 002

PERRY Bertha S d Hopkinton 1898-04-10 age 69yrs 5mos b Maine child of FLINT John Vol: 6 Page: 002

BUSWELL William L d Hopkinton 1898-04-12 age 55yrs 5mos 8dys child of BUSWELL Samuel & Mary Vol: 6 Page: 002

STRAW Mary A d Hopkinton 1898 b Hopkinton Vol: 6 Page: 003 Note: brought from henniker tomp

WRIGHT Mary A d Hopkinton 1898-04-17 age 80yrs b Baltimore MD Vol: 6 Page: 003

CROSS Nettie H d Concord 1898-04-25 age 30yrs 3mos 3dys Vol: 6 Page: 003

TUTTLE Mary J d Hopkinton 1898-05-10 age 76yrs 8mos 12dys b Hopkinton child of BARNARD Joseph & EASTMAN Mirrian J Vol: 6 Page: 003

ORDWAY Frank d Webster 1898-05-15 age 66yrs Vol: 6 Page: 003

HASTINGS Edna May d Hopkinton 1898-05-20 age 28dys b Hopkinton child of HASTINGS Delmer W & CHASE Lena M Vol: 6 Page: 003

BURBANK Albert N d Concord 1898-06-21 age 36yrs Vol: 6 Page: 004

PRINCE ---- d Hopkinton 1898-06-27 b Hopkinton child of PRINCE Heni & LIBBY Stella G Vol: 6 Page: 004

CUTTER Harriet Eliza d Hopkinton 1898-06-27 age 61yrs 11mos b Weston Mass child of CUTTER Jonas & SMITH Elizabeth Vol: 6 Page: 004

FOOTE Irene Melissa d Hopkinton 1898-07-01 age 1yrs 8mos 18dys b Hopkinton child of FOOTE William W & WATTS Helen M Vol: 6 Page: 004

SYMONDS Ann F d Hopkinton 1898-07-24 age 77yrs b Ireland child of FARLEY Thomas & SHERDEN Margaret Vol: 6 Page: 004

CUTLER Hiram d Warner 1898-08-13 age 76yrs 6mos Vol: 6 Page: 004

CORBIT Thomas d Hopkinton 1898-08-24 age 62yrs 10mos 19dys b Ware Mass child of CORBIT Andrew & Hannah Vol: 6 Page: 005

ROWELL Florence S d Hopkinton 1898-10-19 age 37yrs 6mos 5dys child of GOODWIN Benjamin & MIXER Lucy A Vol: 6 Page: 005

CHASE Horace J d Hopkinton 1898-10-24 age 73yrs 13dys b Hopkinton child of CHASE Enoch J Vol: 6 Page: 005

HERSEY Jeremiah d Concord 1898-11-07 age 86yrs 6mos 8dys Vol: 6 Page: 005

CHANDLER Edmund C d Hopkinton 1898-11-20 age 43yrs 28dys b Hopkinton child of CHANDLER Horatio J & CURRIER Susan V Vol: 6 Page: 005

HARDY Judith d Hopkinton 1898-11-26 age 94yrs 1mos 26dys b Hopkinton child of HARDY Benjamin & CLARK Sarah Vol: 6 Page: 005

STORY Sarah d Hopkinton 1898-12-05 age 83yrs 11mos 1dys b Hopkinton child of STORY Moses & CHANDLER Sallie Vol: 6 Page: 006

TRUMBALL Susan W d Hopkinton 1898-12-13 age 84yrs b Boscawen child of JACKMAN Nehemiah & WALKER Sallie Vol: 6 Page: 006

MARSH ---- d Hopkinton 1898-12-22 b Hopkinton child of MARSH Frank & DUSTIN?? Mary Etta Vol: 6 Page: 006

STEVENS Mary A d Hopkinton 1899-01-15 age 63yrs b Tamworth child of PERKINS True & CHAPMAN Mary A Vol: 6 Page: 007

CLOUGH Willard J L d Hopkinton 1899-01-26 b Hopkinton child of CLOUGH George A & ROWE Sara B Vol: 6 Page: 007

SANBORN Jesse D d Webster 1899-02-04 age 84yrs 4mos 2dys Vol: 6 Page: 007

GOULD Ruth d Hopkinton 1899-02-05 age 75yrs 10mos 14dys b Hopkinton child of HILL Thomas & FLOID Ruth Vol: 6 Page: 007

SMITH Charles H d Hopkinton 1899-02-04 age 71yrs 6mos 13dys b Concord child of SMITH Richard K & CHASE Almira Vol: 6 Page: 007

MONTGOMERY Guy d Hopkinton 1899-02-11 age 38yrs 11mos 17dys b Hopkinton child of MONTGOMERY Wm & SAVORY Lucy A Vol: 6 Page: 008

HOOK Harriet N d Hopkinton 1899-02-15 age 81yrs 8mos 11dys b Canterbury child of HOWE Newell Vol: 6 Page: 008

EATON Mary J d Hopkinton 1899-02-17 age 83yrs 5mos b Salisbury Vol: 6 Page: 008

HOLMES Bertha M d Hopkinton 1899-02-22 age 23yrs 8mos 9dys b Hopkinton child of HOLMES Aquilla D & ANDREWS Abbie M Vol: 6 Page: 008

WOOD Sarah F d Manchester 1899-03-01 age 51yrs Vol: 6 Page: 008

DOW Ellen M d Hopkinton 1899-03-15 age 55yrs 10mos b Warner child of COUCH Albert J & SARGENT Ruth Vol: 6 Page: 008

DAVIS Alice T d Hopkinton 1899-03-27 age 24yrs 4mos 9dys b Warner child of DAVIS Eugene & HODGDON Mattie Vol: 6 Page: 009

DAVIS Hiriam N d Warner 1899-03-27 age 73yrs 2mos 20dys Vol: 6 Page: 009

RICHARDSON Sarah d Hopkinton 1899-04-09 age 80yrs 5mos b Wenham Mass child of DODGE Stilman & HILAND Sarah Vol: 6 Page: 009

Hopkinton, NH Deaths 1880

LORD Sarah d Hopkinton 1899-04-20 age 85yrs 7mos 28dys b Hopkinton child of HUBLEND John & CHASE Ruth Vol: 6 Page: 009

BUSWELL Rhney H d Hopkinton 1899-04-26 age 92yrs 9mos 8dys b Hopkinton child of BUSWELL Benjamin & CARTER Joanna Vol: 6 Page: 009

MORRILL George W d Hopkinton 1899-05-10 age 75yrs 8mos b Hopkinton child of MORRILL Joseph & MASTER Permelia Vol: 6 Page: 009

CURRIER Erastus d Hopkinton 1899-05-16 age 82yrs 9mos 4dys b Hopkinton child of CURRIER Amas & PATTERSON Fanny Vol: 6 Page: 010

FOSTER Jonas d Hopkinton 1899-05-28 age 87yrs 9mos b Halifax England Vol: 6 Page: 010

GOULD Charles d Bellingham Mass 1899-05-19 age 76yrs 3mos Vol: 6 Page: 010

HARRIMAN Charles C d Manchester 1899-06-04 age 74yrs 3mos 2dys Vol: 6 Page: 010

SAFFORD George W d Hopkinton 1899-06-10 age 80yrs 10mos 12dys b Exeter child of SAFFORD William & COLCORD Sarah Vol: 6 Page: 010

SARGENT Miriam B d Hopkinton 1899-06-15 age 87yrs 6mos b Warner child of SARGENT Benj & COLBY Eunice Vol: 6 Page: 010

WALKER David d Hopkinton 1899-06-28 age 77yrs 7mos b England Vol: 6 Page: 011

SMITH Willam J d Hopkinton 1899-08-23 age 77yrs 2mos 7dys b Deering child of SMITH Isaac & STEVENS Pamelia Vol: 6 Page: 011

THORNDIKE Wilson d Lyndeborough 1899-08-29 age 71yrs b Concord child of THORNDIKE Thomas W & DOW Ruth Vol: 6 Page: 011

MARSH ---- d Hopkinton 1899-08-30 b Hopkinton child of MARSH Frank P & GUERNEY Marietta Vol: 6 Page: 011

SPOFFORD Nellie Emma d Hopkinton 1899-09-09 age 36yrs 4mos 25dys b Hopkinton child of MILLS Charles & TOWNS Olive Vol: 6 Page: 011

WIGHT Emily H d Salem Mass 1899-09-16 age 17yrs 11mos 4dys child of WIGHT E Oscar & CURRIER Abbie S Vol: 6 Page: 011

SPOFFORD ---- d Hopkinton 1899-10-12 age 1mos 15dys b Hopkinton child of SPOFFORD Eugene & MILLS Nellie Vol: 6 Page: 012

ELLIOTT Emerline C d Hopkinton 1899-10-15 age 53yrs 6mos 21dys b Franklin child of MORSE Samuel & EASTMAN Betsey Vol: 6 Page: 012

DAVIS Walter S d Hopkinton 1899-11-01 age 65yrs 3mos b Warner child of DAVIS Nathaniel & CLOUGH Mary Vol: 6 Page: 012

CULVER Mirando G d Pembroke 1899-11-04 age 66yrs 5mos 2dys b Hopkinton child of KNOWLTON Arial P & LEE Abigail Vol: 6 Page: 012

WEBBER Maggie d Hopkinton 1899-11-21 age 12yrs 6mos 25dys b Hillsboro child of WEBBER Lerman S & REILEY Margaret Vol: 6 Page: 012

CUTLER Rhoda d Warner 1899-11-25 age 95yrs 4mos 18dys b Groton Vt Vol: 6 Page: 012

JACKMAN Benjamin F d Hopkinton 1900-01-14 age 87yrs 11mos 26dys b Boscawenn child of JACKMAN Nemiah & WALKER Sally Vol: 6 Page: 014

MATHEUS Bertha H d Barlbinrigh Mass 1900-01-15 age 34yrs 3mos 6dys Vol: 6 Page: 014

SANBORN Mary d Hopkinton 1900-01-17 b Ireland child of SMITH Peter Vol: 6 Page: 014

PATTERSON Susan H d Hopkinton 1900-01-18 age 88yrs 2mos Vol: 6 Page: 014

TOWNSEND Emma L d Boston Mass 1900-01-29 age 48yrs 5mos 9dys Vol: 6 Page: 014

CHASE Harriet M d Hopkinton 1900-02-05 age 52yrs 4mos 5dys b Warner child of BADGER Sargent & FOSTER Emily F Vol: 6 Page: 014

WILLIAMS Susan d Hopkinton 1900-02-21 age 80yrs 19dys b Henniker child of TUCKER Ezra & HARDY Hannah Vol: 6 Page: 015

FULLER Lucy J d Wakefield Mass 1900-02-23 age 91yrs 11mos 3dys Vol: 6 Page: 015

CONNOR Charles J d Concord 1900-02-03 age 83yrs 10mos 13dys Vol: 6 Page: 015

BOHONAN John W d Hopkinton 1900-02-25 age 52yrs 8mos 29dys b Sutton child of BOHONAN David & BEAN Berlinda Vol: 6 Page: 015

BROWN Addie M d Hopkinton 1900-02-04 age 53yrs 9mos 9dys b Boscawen child of DOW Rufus & BRUCE Maria Vol: 6 Page: 015

DOWNING Frank E d Hopkinton 1900-03-06 age 43yrs 11mos 5dys b Hopkinton child of DOWNING Daniel & BOWMAN Elizabeth Vol: 6 Page: 015

SMART Maude Fiske d Hopkinton 1900-03-19 age 12yrs 3mos 16dys b Hopkinton child of SMART Edward H & FISKE Nellie Vol: 6 Page: 016

STORY Sophronia d Haverhill Mass 1900-03-20 age 78yrs 9mos 11dys Vol: 6 Page: 016

SYMONDS Annie M d Hopkinton 1900-03-25 age 49yrs 2mos 4dys b Weare child of JOHNSON Judith Vol: 6 Page: 016

SANBORN Arvilla d Webster 1900-03-29 age 78yrs 2mos 16dys b Loudon child of BACHELDER L Vol: 6 Page: 016

FARRINGTON Hiram d Concord 1900-03-07 age 94yrs 10mos 24dys Vol: 6 Page: 016

DODGE Abbie A d Webster 1900-04-14 age 59yrs 7mos 15dys b Hopkinton child of WEEKS Charles & HEMPHILL Phebe Vol: 6 Page: 016

BRUCE Isabella d Boston Mass 1900-04-16 age 79yrs 4mos 11dys Vol: 6 Page: 017

MANN Dana J d Salisbury 1900-05-10 age 62yrs 8mos 23dys b Salisbury child of MANN James & TAYLOR Mariam Vol: 6 Page: 017

TILTON Wilhelmina S d Haverhill Mass 1900-05-28 age 9yrs 6mos 18dys Vol: 6 Page: 017

FRENCH Charles d Hopkinton 1900-05-30 age 58yrs b Hopkinton child of FRENCH Reuben E & CHASE Sarah Vol: 6 Page: 017

HEATH Harriet S d Hopkinton 1900-06-16 age 68yrs 8mos b Warner child of CLARKE Stephen B & GOULD Susanna Vol: 6 Page: 017

WEBBER Jeremiah S d Hopkinton 1900-07-01 age 81yrs 3mos 3dys b Boscawen child of WEBBER Jeremiah & FLANDERS Lydia Vol: 6 Page: 017

PERRY True J d Manchester 1900-06-15 Vol: 6 Page: 018

HOYT Harriet Emma d Hopkinton 1900-07-07 age 18yrs 8mos 4dys b Weare child of HOYT Warren & WALDRON Lydia Vol: 6 Page: 018

MILLS Charles H d Hopkinton 1900-07-27 age 65yrs 5mos b Hopkinton child of MILLS Joseph & CLOUGH Celinda Vol: 6 Page: 018

CHANDLER William H d Hopkinton 1900-08-08 b Hopkinton child of CHANDLER George & DWININ Sarah Vol: 6 Page: 018

DODGE Huldah M d Hopkinton 1900-08-08 age 74yrs 2mos 21dys b Winchendon Mass Vol: 6 Page: 018

DANFORTH Emily J d Boston Mass 1900-09-07 age 52yrs 3mos 4dys Vol: 6 Page: 018

GRAY Elmer F d Warner 1900-09-11 age 18yrs 3mos 14dys b Lebanon child of GRAY Chas E & KENDALL Addie Vol: 6 Page: 019

FLANDERS Timothy B d Holyoke Mass 1900-09-13 age 72yrs 9mos 29dys Vol: 6 Page: 019

FOLSOM Maria d Hopkinton 1900-09-15 age 88yrs 5mos 4dys b Deering child of FOLSOM Samuel & LOVERING Anna Vol: 6 Page: 019

BROWN Ivan Frank d Hopkinton 1900-09-17 age 45yrs 3mos 30dys b Manchester child of BROWN Francis & QUIMBY Mary Vol: 6 Page: 019

WAYNE Dorris d Franklin 1900-09-18 age 5mos 18dys child of WAYNE Herny & BARTLETT Cora Vol: 6 Page: 019

DONALDSON George E d Hopkinton 1900-09-19 age 29yrs 11mos 25dys b Enfield N S child of DONALDSON Henry & BROWN Rachel Vol: 6 Page: 019

RUSSELL Lillian May d North Woodstock 1900-09-23 age 3mos 23dys b North Woodstock child of RUSSELL Arthur C & FISH Mabel Vol: 6 Page: 020

PAIGE George W d Hopkinton 1900-10-03 age 51yrs b Henniker child of PAIGE Samuel & PATCH Mary J Vol: 6 Page: 020

SCRIBNER Leonard d Manchester 1900-10-05 age 18yrs Vol: 6 Page: 020

MORRILL Lucy W d Hopkinton 1900-10-06 age 84yrs 1mos 12dys b Saco ME child of WATSON Nichodemon & MORRILL Prudence Vol: 6 Page: 020

HOLMES Edwin J d Hopkinton 1900-10-16 age 23yrs 2mos 14dys b Salisbury child of HOLMES Charles & WEBBER Eva Vol: 6 Page: 020

RAND Harriet N d Hopkinton 1900-10-18 age 85yrs 8mos 6dys b Warner child of DAVIS Paine & DOW Mary Vol: 6 Page: 020

RICHARDSON Bessie Mae d Hopkinton 1900-11-05 age 20yrs 1mos 20dys b Goffstown child of RAND Edson L & KNIGHT Ada F Vol: 6 Page: 021

BURBANK Horace d Boscawen 1900-11-18 age 74yrs b Hopkinton Vol: 6 Page: 021

PINIO Annie D d Dover 1900-11-03 age 45yrs 9mos 5dys Vol: 6 Page: 021

MARSH Thalma Levla d Hopkinton 1900-12-11 b Hopkinton child of MARSH Frank P & DUSTIN Etta R Vol: 6 Page: 021

BLAKE John C d Hopkinton 1900-12-27 age 78yrs b Canada child of BLAKE John & CANFIELD Susan Vol: 6 Page: 021

DOW Charlotte A d Hopkinton 1900-12-28 age 72yrs 5mos 10dys b Hopkinton child of BOUTELLE Calvin & FISK Charlotte Vol: 6 Page: 021

PAIGE John W d Concord 1900-12-15 age 78yrs 11mos 25dys Vol: 6 Page: 022

BLOOD Charles d Hopkinton 1901-01-06 age 74yrs 8mos 5dys b Amherst child of BLOOD Samuel & McINTIER Annie Vol: 6 Page: 023

CUSHION Harriet H d Boscawen 1901-01-08 age 74yrs b Bradford Vol: 6 Page: 023

PAIGE Etta B d Hopkinton 1901-01-17 age 1yrs b Concord child of PAIGE Orvill & DWINNELLS Josie Vol: 6 Page: 023

CHANDLER Mary Jane d Hopkinton 1901-01-24 age 48yrs 1mos 1dys b Warner child of McALPINE Gould Vol: 6 Page: 023

PAIGE Marion d Hopkinton 1901-02-01 b Hopkinton child of PAIGE Thomas W & SHAW Minnie B Vol: 6 Page: 023

DANFORTH Rosannah E d Hopkinton 1901-02-10 age 80yrs 1mos 12dys b Stewartstown child of CAPEN Ebenezer & ABBOTT Mary Vol: 6 Page: 023

PARTRIDGE Harrison d Hopkinton 1901-02-27 age 71yrs 10mos 26dys b Croydon child of PARTRIDGE Elisha & PUTNEY Elvira Vol: 6 Page: 024

BARTON Charles O d Hopkinton 1901-03-17 age 67yrs 1mos 18dys b Hopkinton child of BARTON Charles & STRAW Phebe Vol: 6 Page: 024

TILTON Eunice F d Hopkinton 1901-03-31 age 78yrs 7mos 26dys b Troy NY child of TEWKSBURY John Vol: 6 Page: 024

CURRIER Eliza M d New York City 1901-03-28 age 74yrs Vol: 6 Page: 024

MARSTON Mary A d Hopkinton 1901-04-06 age 85yrs 3mos 3dys b Deerfield child of BARTLETT Nathan & COLBY Nancy Vol: 6 Page: 024

ROGERS Sarah J d Concord 1901-04-19 age 47yrs 7mos Vol: 6 Page: 024

BROCKWAY Fred J d Brattleboro Vt 1901-04-21 age 40yrs child of BROCKWAY John G Vol: 6 Page: 025

KELLY Francis C d Concord 1901-03-20 age 69yrs 7mos 26dys Vol: 6 Page: 025

CHASE Jacob S d Warner 1901-02-26 age 78yrs Vol: 6 Page: 025

PERKINS William D d Concord 1901-04-25 age 68yrs 11mos 27dys Vol: 6 Page: 025

FIFIELD Annie L d Hopkinton 1901-05-17 age 26yrs 2mos 16dys b Hopkinton child of BACON John H & BURBANK Ann P Vol: 6 Page: 025

WEEKS Ida F d Manchester 1901-05-19 age 44yrs Vol: 6 Page: 025

STORY Fred W d Brunswick Me 1901-05-31 age 81yrs 1mos 14dys Vol: 6 Page: 026

DUSTIN Sarah A d Hopkinton 1901-07-09 age 82yrs 3mos 6dys b Hopkinton child of BARNARD Joseph & EASTMAN Marian J Vol: 6 Page: 026

BICKNELL Minnie A d Hopkinton 1901-08-02 age 35yrs b Brooklyn NY child of BICKNELL William J & CROSS Mary M Vol: 6 Page: 026

STRAW Edmund S d Greenfield Mass 1901-03-06 age 81yrs 3mos Vol: 6 Page: 026

JEWELL Ellen C R d Somerville Mass 1901-08-20 age 58yrs 3mos 8dys Vol: 6 Page: 026

FLANDERS Clara A d Hopkinton 1901-09-20 age 50yrs 6mos 25dys b Hopkinton child of FLANDERS Sullivan & ADAMS Maria Vol: 6 Page: 026

CURRIER Josie G d Hopkinton 1901-09-30 age 26yrs 10mos b Concord child of WEBSTR Frank D & DOW Nettie Vol: 6 Page: 027

PERRY ---- d Barre Vt 1901-10-02 age 1dys Vol: 6 Page: 027

STORY Pamelia d Hopkinton 1899-12-15 age 72yrs 2mos 24dys b Weare Vol: 6 Page: 013

BOYCE Ernest G d Dedham Mass 1901-10-09 age 1yrs 6mos 21dys Vol: 6 Page: 027

KIMBALL Clarion Hazen d New York 1901-11-08 age 57yrs 28dys Vol: 6 Page: 027

PERRY Slyvester W d Hopkinton 1901-11-22 age 70yrs 4mos 8dys b Hopkinton child of PERRY William & CRESSEY Aseneth Vol: 6 Page: 027

MONTGOMERY Adaline M B d Concord 1901-11-23 age 82yrs 2mos 13dys Vol: 6 Page: 028

SAFFORD Sarah E H d Hopkinton 1901-11-29 age 78yrs 11mos 25dys b Concord child of EVANS Nathaniel & WIGGIN Harriet Vol: 6 Page: 028

WALKER ---- d Hopkinton 1901-12-15 b Hopkinton child of WALKER Abraham & Mable Vol: 6 Page: 028

BABKIRK Lewis Smith d Hopkinton 1902-01-27 age 66yrs 3mos 27dys b New Brunswick child of BABKIRK James Vol: 6 Page: 029

TERRY George N d Somerville Mass 1902-01-23 age 6mos 29dys Vol: 6 Page: 029

GOODRICH George K d Hopkinton 1902-01-24 age 93yrs 27dys b Springfiled Vt child of GOODRICH Samuel & KIDDER Esther Vol: 6 Page: 029

CLARK Benjamin F d Hopkinton 1902-01-27 age 81yrs 9mos 5dys b Wolfboro child of CLARK Benjamin & Gove Vol: 6 Page: 029

WHYTOCK Mary Edna E d Hopkinton 1902-02-12 age 2mos 2dys b Hopkinton child of WHYTOCK David & FELMING Isabell Vol: 6 Page: 029

BROWN Ellen K d Hopkinton 1902-02-16 age 84yrs 8mos 11dys b Hopkinton child of BROWN Abram & KIMBALL Eunice Vol: 6 Page: 029

BOHONAN Leland d Hopkinton 1902-03-11 age 1yrs 5mos b Weare child of BOHONAN John W & JEWELL Delia A Vol: 6 Page: 030

CHASE Lucinda J d Hopkinton 1902-03-17 age 82yrs 4mos 10dys b Hillsborough child of SEVERENCE Ephraim & Rollins Vol: 6 Page: 030

WIGGIN Ella M d Hopkinton 1902-03-21 age 51yrs 3mos 13dys b Manchester child of COLBY Willard M & KIMBALL Mary B Vol: 6 Page: 030

KEZER Lafayette A d Warner 1902-03-28 age 49yrs 6dys b Hopkinton child of KEZER Moses & Ordway Vol: 6 Page: 030

PIPER George W d Hopkinton 1902-04-09 age 74yrs 7mos 4dys b Henniker child of Crangle & STANLEY Charlotte Vol: 6 Page: 030

DWINNELLS Margret V d Hopkinton 1902-04-13 age 1mos 18dys b Hopkinton child of DWINNELLS Frank P & LIBBY Emma H Vol: 6 Page: 030

PATCH Mary H d Hopkinton 1902-04-09 age 59yrs 3mos 25dys b Hopkinton child of JOHNSON Samuel & HOLMES Charlotte Vol: 6 Page: 031

KIMBALL Madeline d Hopkinton 1902-04-11 age 7mos 4dys b Hopkinton child of KIMBALL Nelson D & PATCH Adalaide M Vol: 6 Page: 031

CLARK Mary Jane d Hopkinton 1902-05-03 age 70yrs 6mos b Hopkinton Vol: 6 Page: 031

FOGG Mirriam S d Hopkinton 1902-05-14 age 80yrs 5mos 24dys b Hopkinton child of EMERSON J J & STRAW Elizabeth Vol: 6 Page: 031

SHEPARD Moses d Hopkinton 1902-05-22 Vol: 6 Page: 031 Note: r r accident

CHASE Charles d Hopkinton 1902-05-26 age 41yrs 6mos 2dys b   child of CHASE Elbridge & Rogers Vol: 6 Page: 031

WING ---- d Hopkinton 1902-05-29 b Hopkinton child of WING Frank & MESSER Clara Vol: 6 Page: 032

ROWELL Alonzo d Concord 1902-05-19 age 66yrs 2mos 8dys Vol: 6 Page: 032

FLANDERS Sullivan d Hopkinton 1902-06-17 age 79yrs 8mos 11dys b Bradford child of FLANDERS Nathaniel & WRIGHT Betsey Vol: 6 Page: 032

HAZELTINE Martha Jane d Hopkinton 1902-07-03 age 48yrs 6mos 14dys b Hopkinton child of HODGDON Charles & HOLMES Harriet M Vol: 6 Page: 032

Hopkinton, NH Deaths 1880

CLOUGH Charles F d Hopkinton 1902-07-06 age 80yrs 7mos 27dys b Hopkinton child of CLOUGH William & COUCH Mary P Vol: 6 Page: 032

CONNOR James W d Hopkinton 1902-07-16 age 73yrs 11mos b Henniker child of CONNOR James & KIMBALL Lydia Vol: 6 Page: 032

LEROY Martha C d Hopkinton 1902-09-01 age 20yrs 1mos 20dys child of PERLEY Charles W & RINIS Rosila Vol: 6 Page: 033

KIRBY Frederick A d Hopkinton 1902-08-23 age 35yrs 5mos 6dys b Uxbridge Mass child of KIRBY George H & GILE Caroline G Vol: 6 Page: 033

BROWN Otis M d Hopkinton 1902-09-16 age 73yrs 9mos 26dys b Hopkinton child of BROWN Bliss & BURBANK Belinda Vol: 6 Page: 033

DOWNING Joshua d Tilton 1902-09-23 age 79yrs 8mos 28dys Vol: 6 Page: 033

BARNARD Abial G d Concord 1902-09-24 age 46yrs b Hopkinton child of BARNARD Joseph & GERRISH Mary Vol: 6 Page: 033

WAYNE Sarah A d Hopkinton 1902-10-18 age 54yrs 4mos b Concord child of SPEED William & STEVENS Maria Vol: 6 Page: 033

CHASE Nathaniel C d Hopkinton 1902-10-25 age 74yrs 8mos 25dys child of CHASE Moses & Wells Vol: 6 Page: 034

KIMBALL Charles H d Concord 1902-10-25 age 79yrs 3mos Vol: 6 Page: 034

COLBY Melvin d Hopkinton 1902-10-31 age 74yrs 4mos 11dys b Hopkinton child of COLBY Moses & ABBOTT Elsie Vol: 6 Page: 034

CAMPBELL Adaline D d Concord 1902-11-04 age 70yrs 10mos 29dys Vol: 6 Page: 034

MORRILL Laura Ann d Hopkinton 1902-11-19 age 76yrs 10mos 3dys b Hopkinton child of BACON John Vol: 6 Page: 034

STRAW William S d Hopkinton 1902-11-20 age 85yrs 5mos 19dys b Hopkinton child of STRAW William & HUSE Hannah Vol: 6 Page: 034

KIMBALL Martha K d Concord 1902-11-27 age 82yrs 8mos 7dys b Hopkinton child of HOLMES John & WHITE Abilla K Vol: 6 Page: 035

DODGE Jonathan d Hopkinton 1900-12-12 age 80yrs 8mos 8dys child of DODGE Grover & FRENCH Lydia Vol: 6 Page: 035

GRAY Jessie May d Hopkinton 1902-12-16 age 7yrs 8mos 3dys b Grantham child of GRAY Charles E Vol: 6 Page: 035

CORLISS Elbridge G d Concord age 71yrs Vol: 6 Page: 035

TASKER Mary J d Hopkinton 1902-12-29 age 70yrs 5mos 28dys b Alton child of Barney & Chamberlain Vol: 6 Page: 035

BAILEY Marion Samantha d Hopkinton 1903-01-04 age 10mos 6dys b Hopkinton child of BAILEY William S & HANNAFORD Ida May Vol: 6 Page: 036

GOODWIN William Knapp d Hopkinton 1903-01-10 age 37yrs 3mos 18dys b New Brunswick Ns child of GOODWIN William Vol: 6 Page: 036

HEATH James A d Hopkinton 1903-01-22 age 74yrs 7mos 7dys b Salisbury Vol: 6 Page: 036

SYMONDS Andrew d Hopkinton 1903-01-16 age 44yrs 9mos 8dys b Hopkinton child of SYMONDS Bryant & FARLEY Ann Vol: 6 Page: 036

SMITH Mary Ann d Hopkinton 1903-01-30 age 79yrs 7mos 12dys b Hopkinton child of MORGAN Nathaniel & COLBY Mehitable Vol: 6 Page: 036

CHASE Curtis B d Hopkinton 1903-02-23 age 60yrs 1mos 28dys b Hopkinton child of CHASE Barach Vol: 6 Page: 036

Hopkinton, NH Deaths 1880

KELLEY Fredeick H d Hopkinton 1903-02-25 age 69yrs 3mos 1dys b Hopkinton child of KELLEY Amos & EVANS Elizabeth Vol: 6 Page: 037

FELCH Marion R d Weare 1903-02-22 age 1yrs 7mos 10dys b Weare child of FELCH Charles T & WHITE Sarah C Vol: 6 Page: 037

MIGNAULT Emma L d Webster 1903-02-28 age 33yrs 8mos 29dys b Hopkinton child of STEVENS Henry S & MORRILL Mary Vol: 6 Page: 037

RICHARDSON Mary d Boscawen 1903-03-03 age 83yrs Vol: 6 Page: 037

COLBY George Forest d Hopkinton 1903-03-14 age 3mos 6dys b Hopkinton child of COLBY Forest & PAIGE Rosa Vol: 6 Page: 037

WHITTIER Sarah Jane d Hopkinton 1903-03-28 age 71yrs 9mos 6dys b Weare child of DANFORTH Gilman & Ruth Vol: 6 Page: 037

KIMBALL Charlie d Webster 1903-04-05 age 47yrs 8mos 23dys b Webster child of KIMBALL Charles & CARPENTER Martha Vol: 6 Page: 038

CHASE Nelson A d Hopkinton 1903-04-05 age 52yrs Vol: 6 Page: 038

HARDY Samuel A d Hopkinton 1903-04-11 age 74yrs 1mos 22dys Vol: 6 Page: 038

BURNS Benjamin A d Hopkinton 1903-04-22 age 84yrs 3mos 17dys Vol: 6 Page: 038

GOODSPEED Helen B d Philadelphia Pa 1903-04-28 age 67yrs Vol: 6 Page: 038

WHITE Judith C d Hopkinton 1903-05-08 age 60yrs 3mos 12dys b Bow child of WHITE Robert W Vol: 6 Page: 038

CHENEY Warren d Hopkinton 1903-06-14 age 82yrs 8mos 14dys b Sandown Vol: 6 Page: 039

WEEKS Josephine M d Hopkinton 1903-06-16 age 59yrs 15dys b Hopkinton child of WEEKS Charles & HEMPHILL Phebe Vol: 6 Page: 039

WALKER ---- d Hopkinton 1903-06-23 b Hopkinton child of WALKER Abrham & BRADBURY Mable Vol: 6 Page: 039

McKENZIE Augis d Henniker 1903-06-17 age 80yrs Vol: 6 Page: 039

JOHNSON Thomas d Hopkinton 1903-06-28 age 86yrs b Ireland Vol: 6 Page: 039

FOOTE Roert M d Hopkinton 1903-07-03 age 71yrs 8mos 3dys b Amesbury Mass child of FOOTE Robert Vol: 6 Page: 039

SPOFFORD Eugene F d Hopkinton 1903-07-18 age 42yrs 8mos 18dys b Hopkinton child of SPOFFORD Frederick & HILAND Sarah Vol: 6 Page: 040

FOOTE Laura E d Hopkinton 1903-07-25 age 57yrs 25dys b Loudon child of BICKFORD C Pierce & LOCKE Martha Vol: 6 Page: 040

THOMAS William H d Hopkinton 1903-08-16 age 53yrs 8mos 27dys b Bath child of THOMAS W C Vol: 6 Page: 040

MERRILL Isaac D d Hopkinton 1903-09-02 age 88yrs 11mos 1dys b Hopkinton child of MERRILL Isaac & WYMAN Mary Vol: 6 Page: 040

SAGE Emeline A H d Hopkinton 1903-10-02 age 86yrs 4mos 4dys b Salem Mass child of GARDNER Joseph & TUCKER Eunice Vol: 6 Page: 040

CURRIER Robert B d New York 1903-10-04 age 84yrs child of CURRIER Stephen Vol: 6 Page: 040

HEATH Huldah d Hopkinton 1903-10-19 age 83yrs 7mos 9dys b Lebanon child of WEBBER Hezekiah & Huldah Vol: 6 Page: 041

COOPER Augusto d Hopkinton 1903-10-24 age 49yrs 3mos 12dys b Concord Vol: 6 Page: 041

COOK William R d Hopkinton 1903-11-11 age 75yrs 8mos 4dys b Wakefield child of COOK John Vol: 6 Page: 041

HEATH Charles d Franklin 1903-11-02 age 80yrs 2mos 7dys Vol: 6 Page: 041

WEBBER Rebecca S d Hopkinton 1903-11-17 age 95yrs b Hopkinton child of WEBBER Wm & BAILEY Rachel Vol: 6 Page: 041

KIMBALL Lavalla M d Hopkinton 1903-11-30 age 88yrs 3mos 7dys b Grafton child of MASON Philip & REED Elizabeth Vol: 6 Page: 041

PUTNAM ---- d Hopkinton 1903-12-02 b Hopkinton child of PUTNAM Charles R & CLOUGH Nancy E Vol: 6 Page: 042

WHITCOMB Hester C d Hopkinton 1903-12-15 age 20yrs 7mos 17dys b Lewiston Me child of HART M B & GRAHAM Lovetta S Vol: 6 Page: 042

DWINNELLS Victoria May d Hopkinton 1903-12-26 age 5mos 12dys b Manchester child of DWINNELLS F & LIBBY Emma Vol: 6 Page: 042

PAGE Minnie V d Hopkinton 1903-12-26 age 8mos b Concord Mass child of PAGE Orrill M & DWINNELLS Josie D Vol: 6 Page: 042

DANFORTH Albert d Hopkinton 1903-12-28 age 84yrs 7dys b Boscawen child of DANFORTH William & PUTNEY Betsey Vol: 6 Page: 042

RAND Warren S d Hopkinton 1904-01-14 age 54yrs 4mos 13dys b Hopkinton Vol: 6 Page: 043

MORRILL Lucia P d Hopkinton 1904-01-24 age 53yrs 11mos 24dys b Hopkinton child of MORRILL Jacob M & ABBOTT Sarah Vol: 6 Page: 043

LIBBIE William T d Hopkinton 1904-02-04 age 81yrs 9mos 19dys b Epsom Vol: 6 Page: 043

ROLLINS William H d Hopkinton 1904-02-05 age 43yrs 4mos 12dys b Hopkinton child of ROLLINS Alfred A & COLBY Mary E Vol: 6 Page: 043

HODGDON Harriet N d Hopkinton 1904-02-06 age 77yrs 7mos 4dys b Hopkinton child of HOLMES John Vol: 6 Page: 043

LOVEREN Ebenezer d Hopkinton 1904-02-14 age 76yrs 11mos b Hopkinton child of LOVEREN Benjamin & BARTLETT Esther Vol: 6 Page: 043

CHASE Mary A d Claremont 1904-02-12 age 81yrs 3mos 1dys Vol: 6 Page: 044

BROWN Geo E d Somerville Mass 1904-03-15 age 60yrs 7mos 4dys Vol: 6 Page: 044

BURPEE Emily S d Hopkinton 1904-03-19 age 83yrs 1mos b Topsham Vt child of BUTTERFIELD Samuel & SCRIBNER Sarah Vol: 6 Page: 044

CHANDLER Augustus R d Hopkinton 1904-03-26 age 71yrs 5mos 20dys b Hopkinton child of CHANDLER Stephen & RIPLEY Mary Vol: 6 Page: 044

PALMER Cora I d Hopkinton 1904-03-31 age 47yrs 1mos 20dys b Antrim child of CLARK Oliver & AYERS Minerva Vol: 6 Page: 044

BLOOD George Calvin d Hopkinton 1904-04-02 age 3dys b Hopkinton child of BLOOD George & MUDGETT Nellie F Vol: 6 Page: 044

WILSON John E d Hopkinton 1904-04-13 age 78yrs 7mos b Pembroke child of WILSON John & EMERY Huldah Vol: 6 Page: 045

ELLIOTT John S d Hopkinton 1904-04-14 age 58yrs 8mos 13dys b Webster child of WILSON George J & SHATTUCK Mary B Vol: 6 Page: 045

KIMBALL Martha d Hopkinton 1904-04-28 age 71yrs 5mos 15dys b Derby Vt child of CARPENTER Joseph & BURR Martha Vol: 6 Page: 045

TUCKER David C d Henniker 1904-04-30 age 58yrs 28dys b Henniker child of TUCKER David & STRAW Mary E Vol: 6 Page: 045

KIMBALL Robert R d Boston Mass 1904-05-02 age 55yrs 1mos 26dys Vol: 6 Page: 045

CLEMENT Betsey M d Hopkinton 1904-05-07 age 89yrs 1mos 8dys b Hopkinton child of CLEMENT John & MORRILL Mirriam Vol: 6 Page: 045

ELLIOTT Angeline P d Hopkinton 1904-05-11 age 75yrs 11mos 28dys b Bow child of SANBORN P Vol: 6 Page: 046

MORRILL Densie E d Hopkinton 1904-05-25 age 28yrs 9mos 14dys b Hill child of SWEATT Horace Vol: 6 Page: 046

KELLEY Julia A d Concord 1904-05-25 age 78yrs 3mos 25dys b Barre Vt child of KETCHUM Silas & DOTY Cyntha Vol: 6 Page: 046

ELLIOTT A Dighton d Hopkinton 1904-05-28 age 66yrs 7mos b Concord child of ELLIOTT Enoch & BOWER Jane Vol: 6 Page: 046

BACON John H d Hopkinton 1904-06-28 age 69yrs 1mos 22dys b Hopkinton child of BACON John Vol: 6 Page: 046

MERRILL Geo E d Manchester Mass 1904-06-25 age 55yrs 4mos 22dys Vol: 6 Page: 046

CLOUGH Mary O d Hopkinton 1904-07-22 age 60yrs 9mos 5dys b Candia child of BEAN Levi & MERRILL Rachel G Vol: 6 Page: 047

HILL Elbridge d Boston Mass 1904-07-22 age 49yrs Vol: 6 Page: 047

WALTERS Eliza Ann d Greenland 1904-07-31 age 86yrs 11dys b Greeland Vol: 6 Page: 047

KIMBALL ---- d Hopkinton 1904-08-05 age 3hrs b Hopkinton child of KIMBALL Nelson D & PATCH Adalade M Vol: 6 Page: 047

BARTLETT Anson A d Hopkinton 1904-08-08 age 21yrs 4mos b Hopkinton child of BARTLETT Henry & HARDY Isabelle Vol: 6 Page: 047

BAILEY Sarah M d Hopkinton 1904-08-22 age 55yrs 6mos 23dys b Hopkinton child of KNOWLTON Francis & HARTWELL Mary Dix Vol: 6 Page: 047

HOLMES Willard M d Hopkinton 1904-08-24 age 77yrs 9mos 4dys b Boscawen child of HOLMES Gardner & MELVIN Betsey Vol: 6 Page: 048

ELLIOTT Ernest E d Hopkinton 1904-08-27 age 26yrs 11mos 1dys b Hopkinton child of ELLIOTT Edson E & COLBY Nettie L Vol: 6 Page: 048

JAMESON Letticia M d Hopkinton 1904-09-11 age 73yrs 11mos 21dys b New Boston child of PRICHARD M Bartlett & GREGG Jane Vol: 6 Page: 048

BAKER Ethel May d Spingfield Vt 1904-09-09 age 9yrs child of BAKER Arthur & Mary Vol: 6 Page: 048

SYMONDS Tilton d Hopkinton 1904-09-20 age 90yrs 2mos 23dys b Hillsborough child of SYMONDS Eliphlet & TILTON Tammy Vol: 6 Page: 048

KIMBALL Fanny T d Hopkinton 1904-09-28 age 86yrs 6mos 24dys b Sutton Vol: 6 Page: 048

WEBBER Cyril T d Hopkinton 1904-09-28 age 63yrs 5mos 16dys b Webster child of WEBBER Jeremiah S Vol: 6 Page: 049

ROWELL Marcia G d Pittsfield 1904-09-29 age 49yrs 3mos 16dys Vol: 6 Page: 049

BEAN Rachel G d Hopkinton 1904-10-12 age 83yrs 8mos 12dys b Hudson child of MERRILL John Vol: 6 Page: 049

FLANDERS Nathaniel d Hopkinton 1904-10-31 age 75yrs 10mos 4dys b Bradford child of FLANDERS Nathaniel & WRIGHT Betsey Vol: 6 Page: 049

COCHRAN Hannah Whipple d Hopkinton 1904-11-01 age 79yrs b New Boston child of COCHRAN Joseph & WILSON Anna Vol: 6 Page: 049

PIERCE Myra F d Hopkinton 1904-11-10 age 72yrs 9mos 6dys b Hopkinton child of COPPS Moses & GEORGE Mary Vol: 6 Page: 049

STERENS Gilman A d Hopkinton 1901-10-22 age 75yrs 3mos 11dys b Goffstown child of STERNS John & TARBOX Susan Vol: 6 Page: 027 Note: ? stevens or sterens

FELLOWS Sarah E d Hopkinton 1889-05-16 age 50yrs 8mos 16dys b Hopkinton child of FELLOWS Ignatious & COPPS Sarah J Vol: 5 Page: 087 Line: 019 Section: 2nd

KIMBALL Benjamin F d Hopkinton 1899-12-21 b Hopkinton child of KIMBALL Carlton & SCRIBNER Martha Vol: 6 Page: 013

BARNARD Joseph d Hopkinton 1899-12-26 age 82yrs 1mos 15dys b Hopkinton child of BARNARD Joseph & EASTMAN Merriam Vol: 6 Page: 013

HUNT Olive A d Hopkinton 1899-12-26 age 60yrs Vol: 6 Page: 013

GERRISH Susan M d Haverhill Mass 1904-11-03 age 75yrs 6mos 10dys b Hopkinton Vol: 6 Page: 050

PUTNEY True J d Hopkinton 1904-11-19 age 55yrs 5dys b Hopkinton child of PUTNEY Ira A & MUZZEY Hannah Vol: 6 Page: 050

SEABORN Winfield F d Hopkinton 1904-11-24 age 34yrs 5mos b Houlton Me child of SEABORN Robert H & WATSON Sarah Vol: 6 Page: 050

LE BARON Mary Phillip d Concord 1904-12-03 age 18yrs 8mos 19dys b Concord child of PHILLIP Ira C & HARDY Angie Vol: 6 Page: 050 Line: Section:

BROWN Daniel E d Hopkinton 1905-01-03 age 68yrs 6mos 14dys b Woodstock child of BROWN Samuel Vol: 6 Page: 051

BARNES Levi N d Hopkinton 1905-01-04 age 72yrs 3mos 17dys b Henniker child of BARNES Levi & PATTERSON Nancy Vol: 6 Page: 051

FENTON Rosa B d Hopkinton 1905-01-13 age 36yrs b Thornton child of ELKINS George W & GLIDDEN Mary E Vol: 6 Page: 051

BOUTWELL Eli A d Hopkinton 1905-01-20 age 71yrs 10mos 25dys b Barre Vt child of BOUTWELL Samuel P & ALLEN Lydia Vol: 6 Page: 051

MORRILL Charles A d Hopkinton 1905-01-26 age 64yrs 27dys b Hopkinton child of MORRILL Ebenezer & SWEATT Phebe Vol: 6 Page: 051

SMITH Nancy J d Hopkinton 1905-02-01 age 73yrs 3mos 20dys b Milton Me Vol: 6 Page: 051

KELLEY Harriet T d Hopkinton 1905-02-11 age 93yrs 5mos 2dys b Hopkinton child of TRUSSELL John Vol: 6 Page: 052

HOWE Etta d Hopkinton 1905-02-16 age 39yrs 3mos 3dys b Bradford child of WYMAN Charles B & CHENEY Jennette Vol: 6 Page: 052

CHASE Ruhanah d Hopkinton 1905-02-16 age 92yrs 11mos 16dys b New Boston child of COCHRAN Joseph & WILSON Anna Vol: 6 Page: 052

ROLLINS Ellen A d Hopkinton 1905-02-17 age 53yrs 9dys b Hopkinton child of SARGENT Abner C & ROGERS Emmeline A Vol: 6 Page: 052

DUNBAR Elmer B d Hopkinton 1905-02-27 age 74yrs 6mos 14dys b Grantham child of DUNBAR Azel & NICHOL Mehitable Vol: 6 Page: 052

Hopkinton, NH Deaths 1880

STRAW Charles H d Hopkinton 1905-03-01 age 45yrs 1mos 9dys b Hopkinton child of STRAW William S & FLANDERS Mary Ann Vol: 6 Page: 052

DANFORTH John d Manchester 1905-02-13 age 76yrs 6mos 16dys Vol: 6 Page: 053

CONNOR Vianna A d Brooklin Mass 1905-03-04 age 62yrs Vol: 6 Page: 053

HARDY Julia A d Hopkinton 1905-03-04 age 81yrs 4mos 8dys b Warner child of HARDY Joseph Vol: 6 Page: 053

ROBERTSON Maria Woods d Quincy Mass 1905-03-10 age 61yrs 10mos 10dys Vol: 6 Page: 053

ALLEN Walton P d Hopkinton 1905-03-27 age 56yrs 1mos 21dys b Chelsea Mass child of ALLEN Willard & STONE Elmira Vol: 6 Page: 053

COLBY Hannah Paige d Hopkinton 1905-04-07 age 74yrs 1mos 23dys b Hopkinton child of EDMUNDS Horace & CILLEY Bridget W Vol: 6 Page: 053

BOUTELLE William H d Hopkinton 1905-04-18 age 79yrs 3mos 17dys b Hopkinton child of BOUTELLE Calvin & FISK Mary Vol: 6 Page: 054

LEARNARD Lucy Ann d Concord 1905-03-05 age 83yrs 7mos Vol: 6 Page: 054

CONNOR Jerome B d Brookline Mass 1905-05-09 age 57yrs Vol: 6 Page: 054

HEATH Clara J d Concord 1905-05-17 age 77yrs 10mos b Boscawen child of HANSON John & ARLIN Alice Vol: 6 Page: 054

CHASE Nancy T d Hopkinton 1905-05-30 age 77yrs 8mos 11dys b Concord Vol: 6 Page: 054

BASCOM Dorothy I d Hopkinton 1905-07-12 age 2mos 26dys b Hopkinton child of BASCOM Fred & FLANDERS Rose Vol: 6 Page: 054

STEVENS George d Boscawen 1905-07-26 age 28yrs b Hopkinton child of STEVENS Henry C & MORRILL Mary Vol: 6 Page: 055

QUIMBY Jonathan d Hopkinton 1905-08-05 age 82yrs 7mos 14dys b Hopkinton child of QUIMBY John & BLANCHARD Hannah Vol: 6 Page: 055

DEARBORN Alice R d New York 1905-08-03 age 25yrs 8mos 10dys Vol: 6 Page: 055

HOLMES Julia A d Hopkinton 1905-08-17 age 72yrs 2mos 22dys b Warner child of CLARK Stephen B Vol: 6 Page: 055

NUDD Warren A d Warner 1905-08-20 age 1yrs 6mos 2dys b Hopkinton child of NUDD John & CHASE Gertrude Vol: 6 Page: 055

MORGAN Mary L d Arlington 1905-02-13 Vol: 6 Page: 055

KELLEY Grace E d Hopkinton 1905-08-30 age 21yrs 11mos 13dys b Hopkinton child of POOR Eri A & BROWN Alice M Vol: 6 Page: 056

PAIGE French d Hopkinton 1905-09-15 age 55yrs 11mos 17dys b Lowell Mass child of PAIGE T E & Clark Vol: 6 Page: 056

JACKMAN Lucretia A d Hopkinton 1905-10-07 age 78yrs 6mos 6dys b Webster child of PILLSBURY John & Sarah Vol: 6 Page: 056

CLOUGH Charles E d Hopkinton 1905-10-09 age 42yrs 2mos 2dys b Hopkinton child of CLOUGH Charles F & HARDY Mary J Vol: 6 Page: 056

HUNT John d Hopkinton 1905-10-18 age 58yrs b Warner child of HUNT Isaac & ORBORN Catherine Vol: 6 Page: 056

WALKER John Thomas d Hopkinton 1905-10-22 age 72yrs 8mos 7dys b Jerico Vt child of WALKER John T & Joy Vol: 6 Page: 056

Hopkinton, NH Deaths 1880

CAMPBELL Harvey d Somerville Mass 1905-10-21 age 79yrs 8mos 27dys Vol: 6 Page: 057

SANBORN Laura d Hopkinton 1905-10-28 age 80yrs 5mos 13dys b Warner child of JONES Daniel & TRUSSELL Judith Vol: 6 Page: 057

BARTON Edwin d Boscawen 1905-10-26 age 89yrs Vol: 6 Page: 057

BRIGGS Ralph Clinton d Hopkinton 1905-11-09 age 5dys b Hopkinton child of BRIGGS John S & WIGGINS Edith Vol: 6 Page: 057

CURRIER Amos H d Hopkinton 1905-11-17 age 57yrs 1mos 9dys b Hopkinton child of CURRIER Edmund E & MORRILL Lulcy Vol: 6 Page: 057

DUNBAR Jonathan N d Hopkinton 1905-11-18 age 83yrs 9mos 8dys b Hopkinton child of DUNBAR Angel Vol: 6 Page: 057

GORMAN Ernest Fred d Hopkinton 1905-11-24 age 20yrs 11mos 24dys b Hopkinton child of GORMAN Thomas & REID Jennie Vol: 6 Page: 058

BURROUGHS Mariah d Hopkinton 1905-12-05 age 86yrs 7mos 20dys b Londonderry child of CORNNING John & CROWELL Sally Vol: 6 Page: 058

FRENCH Clara N d Hopkinton 1905-12-31 age 47yrs 6mos 3dys b Northfield child of FRENCH George & BUSWELL Nancy Vol: 6 Page: 058

WADLEIGH Walter K d Hopkinton 1906-02-07 age 41yrs 10mos b Franklin child of WADLEIGH Jonathan T & THOMAS Betsey Vol: 6 Page: 059 Note: birth Apr 7 1864

MUDGETT Mary Upton d Hopkinton 1906-02-21 age 63yrs 9mos 2dys b Hopkinton child of UPTON Joseph S & MERRILL Clarinda Vol: 6 Page: 059 Note: birth May 18 1842

FAGAN Mary d Hopkinton 1906-02-20 age 44yrs b Ireland Vol: 6 Page: 059 Note: birth 1862

DWINNELLS John G d Hopkinton 1906-03-19 age 71yrs 4mos 6dys b Dunbarton Vol: 6 Page: 059 Note: birth Nov 13 1834

KEZER Lizzie M d Hopkinton 1906-04-14 age 57yrs 6mos 9dys b Sunapee child of JONES Clifton C & RYDER Mary A Vol: 6 Page: 059 Note: birth Oct 5 1849

McALPINE Lucy G d New Boston 1905-02-23 age 85yrs 11mos 4dys Vol: 6 Page: 059

SMITH Philena Prudence d Hopkinton 1906-05-09 age 74yrs 7mos 22dys b Hopkinton child of HAWTHORNE Calvan & JACKMAN Rachel Vol: 6 Page: 060 Note: birth Sep 17 1831

SANBORN Sarah A d Watertown Mass 1906-05-24 age 59yrs 7mos 29dys Vol: 6 Page: 060

COLBY Frank P d Hopkinton 1906-05-31 age 64yrs 10mos 31dys child of COLBY Samuel & STRAW Mary Vol: 6 Page: 060 Note: birth Jul 1841

PAIGE Elizabeth d Hopkinton 1906-06-08 b Hopkinton child of PAIGE Wesley A & HOLMES Lillian Vol: 6 Page: 060

PAIGE Lillian Holmes d Hopkinton 1906-06-08 age 24yrs 8mos 25dys b Gardiner Me child of HOLMES Geo H & WAHLGREW Annie C Vol: 6 Page: 060 Note: birth Sep 13 1881

WHITTEMORE William B d Hopkinton 1906-06-13 age 78yrs 9mos 17dys b Concord Vol: 6 Page: 060 Note: birth Aug 27 1817

GUNNISON Lucene A d Hopkinton 1906-06-19 age 76yrs b New Boston child of WHITE Aaron & CRAIN Louisa Vol: 6 Page: 061 Note: birth Jun 19 1830

Hopkinton, NH Deaths 1880

COGSWELL Georgie A d Concord 1906-07-21 age 46yrs Vol: 6 Page: 061

MONTGOMERY George d Hopkinton 1906-08-05 age 84yrs 3mos 4dys b Salem NY child of MONTGOMERY John & BURBANK Mary Vol: 6 Page: 061 Note: birth May 1,1822

BAILEY Fred H d Hopkinton 1906-08-09 age 73yrs 11mos 9dys b Hopkinton child of BAILEY John Milton & KNOWLTON Lucy P Vol: 6 Page: 061 Note: birth Sep 18 1832

BURNHAM James d Concord 1906-08-19 age 75yrs child of BURNHAM John & WADLEIGH Susan E Vol: 6 Page: 061

DAVIS Mabel d Hopkinton 1906-08-19 b Hopkinton child of FISK Daniel & CHANDLER Dell E Vol: 6 Page: 061 Note: birth Dec 5 1885

SILVER Nancy B d Hopkinton 1906-09-01 age 73yrs 6mos b Bow child of SILVER Isiah & Morrill Vol: 6 Page: 062 Note: birth May 1833

RAND Helen K d Phildadelphia Pa 1906-09-14 age 51yrs 2mos Vol: 6 Page: 062

HARDY Lydia S d Hopkinton 1906-09-11 age 85yrs 9mos 9dys b Epsom child of LANCASTER Jacob & SANDERS Alice Vol: 6 Page: 062 Note: birth Dec 2 1820

BUTNAM George C d Hopkinton 1906-09-16 age 7yrs b Beverly Mass child of BUTNAM George & CLEMONS Sarah P Vol: 6 Page: 062 Note: birth Sep 17 1899

GAGE David L d Concord 1906-10-06 age 69yrs 4dys b Hopkinton child of GAGE John & LONG Mary H Vol: 6 Page: 062 Note: birth Oct 2 1837

HILL Mary E d Hopkinton 1906-10-22 age 68yrs 8mos 26dys b Amesbury Mass child of HARRINGTON Moses B & MORSE Betsey P Vol: 6 Page: 062 Note: birth Jan 26 1828

MITCHELL Valentine J d Hopkinton 1906-11-18 age 61yrs 10mos 23dys b Manchester child of MITHCELL Joseph Jr & SHAW Sarah P Vol: 6 Page: 063 Note: birth Dec 25 1844

SHATTLE Matilda d Hopkinton 1906-12-15 age 60yrs 6mos 15dys b Germany child of SHATTLE Jeremiah & MITCHELE Margdaline Vol: 6 Page: 063 Note: birth May 31 1846

SARGENT Emeline H Hopkinton 1906-12-18 age 87yrs 1mos 18dys b Concord child of ROGERS John Vol: 6 Page: 063 Note: birth Oct 31 1819

BAKER Ralph d Hopkinton 1906-08-25 age 1yrs 1mos b Franklin child of BAKER Fred Vol: 6 Page: 064 Note: birth Jul 25 1905

PUTNAM Lydia C d Hopkinton 1907-01-10 age 75yrs 7mos 15dys b Henniker child of GOSS Luther & COLBY Silva Vol: 6 Page: 065

EMERSON Hanson D d Hopkinton 1907-01-11 age 60yrs 6mos b Hopkinton child of EMERSON James H & FLANDERS Judith Vol: 6 Page: 065

TUCKER David d Hopkinton 1907-01-18 age 92yrs 5mos 16dys b Henniker child of KIMBALL Ezra & HARDY Hannah Vol: 6 Page: 065

COLBY Mary B d Hopkinton 1907-01-19 age 77yrs 7mos 16dys b Hopkinton child of KIMBALL Daniel & HERRICH Asenath Vol: 6 Page: 065

GERRISH Mary S d Hopkinton 1907-01-21 age 49yrs 5mos 13dys b Indiana child of SHEPPARD David & FISHER Rachel Vol: 6 Page: 065

HARRINGTON Rebecca C d Hopkinton 1907-01-30 age 98yrs 9mos 28dys b Concord child of CURRIER Samuel & LEWIS Sarah Vol: 6 Page: 065

Hopkinton, NH Deaths 1880

FOWLER Elizabeth L d Hopkinton 1907-02-04 age 58yrs 1mos 1dys b Newbury child of BROWN Albert Vol: 6 Page: 066

STRAW Gilman J d Hopkinton 1907-02-08 age 70yrs 9mos 13dys b Hopkinton child of STRAW Asahel S & JEWELL Abagail B Vol: 6 Page: 066

WALKER ---- d Hopkinton 1907-02-09 age 28dys b Webster child of WALKER Milton J & ELLIOTT Alice M Vol: 6 Page: 066

FLANDERS Hannah C d Hopkinton 1907-02-22 age 84yrs 11mos 11dys b Hennkier child of CONNOR Abel & WHITNEY Hannah Vol: 6 Page: 066

LIBBY Percy L d Hopkinton 1907-03-06 age 26yrs 3mos 26dys b Gorham Me child of LIBBY C M & Cloutman Vol: 6 Page: 066 Note: birth Nov 8 1880

BARTON Elroy C d Hopkinton 1907-03-12 age 45yrs 2mos 11dys b Hopkinton child of BARTON C O & Cutts Vol: 6 Page: 066 Note: birth Jan 1 1862

LAW ---- d Hopkinton 1907-03-12 b Hopkinton child of LAW Francis & MORRILL Etta Vol: 6 Page: 067

LITTLE Emmeline B d Hopkinton 1907-03-13 age 81yrs 11mos 6dys b Hopkinton child of HARVEY John & Shaw Vol: 6 Page: 067 Note: birth Apr 7 1825

DUNBAR Carrie B d Hopkinton 1907-03-14 age 45yrs 2mos 17dys b Hopkinton child of DUNBAR Elmer B & WEBBER Ann T Vol: 6 Page: 067

GREENLEAF George W d Hopkinton 1907-03-25 age 69yrs 5mos 11dys b Boston Mass child of GREENLEAF William & Emery Vol: 6 Page: 067 Note: birth Oct 14 1837

PERRY William C d Brookline Mass 1907 b Brookline Mass Vol: 6 Page: 067

PERRY ---- d Hopkinton 1907-04-02 b Hopkinton child of PERRY James M & KELLEY Eiditheen Vol: 6 Page: 067

JONES Ruth B d Hopkinton 1907-04-08 age 14yrs 5mos 7dys b Hopkinton child of JONES J Arthur & BAILEY Mabel B Vol: 6 Page: 068

DUNBAR Ann T d Hopkinton 1907-04-06 age 71yrs 1mos 17dys b Hopkinton child of WEBBER Seth & REBEKAH S Vol: 6 Page: 068

COOK Louisa M d Hopkinton 1907-04-21 age 78yrs 9mos 3dys b Vermont child of KENISTON Mariah Vol: 6 Page: 068

TABER Susan K d Holyoke Mass 1907-04-27 age 63yrs Vol: 6 Page: 068

FLANDERS James B d Warner 1907-02-01 age 73yrs 3mos 7dys b Warner Vol: 6 Page: 068

STEVENS Roxanna D d Hopkinton 1907-05-03 age 75yrs 9mos 8dys b Manchester child of Young Vol: 6 Page: 068

CURRIER Alonzo d Concord 1907-05-09 age 45yrs 11mos b Hopkinton child of CURRIER Amos & PATTERSON Fanny Vol: 6 Page: 069

CURRIER Mary Ann d Hopkinton 1907-05-15 age 64yrs 6mos 4dys b Hopkinton child of CURRIER Geo W & FLANDERS Hannah Vol: 6 Page: 069 Note: birth Nov 11 1843

HATCH Lucetta C d Hopkinton 1911-05-14 age 86yrs 1mos 5dys b Hopkinton child of CHASE Cyrus & Jones Vol: 6 Page: 077

ELLIOTT Alma H d Hopkinton 1907-06-27 age 31yrs 9mos 7dys b Gilmanton Vol: 6 Page: 069

SHAW Clara d Hopkinton 1907-06-29 age 66yrs b Lowell Mass Vol: 6 Page: 069

ABBOTT Ezra W d Hopkinton 1907-08-09 age 86yrs 0mos 7dys b Hopkinton Vol: 6 Page: 069

Hopkinton, NH Deaths 1880

FULLER Helen May d Hopkinton 1907-08-14 age 1yrs 5mos 28dys b Hopkinton child of FULLER G Irving & REED Blanch M Vol: 6 Page: 070

FERNALD William J d Hopkinton 1907-08-17 age 61yrs 7mos 17dys b Dover Maine child of FERNALD John & HILTON Eliza Vol: 6 Page: 070

CHANDLER Susan Velona d Hopkinton 1907-08-24 age 73yrs 11mos 16dys b Hopkinton child of CURRIER Carlton & CAMPBELL Dollie Vol: 6 Page: 070

SAWYER Sarah A d Hopkinton 1907-08-29 age 68yrs 11mos 29dys b Hopkinton child of COUCH James & EASTMAN Mary Vol: 6 Page: 070

KIMBALL John S d Hopkinton 1908-01-01 age 62yrs 5mos b Boston Mass child of KIMBALL John S & MARY E S Vol: 6 Page: 074

DENSMORE James A d Hopkinton 1912-01-05 age 59yrs 5mos 13dys b Northfield child of DENSMORE Samuel Vol: 6 Page: 102

CURTICE Grovenor A d Hopkinton 1907-09-29 age 65yrs 5mos 28dys b Lempster child of CURTICE Samuel & SWEATT Lenona Vol: 6 Page: 071

LIBBY Winnifield M d Hopkinton 1907-10-11 b Hopkinton child of LIBBY Percy L & HOOK Alice M Vol: 6 Page: 071

SEVERANCE ---- d Hopkinton 1907-10-12 age 1dys b Hopkinton child of SEVERANCE W J & FOWLER Florence E Vol: 6 Page: 071

BURPEE William Brown d Hopkinton 1907-10-14 age 88yrs 9mos 11dys child of BURPEE J & FLANDERS Zilpha Vol: 6 Page: 071 Note: birth Jun 3 1819

CILLEY Tristram d Norwich Conn 1907-10-27 age 65yrs 4mos 27dys b Weare child of CILLEY John & Judith Vol: 6 Page: 071

SMITH Fred Delno d Hopkinton 1907-10-27 age 2yrs 1mos 6dys b Hopkinton child of SMITH Robert & BOYCE Ardella Vol: 6 Page: 071

MARSH ---- d Hopkinton 1907-11-04 b Hopkinton child of MARSH Frank P & DUSTIN Etta Vol: 6 Page: 072

WATTERSON Gertrude I d Concord 1907-11-21 age 3mos 7dys b Boscawen child of WATTERSON Nathaniel & EMERSON Minnie Vol: 6 Page: 072

HUNT Ella M d Hopkinton 1907-11-24 age 48yrs 4mos 26dys b Nova Scotia child of SPRONL[??] Edward Vol: 6 Page: 072

BURNHAM Charles J d Hopkinton 1907-12-11 age 35yrs 1mos 7dys b Milford child of BURNHAM M Frank & FOLLANSBEE Frances Vol: 6 Page: 072

FOOTE William N d Hopkinton 1907-12-12 age 41yrs 5mos 22dys b Hopkinton child of FOOTE Nelson & Melissa Vol: 6 Page: 072

BARTLETT ---- d Hopkinton 1907-12-30 b Hopkinton child of BARTLETT Clifton & CHASE Lida H Vol: 6 Page: 072

FARRINGTON Ann Mariah d Concord 1907-12-31 age 80yrs 6mos 21dys b Hillsborough child of HARTSHORN Joseph & ELLSWORTH Mary E Vol: 6 Page: 073

FRANKLYLN Eleanor G d Hopkinton 1907-09-07 age 57yrs 2mos 6dys b Rougham England child of THOMAS William M & Catherine Vol: 6 Page: 070

HOOD Ethel L d Hopkinton 1908-01-01 age 12yrs 4mos 4dys b Weare child of HOOD George G & BROWN Fronie E Vol: 6 Page: 074

MacDOUGAL Stuart d Hopkinton 1908-01-10 age 3dys b Hopkinton child of MacDOUGALL James A & LINCOLN Sara Vol: 6 Page: 074

FOSS Emma A d Hopkinton 1908-01-19 age 48yrs 9mos 19dys b Philadelphia Pa child of CLARK Oliver H & AYER Minerva Vol: 6 Page: 074

BOYNTON Elizabeth M d Hopkinton 1908-01-22 age 5mos 18dys b Hopkinton child of BOYNTON Arthur J & CLOUGH Bessie J Vol: 6 Page: 074

CARPENTER Guy d Hopkinton 1908-01-24 age 47yrs 27dys b Hopkinton child of CARPENTER Guy & KIMBALL Mary Vol: 6 Page: 074

SWEATT William M d Hopkinton 1908-02-01 age 95yrs 11mos 11dys b Webster child of SWEATT Isaac & DAVIS Mary Vol: 6 Page: 075

SON Rosa d Hopkinton 1908-01-31 age 69yrs b Ireland child of SANBORN M & Ann Vol: 6 Page: 075

GUERIN Herbert E d Hopkinton 1908-02-03 age 4yrs 11mos 15dys b Hopkinton child of GUERIN Edwin R & LORD Mary E Vol: 6 Page: 075

FOSS Minnie d Hopkinton 1908-01-10 age 28yrs b Hopkinton child of FOSS George E & CLARK Emma A Vol: 6 Page: 075

FOSS John M d Hopkinton 1908-02-11 age 61yrs 2mos 16dys b Hopkinton child of FOSS John M & CONNOR Elvria Vol: 6 Page: 075

ROGERS John d Hopkinton 1908-02-13 age 72yrs 10mos 1dys b Henniker child of ROGERS Hiram & STICKNEY Dorothy Vol: 6 Page: 075

DUSTON Harrison Rufus d Hopkinton 1908-02-18 age 11yrs 4mos 24dys b Hopkinton child of DUSTON Arthur M & CLOUGH Josie C Vol: 6 Page: 076

DOLLOFF Nellie M d Hopkinton 1908-03-20 age 36yrs 5mos 11dys b New Hampton child of SWAIN John D & YEATON Esther A Vol: 6 Page: 076

FOSS George E d Hopkinton 1908-03-23 age 36yrs 9mos 8dys b Hopkinton child of FOSS Jonathan G M & CONNOR Alvira C Vol: 6 Page: 076

FENTON Edna D d Concord 1908-04-15 age 32yrs 4mos 29dys b Thornton child of ELKINS George W & GLIDDEN Mary E Vol: 6 Page: 076

TARR Phoebe d Hopkinton 1908-04-25 age 21yrs 20dys b Gloucester Mass child of TARR George I & Ross Vol: 6 Page: 076

HOYT Sarah C d Hopkinton 1908-04-25 age 87yrs 10mos 14dys b Lakeville Mass Vol: 6 Page: 076

MUDGETT Calvin H d Hopkinton 1908-04-27 age 84yrs 8mos 26dys child of MUDGETT William Vol: 6 Page: 077

BURNHAM Ellen A d Boston Mass 1908-02-16 age 70yrs 19dys Vol: 6 Page: 077

PAIGE Audrey E d Manchester 1908-03-07 age 2mos 27dys b Manchester Vol: 6 Page: 077

HARDY Thomas J d Hopkinton 1908-05-08 age 6mos 17dys child of HARDY Ernest B & Reyno Vol: 6 Page: 077

PAGE Ellen Maria d Hopkinton 1908-05-07 age 80yrs 8mos 5dys b Weston Mass child of CUTTER Jonas P & SMITH Elizabeth Vol: 6 Page: 077

FLETCHER Henry A d Hopkinton 1908-05-14 age 80yrs 5mos 6dys b Washington Vol: 6 Page: 078

BROWN Albert d Hopkinton 1908-05-17 age 92yrs 22dys b Wilmot Vol: 6 Page: 078

CHASE Annie A d Northfield Vt 1908-05-20 age 64yrs 19dys b Concord child of RUNNELS Samuel & ABBOTT Annie Vol: 6 Page: 078

MONTGOMERY William d Hopkinton 1908-05-23 age 84yrs 5dys b Salem NY child of MONTGOMERY John W & BURBANK Mary Vol: 6 Page: 078

HUGHES Thomas d Hopkinton 1908-05-26 age 82yrs b Ireland Vol: 6 Page: 078

COPPS Rufus P d Hopkinton 1908-05-26 age 90yrs 4mos 13dys b Plaistow child of COPPS Moses & GEORGE Mary Vol: 6 Page: 078

DOWNING Elizabeth K d Hopkinton 1908-06-23 age 80yrs 6mos 1dys b Henniker Vol: 6 Page: 079

HOLLAND ---- (Infant) d Concord 1908-06-14 b Concord child of HOLLAND James H & DEARBORN Cornelia H Vol: 6 Page: 079

BLANCHARD Galen E d Hopkinton 1908-06-27 age 56yrs 8mos 2dys b Washington child of BLANCHARD Silas Vol: 6 Page: 079

MORAN Ann d Hopkinton 1908-06-22 age 71yrs b Ireland child of CLANT?? Patrick & FAGAN Elizabeth Vol: 6 Page: 079

BOUTWELL Julia A d Concord 1908-07-29 age 57yrs 10mos 29dys b Hopkinton child of WOODBURY Hiram & WEBSTER Lephie M Vol: 6 Page: 079

SPOFFORD Luther F d Hopkinton 1908-08-14 age 60yrs 22dys b Hopkinton child of SPOFFORD Samuel & FITCH Sarah J Vol: 6 Page: 079

BURBANK Mary F d Hopkinton 1908-09-03 age 70yrs 1mos 3dys b Hopkinton child of PALMER William & ANNA Eliza Vol: 6 Page: 080

ANNIS Paine D d Hopkinton 1908-09-09 age 71yrs 8mos 24dys b Warner child of ANNIS C & Davis Vol: 6 Page: 080

CHASE George d Hopkinton 1908-09-09 age 67yrs 11dys b Hopkinton child of CHASE Ambrose & Gould Vol: 6 Page: 080

CLEMONS Betsey d Hopkinton 1908-09-11 age 84yrs 1mos 7dys b Hopkinton child of DUSTIN Ebenzer & Sarah Vol: 6 Page: 080

MOULTON Amanda F d Hopkinton 1908-09-09 age 49yrs 7mos 22dys b Canterbury child of LYFORD John & HAM Elizabeth Vol: 6 Page: 080

WONDERLICK Edward E d Hopkinton 1908-09-21 age 9mos b Warner child of WONDERLICK Charles & CLARK Alice Vol: 6 Page: 080

COOMBS Adeline M d Woodsville 1908-09-22 age 83yrs 11mos 6dys Vol: 6 Page: 081

ADAMS Joseph H d Hopkinton 1908-09-28 age 72yrs 2mos 17dys b Sutton child of ADAMS Henry & Maxon Vol: 6 Page: 081 Note: birth Jul 11 1836

CLOUGH Benjamin C d Hopkinton 1908-10-04 age 93yrs 8mos 3dys b Hopkinton child of CLOUGH William & Couch Vol: 6 Page: 081

HARDY Laura B d Hopkinton 1908-10-23 age 82yrs 18dys b Warner child of Bartlett Vol: 6 Page: 081

WALKER Jessee d Hopkinton 1908-11-05 age 56yrs Vol: 6 Page: 081

DOW Samuel H d Bow 1908-11-21 age 83yrs 5mos 22dys b Hopkinton child of DOW Samuel & HOYT Sarah E Vol: 6 Page: 081

ELLIOTT Mary E d Lawrence Mass 1908-11-23 age 68yrs 11mos 17dys Vol: 6 Page: 082

PERKINS John S d Hopkinton 1908-11-26 age 71yrs 7mos b Exeter child of PERKINS Joseph & LOCK Louie Vol: 6 Page: 082

STRAW John S d Hopkinton 1908-11-29 age 70yrs 5mos 10dys b Hopkinton Vol: 6 Page: 082

DUSTIN Addie M d Hopkinton 1908-12-06 age 62yrs 4mos 14dys b Hopkinton child of DUSTIN Daniel & BARNARD Sarah Vol: 6 Page: 082

EMERSON Lucretia F d Weare 1908-12-18 age 93yrs 9mos 5dys Vol: 6 Page: 082

CHASE Lucy S d Concord 1909-02-09 age 99yrs 7mos 5dys Vol: 6 Page: 083

BROWN Malvina d Hopkinton 1909-02-08 age 89yrs 10mos 28dys b Hopkinton child of BROWN Abram & KIMBALL Eunice Vol: 6 Page: 083

BLAKE Hannah Hull d Concord 1909-02-10 age 82yrs 13dys b Loudon child of MAXFIELD Joseph R & HULL Sarah Jane Vol: 6 Page: 083

RION Noah M d Warner 1909-02-15 age 56yrs 11mos 1dys b Canterbury child of RION Samuel T & ORDWAY Cynthia Vol: 6 Page: 083

BRADBURY Martha A d Hopkinton 1909-03-03 b Osipee child of MALLARD Ephrim & SEVERANCE Sarah Vol: 6 Page: 083

DANFORTH Helen A d Hopkinton 1909-03-26 age 27yrs 8mos 20dys b Hillsborough child of DANFORTH Charles H & Kempton Vol: 6 Page: 083

WHITTIER Nahum M d Hopkinton 1909-03-27 age 65yrs 4mos 9dys b Danville child of WHITTIER Jacob & SANBORN Harriett Vol: 6 Page: 084

KIMBALL Harry G d Hopkinton 1909-04-05 age 10yrs 3mos 22dys b Hopkinton child of KIMBALL Herbert M & COLBY M Abbie Vol: 6 Page: 084

HOWE Anna M J d Hopkinton 1909-05-01 age 76yrs 10mos 4dys b Deering child of PATTERSON Clara A Vol: 6 Page: 084

DOWNES John N d Boscawen 1909-03-31 age 65yrs Vol: 6 Page: 084

HUBBARD Henry W d Boston Mass 1909-10-21 age 56yrs 4mos 29dys Vol: 6 Page: 084

MERRILL Maria W d Lowell Mass 1909-05-23 age 87yrs 4mos 8dys Vol: 6 Page: 084

HARDON Annie E d Hopkinton 1909-06-05 age 61yrs 6mos 8dys b Winterport Maine child of McFLARITY William & DODGE L Vol: 6 Page: 085

LOCKE Mary A d Hopkinton 1909-06-07 age 61yrs 2mos 10dys b Hopkinton child of WRIGHT James M & WRIGHT Mary A Vol: 6 Page: 085

HARDON Charlotte M d Hopkinton 1909-06-08 age 87yrs 5mos 20dys b Norton Mass child of HODGDON Nathan H & HODGES Sally Vol: 6 Page: 085

CLINE Cecil Ray d Hopkinton 1912-02-10 b Hopkinton child of CLINE Earl O & SHORT Mary V Vol: 6 Page: 103

BOUTWELL Harriet W d Hopkinton 1909-06-17 age 80yrs 17dys b Hopkinton child of WEEKS Thomas J & SMITH Hannah C Vol: 6 Page: 085

FITTS ---- d Hopkinton 1909-07-12 b Hopkinton child of FITTS Jesse L & PRINCE Lida A Vol: 6 Page: 085

ELKINS Fred S d Concord 1909-08-01 age 36yrs 3mos 7dys b Thornton child of ELKINS George & GLIDDEN Mary Vol: 6 Page: 086

BROWN Mary Dunbar d Barre Vt 1909-08-14 age 85yrs 5mos 28dys Vol: 6 Page: 086

TILTON Hazel d Hopkinton 1909-08-25 age 1yrs 1mos 11dys b Hopkinton child of TILTON Joseph & ROLLINS M Alice Vol: 6 Page: 086

CURTICE Augusta W d Hopkinton 1909-08-28 age 60yrs 6mos 2dys b Manchester child of WILSON Robert & HUSE Lucinda Vol: 6 Page: 086

RICHARDSON Frederick G d Hopkinton 1909-09-20 age 55yrs 9mos 13dys b Hopkinton child of RICHARDSON Marsh & BUSWELL Jane W Vol: 6 Page: 086

CLARK Arthur Eugene d Hopkinton 1909-09-24 age 7mos 19dys b Hopkinton child of CLARK Fred & COOPER Mary Vol: 6 Page: 086

Hopkinton, NH Deaths 1880

CLARK Nancy H d Manchester 1909-10-08 age 79yrs 5mos 3dys b Hopkinton Vol: 6 Page: 087

DUSTIN Hannah P d Hopkinton 1909-11-08 age 67yrs 3mos 20dys b Hopkinton child of DUSTIN Cyrus & FISK Edna P Vol: 6 Page: 087

ELKINS Wallace d Hopkinton 1909-12-02 age 85yrs 4mos b Holton Canada child of ELKINS Moses Vol: 6 Page: 087

CHASE Frank Brown d Tilton 1909-12-03 age 64yrs 11mos 24dys Vol: 6 Page: 087

ALLEN Jane N d Boston Mass 1909-12-08 age 59yrs 9mos 18dys Vol: 6 Page: 087

PARKINSON Nettie G d Cambridge Mass 1909-12-16 Vol: 6 Page: 087

PATTERSON William A d Hopkinton 1909-12-19 age 73yrs 7dys b Hopkinton child of PATTERSON David N Vol: 6 Page: 088

CURRIER George W d Hopkinton 1909-12-27 age 93yrs 10mos b Hopkinton child of CURRIER Stephen & STORY Lucy Vol: 6 Page: 088

HOWE Edwin B d Hopkinton 1909-12-28 age 55yrs 9mos 28dys b Warner child of HOWE Joel M & WOODS Elizabeth Vol: 6 Page: 088

PATCH Betsey M d Hopkinton 1910-01-28 age 93yrs 11mos 10dys b Hopkinton child of WEBBER Isaiah & DAVIS Hannah Vol: 6 Page: 089

SMITH Sarah J d Hopkinton 1910-02-07 age 56yrs 10mos 25dys b Hopkinton child of KEZER Moses & ORDWAY Zilpha Vol: 6 Page: 089

HALL Frank E d Hopkinton 1910-02-08 age 58yrs 3mos 15dys b Boscawen child of HALL John Vol: 6 Page: 089

FLANDERS Benjamin d Hopkinton 1910-02-18 age 84yrs 11mos 25dys child of FLANDERS Isarel & HOLMES Olive Vol: 6 Page: 089

KIMBALL Maria P d Waltham Mass 1910-03-03 age 47yrs 5mos 11dys b Hopkinton Vol: 6 Page: 089

DOW Horace M d Hopkinton 1910-04-02 age 77yrs 11mos b Bradford child of DOW John & SHAW Lydia Vol: 6 Page: 089

PILLSBURY Angeline C d W Bridgewater Mass 1910-03-09 age 76yrs 3mos 16dys Vol: 6 Page: 090

DENSMORE Marjorie O d Hopkinton 1910-04-09 age 3dys b Hopkinton child of DENSMORE William E & LIBBY Lillian D Vol: 6 Page: 090

SCRIBNER William d Boscawen 1910-04-19 age 25yrs Vol: 6 Page: 090

CHAMBERLAIN Ellen R B d Hopkinton 1910-04-21 age 74yrs 4mos 20dys b Lubec Me child of RAMSDELL Chas R & CUTTS Elizabeth Vol: 6 Page: 090

KEMPTON Byron E d Hopkinton 1910-05-09 age 64yrs 7mos 7dys b Croydon child of KEMPTON Edward B & HARRIS Mary Vol: 6 Page: 090

COLBY Emma W d Hopkinton 1910-05-13 age 65yrs 7mos 23dys b Hopkinton child of RAND Charles D & DAVIS Harriet N Vol: 6 Page: 090

CHASE Harvey d Hopkinton 1910-05-15 age 81yrs b Hopkinton child of CHASE Enoch J & HOLMES Sarah H Vol: 6 Page: 091

GOODSPEED Annie H d Phildelphia Pa 1910-05-21 age 44yrs Vol: 6 Page: 091

KETCHUM Georgia C d Hyde Park Mass 1910-06-11 age 67yrs 11mos 10dys Vol: 6 Page: 091

THORNTON Nancy C d Hopkinton 1910-06-23 age 71yrs 4mos 27dys b Eaton Canada child of SWEATT Moses & Caroline Vol: 6 Page: 091

POWERS Harry Albert d Boston Mass 1910-06-18 age 39yrs 10mos 15dys Vol: 6 Page: 091

PERKINS Susan d Hopkinton 1910-07-08 age 56yrs 8mos 10dys b Philadelphia Pa Vol: 6 Page: 091

PERRY Ruth d Hopkinton 1910-08-09 age 6mos b Manchester child of PERRY A R & Lane Vol: 6 Page: 092

WEBBER Jennette N d Hopkinton 1910-09-05 age 64yrs 10mos 27dys b Crydon child of JEFFERS Jacob & Kempton Vol: 6 Page: 092

STANLEY Pluma F d Hopkinton 1910-09-07 age 84yrs b Warner child of SAVORY Daniel & STRAW Mary Vol: 6 Page: 092

MONTGOMERY Jerome d Hopkinton 1910-09-14 age 56yrs 2dys b Hopkinton child of MONTGOMERY William & SAVORY Lucy Vol: 6 Page: 092

WHITTIER Otis W d Hopkinton 1910-09-20 age 75yrs 9mos 24dys b Webster child of WHITTIER Phineas & WHITE Hulda Vol: 6 Page: 092

FLANDERS Francis A d Hopkinton 1910-10-05 age 57yrs 29dys b Warner child of FLANDERS J F Vol: 6 Page: 092

WELLS Eliza J d Nashua 1910-10-03 age 65yrs Vol: 6 Page: 093

RICE ---- d Hopkinton 1910-10-20 b Hopkinton child of RICE James G & BOHONAN Bernice Vol: 6 Page: 093

KELLEY Harriet N d Hopkinton 1910-12-01 age 72yrs 1mos 3dys b Wilmot child of HOLLAND Peter & HAINTY Susanna Vol: 6 Page: 093 Note: xx- check orginal

MINER Lottie L d Franklin 1910-11-09 age 67yrs 7mos 6dys Vol: 6 Page: 093

ROSS Sarah L d Somerville Mass 1910 Nov age 75yrs 10mos Vol: 6 Page: 093

LITTLE Charles E d Hopkinton 1910-12-09 age 52yrs 5mos 29dys b Webster child of LITTLE C B & SMITH Susan J Vol: 6 Page: 093

HARRIMAN Delmar W d Hopkinton 1910-12-11 age 41yrs 7mos 14dys b Hopkinton child of HASTINGS Alfred S & PERRY Susan Vol: 6 Page: 094

NOYES James F d Hopkinton 1910-12-16 age 74yrs 5mos 12dys b Boscawen child of NOYES Stewart & FRENCH Olive Vol: 6 Page: 094

HARRIMAN Eliza P d Manchester 1910-12-19 age 86yrs 2mos 2dys b Hopkinton child of NOYES Leonard & STORY Julia Vol: 6 Page: 094

LORD Charles C d Hopkinton 1911-01-01 age 69yrs 5mos 24dys b Berwick Maine child of LORD Charles & HUBBARD Sarah Vol: 6 Page: 095

CURRIER Willie H d Hopkinton 1911-01-04 age 69yrs 8mos 29dys b Hopkinton child of PUTNEY Ira A & MUZZY Hannah Vol: 6 Page: 095

BOUTWELL Alice M d Hopkinton 1911-01-11 age 49yrs 2mos 18dys child of MONTGOMERY George Vol: 6 Page: 095

CHAPMAN Merriam M d Hopkinton 1911-01-20 age 88yrs 8mos 1dys b Weare child of COLLINS Jonathan & Page Vol: 6 Page: 095

PATCH John G d Hopkinton 1911-02-04 age 75yrs 7mos b Hopkinton child of PATCH John & WEBBER Betsey Vol: 6 Page: 095

TILTON Lawrence J d Hopkinton 1911-02-05 age 1yrs 6mos 6dys b Hopkinton child of TILTON Joseph N & ROLLINS M Alice Vol: 6 Page: 095

CHOATE Horace L d Hopkinton 1911-02-11 age 77yrs 9mos 22dys b Henniker child of CHOATE George & DAVIS Betsey Vol: 6 Page: 096

MORRILL Sarah C d Hopkinton 1911-02-20 age 91yrs 1mos 28dys b Hopkinton child of ABBOTT Herman & CURRIER Sally Vol: 6 Page: 096

Hopkinton, NH Deaths 1880

NUDD Frank Horace d Hopkinton 1911-02-22 age 8mos 24dys b Hopkinton child of NUDD John B & CLARK Emma Vol: 6 Page: 096 Note: xx check original

SANDERSON Ina M d Warner 1911-02-26 age 37yrs 2mos 17dys b Warner Vol: 6 Page: 096

HARRINGTON Hattie R d Hopkinton 1911-03-08 age 58yrs 10mos 22dys child of WOODBURY Benj F Vol: 6 Page: 096

BROWN Valarous W d Hopkinton 1911-03-24 age 59yrs 8mos b Hopkinton child of BROWN Gould Vol: 6 Page: 096

BOYCE Melzer D d Hopkinton 1911-04-02 age 59yrs 2mos 26dys b Concord child of BOYCE Isaac C & DAVIS Lorina Vol: 6 Page: 097

EATON Emma C d Hopkinton 1911-04-13 age 65yrs 8mos 24dys b Newbury child of BROWN Albert & ADAMS Lucinda Vol: 6 Page: 097

STRAW M Edith d Hopkinton 1911-05-09 age 41yrs 4mos 15dys b Hopkinton child of STRAW John S & Holmes Vol: 6 Page: 097

LOCKE George H d Hopkinton 1911-05-24 age 68yrs b Hopkinton child of LOCKE David & CHASE Elizabeth Vol: 6 Page: 097

SPAULDING Samantha S d Hopkinton 1911-06-09 age 81yrs 10mos 5dys b Webster child of PUTNEY Stephen & Eastman Vol: 6 Page: 097

WRIGHT Sarah A d Warner 1911 age 72yrs 3mos 13dys b Francestown child of HOLMES Lewis & OSGOOD Mittie Vol: 6 Page: 097

DOW Anna Caroline d Hopkinton 1911-06-28 age 39yrs 4mos b Hopkinton child of CARR Frank H & CHANDLER Mary A Vol: 6 Page: 098

STEVENS Edgar W d Hopkinton 1911-06-30 age 59yrs 6mos b Manchester child of STEVENS Gilman A Vol: 6 Page: 098

CARLSON Carl d Hopkinton 1911-07-04 age 23yrs b Sweden child of NELSON Carl & SWENSON Emma Vol: 6 Page: 098

KELLEY Stella L d Hopkinton 1911-07-27 age 54yrs 10mos 7dys b Hopkinton Vol: 6 Page: 098

MONTGOMERY Julia A d Hopkinton 1911-07-30 age 69yrs 7dys b Salem NY child of MONTGOMERY Charles & BURBANK Adaline Vol: 6 Page: 098

NUDD Bessie Viola d Hopkinton 1911-08-16 age 6yrs 19dys b Webster child of ROBINSON John T & NUDD Alice M Vol: 6 Page: 098

SCRIBNER Carl E d Goshen 1911-07-23 age 20yrs 7mos 3dys Vol: 6 Page: 099

CORTHELL Summner N d Hopkinton 1911-08-15 age 5yrs 13dys b Manchester child of CORTHELL S E & YORK Amy Vol: 6 Page: 099

CROWELL Charles C d Concord 1911-08-18 age 74yrs 9mos 3dys b Hopkinton child of CROWELL Albert & KIMBALL Lydia Vol: 6 Page: 099

BARTLETT Clara B d Hopkinton 1911-08-20 age 49yrs 26dys b Brattleboro Vt child of DAVIS Hiram & HOYT Sarah M Vol: 6 Page: 099

PERKINS Susan G d Hopkinton 1911-09-07 age 72yrs 9mos 20dys b Hopkinton child of PERKINS Hamilton & GEORGE Clara B Vol: 6 Page: 099

FELLOWS Charles F d Melrose Mass 1911-09-11 age 71yrs 6mos 10dys Vol: 6 Page: 099

DRUMIN Thomas J d Hopkinton 1911-09-13 age 65yrs 10mos 29dys b Barbodors child of DRUMIN James J Vol: 6 Page: 100

CAYER Marie A d Hopkinton 1911-09-26 age 4mos 27dys b Hopkinton child of CAYER Thomas & NUDD Bessie Vol: 6 Page: 100

ELLINWOOD Marcus M d Hopkinton 1911-09-27 age 69yrs 11mos 2dys b Hillsborough child of ELLINWOOD John B & Alcott Vol: 6 Page: 100

BARNARD Julia A d Hopkinton 1911-10-13 age 88yrs 4mos 24dys b Hopkinton child of EATON Ichabod & HAZELTON R Vol: 6 Page: 100

WHITE Anson d Weare 1911-10-08 b Hopkinton Vol: 6 Page: 100 Note: died of old age

BURGESS Amos d Hopkinton 1911-11-03 age 75yrs 7mos 7dys b Winslow Me child of BURGESS William & FROST Susan Vol: 6 Page: 100

WIGHT Edwin O d Hopkinton 1911-11-09 age 61yrs 3mos 12dys b West Milan Vol: 6 Page: 101

FRENCH George W d Hopkinton 1911-11-12 age 74yrs 11mos 29dys b Hopkinton child of FRENCH Jonathan & MARY C Vol: 6 Page: 101

SMITH George P d Nashua 1911-11-13 age 64yrs Vol: 6 Page: 101

LOVEJOY Arthur P d Hopkinton 1911-12-28 age 68yrs 10mos 13dys b Littleton child of LOVEJOY Gilman & DRAKE Mary H Vol: 6 Page: 101

BOSSIE Alson Dona d Hopkinton 1907-05-29 age 1mos 24dys b Belmont child of BOSSI Lewis Joseph & CLAIRMONT Edith M Vol: 6 Page: 069

WEBBER I Jewell d Hopkinton 1907-09-26 age 89yrs 2mos 8dys b Hopkinton child of WEBBER Iaaiah & DAVIS Hannah Vol: 6 Page: 070 Note: birth Jul 18 1818

BOUTWELL Henry B A d Hopkinton 1909-06-18 age 46yrs 9mos 21dys b Berlin Ill child of BOUTWELL Eli A & WEEKS Harriet B Vol: 6 Page: 085

CHANDLER Horatio J d Hopkinton 1912-01-01 age 81yrs 4mos 17dys b Hopkinton child of CHANDLER Stephen & RIPLEY Mary A Vol: 6 Page: 102

ROBERTS Ellen Chase d Hopkinton 1912-01-08 age 81yrs 8mos 19dys b Lancaster child of CHASE Benjamin W & WILLIAMS Ann Vol: 6 Page: 102

RICHARDSON Eliza A d Hopkinton 1912-01-16 age 72yrs 8mos 20dys b Copagan Mich child of HARDY Harrison & MORGAN Precilla Vol: 6 Page: 102

RICHARDSON Elizabeth A d Hopkinton 1912-02-06 age 69yrs 5mos 13dys b Bradford child of CRESSEY Edward & JONES Elizabeth Vol: 6 Page: 102

SANVILLE Belle d Hopkinton 1912-02-25 age 35yrs 10mos 2dys b Pittsfield child of COME Peter & WILLETT Mary Vol: 6 Page: 103

WATTS Charles F d Hopkinton 1912-03-04 age 57yrs 3mos b Warner child of WATTS William & SARGENT Sarah E Vol: 6 Page: 103

STRAW Horace d Hopkinton 1912-04-06 age 83yrs 1mos 3dys b Hopkinton child of STRAW Jacob & FLANDERS Mariam Vol: 6 Page: 103

DOW Eliza H E d Hopkinton 1912-04-07 age 12yrs 4mos 11dys child of MURDOUGH William & AYER Caroline S Vol: 6 Page: 103

STARK Clarinda N F d Manchester 1912-03-12 age 92yrs Vol: 6 Page: 103

STEVENS Myrtie E d Pembroke 1912-05-02 age 35yrs 10mos 9dys b Hopkinton child of STEVENS Henry & CURRIER Allie A Vol: 6 Page: 104

DAY Henry C d Hopkinton 1912-05-04 age 81yrs 7mos 7dys b East Weare child of DAY George & CHASE Sarah Vol: 6 Page: 104

JACKMAN George W d Hopkinton 1912-05-10 age 84yrs 3mos 11dys b Hopkinton child of JACKMAN Hazen & KIMBALL Charlot Vol: 6 Page: 104

MORRILL Theresa F d Goffstown 1912-05-20 age 73yrs 7mos 21dys b Derry Vt child of KIMBALL Iddo & RICHARDSON Fannie Vol: 6 Page: 104

MUDGETT Mary J d Concord 1912-02-26 age 86yrs 7mos 24dys Vol: 6 Page: 104

Hopkinton, NH Deaths 1880

BROWN Mary E d Hopkinton 1912-06-17 age 79yrs 4mos 5dys b Hopkinton child of ORDWAY George & CROWELL Nancy Vol: 6 Page: 104

HALE Harry E d Hopkinton 1912-06-07 age 23yrs 1mos 27dys b Boscawen child of HALE George C & Champain Vol: 6 Page: 105

BROWN d Hopkinton 1912-07-01 child of BROWN Alanson & FLEMING Melissa Vol: 6 Page: 105

WHITE Ida May d Hopkinton 1912-08-14 age 29yrs 7mos 17dys b Webster child of ELLIOTT Edson E & COLBY Nellie L Vol: 6 Page: 105

HEATH Max M d Newport 1912-08-14 age 8mos 5dys b Newport child of HEATH Elizabeth Vol: 6 Page: 105

ADAMS Judith d Hopkinton 1912-08-15 age 80yrs 6mos 28dys b Warner child of SARGENT Merriman Vol: 6 Page: 105

BACON Edwin A d Concord 1912-08-25 age 74yrs 7mos 28dys b Hopkinton child of BACON John & PATTERSON Sylvia Vol: 6 Page: 105

DUNBAR Mattie B d Hopkinton 1912-04-28 age 44yrs 2mos 14dys b Gilmanton child of FLANDERS Rufus L & HACKETT Mary J Vol: 6 Page: 106

BLAKE Charles N d Hopkinton 1912-08-31 age 63yrs 2mos 9dys b Hopkinton child of BLAKE John & Maxfield Vol: 6 Page: 106

HASTINGS Susan E d Concord 1912-08-30 age 72yrs 8mos 12dys b Hopkinton child of PERRY William & PRESSEY Asenith Vol: 6 Page: 106

LONG Mary J d Chicago Ill 1912-06-12 age 92yrs 1mos 21dys Vol: 6 Page: 106

FULLER Julia F d Hopkinton 1912-10-07 age 58yrs 9mos 5dys b Hopkinton child of MORRILL Jacob M & ABBOTT Sarah C Vol: 6 Page: 106

PAIGE Van R d Hopkinton 1912-10-16 age 69yrs 8mos 5dys b Henniker child of PAIGE Samuel & PATCH Mary J Vol: 6 Page: 106

RICHARDSON Thomas B d Hopkinton 1912-10-19 age 82yrs 3mos 6dys b Deering child of RICHARDSON Thomas R & BLOOD Mary Vol: 6 Page: 107

DOWNS Eunice Elizabeth d Hopkinton 1912-11-21 age 3mos 26dys b Hopkinton child of DOWNS Wm M & COUCH Stella N Vol: 6 Page: 107

PUTNAM William F d Concord 1912-11-20 age 68yrs 6mos 9dys child of PUTNAM Rufus Vol: 6 Page: 107

KAY James E d Hopkinton 1912-11-16 age 27dys b Hopkinton child of KAY James & CLARK Lillian Vol: 6 Page: 107

STEVENS Caroline L d Hopkinton 1912-12-06 age 55yrs 2mos b Wakefield child of HUBBARD Benj & BIXBY Lucy J Vol: 6 Page: 107

CHASE ---- d Hopkinton 1912-12-09 b Concord child of CHASE Hubert S & LIBBY Emily H Vol: 6 Page: 107

CHASE Emily H d Concord 1912-12-11 age 35yrs 7mos 25dys b Hopkinton child of LIBBY George A & KENISTON Stella Vol: 6 Page: 108

WEEKS Hannah J d Hopkinton 1912-12-14 age 70yrs 8mos 15dys b Webster child of HUBBARD Dudley C & SIMPSON Hannah T Vol: 6 Page: 108

TUFTS Elsie G d Hopkinton 1912-12-26 age 5mos 11dys b Hopkinton child of TUFTS Jerome W & COUCH Mertie G Vol: 6 Page: 108

MINER ---- d Hopkinton 1912-12-27 b Hopkinton child of MINER Wm & ANNIS Hattie Vol: 6 Page: 108

LADD Dexter d Hopkinton 1913-01-13 age 40yrs 11mos 28dys b Epping child of LADD Samuel & DODGE Sarah J Vol: 6 Page: 109

CLOUGH Geo A d Hopkinton 1913-01-25 age 44yrs 1mos 11dys b Hopkinton child of CLOUGH Moses T & BEAN Mary O Vol: 6 Page: 109

ELLIOTT Marcia H d Hopkinton 1913-01-26 age 40yrs 1mos 23dys b Hopkinton child of ELLIOTT George W & HOYT Ellen Vol: 6 Page: 109

COTA Lottie M d Hopkinton 1913-01-28 b Barton Vt child of HYDE Horace H & PROVINACHA Carrie Vol: 6 Page: 109

SPAULDING Dustin A d Hopkinton 1913-01-28 age 83yrs 5mos 13dys b Nashua child of SPAULDING Reuben & BARRETT Susan Vol: 6 Page: 109

DUSTIN Herbert C d Hopkinton 1913-01-30 age 58yrs 2dys b Hopkinton child of DUSTIN Cyrus & FISKE Edna Vol: 6 Page: 110

FIFIELD Mary E d Hopkinton 1913-02-01 age 84yrs 11mos 26dys b Antrim child of HOLMES Thomas S & DINSMORE Sarah Vol: 6 Page: 110

CHASE Horace G d New York Ny 1911-02-03 age 85yrs 6mos 25dys Vol: 6 Page: 110

CLARKE Leslie Wm d Hopkinton 1913-02-03 b Hopkinton child of CLARKE James F & DROWN Mabel Vol: 6 Page: 110

KELLEY Roxanna W d Hopkinton 1913-02-09 age 77yrs 6mos 24dys child of JONES Peter & LOCKE Anna E Vol: 6 Page: 110

COCHRAN Augusta K d Hopkinton 1913-02-09 age 82yrs 5mos 24dys b New Boston child of COCHRAN Joseph & WILSON Anna Vol: 6 Page: 110

PAGE George Henry d Worcester Mass 1913-02-13 age 60yrs 5mos 8dys Vol: 6 Page: 111

HARDY Carlos Frank d Hopkinton 1913-02-15 age 76yrs 2mos 10dys b Hopkinton child of HARDY Benjamin & PUTNEY Lydia Vol: 6 Page: 111

COLBY Myron M d Hopkinton 1913-02-17 age 57yrs 8mos 5dys b Warner child of COLBY Timothy F & ELSWORTH Ruth Vol: 6 Page: 111

HOYT Mahala d Hopkinton 1913-02-16 age 91yrs 10mos 24dys b Hopkinton child of FLANDER Israel & HOLMES Olive Vol: 6 Page: 111

HOOK Charles F d Hopkinton 1913-02-19 age 31yrs 5mos 18dys b Hopkinton child of HOOK James M & DOYEN Mary A Vol: 6 Page: 111

GOULD Elizabeth B d Hopkinton 1913-02-25 age 83yrs 11mos 28dys b So Berwick Me child of NEAL Brackett Vol: 6 Page: 111

WAYNE Edward d Hopkinton 1913-02-25 age 64yrs 5mos 15dys Vol: 6 Page: 112

HARDY Olevia J d Hopkinton 1913-03-05 age 73yrs 3mos 4dys b Manchester child of JOHNSON Nathan & CLOGSTON Clemina Vol: 6 Page: 112

CURRIER Mary S d Somerville Mass 1913-03-08 age 73yrs 10mos 23dys b Hopkinton child of NICHOLS David & STORY Mary S Vol: 6 Page: 112

SMITH Lavonia L d Hopkinton 1913-03-13 age 74yrs 3mos 4dys b Warner child of FLANDERS Rhoda Vol: 6 Page: 112

WHEELER Elizabeth A d Hopkinton 1913-03-19 age 79yrs 10mos 24dys b Warner child of EASTMAN Timothy & SIBLEY Polly Vol: 6 Page: 112

CHANDLER Caroline E d Concord 1913-04-06 age 87yrs Vol: 6 Page: 112

CARPENTER Mary A d Hopkinton 1913-04-11 age 79yrs 5mos 11dys b Hopkinton child of JACKMAN Hazen & BAKER Mary A Vol: 6 Page: 113

DYER Estella D d Boston Mass 1913-04-20 age 64yrs 6mos 5dys Vol: 6 Page: 113

NELSON David Homer d Concord 1913-05-17 age 31yrs 6mos 2dys b Hopkinton child of NELSON John & SEAVEY Nettie Vol: 6 Page: 113

Hopkinton, NH Deaths 1880

HOOK James M d Hopkinton 1913-05-26 age 75yrs 2mos 24dys b Concord child of HOOK James & HOW Hannah M Vol: 6 Page: 113

DAVIS Dollie Jones d Hopkinton 1913-06-02 age 80yrs 9mos 29dys b Warner child of JONES Daniel & TRUSSELL Judith Vol: 6 Page: 113

GREEN?? Mary Catherine d Hopkinton 1913-06-23 age 74yrs 1mos b Boston Mass child of DOWNER Samuel & DEWOLFE Mary L Vol: 6 Page: 113

BEBBER Joel d Hopkinton 1913-06-12 age 90yrs 9mos 16dys b Freeport Me child of BEBBER Joel & JOHNSON Hannah Vol: 6 Page: 114 Note: birth 1822 Aug 26

PURINGTON James A d Hopkinton 1913-06-22 age 54yrs 1mos b Farnum Canada child of PURINGTON James A & ROCKWELL Angeline Vol: 6 Page: 114

GOLD Finley B d Hopkinton 1913-06-23 age 13yrs 9mos 10dys b Nashua child of GOLD Robert & BICKFORD Gertrude Vol: 6 Page: 114

GREENLEAF Sarah B d Hopkinton 1913-06-19 age 74yrs 6mos 24dys b Watertown Mass child of BATES E W & WHITMAN Mary A Vol: 6 Page: 114

DAVIS Eliza J d Hopkinton 1913-07-15 age 58yrs 6mos 11dys b Middleton Mass child of COOK Hugh Vol: 6 Page: 114

BROWN Charles W d Concord 1913-07-18 age 66yrs 11dys b Hopkinton child of BROWN Mark & CHASE Estha M Vol: 6 Page: 114

PERKINS Susan d Canterbury 1913-06-09 age 76yrs 29dys b Albany Vt child of CARLTON George & TRIP Nancy Vol: 6 Page: 115

HAGER Mary Ann d Hopkinton 1913-07-25 age 94yrs 26dys b Blandford Mass Vol: 6 Page: 115

SMITH Harriott J d Hopkinton 1913-08-14 age 77yrs 2mos 21dys b Boston Mass child of SMITH Charles & Bryant Vol: 6 Page: 115

BARTON Warren B d Hopkinton 1913-08-18 age 55yrs b Hopkinton child of BARTON Charles O & CUTTS Philander Vol: 6 Page: 115

GUILD Abbie M d Hopkinton 1913-08-15 age 67yrs 3mos 17dys b Hopkinton child of STORY Luther & CROWELL Mary Vol: 6 Page: 115

SANBORN Edgar F d Concord 1913-09-04 age 51yrs 3mos 27dys child of SANBORN Jessie D & BATCHELDER Arvilla Vol: 6 Page: 115

KELLLEY Andrew J d Hopkinton 1913-09-13 age 78yrs 7mos 22dys b Webster child of KELLEY Timothy & BURBANK Jane Vol: 6 Page: 116

HACKETT Nellie M d Hopkinton 1913-09-05 age 48yrs 5mos 20dys b Hopkinton child of CROWELL Joseph & ASH Nancy Vol: 6 Page: 116

ROUSE John D Jr d Hopkinton 1913-10-04 age 7mos 13dys b Hopkinton child of ROUSE Loren L & NOVEEN Annie J Vol: 6 Page: 116

ROUSE James L d Hopkinton 1913-10-06 age 7mos 15dys b Hopkinton child of ROUSE Loren L & NOVEEN Annie J Vol: 6 Page: 116

HILAND Priscilla A d Concord 1913-10-15 age 68yrs 8mos 15dys b Hopkinton child of KIMBALL Moses & EMERSON Harriet Vol: 6 Page: 116

MUDGETT Anna d Boston Mass 1913-10-15 age 72yrs Vol: 6 Page: 116

FLANDERS Samuel B d Canterbury 1913-10-22 age 57yrs 11mos 13dys b Concord child of FLANDERS Charles & SMART Adeline Vol: 6 Page: 117

DANFORTH Henry P d Lawrence Mass 1913-10-12 age 67yrs 11mos b Hopkinton child of DANFORTH John P & HASTINGS Emeline Vol: 6 Page: 117

CILLEY William N d Concord 1913-11-03 age 58yrs b Andover child of CILLEY Phillip & COTE Sarah J Vol: 6 Page: 117

DAVIS Nellie G d Boston Mass 1913-11-10 age 47yrs 3mos 2dys b Wilmot child of PUTNAM Addison S Vol: 6 Page: 117

ELKINS George W d Concord 1913-11-15 age 73yrs 8mos 27dys b Thornton child of ELKINS Eben & GLIDDEN Emily Vol: 6 Page: 117

SKILLEN William W d Henniker 1913-11-23 age 69yrs 9mos 11dys b Montreal Canada child of SKILLEN Willian W Vol: 6 Page: 117

PUNTENNEYE Isabel K d Plymouth 1913-12-08 age 40yrs b Hopkinton child of KEMPTON Warren M & HOWARD Orintha Vol: 6 Page: 118

KIMBALL Charles Carrol d Hopkinton 1913-12-21 age 82yrs 9mos 27dys b Hopkinton child of KIMBALL Hazen & BAKER May Ann Vol: 6 Page: 118

FOLLANSBEE Agusta d Hopkinton 1913-12-20 age 54yrs 9mos 5dys b Weare child of SCRUTON Geo & CURRIER Mary M Vol: 6 Page: 118

GUILD Glenice B d Concord 1913-12-26 age 1yrs 6mos 20dys b Concord child of GUILD Frank E & CURRIER Jennie B Vol: 6 Page: 118

PUTNEY Elllen W d Hopkinton 1913-12-31 age 62yrs 2mos 24dys b Hopkinton child of AYERS Isaac & SILVER Elizabeth Vol: 6 Page: 119

CHASE Susan Stanwood d Concord 1912-01-29 age 74yrs 1mos 4dys b Hopkinton child of STANWOOD Joseph & PERKINS Louisa Vol: 6 Page: 102

CAMPBELL Julia A d Hopkinton 1913-01-17 b Chimney Point NY child of TITCHEL? Orin T & LITTLE Adaline Vol: 6 Page: 109 Note: xx fitchel or titchel

PERRY James Earle d Hopkinton 1882-10-13 age 1yrs 9dys b Hopkinton child of PERRY James M & KELLEY Thinnie Vol: 5 Page: 039 Line: 025 Section: 1st

DODGE Mary d Hopkinton 1890-03-12 age 73yrs 6mos b Hopkinton child of STERE?? David & CURRIER Mehitable Vol: 5 Page: 091 Line: 013 Section: 2nd Note: it could be story??

SOUTHWICK Grace Bell d Hopkinton 1881-12-29 age 7mos b Hopkinton child of SOUTHWICK William & COLBY Mittien ?? Vol: 5 Page: 035 Line: 028 Section: 1st

LANCASTER Jacob d Hopkinton 1879-11-04 age 69yrs b Canada East child of LANCASTER Thomas & SARGENT Sarah Vol: 5 Page: 029 Line: 018 Section: 1st

DWINELLS Edith M d Hopkinton 1884-01-07 age 1yrs 3mos b Hopkinton child of DWINELLS John G & CHASE Carrie M Vol: 5 Page: 067 Line: 001 Section: 2nd

MERRILL Amanda M d Hopkinton 1880-12-20 age 33yrs b Hopkinton child of MERRILL Stephen & HOLMES Maria W Vol: 5 Page: 033 Line: 020 Section: 1st

CONNOR Arthur N d Hopkinton 1888-11-22 age 26yrs 7mos 28dys child of CONNOR Frederick W & FLANDERS Sophiah C Vol: 5 Page: 085 Line: 003 Section: 2nd

SANBORN Abagial d Hopkinton 1882-07-12 age 70yrs b Washington child of NEWMANS Benjamin & GORDEN Sally Vol: 5 Page: 039 Line: 011 Section: 1st

Hopkinton, NH Deaths 1880

CURRIER Jennie S d Hopkinton 1882-11-08 age 17yrs 7mos 22dys b Concord child of DOW Henry E & BOUTELLE Charlotte Vol: 5 Page: 041 Line: 005 Section: 1st

MOULTON Clara A d Hopkinton 1883-01-07 age 27yrs 3mos 10dys b Concord child of MOULTON William A & STRAW Susan L Vol: 5 Page: 041 Line: 012 Section: 1

KIMBALL Cyntha F d Hopkinton 1883-03-26 age 80yrs 7mos 6dys b Hopkinton child of FELLOWS Obediah & EMERSON Sarah Vol: 5 Page: 041 Line: 019 Section: 1st

RIDER Mary Rebecca d Hopkinton 1884-05-25 age 47yrs 10mos 11dys b Hopkinton child of HUNT Ephriam & EATON Susan Vol: 5 Page: 067 Line: 011 Section: 2nd

FAGAN Margrette d Hopkinton 1884-05-25 age 63yrs b Ireland child of MORAN Christopher & SMITH Elizabeth Vol: 5 Page: 067 Line: 012 Section: 2nd

CHANDLER Abial R d Hopkinton 1884-11-04 age 60yrs 10mos b Hopkinton child of CHANDLER Stephen & RIPLEY Mary Vol: 5 Page: 069 Line: 001 Section: 2nd

STRAW Percey W d Hopkinton 1885-02-25 age 3yrs 4mos 10dys b Hopkinton child of STRAW James O & WHITTIMORE Ada M Vol: 5 Page: 071 Line: 010 Section: 2nd

BOUTWELL Ella R d Hopkinton 1885-03-24 age 32yrs 10mos b Hopkinton child of BOUTWELL Eli A & WEEKS Harriet W Vol: 5 Page: 071 Line: 013 Section: 2nd

BARTLETT ---- d Hopkinton 1885-05-10 age 5mos b Hopkinton child of BARTLETT Henry & HARDY Isabella M Vol: 5 Page: 071 Line: 024 Section: 2nd

CLOUGH Charlotte d Hopkinton 1885-11-03 age 69yrs 8mos 15dys b Hopkinton child of DUSTIN Ebenezer & PIERCE Sarah Vol: 5 Page: 073 Line: 010 Section: 2nd

MORGAN Arthur B d Hopkinton 1885-11-19 age 18yrs 8mos 5dys b Hopkinton child of MORGAN Frank N & JONES Fannie A Vol: 5 Page: 073 Line: 012 Section: 2nd

SARGENT Cora F d Hopkinton 1886-01-19 age 18yrs 8mos 4dys b Hopkinton child of SARGENT John B & NUTTER Harriet M Vol: 5 Page: 075 Line: 004 Section: 2nd

MONTGOMERY ---- d Hopkinton 1886-01-29 b Hopkinton child of MONTGOMERY Guy & MARTIN Nellie E Vol: 5 Page: 075 Line: 005 Section: 2nd

EVANS Isabel P d Hopkinton 1886-02-04 age 53yrs 11mos b Hopkinton child of TYLER Cyril C (md) & PUTNAM Sarah Vol: 5 Page: 075 Line: 008 Section: 2nd

ROGERS Alexander d Hopkinton 1886-10-04 age 72yrs 5mos 21dys b Exeter child of ROGERS Robert & SULLIVAN Margery Vol: 5 Page: 077 Line: 008 Section: 2nd

DUSTIN Ednah Fisk d Hopkinton 1887-02-15 age 75yrs 9mos 25dys b Salisbury child of FISK Ebenezer & PROCTOR Hannah Vol: 5 Page: 079 Line: 005 Section: 2nd

FELLOWS Ignations W d Hopkinton 1887-02-21 age 81yrs 2mos b Hopkinton child of FELLOWS Benjamin & LADD Betsey Vol: 5 Page: 079 Line: 008 Section: 2nd

SPOFFORD Abbie A d Hopkinton 1887-03-14 age 41yrs 11mos b Hopkinton child of PAIGE John W & BERRY Elizabeth Vol: 5 Page: 079 Line: 009 Section: 2nd

RICHARDS Martha B d Hopkinton 1887-07-07 age 80yrs 6mos 14dys b Newport child of DOW Nathaniel & BUSWELL Martha Vol: 5 Page: 079 Line: 025 Section: 2nd

TAYLOR Charles E d Hopkinton 1887-07-25 age 55yrs 11mos 25dys b Hancock child of TAYLOR Edward & WHITCOMB Hannah Vol: 5 Page: 079 Line: 027 Section: 2nd

HARDY George B d Hopkinton 1888-06-18 age 78yrs 8mos 10dys b Hopkinton child of HARDY Isaac Jr & BODWELL Hannah Vol: 5 Page: 083 Line: 018 Section: 2nd

CHANDLER William d Hopkinton 1889-04-30 age 77yrs 1mos 4dys b Albany Me child of CHANDLER Phileman & CASE Asenath Vol: 5 Page: 087 Line: 014 Section: 2nd

FLANDERS Parker M d Hopkinton 1889-08-24 age 73yrs 6mos 29dys b Hopkinton child of FLANDERS Phillip & SMITH Sarah Vol: 5 Page: 089 Line: 003 Section: 2nd

CLOUGH Elvira W d Hopkinton 1889-12-13 age 86yrs 7mos 26dys b Hopkinton child of HILLDRETH Levi & DARLING Sarah Vol: 5 Page: 089 Line: 018 Section: 2nd

WILLIAMS Luther d Hopkinton 1889-12-17 age 69yrs 5mos 15dys b Pepperell Mass child of WILLIAMS Peter & LAKIN Anna Vol: 5 Page: 089 Line: 021 Section: 2nd

KEMPTON Warren M d Hopkinton 1890-01-30 age 75yrs 11dys b Charlestown child of KEMPTON Edward & BISHOP Ruth Vol: 5 Page: 091 Line: 008 Section: 2nd

FLANDERS Nellie d Hopkinton 1890-02-04 age 28yrs 7mos b Hopkinton child of WHITTIER Amos H & DANFORTH Sarah J Vol: 5 Page: 091 Line: 009 Section: 2nd

CHANDLER Martha F d Hopkinton 1890-09-17 age 68yrs 1mos 10dys b Concord child of ELLIOTT Joseph F & FISKE Anna S Vol: 5 Page: 093 Line: 003 Section: 2nd

KIMBALL Iddo K d Hopkinton 1891-09-28 age 78yrs 3mos 24dys b Bradford Mass child of KIMBALL Amos & HASTINGS Affa Vol: 5 Page: 097 Line: 004 Section: 2nd

WEBBER Roxanna D d Hopkinton 1891-10-24 age 70yrs 10mos 10dys b Hopkinton child of TOWNE Rodney & ORDWAY Hannah Vol: 5 Page: 097 Line: 007 Section: 2nd

NICHOLS George H d Hopkinton 1892-04-08 age 52yrs 5mos b So Boston Mass child of NICHOLS Killy & GREEN Eliza Vol: 5 Page: 099 Line: 023 Section: 2nd

RUTHERFORD ---- d Hopkinton 1892-08-12 b Hopkinton child of RUTHERFORD George R & COLBY Mattie Vol: 5 Page: 101 Line: 017 Section: 2nd

Hopkinton, NH Deaths 1880

HOLMES Sherman F d Hopkinton 1892-09-10 age 58yrs 11mos 10dys b Boscawen child of HOLMES Gardner & MELVIN Betsey Vol: 5 Page: 101 Line: 020 Section: 2nd

RAND Charles D d Hopkinton 1893-01-05 age 80yrs 5mos 20dys b Hopkinton child of RAND Jonathan & DAVIS Elizabeth Vol: 5 Page: 105 Line: 001 Section: 2nd

MORGAN Mehitable d Hopkinton 1893-01-11 age 95yrs 11mos 17dys b Hennkier child of COLBY Daniel & GILMAN Elizabeth Vol: 5 Page: 105 Line: 002 Section: 2nd

KEZER Nathaniel J d Hopkinton 1893-10-07 age 83yrs b Hopkinton child of KEZER Nathaniel & ELLIOTT Rachel Vol: 5 Page: 107 Line: 003 Section: 2nd

TERRY Katherine d Hopkinton 1894-01-08 age 77yrs 10mos b Hopkinton child of BUSWELL Benjamin & CARTER Joana Vol: 5 Page: 109 Line: 002 Section: 2nd

RICHARDSON Jane W d Hopkinton 1894-01-09 age 82yrs 11mos 28dys b Hopkinton child of BUSWELL Bejamin & CARTER Jane Vol: 5 Page: 109 Line: 005 Section: 2nd

EDMUNDS H Mairon d Hopkinton 1894-03-08 age 50yrs 7mos b Hopkinton child of STRAW William S & FLANDERS Mary Vol: 5 Page: 109 Line: 009 Section: 2nd

EASTMAN Elizabeth d Hopkinton 1894-04-17 age 85yrs 10mos 7dys b Hopkinton child of ROWELL Moses & EASTMAN Tamson Vol: 5 Page: 109 Line: 014 Section: 2nd

GREENE Ellen Chase d Hopkinton 1894-07-12 age 80yrs b Norwich Vt child of LITTLE William & WIGGIN Elisa Vol: 5 Page: 109 Line: 023 Section: 2nd

BRUCE Samuel C d Hopkinton 1894-08-11 age 47yrs b Boston Mass child of BRUCE George W & MORRISON Isabel Vol: 5 Page: 109 Line: 025 Section: 2nd

DUSTIN Sarah A d Hopkinton 1894-08-26 age 6mos 12dys b Hopkinton child of DUSTIN Cyrus & SPAULDING S Nelie Vol: 5 Page: 109 Line: 028 Section: 2nd

COPPS Melissa F d Hopkinton 1894-09-15 age 73yrs 1mos 3dys b Bradford child of FLANDERS Nathaniel & WRIGHT Betsey Vol: 5 Page: 111 Line: 005 Section: 2nd

BALL Melvina G d Hopkinton 1894-11-21 age 21yrs 2mos 7dys b Canada child of GILMORE Lucius H & BURNAM Melvinaa Vol: 5 Page: 111 Line: 019 Section: 2nd

CHANDLER ---- d Hopkinton 1895-01-02 b Hopkinton child of CHANDLER Frank W & ROGERS Margary S Vol: 5 Page: 113 Line: 001 Section: 2nd

FULLER Adeline C d Hopkinton 1895-01-28 age 76yrs 1mos 3dys b Hopkinton child of FELLOWS Obediah & EMERSON Sarah Vol: 5 Page: 113 Line: 005 Section: 2nd

FRYE Harriet Newell d Hopkinton 1895-01-28 age 66yrs 5mos 2dys b Northfield child of BUSWELL James & CLOUGH Mary Vol: 5 Page: 113 Line: 006 Section: 2nd

MONTGOMERY Charles d Hopkinton 1895-06-14 age 76yrs 9mos b Salem Ny child of MONTGOMERY John W & BURBANK Mary Vol: 5 Page: 113 Line: 021 Section: 2nd

DUNBAR Grace Mand d Hopkinton 1895-10-08 age 21yrs 1mos 18dys b Hopkinton child of DUNBAR Elmer B & WEBBER Ann T Vol: 5 Page: 115 Line: 003 Section: 2nd

BARNARD Charles L d Hopkinton 1895-12-27 age 25yrs 8mos b Hopkinton child of BARNARD Joseph & GERRISH Maria Vol: 5 Page: 115 Line: 008 Section: 2nd

FULLER Walter D d Hopkinton 1896-08-08 age 21yrs 6mos 12dys b No Salem Ny child of FULLER Wm J & LAMONTE Jennie Vol: 5 Page: 117 Line: 026 Section: 2nd

HARWOOD Maria R d Hopkinton 1896-09-21 age 30yrs 10mos 21dys b Hopkinton child of CLOUGH Charles F & HARDY Mary J Vol: 5 Page: 119 Line: 003 Section: 2nd

CONNOR Charles N d Hopkinton 1896-10-18 age 24yrs 24dys b Hopkinton child of CONNOR James M & PUTNEY Judith Vol: 5 Page: 119 Line: 006 Section: 2nd

MORRILL Jacob M d Hopkinton 1896-10-22 age 77yrs 3mos 8dys b Hopkinton child of MORRILL Joseph & MARTIN Parmelia Vol: 5 Page: 119 Line: 007 Section: 2nd

WHITE Jacob A d Hopkinton 1897-01-03 age 74yrs 11mos 28dys b Topsfield Mass child of WHITE O G & BROWN Rebecca Vol: 5 Page: 121 Line: 001 Section: 2nd

THOMPSON Ruth M d Hopkinton 1897-06-08 age 3dys b Hopkinton child of THOMPSON William & BERRY Alice Mable Vol: 5 Page: 121 Line: 018 Section: 2nd

KIMBALL Gilman B d Hopkinton 1897-06-16 age 42yrs 8mos 23dys b Hopkinton child of KIMBALL Moses T & SMITH Mary H Vol: 5 Page: 121 Line: 019 Section: 2nd

Hopkinton, NH Marriages 1898-1913

DOW Myron W & SHATTUCK Nettie M m Dec 30, 1897 Hopkinton. Groom: age 29 b Henniker s/o DOW Wallace b Newbury & SAWYER Emilya b Henniker. Bride: age 28 b Weare d/o VITTY Jonathan b Weare & HOWE Elizabeth b Weare. Vol: 6 Page: 001

SPOFFORD Eugene L & MILLS Nellie E m Jan 21, 1898 Hopkinton. Groom: age 38 b Hopkinton s/o SPOFFORD Fred b Auburn & HILAND Sarah b Hopkinton. Bride: age 36 b Hopkinton d/o MILLS Charles. Vol: 6 Page: 001

DERRY Joseph & PAGE Elvira m Jan 24, 1898 Concord. Groom: age 21 b Concord s/o DERRY Joseph b Canada & FAGAN Julia b Ireland. Bride: age 19 b Dunbarton d/o PAIGE Edson & SIMONDS Mary A b Bow. Vol: 6 Page: 001

DANFORTH Edmund G & FOSS Lucy A m Jan 11, 1899 Hopkinton. Groom: age 24 b Hopkinton s/o DANFORTH Enoch b Webster & CONNOR Lydia A b Henniker. Bride: age 21 b Hopkinton d/o FOSS Geo E b Hopkinton & Emma b Hopkinton. Vol: 6 Page: 007

PUTNAM George M & CLOUGH Flora E m Jan 19, 1899 Hopkinton. Groom: age 35 b Hopkinton s/o PUTNAM Charles b Hopkinton & EASTMAN Almira b Hopkinton. Bride: age 37 b Hopkinton d/o CLOUGH Charles F b Hopkinton & HARDY Mary J b Warner. Vol: 6 Page: 007

STRAW True J & MILLS Alice Bertha m May 15, 1899 Somerville Mass. Groom: age 27 b Hopkinton s/o STRAW Gilman J b Hopkinton & HOYT Weltha b Henniker. Bride: age 25 b Lynn Mass d/o MILLS Charles W b Lynn Mass & BEAN Nellie H b Andover Mass. Vol: 6 Page: 007

PERRY Sylvester W & JOSLIN Mary A (Mrs) m Feb 7, 1899 Hopkinton. Groom: age 66 b Hopkinton s/o PERRY William b Henniker & PRESSEY Asenath b Hopkinton. Bride: age 60 b Gardner Mass d/o SANDERS William & CAPIN Rosanna. Vol: 6 Page: 008

SPOFFORD Arthur F & DODGE Maude E m Feb 8, 1898 Hopkinton. Groom: age 27 b Hopkinton s/o SPOFFORD S Alfred b Hopkinton & PAIGE M Abbie b Hopkinton. Bride: age 22 b Hopkinton d/o DODGE William F b Hopkinton & EDGERLY Martha J b New Hampton. Vol: 6 Page: 002

WHEELER John F & SWINNINGTON Etta M m Feb 15, 1898 Hopkinton. Groom: age 21 b Concord s/o WHEELER Felix b Quebec Canada & ST John Lizzie b Vermont. Bride: age 16 b Nelson d/o ---- ---- b Lyndeboro & ---- ---- b Sutton. Vol: 6 Page: 002

KIMBALL Elbridge G & HOYT Lydia A m Mar 22, 1898 Sutton. Groom: age 66 b Hopkinton s/o KIMBALL David b Hopkinton & HERRICK Asenath b Hopkinton. Bride: age 54 b Exeter d/o WALDRON George b Rye & LADD Hulda b Brentwood. Vol: 6 Page: 002

GRIFFIN Edwin A & CARTER L Della m Apr 6, 1898 Hopkinton. Groom: age 43 b Concord s/o GRIFFIN Joshua A b Pembroke & CURRIER Emily b Concord.

Hopkinton, NH Marriages 1898

Bride: age 35 b Hopkinton d/o STRAW John S b Hopkinton & HOLMES Mary A b Hopkinton. Vol: 6 Page: 003

HASTINGS Delmer W & CHASE Lena M m Apr 21, 1898 Hopkinton. Groom: age 28 b Hopkinton s/o HASTINGS Alfred S b Hopkinton & PERRY Susan b Hopkinton. Bride: age 23 b Hopkinton d/o CHASE Orrin b Hopkinton & BADGER Hattie M b Warner. Vol: 6 Page: 003

ADAMS Claud D & GETCHEL Cora B m Jul 24, 1898 Hopkinton. Groom: age 28 b Hopkinton s/o ADAMS Joseph H b Sutton & SARGENT Judith P b Warner. Bride: age 16 b Hopkinton d/o GETCHEL Charles P & SEAVEY Charlotte. Vol: 6 Page: 003

HARRINGTON Moses B & BARKER Lillian B m Oct 12, 1898 Hopkinton. Groom: age 21 b Hopkinton s/o HARRINGTON Thomas O b Concord & WOODBURY Hattie b Minn. Bride: age 19 b Lebanon d/o BARKER Orril b Windsor Vt & WALKER Adalade b Meridin. Vol: 6 Page: 004

KEMPTON Hiram J & LANDRY Eva m May 30, 1907 Hopkinton. Groom: age 25 b Newport s/o KEMPTON Freeman b Croydon & TANDY Flora B b Goshen. Bride: age 19 b Newport d/o LANDRY W & COUTT Mary. Vol: 6 Page: 043

ROACH John Jr & FEELY Margret m Oct 12, 1898 Concord. Groom: age 30 b Hopkinton s/o ROACH John b Ireland & ROONY Ann b Ireland. Bride: age 30 b Ireland d/o FEELY Patrick. Vol: 6 Page: 004

CHASE Marl Delbert & HARDY Clara M m Oct 26, 1898 Henniker. Groom: age 26 b Warner s/o CHASE Alonzo b Hopkinton & COLBY Kate E b Warner. Bride: age 27 b Hopkinton d/o HARDY Woodbury b Hopkinton & PRICE Ellen M b Peabody Mass. Vol: 6 Page: 005

SYMONDS William M & BURNHAM Alice M m Nov 5, 1898 Hopkinton. Groom: age 26 b Concord s/o SYMONDS George b Concord & WEBSTER Lucy A. Bride: age 30 b Hillsborough d/o BURNHAM George W & WYMAN Loella M b Deering. Vol: 6 Page: 005

FLANDERS Fred & LEWIS Ora M m Nov 20, 1898 Hillsborough. Groom: age 37 b Hopkinton s/o FLANDERS Rufus b Hopkinton & GALE Mary C. Bride: age 23 b Hillsboro d/o LEWIS Alba O b Laconia & ROBERST Mary E b Meridith. Vol: 6 Page: 005

COLBY Mark R & LAW Arminda M m Dec 25, 1898 Hopkinton. Groom: age 21 b Dunbarton s/o COLBY Forest b Litchfield & BARNARD Abbie H b Dunbarton. Bride: age 19 b Dunbarton d/o LAW Orrin b Warner. Vol: 6 Page: 006

BLOOD George & EASTMAN Nellie F m Dec 31, 1898 Hopkinton. Groom: age 24 b Andover Mass s/o BLOOD George W b Andover Mass & REA Mary E b Andover Mass. Bride: age 33 b Bristol d/o MUDGETT Calvin H b Bristol & FISHER Julia. Vol: 6 Page: 006

HARDY Lewis B & HAZELTON Grace M m May 18, 1899 Hopkinton. Groom: age 21 b Hopkinton s/o HARDY Samuel A b Hopkinton & PUTNEY Abbie b Hopkinton. Bride: age 17 b   d/o HAZELTIN Herman R b Groton & DWINNELLS Nellie M b Warner. Vol: 6 Page: 008

BLAKE Albert H & EMERSON Grace A m Jun 14, 1899 Warner. Groom: age 27 b Weare s/o BLAKE Charles H b Hopkinton & FOSTER Ella F b Bradford. Bride: age 23 b Weare d/o EMERSON J Frank b Hopkinton & PARKER Hattie M b Vermont. Vol: 6 Page: 008

CILLEY Elden G & WIGHT Florence A m Jun 26, 1899 Hopkinton. Groom: age 30 b Weare s/o CILLEY Benj F b Weare & CUSHING Mary S b Lowell Mass. Bride: age 24 b Hopkinton d/o WIGHT Edwin O & CURRIER Abbie S b Hopkinton. Vol: 6 Page: 009

MITCHEL Dolf & LIBBY Stella G m Jul 1, 1899 Hopkinton. Groom: age 28 b Milton Falls Vt s/o MITCHEL George. Bride: age 26 b Hopkinton d/o LIBBY George A b Webster & KENNISTON Estella b Franklin. Vol: 6 Page: 009

CHANDLER George W & DURNIN Sarah m Oct 25, 1899 Hopkinton. Groom: age 26 b Hopkinton s/o CHANDLER Horatio J b Hopkinton & CURRIER Susan V b Hopkinton. Bride: age 28 b Scotland d/o DURNIN John b Scotland & BREEN Ann b Scotland. Vol: 6 Page: 009

CHASE Fred J & HARDY Emma A m Nov 30, 1899 Contoocook. Groom: age 29 b Hopkinton s/o CHASE Orrin b Hopkinton & BADGER Hattie M b Warner. Bride: age 17 b Warner d/o HARDY Ira J b Hopkinton & GETCHEL Celia F b Carthage Me. Vol: 6 Page: 010

BLAKE Frank A & PADDLEFORD Susie M m Jan 14, 1900 Hopkinton. Groom: age 20 b Hopkinton s/o BLAKE Charles H b Hopkinton & FOSTER Ella b Weare. Bride: age 24 b Canada Ont d/o PADDLEFORD James & MORRILL Nellie b Henniker. Vol: 6 Page: 011

GLEASON Fred H & MALONEY Lena M m Mar 31, 1900 Hopkinton. Groom: age 23 b Athol Mass s/o GLEASON James H b Hardwick Mass & LEE Addie E b Springfield Mass. Bride: age 16 b Boston Mass d/o MALONY Lucy M. Vol: 6 Page: 011

HILAND John M & LAW Susie M m Apr 18, 1900 Hopkinton. Groom: age 26 b Hopkinton s/o HILAND George B b Hopkinton & KIMBALL Priscilla A b Hopkinton. Bride: age 23 b Dunbarton d/o LAW Orrin b Dunbarton & BUTTERS Sarah A ?? b Dunbarton. Vol: 6 Page: 011

NELSON John H & CORSER Blanche A m May 2, 1900 Hopkinton. Groom: age 49 b Hopkinton s/o NELSON Joseph P b Sutton & HUBBARD Esther b Hopkinton. Bride: age 20 b Hopkinton d/o CORSER Handet?? b Webster & HOLMES M Belle. Vol: 6 Page: 012

STORY Charles M & TUCKER Minnie A m May 1, 1900 Henniker. Groom: age 42 b Hopkinton s/o STORY Moses b Hopkinton & DIMOND Harriet b Warner. Bride: age 31 b Hopkinton d/o TUCKER David C b Henniker & PERRY Carrie b Hopkinton. Vol: 6 Page: 012

BROWN Lamson O & FLEMING Melissa m May 30, 1900 Hopkinton. Groom: age 24 b Thornton s/o BROWN Daniel E b Woodstock & ELKINS Laura A b Woodstock. Bride: age 22 b Ontario d/o FLEMING Robert b Scotland & REID Samantha b Canada. Vol: 6 Page: 012

FULLER William Francis & ELKINS Eva Bertha m Jun 28, 1900 Concord. Groom: age 24 b Hopkinton s/o FULLER John A b Bridgewater & MORRILL Julia F b Hopkinton. Bride: age 18 b Thornton d/o ELKINS George W b Thornton & GLIDDEN Mary E b Pembroke. Vol: 6 Page: 013

LIBBY Frank D & McINTIRE Dora M m Jul 18, 1900 Hopkinton. Groom: age 52 b Hopkinton s/o LIBBY William T b Epsom & SMART Elliner b Epsom. Bride: age 30 d/o NICKELSON Charles b Quebec & BROWN Melissa b Northwood. Vol: 6 Page: 013

Hopkinton, NH Marriages 1898

CURRIER James G & DURIAN M A M Laure m Oct 10, 1900 Ashland. Groom: age 26 b Portland Me s/o CURRIER James b Barrhead Scotland & ELLIOTT Mary b Londery Ireland. Bride: age 25 b St Andrews Pq d/o DURIAN Thomas A b St Andrews P Q & Marie b Canada. Vol: 6 Page: 013

KIMBALL Harry H & GRIFFIN Jessamine M m Oct 24, 1900 Hopkinton. Groom: age 23 b Hopkinton s/o KIMBALL Charles C b Hopkinton & CARPENTER Martha b Derby Vt. Bride: age 29 b Hopkinton d/o GRIFFIN Albert E b Bow & HELEN J b Lowell Mass. Vol: 6 Page: 014

WING Fred C & HAMMOND Anna E m Feb 27, 1901 Hopkinton. Groom: age 21 b West Summer Me s/o WING Clark A & PUTNAM Lydia. Bride: age 17 b Carthage Me d/o HAMMOND Albert F & THOMPSON Sarah E. Vol: 6 Page: 016

MONTGOMERY Scott & CLOUGH Mary R m Nov 8, 1900 Hopkinton. Groom: age 43 b Hopkinton s/o MONTGOMERY William b Salem NY & SAVORY Lucy A b Warner. Bride: age 29 b Hopkinton d/o CLOUGH Moses T b Hopkinton & BEAN Oristio b Candia. Vol: 6 Page: 014

MILLS Charles & CLARK Effie M m Dec 20, 1900 Hopkinton. Groom: age 33 b Hopkinton s/o MILLS Charles H b Hopkinton & TOWNE Olive H b Weare. Bride: age 17 b Weare d/o CLARK Addison H b Londonderry & BROWN Ida M b Waterbury Vt. Vol: 6 Page: 014

CONNOR Herbert J & DOW May B m Jan 14, 1901 Henniker. Groom: age 28 b Concord s/o CONNOR Frederick W b Hill & FLANDERS Sophia b Concord. Bride: age 27 b Bradford d/o DOW Horace M b Weare & MURDER Eliza b Bradford. Vol: 6 Page: 015

SMITH Robert & BOYCE Ardelle L m Apr 6, 1901 Hopkinton. Groom: age 28 b Boscawen s/o SMITH Charles W b Canterbury & FLANDERS Levonia L b Warner. Bride: age 18 b Concord d/o BOYCE Melzer D b Concord & ORDWAY Alice C b Concord. Vol: 6 Page: 016

CHASE Walter B & HANNAFORD Sarah E m Apr 13, 1901 Hopkinton. Groom: age 20 b Hopkinton s/o CHASE Orrin b Hopkinton & BADGER Harriet M b Warner. Bride: age 17 b Old Orchard Me d/o HANNAFORD Edward N b Peterboro & HUCHINS Lucy E b Kennebunk Me. Vol: 6 Page: 016

COLBY Forest & BUNTEN Rosa B m Jun 2, 1901 Hopkinton. Groom: age 51 b Litchfield s/o COLBY Abram & KIMBALL Adaline. Bride: age 39 b Dunbarton d/o PAIGE John & Clemena. Vol: 6 Page: 017

SHALLIES Leon Leforest & BUSWELL Mand D m Jul 3, 1901 Hopkinton. Groom: age 21 b Great Falls s/o SHALLLIES Ira B & HAM Ella F. Bride: age 22 b Concord d/o BUSWELL Samuel & DEBORAH D b Mechias Me. Vol: 6 Page: 017

BROWN John T & HEMPHILL Laura N m Aug 18, 1901 Hopkinton. Groom: age 29 b Thornton s/o BROWN Daniel E b Woodstock & ELKINS Laura A b Thornton. Bride: age 22 b Henniker d/o MUZZY Horace E b Henniker & HEMPHILL Capitola B b Henniker. Vol: 6 Page: 017

CHASE Harry A & BURGESS Lilla M m Sep 18, 1901 Hopkinton. Groom: age 29 b Hopkinton s/o CHASE Orren b Warner & BADGER Hattie M b Warner. Bride: age 21 b Charlestown d/o BURGESS Amos b Winslow Me & Martha b Teszisle Me. Vol: 6 Page: 018

Hopkinton, NH Marriages 1898

RUNNELLS Albert F & BURNHAM Nellie M m Sep 18, 1901 Hopkinton. Groom: age 26 b Hopkinton s/o RUNNELLS Edward G b Webster & MILLS Mary J b Concord. Bride: age 22 b Hillsborough d/o BURNHAM George W b Hillsborough & WYMAN Loella b Deering. Vol: 6 Page: 018

CHASE Samuel Myron & FORD Etta Elizabeth m Sep 28, 1901 Hopkinton. Groom: age 39 b Chicago Ill s/o CHASE Horace G b Hopkinton & SHERWIN Ellen M b Aurira Ny. Bride: age 31 b Brooklin Ny d/o FORD Samuel R b New York & WILKINSON Delia B b Smithville RI. Vol: 6 Page: 018

SPOFFORD F Eugene & JEPSON Hygia m Oct 9, 1901 Hopkinton. Groom: age 41 b Hopkinton s/o SPOFFORD Fred b Hopkinton & HILAND Sarah b Hopkinton. Bride: age 28 b Warner d/o JEPSON Henry & SARGENT Namoia b Warner. Vol: 6 Page: 019

WILLIAM M Burton & SANBORN A May m Oct 16, 1901 Melrose Mass. Groom: age 24 b Manchester s/o WILLIAM Marcus C b Morrill Me & BROWN Emma L b Hopkinton. Bride: age 26 b Gilmanton d/o SANBORN Frank E b Gilmanton & BACHELDER Jennie b Chichester. Vol: 6 Page: 019

PATCH George E & FRENCH Elsie B m Nov 27, 1901 Deerfield. Groom: age 25 b Hopkinton s/o PATCH John G b Hopkinton & JOHNSON Mary H b Hopkinton. Bride: age 23 b Deerfield d/o FRENCH M Frank b Deerfield & NORCROSS Lucy C b Bethelhem. Vol: 6 Page: 019

CLINTON Winfield M & BARTLETT Cora M m Dec 2, 1901 Hopkinton. Groom: age 21 b Hopkinton s/o CLINTON John D b Lynn Mass & SARAH J b Hopkinton. Bride: age 20 b Warner d/o BARTLETT Josiah H b Warner & BAILEY Eva E b Warner. Vol: 6 Page: 020

LIBBY Walton & DOW Della M m Dec 2, 1901 Hopkinton. Groom: age 19 b Hopkinton s/o LIBBY George A b Hopkinton & KENNISTON Stella b Andover. Bride: age 20 b Hopkinton d/o WEBSTER Frank & DOW Nettie b Concord. Vol: 6 Page: 020

WESCOTT Benjamin & GRAY Emma F m Dec 12, 1901 Hopkinton. Groom: age 26 b Bristol s/o WESCOTT Charles H b Andover & NUDD Mary P b Loudon. Bride: age 30 b Weare d/o GRAY George A b Lowell Mass & SARAH L b Bow. Vol: 6 Page: 020

CLOUGH Harry Rupert & ILLSLEY Florence Coburn m Sep 8, 1909 Worcester Mass. Groom: age 25 b Lebanon. Bride: age 26 b West Farley Vt. Vol: 6 Page: 048

STEVENS Bert C & NORRISS Almeda M m Mar 26, 1902 Hopkinton. Groom: age 27 b Amherst s/o STEVENS Alphons b Amherst & HACKETT Sarah L b Amherst. Bride: age 21 b Derby Vt d/o NORRISS George W b Derby Vt & Ida E b Derby Vt. Vol: 6 Page: 021

BLANCHARD Harry E & GUILD Grace E m May 14, 1902 Henniker. Groom: age 23 b Hillsborough s/o BLANCHARD Galen E b Washington & ROACH Nellie M b Hillsborough. Bride: age 19 b Hopkinton d/o GUILD Edmund R b West Farley Vt & STORY Abby. Vol: 6 Page: 021

CORLISS Charles H & LIBBY Myrtie M m May 17, 1902 Hopkinton. Groom: age 34 b Hopkinton s/o CORLISS Elbridge G b Grafton & STEVENS Mary J b Warner. Bride: age 23 b Hopkinton d/o LIBBY George A b Hopkinton & KENNISTON Estella b Andover. Vol: 6 Page: 022

Hopkinton, NH Marriages 1898

BARTON Warren B & FOGG Lizzie A m Jul 8, 1902 Concord. Groom: age 44 b Hopkinton s/o BARTON Charles O b Hopkinton & CUTTS Philanda b Goshen. Bride: age 46 b Manchester d/o FOGG Sherburne b Meridith & EMERSON Miriam S b Hopkinton. Vol: 6 Page: 022

KIMBALL Robert Warren & ELLIOTT Susie m Sep 16, 1902 Hopkinton. Groom: age 21 b Pittsfield s/o KIMBALL George A S b Boston Mass & GREEN Theresa b Pittsfield. Bride: age 23 b Haverhill Mass d/o ELLIOTT Christopher & Annie. Vol: 6 Page: 022

CRESSEY Myron Greely P & PUTNAM Helen Bickford m Oct 8, 1902 Hopkinton. Groom: age 25 b Bradford s/o CRESSEY George W W b Nashua & PRESBY Ella F b Bradford. Bride: age 24 b Hopkinton d/o PUTNAM Joseph E b Hopkinton & STRAW Margret b Hopkinton. Vol: 6 Page: 023

KELLEY Arthur J & BROWN Ethelyn Grace m Nov 12, 1902 Hopkinton. Groom: age 28 b Hopkinton s/o KELLEY Andrew J b Webster & JONES Roxanna W b Charlestown Mass. Bride: age 19 b Hopkinton d/o POOR Eri A b Hooksett & BROWN Alice H b Hopkinton. Vol: 6 Page: 023

NELSON Lewis A & CHASE Maud B m Jan 14, 1903 Hopkinton. Groom: age 18 b Warner s/o NELSON John H b Hopkinton & SEAVEY Nettie M b Hopkinton. Bride: age 19 b Hopkinton d/o CHASE George b Hopkinton & FISK Jennie M b Hopkinton. Vol: 6 Page: 024

ROWELL Charles S & HUNTOON Ada M m Feb 4, 1903 Hopkinton. Groom: age 45 b Hopkinton s/o ROWELL Isaac b Hopkinton & ADAMS Harriet b Henniker. Bride: age 28 b Eat Unity d/o HUUNTOON Ora M b East Unity & CURTICE M Velona b Windsor. Vol: 6 Page: 024

MELCHER Maurice C & LIBBY Alice M m Mar 14, 1903 Hopkinton. Groom: age 20 b Thornton s/o MELCHER George & BROWN Laura A b Thornton. Bride: age 16 b Hopkinton d/o LIBBY George A b Hopkinton & KENNISTON Estella b Franklin. Vol: 6 Page: 024

GEER Calvin R & PERRY Bertha May m Mar 25, 1903 Hopkinton. Groom: age 28 b Canada s/o GEER Andrew b Canada & GEORGE Sarah. Bride: age 19 b Hopkinton d/o PERRY James M b Hopkinton & KELLEY Edithen E b Hopkinton. Vol: 6 Page: 025

BURGESS Walter O & ROBIE Annie P m Apr 16, 1903 Hopkinton. Groom: age 19 b Claremont s/o BURGESS Amos b Winslow Me & ELLIS Martha J b Presque Isle Me. Bride: age 17 b Boscawen d/o ROBIE Charles E b Colebrook & INGERSON Chloe M b Lisbon. Vol: 6 Page: 025

AUSTIN Carlos & LULL Bessie E m Jun 11, 1903 Hopkinton. Groom: age 34 b Sheldon Vt s/o AUSTIN George b Highgate Vt & Mary A. Bride: age 24 b Weare d/o LULL Augustus & Carrie A b Weare. Vol: 6 Page: 025

HUNTOON Frank F W & AUSTIN Adeline L m Jul 4, 1903 Hopkinton. Groom: age 22 b Hopkinton s/o HUNTOON Warren b Salisbury & MORRILL Nellie b Andover. Bride: age 17 b Sheldon Vt d/o AUSTIN George b Highgate Vt & Mary A. Vol: 6 Page: 026

BLANCHARD Walter R & RAY Ola M m Sep 16, 1903 New Boston. Groom: age 20 b Greenfield s/o BLANCHARD Charles b Bennington & SAVAGE Etta b Greenfield. Bride: age 24 b Vermont d/o RAY Levi N b Vertmont & BORDEN Anna A b Hanover. Vol: 6 Page: 026

FIFIELD Frank A & ADAMS Laura A m Oct 18, 1903 Hopkinton. Groom: age 36 b Alstead s/o FIFIELD Abram & COLBY Lydia J b Hopkinton. Bride: age 40 b Thornton d/o BROWN Daniel E b Woodstock & ELKINS Laura A b Thornton. Vol: 6 Page: 026

FAVOR Charles D & LOCKE Annie E m Oct 25, 1903 Hopkinton. Groom: age 26 b Weare s/o FAVOR Ellen b Weare. Bride: age 25 b Hopkinton d/o LOCKE George H b Hopkinton & WRIGHT Mary E b Hopkinton. Vol: 6 Page: 027

FULLER George Irving & READE Blanche Minetta m Oct 26, 1903 Hopkinton. Groom: age 24 b Hopkinton s/o FULLER Orren F b New Hampton & CAMPBELL Lillian E b Hopkinton. Bride: age 21 b Weare d/o READE Henry b Trowbridge England & Sarah b Harrisville. Vol: 6 Page: 027

CLARK Fred & COOPER Mabel m Nov 10, 1903 Hopkinton. Groom: age 40 b Hopkinton s/o CLARK Benjamin b Hopkinton & KEAZER Mary J b Henniker. Bride: age 25 b Hopkinton d/o COOPER Joseph A b Sunapee & POWELL Augusta J b Concord. Vol: 6 Page: 027

HALL Frank E & WEEKS Annie M m Dec 31, 1903 Hopkinton. Groom: age 52 b Boscawen s/o HALL John & KIMBALL Olive J b Salisbury. Bride: age 25 b Hopkinton d/o RAND Mary b Manchester. Vol: 6 Page: 028

DETTE William & KNIGHT Frances Rice m Jan 2, 1904 Hopkinton. Groom: age 32 b Buffalo Ny s/o DETTE Theodore J b Buffalo NY & HEILBRON Mary b Hamburg NY. Bride: age 28 b Des Moines Iowa d/o KNIGHT John M b Dummerston Vt & RICE Frances b Millville Mass. Vol: 6 Page: 029

WALKER John T & PIPER Jane m Jan 19, 1904 Hopkinton. Groom: age 70 b Jerico Vt s/o WALKER John T b England & JOY Lydia b Jerico Vt. Bride: age 70 b Hillsborough d/o CARTER Samuel & RAY Mary. Vol: 6 Page: 029

CHASE Herbert S & DENSMORE Emily H m Mar 12, 1904 Hopkinton. Groom: age 37 b Warner s/o CHASE Alonzo b Hopkinton & WELLS Mary J T b Sutton. Bride: age 27 b Hopkinton d/o LIBBY George A b Webster & KENNINSTON Estella b Andover. Vol: 6 Page: 029

CHANDLER Harry G & MARTIN Mabel A m Mar 23, 1904 Weare. Groom: age 23 b Henniker s/o CHANDLER Charles H b Nashua & McALPINE Mary J b Warner. Bride: age 22 b Weare d/o MARTIN Donald b Scotland & MORSE Hannah B b Londonderry. Vol: 6 Page: 030

NELSON Eddie L & BOHONAN Etta L m Apr 6, 1904 Hopkinton. Groom: age 24 b Hillsborough s/o NELSON David L & CHASE Clara. Bride: age 19 b Hopkinton d/o BOHONAN John W b Sutton & JEWELL Delia A b Weare. Vol: 6 Page: 030

TILTON Joseph N & ROLLINS M Alice m May 18, 1904 Hopkinton. Groom: age 27 b Hopkinton s/o TILTON George F b Concord & NADEAU Minnie J b Shipton Canada. Bride: age 23 b Hopkinton d/o ROLLINS John b Berlin Vt & SARGENT Ellen A b Hopkinton. Vol: 6 Page: 030

CARR John F & SYMONDS Edna A m Jun 1, 1904 Hopkinton. Groom: age 26 b Hopkinton s/o CARR Frank H b Hopkinton & BOYNTON Mary A W b Hopkinton. Bride: age 26 b Hopkinton d/o SYMONDS Samuel T b Hillsborough & JOHNSON Annie N b Weare. Vol: 6 Page: 031

BURNHAM George W & KIMBALL A Jennie m Sep 8, 1904 Concord. Groom: age 66 b Hillsborough s/o BURNHAM Albert G b Hillsborough & SYMONDS

Tammey b Hillsborough. Bride: age 52 b Hopkinton d/o KIMBALL Moses Warren b Sanbornton & Judith b Alton. Vol: 6 Page: 031

BRYAN John H Jr & COLBY Helen N m Oct 18, 1904 Hopkinton. Groom: age 47 b Plymouth Conn s/o BRYAN John H b Watertown Conn & TAT?? Mary A b New York. Bride: age 50 b Hopkinton d/o COLBY Melvin b Hopkinton & PAGE Hannah b Hopkinton. Vol: 6 Page: 031

FRYE Amos F & SANBORN Clara May m Jun 14, 1905 Warner. Groom: age 23 b Worcester Mass s/o COBURN Henry A b Worcester Mass & FRYE Bertie b Concord. Bride: age 18 b Hopkinton d/o SANBORN Herman C b Webster & FRENCH Lizzie b Northfield. Vol: 6 Page: 034

FRAZIER Shirley W & NELSON Clara J m Jun 21, 1905 Hillsborough. Groom: age 23 b Warner s/o FRAZIER William C b Salisbury & LESLIE Francis J b Hillsborough. Bride: age 28 b Warner d/o CHASE Alonzo b Warner & COLBY Kate E b Warner. Vol: 6 Page: 034

BARTLETT Clifton J & CHASE Lida H m Sep 20, 1905 Hopkinton. Groom: age 19 b Warner s/o BARTLETT Joseph** b Warner & BAILEY Eva E b Warner. Bride: age 17 b Hopkinton d/o CHASE Nelson A b Hopkinton & CLARK Annie J b Warner. Vol: 6 Page: 034 Note: fam record name is Josiah

BOHANAN Lester J * & EATON Blanche B m Jun 30, 1910 Hopkinton. Groom: age 28 b Hopkinton s/o BOHONANA John W b Sutton & JEWELL Delia A b Weare. Bride: age 29 b Bradford d/o EATON Albert S & ---- ---- b Bradford. Vol: 6 Page: 052 Note: also record on pg 49 -marriage date Jun 30 1911

BOYCE Harley Anson & CURRIER Augusta May m Dec 21, 1909 Hopkinton. Groom: age 21 b Hopkinton s/o BOYCE Melzer D b Concord & ORDWAY Alice C b Concord. Bride: age 21 b Tilton d/o CRONIN John J & BAKER Anastasia b Tilton. Vol: 049 Page: 049

DOW Harvey M & SWEATT Alice Etta m Jun 25, 1906 Hopkinton. Groom: age 50 b Hopkinton s/o DOW Samuel H b Concord & HOYT Sarah b Hopkinton. Bride: age 40 b Canada d/o LOCKE ?? & Sarah. Vol: 6 Page: 037

CLIFFORD Harry F & WARD Pamelia I m Jan 1, 1906 Hopkinton. Groom: age 28 b Boston Mass s/o CLIFFORD Francis b England & Nellie b Scotland. Bride: age 22 b Boston Mass d/o WARD Gardner I b Everett Mass & WOODWARD Martha S b Sanbornton. Vol: 6 Page: 036

CORSER Elmer Elsworth & LIBBY Jesse Elizabeth m Mar 13, 1906 Hopkinton. Groom: age 43 b Webster s/o CORSER Rice b Boscawen & PAIGE Sarah b Windsor. Bride: age 17 b Hopkinton d/o LIBBY George A b Hopkinton & KENNISTON Estella A b Andover. Vol: 6 Page: 036

HUNT William O & PERKINS Sara Ethel m Jun 9, 1906 Sanborton. Groom: age 27 b Salem Mass s/o HUNT Charles b Warner & SPROWL Ella A b Nova Scotia. Bride: age 28 b Dunbarton d/o PERKINS Moses J b Freemont & STEVENSON Amanda J b Freemont. Vol: 6 Page: 036

ADAMS Claud D & FLATHERS Ida May m May 17, 1906 Hopkinton. Groom: age 36 b Hopkinton s/o ADAMS Joseph H b Sutton & SARGENT Judith b Warner. Bride: age 24 b Lawrence Mass d/o FLATHER Samuel K b Fall River Mass & ARNOLD Carrie Bell b Schenectady Ny. Vol: 6 Page: 037

WHITE Percey Edward & ELLIOTT Ida May m Jun 20, 1906 Hopkinton. Groom: age 21 b Amherst s/o WHITE Enos S b Waterford Vt & WRIGHT Marietta A b

Amherst. Bride: age 22 b Webster d/o ELLIOTT Edson E b Webster & COLBY Nettie L b Deering. Vol: 6 Page: 037

GUERIN George & WELCOME Sarah m Sep 12, 1906 Weare. Groom: age 22 b Manchester s/o GUIRIN Edward b Canada & CHAMPAGNE Mary b Canada. Bride: age 17 b Canada d/o WELCOME Benjamin b Canada & CHAMPAGNE Cordetia b Canada. Vol: 6 Page: 038

STRAW Ernest Gale & SYMONDS Mildred Grace m Sep 12, 1906 Hopkinton. Groom: age 21 b Hopkinton s/o STRAW Andrew L F b Hopkinton & CHANDLER Dolly V b Hopkinton. Bride: age 18 b Hopkinton d/o SYMONDS Samuel T b Hillsborough & JOHNSON M Ann b Weare. Vol: 6 Page: 038

PALMER Albert O & ROLLINS Edith F m Sep 15, 1906 Hopkinton. Groom: age 25 b Hopkinton s/o PALMER Willie O b Hopkinton & CLARK Cora I b Auburn. Bride: age 21 b Hopkinton d/o ROLLINS John b Hopkinton & SARGENT Ellen A b Hopkinton. Vol: 6 Page:

KELLEY Leowen H & HOLMES Stella L m Sep 19, 1906 Hopkinton. Groom: age 31 b Hopkinton s/o KELLEY Frederick H b Hopkinton & HOLLAND Harriet N b Wilmont. Bride: age 49. Vol: 6 Page: 039

HOUGH Hazen Purmont & MORRILL Laura Sylvia m Sep 29, 1906 Hopkinton. Groom: age 28 b Lebanon s/o HOUGH Henry B b Lebanon & PURMONT Ellen M. Bride: age 26 b Newtonville Mass d/o MORRILL Frank I b Hopkinton & STEVEN Hattie F b Piermont. Vol: 6 Page: 039

BAKER Harry A & GILCHRIST Alice L m Oct 4, 1906 Henniker. Groom: age 23 b Andover s/o BAKER Frank E & WHITAKER Alma C b Salisbury. Bride: age 21 b Henniker d/o GILCHRIST John G & WHITNEY Lizzie M b Henniker. Vol: 6 Page: 039

BUNTEN Arthur Webster & FULLER Eva Lillian m Oct 17, 1906 Hopkinton. Groom: age 25 b Dunbarton s/o BUNTEN Edgar b Dunbarton & PAGE Rosa b Dunbarton. Bride: age 22 b Hopkinton d/o FULLER Orren F b New Hampton & CAMPBELL Lillian E b Hopkinton. Vol: 6 Page: 040

SYMONDS Samuel T & HARDY Lillian J m Oct 31, 1906 Hopkinton. Groom: age 57 b Hillsborough s/o SYMONDS Tilton b Hillsborough & DUTTON Catherine B b Hillsborough. Bride: age 43 b Nova Scotia d/o HARDY Benjamin b Nova Scotia & MARSHALL Sarah C b Nova Scotia. Vol: 6 Page: 040

LOCKE Charles Edward & FLANDERS Minnie Caroline m Sep 26, 1906 Manchester. Groom: age 23 b Hopkinton s/o LOCKE George H b Hopkinton & MARY Ann b Hopkinton. Bride: age 22 b Henniker d/o FLANDERS Abraham M b Henniker & CURRIER Olive S b Warner. Vol: 6 Page: 040

CHURCHILL Leo R & FRANKLYN Lucy Jame m Nov 2, 1906 Hopkinton. Groom: age 25 b Lovestdale Vt s/o CHURCHILL George H b Lovestdale Vt & SARGENT Mary J b Danby Vt. Bride: age 25 b Farrburg Neb d/o FRANKLYN Frederick J b England & THOMAS Elenor Gyles b England. Vol: 6 Page: 041

LIBBY Percy Leroy & HOOK Alice M m Nov 29, 1906 Hopkinton. Groom: age 25 b Gorham Me s/o LIBBY Charles M b Gorham Me & CLONDMAN Clara b Little Falls Me. Bride: age 20 b Hopkinton d/o HOOK James M b Concord & DOYEN Mary A b Canada. Vol: 6 Page: 041

JACKMAN George W & WHIPPLE Mary E m Dec 19, 1906 Hopkinton. Groom: age 78 b Hopkinton s/o JACKMAN Hazen b Hopkinton & KIMBALL Charlotte

Hopkinton, NH Marriages 1898

b Hopkinton. Bride: age 58 b Lyme d/o WHIPPLE Jonathan b Lyme & FLINT Elizabeth B b Lyme. Vol: 6 Page: 041

MARSH Frank P & GURNEY Marietta R m Sep 5, 1898 Henniker. Groom: age 24 b Weare s/o MARSH Benj F b Concord & STRATON Lorena b Lisbon. Bride: age 25 b Antrim d/o DUSTIN B Frank & ROBB Roxie A b Stoddard. Vol: 6 Page: 004

TIRRELL Perley C & ROSS Hester Louise m Jan 22, 1901 Hopkinton. Groom: age 20 b Manchester s/o TERRILL George H b Manchester & CLARK Georgie A b Warner. Bride: age 21 b Bedford Que d/o ROSS Henry L b St Albans & WHITE Wealtha Cardelia b Canada. Vol: 6 Page: 015

CONERN Joseph F & GEORGE Grace I m Feb 26, 1901 Warner. Groom: age 24 b Wolinhamton Eng ? s/o CONERN John b Wolverhampton Eng & HOPKINS Agnes H b Bedford Eng. Bride: age 25 b Warner d/o GEORGE Darins b Warner & UPTON Emma b Wilmot. Vol: 6 Page: 015 Note: x

GOODWIN Walter E & HOWE Eva M m Jan 8, 1902 Hopkinton. Groom: age 25 b Hopkinton s/o GOODWIN Charles P b Hopkinton & CROWELL Etta M b Hopkinton. Bride: age 22 b Rowley Mass d/o HOWE Amos & Josephine. Vol: 6 Page: 021

PALMER Albert O & ROLLINS Edith F m Sep 15, 1906 Hopkinton. Groom: age 25 b Hopkinton s/o PALMER Willie O b Hopkinton & CLARK Cora I b Antrim. Bride: age 21 b Hopkinton d/o ROLLINS John b Hopkinton & SARGENT Ellen A b Hopkinton. Vol: 6 Page: 038

ORDWAY Augustine C & CHASE Martha J m Jan 2, 1907 Concord. Groom: age 48 b Goshen s/o ORDWAY John & WHITTENDER Mary E b Newbury. Bride: age 57 b Hopkinton d/o CHASE Barach b Hopkinton & MORRISON Lydia b Hopkinton. Vol: 6 Page: 042

MOSHER Edwin St M & FULLER Carrie Adeline m Jan 9, 1907 Hopkinton. Groom: age 29 b Presque Isle Me s/o MOSHER George W b Moshville N S & McDEVITT Augusta b Howard Me. Bride: age 24 b Hopkinton d/o FULLER Orren b New Hampton & CAMPBELL Lilla E b Hopkinton. Vol: 6 Page: 042

COOPER Adelbert & GARLAND Della S m Jan 9, 1907 Suncook. Groom: age 31 b Concord s/o COOPER Joseph A b Sunapee & POWELL Harriet A b Concord. Bride: age 31 b Enfield d/o ROLLINS James b Enfield & Nellie b Enfield. Vol: 6 Page: 042

HOYT Frank French & HUNT Edith Nettie m Sep 11, 1907 Hopkinton. Groom: age 23 b Hopkinton s/o HOYT Walter F b Hopkinton & PHELPS Sarah b Tilton. Bride: age 22 b Salem Mass d/o HUNT Charles b Warner & SPROWL Ella A b Nova Scotia. Vol: 6 Page: 043

TAYLOR L Howard & MELCHER Eva M m Nov 9, 1907 Concord. Groom: age 23 b W Townsend Mass s/o TAYLOR Edgar N b Parsonfield Me & DOW Georgia A b Concord. Bride: age 22 b Thornton d/o MELCHER George b Thornton & BROWN Laura A b Thornton. Vol: 6 Page: 043

ROLLINS John & LEARD Annie D m Apr 2, 1908 Templeton Mass. Groom: age 57 b Berlin Vt s/o ROLLINS Alfred A b Antrim & COLBY Mary E b Hopkinton. Bride: age 39 b Prince Edward Isl d/o LEARD Lewis b Prince Edward Isl & MUTTART Mary Ann b Prince Edward Isl. Vol: 6 Page: 044

MORAN Reginald T & STRAW Blanche Maud m Sep 5, 1908 Goffstown. Groom: age 23 b Concord s/o MORAN Thomas J b Concord & O'RILEY Catherine b Ireland. Bride: age 21 b Hopkinton d/o STRAW Andrew L b Hopkinton & CHANDLER Dolly V b Hopkinton. Vol: 6 Page: 044

PRESTON Frank Loring & PARRISH Alice Roberts m Sep 12, 1908 Hopkinton. Groom: age 22 b Boston Mass s/o PRESTON Frank A b Boston Mass & LORING Marin W b Weston Mass. Bride: age 19 b Atlantic City NJ d/o PARRISH Richard Price b Philadelphia Pa & ROBERTS Alice May b Philadelphia Pa. Vol: 6 Page: 044

DOW Perley D & CURRIER Helen m Oct 12, 1908 Hopkinton. Groom: age 19 b Weston Mass s/o DOW George P b Hopkinton & STEWART Carrie M. Bride: age 16 b Hopkinton d/o CURRIER Willie A b Hopkinton & WEBSTER Gertie J b Concord. Vol: 6 Page: 045

DUSTIN Daniel Herbert & ASHBY Sylvia Earline m Oct 21, 1908 Bradford. Groom: age 23 b Hopkinton s/o DUSTIN Herbert C b Hopkinton & RICHARDSON S Addie b Hopkinton. Bride: age 22 b Concord d/o ASHBY Charles F b Bradford & CLOUGH Ruhannah b Lyman Me. Vol: 6 Page: 045

PAIGE Ralph Samuel & ELLIOTT Verena Irene m Oct 24, 1908 Hopkinton. Groom: age 24 b Weare s/o PAIGE Alfred F b Weare & GILLIS Eliza A b Bennington. Bride: age 20 b Chief Mich d/o ELLIOTT Edson E b Webster & COLBY Nettie L b Deering. Vol: 6 Page: 045

DOWNS William Myron & COUCH Stella Hazel m Jan 2, 1909 Boscawen. Groom: age 18 b Harverhill s/o DOWNS Charles b Woodsville & WETHERBEE Nellie b Ryegate Vt. Bride: age 16 b Salisbury d/o COUCH Eugene C b Salisbury & PAIGE Georgianna b Sutton. Vol: 6 Page: 046

BAILEY William S & PAIGE Josie E m Feb 7, 1909 Hopkinton. Groom: age 28 b Hopkinton s/o BAILEY Wiliam P & DOW Annie P b Warner. Bride: age 30 b Hopkinton d/o DWINNELLS John G b & CHASE Caroline M b Warner. Vol: 6 Page: 046

WHITTIER Louis P & PETERS Rose F m Jun 23, 1909 Hopkinton. Groom: age 28 b Bow s/o WHITTIER Otis M b Webster & WILKINSON Iva b Concord. Bride: age 22 b Canaan d/o PETERS William F b Canaan & WEEKS Emily F b Northwood. Vol: 6 Page: 046

SCRIGGINS Arthur C & WHEDEN Annie B m Jul 26, 1909 Hopkinton. Groom: age 37 b Sandwich s/o SCRIGGINS Charles B b Pittsfield & MASON Julia b Sandwich. Bride: age 41 b Sandwich d/o MUDGETT Charles E b Sandwich & WALLINGFORD Mary J b Alton. Vol: 6 Page: 047

SEVERANCE Herbert D & COLBY Lena M m Aug 24, 1909 Concord. Groom: age 48 b Stoddard s/o SEVERANCE Joseph b Washington & PUTNEY Adeline b Bradford. Bride: age 34 b Bradford d/o COLBY Abram P & RICHARDS ---- b New Boston. Vol: 6 Page: 047

SANBORN Smith B & BUSWELL Mary Esther m Sep 9, 1909 Manchester. Groom: age 49 b Webster s/o SANBORN Jesse D b Webster & BACHELDER Arvilla b Loudon. Bride: age 50 b Hopkinton d/o BUSWELL Smith S b Hopkinton & ELDER Deberah D b Maine. Vol: 6 Page: 047

COLBY Frank H & BURNHAM Carrie L m Oct 14, 1909 Hopkinton. Groom: age 51 b Bow s/o COLBY Francis W b Bow & WHEELER Paulina P b Dunbarton.

Hopkinton, NH Marriages 1898

Bride: age 33 b Hillsborough d/o BURNHAM George W b Hillsborough & WYMAN Loella M b Deering. Vol: 6 Page: 048

DENSMORE William E & LIBBY Lillian D m Oct 16, 1909 Billerica Mass. Groom: age 21 b Hopkinton. Bride: age 18 b Hopkinton. Vol: 6 Page: 048

COOPER Joseph A & COLBY Mary W m Apr 9, 1910 Bradford. Groom: age 63 b Sunapee s/o COOPER David b Sunapee & ROGER Mary b Sunapee. Bride: age 64 b Roxbury Mass d/o CASS Aaron b Candia & BROWN Hannah A b Wilmot. Vol: 6 Page: 049

KIMBALL Charles C & COLBY Elsie J m Jul 26, 1910 Hopkinton. Groom: age 21 b Canterbury s/o KIMBALL Lucien C b Webster & STANYAN Edna P b Wentworth. Bride: age 18 b Hopkinton d/o COBLY Arthur P b Hopkinton & WHIPPLE Elida W b Manchester. Vol: 6 Page: 049

CLOUGH Francis & BODWELL Dorothy Caroline m Aug 4, 1910 Nashua. Groom: age 22 b Hopkinton s/o CLOUGH Moses T b Hopkinton & BEAN Mary O b Candia. Bride: age 23 b Rockville Ns d/o BODWELL Newton P b Salem & McMASTER Ida T b Wilmot Ns. Vol: 6 Page: 049

LEAVITT Ralph Jerome & SMART Stella Gertrude m Feb 16, 1910 Hopkinton. Groom: age 24 b Sandwich s/o LEAVITT William S b Milton Mass & SCRIGGINS Annie B b Sandwich. Bride: age 31 b Warner d/o BARTLETT Woodbury b Warner & DAVIS Clara Bell b Hartland VT. Vol: 6 Page: 050

COOLEDGE Charles W Jr & DANFORTH Mabel Kempton m Mar 28, 1910 Warner. Groom: age 32 b Hancock s/o COOLEDGE Charles W b Leominster Mass & BROWN Kate Lucy b Independance Ohio. Bride: age 33 b Reeds Ferry d/o DANFORTH Charles H b East Weare & KEMPTON Marietta H b Croydon. Vol: 6 Page: 050

MILLS Walter Brown & POTHOFF Annie J m Mar 28, 1910 Hopkinton. Groom: age 32 b Hopkinton s/o MILLS George W b Hopkinton & BROWN Unice b Concord. Bride: age 32 b Holland d/o POTHOFF John b Holland & SCHONLTON Angelina b Holland. Vol: 6 Page: 050

COOPER Joseph & COLBY Mary W m Apr 9, 1910 Bradford. Groom: age 63 b Sunapee s/o COOPER David b Sunapee & ROGERS Mary b Sunapee. Bride: age 64 b Roxbury Mass d/o CASS Aaron b Candia & BROWN Hannah A b Wilmot. Vol: 6 Page: 051

KIMBALL Charles C & COLBY Elsie J m Jul 26, 1910 Hopkinton. Groom: age 21 b Canterbury s/o KIMBALL Lucien C b Webster & STANYAN Edna P b Wentworth. Bride: age 18 b Hopkinton d/o COLBY Arthur P b Hopkinton & WHIPPLE Elida W b Manchester. Vol: 6 Page: 051

CLOUGH Francis & BODWELL Dorothy C m Aug 4, 1910 Nashua. Groom: age 22 b Hopkinton s/o CLOUGH Moses T b Hopkinton & BEAN Mary O b Candia. Bride: age 23 b Rockville N S d/o BODWELL Newton P b Salem & McMASTER Ida T b Wilmot. Vol: 6 Page: 051

BELKNAP Charles J & BARBER Esther M m Aug 10, 1910 Hopkinton. Groom: age 68 b Newport s/o BELKNAP Sawyer & AIKEN Mary Martha b Bedford. Bride: age 48 b Chelsea Mass d/o BARBER Robert b England & WOL-STENTHOLMS Zillah b England. Vol: 6 Page: 052

BLAKE Willie C & SULLIVAN Bridgett Anna m Sep 10, 1910 Concord. Groom: age 20 b Thornton s/o BLAKE William E b Thornton & BROWN Clara B b

Thornton. Bride: age 23 b New Brunswick d/o SULLIVAN Mitchell b Biddeford Me & Margarett b Biddeford Me. Vol: 6 Page: 052

HOOK Edward M & HASELTON Lucy E m Oct 8, 1910 Warner. Groom: age 33 b Canada s/o HOOK James M b Concord & DOYING Mary A b Canada. Bride: age 26 b Chester d/o HASELTON Benjamin F b Manchester & GARLAND Lucy A b Hampton. Vol: 6 Page: 053

KING Earl F & ADAMS Bernice May m Dec 26, 1910 Concord. Groom: age 24 b Richforst Vt s/o KING H H b Berkshire Vt & BOMBARD Roxey E b Bakersfield Vt. Bride: age 22 b Concord d/o ADAMS Benjamin F b Wolfeboro & HAYES Mary A b Alton. Vol: 6 Page: 053

DENSMORE Harlen & PINARD Clara Bell m Apr 23, 1910 Hopkinton. Groom: age 20 b Hopkinton s/o DENSMORE James A b Hopkinton & LIBBY Ellen J b Salisbury. Bride: b Andover d/o PINARD Lewis b Andover. Vol: 6 Page: 053 Note: records states a duplicate

SYMONDS Charles D & PARKER Grace E m Feb 27, 1911 Hopkinton. Groom: age 20 b Hopkinton s/o SYMONDS George b Concord & WEBSTER Lucy A b Glastonbury Conn. Bride: age 21 b Manchester d/o PARKER John b Manchester & Evelyn b Manchester. Vol: 6 Page: 054

DAVIS Henry Russell & LINCOLN Mildred m Jun 7, 1911 Taunton Mass. Groom: age 21 b Warner s/o DAVIS Henry C b Warner & WHITTIER Alice b Webster. Bride: age 22 b Taunton Mass d/o LINCOLN Benjamin C b Taunton Mass & DEANE Annah b Newton Mass. Vol: 6 Page: 054

BARBER David Andrew & BATES Cara Margaret m Jul 19, 1911 Hopkinton. Groom: age 54 b Boston Mass s/o BARBER Robert b England & WOLSTEN-HOLM Zilah b England. Bride: age 39 b Chicago Ill d/o McCONOR Dougall & SWENEY Rose. Vol: 6 Page: 054

MONTGOMERY William Lee & OMAN Agenes S V m Jul 23, 1911 Hopkinton. Groom: age 23 b Warner s/o MONTGOMERY Jerome b Hopkinton & DUNBAR Eliza J b Warner. Bride: age 16 b Boston Mass d/o OMAN Andrew G b Sweeden & MAGNUSON Caroline b Sweeden. Vol: 6 Page: 055

SHREWE Henry Mason & PIERCE Eva Adaline m Sep 7, 1911 Riverside Ill. Groom: age 31 b Salem Mass s/o SHREWE Benjamin b Salem Mass & GARDNER Mary b Bristol RI. Bride: age 24 b Chicabo Ill d/o PIERCE Charles Barnes b Boston Mass & SMITH Lillian C b Indianopolis Ind. Vol: 6 Page: 055

STANLEY Clinton J & HALL Annie M m Sep 21, 1911 Hopkinton. Groom: age 33 b Hopkinton s/o STANLEY Edward W b Hopkinton & CLOUGH Mary E b Hopkinton. Bride: age 32 b Hopkinton. Vol: 6 Page: 055

ELLIOTT Clarence T & STEEVENS Margarette m Oct 3, 1911 Hopkinton. Groom: age 43 b Webster s/o ELLIOTT Thomas b Webster & DUSTIN Sarah E b Hopkinton. Bride: age 38 b Nova Scotia d/o McDONALD Henry & CONDON Annie. Vol: 6 Page: 056

PUTNEY Ira M & BARKER Bessie m Oct 14, 1911 Nelson. Groom: age 33 b Hopkinton s/o PUTNEY True J b Hopkinton & AYERS Ellen M b Manchester Mass. Bride: age 31 b Nelson d/o BARKER Thadeus W b Dublin & HARDY Rose M b Nelson. Vol: 6 Page: 056

ALDEN Carroll Storrs & GRAHAMA Meeta Campbell m Oct 21, 1911 Hopkinton. Groom: age 35 b Mediana Ohio s/o ALDEN Ezra Judson b Lyme & STORRS

Helen Frances b Hanover. Bride: age 41 b Fort Riley Kan d/o GRAHAM William M b Washington D C & RICKETTS Mary B b Fort Fairfield Me. Vol: 6 Page: 056

SYMONDS Arthur G & CHASE L Winnifield m Dec 19, 1911 Hopkinton. Groom: age 30 b Hopkinton s/o SYMONDS Samuel T b Hillsborough & JOHNSON Mary A b Deering. Bride: age 23 b Hopkinton d/o CHASE George b Hopkinton & FISKE Jennie b Hopkinton. Vol: 6 Page: 057

GAGNON Omar A & CURRIER Mary D m Dec 21, 1911 Manchester. Groom: age 24 b Goffstown s/o GAGNON Francis b Canada & ELIE Hartimise b Canada. Bride: age 19 b Hopkinton d/o CURRIER William A b Hopkinton & WEBSTER Gertrude b Hopkinton. Vol: 6 Page: 057

BOHANAN John H & MARCY Esther G m Jan 1, 1912 Hopkinton. Groom: age 22 b Hopkinton s/o BOHANAN John W b Sutton & JEWELL Delia A b Weare. Bride: age 18 b Cambridge Mass d/o MARCY Henry E b Southbridge Mass & GREENLEAF Hattie R b Cambridge Mass. Vol: 6 Page: 058

WESCOTT Benjamin & AYER Flora A m Jan 1, 1912 Hopkinton. Groom: age 36 b Bristol s/o WESCOTT Charles H b Andover & NUDD Mary R b Loudon. Bride: age 31 b Hopkinton d/o AYER Walter C & CLOUGH Maria b Hopkinton. Vol: 6 Page: 058

MARCY John & BAKER Mildred Fay m Mar 13, 1912 Hopkinton. Groom: age 21 b Cambridge Mass s/o MARCY Henry E b Southbirdge Mass & GREENLEAF Hattie R b Cambridge Mass. Bride: age 23 b Hopkinton d/o BAKER William A b Concord & PALMER Effie V b Hopkinton. Vol: 6 Page: 058

AMES George P & STRAW Flora M m May 8, 1912 Manchester. Groom: age 46 b Guilford s/o AMES Thompson b Guilford & PIPER Hannah b Gilmanton. Bride: age 48 b Hopkinton d/o STRAW John S b Hopkinton & HOLMES Mary A b Hopkinton. Vol: 6 Page: 059

GUIMOND Fred & CURRIER Donna Frances m May 25, 1912 Hillsborough. Groom: age 25 b Hopkinton s/o GUIMOND Zoel b Canada & PAGE Laura b Canada. Bride: age 18 b Warner d/o CURRIER Charles b Warner & EDMUNDS Agnes b Warner. Vol: 6 Page: 059

MILLS Lerman H & CHARLES Jennie m Jun 15, 1912 Hopkinton. Groom: age 42 b Hopkinton s/o MILLS Charles N b Hopkinton & TOWNES Olive b Dunbarton. Bride: age 36 b Scotland d/o CHARLES James b Scotland & ROBERTSONS Jane b Scotland. Vol: 6 Page: 059

HASELTON Homer H & CARTER Susie W m Aug 8, 1912 Hopkinton. Groom: age 25 b Hopkinton s/o HASELTON Herman R b Groton & DWINNELLS Nellie M b Hopkinton. Bride: age 24 b Concord d/o CARTER James b Warner & ---- ---- b Concord. Vol: 6 Page: 060

BRUCE Harry George & BIGELOW Charlotte E m Aug 13, 1912 Hopkinton. Groom: age 19 b Groveton s/o BRUCE John M b Buckfield Me & McMANN Nellie b Stark. Bride: age 18 b Orford d/o BIGELOW James b Woodstock & HICKS Ella b Bradford. Vol: 6 Page: 060

DOWNES Daniel & SARGENT Alice E m Sep 2, 1912 Warner. Groom: age 22 b Wilmot s/o DOWNES Edwin D b Andover & KENISTON Elzira A b Wilmot. Bride: age 21 b Warner d/o SARGENT Fred E b Warner & ANNIS Nellie b Warner. Vol: 6 Page: 060

Hopkinton, NH Marriages 1898

GRIFFIN Clement A & DUNBAR Mildred F m Oct 2, 1912 Hopkinton. Groom: age 29 b Hopkinton s/o GRIFFIN Alfred E b Bow & MORRILL Helen J b Lowell Mass. Bride: age 20 b Hopkinton d/o DUNBAR Eugene b Hopkinton & PAGE Mary E b Dunbarton. Vol: 6 Page: 061

BURBANK Walter F & MORRISON A Elmira m Nov 21, 1912 Concord. Groom: age 23 b Hopkinton s/o BURBANK Irvin D b Hopkinton & FRENCH Augusta G b Hopkinton. Bride: age 26 b Londonderry d/o MORRISON Royal R b New London & TOWNES Ella b New Boston. Vol: 6 Page: 061

O'NEAL Frank Wilson & BLANCHETTE Alice m Dec 4, 1912 Hopkinton. Groom: age 28 b Salisbury s/o O'NEAL James b Hillsborough & HOAR Mary b Salisbury. Bride: age 19 b Goffstown. Vol: 6 Page: 061

ARCHIBALD George Wm & LOTHROP Marion Harrison m Mar 1, 1913 Hopkinton. Groom: age 27 b Nova Scotia s/o ARCHIBALD George b Nova Scotia & CROUSE Louisa b Nova Scotia. Bride: age 24 b Charlestown Mass d/o LOTHROP George b Hyannis Mass & HUTCHINSON Adelaid b Charlestown Mass. Vol: 6 Page: 062

CORLISS Hosea F & HAYES Elizabeth D m Jun 18, 1913 Everett Mass. Groom: age 32 b Hudson s/o CORLISS James M F b Hudson & BUNKER Hattie E b Maine. Bride: age 30 b Chelsea Mass d/o HAYES George R b England & Isabel b Scotland. Vol: 6 Page: 062

HOWLETT James D & MORRILL Mary Agnes m Jun 21, 1913 Hopkinton. Groom: age 38 b Prince Edward Island s/o HOWLETT George b New York & Flora b Prince Edward Isl. Bride: age 36 b Concord d/o MORRILL Luther S b Concord & GAGE Mary A b Hopkinton. Vol: 6 Page: 062

DUNBAR George E & GUILD Grace E m Jul 6, 1913 Dunbarton. Groom: age 46 b Hopkinton s/o DUNBAR Elmer B b Hopkinton & WEBBER Ann T b Hopkinton. Bride: age 30 b Hopkinton d/o GUILD Royal E b Hopkinton & STORY Abbie A b Hopkinton. Vol: 6 Page: 063

HACKETT Edwin Joseph & HOWLETT Florence Imogene m Jul 1, 1913 Penacook. Groom: age 26 b Hopkinton s/o HACKETT Walter C b Sanbornton & CROWELL Nellie M b Hopkinton. Bride: age 31 b Keene d/o SYMONDS Walter b California & SANBORN Sarah A b Alexandria. Vol: 6 Page: 063

CHASE Carroll T & SHURTLEFF Emma May m Jul 26, 1913 Warner. Groom: age 20 b Hopkinton s/o CHASE Charles T b Salisbury & WEBBER Florence W b Hopkinton. Bride: age 21 b Webster d/o SHURTLETT John J b Lebanon & ELLINWOOD Fannie E b Manchester. Vol: 6 Page: 063

DAVIS Nathaniel Francis & BALL Nina May m Sep 15, 1913 Washington. Groom: age 37 b Warner s/o DAVIS Henry C b Warner & WHITTIER Alice b Webster. Bride: age 24 b Washington d/o BALL S N b Washington & BROOKS Carrie b Antrim. Vol: 6 Page: 064

KRZYZINICH John T & CARTER Grace I m Oct 4, 1913 Hopkinton. Groom: age 22 b Poland s/o KRZYZINICH Antoni b Poland & WELGARECKA Magdoliana b Poland. Bride: age 18 b Concord d/o CARTER James b Warner & CALIEF Mary b Concord. Vol: 6 Page: 064

BOHANAN Percy Ralph & FOWLER Alice Naomi m Oct 5, 1913 Hopkinton. Groom: age 21 b Hopkinton s/o BOHANAN John W b Sutton & JEWELL Delia

Hopkinton, NH Marriages 1898

A b Weare. Bride: age 21 b Newbury d/o FOWLER Elmer O b Newbury & LUND Leona b Piermont. Vol: 6 Page: 064

BLANCHETTE Harry & O'NEAL Mabel m Nov 12, 1913 Hopkinton. Groom: age 25 b New Boston s/o BLANCHETTE Joseph b Canada & BANGER Mary b Canada. Bride: age 18 b Kilmans Mills N B d/o O'NEAL Joseph b Kilmans Mills Nb & Minnie b Kilmans Mils Nb. Vol: 6 Page: 065

NICHOLS Elwin B & COLBY Sarah E m Nov 27, 1913 Hopkinton. Groom: age 51 b Weare s/o NICHOLS Joshua M b Henniker & COLLINS Mary. Bride: age 47 d/o COLBY Bailey K b Warner & SMITH Rosina b Hardwick Vt. Vol: 6 Page: 065

TALLANT Eugene A & LITTLE Emma J m Nov 30, 1913 Hopkinton. Groom: age 28 b Pelham s/o TALLANT Andrew b Meredith & ROBEY Angie b Lawrence Mass. Bride: age 23 b Hopkinton d/o LITTLE Charles E b Webster Nh & MATTIE B b Webster. Vol: 6 Page: 065

WILSON Edward R & LORD Cora May m Dec 15, 1913 Hopkinton. Groom: age 22 b Salem Mass s/o WILSON George A b Peabody Mass & BURTON Josephine H b Salem Mass. Bride: age 21 b Hopkinton d/o LORD George b New Market & HODGDON Hattie M b Hopkinton. Vol: 6 Page: 066

CLINE Earl O & SHORT Mary V m Oct 25, 1904 Franklin. Groom: age 18 b Swanton Vt s/o CLINE Frank C b Swanton Vt & LORD Hattie M. Bride: age 19 b Tilton d/o SHORT Harry L & CAMPBELL Addie. Vol: 6 Page: 032

KIMBALL Arthur C & BOHONAN Elsie D m Oct 29, 1904 Hopkinton. Groom: age 24 b Hopkinton s/o KIMBALL Charlie b Webster & WEBBER M Ella b Webster. Bride: age 25 b Hopkinton d/o BOHONAN John W b Sutton & JEWELL Delia A b Weare. Vol: 6 Page: 032

SHURTLEFF Charles A & MORAN Mary K m Oct 11, 1905 Concord. Groom: age 26 b Hopkinton s/o SHURTLEFF Samuel S b Waldron Vt & MILTON Mary b Hopkinton. Bride: age 17 b Hopkinton d/o MORAN Christopher b Concord & Mary b Ireland. Vol: 6 Page: 035

BOUTILIER Ernest Gray & WILCOX Bessie F m Nov 16, 1905 Hopkinton. Groom: age 21 b Halifax Ns s/o BOUTILIER William b Nova Scotia & Salena b Nova Scotia. Bride: age 18 b Petersham Mass d/o WILCOX Edward b Mass & WILCOX Mary b Leominster. Vol: 6 Page: 035

DEMSMORE Harlen W & PINARD Clara Bell m Apr 23, 1909 Hopkinton. Groom: age 20 b Hopkinton s/o DENSMORE James A b Tilton & LIBBY Ella J b Salisbury. Bride: age 17 b Andover d/o PINARD Lenis b Claremont & ---- ---- b Grafton. Vol: 049 Page: 049

CLOUGH M Tenney & MOFFETT Adalade D m Mar 14, 1905 Hopkinton. Groom: age 66 b Hopkinton s/o CLOUGH Willard b Hopkinton & DUSTIN Charotte b Hopkinton. Bride: age 48 b Fall River Mass d/o BASSETT Davis T b Maine & SHERMAN Hannah b Rhode Island. Vol: 6 Page: 033

HAZELTINE Joseph W & HARDON Annie May m Apr 2, 1905 Hopkinton. Groom: age 31 b Concord s/o HAZELTINE John b Concord & BAKER Mary Annie b Concord. Bride: age 29 b Hopkinton d/o HARDON Charles b Mansfeild Mass & MCCARTHY Anne Eaton b Winteport Me. Vol: 6 Page: 033

HIBBARD James A & JEROLD Sarah Jane m May 3, 1905 Hopkinton. Groom: age 64 b Charlestown Mass s/o HIBBARD James C b Lebanon & SCOTT Emily b Albany Vt. Bride: age 69 b Loudon d/o CHASE William F b Loudon & HAINES Mary b Loudon. Vol: 6 Page: 033

Hopkinton, NH Births 1902-1937

Format for this chapter: Birth year/month/day, Child's name, Where <u>recorded</u>, Father's name, Mother's name, Father's birthplace, Mother's birthplace. The child's actual place of birth was not given in most years.

1917/01/07, Smith Morris W, Hopkinton, Smith Harold, Braley Bessie S, Hopkinton, Grafton

1917/04/02, Hook Claribel, Hopkinton, Hook Wm. I, Walsh Catherine, Fallas City Neb, Ireland

1912/01/28, Bartlett Ruth Orrall, Hopkinton, Bartlett Clifton J, Chase Lida H, Warner, Hopkinton

1912/02/10, Cline Cecil Ray, Hopkinton, Cline Earl O, Short Mary V, Swanton VT, Tilton

1912/04/09, Guerin Mamie Alice, Hopkinton, Guerin George, Welcome Sarah, Manchester, Canada

1912/04/14, Hardy Alta May, Hopkinton, Hardy Ernest B, Rayno Susie I, Ben Bow MO, Hopkinton

1912/05/01, Parfitt Wiliam Andrew, Hopkinton, Parfitt William J, Tallant Laura A, Stowe VT, Pelham

1917/04/09, Taylor Dorris Roberta, Hopkinton, Taylor Howard, Melcher Eva, W. Townsend MA, Thornton

1917/01/04, Kay Albert E, Hopkinton, Kay James, Clark Lillian,

1917/04/15, Provencher Evelyn Mary, Hopkinton, Provencher Albert, Bean Florence, Michigan, Johnstown NY

1917/04/26, Dwinnells Jennie Ella, Hopkinton, Dwinnells George, Smith Lena, Hopkinton, Quebec CAN

1921/01/02, Barton Maurice Wilson, Hopkinton, Barton Leslie C, Severence Isabelle D, Concord, Washington

1917/06/07, Howley Mary Ellen, Hopkinton, Howley James, Corcoran Mary, Augusta ME, Keysville NY

1917/07/17, Putney Grace Elizabeth, Hopkinton, Putney Ira, Barker Bessie, Hopkinton, Dublin

1917/07/23, Ripley Katherine Lena, Hopkinton, Ripley George, Davis Abberta, Hopkinton, Berlin

1917/08/09, Hood Laurence Francis, Hopkinton, Hood George, Brown Fronie, Warner, Manchester

1917/08/19, Nudd Carol Eugenia, Hopkinton, Nudd Charles, Martel Charlotte, Warner, Manchester

1917/08/20, Woodbury Barbara Mary, Hopkinton, Woodbury Nathaniel, Moran Margaret, No Weare, Hopkinton

1917/11/03, Flanders Maurice Henry, Hopkinton, Flanders Maurice, Makepeace Cora, Sutton, Concord

1917/11/20, Davis Thomas Maisom, Hopkinton, Davis Thomas, Oman Florence, Hopkinton, Dorchester

1917/12/21, Watts Frances Edith, Hopkinton, Watts John A, Kimball Edith, Hopkinton, Hopkinton

1918/01/16, Emerson Jean, Hopkinton, Emerson Roy D, Currier Florence G, Warner, Hopkinton

1918/01/28, Hathaway-No Name, Hopkinton, Hathaway Charles H, Murphy Margaret, Montreal Canada, New York NY

1918/02/03, Cooper Baby, Hopkinton, Cooper Herbert D, Burgess Gertrude V, Concord, Caribou ME

1918/03/03, Sweatt Eugene A, Hopkinton, Sweatt Jesse J, Lord Mabel E, Millfield, Hopkinton

1918/03/10, Barton Eugene A, Hopkinton, Barton Leslie C, Severence Isabelle D, Hopkinton, Washington

1918/03/27, Griffin Roy Goodhue, Hopkinton, Griffin Daniel A, Goodhue Marguerite A, Hopkinton, Webster

1918/03/31, Davis Norman Francis, Hopkinton, Davis Nathaniel, Ball Nina May, Warner, Washington

1918/04/13, Guimond Lawrence E, Hopkinton, Guimond Fred Z, Currier Donna F, Manchester, Warner

1918/04/25, McMalon Edith Harriet, Hopkinton, McMalon William F, Dunn Bertha M, Moretown VT, Fitzwilliam

1918/04/27, Severence Josephine F O, Hopkinton, Severence Will J, Fowler Florence, Washington, Washington

1918/05/06, Wescott Marion, Hopkinton, Wescott Benj C, Ager Flora M, Bristol, Hopkinton

1918/05/14, Weast John James, Hopkinton, Weast James A, Barlow Bessie M, Princenton NY, Mariaville NY

1918/05/18, Hoyt Clara Bernice, Hopkinton, Hoyt Jesse J, Grace Etta M, Hillsboro, Bradford

1918/06/25, Holmes - No Name, Hopkinton, Holmes Myron W, Flanders Lucy J, Hopkinton, Warner

1918/08/20, Stamiels Elinor, Hopkinton, Stamiels Arthur H, Healey Belle M, Croydon, North Dakota

1918/09/01, Straw Arlee Mae, Hopkinton, Straw Clayton B, Rollins Agnes M, Hopkinton, Hopkinton

1918/10/01, Pepler Marjorie Enid, Hopkinton, Pepler Alfred W, Daniels Harriet E, Canterbury, Webster

1918/10/01, Rouse Vera Virginia, Hopkinton, Rouse Loren L, Noreen Annie J, Canada, Sweden

1918/10/06, Montgomery- No Name, Hopkinton, Montgomery William I, Omnan Agnes, Warner, Boston MA

1918/10/10, Tilton Raymond Wendell, Hopkinton, Tilton Joseph N, Rollins M Alice, Hopkinton, Hopkinton

1918/12/01, Blanchard- No Name, Hopkinton, Blanchard Bert G, Bohanan Edna, Greenfield, Hopkinton

1918/12/14, Marcy Ethel Rebecca, Hopkinton, Marcy John H, Baker Mildred F, Cambridge MA, Hopkinton

1918/12/17, Champney Alfred James, Hopkinton, Champney Louis F, Moore Laura E, Sharon VT, London VT

1918/12/17, Bohanan Percy R, Hopkinton, Bohanan Roy Irving, Fowler Alice M, Hopkinton, Newbury
1918/12/19, Gomes Hugo Reinhold Jr, Hopkinton, Bomes Hugo Reinhold, Carlson Alma T, Sweden, Providence RI
1918/12/25, Mudge Lillian Christina, Hopkinton, Mudge Frand C, Sargent Mary A, Bedford, Goffstown
1919/01/27, Lindquist Paul Alexander, Hopkinton, Lindquist Carl, Nilson Hilda, Sweden, Sweden
1919/02/11, Bohanan Lois Ruth, Hopkinton, Bohanan J Harry, Marcy Esther G, Hopkinton, Cambridge MA
1919/02/15, Guerin Etta May, Concord, Guerin Edward R, Chase Susie M, Raymond, Hopkinton
1919/02/20, Provencher Doris Florence, Hopkinton, Provencher Albert J, Bean Florence E, Bay City Mich, Johnstown NY
1919/03/11, Cooper Milo, Hopkinton, Cooper Clarence C, Crockett Lena B, Concord, Laconia
1919/03/23, Derry Angus Joseph, Hopkinton, Derry Angus P, Leet Mary H, Hopkinton, Nova Scotia
1919/04/08, Hopkins Christobel Hattie, Hopkinton, Hopkins Wm. B, Grace Hattie B, Canada, Wilmot
1919/04/12, Howley-No Name, Hopkinton, Howley James, Corcoran Mary, Portland ME, Keysville NY
1919/04/18, Putney Margaret Maria, Hopkinton, Putney Ira A, Barker Bessie, Hopkinton, Dublin
1919/05/11, Davis Esther, Concord, Davis Willie N, Emerson Florence, Warner, Webster
1919/05/17, Bunten John, Hopkinton, Bunten John, Barnard Mary, Concord, Dunbarton
1919/05/27, Bailey Frances Viola, Hopkinton, Bailey George W, Chase Gertrude, Warner, Hopkinton
1919/06/08, Barton Lloyd Alfred, Hopkinton, Barton Leslie C, Severence Isabelle, Concord, East Washington
1919/08/06, Kay Harold Donald, Hopkinton, Kay James, Clark Lillian F, Fall River MA, Warner
1919/08/07, Flanders Frank Irving, Hopkinton, Flanders Frank W, Burbank Helen A, Goshen, Hopkinton
1919/08/18, Holmes Edwin C, Hopkinton, Holmes Myron W, Flanders Lucy J, Hopkinton, Warner
1919/09/03, Boutwell Russell, Concord, Boutwell Ralph E, Hackett Jennie M, Concord, Hopkinton
1919/09/30, Dwinnells Lucillie Estelle, Hopkinton, Dwinnells George A, Smith Lena M, Hopkinton, Canada
1919/11/05, Archibald Norma Adelaide, Hopkinton, Archibald George W, Lothrop Marion H, Nova Scotia, Charlestown MA
1919/11/22, Drown- No Name, Hopkinton, Drown Dorothy A, Warner
1919/11/24, Hoyt Maurice Edward, Hopkinton, Hoyt Jesse J, Grace Etta M, Hillsboro, Bradford

1919/12/20, Wunderlich Ruth May, Hopkinton, Wunderlich Charles, Clark Alice K, Worcester MA, Warner

1919/11/20, Dustin Daniel E, Hopkinton, Dustin Daniel H, Ashby Sylvia, Hopkinton, Concord

1920/01/12, Adams Velna C, Newport, Adams Ralph, Harding Jennie, Sunapee

1920/02/15, Barnard Clifford J, Hopkinton, Barnard Raymond J, Farnum Ruth, Hopkinton, Lancaster

1920/02/23, Bohman Russell Wallace, Concord, Bohman J Harry, Marcy Esther G, Hopkinton, Cambridge MA

1920/02/28, Blake Lewis William, Hopkinton, Blake Willie C, Towne Chassie I, Thornton, Weare

1920/02/29, Hoyt Elisabeth Emma, Hopkinton, Hoyt Edward, Blanchette Delia, Bradford, Goffstown

1920/03/22, Hoyt Lyman Leslie, Hopkinton, Hoyt Charles S, Severence Effie, Hopkinton, East Washinton

1920/03/29, Greenly Norman Earl, Hopkinton, Greenly Vernon M, Wilson Isabel M, Oxford, Deering

1920/04/11, Derry Charles William, Hopkinton, Derry Augus P, Leet Mary H, Hopkinton, Nova Scotia

1920/04/21, Emerson Sterling Parker, Hopkinton, Emerson Walter, Teakles Effie B, Goffstown, New Brunswick

1920/04/24, Merrill Frederick George, Hopkinton, Merrill Fred A, Hayford Arlene, Franklin, Goffstown

1920/05/11, Dockham -No Name, Hopkinton, Dockham Forrest E, Bletcher Vera, Guilford, Dover

1920/05/19, Martin Catherine E, Hopkinton, Martin Edward, Dwinels Edna M, Prince Edward Is, Hopkinton

1920/06/04, Fields-No Name, Hopkinton, Fields Evan S, Rolloff Margaret E, Barhadoes W I, Dunkirk NY

1920/07/11, Goodwin Genievieve, Hopkinton, Goodwin William E, Smith Susie, Manchester, Halifax N. S.

1920/08/16, Day Lewis Reginald, Hopkinton, Day Charles E, Corliss Ruth A, Northwood, Northwood

1920/08/28, Marcy Dorothy Mildred, Hopkinton, Marcy John, Baker Mildred, Cambridge MA, Hopkinton

1920/09/04, Oslund Alma, Concord, Oslund Carl E, Pierce Helen A, Worcester MA, Orvoidville

1920/09/11, Hurd Gertrude Winifred, Hopkinton, Hurd Walter B, Nuttall Annie F, England, New Brunswick

1920/09/14, Flanders Lawrence Earle, Hopkinton, Flanders Charles O, Drew Florence, Warner, Concord

1920/09/27, Montgomery Elizabeth, Hopkinton, Montgomery William L, Oman Agnes, Warner, Boston MA

1920/10/02, Boman Elizabeth Eudora, Hopkinton, Boman Lester J, Eaton Blanche B, Weare, Newbury

1920/10/04, Ripley Grace Ellen, Hopkinton, Ripley George H, Davis May, Hopkinton, Berlin

1920/10/09, Clay Anna Iola, Hopkinton, Clay Edward H, Sargent Agnes I, Franklin, Warner

1920/10/15, Blanchette Philip Harold Jr, Hopkinton, Blanchette Philip H, Hardy Linnie F, Franklin, Warner

1920/10/22, Sornberger Cyril Wallace, Hopkinton, Sornberger Eddie M, McCoubrey Mary J, Canada, Salisbury

1920/10/29, Dorrey Lela West, Hopkinton, Dorrey Howard, Weeks Lela, Victory N. S., Nottingham

1920/11/15, Bunten Mary Frances, Hopkinton, Bunten John, Barnard Mary, Concord, Dunbarton

1920/12/20, Gomes-No Name, Hopkinton, Gomes Hugo R, Carlson Alma, Sweden, Providence RI

1920/12/23, Burbee No Names#, Hopkinton, Burbee Eligeh, Norris Annie B, Canada, Weare

1921/01/16, Lord Stanley A, Hopkinton, Lord Harold B, Corsen H Josephine, Lynn MA, Contoocook

1909/02/01, Ladd Margaret, Hopkinton, Ladd Dexter, Davis Maud, Epping, Raymond

1921/02/12, Geer Ruby Etta, Hopkinton, Geer Bert L, Bryant Candice, Canada, Moira NY

1921/02/12, Densmore Helen May, Hopkinton, Densmore Edward J, Libby Captola, Hopkinton, Hopkinton

1921/03/03, Barnard-No Name, Hopkinton, Barnard Raymond J, Farnham Ruth, Hopkinton, Lancaster

1921/03/17, Bohanan No Name, Hopkinton, Bohanan J Harry, Marcy Esther A, Hopkinton, Cambridge MA

1921/04/03, Meatly Helen, Hopkinton, Meatly Israel, Woodridge Ella M, Fitzwilliam, Lowell MA

1921/04/18, MmMahon Doris May, Hopkinton, MmMahon Wm L, Dunn Bertha M, Moretown VT, Fitzwilliam

1921/05/09, Hoyt Alice Helen, Hopkinton, Hoyt Edward J, Blanchette Delia, Bradford, Goffstown

1921/05/22, Elliott Eva E, Hopkinton, Elliott Eden, Glasier Annie, Michigan, New York

1921/05/26, Harris Florence May, Hopkinton, Harris Wm F, Seaberg Matilda, Watertown MA, Sweden

1921/05/30, Young Peter Milton, Concord, Young Waldo N, Milton Dorothy, Manchester, Hopkinton

1921/07/19, Story Harry O Jr, Hopkinton, Story Harry O, Foster Mertie E, Canaan, Rummney

1921/07/21, Boutwell Lawrence, Hopkinton, Boutwell Ralph E, Hackett Jennie M, Concord, Hopkinton

1921/08/26, Cooper Wallace Elmer, Hopkinton, Cooper Clarence C, Crockett Lena B, Concord, Laconia

1921/08/26, Derry Mary Teresa, Hopkinton, Derry Angus P, Leet Mary H, Hopkinton, Nova Scotia

1921/09/06, Putney John Sanborn 3rd, Hopkinton, Putney John S Jr, Houston Dorothy, Chicago, Roxbury MA

1921/10/10, Hoyt Flora E, Hopkinton, Hoyt Charles S, Severence Effie E, Bradford, East Washington

1921/10/10, Hoyt Florence E, Hopkinton, Hoyt Charles S, Severence Effie E, Bradford, East Washington

1921/11/10, Champney Caroline M, Hopkinton, Champney Roger E, Clark Hester A, Boscawen, Hopkinton

1921/12/29, Flanders Hazel Augusta, Hopkinton, Flanders Fred W, Burbank Helen A, Goshen, Hopkinton

1922/01/02, Burber Dorothy Anne, Hopkinton, Burber Elijah, Norris Anna B, Canada, Weare

1922/01/04, Brown Barbara Louise, Hopkinton, Brown Lanson O, Carter Susie W, Thornton, West Concord

1922/01/16, Goodwin Madeline, Hopkinton, Goodwin Wm E, Smith Susie, Manchester, Halifax N. S.

1922/03/08, Buntin Forrest Kinsley, Hopkinton, Buntin John E, Barnard Mary W, Concord, Dunbarton

1922/03/13, Little Thelma Vivian, Hopkinton, Little William B, Mould Emma, Hopkinton, England

1922/03/21, Straw Margaret Gertrude, Hopkinton, Straw Clayton B, Rollins Agnes M, Hopkinton, Hopkinton

1922/03/21, Whittier Olive Etta, Hopkinton, Whittier Wesley P, Green Rachel I, Concord, Dunbarton

1922/03/24, Libby Arthur Francis, Hopkinton, Libby George K, Manning Ellen G, Hopkinton, Cambridge MA

1922/04/07, Montgomery June, Hopkinton, Montgomery Wm L, Donovan Agnes, Warner, Boston MA

1922/04/10, Dockman George Elmore, Hopkinton, Dockman Forrest E, Blatcher Vera, Gilford, Dover

1922/04/14, Hoyt -No Name, Hopkinton, Hoyt Jesse J, Grace Etta M, Hillsboro, Bradford

1922/05/11, Dony Earl, Hopkinton, Dony Howard, Demerit Lela E, Victory N. S., Nottingham

1922/08/13, Provenchier Marion L, Hopkinton, Provenchier Albert, Bean Florence C, Bay City Mich, Johnstown NY

1922/06/17, Barnard Dean Clinton, Hopkinton, Barnard Raymond, Farnum Ruth, Hopkinton, Lancester

1922/06/19, Bergstrom Edna May, Hopkinton, Bergstrom Sexton, Dalyrimple Edna, Maynard MA, Chelsea MA

1922/07/04, Langlev Donald Chase, Hopkinton, Langlev Howard G, Nelson Laura, Gilmanton, Perth Amboy NJ

1919/06/24, Goodrich John Prescott, Hopkinton, Goodrich John P, Wright Pauline, Fall River MA, Warner

1937/01/03, Dexter Priscilla Ann, Hopkinton, Dexter Stanley, Cooper Lena, Concord, Hopkinton

1922/09/04, Lord Donald Edgar, Hopkinton, Lord Harold B, Corsen H Josephine, Lynn MA, Hopkinton

1927/01/01, Montgomery Roger William, Hopkinton, Montgomery Wm L, Oman Agnes, Warner, Boston MA

1922/10/29, Thompson Elmer John, Hopkinton, Thompson Elmer J, Lyon Rose M, Webster, Whitman MA

1922/10/29, Morand Jacqueline Edith, Hopkinton, Morand Leroy, Segall Ruth, Brooklyn NY, Rumania

1922/11/04, Huniston Bernard Elmer, Hopkinton, Huniston Herbert, Speers Victoria, Powers Court CAN, Warehouse Pt CT

1922/11/22, Oslund Carol Evelyn, Hopkinton, Oslund Carl, Pierce Helen A, Worcester MA, Orford

1922/11/24, Mudge Henry Louis, Hopkinton, Mudge Frank, Sargent Mary, Bedford, Goffstown

1922/12/22, Densmore Sadie Dean, Hopkinton, Densmore Edward J, Libby Captola Dean, Hopkinton, Hopkinton

1923/02/23, Geer Neal Andrew, Hopkinton, Geer Bert L, Bryant Candice A, Canada, Moria NY

1923/03/20, Moulton Ruth Edna, Hopkinton, Moulton Augustus, Mignault Edna, Bridgewater, Webster

1923/03/20, Symonds Bruce K, Hopkinton, Symonds Arthur G, Chase Winnifred, Hopkinton, Hopkinton

1923/03/22, Clark Arlene Myrtle, Hopkinton, Clark James F, Drowns Lilla M, Warner, Warner

1923/04/05, Adams Cynthia J, Newport, Adams Ralph, Harding Jennie, Franklin, Newport

1923/05/22, Bean Myla Grace, Hopkinton, Bean Maurice, Sanborn Hazel, Bristol, Meredith

1923/05/25, Greenly Dana Fay, Hopkinton, Greenly V. Merrill, Wilson Isabel, Orford, Deering

1923/06/02, Clifford James, Lowell MA, Clifford James E, McCoffey Mary, Watertown MA, Lowell MA

1923/06/15, Clay Edw Athur, Hopkinton, Clay Edward Henry, Sargent Agnes Iola, Franklin, Warner

1923/06/24, Bailey Everett Chas, Hopkinton, Bailey George W, Chase Gertrude M, Warner, Hopkinton

1923/06/28, Harris Jennie Eliz, Hopkinton, Harris Wm. F, Sealy Mathilda, Watertown MA, Sweden

1923/06/29, Billings Herbert S, Hopkinton, Billings Herbert S, Whittemore Emily, Manchester, Penacook

1923/07/07, Dockham Verne Bletcher, Hopkinton, Dockham Forrest E, Bletcher Vera, Gilford, Dover

1923/07/16, Hoyt Carl Edward, Hopkinton, Hoyt Edward F, Blanchette Delia, Bradford, Goffstown

1923/07/25, Fogg Laura Eva, Hopkinton, Fogg Clifton W, Bean Bessie M, Laconia, Gilford

1923/08/11, Deney Margaret Frances, Hopkinton, Deney Angus P, Leet Mary H, Hopkinton, Nova Scotia

1923/09/09, Bohanan Meta, Hopkinton, Bohanan J Harry, Marcey Esther G, Hopkinton, Cambridge MA

1923/09/14, Barnard Reta Lucila, Hopkinton, Barnard Pearl D, Craig Eulalie M, Hopkinton, Dixmont ME

1923/09/27, Shampany John Robert, Hopkinton, Shampany Will G, Clark Mary V, Sharon VT, Hopkinton

1923/10/03, Hastings Alfred Floyd, Hopkinton, Hastings Floyd D, Hardy Mildred P, Hopkinton, Hopkinton

1923/12/01, Dwinells Walter, Hopkinton, Dwinells George A, Smith Lena M, Hopkinton, Canada

1923/12/03, Barnard Nila Mabelle, Hopkinton, Barnard Raymond J, Farnham Ruth, Hopkinton, Lancaster

1924/01/01, Perry Clara Ella, Hopkinton, Perry Charles H, Beals Gladys E, Hopkinton, Goffstown

1924/01/04, Emerson Constance Chase, Hopkinton, Emerson Lloyd S, Chase Miriam, Providence RI, Hopkinton

1924/01/09, Clausen Mary, Boston MA, Clausen Albert V, Bailey Alice, Medford MA, Brookfield MA

1924/03/10, Cooper Carrie Eva, Hopkinton, Cooper Clarence C, Crockett Lena B, Concord, Laconia

1924/03/25, Burgess Florence Evelyne, Hopkinton, Burgess Walter O, Roby Annie P, Concord, Boscawen

1924/04/03, Moram Dean Straw, Hopkinton, Moram Reginald, Straw Blanche M, Concord, Hopkinton

1924/04/06, Dorry Hazel Avis, Hopkinton, Dorry Howard, Weeks Lela E, Nova Scotia, Nottingham

1924/04/10, Bumpus Harriet Janet, Hopkinton, Bumpus Charles, King Marion L, Westminster MA, Sutton MA

1924/06/06, Sweatt Viola May, Hopkinton, Sweatt Jesse J, Lord Mabel E, Millsfield, Hopkinton

1924/06/10, Northrup Alice Audrey, Hopkinton, Northrup Jay, Judd Mildred, Lisborn NY, Canada

1924/06/28, Darling Dana Brock, Lowell MA, Darling Millard S, Beals Mildred, Lowell MA, Lowell MA

1924/08/10, Densmore Alice Viola, Hopkinton, Densmore Edward, Libby Captola, Hopkinton, Hopkinton

1924/08/16, Hoyt Isiac F, Hopkinton, Hoyt Edward, Blanchette Delia, Bradford, Goffstown

1924/08/24, Colt-No Name, Hopkinton, Colt Loren R, Harris Ruth M, Canada, Newport VT

1924/08/31, Hanks Eric Wallace, Hopkinton, Hanks William E, Sealey Matilda, Watertown MA, Sweden

1924/10/03, Hurd Audrey Caroline H, Hopkinton, Hurd Walter B, Nuttall Annie, England, St Johns N. B.

1925/01/13, Sonerberger Muriel Verbal, Hopkinton, Sonerberger Eddie, McCoubrey Mary J, Canada, Canada

1925/02/18, Sullivan John Hugh, Contoocook, Sullivan Edward, Dwinnells Manoie, Chester VT, Hopkinton

1925/04/17, Bohonan Margaret Elinor, Hopkinton, Bohonan Percy, Fowler Alice N, Hopkinton, Newbury

1925/04/28, Brown Olive Muriel, Contoocook, Brown Lanson O, Carter Susie W, West Thornton, Concord

1925/06/20, Boynton Gordon Farnham Jr, Concord, Boynton Gordon F, Peaslee Grace E, Howell NY, Weare

1925/07/20, Graves Doris Irene, Hopkinton, Graves Burt W, Tenney Harriet I, Sheldon VT, So Royalston VT

1925/08/11, Clifford Edward, Lowell MA, Clifford James, McCaffrey Mary G, Watertown MA, Lowell MA

1925/08/19, Rice Donald Neal, Concord, Rice Neal J, Haven Unice M, Hopkinton, Penacook

1925/08/26, Prescott Theresa Myrtle, Contoocook, Prescott Wilfred M, Goodwin Edna E, Wilmont, Newport

1925/09/30, Mitchell Priscilla Agnes, Concord, Mitchell Wallace H, Fletcher Pearl A,

1925/10/13, Fitts Thelma Loie, Hopkinton, Fitts Geo F, Hardy Bertha I, Alexandria, Salisbury

1925/10/25, Kimball Frank E Jr, Hopkinton, Kimball Frank E, Derry Hazel J, Canterbury, Hopkinton

1925/11/13, Severance George Leslie, Hopkinton, Severance Alfred T, Cooper Ethel A, Hopkinton, Hopkinton

1925/12/21, Stevens Ernest L Jr, Hopkinton, Stevens Ernest L, Hathaway Rita V, Hopkinton, Canada

1925/12/22, Cooper-No Name, Hopkinton, Cooper Clarence C, Crockett Lena, Concord, Laconia

1925/12/23, Glanville Manley A Jr, Concord, Glanville Manley A, Devine Helen, Everett MA, Newark NJ

1925/12/31, Sweatt Harriet M, Hopkinton, Sweatt Jesse J, Lord Mabel E, Millsfield, Hopkinton

1926/03/06, Maschino Mary Frances, Contoocook, Maschino Emil, Thornton Margaret, Roslindale MA, Gardner MA

1926/03/06, Sullivan Norma Ruth, Hopkinton, Sullivan Homer A, Frye Doris E, Quebec, Hopkinton

1926/05/03, Downes Arleen Ann, Hopkinton, Downes Daniel, Sargent Alice E, Andover, Warner

1926/05/01, Burgess Fayette Delmo, Contoocook, Burgess Royal F, Adams Hazel E, Plymouth MA, Contoocook

1926/05/06, Barton - No Name, Hopkinton, Barton Leslie, Severence Isabelle, Hopkinton, Washington

1926/06/25, Emerson Russell Stone, Contoocook, Emerson Lloyd S, Chase Miriam, Providence RI, Hopkinton

1926/08/23, Little Charles Edward, Hopkinton, Little William B, Mould Emma L, Hopkinton, England
1926/09/06, Dorry Avis Eunice, Hopkinton, Dorry Howard, Demerritt Lela, Nova Scotia, Nottingham
1926/09/20, Harris John Henry, Hopkinton, Harris William F, Seabury Matilda, Watertown MA, Sweden
1926/09/24, Hoyt Thelma Clara, Hopkinton, Hoyt Edward, Blanchette Delia, Bradford, Goffstown
1926/09/25, Straw Mary Ann, Hopkinton, Straw Clayton B, Rollins Agnes M, Hopkinton, Hopkinton
1926/09/29, Clay John Laughton, Hopkinton, Clay Edward H, Sargent Agnes I, Franklin, Warner
1926/10/23, Boynton Elizabeth Ann, Concord, Boynton Gordon F, Peaslee Grace E, Hornnell NY, Weare
1927/04/01, Montgomery Roger William, Contoocook, Montgomery Wm. L, Oman Agnes, Warner, Boston MA
1927/01/04, Robertson June Clarice, Contoocook, Robertson Moses P, Brill Muriel H, Henniker, Carroll
1927/01/15, Mitchell -No Name, Contoocook, Mitchell Wallace H, Fletcher Pearl A, Contoocook, Laconia
1929/02/19, Duclos-No Name, Hopkinton, Duclos Francis, Robar Laura, Lewis NY, Chesterfield NY
1927/02/12, Billings Beverly Ann, Contoocook, Billinsg Herbert S, Whittemore Emily M, Manchester, Concord
1927/03/22, Brassau Eleanor, Hopkinton, Brassau Curtis E, Straw Doris L, Fitzwilliam, Franklin
1927/04/30, Burgess Edward Winston, Contoocook, Burgess Royal F, Adams Hazel E, Plymouth MA, Contoocook
1927/02/26, Porter Mabelle Irene, Hopkinton, Porter William A, Harvey Isabel A, Nova Scotia, Nova Scotia
1927/06/19, Carns Marjorie Frances, Concord, Carns Herbert C, Bell Irene F, Hopkinton, Portchester NY
1927/05/03, Geer Herrick E, Hopkinton, Geer Bert L, Bryant Candice A, Quebec, Moria NY
1927/06/21, Barton Norma Mary, Concord, Barton Elmar Ray, O'Brien Catherine, West Concord, Boston MA
1927/06/27, Hall Rita May, Concord, Hall Charles, Willard Josephine, Warner
1927/08/30, Clough Marilyn, Contoocook, Clough Harold R, Sawyer Raeline R, Hopkinton, Hopkinton
1927/09/05, Bartlett Raymond Joseph, Hopkinton, Bartlett Roy O, Hanks Esther, Hopkinton, No Stratford
1927/09/16, Perry Edward Herbert, Hopkinton, Perry Charles, Beals Gladys, Hopkinton, Goffstown
1927/11/02, Smart Muriel Dawn, Contoocook, Smart Harold B, Hood Ruth M, Warner, Hopkinton
1928/02/04, Kimball Lewis Butler, Concord, Kimball Lewis B, Foley Grace A, Hopkinton, Blackville N. B.

1928/04/03, Dorrey Pearl Edith, Hopkinton, Dorrey Howard, Demeritt Lela, Bear River N. S., Nottingham

1928/04/18, Graves Donald Earle, Hopkinton, Graves Burl W, Tenney Harriet J, Sheldon VT, S. Royalton VT

1928/06/20, Cooper Nellie Viola, Hopkinton, Cooper Clarence E, Crockett Lena B, Concord, Laconia

1928/07/10, Bergstrom Walter Mark, Hopkinton, Bergstrom Oscar R, Osland Clara M, Maynard MA, Providence

1928/08/23, Little William Burton, Hopkinton, Little William B, Mould Em L., Hopkinton, England

1928/08/27, Ripley Richard Arthur, Hopkinton, Ripley George, Davis May A, Hopkinton, Berlin

1928/02/05, Brown Barbara May, Concord, Brown Gilman D, Tucker Katherine M, Dunbarton, Warner

1928/04/04, Gray Murial Alice, Concord, Gray Arthur W, Pema Teckla, Gloucester MA, Gloucester MA

1930/09/15, Flamand-No Name, Hopkinton, Flamand William J, Giguere Evelyn L, Canada, Concord

1928/06/27, Reed Stanton Kimball, Concord, Reed Robert G, Kimball Elizabeth, Contoocook, Concord

1928/09/19, Harris Dorothy Gertrude, Hopkinton, Harris Wm F, Seaberry Matilda, Watertown, Sweden

1928/09/05, Cressy William Manley, Royalton MA, Cressy Chas Byron, Redington Muriel B, Bradford, Warner

1928/11/14, Libby Ruth Elizabeth, Contoocook, Libby Geo K, Manning Ellen G, Contoocook, Cambridge MA

1937/01/11, Johnson Olive Danice, Hopkinton, Johnson Oliver D, Wells Margaret, Acton Maine, Franklin

1928/09/22, Nedeau Frances Raymond, Concord, Nedeau Ernes H, Ballow Dorothy, Meredith, Holyoke MA

1928/10/29, Barton Raylene Louise, Concord, Barton Elmer Ray, O'Brien Catherine, W. Hopkinton, Boston MA

1928/09/09, Barnard Cora Frances, Concord, Barnard Raymond, Farnham Ruth, Hopkinton, Lancaster

1937/01/13, Derry Everett John, Hopkinton, Derry Angus J, Bartlett Marjorie, Hopkinton, Warner

1929/01/31, Bartlett Ruth Ann, Contoocook, Bartlett Roy O, Hanks Esther B, Concord, Stratford

1929/02/19, Conant Blanch Mable, Concord, Conant Hiram E, Flanders Hilda, Contoocook, Warner

1929/03/30, Duclos-No Name, Hopkinton, Duclos Francis, Robar Laura, Lewis N Y, Chesterfield NY

1929/04/20, Story Robert Foster, Concord, Story Ralph N, Bolivar Violet, Canaan, Auburn

1929/08/07, Danielson Gordon Wesley, Contoocook, Danielson Henning E, Clarkson Ruth, Worcester MA, Worcester MA

237

1929/09/10, Flammand Jeanette Evelyn, Hopkinton, Flammand William J, Giguere Evelyn, Concord, Concord

1929/09/30, Cooper Eloise Florence, Concord, Cooper Robert A, Cowdrey Florence M, Hopkinton, Lowell MA

1929/10/09, Burbank Mary Alvis, Concord, Burbank Carl Henry, Stevens Evelyn May, Hopkinton, East Weare

1929/10/26, Barton Charles Henry, Hopkinton, Barton Leslie C, Severence Isabelle, Concord, Washington

1929/11/22, Richardson Edith Viola, Hopkinton, Richardson Leslie A, Hamilton Jennie W, Mcgallaway Md, Cumberland ME

1929/11/26, Hoyt Geneve Ruth, W. Hopkinton, Hoyt Edward, Blanchette Delia, Bradford, Goffstown

1929/05/28, Townes Audrey Faye, Pittsfield, Townes Shirley O, Emerson Nora B, Weare, Pittsfield

1929/06/09, Holmes Lyle Allen, Concord, Holmes Leon A, Young Irene B, Bridgewater MA, Warner

1929/12/08, Rice-No Name, Concord, Rice Neal J, Haven Eunice M, Hopkinton, Peancook

1929/12/09, Reddy Samuel Jr, Concord, Reddy Samuel, Gillingham Catherine, Scituate MA, Jacksonville FL

1930/01/05, Hathaway Gary, Concord, Hathaway George, Smart Dorothy, Montreal, Ossipee

1930/01/11, Hardy Lucy Marie, W. Hopkinton, Hardy Francis Anzel, Cooper Ruth May, Webster, Hopkinton

1930/02/05, Feltis Jacqueline, Concord, Feltis Wendall E, Machino Rose Anna, Quincy MA, Roislindal MA

1930/02/25, Archibald-No Name, Concord, Archibald Stewart G, Chase Bertha M, Nova Scotia, No Charlestown

1930/02/26, Derry Anne Elizabeth, Concord, Derry Angus P, Leet Mary Helen, Hopkinton, Nova Scotia

1937/01/20, Bailey William S Jr, Hopkinton, Bailey William S, Lowe Alice, Contoocook, Fitchburg MA

1930/05/30, Cooper Joseph Albert, Hopkinton, Cooper Clarence C, Crockett Lena, Concord, Laconia

1930/05/31, Turgeon Pauline E, Hopkinton, Turgeon Paul, Shaw Florence E, Somersworth, Augusta ME

1930/06/19, Smith Lucille Ottalia, Concord, Smith Warren J, Lynch Ruby, Whitefield, Charlestown WV

1930/06/30, Stevens Mary Louise, Concord, Stevens Shirley, Flanders Ellen, Portland ME, Hopkinton

1930/07/19, Hastings Elsie Helen, Hopkinton, Hastings Wesley H, Rosebrook Elsie H, Grantham, Guildhall VT

1930/07/19, Johnson-No Name, Hopkinton, Johnson A J, Ineson Marion E, Melrose MA, Weare

1930/07/08, Patch Cynthia Mae, Concord, Patch Guy Johnson, Danforth Emma M, Hopkinton, Hopkinton

1930/08/07, Clough Charles Elmer, Concord, Clough Harold R, Sawyer Raeline, Contoocook, Contoocook

1930/08/12, Sturtevant Evelyn F, Contoocook, Sturtevant Cecil O, Gould Doris E, Manchester, Bedford

1930/08/24, Nolan Leona Irene, Hopkinton, Nolan James Kenneth, Connelly Bernice G, Sutton, Halifax N. S.

1930/09/01, Call Roderic Arthur, Concord, Call Everett H, Mansur Helen, Webster, Concord

1930/10/06, Bartlett-No Name (James), Concord, Bartlett Roy O, Hanks Ester, Contoocook, Stratford

1930/11/29, Glanville-No Name, Concordon, Glanville Manley A, Devine Helen A, Everett MA, Newark NJ

1930/11/30, Straw Phyllis Una, Hopkinton, Straw Clayton Bayard, Rollins Agnes May, N H, N H

1931/02/04, Clark Sylvia Roselle, Hopkinton, Clark Floyd E, Field Eva A, Fitzwilliam, Merimack

1931/02/20, Brown Gilman Arthur, Concord, Brown Gilman D, Tucker Catherine M, Dunbarton, Warner

1931/03/23, Nyberg Gail Marilyn, Hopkinton, NYberg Russell T, Tebbetts Edna L, Manchester, Nashua

1931/05/07, Boynton Janice Gwendolyn, Concord, Boynton Gordon F, Peaslee Grace E, Hornell NY, Weare

1931/05/09, Duclos-No Name, Concord, Duclos Francis, Robar Laura, Willsboro NY, Keesiville NY

1931/06/02, Cooper Lloyd Chester, Penacook, Cooper George E, Keaton Annabel M, Hopkinton, Webster

1931/06/13, Smith Geraldine Dorothy, Concord, Smith Roy, Lessard Eugenia, Contoocook, Raymond

1931/06/24, Starkey Frank Richard, Newport, Starkey Frank E, Miller Evelena, Newbury, Newport

1937/02/16, Sargent Arthur F Jr, Hopkinton, Sargent Arthur F, Hurd Gertrude, Roxbury MA, Hopkinton

1931/07/16, Barton Elisabeth M, Hopkinton, Barton Leslie, Severence Isabelle, Concord, East Washington

1931/08/02, Smith Elizabeth Emma, Hopkinton, Smith Warren J, Lynch Robie A, Whitefield, Huntington WV

1931/11/20, Austin Leona Beatrice, Concord, Austin William A, Caswell Leona B, Cambridge MA, Cochituate MA

1931/09/09, Harris - No Name, Concord, Harris William F, Seaberg Matilda, Watertown MA, Sweden

1931/10/08, Fellows Joseph Byron, Hopkinton, Fellows Joseph A, Cooper Eva M, Washington VT, Bradford

1931/10/10, Hardy Ansel Francis, W. Hopkinton, Hardy Francis A, Cooper Ruth M, Salisbury, Hopkinton

1931/10/21, Childs Cynthia Jane, Concord, Childs Stewart I, Rice Ruth E, Sunderland, Warren MA

239

1931/10/31, Billings-baby#, Concord, Billings Herbert S, Whittemore Emily, Manchester, Concord

1931/11/03, Emery Beverly Jean, Concord, Emery Floyd C, Frost Susie B, Plymouth, Concord

1931/11/18, Call Joan Mansur, Contoocook, Call Everett H, Mansur Helen M, Webster, Concord

1937/02/22, Wunderlich Paul H, Hopkinton, Wunderlich Frank, Wunderlich Evelyn, W. Hopkinton, W. Hopkinton

1931/12/10, Bohanan David March, Hopkinton, Bohanan J Harry, Marcy Esther C, Hopkinton, Cambridge MA

1931/12/25, Sturtevant Carol Anne, Concord, Sturtevant Orlando, Gould Doris, Manchester, Bradford

1937/02/27, Call Bernice C, Hopkinton, Call Robert L, Hoyt Clara B, Caboll Missouri, Hopkinton

1932/01/07, Hodge Rita May, Contoocook, Hodge Barker M, Sargent Dorothy M, Jackson, Boston MA

1932/01/15, Haley Ella Corinne, Hopkinton, Haley Louis W, Curtis Ann A, N. Adams MA, Cheshire MA

1932/02/20, Blanchette Donivan Arthur, W. Hopkinton, Blanchette Philip J, Clark Evelyn M, NH, W. Hopkinton

1932/03/01, Story Theodore Allen, Concord, Story Ralph N, Bolivar Violet, NH

1932/04/16, Oslund-No Name, Concord, Oslund Carl E, Pierce Helen A, Worcester MA, Orford

1937/05/24, Mclaren Donald, Hopkinton, McLaren Walter E, Graham Freda J, Waterwon MA, Truro N. S.

1932/05/09, Clark Edith Marion, W. Hopkinton, Clark James F, Drown Lilla Mabel, Warner, Warner

1932/05/25, Rice Fay Anne, Concord, Rice Earl J, Melcher Evelyn R, Hopkinton, Hopkinton

1932/05/30, Hoyt David Crosby, Hopkinton, Hoyt Clair F, Crosby Phebe, Hillsboro, Wentworth

1937/06/15, Bohanan Clifton M, Hopkinton, Bohanan Clifton R, Dunham Florence, Hopkinton, S. Shafsbury VT

1932/08/02, Holmes-No Name, Concord, Holmes Leon A, Young Irene D, Bridgewater MA, Warner

1932/08/14, Clark-No Name #, W. Hopkinton, Clark Georgiana M, W. Hopkinton

1932/08/21, Blakey-No Name, Concord, Blakey Richard B, Spurlin Heather L, Manchester, Biddeford ME

1932/08/24, Bartlett -No Name (Kenneth Harold), Concord, Bartlett Roy O, Hanks Esther, Concoord- Davisville, Stratford

1932/08/25, Chase Margaret Eva, Concord, Chase Edward, Houde Eva M A, Contoocook, Lowell MA

1932/08/26, Grazino Rita Odelle, Concord, Grazino Thomas A, Nelson Margery L, Concord, Concord

1932/09/03, Rollins-No Name, Hopkinton, Rollins Wm H L, Chase Mildred,

1932/09/15, Wunderlich John Timothy, Henniker, Wunderlich Frank, Robertson Evelyn T, Hopkinton, Hopkinton

240

1932/09/18, Sullivan Barbara Jean, Concord, Sullivan Edward, Dwinnells Marion S, Chester V, Contoocook

1932/09/02, Starkey - No Name, Hopkinton, Starkey Frank E, Miller Evelena, Newbury, Newport

1932/09/23, George Charlie Edward, Hopkinton, George Earl E, Bartlett Alice I, Concord, Hopkinton

1937/08/12, Babson Jerole Lee, Hopkinton, Babson John L, Carruthers Jean, Gloucester MA, Orano ME

1932/10/10, Bailey William Hall, Concord, Bailey George N, Matherson Alice E, Somerville MA, Concord

1932/10/12, Reed Robert George, Concord, Reed Robert G, Kimball Elisabeth, Contoocook, Hopkinton

1932/10/22, Turgeon Evelyn Grace, Hopkinton, Turgeon Paul, Shaw Florence E, Somersworth, York ME

1932/11/29, Densmore Ruth Agnes, Contoocook, Densmore Edw J, Libby Captola D, Contoocook, Contoocook

1932/12/05, Stevens Charles Albert, Hopkinton, Stevens Chas. A, Shaw Bertha Am, Hopkinton, Salisbury

1932/12/05, French Joseph Nathaniel, Concord, French Joseph N, Tanberg Yoland, Boston MA, Norway

1937/09/05, Tilton Erdine Anona, Hopkinton, Tilton Robert E, Mount Anoma, Concord, Brockton MA

1932/12/17, Haley Millicent May, Contoocook, Haley Louis W, Curtis Anna A, N. Adams MA, Cheshire MA

1932/12/29, Hardy-No Name, Hopkinton, Hardy Ansel Francis, Cooper Ruth May, Webster, Hopkinton

1933/01/16, Allen Patricia Ann, Concord, Allen Charles L, Little Beatrice E, Ctr Harbor, Mt Dors FL

1933/01/16, Severence Norman Richard, Pembroke, Severence Archie, Gagnon Odena, Hopkinton, Pembroke

1933/02/08, Smith Robert Harold, Concord, Smith Leroy, Lessard Eugenia, Contoocook, Raymond

1933/03/12, Patch Everett Edmund, Concord, Patch Guy J, Danforth Emma M, Hopkinton, Hopkinton

1933/03/14, Chase Walter Carroll, Concord, Chase Walter B, Harriet Andrews, Brooklyn NY, New Boston

1933/03/23, Jameson Ellinor Marie, Hopkinton, Jameson Henry B, Dunlap Mabel, Bow, Hillsboro

1933/03/28, Sawyer Baby #, Concord, Sawyer Harry B, Cody Ruth, Thetford VT, Canaan

1937/09/29, Northup Richard W, Hopkinton, Northup Leon J, Whitney Mildred, Lisbon NY, Antrim

1933/04/23, Coen Barbara Ann, Concord, Coen Scott J, Ladd Doris, Tilton, Contoocook

1933/01/13, Hastings Loren A, Cornish, Hastings Herbert, Rosebrook Elsie H, Grantham, Guildhall VT

1933/05/05, Martin Beverly Ann, Concord, Martin Edward, Dwinnells Edna, Prince Edw Is, Contoocook

1933/06/22, Stevens Mary Elizabeth, Concord, Stevens Howard A, Ineson Mary E, Hopkinton, East Weare

1933/06/29, Mccarthy Wm. Francis, Manchester, McCarthy Mary, Contoocook

1933/06/30, Bieber Robert Engel, Concord, Bieber Geo W, Engel Marion, Lisborn Falls ME, Penacook

1933/07/09, Nyberg Richard Allen, Hopkinton, NYberg Russell T, Tibbetts Edna L, Manchester, Nashua

1933/07/31, Bean Robert Morrison, Concord, Bean John E, Prichard Doris, Johnstown NY, Hillsboro

1933/08/26, Call Barbara, Contoocook, Call Everett H, Mansur Helen, Webster, Concord

1937/10/25, Blanchette Beverly Ann, Hopkinton, Blanchette Philip J, Clark Evelyn M, Goffstown, Hopkinton

1933/09/08, Brown Chas. Willis Jr, Concord, Brown Chas. W, Eddy Barbara, Lebanon, Northfield MA

1933/10/04, Cooper Marjorie Rose, Concord, Cooper Geo E, Keaton Annabelle, Hopkinton, Webster

1933/10/13, Oslund Carl Enar, Concord, Oslund Carl E, Pierce Helen A, Worcester MA, Orford

1933/11/16, Barnard Maurice Edgar, Hopkinton, Barnard Raymond J, Farnham Ruth, Hopkinton, Lancaster

1934/01/16, Blanchette Zelma Dorothea, W. Hopkinton, Blanchette Harry, Morton Nellie May, New Boston, New Brunswick

1934/01/27, Severance Norma Florence, Pembroke, Severance Archie, Gagnon Odina, Hopkinton, Suncook

1934/02/03, Townes Baby, Concord, Townes Shirley O, Emerson Nora B, East Weare, Pittsfield

1934/02/26, Cressey Bryon George, Concord, Cressy Wm. A, Hall Olive M, Bradford, Contoocook

1934/02/27, Barnard George Richard, Concord, Barnard Perley, Craig Eulala, Hopkinton, Dixmont ME

1934/03/10, Cressy Clifton Neal, Concord, Cressy Chas. B, Reddington Muriel, Bradford, Warner

1934/01/29, Smart Alice Elaine, Concord, Smart Francis, Stevens Olive, Wolfeboro, Hopkinton

1934/04/15, Coen Robert Scott, Concord, Coen Scott, Ladd Dois, Tilton, Contoocook

1934/04/24, Disconoff Peter Andre, Concord, Disconoff Andre, Hotian Evelyn, Moscow Russia, Austria

1934/06/20, Estey Leona Jane, Concord, Estey Raymond C, Mount Eleanor, Providence RI, Brockton MA

1934/06/21, Farrar Beulah Aimee, Concord, Farrar Elbert R, Floyd Iva S, Hillsboro, Concord

1934/06/26, Courchene Beverly An, Concord, Courchene Anatole, Aldrich Doris, VT, Concord

1934/06/30, Macdonald Weldon Lee, Concord, MacDonald Grant, Maylan Dorothy, New Brunswick, Laconia

1934/07/02, Tyler Rosalie May K, E. Lempster, Tyler Elwin, Krzyzaniak Helen, NY, Contoocook

1934/07/24, Johnson Thomas H Jr, Concord, Johnson Thomas H, Downes Isabelle, Concord

1934/08/02, Bailey Norman Ralph, W. Hopkinton, Bailey Ralph G, Clark Nellie V, Contoocook, Weare

1934/08/24, Graziano Gary Stanley, Contoocook, Graziano Thomas, Nelson Margery, Concord, Concord

1934/08/31, Brown Burton Earl, Concord, Brown Chas. W, Eddy Barbara, Enfield, Northfield MA

1934/09/17, Mills Beverly Ann, Concord, Mills Harry C, Brown Nettie, Salisbury, Concord

1934/09/27, Smith Oris, Concord, Smith Leroy, Lessard Eugenia V, Contoocook, Raymond

1934/11/03, Robinson -No Name, W. Hopkinton, Robinson Everett B, Page Dorothy G, W. Hopkinton, Hillsboro

1937/11/01, Howley Robert Jordon Jr, Hopkinton, Howley Robert W, Jordan Shirley, Contoocook, Ireland

1934/12/06, Hardy Betty Ann, W. Hopkinton, Hardy Ansel F, Cooper Ruth M, Webster, Hopkinton

1937/11/05, Hammond David H, Hopkinton, Hammond J H (Rev), Goodwin Helen J, Indiana, Bridgewater MA

1934/12/28, George Leonard Lutherd, W. Hopkinton, George Earl E, Bartlett Alice I, Concord, W. Hopkinton

1934/11/16, Gray Lois, Concord, Gray C Maurice, Page Evelyn, Alton, Gilford

1934/11/22, Starkey Sally Lou, Concord, Starkey John C, Bartlett Marjorie S, Sutton, No Anson IN

1934/12/14, Morgan Albert Leon Jr, Concord, Morgan Albert L, Hurlbutt Ruth, Warner, Groveton

1935/01/04, Byers Joann Alice, Hopkinton, Byers Eldon D, Wunderlich Alice, Mars Hill ME, Hopkinton

1935/01/11, Cayer Neil Thomas, W. Hopkinton, Cayer Horace T, Miller Arline, W. Hopkinton, Newport

1935/02/10, Hall Kristin, Concord, Hall Lawrence W, Allen Phyllis, Freeport Me, Portland ME

1937/11/23, Smith Virginia Gail, Hopkinton, Smith Leroy C, Lessard Eugenia, Contoocook, Concord

1935/04/09, Plourde-No Name, Concord, Plourde Edward F, Reardon Helen, Manchester, Hampstead L I

1935/05/01, Stevens Della May, Hopkinton, Stevens Charles A, Shaw Bertha M, Hopkinton, Salisbury

1935/05/13, Houle William J, Concord, Houle William E, Gilman Mona, Concord, Alton

1935/05/19, Blanchard Sheldon G, Concord, Blanchard Francis G, Gillingham Ruth, New Boston, New Hampton

1935/06/05, Leavitt Thomas W, Concord, Leavitt Charles T, Lampron Irene C, Northwood, Concord

1935/06/05, Bean Sara Lucille, Concord, Bean John E, Prichard Doris, Johnstonw NY, Hillsborough

1935/06/21, Crowley Joanne Louise, Concord, Crowley William H, King Lean, Concord, Orange MA

1935/07/17, Call Nathan Perry, Contoocook, Call Everett H, Mansur Helen, Webster, Concord

1935/08/09, Brown Joan Danice, Concord, Brown John D, Sargent Eveleen D, Hopkinton, Roxbury MA

1935/08/19, Crawford Arnold Hanson, Concord, Crawford Ralph E, Bletcher Lena, Enfield MA, Dover

1935/08/20, Lawson Jeanne Marie, Concord, Lawson Arthur O, Provencher Mary, Contoocook, Warner

1935/08/23, Coen Richard Allen, Concord, Coen Scott J, Ladd Doris M, Tilton, Contoocook

1935/09/26, Suszynski Joseh Felex, W. Hopkinton, Suszynski Felix, Przybylska Helen, Poland, Poland

1935/10/12, Martin Marlene Ann, Manchester, Martin Harold, Farmer Vivian, Hillsboro, Weare

1935/10/19, Farrar Alice Julia, Concord, Farrar Elbert R, Floyd Iva, Hillsboro, Concord

1935/11/12, Fuller Nancy Jean, Concord, Fuller Robert R, Colby Madeline, Contoocook, Warner

1935/11/29, Moore Elaine Emily, Contoocook, Moore Andrew G, Hardy Myrtle, Loudon, Henniker

1935/12/18, Smith Lorraine Deleno, Concord, Smith Leroy C, Lessard Eugenia, Contoocook, Raymond

1937/12/02, Brown Bruce A, Hopkinton, Brown Charles W, Eddy Barbara E, Lebanon, Northfield MA

1936/01/16, Bailey Ellen Elizabeth, Hopkinton, Bailey Ralph G, Clark Nellie V, Hopkinton, No Weare

1936/03/14, Robertson Dorothy Ann, W. Hopkinton, Robertson Everett, Page Dorothy G, W. Hopkinton, Hillsboro

1936/02/14, Campbell Sylvia Howell, Concord, Campbell Howell P, Belrose Elsie D, Concord, Boston MA

1936/02/26, Leavitt Donald Brian, Concord, Leavitt Wilfred, Story Pauline, Concord

1936/02/27, Severance William, Concord, Severance Archie, Gagne Odina, Hopkinton, Suncook

1936/02/28, Graziano Nora Etta, Concord, Graziano Thomas, Nelson Margery, Concord, Concord

1936/03/05, Howley Jane Ellen, Concord, Howley Robert W, Jordan Shirley, Contoocook, Irleand

1937/12/13, Johnson Frank D, Hopkinton, Johnson Thomas H, Downes Isabele, Mt Holly VT, Concord

1936/03/31, Babson Jean Lois, Concord, Babson John L, Carruthers Jean C, Gloucester MA, Orano ME

1936/04/12, Ballam Carlton D, Hopkinton, Ballam John, Warren Mary, Chelsea MA, Robinston ME

1936/04/14, Owen Megan, Concord, Owen Harold H, Guyol Louise, Portsmouth, Concord

1936/06/25, Jenkins Baby #, Concord, Jenkins Carol, Garland Grace, Davisville, Tilton

1936/07/11, Page Victor Leslie, Concord, Page Lester, Krzyaniak Helen, Henniker, Contoocook

1936/07/17, Clough Dennis Joseph, Hopkinton, Clough Augusta K, Bailey Hazel M, Wentworth, Wh. River Jct VT

1936/07/27, Mignault George Richard, Concord, Mignault Edward A, Drouin Rose, Webster, Concord

1937/12/22, Stevens Marguerite L, Hopkinton, Stevens Chas A, Shaw Bertha M, Hopkinton, Salisbury

1936/08/18, George Richard Erving, Henniker, George Earl E, Bartlett Alice I, Concord, W. Hopkinton

1936/09/03, Crowley William Harold, Concord, Crowley William H, King Leah, Concord, Orange MA

1936/09/09, Estey Donald Raymond, Concord, Esty Raymond C, Mount Eleanor, Providence RI, Brockton MA

1936/09/13, Bergstrom - No Name, Concord, Bergstrom Ernest, Prentiss Florence, Saugus MA, Concord

1936/10/31, Barton - No Name, W. Hopkinton, Barton Leslie C, Severance Isabelle, Concord, East Washington

1936/11/02, Morgan Wayne Wilfred, Concord, Morgan Albert L, Hurlbutt Ruth, Warner, Groveton

1936/11/29, Stevens Priscilla, Concord, Stevens Ernest Lee, Stevens Rita V, Hopkinton, Farnham Quebec

1936/11/29, Brown Baby Girl#, Concord, Brown John Daniel, Sargent Eveleen, Contoocook, Roxbury MA

1902/02/10, Boutwell Esther May, Hopkinton, Boutwell Arthur J, Fitts Carrie J, Hopkinton, Dunbarton

1902/02/15, Clough Harold Roland, Hopkinton, Clough Charles E, Hastings Gertrude, Hopkinton, Hopkinton

1902/02/15, Dwinnells Margaret V, Hopkinton, Dwinnells Frank P, Libby Emma H, Hopkinton, Hopkinton

1937/05/24, Mckenna Francis G, Hopkinton, Mckenna France E, Gilbert Carmen, Concord, Stewartstown

1902/03/08, Libby Captolia D, Hopkinton, Libby Frank D, Mcintire Dora, Hopkinton, New Brunswick

1902/05/02, Cameron Claude, Hopkinton, Cameron Oscar A, Fisk Florence, Coaticook P Q, Concord N. S.

1902/05/29, Wing-No Name#, Hopkinton, Wing Frank, Messer Clara, Woburn MA, New York

1902/06/26, Brassau Frank, Hopkinton, Brassau Frank, Emma, Northfield VT, Stanberge P Q

1902/07/12, Fuller Roland F, Hopkinton, Fuller William F, Elkins Eva B, Hopkinton, Thornton

1937/08/09, Bailey Norma Frances, Hopkinton, Bailey Ralph G, Clark Nellie V, Contoocook, Weare

1902/10/10, Severance Archie W, Hopkinton, Severance Will, Fowler Florence E, Washington, Washington

1902/11/09, Stevens Viola Lovisa, Hopkinton, Stevens Edgar W, Manchester, P E Island

1902/11/22, Hood No-name, Hopkinton, Hood George G, Brown Fannie E, Peterborough, Goffstown

1902/12/01, Colby No Name, Hopkinton, Colby Forest, Paige Ross Belle, Litchfield CAN, Dunbarton

1902/12/09, Short -No Name, Hopkinton, Short Harry L, Campbell Addie, Sherbrooke, Manchester

1902/12/22, Goodwin -No Name, Hopkinton, Goodwin Walter E, Howe Eva M, Hopkinton, Rowley MA

1902/12/30, Guimond -No Name, Hopkinton, Guimond Zoel, Paige Lura, Canada, Canada

1903/02/01, Cooper Robert Albert, Hopkinton, Cooper Herbert D, Burgess Gertrude Viola, Concord, Caribou ME

1903/03/15, Rice Earl Jacob, Hopkinton, Rice James G, Bohonan Bernice M, Henniker, Hopkinton

1903/04/27, Huntoon Grovenor Aril, Hopkinton, Huntoon Arthur C, Eastman Ethel E, Unity, Warner

1903/04/30, Nelson Mildred, Hopkinton, Nelson Lewis Arthur, Chase Bertha Maude, Warner, Hopkinton

1903/06/14, Smith Harold Robert, Hopkinton, Smith Robert, Boyce Ardelia, Boscawen, Concord VT

1903/06/23, Walker - No Name, Hopkinton, Walker Abraham S, Bradbury Mabel, Canada, Washington

1903/06/24, Marshall Marjorie E, Hopkinton, Marshall Harry W, Cressey Nettie M, Webster, Bradford

1903/08/12, Spiers Virginia, Hopkinton, Spiers Junius B, Haskins Mabel, Reams VA, Boston MA

1903/08/18, Flanders Abial Carter, Hopkinton, Flanders Walter H, Thompson S. Lizzie, Warner, Concord

1903/08/27, Davis Audrey Aline, Hopkinton, Davis Horace J, Carroll Junie B, Warner, Sutton

1903/08/31, Kimball George R G, Hopkinton, Kimball Robert W, Elliott Susie, Pittsfield, Haverhill MA

1903/08/31, Reed Robert George, Hopkinton, Reed Frank H, George Helen, Boston MA, Barnstead

1903/09/15, Merrill Leon Stanley, Hopkinton, Merrill Harry E, Callaghan Alice L, Concord, Canada

1903/11/16, Baker-No Name, Hopkinton, Baker Fred Leon, Woodward Lula G, Andover, Wilmot

1903/12/02, Putnam - No Name, Hopkinton, Putnam Charles R, Clough Nancy E, Hopkinton, Hopkinton

1903/12/05, Howe Florence Hazel, Hopkinton, Howe Edwin B, Eyman Etta, Warner, Bradford

1903/12/12, Sargent Lizzie Irene, Hopkinton, Sargent Arthur H, Pickering Dora, Canterbury, Meredith

1903/12/14, Chandler Lizzie Irene, Hopkinton, Chandler Arthur O, Miller Jennie C, Vermont, Dundee Scot

1903/12/14, Chandler Mary Jean, Hopkinton, Chandler Arthur O, Miller Jennie C, Vermont, Dundee Scot

1904/02/18, Nudd Warren Alfred, Hopkinton, Nudd John B, Chase Gertrude M, Warner, Hopkinton

1904/02/23, Dwinnells Marion Sarah, Hopkinton, Dwinnells George A, Howley Mary, Hopkinton, Portland ME

1904/03/31, Blood George Calvin, Hopkinton, Blood George, Mudgett Nellie F, Ballardvale MA, Bristol

1904/04/09, Fenton Agnes M, Hopkinton, Fenton Leander, Elkins Rosa B, Nova Scotia, Thornton

1904/04/17, Sleeper Everts M, Hopkinton, Sleeper C Everts, Morrill Elsie L, Franklin, Springfield

1904/04/30, Elliott Elsie Arline, Hopkinton, Elliott Clarence T, Collins Alma H, Webster, Gilmanton

1904/05/04, Case Lilliam May, Hopkinton, Case George A, Quimby Jennie N, Francestown, Enfiled

1904/05/17, Patch Frank George, Hopkinton, Patch George E, French Elsie B, Hopkinton, Derrfield

1904/06/20, Blanchard Aline, Hopkinton, Blanchard Walter R, Ray Ola M, Greenfeild, Orange

1904/06/30, Montgomery Willard Clough, Hopkinton, Montgomery Scott, Clough Mary R, Hopkinton, Hopkinton

1904/08/05, Kimball- No Name, Hopkinton, Kimball Nelson, Patch Adalade M, Hopkinton, Newfield ME

1904/08/24, Cooper Ralph Herbert, Hopkinton, Cooper Herbert D, Burgess Gertrude V, Concord, Caribou ME

1904/08/24, Guildbault -No Name, Hopkinton, Guildbault Ovid, Guerin Mary, Canada, Manchester

1904/10/23, Huntoon Marguerite May, Hopkinton, Huntoon Frank W, Austin Adeline, Hopkinton, Highgate VT

1904/11/02, Clark Hester A, Hopkinton, Clark Fred, Cooper Mabel E, Hopkinton, Concord

1904/11/09, Geer Harold Herman, Hopkinton, Geer Calvin R, Perry Bertha M, Canada, Hopkinton

1904/12/09, Sawyer Raelene Richards, Hopkinton, Sawyer Elmer E, Mudgett Lillian M, Warner, Weare

1905/01/17, Ward Harvey Ernest, Hopkinton, Ward Gardner M, Hazard Ida J, Franklin, Milford MA

1905/02/19, Littlefield Howard A Watts, Hopkinton, Littlefield Burt, Watts Ida M, Kennnebunk ME, Hopkinton
1905/02/22, Severance Alfred T, Hopkinton, Severance Willie J, Fowler Florence E, Washington, Washington
1905/03/10, Wing Harold Mason, Hopkinton, Wing Frank B, Messer Clara C, MA, Saratoga NY
1905/03/15, Carr John Sheldon, Hopkinton, Carr John, Symonds Edna, Hopkinton, Hopkinton
1905/03/18, Cooper Lizzie Augusta, Hopkinton, Cooper Clarence C, Crockett Lena M, Concord, Laconia
1905/03/28, Flanders Ellen French, Hopkinton, Flanders Fred W, Burbank Helen, Goshen, Hopkinton
1905/04/10, Chandler Ralph Wellman, Hopkinton, Chandler George W, Durnin Sarah, Hopkinton, Scotland
1905/04/16, Bascom Dorothea I, Hopkinton, Bascom Fred, Flanders Rosa, Canada, Hopkinton
1905/05/01, Morrill Annie C, Hopkinton, Morrill Ernest L, Cookson Hattie E, Springfield, Burnham ME
1905/06/07, Perry Carroll F, Hopkinton, Perry Walter G, Barnard Flora J, Campton, Weare
1905/07/09, Preston Dorothy, Hopkinton, Preston Charles A, Davis Mary A, New Boston, Warner
1905/07/17, Kelley Grace Ethelyn, Hopkinton, Kelley Arthur J, Brown Ethelyn G, Hopkinton, Hopkinton
1905/08/19, Cilley Raymond G, Hopkinton, Cilley Elden Gardner, Wight Florence A, Weare, Hopkinton
1905/08/19, Spofford Frank Lincoln, Hopkinton, Spofford Arthur F, Dodge Maud E, Hopkinton, Hopkinton
1905/08/31, Chandler Florence Mildred, Hopkinton, Chandler Arthur O, Miller Jennie C, Vermont, Scotland
1905/09/21, Smith Fred D, Hopkinton, Smith Robert, Boyce Ardelle E, Webster, Concord
1905/09/28, Kimball Mildred Ella, Hopkinton, Kimball Arthur C, Bohonan Elsie B, Hopkinton, Weare
1905/10/04, Briggs Ronald, Hopkinton, Briggs John L, Higgins Edith B, Wilmot, Manchester
1905/10/04, Briggs Ralph Clinton, Hopkinton, Briggs John L, Higgins Edith B, Wilmot, Manchester
1905/10/31, Stevens Marjorie Frances, Hopkinton, Stevens Waldron F, McLane Alice W, Manchester, New Boston
1905/11/04, Clinton Ralston Dewitt, Hopkinton, Clinton Winfield M, Bartlett Cora M, Hopkinton, Warner
1905/11/05, Bartlett Roy Osborne, Hopkinton, Bartlett Clifton J, Chase Lida H, Warner, Hopkinton
1905/11/09, Burgess Fred Louis, Hopkinton, Burgess Walter O, Robie Annie P, Claremont, Boscawen

1905/11/21, Mitchell Wallace Harold, Hopkinton, Mitchell Dolph, Libby Stella G, Burlington VT, Hopkinton

1905/12/09, Kimball - No Name, Hopkinton, Kimball Robert W, Elliott Susie, Pittsfield, Exeter

1906/01/26, Mcleod -No Name, Hopkinton, McLeod Kenneth A, Bryer Bertha A, Nova Scotia, Surry

1906/02/16, Fuller-No Name, Hopkinton, Fuller G Irving, Reade Blanche M, Hopkinton, Marlborough

1906/02/23, Montgomery-No Name, Hopkinton, Montgomery Scott, Clough Mary R, Concord, Caribou ME

1906/03/24, Cooper Maud Ellen, Hopkinton, Cooper Herbert D, Cooper Gertrude V, Concord, Caribou ME

1906/03/25, Stevens Edgar Aaron, Hopkinton, Stevens Edgar W, Mcdonald Margarett L, Manchester, Prince Edward Island

1906/04/11, Card Maud Mildred, Hopkinton, Card Thomas B, Emerson Blanche M, St Croix N. S., Hopkinton

1906/04/13, Page Electa May, Hopkinton, Page Orrill, Dwinnells Josie D, Woodstock, Hopkinton

1906/05/25, Melcher Evelyn Ruth, Hopkinton, Melcher Maurice C, Libby Alice M, Thornton, Hopkinton

1906/05/22, Foote-No Name, Hopkinton, Foote William N, Watts Helen M, Farmington ME, Hopkinton

1906/06/08, Paige Elizabeth, Hopkinton, Paige Wesley A, Holmes Lillian, Franklin, Gardiner ME

1906/06/24, Lindquist Lillie Marion, Hopkinton, Lindquist Carl, Nelson Hilda, Sweden, Sweden

1906/08/19, Davis Mabel Fisk, Hopkinton, Davis H Russell, Fisk Mabel D, Warner, Hopkinton

1906/09/10, Morrill Dorothy Angie, Hopkinton, Morrill Ernest I, Cookson Hattie E, Springfield,

1906/09/30, Howley- No Name, Hopkinton, Howley James, Corcoran Mary, Manchester, Keeseville NY

1906/10/01, Richards Gladys Ruth, Hopkinton, Richards Wm. W, Page Abba A, Charlestown, Whiting ME

1906/04/20, Chase-No Name, Hopkinton, Chase Marl D, Hardy Clara M, Warren, Hopkinton

1906/11/08, Severance Dorothy Ada, Hopkinton, Severance Willie J, Fowler Florence, Washington, Washington

1906/12/08, Cooper George E, Hopkinton, Cooper Clarence C, Crockett Lena M, Concord, Laconia

1906/12/31, Libby Horace D, Hopkinton, Libby Frank D, Nichols Eldoro M, Hopkinton, New Brunswick N. S.

1907/01/04, Elliott Lawrence Sherman, Hopkinton, Elliott Clarence T, Collins Alma H, Webster, Gilmanton

1907/01/10, Clark Mary Viola, Hopkinton, Clark Fred, Cooper Mabel Eliza, Hopkinton, Concord

249

1907/03/05, Shurtleff Joseph Samuel, Hopkinton, Shurtlett Chas A, Moran Mary R, Hopkinton, Hopkinton
1907/03/06, Adams Hazel Emily, Hopkinton, Adams Claude D, Flathers Ida M, Hopkinton, Lawrence MA
1907/03/12, Law-No Name, Hopkinton, Law Francis P, Morrill Etta, Vermont, Springfield
1907/03/27, Fitts Clyde Ellsworth, Hopkinton, Fitts Jesse L, Prim Lula M, Dunbarton, Lynn MA
1907/04/02, Perry-No Name, Hopkinton, Perry James M, Kelly Editheen, Hopkinton, Hopkinton
1907/04/02, Patch John Norris, Hopkinton, Patch George E, French Elsie B, Hopkinton, Derrfield
1907/04/20, Giddings Hazel Ida, Hopkinton, Giddings John, Sawyer Ethel M, New Boston, Peterborough
1907/02/15, Hood Wallace Raymond, Hopkinton, Hood George G, Brown Phronie E, Peterborough, Goffstown
1907/04/29, Cline Donald, Hopkinton, Cline Earl O, Short Mary Victoria, Swanton VT, Tilton
1907/05/10, Baker Max Gilchrist, Hopkinton, Baker Harry A, Gilchrist Alice I, Andover, Henniker
1907/05/16, Smith Edgar Jesse, Hopkinton, Smith Jesse W, Flanders Mary S, Sutton VT, Bradford
1907/07/07, Kimball Frank Moses, Hopkinton, Kimball Herbert M, Colby Mary A, Hopkinton, Bow
1907/06/10, Tilton Sherburn G, Hopkinton, Tilton Joseph N, Rollins Mary A, Concord, Hopkinton
1907/07/07, Mayo-No Name, Hopkinton, Mayo David, Guillette Elsie, Champlain NY, Canada
1907/07/17, Kimball Ralph Harold, Hopkinton, Kimball Nelson D, Patch Adelaide M, Hopkinton, Newfield ME
1907/07/24, Elliott Charles, Hopkinton, Elliott Charles E, Howe Gertrude, Hopkinton, Jamaica Plain MA
1907/07/31, Dwinnell George Leroy, Hopkinton, Dwinnell Geo A, Howley Mary, Hopkinton, Portland ME
1907/08/20, Ladd Doris Marguerite, Hopkinton, Ladd Dexter, Davis Maud, Epping, Raymond
1907/08/04, Boynton Elizabeth M, Hopkinton, Boynton Arthur J, Clough Bessie J, Weare, Concord
1907/08/28, Locke Ruth Caroline, Hopkinton, Locke Edward C, Flanders Minnie C, Hopkinton, Henniker
1907/09/18, Carr Thoms Symonds, Hopkinton, Carr John Frank, Symonds Edna A, Hopkinton, Hopkinton
1907/10/11, Libby Winnifred M, Hopkinton, Libby Percy L, Hook Alice M, Maine, Hopkinton
1907/10/11, Severance-No Name, Hopkinton, Severance Wm. J, Fowler Florence E, Washington, Washington

1907/10/25, Huntoon Dorris M, Hopkinton, Huntoon Frank W, Austin Adeline, Hopkinton,

1907/11/04, Marsh-No Name, Hopkinton, Marsh Frank P, Dustin Etta, Dunbarton, Antrim

1907/03/23, Hardy-No Name, Hopkinton, Hardy Stillman A, Bagley Pauline, Hopkinton, Sydney Australia

1907/11/28, Hoyt Arnold Elwin, Hopkinton, Hoyt Harry I, Johnson Lillian M, Hopkinton, Canada

1907/12/02, Nelson Ruth Elinor, Hopkinton, Nelson Lewis A, Chase Bertha M, Warner, Hopkinton

1907/12/04, Guerin Dora Sarah, Hopkinton, Guerin George, Welcome Sarah, Manchester, Canada

1907/12/25, Morrill Lois Agnes, Hopkinton, Morrill Ernest L, Cookson Hattie E, Springfield, Burnham ME

1907/12/29, Bartlett -No Name, Hopkinton, Bartlett Clifton J, Chase Lida H, Warner, Hopkinton

1908/01/07, MacDougal Stuart, Hopkinton, MacDougal James A, Lincoln Sara M, Nova Scotia, Taunton MA

1908/01/26, Howley James Thomas, Hopkinton, Howley James, Corcoran Mary, Maine, Keesevilley NY

1908/03/07, Montgomery Grace Evelyn, Hopkinton, Montgomery Scott, Clough Mary C, Hopkinton, Hopkinton

1908/04/17, Danforth Emma May, Hopkinton, Danforth Edmund G, Foss Lucy A, Hopkinton, Hopkinton

1908/04/21, Hall George Edward, Hopkinton, Hall Frank E, Weeks Annie M, Hopkinton, Hopkinton

1908/05/06, Lindquest Ruth Evelyn, Hopkinton, Lindquest Carl J, Nelson Hilda, Sweden, Sweden

1908/05/19, Stevens Gertrude, Hopkinton, Stevens Arthur W, Watts Ida M, Manchester, Hopkinton

1908/05/27, Melcher Lyle Waldron, Hopkinton, Melcher Maurice C, Libby Alice W, Thornton, Hopkinton

1908/06/12, Kimball Bernerd Arthur, Hopkinton, Kimball Arthur C, Bohonan Elsie D, Hopkinton, Weare

1908/07/14, Tilton Mary Hazel, Hopkinton, Tilton Joseph N, Rollins Mary A, Concord, Hopkinton

1908/08/31, Cheney Charles Henry, Hopkinton, Cheney Charles H, Martin Ethel A, Bradford, Grafton

1908/09/03, Patch Guy Johnson, Hopkinton, Patch George E, French Elsie B, Hopkinton, Deerfield

1908/11/22, Chandler-No Name, Hopkinton, Chandler Geo W, Dimin Sarah, Hopkinton, Scotland

1908/12/14, Dow Lawrence Robert, Hopkinton, Dow Perley D, Currier Helen, Loudon, Hopkinton

1908/12/19, Hardy Charles Andrew, Hopkinton, Hardy Ernest B, Rayno Susie I, Ben Bow Mo, Hopkinton

1909/01/20, Moran Reginald Paul, Hopkinton, Moran Reginald T, Straw Blanche M, Concord, Hopkinton

1909/01/21, Taylor Leslie Edgar, Hopkinton, Taylor Howard L, Melcher Eva M, Townsend, Thornton

1909/01/31, Hardy Ellen Josephine, Hopkinton, Hardy Stillman A, Pauline S, Hopkinton, India

1909/02/05, Clark Harold Eugene, Hopkinton, Clark Fred, Cooper Mabel E, Hopkinton, Concord

1909/02/19, Corliss Viola Evanga, Hopkinton, Corliss James A, Stone Grace M, Hudson, Claremont

1909/03/18, Guerin Arthur Joseph, Hopkinton, Guerin Morrill, Guilbault Rosanna, New Boston, Canada

1909/03/18, Guerin Normand Morrill, Hopkinton, Guerin Morrill, Guilbault Rosanna, New Boston, Canada

1909/03/23, Austin Everett Carlos, Hopkinton, Austin Carlos G, Lull Bessie E, Swanton VT, Weare

1909/03/24, Fuller Doris Julia, Hopkinton, Fuller William F, Elkins Eva B, Hopkinton, Thornton

1909/04/28, Boutwell Allen Taft, Hopkinton, Boutwell Arthur J, Fitts Carrie J, Hopkinton, Dunbarton

1909/04/28, Guerin Laurence George, Hopkinton, Guerin George, Welcome Sarah, Manchester, Canada

1909/04/28, Kenney Frank Amos, Hopkinton, Kenney William A, Button Vernie E, Concord, Jefferson

1909/05/02, Cayer Horace Triffle, Hopkinton, Cayer Thomas E, Nudd Bessie, Manchester, Warner

1909/05/09, Wunderlich Anna Jane, Hopkinton, Wunderlich Charles, Clark Alice, Worcester MA, Warner

1909/07/12, Fitts - No Name #, Hopkinton, Fitts Jesse L, Prune Linda, Dunbarton, Lynn MA

1909/07/22, Bailey Ralph George, Hopkinton, Bailey George W, Chase Gertrude M, Warner, Hopkinton

1909/07/25, Cooper Mildred Irene, Hopkinton, Cooper Herbert D, Burgess Gertrude, Concord, Caribou ME

1909/07/30, Tilton Lawrence, Hopkinton, Tilton Joseph N, Rollins M Alice, Hopkinton, Hopkinton

1909/08/09, Howley-No Name, Hopkinton, Howley James, Corcoran Mary, Augusta ME, Keesville NY

1909/09/02, Nelson Barbara, Hopkinton, Nelson Lewis A, Chase Bertha M, Hopkinton, Hopkinton

1909/09/30, Morrill Nerna F, Hopkinton, Morrill Ernest L, Cookson Emma, Springfield, Burnham ME

1909/10/05, Peel Dorothy Lucille, Hopkinton, Peel Joseph G, Chase Jessie A, Lowell MA, Franklin

1909/10/26, Gilman Joseph Edward, Hopkinton, Gilman Warren G, Labontee Jennie, Newport RI, Henniker

1909/11/12, Drown Glennis Myrtle, Hopkinton, Drown Bert D, Leslie Mabel, Canada, Manchester

1909/11/20, Boynton Josephine Louise, Hopkinton, Boynton Arthur J, Clough Bessie J, Weare, Concord

1909/12/13, Parnell Annie, Hopkinton, Parnell Oscar, Evans Amanda E, North Carolina, Maxton NC

1910/01/30, Whitford Evelyn Ordway, Hopkinton, Whitford Richmond O, Davis Shirlie M, Bismarck ND, Warner

1910/02/17, Nelson Carl H, Hopkinton, Nelson John H, Corser Blanche A, Hopkinton, Hopkinton

1910/03/04, Montgomery Gladys May, Hopkinton, Montgomery Scott, Clough Mary R, Hopkinton, Hopkinton

1910/03/11, Hoyt- No Name, Hopkinton, Hoyt Harry I, Johnson Lillan May, Hopkinton, Canada

1910/03/29, Partridge Rose, Hopkinton, Partridge William, Swallow Minnie W, Waterville ME, Dorchester MA

1910/04/07, Densmore Marjorie Ollie, Hopkinton, Densmore William E, Libby Lillian, Hopkinton, Hopkinton

1910/03/30, Guerin-No Name, Hopkinton, Guerin George, Welcome Sarah, Manchester, Canada

1910/05/03, Winslow William H, Hopkinton, Winslow William H, Miller Bessie L, Fairfield ME, Page VA

1910/05/25, Boyce Gerald, Hopkinton, Boyce Harley A, Cronin Augusta, Hopkinton, Tilton

1910/05/29, Nudd Frank Horace, Hopkinton, Nudd John B, Clark Emma J, Warner, Warner

1910/06/10, Brown Gardner Albert, Hopkinton, Brown Lanson O, Fleming Melissa, Thornton, Canada

1910/06/14, Severance Harry Arthur, Hopkinton, Severance Herbert D, Colby Lena M, Manchester, Stoddard

1910/08/02, Hall Olive May, Hopkinton, Hall Frank E, Weeks Annie M, Hopkinton

1910/08/14, Cornett Elizabeth Frances, Hopkinton, Cornett Newton, Moran Mary, Jackson KY, Concord

1910/08/18, Bunten Shirlie Elizabeth, Hopkinton, Bunten Arthur W, Fuller Eva L, Manchester, Hopkinton

1910/10/04, Fitts Raymond Charles, Hopkinton, Fitts Jesse L, Prince Lilla M, Dunbarton, Lynn MA

1910/10/20, Rice-No Name #, Hopkinton, Rice James G, Bohonan Bernice, Henniker, Weare

1910/10/23, Elliott Edson Esau, Hopkinton, Elliott Eden E, Glazier Anna, Michigan, New York NY

1910/10/28, Taylor Lawrence Earl, Hopkinton, Taylor Howard, Melcher Eva, Townsend MA, Thornton

1910/11/16, Barnard Frederick Grover, Hopkinton, Barnard Grover C, Cushing Ines M, Dunbarton, Goffstown

1910/11/28, Cooper Ruth May, Hopkinton, Cooper Clarence C, Crockett Lena M, Concord, Laconia

1910/12/03, Cline Richard Emery, Hopkinton, Cline Earl O, Short Mary V, Swanton VT, Tilton

1910/12/12, Palmer Russell Freeman, Hopkinton, Palmer Albert O, Rollins Edith, Hopkinton, Hopkinton

1910/12/23, Huntoon-No Name, Hopkinton, Huntoon Frank, Austin Adeline, Hopkinton, Swanton VT

1911/01/08, Frye Doris Evelyn, Hopkinton, Frye Amos F, Sanborn Clara M, Worcester MA, Hopkinton

1911/01/12, Bunnell Eleanor, Hopkinton, Bunnell Alva S, Murray Ethel B, Henniker, Nova Scotia

1911/02/14, Tilton Doris Marion, Hopkinton, Tilton Joseph N, Rollins M Alice, Hopkinton, Hopkinton

1911/02/18, Dustin Elden Herbert, Hopkinton, Dustin Daniel H, Ashby Sylvia, Hopkinton, Concord

1911/02/28, Merrill Grace Elizabeth, Hopkinton, Merrill Edward L, Lepage Sarah Elizabeth, Somerville MA, Cambridge MA

1911/02/26, Prince Clara Louise, Hopkinton, Prince Roscoe P, Pearson Carrie G, Orange, Salisbury

1911/02/27, Kimball Carroll Colby, Hopkinton, Kimball Charles C, Colby Elsie J, Canterbury, Hopkinton

1911/02/28, Kimball Raymond Sheldon, Hopkinton, Kimball Nelson D, Patch Adelaide, Hopkinton, Newfield ME

1911/03/13, Geer Gladys Ruth, Hopkinton, Geer Bert L, Bryant Candice, Canada, New York

1911/03/17, Hook Lester James, Hopkinton, Hook Charles F, Underhill Bertha I, Hopkinton, Chester

1911/04/17, Thompson Lucie Elzira, Hopkinton, Thompson Clarence, Drown Idella A, Webster, Wilmot

1911/04/29, Cayer Marie Anna, Hopkinton, Cayer Thomas E, Nudd Bessie M, Manchester, Warner

1911/04/26, Guerin Armond Joseph, Hopkinton, Guerin George, Welcome Sarah, Hopkinton, Canada

1911/05/16, Boyce John Melzer, Hopkinton, Boyce Harley A, Cronin Augusta, Hopkinton, Tilton

1911/05/18, Stevens Charles Arthur, Hopkinton, Stevens Arthur W, Watts Ida M, Manchester, Hopkinton

1911/05/18, Wunderlick Alice L, Hopkinton, Wonderlick Charles, Clark Alice, Worcester MA, Warner

1911/05/19, Bartlett Charles Richard, Hopkinton, Bartlett Luther, Nudd Nellie, Warner, Hopkinton

1911/07/18, Gunn Arlene Frances, Hopkinton, Gunn George M, Tilton Hazel F, Concord, Rochester

1911/08/07, Nudd- No Name, Hopkinton, Nudd Archie H, Blanchette Clara, Warner, New Boston

1911/08/20, Clark Freddie A, Hopkinton, Clark Fred, Cooper Mabel E, Hopkinton, Concord

1911/08/25, Chase Edwin Oscar, Hopkinton, Chase Oscar N, Thornton Maggie, Hopkinton, England
1911/09/29, Symonds -No Name, Hopkinton, Symonds Chas D, Parker Grace E, Hopkinton, Manchester
1911/10/06, Miner Jennie E, Hopkinton, Miner William H, Annis Hattie E, Norwood NY, Warner
1911/10/06, Davis-No Name, Hopkinton, Davis Joseph F, Hacket Grace A, Hudson, Hopkinton
1911/11/20, Boynton-No Name, Hopkinton, Boynton Arthur J, Clough Bessie J, Weare, Concord
1911/12/21, Heaps- No Name, Hopkinton, Heaps Joseph, Haigh Carrie, England, Salem
1915/03/18, Blanchard Lloyd William, Hopkinton, Blanchard Walter R, Abell Lottie H, Greenfield, Manchester
1915/03/20, Libbey Sumner A, Hopkinton, Libbey Fred S, Burdick S Beatrice, Wolfeboro, Winthay CT
1915/03/25, Clark Georgianna Mabel, Hopkinton, Clark James, Drown Lilla M, Warner, Warner
1915/03/14, Ward Barbara Alice, Hopkinton, Ward G Miles, Hazard Ida J, Franklin, Milford MA
1915/04/01, Straw Helen Flagg, Hopkinton, Straw Forest G, Flagg Marion A, Hopkinton, Allston MA
1915/04/11, Hook Arlen Mary, Hopkinton, Hook William I, Burgland Katherine, Hopkinton, Ireland
1912/05/07, Cornet Joseph Clair, Hopkinton, Cornet Newton, Moran Mary C, Jackson KY, Concord
1912/05/12, Hardy Alexander, Hopkinton, Hardy Stillman A, Bagley Pauline, Hopkinton, Melbourne Australia
1912/06/14, Clough Doris Virginia, Clough Harry R, Clough Harry R, Illsley Florence, Lebanon, Fairlee VT
1912/06/24, Robertson Evelyn Viola, Hopkinton, Robertson John T, Nudd Alice M, Warner, Warner
1912/07/01, Brown -No Name #, Hopkinton, Brown Lanson O, Fleming Melissa, Thornton, Canada
1912/07/15, Tufts Elsie J, Hopkinton, Tufts Jerome W, Couch Mertie G, Chester VT, Salisbury
1912/07/26, Elliott Elim Etis, Hopkinton, Elliott Eden E, Glazier Anna, Michigan, Arkwright NY
1912/07/26, Downs Eunice E, Hopkinton, Downs William M, Clouch Stella H, Haverhill, Salisbury
1912/07/29, Merrill Gertrude Estella, Hopkinton, Merrill Edward L, Lafage Sarah E, Somerville MA, Cambridge MA
1912/08/08, Corliss Ervin Elliott, Hopkinton, Corliss Walter, Elliott Nellie, Nashua, Webster
1912/09/05, Blanchard Edna F, Hopkinton, Blanchard Bert G, Bohanan Edna F, Greenfield, Hopkinton

1912/09/12, Nudd Ella May, Hopkinton, Nudd John B, Clark Emma J, Warner, Warner

1912/10/05, Lindquist Theodore Augustus, Hopkinton, Lindquist Carl J, Nelson Hilda, Sweden, Sweden

1912/10/09, Stanley Horace C, Hopkinton, Stanley Clinton J, Hall Annie M, Hopkinton, Hopkinton

1912/10/19, Kay James Earnest, Hopkinton, Kay James, Clark Lillian F, Fall River MA, Warner

1912/11/18, Somborger -No Name, Hopkinton, Somborger Eddie M, McCoubrey Mary J, Canada, Canada

1912/12/04, Elliott Thomas Carlton, Hopkinton, Elliott Clarence T, Mcdonald Margaret A, Webster, Prince Edward Island

1912/12/21, Coombs Elizabeth Elliott, Hopkinton, Coombs John L, Elliott Julia, Rumney, Bow

1912/12/27, Miner-No Name#, Hopkinton, Miner William H, Annis Hattie E, Norwood NY, Warner

1913/01/08, Putney True Barker, Hopkinton, Putney Ira A, Barker Bessie I, Hopkinton, Dublin

1913/01/13, Cota Gladys, Hopkinton, Cota Fred, Hyde Lotta, St Johnsbury VT, Barton VT

1913/02/03, Clark Leslie W, Hopkinton, Clark James F, Drown Mabel, Warner, Warner

1913/02/06, Muzzy Gladys B, Hopkinton, Muzzy Harrison D, Brown Gladys A, Sunapee, Sunapee

1913/02/17, Rouse John D, Hopkinton, Rouse Loren L, Novren Annie I, Canada, Sweden

1913/02/17, Rouse James L, Hopkinton, Rouse Loren L, Novren Annie I, Canada, Sweden

1913/02/27, Perkins - No Name, Hopkinton, Perkins John, Smith Lena, Canada, Canada

1913/03/04, Howley Ruth Agnes, Hopkinton, Howley James, Corcoran Mary, Manchester, Keesville NY

1913/03/04, Bohanon Flora Margaret, Hopkinton, Bohanon J Harry, Marcy Esther G, Hopkinton, Cambridge MA

1913/03/08, Raymond-No Name, Hopkinton, Raymond Dana C, Welch Annie, Milford, Portsmouth

1913/04/11, Bailey Arnold Elwin, Hopkinton, Bailey George W, Chase Gertrude, Warner, Hopkinton

1913/05/08, Davis Grant L, Hopkinton, Davis Arthur G, Livingston Cecile F, East Jaffrey, Peterborough

1913/04/11, Burbank Dorothy, Hopkinton, Burbank Ray C, Davis Barbara J, Webster, Warner

1913/05/13, Marcy Sidney Paul, Hopkinton, Marcy John H, Baker Mildred, Cambridge MA, Hopkinton

1913/06/13, Montgomery George Fremont, Hopkinton, Montgomery Scott, Clough Mary, Hopkinton, Hopkinton

1913/07/01, Wunderlich Frank Henry, Hopkinton, Wunderlich Charles, Clark Alice K, Worcester MA, Warner

1913/07/10, Mills James Charles, Hopkinton, Mills Lerman H, Charles Jemima, Hopkinton, Scotland

1913/06/21, Downs Pauline Mae, Hopkinton, Downes Daniel, Sargent Alice E, Wilmot, Warner

1913/07/28, Sweatt Catherine Doris, Hopkinton, Sweatt Lewis H, Macpher Carrie A, Hill, Boston MA

1913/08/28, Montgomery Eleanor Alice, Hopkinton, Montgomery Wm. I, Oman Agnes S. V, Warner, Boston MA

1913/09/01, Clark Emma Elizabeth, Hopkinton, Clark Lewis, Parker Henrietta, Meriden, Lebanon

1913/09/26, Case Barbara Olive, Hopkinton, Case Ernest E, Allin Bernice, Francestown, New Boston

1913/10/08, O'neal Alan Walter, Hopkinton, O'Neal Frank W, Blanchette Alice, Salisbury N. B, Goffstown

1913/11/07, Archilbald George Wm Jr, Hopkinton, Archibald George W, Lothrop Marion H, Nova Scotia, Charlestown MA

1913/11/07, Kay Etta Frances, Hopkinton, Kay James, Clark Lillian F, Fall River MA, Warner

1913/11/12, Tilton Willard John, Hopkinton, Tilton Joseph N, Rollins M Alice, Hopkinton, Hopkinton

1913/12/04, Cooper Clarence Herber, Hopkinton, Cooper Clarence C, Crockett Lena M, Concord, Laconia

1913/12/09, Symonds Carol Evelyn, Hopkinton, Symonds Chauncy J, Smith Viola E, Parishville NY, Hopkinton

1913/12/13, Taylor Gladys Ruth, Hopkinton, Taylor Howard, Melcher Eva, Townsend MA, Thornton

1913/12/15, Brown John Daniel, Hopkinton, Brown John T, Hemphill Laura M, Thornton, Henniker

1913/12/31, Coombs Irving James, Hopkinton, Coombs Stephen W, Hook Alice M, Chatham MA, Hopkinton

1914/01/14, Clark Evelyn May, Hopkinton, Clark James, Drown I Mabel, Warner, Warner

1914/01/27, Geer Earl Anderson, Hopkinton, Geer Bert L, Bryant Candice, North Troy VT, Moiria NY

1914/01/31, Guerin-No Name, Hopkinton, Guerin George, Welcome Sarah, Manchester, Canada

1914/04/01, Fuller Barbara May, Hopkinton, Fuller William, Elkins Eva B, Hopkinton, Thornton

1914/03/27, Bassett - No Name, Hopkinton, Bassett Williama, Fannie Mary A, Elgin MA, Canada

1914/08/28, Howlet Elizabeth Townsend, Hopkinton, Howlet James D, Morrill Mary A, Prince Edward Island, Concord

1914/04/08, Krzyzamiak John Victor, Hopkinton, Krzyzamiak John T, Carter Grace I, Poland, Concord

1914/05/14, Elliott Edgar Elwin, Hopkinton, Elliott Eden E, Glasier Anna, Brontown Mich, New York NY

1914/05/17, Bartlett Clifton Ray, Hopkinton, Bartlett Clifton J, Chase Lida H, Warner, Hopkinton

1914/05/19, Brown Shilie Winnifred, Hopkinton, Brown Lanson O, Fleming Melissa F, Thornton, Canada

1914/06/23, Bunnell Pearl Webster, Hopkinton, Bunnell Harry E, Harriman Sarah G, Concord, Warner

1914/06/25, Nudd-No Name, Hopkinton, Nudd John B, Clark Emma J, Webster, Warner

1914/07/22, Eagles - No Name, Hopkinton, Eagle Arthur, Ryan Maud, Nova Scotia, Nova Scotia

1914/05/22, Roberson Shirley Carl, Hopkinton, Roberson Milo B, Blanchette Emma M, Henniker, Goffstown

1914/05/31, Bohonan John Harry Jr, Hopkinton, Bohonan Harry, Marcy Ester G, Hopkinton, Cambridge MA

1914/06/15, Mcginnis Charlotte Lucile, Hopkinton, McGinnis Charles, Sanborn Sadie M, Montana, Hopkinton

1914/08/16, Haselton Maurice Horner, Hopkinton, Haselton Homer H, Carter Susie W, Hopkinton, Concord

1914/08/21, Fuller Robert Reade, Hopkinton, Fuller George L, Reade Blanche, Hopkinton, Weare

1914/09/02, Bohonan Clifton Earl, Hopkinton, Bohonan Percy R, Fowler Alice M, Hopkinton, Newbury

1914/09/03, Bartlett Alice Isabelle, Hopkinton, Bartlett Luther, Nudd Nettie R, Warner, Warner

1914/10/09, Wilson Ruth Franklin, Hopkinton, Wilson Rupert F, Louise E, Mcindoes Falls VT

1914/06/10, Lawson Arthur Olof, Hopkinton, Lawson Arthur, Olson Anna, Sweden, Sweden

1914/10/29, Flanders Howard Edger, Hopkinton, Flanders Carleton, Whitney Mary E, Henniker, Merrimack FL

1914/11/22, Brackett Sadia Beatrice, Hopkinton, Brackett Amos, Wall Lottie, Riverton Conn, St Albans VT

1914/11/28, Stevens Olive Francis, Hopkinton, Stevens Arthur W, Watts Ida M, Hopkinton

1914/12/08, Gough Williama Everett, Hopkinton, Gough Edward T, Robbins Edna, Bristow Iowa, Nebraska

1914/12/13, Kay James Irving, Hopkinton, Kay James, Clark Lillian F, Fall River MA, Warner

1914/12/19, Sounberger- No Name, Hopkinton, Sounberger Eddie M, McCoubrey Mary J, Canada, Canada

1922/08/20, Barton Walter Wallace, Hopkinton, Barton Leslie C, Severance Isabelle D, Concord, East Washinton

1915/05/10, Howley Edward John, Hopkinton, Howley James, Corcoran Mary, Augusta ME, Keesville NY

1915/05/14, Ward Barbara Priscilla, Hopkinton, Ward Roger R, Wilson Lilie, Wilminton MA, Canada

1915/06/20, Page-No Name, Hopkinton, Page William H, Howley Mary, Henniker, Portland ME

1915/03/18, Shreve Jane, Hopkinton, Shreve Henry A, Pierce Eva A, Salem MA, Chicago IL

1915/07/19, Robertson Frances Emma, Hopkinton, Robertson Milo B, Blanchette Emma, Henniker, Goffstown

1915/08/20, Hoit Agnes, Hopkinton, Hoit Charles S, Severance Effie E, Bradford, Manchester

1915/09/01, Bender Mary Evelyn, Hopkinton, Bender Harold M, Johnson Bertha E, Manchester, Manchester

1915/07/15, Corliss Welcome P, Hopkinton, Corliss Hosea F, Hayes Elizabeth D, Nashua, Prince Edward Island

1915/08/26, Benton Rosaline, Hopkinton, Benton Joseph S, Burham Dorothy, Newton MA, Lowell MA

1915/09/06, Sawtelle Fred Barnes, Hopkinton, Sawtelle Carroll, Jordan Hattie, Stannard VT, Warner

1915/09/23, Spiller Robert Orris, Hopkinton, Spiller Robert, Fifield Alice I, Hopkinton

1915/10/01, Guerin - No Name, Hopkinton, Guerin George, Welcome Sarah, Manchester, Montreal Canada

1915/10/08, Wunderlich James Otis, Hopkinton, Wunderlich Charles, Clark Alice K, Worcester MA, Warner

1915/10/27, Symonds Edson Smith, Hopkinton, Symonds Chauncey, Smith Vioia E, Plaushville N Y, Hopkinton

1915/10/27, Kay Dorris May, Hopkinton, Kay James, Clark Lillian F, Fall River MA, Warner

1915/11/12, Rouse Mabel Rose, Hopkinton, Rouse Loren L, Noreen Annie J, Canada, Sweden

1915/12/12, Staniels-No Name, Hopkinton, Staniels Arthur, Healey Belle M, Croydon, North Dakota

1915/12/22, Mitchell Francis Elwell, Hopkinton, Mitchell Everett J, Roby Mamie P, Warner, Sutton

1915/12/28, Nelson Christine, Hopkinton, Nelson Lewis A, Chase B Maud, Warner, Hopkinton

1915/12/29, Little Alice Louise, Hopkinton, Little William B, Mould Emmie S, Hopkinton, England

1916/01/04, Guimond Donna Alice, Hopkinton, Guimond Fred, Currier Donna F, Manchester, Warner

1916/01/07, Krzyzamiak Helen Marjorie, Hopkinton, Krzyzamiak John, Carter Grace, Poland, Concord

1916/01/29, Mills Olive Jean, Hopkinton, Mills Lerman H, Charles Germain, Hopkinton, Scotland

1916/02/08, Cayer Albert Thomas, Hopkinton, Cayer Thomas, Welch Grace, Manchester, Hopkinton

1916/02/23, Cate Zona Marie, Hopkinton, Cate George A, McCutchun Isabel M, Methuen MA, Leeds P Q

1916/02/09, Symonds Virginia Chase, Hopkinton, Symonds Arthur G, Chase Winnifred, Hopkinton, Hopkinton

1916/02/21, Brown- No Name #, Hopkinton, Brown Lanson O, Felming Melissa, Thornton, Canada

1916/03/15, Chandler Alfred Norman, Hopkinton, Chandler Arthur O, Miller Jennie, W.farlee VT, Dundee Scotland

1916/03/24, Lawson Erick Reinhold, Hopkinton, Lawson Arthur V, Olson Anna, Sweden, Sweden

1916/03/24, Elliott Elmer Eugen Esek, Hopkinton, Elliott Eden E, Glasier Anna, Browntown Mich, Arkwright NY

1916/04/12, Barton Howard Leslie, Hopkinton, Barton Leslie C, Severance Isabell, Concord, Washinton

1916/04/24, Wescott Benjamin Walter, Hopkinton, Wescott Benj. C, Ager Flora M, Bristol, Hopkinton

1916/04/25, Thompson Luther Frank, Hopkinton, Thompson Clarence V, Downes Idelia A, Webster, Wilmot

1916/04/27, Emerson Gertrude D, Hopkinton, Emerson Roy D, Currier Florence G, Warner, Hopkinton

1916/05/01, Bartlett Winnifred Louise, Hopkinton, Bartlett Luther, Richards Nellie, Warner, Warner

1916/05/02, Flanders Albert James, Hopkinton, Flanders Albert J, Libby Hazel Dell, Hopkinton, Hopkinton

1916/05/11, Bartlett Joseph Augustine, Hopkinton, Bartlett Clifton J, Chase Lida, Hopkinton, Hopkinton

1916/06/09, Locke Geraldine Mary, Hopkinton, Locke James W, Purlington Gladys A, Hopkinton, Weare

1916/06/11, Libby George Kenneth, Hopkinton, Libby George K, Manning Ellen G, Hopkinton, Cambridge MA

1916/07/14, Burbank Dorothea Evelyn, Hopkinton, Burbank Walter L, Morrison Elmira A, Hopkinton, Londonderry

1916/07/24, Bohanan Ruby Alice, Hopkinton, Bohanan Percy R, Fowler Alice M, Hopkinton, Newbury

1916/07/27, Hathaway Warren Thomas, Hopkinton, Hathaway Chas H, Murphy Margaret, Montreal Canada, New York NY

1916/08/16, Davis Alice Margaret, Hopkinton, Davis Nathaniel F, Ball Nina B, Warner, Washington

1916/08/20, Cooper Lena Beatrice, Hopkinton, Cooper Clarence C, Crockett Lena, Concord, Laconia

1916/08/27, Kezer James W, Hopkinton, Kezer Frank H, Farnum Alda B, Hopkinton, Nova Scotia

1916/10/11, Goodrich Florence Mae, Hopkinton, Goodrich John P, Wright Pauline C, Hopkinton, Merrimack

1916/10/19, Dustin Adelaide, Hopkinton, Dustin Daniel H, Ashby Sylvia E, Hopkinton, Concord

1916/10/15, Somberger Viola Ruby Olive, Hopkinton, Somberger Eddie M, McCoubrey Mary J, Canada, Canada

1916/11/13, Bohanan Ashton Jewel, Hopkinton, Bohanan Lester J, Eaton Blanche E, Hopkinton, Newbury

1916/11/19, Burbank Bertha June, Hopkinton, Burbank Alonzo P, Gault Sadie S, Gloucester MA, Bridgewater

1916/12/16, Marcy Lloyd Stephen, Hopkinton, Marcy John H, Baker Mildred F, Cambirge MA, Hopkinton

1916/12/20, Wickstrom Marjory Alberta, Hopkinton, Wickstrom Carl J, Wolfreys Olive M, Finland, Charlestown MA

1916/12/29, Guimond Henry Robert, Hopkinton, Guimond Fred, Currier Donna F, Manchester, Warner

1917/07/30, Archibald Marie Louise, Hopkinton, Archibald George, Lothrope Marion, Nova Scotia, Charlestown MA

1920/05/09, Whittemore Hollie Leon Jr, Manchester, Whittemore Hollie L, Pillsbury Marion, Colebrook, Londonderry

1921/01/30, Severence Jennie Mary, Hopkinton, Severance Howard C, Blanchette Mary V, Washington NH, Goffstown

1922/05/14, Bergstrom Robert Carl, Hopkinton, Bergstrom Oscar R, Oshurd Clara M, Maynard MA, Providence RI

1922/05/18, Wunderlich Frederick Agustive, Hopkinton, Wunderlich Charles, Clark Alice, Worcester MA, Warner

1927/01/22, Goodwin William Ellsworth Jr, Hopkinton, Goodwin William E, Smith Susan, Manchester, Halifax N. S.

1928/04/16, Whittemore -No Name, Concord, Whittemore John K, Nicholson Doris E, Colebrook, New Bedford MA

1928/09/19, Reddy Charlotte Ann, Concord, Reddy Samuel, Gillinghama Catherine, Scituate MA, Jacksonville Fla

1930/03/05, Blanchette Pauline M, W. Hopkinton, Blanchette Philip J, Clark Evelyn May, Goffstown, West Hopkinton

1931/07/01, Provencher Nina Annette, Concord, Provencher Albert, Bean Florence, Bay City Mich, Johnstown NY

1931/09/06, Putney Mary Lou Alberta, Hopkinton, Putney John S Jr, Houston Dorothy R, Chicago IL, Roxbury MA

1931/09/26, Robertson Everett Blanchette, Hopkinton, Robertson Everett B, Page Dorothy C, Hopkinton, Hillsboro

1932/01/05, Shurtleff Patricis, Concord, Shurtleff Joseph S, Grant Janet Cadelle, Contoocook, Edinboro Scotland

1932/04/28, Swindlehurst John Robert, Hopkinton, Swindlehurst John, Boynton Josephine, Peterboro, Hopkinton

1932/07/20, Susynski Helen Maxine, W. Hopkinton, Susynski Felix, Pizbylski Helen P, Konin Poland, Konin Poland

1932/09/25, Houston William Edward, Concord, Houston William Edward, Allen Blanche, Concord, Swampscott MA

1932/12/09, Blanchard Dorothea Ruth, Concord, Blanchard Francis, Gillingham Ruth J, New Boston, New Hampton

1933/04/03, Blanchette Norma Lois, W. Hopkinton, Blanchette Philip J, Clark Evelyn M, Goffstown, W. Hopkinton
1933/09/05, Roberston Frederick Arthur, W. Hopkinton, Roberston Everett, Page Dorothy G, W. Hopkinton, Hillsboro
1934/11/28, Carroll Arelen Rita, Hopkinton, Carroll James E, Wilcox Viola M, Gloucester MA, Dartmouth MA
1934/12/09, Leavitt Geraldine May, Contoocook, Leavitt Lawrence, Page Mary Etta, Springfield MA, Henniker
1935/02/22, Blanchette Freddie J, W. Hopkinton, Blanchette Philip J, Clark Evelyn M, Goffstown, W. Hopkinton
1936/01/08, Blanchette Harvey Isaac, W. Hopkinton, Blanchette Philip J, Clark Eveleyn M, Goffstown, W. Hopkinton
1936/02/08, Huntoon Arthur Cutis 2nd, Concord, Huntoon Grovenor A, Stone Emma Louise, Contoocook, Wakefield MA
1936/02/11, Carroll Raymond William, Hopkinton, Carroll James E, Wilcox Viola, Gloucester MA, Dartmouth MA
1936/08/14, Foster Virginia Bellevue, Merrimack County Farm, Foster Carol, Bellevue Geraldine, Skowhegan ME, Rochester
1902/02/28, Bailey Marion Samntha, Hopkinton, Bailey William S, Hannaford Ida May, Hopkinton, Old Orchard ME
1902/08/04, Tirrell Percy Regnald, Hopkinton, Tirrell Perley Clark, Ross Esther Louise, Manchester, Bedford P Q
1906/04/16, Shurtleff Charles Christopher, Hopkinton, Shurtleff Charles A, Moran Mary K, Hopkinton, Hopkinton
1908/12/22, Partridge Alvin Henry, Hopkinton, Partridge William, Swallow Minnie W, Hallowell ME, Boston MA
1909/10/07, Saltmarsh William Rollins, Hopkinton, Saltmarsh William A, Rollins Gertrude, Concord, Providence RI
1910/03/29, Partridge Charles P, Hopkinton, Partridge William, Swallow Minnie W, Waterville ME, Dorchester MA
1910/04/15, Guerin Margaret Anna, Hopkinton, Guerin Joseph, Marcie Prosper, Saint Alexander, Saint Alexander
1910/05/06, Sleeper Benerd Sylvanious, Hopkinton, Sleeper Charles E, Morrill Elsie L, Franklin, Springfield
1912/08/11, Robinson Everett Blanchette, Hopkinton, Robinson Milo B, Blanchette Emma M, Henniker, Goffstown
1912/09/13, Chandler Warren Gilbert, Hopkinton, Chandler Arthur O, Miller Jennie O, Fairlee VT, Dundee Scotland
1914/01/29, Hathaway Elsie Irene, Hopkinton, Hathaway Charles, Murphy Margaret, Montreat P Q, New York NY
1914/03/29, Burnham Martha Ellen, Hopkinton, Burnham Arthur M, Newman Blanche B, Hillsborough, Hillsborough
1914/04/06, Corliss Noise Frederick, Hopkinton, Corliss Hosea F, Hayes Elizabeth D, Hudson, Charlottston N B
1914/11/04, Blanchette Jennie Minnie, Hopkinton, Blanchette Henry, O'Neal Mabel E, New Boston, New Brunswick

1922/09/14, Elliott Ethel Elffn Cloes, Hopkinton, Elliott Eden, Glasier Annie, Browntown Mich, Arkwright NY
1915/06/24, Archibald Doris Lothrop, Hopkinton, Archbald George W, Lothrop Marion B, Nova Scotia, Charleston MA
1917/05/10, Treen Anna Gertrude, Hopkinton, Treen Ernest, Mclean Josephine, Nova Scotia, Prince Edward Island
BURBANK Harriett N D Hopkinton

Hopkinton, NH Marriages 1914-1937

WHITTIER Wesley P of Hopkinton & GREER Rachel I of Dunbarton m Jan 30, 1915 Hopkinton. Groom: age 21, marr 1st time, b Concord s/o WHITTIER Parker C b Canaan & PLUMMER Mary E b Concord. Bride: age 18, marr 1st time, b Dunbarton d/o GREER Otis B b Hookset & SMITH Olive L b Weare. Vol: 7 Page: 007

MITCHELL Everett Johnson of Hopkinton & ROBY Mannie P of Warner m Feb 2, 1915 Sutton. Groom: age 26, marr 1st time, b Waraner s/o MITCHELL Francis C b Andover & JOHNSON Belle N b Warner. Bride: age 24, marr 1st time, b Sutton d/o ROBY Robert E b Sutton & BARBER Nellie L b Sutton. Vol: 7 Page: 007

EMERSON Ray Darling of Hopkinton & CURRIER Florence of Hopkinton m May 22, 1915 Hopkinton. Groom: age 23, marr 1st time, b Warner s/o EMERSON Fred H b Hopkinton & KIMBALL Nellie F b Maine. Bride: age 21, marr 1st time, b Hopkinton d/o CURRIER Wilie A b Hopkinton & WEBSTER Josie G b Hopkinton. Vol: 7 Page: 007

GREENE Gardner Bailey of Hopkinton & CONWAY Marjorie M of Manchester m May 31, 1915 Manchester. Groom: age 27, marr 1st time, b Hopkinton s/o GREENE Willard T b Hopkinton & BAILEY Etta C b Chelsea Ma. Bride: age 21, marr 1st time, b Manchester d/o CONWAY John F b Manchester & CURRIER Mary E b Deering. Vol: 7 Page: 008

UNDERHILL Elmer M of Bellow Falls Vt & WESSMAN Anna E of Hopkinton m Jul 20, 1915 Windson Vt. Groom: age 52, marr 2nd time, b Piermont s/o UNDERHILL Alanson S b Piermont & MEAD Hannah B b Piermont. Bride: age 40, marr 2nd time, b Sweeden d/o WESSMAN August b Sweeden & Maria b Sweeden. Vol: 7 Page: 008

McPHERSON Kenneth James of Concord & LIBBY Myrtle Mae of Contoocook m Feb 14, 1917 Concord. Groom: age 23, marr 1st time, b Manchester s/o McPHERSON James b Manchester & HIGGINS Edith B b Manchester. Bride: age 24, marr 1st time, b Contoocook d/o LIBBY George A b Hopkinton & CURTICE Estella b Wilmot. Vol: 7 Page: 019

BUNTEN John E of Hopkinton & BARNARD Mary W of Dunbarton m Jun 30, 1917 Dunbarton. Groom: age 22, marr 1st time, b Concord s/o BUNTEN Edgar b Dunbarton & PAGE Rosa B b Dunbarton. Bride: age 20, marr 1st time, b Dunbarton d/o BARNARD Aaron C b Dunbarton & CALDWELL Amy b Dunbarton. Vol: 7 Page: 019

CHASE Walter J of Henniker & ROBERTS Edna J of Hopkinton m Jun 20, 1917 Hopkinton. Groom: age 42, marr 2nd time, b Henniker s/o CHASE Ezra b Henniker & ROGERS Nancy B b Canterbury. Bride: age 21, marr 2nd time, b Cambridge Ma d/o BROOKS Abbott L b Ne Harbor Me & GORDON Annie b Boston Ma. Vol: 7 Page: 019

Hopkinton, NH Marriages 1914

McDIARMID Joseph of Hopkinton & SANFERN Hallie P of Hopkinton m Feb 22, 1917 Worcester Ma. Groom: age 38, b Montville Conn s/o Hugh & ADAMS Anna. Bride: age 28, b St Lewis Ma?? d/o POPE Clarence & RETA Emma. Vol: 7 Page: 020

GRIFFIN Daniel A of Hopkinton & GOODHUE Margerite A of Webster m May 30, 1917 Webster. Groom: age 26, marr 1st time, b Hopkinton s/o GRIFFIN Alfred E b Bow & MORRILL Helen b Lowell Ma. Bride: age 23, marr 1st time, b Webster d/o GOODHUE Senter b Webster & WRIGHT Nellie A b Berlin Wis. Vol: 7 Page: 020

COOLEY Lean Weston of Dana Ma & MILTON Olive B of Hopkinton m Aug 25, 1919 Manchester. Groom: age 25, marr 1st time, b Hardwick Ma s/o COOLEY Dwight W b Dana Ma & THAYER Florence b Hardwick Ma. Bride: age 24, marr 1st time, b Hopkinton d/o MILTON William H b Hopkinton & MOORE Carrie b Otis Ma. Vol: 8 Page: 4

HOYT Jesse J of West Hopkintn & GRACE Etta M of West Hopkinton m Jul 7, 1918 Contoocook. Groom: age 26, marr 1st time, b Hillsboro s/o HOYT Edward F b Bradford & BUTTRICK Charlotte b W Deering. Bride: age 17, marr 1st time, b Bradford d/o GRACE George b Wilmont & HUNT Addie B b Washington. Vol: 7 Page: 022

HARDY Francis A of West Hopkinton & COOPER Ruth M of Contoocook m Oct 26, 1929 Hopkinton. Groom: age 22, marr 1st time, b Webster s/o HARDY Elwell b Webster & WIGGINS Lucy b Webster. Bride: age 18, marr 1st time, b Contoocook d/o COOPER Clarence b Hopkinton & CROCKETT Lena May b Laconia. Vol: 9 Page: 014

EATON Ablert E of Hopkinton & KIMBALL Jennie E of Hopkinton m Jan 1, 1914 Hopkinton. Groom: age 73, marr 2nd time, b Newbury s/o EATON Eben b Newbury & CROSS Hannah b Salem Ma. Bride: age 44, marr 2nd time, b N Berwick Me d/o KIMBALL Clarion H b Hopkinton & CHALLAN Lucy C b Hopkinton. Vol: 7 Page: 001

GUERIN Edward R of Hopkinton & CHASE Susie May of Hopkinton m Jan 24, 1914 Hopkinton. Groom: age 43, marr 2nd time, b Raymond s/o GUERIN Edward b Canada & CHAMPAGNE Mary b Canada. Bride: age 25, marr 2nd time, b Hopkinton d/o CHASE Edward E b Hopkinton & MOULTON Etta b Hopkinton. Vol: 7 Page: 001

HOOK William J of Hopkinton & BURGLAND Catherine of Lynn Ma m Feb 7, 1914 Lynn Ma. Groom: age 30, marr 1st time, b Hopkinton s/o HOOK James M b Concord & DOYING Mary A b Danville Canada. Bride: age 27, marr 1st time, b Galway Ireland d/o WELSH John P b Dublin Ireland & CURLEY Delia J b Galway Ireland. Vol: 7 Page: 001

CASSAVAUGH Emery A of Concord & MITCHELL Gladys D of Hopkinton m Jan 26, 1914 Penacook. Groom: age 23, marr 1st time, b Boscawen s/o CASSAVAUGH Albert b Chazy N Y & DUCAT Ellen b Plattsbury Ny. Bride: age 19, marr 1st time, b Hopkinton d/o MITCHELL Dolf b Lowell Ma & LIBBY Stella G b Hopkinton. Vol: 7 Page: 002

BOUTWELL Ernest A of Hopkinton & COLBY Bertha E of Warner m Mar 2, 1914 Warner. Groom: age 22, marr 1st time, b Hopkinton s/o BOUTWELL Henry B A b Ill & MONTGOMERY Alice b Hopkinton. Bride: age 22, marr 1st time, b

Warner d/o COLBY Edward K & KIMBALL Jennie L b New Jersey. Vol: 7 Page: 002

FELCH James B of Hopkinton & WILSON Augusta of Manchester m Mar 17, 1914 Hopkinton. Groom: age 58, marr 2nd time, b Weare s/o FELCH Square b Weare & SILVER Laura b Bow. Bride: age 57, marr 2nd time, b Manchester d/o ROBINSON S Franklin b Epsom & BATCHELDER Mary A b Pembroke. Vol: 7 Page: 002

STRAW Forest G of Hopkinton & FLAGG Marion Adeline of Melrose Ma m Apr 8, 1914 Melrose Ma. Groom: age 31, marr 1st time, b Hopkinton s/o STRAW Gilman J b Hopkinton & HOYT Weltha A b Henniker. Bride: age 23, marr 1st time, b Allston Ma d/o FLAGG Gardner W b Wellesley Ma & SARGENT May b Bow. Vol: 7 Page: 003

KINGSTON George J of Newburyport Ma & KIMBALL Ruth N of Hopkinton m Jun 21, 1914 Hopkinton. Groom: age 30, marr 1st time, b Newburyport Mas s/o KINGSTON William b Saint John Nb & Martha b Saint John Nb. Bride: age 22, marr 1st time, b Hopkinton d/o KIMBALL Nelson D b Hopkinton & Adelaide M b Newfield Me. Vol: 7 Page: 003

MUDGETT J Frank of Hopkinton & MARCY Hattie R of Hopkinton m Jun 21, 1914 Hopkinton. Groom: age 71, marr 2nd time, b Weare s/o MUDGETT Moses b Weare & BOYNTON Aurinda b Weare. Bride: age 48, marr 2nd time, b Cambridge Ma d/o GREENLEAF George W b Boston Ma & BATES Sarah B b Watertown Ma. Vol: 7 Page: 003

PERRY Arthur B of Boston Ma & ALLEN Olive A of Hopkinton m Aug 7, 1914 Hopkinton. Groom: age 23, marr 1st time, b Boston Ma s/o PERRY Edward B b Rayham Ma & BRANCH Ella F b Boston Ma. Bride: age 22, marr 1st time, b Hopkinton d/o ALLEN Walton b Chelsa Ma & MONTGOMERY Martha b Hopkinton. Vol: 7 Page: 004

DWINNELLS George A of Hopkinton & SMITH Lena May of Hopkinton m Aug 24, 1914 Hopkinton. Groom: age 39, marr 2nd time, b Hopkinton s/o DWINNELLS John G b Dunbarton & CHASE Caroline M b Hopkinton. Bride: age 27, marr 2nd time, b Canada d/o SMITH Allie b Canada & Nettie b Canada. Vol: 7 Page: 004

FRENCH Albert H of Hopkinton & BOUTWELL Helen A of Hopkinton m Aug 25, 1914 Hopkinton. Groom: age 35, marr 1st time, b Hopkinton s/o FRENCH Charles b Hopkinton & HARDY Sarah A b Hopkinton. Bride: age 16, marr 1st time, b Hopkinton d/o BOUTWELL Wallace E b Mass & WARD Lillie A b Hopkinton. Vol: 7 Page: 004

RENDER Harold Merrill of Manchester & JOHNSON Bertha E of Hopkinton m Oct 10, 1914 Hopkinton. Groom: age 35, marr 1st time, b Manchester s/o DAVIDSON Charles F & MERRILL Emma F b Manchester. Bride: age 41, marr 1st time, b Manchester d/o JOHNSON Franklyn P b Northfield & CHENEY Evelyn b Manchester. Vol: 7 Page: 005

GOODWIN Ernest Lauren of Concord & MILLS Gerrude E of Hopkinton m Oct 22, 1914 Nashua. Groom: age 52, marr 1st time, b Lake Village s/o GOODWIN Jeremiah S b Athens Me & VINCENT Lucy N b Woodstock. Bride: age 47, marr 1st time, b Woodstock Vt d/o THORTON Albert C b Croydon & NEWELL Mary E b Stockbirdge Vt. Vol: 7 Page: 005

Hopkinton, NH Marriages 1914

WEEKS N Cogswell of Hopkinton & ROLLINS Clara A of Pittsfield m Nov 26, 1914 Pittsfield. Groom: age 74, marr 2nd time, b Hopkinton s/o WEEKS Thomas J b Hopkinton & SMITH Hannah C b Rowley Ma. Bride: age 60, marr 2nd time, b Strafford d/o SANDERS William b Strafford & REYNOLDS Addie b Durham. Vol: 7 Page: 005

LIBERTY Joseph of Hopkinton & DENNIS Gretchen May of Hopkinton m Jan 4, 1919 Hopkinton. Groom: age 28, marr 1st time, b Canada s/o LIBERTY Hanorie b Canada & Dalila b Canada. Bride: age 16, marr 1st time, b Webster d/o DENNIS Napolon b Penacook & HARDY Grace b Manchester. Vol: 8 Page: 001

DAVIS Willie Neal of Hopkinton & EMERSON Florence M of Hopkinton m Dec 31, 1914 Hopkinton. Groom: age 53, marr 2nd time, b Warner s/o DAVIS Paine b Warner & BABCOCK Esther b Easport Me. Bride: age 32, marr 2nd time, b Webster d/o EMERSON Fred N b Hopkinton & KIMBALL Nellie F b Turner Me. Vol: 7 Page: 006

BURKE Floyd William of Hopkinton & CAMPBELL Gladys M of Stowe Ma m Jan 18, 1915 Nashua. Groom: age 22, marr 1st time, b Marlboro Ma s/o BURKE William F b Boston Ma & WILKINS Carrie M b Marlboro Ma. Bride: age 18, marr 1st time, b Canning N S d/o CAMPBELL William A b Billtown Ns & BLANKHORN Maria b Hals Harbor N S. Vol: 7 Page: 006

FLANDERS Maurice of Concord & MAKEPEACE Cora M of Hopkinton m Jan 6, 1917 Bellow Falls Vt. Groom: age 24, marr 1st time, b Sutton s/o FLANDERS Wilson B b Warner & ADAMS Flora B b Sutton. Bride: age 20, marr 1st time, b Hopkinton d/o MAKEPEACE George A b Concord & POLAND Evangie M b Hopkinton. Vol: 7 Page: 018

YOUNG Waldo N of Manchester & MILTON Dorothy of Hopkinton m May 1, 1917 Hopkinton. Groom: age 25, marr 1st time, b Manchester s/o YOUNG Frank N b Manchester & HAZELTON Lizzie. Bride: age 19, marr 1st time, b Hopkinton d/o MILTON Will H b Hopkinton & THOMPSON Carrie A T b Otis Ma. Vol: 7 Page: 018

BLANCHETTE Frank F of Hopkinton & WHITNEY Stephenetta of Hillsboro m Apr 28, 1917 Henniker. Groom: age 19, marr 1st time, b Goffstown s/o BLANCHETTE Jos. b Chicopee Falls & BURAGUARD Selina b Montreal Canada. Bride: age 16, marr 1st time, b Hillsboro d/o WHITNEY Stephen J b Newport & CHALMERS Carrie E b Claremont. Vol: 7 Page: 018

WHITTIER Lester Ruben of Hopkinton & HESLEY Blanche M of Hopkinton m Jun 6, 1917 Hopkinton. Groom: age 29, marr 1st time, b Concord s/o WHITTIER Parker C b Hebron & PLUMNER Mary E b Hebron. Bride: age 31, marr 1st time, b North Docato d/o HESLEY James C b Bristol & BEAN Orissa A b Rumford Me. Vol: 7 Page: 020

INGRAM Glendon Beryl of Laconia & ELLIOTT Marian Kate of Contoocook m 1919 Hopkinton. Groom: age 22. Bride: age 21. Vol: 8 Page: 5

CAYER Thomas Ernest of Hopkinton & WELCH Grace Hazel of Hopkinton m Aug 25, 1915 Hillsboro. Groom: age 29, marr 2nd time, b Manchester s/o CAYER Triffle b Canada & RENNIE Mary b Canada. Bride: age 18, marr 2nd time, b Warner d/o WELCH William b Concord & STORY Sadie b Boscawen. Vol: 7 Page: 008

Hopkinton, NH Marriages 1914

LIBBY George K of Hopkinton & MANNING Ellen G of Boston Ma m Sep 7, 1915 Manchester. Groom: age 19, marr 1st time, b Hopkinton s/o LIBBY George A b Hopkinton & KENNISTON Estella b Andover. Bride: age 20, marr 1st time, b Cambridge Ma d/o MANNING Michael J b Galaway Ireland & O'BRIEN Mary E b Boston Ma. Vol: 7 Page: 009

GOMES Hugo R C of Hopkinton & CARLSON Alma T of Cranston RI m Sep 21, 1915 Hopkinton. Groom: age 27, marr 1st time, b Sweeden s/o GOMES John b Portugal & JOHNSON Emma C b Sweeden. Bride: age 21, marr 1st time, b Providence RI d/o CARLSON Gustf A b Sweeden & CARLSON Behardena M b Sweden. Vol: 7 Page: 009

FULLER John F of Hopkinton & READ Ada Isabel of Hillsborough m Oct 12, 1915 Hillsborough. Groom: age 28, marr 1st time, b Hopkinton s/o FULLER Orren J b Bristol & CAMPBELL Lillian E b Hopkinton. Bride: age 27, marr 1st time, b Hillsborough d/o READ Ambrose b Trowbridge Eng & DOWNEY Annie b Boston Ma. Vol: 7 Page: 009

MOORE Thomas F of Hopkinton & TAYLOR Hattie M of Derry m Jul 22, 1915 Derry. Groom: age 33, marr 1st time, b Manchester s/o MOORE Thomas b Ireland & KENNEDY Mary b Ireland. Bride: age 39, marr 1st time, b Hudson d/o CORLISS James M & BUNKER Hattie E b Moultonborough. Vol: 7 Page: 010

SYMONDS Benjiman of Hopkinton & BAVIS Grace of Hopkinton m Nov 16, 1915 Hopkinton. Groom: age 25, marr 1st time, b Hopkinton s/o SYMONDS Benjamin b Hillsborough & PORTER Emma J b Hartford Vt. Bride: age 26, marr 1st time, b Hopkinton d/o HACKETT Walter b Sanbornton & CROWELL Nellie b Hopkinton. Vol: 7 Page: 010

EMERSON Arthur S of Hopkinton & DAVIS Bernice A of Concord m Nov 26, 1915 Concord. Groom: age 33, marr 1st time, b Hopkinton s/o EMERSON Hanson D b Hopkinton & MILLS Mary F b Hopkinton. Bride: age 16, marr 1st time, b Concord d/o DAVIS Fred N b Concord & HEATH Bertha b Concord. Vol: 7 Page: 010

GOODRICH John P of Hopkinton & WRIGHT Pauline C of Concord m Dec 21, 1915 Hopkinton. Groom: age 37, marr 1st time, b Hopkinton s/o GOORICH George K b Springfield Vt & LORD Lydia b New Market. Bride: age 20, marr 1st time, b Merrimack d/o WRIGHT Frank E b Athol Ma & FERGUSON Mae L b Merrimack. Vol: 7 Page: 011

MAGNAN Telesphore of Hopkinton & WALKER Jane of Hopkinton m Dec 27, 1915 Hopkinton. Groom: age 30, marr 1st time, b Granby Canada s/o MAGNAN Glasphore b Montreal Canada & ROCHON Marseline b Miltown Canada. Bride: age 82, marr 1st time, b Hillsborough d/o CARTER Samuel b Henniker & RAY Mary b Henniker. Vol: 7 Page: 011

WIKSTROM Carl Jeremiah of Hopkinton & WELFRYS Olive M of Boston Ma m Feb 5, 1916 Manchester. Groom: age 28, marr 1st time, b Finland s/o WIKSTROM Carl August b Finland & LINDERSTROM Hilder b Finland. Bride: age 24, marr 1st time, b Boston Ma d/o WELFRYS Frances Joseph b Boston Ma & PLOYER Margaret E b P E Island. Vol: 7 Page: 012

MARTIN Edward of Windsor Vt & DWINNELLS Edna of Hopkinton m Mar 18, 1916 Windsor Vt. Groom: age 23, marr 1st time, b P E Ireland s/o MARTIN

Savin b P E Island & DERRING Katherine. Bride: age 18, marr 1st time, b Hopkinton d/o DWINNELLS Geo & ---- ---- b Portland Me. Vol: 7 Page: 012

BOUTWELL Earle F of Hopkinton & BARNARD Florence M of Weare m Apr 18, 1916 Goffstown. Groom: age 22, marr 1st time, b Hopkinton s/o BOUTWELL Arthur J b Hopkinton & FITTS Carrie J b Dunbarton. Bride: age 23, marr 1st time, b Weare d/o BARNARD Edmund B b Weare & HODGDON Alice M b Manchester. Vol: 7 Page: 012

DAVIS Thomas E of Hopkinton & OMAN Florence of Hopkinton m Apr 23, 1916 Hopkinton. Groom: age 28, marr 1st time, b Hopkinton s/o DAVIS Henry B b Hopkinton & COOK Eliza b Middleton Ma. Bride: age 24, marr 1st time, b Boston Ma d/o OMAN Andrew G b Sweden & MAGNUSON Caroline b Sweden. Vol: 7 Page: 013

BARTON Leslie C of Henniker & SEVERANCE Isabel of Hopkinton m May 10, 1916 Concord. Groom: age 19, marr 1st time, b Concord s/o BARTON Robert b Hopkinton & THOMPSON Mabel b Springfield. Bride: age 17, marr 1st time, b Washington d/o SEVERANCE William b Stoddard & FOWLER Florence b Washington. Vol: 7 Page: 013

STRAW Claton B of Hopkinton & ROLLINS Agnes May of Hopkinton m Jun 3, 1916 Hopkinton. Groom: age 21, marr 1st time, b Hopkinton s/o STRAW James O b Hopkinton & WHITTIER Ada W b Hopkinton. Bride: age 21, marr 1st time, b Hopkinton d/o ROLLINS William N b Hopkinton & PERNELLO Margaret b Beauport Cty Ireland. Vol: 7 Page: 013

LANGLEY Alexander L of Pembroke Me & PARTRIDGE Sarah M of Hopkinton m Jul 22, 1916 Hopkinton. Groom: age 40, b Pembroke Me s/o LANGLEY Alexander b Pembroke Me & KING Josephine O b Pembroke Me. Bride: age 22, b Concord d/o PARTRIDGE William b Hallowell Me & SNALLOW[??] Minnie b Boston Ma. Vol: 7 Page: 014

HARDY Orin Henry of Concord & WATTS Mildred E of Hopkinton m Jul 4, 1916 Pembroke. Groom: age 27, marr 1st time, b Concord s/o HARDY Henry G b Concord & MORRILL Mary E b Boscawen. Bride: age 21, marr 1st time, b Hopkinton d/o WATTS Charles b Warner & RYAN Mary b Webster. Vol: 7 Page: 014

DENSMORE Edward J of Hopkinton & WHEELER Mary Maud of Bristol m Sep 2, 1916 Hopkinton. Groom: age 27, marr 1st time, b Hopkinton s/o DENSMORE James A b Northfield & LIBBY Elanor b Salisbury. Bride: age 20, marr 1st time, b Andover d/o WHEELER Allie b Springfield Vt & MCVEY July Ann b Andover. Vol: 7 Page: 014

HARRIS Oliver Gordon of Hopkinton & FULLER Irma M of Hopkinton m Sep 30, 1916 Goffstown. Groom: age 23, marr 1st time, b Salem s/o HARRIS Hubert W b Blackstone Ma & WOODBURY Mary F b West Moreland. Bride: age 27, marr 1st time, b Hopkinton d/o FULLER Orren F b Bristol & CAMPBELL Lilla E b Hopkinton. Vol: 7 Page: 015

BLAKE Willie C of Hopkinton & TOWNS Chassie L of Weare m Oct 14, 1916 Weare. Groom: age 26, marr 2nd time, b Thornton s/o BLAKE William E b Thornton & BROWN Clara B b Thornton. Bride: age 22, marr 2nd time, b Weare d/o TOWNES Lewis b Weare & JEWELL Etta M b Weare. Vol: 7 Page: 015

CALL Everett H of Hopkinton & BAILEY Ruby S of Dunbarton m Oct 21, 1916 Dunbarton. Groom: age 26, marr 1st time, b Webster s/o CALL Arthulr C b Webster & McEWEN Nettie b Calton Ny. Bride: age 25, marr 1st time, b Dunbarton d/o BAILEY George O b Dunbarton & SARGENT Mary E b Dunbarton. Vol: 7 Page: 015

BOYNTON John Merton of Hopkinton & BOYNTON Ruby Maud of Dunbarton m Oct 30, 1916 Hopkinton. Groom: age 24, marr 2nd time, b Weare s/o BOYNTON Henry George b Weare & WEED Jennie May b New York. Bride: age 19, marr 2nd time, b Dunbarton d/o BOYNTON Ella b Dunbarton. Vol: 7 Page: 016

COOK Ralph M of Concord & COOLIDGE Donna B of Hopkinton m Nov 23, 1916 Hopkinton. Groom: age 27, marr 1st time, b North Walpole s/o COOK Millard F b Westmoreland & HYDE Lizzie D b Ireland. Bride: age 32, marr 1st time, b Bristol d/o COOLIDGE Charles W b Leominster Ma & BROWN Katherine L b Indendence Ohio. Vol: 7 Page: 016

PEASLEE Roy William of Hopkinton & HALL Alta B of Brewer Me m Dec 27, 1916 Brewer Me. Groom: age 25, marr 1st time, b Randolph Me s/o PEASLEE Henry W b Whitefield Me & LOW Addie P b Boston Ma. Bride: age 23, marr 1st time, b Brewer Me d/o HALL Hudron?? A b Darryascroft Me & ANDERSON Maggie S b Aberdeenshier Scot. Vol: 7 Page: 016

WATTS John Alred of Hopkinton & KIMBALL Edith G of Hopkinton m Dec 25, 1916 Hopkinton. Groom: age 23, marr 1st time, b Hopkinton s/o WATTS Charles F b Webster & RYAN Mary A b Hopkinton. Bride: age 23, marr 1st time, b Hopkinton d/o KIMBALL Nelson D b Hopkinton & Adelaide M b Hopkinton. Vol: 7 Page: 017

JONES S Harris of Canton Me & RUSS Margarite of Hopkinton m Dec 13, 1917 Hopkinton. Groom: age 30, marr 1st time, b Canton Me s/o JONES S C b Canton Me & HARRIS Julia b Green Me. Bride: age 22, marr 1st time, b Hopkinton d/o RUSS William C b Nashua & COLBY Margaret b S. Seekonk RI. Vol: 7 Page: 021

BOUTWELL Ralph E of Hopkinton & HACKETT Jennie M of Hopkinton m Nov 1, 1917 Hopkinton. Groom: age 21, marr 1st time, b Concord s/o BOUTWELL Wallace E b Pelham & WARD Lily A b Boston Ma. Bride: age 22, marr 1st time, b Hopkinton d/o HACKETT Walter C b Sanbornton & CROWELL Nellye M b Hopkinton. Vol: 7 Page: 021

WOODWARD Grover C of Boston Ma & CLARK Harriett Bella of Newton Ma m Jan 26, 1918 Hopkinton. Groom: age 33, marr 1st time, b Antrim s/o WOODWARD John W b Woodstock Vt & KIMBALL Lillian A b Hillsborough. Bride: age 33, marr 1st time, b Medford Ma d/o CLARK Sarah E b Charlestown. Vol: 7 Page: 022

OLSON Elmer William of Concord & GOODRICH Gladys of Hopkinton m Feb 19, 1918 Hopkinton. Groom: age 21, marr 1st time, b Sweden s/o OLSON August b Sweden & SJORN Nellie b Sweden. Bride: age 21, marr 1st time, b Concord d/o GOODRICH Leman b Hopkinton & POWELL Jennie V b Loudon. Vol: 7 Page: 022

DUNBAR Arthur S of Hopkinton & SPENCER Annie of Cambridge Ma m Jan 17, 1919 Hopkinton. Groom: age 24, marr 1st time, b Hopkinton s/o DUNBAR

Elmer E b Hopkinton & PAIGE Mary E b Dunbarton. Bride: age 24, marr 1st time, b Bay Roberts N F d/o SPENCER William b Bay Roberts N F & ADAMS Finnie b Bay Roberts N F. Vol: 8 Page: 001

MILLS Frank H of Hopkinton & HAYNES Lillian of Wilmot m Mar 19, 1919 Concord. Groom: age 34, marr 1st time, b Hopkinton s/o MILLS George W b Hopkinton & WHEELER Eunice B b Concord. Bride: age 27, marr 1st time, b Concord d/o HAYNES William b Concord & DAVIS Bertha b Pittsfield. Vol: 8 Page: 001

EMERSON Lloyd S of Hopkinton & CHASE Miriam of Hopkinton m Mar 25, 1919 Contoocook. Groom: age 24, marr 1st time, b Providence RI s/o EMERSON William C b Hopkinton & STONE Ella J b Providence RI. Bride: age 21, marr 1st time, b Hopkinton d/o CHASE Charles T b Charlestown Ma & WEBBER Florence D b Hopkinton. Vol: 8 Page: 002

BARNARD Raymond J of Hopkinton & FARNHAM Ruth of Lancaster m Apr 29, 1919 Lancester. Groom: age 28, marr 1st time, b Hopkinton s/o BARNARD George E b Hopkinton & TYLER Bertha S b Hopkinton. Bride: age 21, marr 1st time, b Lancaster d/o FARNHAM John M b Guildhall Vt & HARRIS Cora A b Northfield Ma. Vol: 8 Page: 002

DUSTIN Ebenezer F of Hopkinton & SHARPLESS Laura M S of W Chester Pa m Jul 12, 1918 Brooklyn Ny. Groom: age 74, marr 3rd time, b Hopkinton s/o DUSTIN Cyrus b Warner & FISK Ednah P b Wilmot. Bride: age 60, marr 3rd time, b Centereville Del d/o SHARPLESS Walter b Us & HOLT Maria b Us. Vol: 7 Page: 023

LITTLE Robert B of Mt Dora Fla & HOWE Edna S of Hopkinton m Aug 7, 1918 Hopkinton. Groom: age 26, marr 1st time, b Hopkinton s/o LITTLE Charles Edson b Webster & KIMBALL Mattie b Webster. Bride: age 24, marr 1st time, b New York d/o HOWE Jonas b Liconderogg Ny & SHARPE Annetta b Chilson Hill Ny. Vol: 7 Page: 023

BARTON Herman of Hopkinton & FRENCH Myrtie D of Hopkinton m Aug 25, 1918 Hopkinton. Groom: age 44, marr 1st time, b Hopkinton s/o BARTON Charles O b Hopkinton & CUTTS Philinda b Goshen. Bride: age 36, marr 1st time, b Warner d/o ROBERTS Charles O b Warner & BARTLETT Hattie M b Warner. Vol: 7 Page: 023

CANFIELD H William of Hopkinton & JACOBS Gladys C M of Rochester m Aug 28, 1918 Rochester. Groom: age 23, marr 1st time, b Thornton s/o CANFIELD Edward J b Franklin & GILES Addie E b Epsom. Bride: age 20, marr 1st time, b Rochester d/o JACOBS William F b Rochester & NICHOLS Mary L b Rochester. Vol: 7 Page: 024

SEVERENCE Howard C of Hopkinton & BLANCHETTE Mary of Hopkinton m Sep 4, 1918 Henniker. Groom: age 21, marr 1st time, b Washington s/o SEVERENCE William J b Washington & FOWLER Florence b Washington. Bride: age 16, marr 1st time, b Goffstown d/o BLANCHETTE Joseph b Canada & Jennie b Canada. Vol: 7 Page: 024

DUSTON Freeman C of Hopkinton & SWEATT Lena M of Concord m Oct 22, 1918 Concord. Groom: age 26, marr 1st time, b Hopkinton s/o DUSTON Arthur M b Boscawen & CLOUGH Josie E b Hopkinton. Bride: age 25, marr

Hopkinton, NH Marriages 1914

1st time, b Webster d/o SWEATT Frank Leon b Webster & CHASE Maude b Webster. Vol: 7 Page: 024

KIMBALL John Prescott of Hopkinton & WEST Nettie W of Manchester m Oct 28, 1918 Hudson. Groom: age 39, marr 2nd time, b Hopkinton s/o KIMBALL John b Boston Ma & FRENCH Sara b Hopkinton. Bride: age 29, marr 2nd time, b Essex Jct Vt d/o WAKEFIELD Searles G b Linden Vt & COLE Beatrice b Canada. Vol: 7 Page: 025

LIBERTY Joseph of Hopkinton & DENNIS Gretchen May of Hopkinton m Jan 4, 1919 Hopkinton. Groom: age 28, marr 1st time, b Canada s/o LIBERTY Howorie b Canada & Dalila b Canada. Bride: age 16, marr 1st time, b Webster d/o DENNIS Napolone b Penacook & HARDY Grace b Manchester. Vol: 7 Page: 026

DUNBAR Arthur E of Hopkinton & SPENCER Annie of Cambridge Ma m Jan 17, 1919 Hopkinton. Groom: age 24, marr 1st time, b Hopkinton s/o DUNBAR Elmer E b Hopkinton & PAIGE Mary E b Dunbarton. Bride: age 24, marr 1st time, b Bay Roberts N F d/o SPENCER William b Bay Roberts N F & ADAMS Finnie b Brigus N F. Vol: 7 Page: 026

O'NEAL Percy of Hopkinton & BEHRN'S Ruth C of Pepperell Ma m Dec 26, 1914 Nashua. Groom: age 21, marr 1st time, b Dobsins Crn Nb s/o O'NEAL Alfred b Canada & STONE Annie b Canada. Bride: age 21, marr 1st time, b Pepperell Ma d/o BEHRN'S Frank b Maine & BASS Hattie b Pepperell Ma. Vol: 7 Page: 006

BAILEY William S of Hopkinton & LOWE Alice of Boston Ma m Jan 24, 1931 Nashua. Groom: age 50, marr 3rd time, b Hopkinton s/o BAILEY William P b Boston Ma & DOW Annie b Warner. Bride: age 37, marr 3rd time, b Fitchburg Ma d/o LOWE Walter b England & DONNELLY Mary b Fitchburg Ma. Vol: 9 Page: 022

SARGENT Gustin H of Concord & KIMBALL Grace P of Hopkinton m Oct 18, 1930 Manchester. Groom: age 28, marr 1st time, b Norwich Vt s/o SARGENT Seymour O b Norwich Vt & WATKINS Mary A b Merrimack. Bride: age 35, marr 1st time, b Hopkinton d/o KIMBALL Herbert M b Hopkinton & COLBY Mary A b Bow. Vol: 9 Page: 022

BUSWELL Frank P of Hopkinton & SLACK Etta of Concord m Dec 24, 1930 Goffstown. Groom: age 62, marr 1st time, b Concord s/o BUSWELL Samuel S b Hopkinton & EDLER Deborah b Machias Me. Bride: age 65, marr 1st time, b Webster d/o ROBY Hiram b Warner & HOWARD Angie J b Lyme. Vol: 9 Page: 022

SMITH Leroy Charles of Hopkinton & LESSARD Eugenia V of Hopkinton m Feb 14, 1931 Concord. Groom: age 29, marr 1st time, b Hopkinton s/o SMITH Robert b Webster & BOYCE Ardelle L b Concord. Bride: age 20, marr 1st time, b Raymond d/o LESSARD Lewis b Canada & RIVERS Lionie b Canada. Vol: 9 Page: 023

TONKIN Lawrence of Concord & CHASE Merle Estelle of Hopkinton m Jun 20, 1931 Concord. Groom: age 25, marr 1st time, b Concord s/o TONKIN George b England & PROWSE Nannie b England. Bride: age 25, marr 1st time, b Hopkinton d/o CHASE Marl b Warner & HARDY Clara M b Hopkinton. Vol: 9 Page: 024

Hopkinton, NH Marriages 1914

CLOUGH Wendell of Contoocook & GILE Catherine of Tilton m Apr 9, 1919 Tilton. Groom: age 25, marr 1st time, b Contoocook s/o CLOUGH Charle F b Hopkinton & HASTINGS Gertrude b Hopkinton. Bride: age 28, marr 1st time, b Belmont d/o GILE Asa E b Belmont & WOODWARD Etta J. Vol: 8 Page: 002

MEAD C Stanley of Everett Ma & LADD Olive A of Contoocook m Jul 9, 1919 Contoocook. Groom: age 28, marr 1st time, b Everett Ma s/o MEAD Charles H b Concord & HAPGOOD Clara A b Chelsea Ma. Bride: age 18, marr 1st time, b Contoocook d/o LADD Dexter b Epping & DAVIS Maud b Raymond. Vol: 8 Page: 003

BROWN Lanson O of Hopkinton & HASELTON Susie W of Hopkinton m Aug 23, 1919 Hopkinton. Groom: age 43, marr 2nd time, b Thornton s/o BROWN Daniel E b Thornton & ELKINS Laura A b Thornton. Bride: age 31, marr 2nd time, b West Concord d/o CARTER J S b Warner & CALEF Mary G b W Concord. Vol: 8 Page: 003

WASHBURN Russell W of Hopkinton & ELLIOTT Gertrude H of Hopkinton m Sep 3, 1919 Hopkinton. Groom: age 25, marr 1st time, b Caribou Me s/o WASHBURN Ernest b Caribou Me & GOOD Emily J b Caribou Me. Bride: age 25, marr 1st time, b Hopkinton d/o ELLIOTT Charles E b Hopkinton & HOWE Ann G b Hopkinton. Vol: 8 Page: 003

WELLMAN Marcus B of Manchester & EMMONS Bertha Alice of Portland Me m Oct 22, 1919 Hopkinton. Groom: age 42, marr 2nd time, b Manchester s/o WELLMAN Marcus C b Morrill Me & BROWN Emma L b Contoocook. Bride: age 44, marr 2nd time, b Greenwood Me d/o EMMONS Isreal E b Biddeford Me & BISHOP Franacina J b Leeds Me. Vol: 8 Page: 4

HALL Charles G of Epsom & ELLIOTT Carrie F of Hopkinton m Nov 27, 1919 Hopkinton. Groom: age 25, marr 1st time, b Pembroke s/o HALL Warren J b Salisbury & BROWN Fannie b Barrington. Bride: age 21, marr 1st time, b Hopkinton d/o ELLIOTT Edson F b Webster & COLBY Nettie L b West Deering. Vol: 8 Page: 4

COLBY Myron H of Contoocook & FINNO Francis Jane of Manchester m Dec 11, 1919 Contoocook. Groom: age 35, marr 1st time, b Hopkinton s/o COLBY Forrest b Litchfield & BARNARD Abbie H b Dunbarton. Bride: age 25, marr 1st time, b Little Branch Nb d/o FINNO James S b Kichibovguac & McDONALD Isabel b Little Branch Nb. Vol: 8 Page: 005

STEVENS Ernest Lee of Hopkinton & HATHAWAY Rita V of Hopkinton m Jan 11, 1920 Hopkinton. Groom: age 23, marr 1st time, b Hopkinton s/o STEVENS Ernest L b Manchester & RICHARDSON Nettie b Hopkinton. Bride: age 21, marr 1st time, b Farnum Quebec d/o HATHAWAY Charles H b Montreal & MURPHY Margaret b New York City. Vol: 8 Page: 6

STANLEY Edward W of Hopkinton & EMERY Abbie E of Raymond m Jan 21, 1920 Milford. Groom: age 71, marr 3rd time, b Hopkinton s/o STANLEY Horace C b Hopkinton & KIMBALL Mary A b Hopkinton. Bride: age 59, marr 3rd time, b Greenfield d/o DRAPER James C P b Greenfield & PARKER Anstis W b Francestown. Vol: 8 Page: 6

MARSTON Leon A of Deerfield & AHALE Flossie O of Hopkinton m May 12, 1920 Weare. Groom: age 35, marr 1st time, b Derrfield s/o MARSTON Levi B b Deerfield & YARLAND Ariscena C b Maine. Bride: age 25, marr 1st time, b Hopkinton d/o ELLIOTT Edson E b Webster & COLBY Nettie L b Hopkinton. Vol: 8 Page: 6

KENYON Frank F of Hopkinton & ROBIE Mary L K J of Hopkinton m Jun 26, 1920 Franklin. Groom: age 52, marr 2nd time, b Pomfret Vt s/o KENYON Albert b Pomfret Vt & KEMPTON Lucy b Pomfret Vt. Bride: age 54, marr 2nd time, b Andover d/o SEAVEY John b Andover & STEWART Priscilla b Piermont. Vol: 8 Page: 7

DERBY Walter Thatcher of Hopkinton & HAYFORD Arlene Viola of Hopkinton m Jun 30, 1920 Hopkinton. Groom: age 27, marr 1st time, b Toledo Ohio s/o DERBY Dana R b Lyme & THATCHER Mary E b Defiance Ohio. Bride: age 18, marr 1st time, b Goffstown d/o HAYFORD George A b Weare & COLBY Octavia B b Portsmouth. Vol: 8 Page: 7

BLANCHETTE Philip of West Hopkinton & HARDY Linny of West Hopkinton m Jul 17, 1920 Contoocook. Groom: age 24, marr 1st time, b Goffstown s/o BLANCHETTE Joseph b Lom Canada & BUREGARD Jeannette b Lom Canada. Bride: age 16, marr 1st time, b Salisbury d/o HARDY Elewell b Springfield Ma & WIGGIN Lucy b Salisbury. Vol: 8 Page: 7

INGRAM Glendon B of Laconia & ELLIOTT Marian K of Contoocook m Aug 3, 1920 Contoocook. Groom: age 22, marr 1st time, b Laconia s/o INGRAM Walter E b Vermont & SHEPARD Hattie E b Rumney Vt. Bride: age 21, marr 1st time, b Contoocook d/o ELLIOTT Charles b Contoocook & HOWE Gertrude b Jamaica Plains Ma. Vol: 8 Page: 8

CONANT Dwight L of Contoocook & McGUIRE Helen of Portland Me m Jun 21, 1920 Portland Me. Groom: age 23, marr 1st time, b Contoocook s/o CONANT Dwight E b Willimantic Conn & KEMP Blanche L b Concord. Bride: age 22, marr 1st time, b Berlin d/o McGUIRE Thomas W b Quebec P Q & DOOLEY Mary E b Whitefield. Vol: 8 Page: 8

HALL Raymond C of Candia & LESSARD Marie B of Contoocook m Sep 5, 1920 Raymond. Groom: age 21, marr 1st time, b Derrfield s/o HALL Frank P b Orford & ABBOTT Susie M b Suncook. Bride: age 19, marr 1st time, b Auburn d/o LESSARD Louis b Montreal P Q & RIVERS Leonie b Quebec. Vol: 8 Page: 8

PUTNEY John S Jr of Contoocook & HOUSTON Dorothy R of West Campton m Oct 20, 1920 Concord. Groom: age 25, marr 1st time, b Chicago Ill s/o PUTNEY John S b Webster & MILTON Lucille b Norfolk Va. Bride: age 22, marr 1st time, b Roxbury Ma d/o HOUSTON William C b Boston Ma & GEORGETTE R b Denver Colorada. Vol: 8 Page: 9

BARNARD Perley D of Hopkinton & CRAIG Eulalie of Hopkinton m Nov 3, 1920 Hopkinton. Groom: age 28, marr 1st time, b Hopkinton s/o BARNARD George E b Hopkinton & TYLER Bertha b Hopkinton. Bride: age 21, marr 1st time, b Dixmont Me d/o CRAIG Sewell E b Dixmont Me & ROLLINS Della L b Grafton. Vol: 8 Page: 9

EMERSON Frank D of Contoocook & HARTZ Mabel E of Warner m Nov 6, 1920 Warner. Groom: age 25, marr 1st time, b Hopkinton s/o EMERSON Fred H b Hopkinton & KIMBALL Nellie b Concord. Bride: age 23, marr 1st time, b

Cambridge Ma d/o HARTZ Edward b Cambridge Ma & BURNS Alberta b Edinburg Scotland. Vol: 8 Page: 9

THOMPSON Elmer J of Contoocook & LYON Rose Mable of Lowell Ma m Dec 25, 1920 Lowell Ma. Groom: age 23, marr 1st time, b Webster s/o THOMPSON Frank V b Suncook & ELLIOTT Josephine. Bride: age 25, marr 1st time, b Whitman Ma d/o LYON Arthur G b Rainham Ma & LANE Martha T b Hanson Ma. Vol: 8 Page: 10

WARD E Harvey of Hopkinton & PIPER Clara J of Plymouth m Jan 8, 1927 Contoocook. Groom: age 21, marr 1st time, b Hopkinton s/o WARD G Miles b Franklin & HOWARD Ida b Milford Ma. Bride: age 21, marr 1st time, b Northfield d/o PIPER Henry A b Northfield & MOSES Mary b Groton. Vol: 9 Page: 001

KIMBALL F Everett of Canterbury & DERRY Hazel Julia of Hopkinton m Jan 6, 1921 Hopkinton. Groom: age 27, marr 1st time, b Canterbury s/o KIMBALL Edwin F b Canterbury & BEVERLY Ida M b Canterbury. Bride: age 21, marr 1st time, b Hopkinton d/o DERRY Joseph E b Concord & PAGE Elvira C b Dunbarton. Vol: 8 Page: 11

SIMINO Charles M of Hopkinton & DEGREENIA Gladys of Island Pond Vt m Mar 12, 1921 Hopkinton. Groom: age 25, marr 2nd time, b Iresburg Vt s/o SIMINO Charles H b Canada & CLIFFORD Phoebe b Eden Vt. Bride: age 26, marr 2nd time, b So Albany Vt d/o COPELAND Charles b Canada & COBB Pansy b Albany Vt. Vol: 8 Page: 11

PURINGTON Roger Winthrop of Weare & HOOD Edith May of Hopkinton m May 12, 1921 Reeds Ferry. Groom: age 21, marr 1st time, b Weare s/o PURINGTON Chas F Jr b Weare & RAND Etta M b Wolfeboro. Bride: age 21, marr 1st time, b Weare d/o HOOD George G b Peterboro & BROWN Fronie E b Goffstown. Vol: 8 Page: 11

WHITE Chancey Walter of Concord & BLAKE Lillian Pearl* of Contoocook m Jun 11, 1921 Contoocook. Groom: age 24, marr 1st time, b Antrim s/o WHITE William C b Antrim & BUCHANAN Nettie L b Newbury Vt. Bride: age 25, marr 1st time, b Thornton d/o TOBYNE Rodney & Mary. Vol: 8 Page: 12

BLAKE James of Hopkinton & BLUE Lizzie J P of Hopkinton m Jul 9, 1921 Concord. Groom: age 55, marr 3rd time, b Newport Vt s/o BLAKE Elijah b Walden Center Vt & YOUNG Sarah b Edenborough Scotland. Bride: age 47, marr 3rd time, b Dundee Scotland d/o PEDDIE Daniel b Stanley Scotland & JEFFERS Lizzie b Dundee Scotland. Vol: 8 Page: 12

GAGE Frank S of Greenfield & CONANT Blanche of Hopkinton m Jul 23, 1921 Roby's Corner. Groom: age 49, marr 2nd time, b Norwich Ny s/o GAGE Roger S b Washington & NEASKERN Jennie b Sequoit Ny. Bride: age 47, marr 2nd time, b Concord d/o KEMP Frank P b Suncook & EASTMAN Jennie b Stoneham Ma. Vol: 8 Page: 12

NEWELL George H of Manchester & MONTGOMERY Lucy of Hopkinton m Aug 21, 1921 Hopkinton. Groom: age 28, marr 1st time, b Harrisville Ny s/o NEWELL Chauncey J b Harrisville Ny & SILL Addie b Hartwick Ny. Bride: age 28, marr 1st time, b Hopkinton d/o MONTGOMERY Guy b Hopkinton & MARTIN Nellie b Salem Ny. Vol: 8 Page: 13

Hopkinton, NH Marriages 1914

GILMORE Lew Weston of Concord & HARDY Marion Grace of Contoocook m Aug 31, 1921 Center Sandwich. Groom: age 26, marr 1st time, b Concord s/o GILMORE Charles L b Concord & MINNIE M b Henniker. Bride: age 21, marr 1st time, b Contoocook d/o HARDY Lewis B b Contoocook & HASELTON Grace M b Contoocook. Vol: 8 Page: 13

HOYT Edward F of West Hopkinton & BLANCHETTE Delia of West Hopkinton m May 19, 1921 Hopkinton. Groom: age 55, marr 2nd time, b Bradford s/o HOYT James M b Hillsboro & BUMFORD Mary E b Alexander. Bride: age 23, marr 2nd time, b Goffstown d/o BLANCHETTE Joseph b Canada & BUREAUGARD Jennie b Canada. Vol: 8 Page: 13

HACKETT Walter of Hopkinton & MURPHY Jennie of New Bedford Ma m Sep 14, 1921 Contoocook. Groom: age 58, marr 2nd time, b Sanborton s/o HACKETT Edwin L b Meredith & GLYNN Corlista F b Haverhill. Bride: age 60, marr 2nd time, b Hopkinton d/o CROWELL Joseph b Hopkinton & ASH Nancy b Hopkinton. Vol: 8 Page: 14

RICE Neal J of Hopkinton & HAVEN Eunice M of Hopkinton m Oct 25, 1921 Hopkinton. Groom: age 20, marr 1st time, b Hopkinton s/o RICE James G b Henniker & BOHANAN Bernice b Hopkinton. Bride: age 19, marr 1st time, b Penacook d/o HAVEN Frank B b Newport & NELSON Ida M b Hillsboro. Vol: 8 Page: 14

PERRY Ralph Howard of Hopkinton & COLBY Marion Viola of Hopkinton m Oct 30, 1921 Hopkinton. Groom: age 20, marr 1st time, b Hopkinton s/o PERRY James M b Hopkinton & KELLEY Editheen E b Hopkinton. Bride: age 18, marr 1st time, b Manchester d/o DWINNELLS Frank P b Hopkinton & LIBBY Emily H b Hopkinton. Vol: 8 Page: 14

KETCHUM Perley A of Boscawen & BROWN Marguerite of Contoocook m Nov 21, 1921 Concord. Groom: age 27, marr 1st time, b Boscawen s/o KETCHUM John b Champlain Ny & MINER Rosanna b Randolph Vt. Bride: age 20, marr 1st time, b Contoocook d/o BROWN Lanson O b Thornton & FLEMMING Melissa b Ontario Canada. Vol: 8 Page: 15

HUNTINGTON Arthur N of Henniker & FOWLER Mary R of Hopkinton m Nov 12, 1921 Sunapee. Groom: age 42, marr 2nd time, b Henniker s/o HUNT-INGTON Joseph J b Henniker & GORDON Mary T b Henniker. Bride: age 36, marr 2nd time, b Croydon d/o FOWLER Horace b Kelleyville & BROWN Elizabeth b Newbury. Vol: 8 Page: 15

DENSMORE Edward John of Hopkinton & LIBBY Capitola Dean of Hopkinton m Apr 16, 1921 Providence RI. Groom: age 31, marr 2nd time, b Hopkinton s/o DENSMORE James A b Northfield & LIBBY Eleanor Jane b Webster. Bride: age 19, marr 2nd time, b Hopkinton d/o LIBBY Frank D b Hopkinton & NICHOLS Eldora b Sweden. Vol: 8 Page: 15

DOHERTY James Wifird Jr of West Hopkinton & MERRILL Hazel of West Hopkinton m Feb 27, 1922 Contoocook. Groom: age 21, marr 1st time, b Somerville Ma s/o DOHERTY James Wilfird b N B & GORDON Nellie b Gasgow Scotland. Bride: age 19, marr 1st time, b Fitzwilliam d/o MERRILL Rodney Thomas b Franklin & TATRO Mattie b Swanton Vt. Vol: 8 Page: 16

HASTINGS Floyd D of Contoocook & HARDY Mildred P of Contoocook m Mar 8, 1922 Contoocook. Groom: age 21, marr 1st time, b Contoocook s/o

277

Hopkinton, NH Marriages 1914

HASTINGS Delman W b Hopkinton & CHASE Lena M b Contoocook. Bride: age 22, marr 1st time, b Contoocook d/o HARDY Lewis B b Hopkinton & HASELTON Grace b Contoocook. Vol: 8 Page: 16

PERRY Charles H of Hopkinton & BEALS Gladys E of Goffstown m Apr 16, 1922 Goffstown. Groom: age 29, marr 1st time, b Contoocook s/o PERRY James b Contoocook & KELLEY Edithren E b Contoocook. Bride: age 22, marr 1st time, b Goffstown d/o BEALS William H b N B & BUTTERFIELD Ella T b New Boston. Vol: 8 Page: 16

KENYON Frank F of Hopkinton & CARSWELL Annie B of Manchester m May 6, 1922 Hopkinton. Groom: age 53, marr 3rd time, b Pomford Vt s/o KENYON Albert b Pomford Vt & KEMPTON Lucy b Pomford Vt. Bride: age 54, marr 3rd time, b Manchester d/o LAMPREY David C b Deerfield & WHITE Annie B b Porstsmouth. Vol: 8 Page: 17

KIMBALL Leroy H of Hopkinton & GILLINGHAM Mariam of Hopkinton m Jun 16, 1922 Hopkinton. Groom: age 26, marr 1st time, b Middlefield Mas s/o KIMBALL Lucian C b Webster & STANYAN Edna b Wentworth. Bride: age 22, marr 1st time, b Newport RI d/o GILLINGHAM John W b Newport RI & COOKMAN Sarah b Eli P Q Canada. Vol: 8 Page: 17

DINMAN Henry J of Hopkinton & FISK Lydia A of Hopkinton m Aug 23, 1922 Contoocook. Groom: age 33, marr 1st time, b New Bedford Ma s/o DINMAN Henry B b Bristol RI & SIMMONS Ella R b Fairhaven Ma. Bride: age 33, marr 1st time, b Hopkinton d/o FISK Daniel F b Hopkinton & CHANDLER Delta E b Hopkinton. Vol: 8 Page: 17

DUSTON Arthur S of Hopkinton & FITTS Charlotte H of Dunbarton m Aug 23, 1922 Dunbarton. Groom: age 28, marr 1st time, b Hopkinton s/o DUSTON Arthur M b Boscawen & CLOUGH Josephine E b Hopkinton. Bride: age 21, marr 1st time, b Dunbarton d/o FITTS Benjamin E b Dunbarton & EMERSON Charlotte b Dunbarton. Vol: 8 Page: 18

KILBORN Robert Parker of Derby Vt & DAVIS Doris of Hopkinton m Aug 30, 1922 Contoocook. Groom: age 24, marr 1st time, b Derby Vt s/o KILBORN Willey T b Derby Vt & HOPKINSON Catherie b Derby Vt. Bride: age 25, marr 1st time, b Warner d/o DAVIS Willie N b Warner & PUTNAM Nellie L b Wilmont. Vol: 8 Page: 18

ARCHIBALD Stewart G of Hopkinton & CHASE Bertha May of Hopkinton m Sep 16, 1922 Warner??. Groom: age 23, marr 1st time, b N B s/o ARCHIBALD Ambrose b N B & SNYDNER Jennie b Upper Branch Nb. Bride: age 19, marr 1st time, b North Charlestown d/o CHASE Henry A b Hopkinton & BURGESS Lila May b Springfield Vt. Vol: 8 Page: 18

FELTIS Wendall E of Hopkinton & WEEKS Rose A of Somerville Ma m Oct 27, 1922 Contoocook. Groom: age 26, marr 1st time, b Quincy Ma s/o FELTIS Horace A b Quincy Ma & TANNER Mary b Abington Ma. Bride: age 26, marr 1st time, b Rosindale Ma d/o MACHINO George b Germany & Mary b France. Vol: 8 Page: 19

SMITH Charles B of Hopkinton & BUNNELL Roxie A of Hopkinton m Dec 21, 1922 Manchester. Groom: age 33, marr 1st time, b Chester Vt s/o SMITH Harlow J b Chester Vt & BLAKE Lizzie b Keene. Bride: age 19, marr 1st time,

Hopkinton, NH Marriages 1914

b Warner d/o BUNELL Harry E b Henniker & HARRIMAN Sadie b Warner. Vol: 8 Page: 19

ALDEN Chester H of Plymouth Ma & HOUGHTON Mable J of Walpole m Dec 25, 1922 Walpole. Groom: age 36, marr 2nd time, b Avon Ma s/o ALDEN Frederick E b Randolpy Vt & GANDWELL Ovilla. Bride: age 27, marr 2nd time, b Walpole d/o HOUGHTON Algeion b Walpole & SELKISH Jennis S b Surry. Vol: 8 Page: 19

SMART Harold B of Hopkinton & HOOD Ruth of Hopkinton m Jan 6, 1923 Contoocook. Groom: age 20, marr 1st time, b Warner s/o SMART Benjamin b Warner & BARTLETT Gertrude b Warner. Bride: age 17, marr 1st time, b Hopkinton d/o HOOD George b Peterboro & BROWN Fannie b Goffstown. Vol: 8 Page: 20

DALBY James Martin of Hopkinton & KOON Penniah Ellen of Syracuse Ny m Jan 17, 1923 Hopkinton. Groom: age 42, marr 2nd time, b Scituate Ma s/o DALBY John Franklin b Scituate Ma & MARTIN Jennie b Halifax N S. Bride: age 40, marr 2nd time, b Auburn Ny d/o KOON Joseph M b Auburn Ny & HOWARD Elizabeth H b Aubury Ny. Vol: 8 Page: 20

PERKINS Leroy J of Brooklin & DAVIS Lillian S of Hopkinton m Feb 8, 1923 Hopkinton. Groom: age 23, marr 1st time, b Andover s/o PERKINS Boney b Wilmont & Jennie b Andover. Bride: age 17, marr 1st time, b Salisbury d/o DAVIS Willie E b Canterbury & WATSON Sarah E b Northfield. Vol: 8 Page: 20

EASTMAN Harold of Liberty Me & CHANDLER Mary Jean of Hopkinton m Mar 17, 1923 Hopkinton. Groom: age 21, marr 1st time, b Liberty Me s/o EASTMAN Burton A b Libert Me & McGOWAN Helen b Scotland. Bride: age 19, marr 1st time, b Hopkinton d/o CHANDLER Arthur O b West Fairley Vt & MILLER Jean C b Scotland. Vol: 8 Page: 21

CHASE Leon P of Hopkinton & RICE Ethlyn of Milford m Apr 3, 1923 Contoocook. Groom: age 27, marr 1st time, b Hopkinton s/o CHASE Oscar N b Hopkinton & THORNTON Margaret b Hopkinton. Bride: age 21, marr 1st time, d/o RICE Blanchard F b Hygate Vt & PATTERSON Mary L b Canada. Vol: 8 Page: 21

PROCTOR William H of Beverly Ma & VONHAAS May L of Beverly Ma m Jun 27, 1923 Hopkinton. Groom: age 40, marr 2nd time, b Salem Ma s/o PROCTOR William b Salem Ma & FLAKE Mattie b Nova Scotia. Bride: age 43, marr 2nd time, b Chicago Ill d/o HAWLEY J b Ireland & FORD Anna b Ireland. Vol: 8 Page: 21

TARBALL Wallace H of Hopkinton & ELLIOTT Clarice M of Concord m Jul 15, 1923 Bridgewater. Groom: age 51, marr 2nd time, b Pepperell Ma s/o TARBALL Chales H b Pepperell Ma & ESKRIDGE Mary E b Shelby Ma. Bride: age 35, marr 2nd time, b Concord d/o ELLIOTT Henry F b Lisbon & DOLLOF Myra Etta b Bridgewater. Vol: 8 Page: 22

MORSE Clayton Harold of Hooksett & READ Elsie Ellen of Contoocook m Jun 30, 1923 Manchester. Groom: age 31, marr 1st time, b Derry s/o MORSE Edwin J b Auburn & POOR Grace E b Manchester. Bride: age 25, marr 1st time, b Hillsboro d/o READ Henry b Trowbridge Eng & SEAVER Sarah b Harrisville. Vol: 8 Page: 22

SHAMPNEY Will G of Hopkinton & CLARK Mary Viola of Hopkinton m Aug 31, 1923 Hopkinton. Groom: age 40, marr 1st time, b Sharon Vt s/o SHAMPNEY John b Canada & HOUSTIER Caroline b Canada. Bride: age 17, marr 1st time, b Hopkinton d/o CLARK Fred b Hopkinton & COOPER Mable Elina b Concord. Vol: 8 Page: 22

GLANVILLE Manley H of Contoocook & DEVINE Helen A of Dorchester Ma m Jun 30, 1923 Dorchester Ma. Groom: age 27, marr 1st time, b Everett Ma s/o GLANVILLE Charles F b England & Susiar b Boston Ma. Bride: age 27, marr 1st time, b Newark NJ d/o DEVINE William P b Norwalk Conn & Bertha b Newark NJ. Vol: 8 Page: 23

REID Charles Allen of Boston Ma & WEINZEIRL Mildred C of Contoocook m Sep 16, 1923 Contoocook. Groom: age 20, marr 1st time, b Somerville Ma s/o REID Clarence A b Canada & DENOVAN Kathleen b Montreal Canada. Bride: age 20, marr 1st time, b Boston Ma d/o WEINZEIRL Julius b Austria & FEST Hetty b Germany. Vol: 8 Page: 23

SEVERANCE Archie W of Hopkinton & CILLEY Ardis M of Franklin m Oct 7, 1923 Franklin. Groom: age 20, marr 1st time, b Hopkinton s/o SEVERANCE Will J b Washington & FOWLER Florence b Washington. Bride: age 16, marr 1st time, b Franklin d/o CILLEY Leonard W b Orange & FLANDERS Lina M b Orange. Vol: 8 Page: 23

TUCKER John F of Hopkinton & BOWERS Nancy B of Harrisville m Oct 6, 1923 Contoocook. Groom: age 47, marr 1st time, b Hopkinton s/o TUCKER Samuel G b Henniker & CHASE Nancy b Ryegate Vt. Bride: age 47, marr 1st time, b NY d/o BLAIR John b Ireland & SWEENEY Eliza b NY. Vol: 8 Page: 24

BOYNTON Gordon F of River Point RI & PEASLEE Grace E of Hopkinton m Oct 13, 1923 Hopkinton. Groom: age 34, marr 1st time, b Howell Ny s/o BOYNTON Edgar A b Cincinnati Ohio & FOSTER Lenor b Howell Ny. Bride: age 31, marr 1st time, b Weare d/o PEASLES Charles H b Weare & CARPENTER Susie b Hopkinton. Vol: 8 Page: 24

EMERSON F Harold of Hopkinton & COBURN Bernice F of Warner m Oct 15, 1923 Warner. Groom: age 27, marr 1 timest, b Hopkinton s/o EMERSON Fred H b Hopkinton & KIMBALL Nellie b Concord. Bride: age 25, marr 1st time, b Webster d/o FORSYTH Edward L b Manchester & BRACKETT Alma b Webster. Vol: 8 Page: 24

KIMBALL Howard A of Littleton & CHANDLER Elizabeth of Hopkinton m Nov 3, 1923 Hopkinton. Groom: age 21, marr 1st time, b Littleton Ma s/o KIMBALL Walter b Waltham Ma & McKINLEY Mable b St John. Bride: age 19, marr 1st time, b Hopkinton d/o CHANDLER Arthur O b Hopkinton & MILLER Jennie C b Dundee Scotland. Vol: 8 Page: 25

SADLOW James of Hartford Conn & BEALS Estella Maud of Middleton N S m Nov 24, 1923 Hopkinton. Groom: age 36, marr 2nd time, b Chicago Ill s/o SADLOW John b Bohemia & GLAYDIA Anna b Bohemia. Bride: age 40, marr 2nd time, b Middleton Nc d/o BEALS Albert b Nova Scotia & MIDDLEN Henrietta b Brooklyn Ny. Vol: 8 Page: 25

BRENNELL Harry E of Hopkinton & LEAVITT Stella G of Hopkinton m Jan 19, 1924 Concord. Groom: age 49, marr 2nd time, b Concord s/o BRENNELL Seth A b Bristol & EASTMAN Helen J b Henniker. Bride: age 44, marr 2nd time, b

Warner d/o BARTLETT Woodbury b Warner & DAVIS Clara b Brattleboro Vt. Vol: 8 Page: 26

McCONNELL James E of Suncook & BLANCHARD Ina E of Hopkinton m Feb 12, 1924 Contoocook. Groom: age 23, marr 1st time, b Concord s/o McCONNELL Samuel b Hillsboro & COLBY Ola b Bow. Bride: age 18, marr 1st time, b Weare d/o BLANCHARD Walter R & RAY Olaa M. Vol: 8 Page: 26

STEVENS Sherley of Hopkinton & FLANDERS Elen of Hopkinton m Jun 21, 1924 Concord. Groom: age 21, marr 1st time, b Me s/o STEVENS Geo M b Conway & ALLEN Etta B b Northfield. Bride: age 19, marr 1st time, b Warner d/o FLANDERS Fred W b Goshen & BURBANK Helen b Hopkinton. Vol: 8 Page: 26

FARNHAM Walter E of Watertown Ma & SCHRIBER Rose of East Dedham Ma m Jun 25, 1924 Hopkinton. Groom: age 19, marr 1st time, b Boston Ma s/o FARNHAM Ernest & PRESCOTT Edith b Maine. Bride: age 19, marr 1st time, b Germany d/o SCHRIBER Jacob b Germany & WEISBECKER Maria A b Germany. Vol: 8 Page: 27

ROBINSON Roland C of Hopkinton & STEVENS Mildred S of Hopkinton m Jul 26, 1924 Hopkinton. Groom: age 20, marr 1st time, b Concord s/o ROBINSON Frank H b Concord & CHARD Jennie b Gloucester Ma. Bride: age 16, marr 1st time, b Lyme d/o STEVENS George M b Fryeburg Me & ALLEN Etta B b Gilmanton. Vol: 8 Page: 27

EMERSON James H of Hopkinton & LITTLE Edna E of Hopkinton m Feb 12, 1927 Concord. Groom: age 42, marr 1st time, b Hopkinton s/o EMERSON Hanson D b Hopkinton & MILLS Mary F b Hopkinton. Bride: age 23, marr 1st time, b Newport d/o HOW Jonah C b Scharoom Vt & SHARP Emily A. Vol: 9 Page: 001

HARDY Elwin L of Hopkinton & DANIELLS Marion L of Weare m Oct 18, 1924 Weare. Groom: age 23, marr 1st time, b Hopkinton s/o HARDY Lewis B b Hopkinton & HASELTON Grace b Hopkinton. Bride: age 21, marr 1st time, b Weare d/o DANIELS George S b Weirs?? & MERRILL Lottie b Goffstown. Vol: 8 Page: 28

FIELD Franklin A W Jr of Boston Ma & MURPHY Mildred V of Boston Ma m Nov 2, 1924 Hillsboro. Groom: age 23, marr 1st time, b Bangor Me s/o FIELD Franklin A W b Florida & McCAW Mabel b Me. Bride: age 24, marr 1st time, b Boston Ma d/o MURPHY Michal J b Ireland & CROOPOOR[??] Margarett b Rockport Ma. Vol: 8 Page: 28

GEORGE Harry W of Manchester & BEAL Jennie W of Manchester m Dec 24, 1924 Contoocook. Groom: age 47, marr 3rd time, b Barnstead s/o GEORGE Henry W b Barnstead & THOMPSON Lizzie E b Gilmanton. Bride: age 41, marr 3rd time, b Bedford d/o BEAL Charles B b Manchester & ANNE E b Norwich Vt. Vol: 8 Page: 28

KIMBALL Richard H of Webster & CARD Maud M of Hopkinton m Feb 11, 1925 Hopkinton. Groom: age 23, marr 1st time, b Webster s/o KIMBALL Harry H b Webster & GRIFFIN Jessie b Hopkinton. Bride: age 18, marr 1st time, b Hopkinton d/o CARD Thomas B b Nova Scotia & EMERSON Blanche b Hopkinton. Vol: 8 Page: 29

BARTLETT Roy O of Hopkinton & HANKS Ester of Franklin m May 5, 1925 Warner. Groom: age 19, marr 1st time, b Hopkinton s/o BARTLETT Clifton J b Warner & CHASE Lida H b Hopkinton. Bride: age 19, marr 1st time, b Stratford d/o HANKS Gilbert b Stratford & DEMARS Leda L b Newport. Vol: 8 Page: 29

BAUMEISTER William H of Boston Ma & SCHMITT Hedwig of Hopkinton m Jun 3, 1925 Contoocook. Groom: age 49, marr 2nd time, b Germany s/o BAUMEISTER Henri b Germany & Elizabeth b Germany. Bride: age 44, marr 2nd time, b Germany d/o FEST Frederick b Germany & FABIAN Marie b Germany. Vol: 8 Page: 29

WALKER Milton J of Hopkinton & CRAM Helen E of Laconia m May 25, 1925 Laconia. Groom: age 59, marr 2nd time, b Danbury s/o WALKER David P b Wilmont & HAZELTINE Lydia A b Rumney. Bride: age 34, marr 2nd time, b Laconia d/o CRAM William b Boston Ma & PATCH Georgianna F b Lakeport. Vol: 8 Page: 30

MITCHELL Wallace H of Hopkinton & FLETCHER Pearl A of Laconia m Jun 20, 1925 Concord. Groom: age 19, marr 1st time, b Hopkinton s/o MITCHELL Dolf b Burlington Vt & LIBBY Estella b Hopkinton. Bride: age 19, marr 1st time, b Laconia d/o FLETCHER William E b Canada & McCLELLEN Lydia b Nova Scotia. Vol: 8 Page: 30

BURNBANK Carl of Hopkinton & STEVENS Evelyn of Hopkinton m Jul 10, 1925 Bradford. Groom: age 32, marr 1st time, b Hopkinton s/o BURNBANK Iving D b Hopkinton & FRENCH Augusta b Hopkinton. Bride: age 18, marr 1st time, b East Weare d/o STEVENS Arthur b Manchester & Ida b Hopkinton. Vol: 8 Page: 30

DODGE Charles Frank of Contoocook & ABBOTT Mildred S of Concord m Aug 8, 1925 Concord. Groom: age 25, marr 1st time, b Vt s/o DODGE Frank Everett b Webster & McFOSTER Annie L b Sheldon Vt. Bride: age 24, marr 1st time, b Concord d/o ABBOTT Joseph Newton b Concord & CHASE Martha O b Hopkinton. Vol: 8 Page: 31

NUDD Archie H of Hopkinton & CRAIG Jennie B of Antrim m Aug 30, 1925 Warner. Groom: age 38, marr 2nd time, b Warner s/o NUDD Horace G b Canterbury & BROWN Alice B b Hopkinton. Bride: age 23, marr 2nd time, b Antrim d/o CRAIG George b Newport & ROGERS Edith b Antrim. Vol: 8 Page: 31

BANKS Joseph of Greenwood Ma & JONES Ruth M of Melrose Ma m Sep 21, 1925 Contoocook. Groom: age 38, marr 1st time, b England s/o BANKS Harry b Scotland & ETCHELLS Elizabeth b Scotland. Bride: age 24, marr 1st time, b Melrose Ma d/o GIBBONS Frank b Melrose Ma & ELLIS Mary b England. Vol: 8 Page: 31

BURGESS Royal F of Hopkinton & ADAMS Hazel of Hopkinton m Dec 8, 1925 Contoocook. Groom: age 21, marr 1st time, b Plymouth Ma s/o PIERCE John b Carver Ma & BURGESS Martha F b Plymouth Ma. Bride: age 18, marr 1st time, b Hopkinton d/o ADAMS Claud D b Hopkinton & FLANDERS Ida b Lawrence Ma. Vol: 8 Page: 32

STORY Rapha N of Hopkinton & BOLIVER Violet V of Hopkinton m Dec 10, 1925 Hopkinton. Groom: age 21, marr 1st time, b Canaan s/o STORY Harry O b Canaan & FOSTER Mirtie b Rumney. Bride: age 16, marr 1st time, b Auburn d/o BOLIVER Allen b Nova Scotia & ARCHIBALD Dora b Nova Scotia. Vol: 8 Page: 32

STILES Archie J of Hopkinton & YOUNG Ida B of Newport Vt m Dec 14, 1925 Warner. Groom: age 42, marr 2nd time, b Newport Vt s/o STILES John B b Hyde Part Vt & BOWLEY Unice H b Newport Vt. Bride: age 46, marr 2nd time, d/o BEAN Frank & WARD Mary Ann b Farfax Vt. Vol: 8 Page: 32

STEVENS Sylvester of Hopkinton & REYNOLDS ? Mary L of Penacook m Jan 14, 1926 Hillsboro. Groom: age 78, marr 3rd time, b Franklin s/o STEVEN Reuben b Sutton & CLAY Mary Jane b New Boston. Bride: age 60, marr 3rd time, b Penacook d/o LeCLAIR John b Canada & OSIA Phebia b Canada. Vol: 8 Page: 33

PATCH Frank G of Hopkinton & DUNBAR Grace M of Hopkinton m Jun 14, 1927 Concord. Groom: age 23, marr 1st time, b Hopkinton s/o PATCH George E b Hopkinton & FRENCH Elsie D b Deerfield. Bride: age 31, marr 1st time, b Hopkinton d/o DUNBAR Eugene E b Hopkinton & PAGE Mary E b Dunbarton. Vol: 9 Page: 002

SULIVAN Homer A of Hopkinton & FRYE Doris E of Hopkinton m Mar 25, 1926 Contoocook. Groom: age 20, marr 1st time, b Quebec s/o SULLIVAN Arthur E b Canada & WALKER Cora E b Quebec. Bride: age 16, marr 1st time, b Contoocook d/o FRY Amos F b Worcester Ma & SANBORN Clara May b Hopkinton. Vol: 8 Page: 33

KINNE Lewis C of Hopkinton & LEROUX Florence of Hopkinton m Jun 22, 1926 Contoocook. Groom: age 30, marr 1st time, b Lelbanon s/o KINNE Charles b Methuen Ma & WELCH Nellie b Conn. Bride: age 21, marr 1st time, b Laconia d/o LEROUX Donald W b Canada & MARSTON Lula D b Meridith. Vol: 8 Page: 34

STEEL Thomas Albert of Boxborough Ma & BURNS Gertrude May of Hopkinton m Jul 10, 1926 Hopkinton. Groom: age 23, marr 1st time, b Boxborough Ma s/o STEEL Burpee b Boxborough Ma & WALKER Martha Jane b Boxborough Ma. Bride: age 29, marr 1st time, b Plainfield d/o MILNER Edward b Nova Scotia & JORDAN Emma J b Plainfield. Vol: 8 Page: 34

KIMBALL Lewis R of Hopkinton & FOLEY Grace A of Newburyport Ma m Jun 18, 1926 Newburyport Ma. Groom: age 28, marr 1st time, b Hopkinton s/o KIMBALL Nelson b Hopkinton & KIMBALL Adelaide M b Newfield. Bride: age 38, marr 1st time, b Blackville Nb d/o FOLEY James b St Johns N B & MARY A b Blackville N B. Vol: 8 Page: 34

BURGESS Fred L of Hopkinton & COMIEAU Elsie May of Webster m Aug 16, 1926 Hillsboro. Groom: age 20, marr 1st time, b Hopkinton s/o BURGESS Walter O b Claremont & ROBY Annie P b Boscawen. Bride: age 20, marr 1st time, b Nova Scotia d/o COMEAU Leo M b Nova Scotia & MELANSO Agnes b Nova Scotia. Vol: 8 Page: 35

HEINEKEN John E of Milltown NJ & ELLIOTT Elsie A of Hopkinton m Aug 25, 1926 Contoocook. Groom: age 23, marr 1st time, b Millstown NJ s/o HENINEKEN John F D b Columbia NJ & Emily S b Smith River NJ. Bride: age 22, marr 1st time, b Contoocook d/o ELLIOTT Clarence T b Webster & Alena b Gilmanton. Vol: 8 Page: 35

Hopkinton, NH Marriages 1914

CLOUGH Harold R of Hopkinton & SAWYER Raelene of Hopkinton m Sep 20, 1926 Hopkinton. Groom: age 24, marr 1st time, b Hopkinton s/o CLOUGH Charles E b Hopkinton & HASTINGS Gertrude b Hopkinton. Bride: age 21, marr 1st time, b Hopkinton d/o SAWYER Elmer E b Sutton & MUDGETT Lillian C b Weare. Vol: 8 Page: 35

HALL Charles G of Hopkinton & WILLARD Josephine of Hillsboro m Oct 6, 1926 West Hopkinton. Groom: age 32, marr 2nd time, b Pembroke s/o HALL Warren J b Salisbury & BROWN Fannie b Barrington. Bride: age 22, marr 2nd time, b Warner d/o WILLARD Joseph G b Newport & ORDWAY Arville b Warner. Vol: 8 Page: 36

COOPER Robert Albert of Hopkinton & COWDRAY Florence of Lowell Ma m Nov 24, 1926 Lawrence Ma. Groom: age 23, marr 1st time, b Hopkinton s/o COOPER H D b Concord & BURGESS Gertrude V b Caribou Me. Bride: age 26, marr 1st time, b Lowell Ma d/o COWDRAY F F b Norfolk Eng & COX Mary A b Loundon Eng. Vol: 8 Page: 36

NORTHRUP George M of Hopkinton & NORTHRUP May A of Hopkinton m Dec 20, 1926 Hopkinton. Groom: age 57, marr 3rd time, b Lisbon Ny s/o NORTHRUP Albert & WILLIAMSON Sarah J b Canton Ny. Bride: age 44, marr 3rd time, b Lisbon Ny d/o NORTHRUP Henry b Lisbon Ny & HEDDING Jamima b Canton Ny. Vol: 8 Page: 36

HOYT Charles of Hopkinton & LAMSLEY Rosetts of Henniker m Dec 25, 1926 Henniker. Groom: age 39, marr 2nd time, b Bradford s/o HOYT Edward F b Bradford & BUTRICK Charlotte b Deering. Bride: age 25, marr 2nd time, b Weare d/o MITCHELL Charles b Topsam Vt & FOLANSBEE Stella C b Weare. Vol: 8 Page: 37

DOWNS William W Jr of Scituate Mass & REDDY Elizabeth of Contocoook m Sep 18, 1926 Bridgewater Ma. Groom: age 23, marr 1st time, b Scituate Ma s/o DOWNS William W & NAY Flora C. Bride: age 19, marr 1st time, b Scituate Ma d/o REDDY Albert S & WOOD Cora. Vol: 8 Page: 37

CLARK Moses D of Hopkinton & SEVERANCE Dorothy of Hopkinton m Nov 20, 1926 Concord. Groom: age 39, marr 1st time, b Warner s/o CLARK Frank b Warner & McDOLE Georgianna. Bride: age 19, marr 1st time, b Hopkinton d/o SEVERANCE Willie J b Washington & FOWLER Florence b Washington. Vol: 8 Page: 37

COMES Herbert C of Hopkinton & BELL Irene of Portchester Ny m Sep 4, 1926 Hopkinton. Groom: age 30, marr 1st time, b Hopkinton s/o COMES Herbert C b Henniker & KEMP Clara May b Concord. Bride: age 24, marr 1st time, b Portchester Ny d/o BELL Abraham b Portchester Ny & HAYES Addie b Portchester Ny. Vol: 8 Page: 38

STACY Frank M of Henniker & HIGGINS Helen of Contoocook m Dec 30, 1920 Henniker. Groom: age 23, marr 1st time, b So Rayegate Vt s/o STACY Frank M & BEATON Margaret. Bride: age 19, marr 1st time, b E Boston Ma d/o HIGGINS Edmund A b E Boston Ma & BELCHER Ethel L b Winthrop Ma. Vol: 8 Page: 10

MONTGOMERY Henry B of Goffstown & DAVIS Florence O of Hopkinton m Oct 15, 1924 Contoocook. Groom: age 35, marr 1st time, b Manchester s/o MONTGOMERY Albert b Warner & RUSSELLL Sue I b Vermont. Bride: age

33, marr 1st time, b Boston Ma d/o OMAN A G b Sweden & MAJERSON Caroline b Sweden. Vol: 8 Page: 27

KRAPAHL Fredrick of Boston Ma & DEXTER Elizabeth of Boston Ma m Mar 5, 1926 Contoocook. Groom: age 22, marr 1st time, b Boston Ma s/o KARPAHL William b Germany & NOSEN Dorothea b Germany. Bride: age 23, marr 1st time, b Boston Ma d/o DEXTER Andrew b Scotland & BURNS Jane b Scotland. Vol: 8 Page: 33

BARTON Elmer of Hopkinton & O'BRIEN Catherine of Boston Ma m Mar 22, 1927 Contoocook. Groom: age 35, marr 2nd time, b Concord s/o BARTON Elmer C b Hopkinton & CURRIER Mary b Hopkinton. Bride: age 29, marr 2nd time, b Boston Ma d/o O'BRIEN John b Ireland & CROWLEY Bridgett b Ireland. Vol: 9 Page: 001

YOUNG Joseph H of Hopkinton & OLSEN Ivy M of Hopkinton m Jun 8, 1927 Concord. Groom: age 28, marr 1st time, b Sanford Me s/o YOUNG Joseph H b Boston Ma & FLANDERS Alice b Hopkinton. Bride: age 24, marr 1st time, b Saugus Ma d/o MITCHELL John H b Saugus Ma & MERCER Helen b England. Vol: 9 Page: 002

HOLMES Leon A of Middleboro Ma & YOUNG Irene B of Hopkinton m Jun 18, 1927 Concord. Groom: age 22, marr 1st time, b Bridgewater Ma s/o HOLMES Roy A b Bridgewater Ma & TINKHAM Nellie b Middleboro Ma. Bride: age 16, marr 1st time, b Warner d/o YOUNG Ira V b Cornish & BARTLETT Bernice M b Newport. Vol: 9 Page: 002

CRESSY Charles B of Hopkinton & REDINGTON Muriel B of Warner m Jun 29, 1927 Bradford. Groom: age 19, marr 1st time, b Bradford s/o CRESSY Byron A b Bradford & RING Gertrude L b Deering. Bride: age 20, marr 1st time, b Warner d/o REDINGTON Manley & PIERCE Martha b Warner. Vol: 9 Page: 003

STRAW True J of Hopkinton & CARTER Elsie M of Hopkinton m Jul 3o 1927 Warner. Groom: age 56, marr 2nd time, b Hopkinton s/o STRAW Gilman J b Hopkinton & HOYT Wealthy A b Bradford. Bride: age 38, marr 2nd time, b Concord d/o CARTER James W b Warner & CALEF Mary G b Concord. Vol: 9 Page: 003

LOWE Max of No Attleboro Ma & PRINCE Katherine of No Attleboro Ma m Aug 14, 1927 Contoocook. Groom: age 59, marr 1st time, b Germany s/o LOWE Frederick b Germany & Maria b Germany. Bride: age 60, marr 1st time, b Germany d/o MERKLE Christian b Germany. Vol: 9 Page: 003

BALL Phillip B of Hopkinton & CONANT Lena M of Hopkinton m Aug 22, 1927 Contoocook. Groom: age 27, marr 1st time, b Washington s/o BALL Sumner N b Washington & BROOKS Carrie b Antrim. Bride: age 29, marr 1st time, b Hopkinton d/o CONANT Dwight E b Willimantic Conn & KEMP Blanch b Concord. Vol: 9 Page: 004

COOPER Ralph H of Hopkinton & WILLEY Irene of Rochester m Jan 1, 1934 Hopkinton. Groom: age 29, marr 1st time, b Hopkinton s/o COOPER Herbert D b Concord & BURGESSS Gertrude b Caribou Me. Bride: age 21, marr 1st time, b Rochester d/o WILLEY B F b Dover & BAILEY Mary E b Somersworth. Vol: 10 Page: 001

Hopkinton, NH Marriages 1914

REDDY Samuel Jr of Hopkinton & GILLINGHAM Catherine of Hopkinton m Sep 3, 1927 Contoocook. Groom: age 21, marr 1st time, b No Situate Ma s/o REDDEY Samuel b Portland Me & COLDWELL Lydia A b Stoneham Ma. Bride: age 18, marr 1st time, b Stoneham Ma d/o GILLINGHAM John W b Newport RI & COOKMAN Sarah b Canada. Vol: 9 Page: 004

FELLOWS Joseph of Bradford & CRESSEY Eva M of Hopkinton m Sep 3, 1927 Bradford. Groom: age 29, marr 1st time, b Washington Vt s/o FELLOWS Don A b Plainfield & WALKER Alice B b Plainfield. Bride: age 20, marr 1st time, b Bradford d/o CRESSEY Byron b Bradford & RING Gertrude L b Deering. Vol: 9 Page: 005

CONANT Hiriam of Hopkinton & FLANDERS Hilda of Warner m Sep 6, 1927 Concord. Groom: age 35, marr 1st time, b Hopkinton s/o CONANT Dwight E b Willimatic Conn & KEMP Blanch b Concord. Bride: age 28, marr 1st time, b Warner d/o FLANDERS Herbert b Warner & GLOVER Mary G b Warner. Vol: 9 Page: 005

BERWICK George W of Hopkinton & FORD Luella S of Concord m Oct 8, 1927 Concord. Groom: age 20, marr 3rd time, b Manchester s/o BERWICK William H b Canada & DROINCE Josephine b Canada. Bride: age 20, marr 3rd time, b Orange d/o FORD Henry b Orange & LANGLEY Bernice I b Wilmont. Vol: 9 Page: 006

REED Robert G of Contoocook & KIMBALL Sarah of Concord m Jul 19, 1927 Portsmouth. Groom: age 23, marr 1st time, b Contoocook s/o REED Frank H b Boston Ma & GEORGE Helen b Pittsfield. Bride: age 21, marr 1st time, b Hopkinton d/o KIMBALL Robert W b Pittsfield & ELLIOTT Susan b Exeter. Vol: 9 Page: 005

HATHAWAY George J of Hopkinton & SMART Dorothy E of Hopkinton m Nov 23, 1927 Hillsboro. Groom: age 21, marr 1st time, b Canada s/o HATHAWAY Charles N b Canada & MURPHY Margaret b New York. Bride: age 23, marr 1st time, b Ossipee d/o SMART N S b Gilmanton & HAYDEN Margaret b Haverhill Ma. Vol: 9 Page: 006

ARCHIBALD Ernest S of Hopkinton & MORAN Tiresa E of Hopkinton m Dec 28, 1927 Hillsboro. Groom: age 26, marr 1st time, b New Boston s/o ARCHIBALD Joseph b Nova Scotia & VEINO Rose E b Nova Scotia. Bride: age 30, marr 1st time, b Hopkinton d/o MORAN Christopher b Concord & MALIAN Mary b Ireland. Vol: 9 Page: 006

MILLS Arthur P of Hopkinton & GUEST Mable Ellen of Short Hills NJ m Apr 7, 1928 Hopkinton. Groom: age 44, marr 1st time, b Hopkinton s/o MILLS Charles H b Hopkinton & TOWNES Olive b Dunbarton. Bride: age 46, marr 1st time, b England d/o GUEST Harry J b England & WATERS Frances J b England. Vol: 9 Page: 007

HARRIMAN Carl E of Salem & STORY Dorothy of Hopkinton m Jun 8, 1928 Grantham. Groom: age 26, marr 1st time, b Ashland s/o HARRIMAN Roy C b Plymouth & BARNABY Addie M b Nova Scotia. Bride: age 22, marr 1st time, b Concord d/o STORY Harry O b Canaan & FOSTER Mertie E b Rumney. Vol: 9 Page: 007

SERGEANT Henry G of Hopkinton & BAKER Dorothy E of Concord m Jun 20, 1928 Hopkinton. Groom: age 61, marr 2nd time, b Kent Hill Ill s/o SARGENT

James W b New York & GILL Harriett G b New Haven Conn. Bride: age 35, marr 2nd time, b Thetford England d/o BAKER Jonathan b England. Vol: 9 Page: 007

SWALLOW Parker of Mattapan Ma & McLEOD Margaret of Mattapan Ma m Jul 14, 1928 Contoocook. Groom: age 27, marr 1st time, b Canada s/o SWALLOW Ulysesses D b P E Island & BURKER Rebekah b Brockton Ma. Bride: age 27, marr 1st time, b Boston Ma d/o McLEOD Daniel b P E Island & STEWART Sadie A b P E Island. Vol: 9 Page: 008

COOPER George Edward of Hopkinton & KEATON Annabell May of Concord m Jul 14, 1928 Canterbury. Groom: age 21, marr 1st time, b Hopkinton s/o COOPER Clarence b Concord & CROCKETT Lena b Laconia. Bride: age 15, marr 1st time, b Webster d/o KEATON Frank & MOORE Bertha K b Webster. Vol: 9 Page: 008

BARTLETT Lewis A of Hopkinton & TAULKINGHAM Daisy of Hopkinton m Sep 23, 1928 Hopkinton. Groom: age 21, marr 1st time, b Warner s/o BART-LETT Luther b Warner & NUDD Nellie R b Warner. Bride: age 19, marr 1st time, b Machias Me d/o TAULKINGHAM George b Machias Me & O'BRIAN Agnes b Kittery Me. Vol: 9 Page: 008

SMITH John C of Hopkinton & HILAND Susie M of Hopkinton m Nov 14, 1928 Contoocook. Groom: age 66, marr 2nd time, b Hopkinton s/o SMITH Charles H b Hopkinton & DELINO Nancy J b Maine. Bride: age 51, marr 2nd time, b Dunbarton d/o LAW Orin & BUTTERS Sarah M. Vol: 9 Page: 009

GOOLY?? George of Londonderry & CLARK Gertrude of Hopkinton m Jan 1, 1929 Londonderry. Groom: age 27, marr 1st time, b Londonderry s/o GREELEY?? Charley b Derry & ALLEN Harrott ?? b Jeffery. Bride: age 23, marr 1st time, b Middlebury Vt d/o CLARK Harmon b Vertmont & SUMNER Alice b Middlebury Vt. Vol: 9 Page: 010

SMITH Alfred W of Lowell Ma & FULTON Wilhelmina F of Concord m Jan 26, 1929 Manchester. Groom: age 25, marr 1st time, b Exeter s/o SMITH Albert F b Germany & WANZEL Katherine b Brooklyn Ny. Bride: age 23, marr 1st time, b Newville N S d/o FULTON Samuel O b Newville N S & ---- ---- b Sherbrook N S. Vol: 9 Page: 010

CURRIER Harland H of Hopkinton & LESSARD Lucia of Hopkinton m Feb 2, 1929 Penacook. Groom: age 28, marr 1st time, b Hopkinton s/o CURRIER Willie H b Hopkinton & WEBSTER Gertrude b Hopkinton. Bride: age 17, marr 1st time, b Candia d/o LESSARD Lewis b Canada & RIVERS Lenora b Canada. Vol: 9 Page: 010

MOULTON Will H of Concord & TIERNEY Mary A of Hopkinton m Apr 24, 1929 Hillsboro. Groom: age 67, marr 2nd time, b Hopkinton s/o MILTON Geo W b Hopkinton & CUMMINGS Mary A b Nova Scotia. Bride: age 45, marr 2nd time, b Concord d/o TIERNEY Thomas J b Concord & DRISCALL Mary b Ireland. Vol: 9 Page: 011

NELSON Carl Hamblet of Hopkinton & MESSIER Mable M of Warner m Apr 24, 1929 Hopkinton. Groom: age 19, marr 1st time, b Contoocook s/o NELSON John H b Hopkinton & CORSER Blanche b Hopkinton. Bride: age 24, marr 1st time, b Warner d/o MARSHALL Albert C b Washington & ROBY Hattie E b Warner. Vol: 9 Page: 011

Hopkinton, NH Marriages 1914

LaBONTY Jesse of Loudon & FOOTE Marion of Hopkinton m Apr 13, 1929 Concord. Groom: age 41, marr 2nd time, b Pittsfield s/o LABONTY Frank C b Highgate Vt & OSIER Nellie b Canada. Bride: age 26, marr 2nd time, b Hopkinton d/o FOSTER William Nelson b Portland Me & WATTS Helen Mary b Hopkinton. Vol: 9 Page: 011

SIGRIST Andrew E of Manchester & DUGAN Gertrude H of Contoocook m Apr 1, 1929 Hillsboro. Groom: age 24, marr 1st time, b Manchester s/o SIGRIST Eugene b Canada & GAUDET Eugenie b Canada. Bride: age 21, marr 1st time, b Bedford d/o DUGAN Francis b Manchester & HARRINGTON Mary O b Manchester. Vol: 9 Page: 012

MINIUTTE Sante of Concord & WHEELER Marshia L of Hopkinton m Jun 16, 1929 Hopkinton. Groom: age 41, marr 2nd time, b Italy s/o MINIUTTE Pasquale b Italy & COZZE Ragina b Italy. Bride: age 38, marr 2nd time, b Hopkinton d/o AUSTIN Oliver b Hopkinton & MOODY Bertha b Bow. Vol: 9 Page: 012

DAVIS Edward R of Portland Me & JOHNSON Pauline O of Contoocook m Aug 4, 1929 Walpole. Groom: age 24, marr 1st time, b Boston Ma s/o DAVIS William S b Boston Ma & DENNETT Annie b No Berwick Me. Bride: age 24, marr 1st time, b Newbury d/o JOHNSON Ralph W b Newbury & PAUL Isabelle H b Newport. Vol: 9 Page: 012

CHASE Fred J of Contoocook & ADAIR Ida Ann of Contoocook m Aug 26, 1929 Contoocook. Groom: age 58, marr 2nd time, b Contoocook s/o CHASE Orrin b Contoocook & BADGER Hattie May b Warner. Bride: age 62, marr 2nd time, b New London d/o FISKE Benjamin & PHILBRICK Mary Ann b Sutton. Vol: 9 Page: 013

QUIGLEY John W of Concord & GEER Gladys of Hopkinton m Sep 16, 1929 Contoocook. Groom: age 36, marr 1st time, b Frankfort Me s/o QUIGLEY John b Winterport Me & AVERILL Ada B b Frankford Me. Bride: age 18, marr 1st time, b Hopkinton d/o GEER Bert L b & BRYANT Candice A b Maria Ny. Vol: 9 Page: 013

ANDERSON George of Contoocook & MILLER Mabel of Pembroke m Sep 21, 1929 Concord. Groom: age 21, marr 1st time, b Brookline Ma s/o ANDERSON August b Sweden & McMANARA Mary b Ireland. Bride: age 24, marr 1st time, b Mccrimmon Ont d/o MILLER William b Brookline Ma & McDONALD Sarah b Ontario. Vol: 9 Page: 014

CHASE Walter B of Hopkinton & ANDREWS Harriett C of New Boston m Nov 5, 1929 New Boston. Groom: age 27, marr 1st time, b New York s/o CHASE Carroll b Windham NY & MORSE Charlotte C b Winchester Ma. Bride: age 19, marr 1st time, b New Boston d/o ANDREWS Charles b New Boston & HANSON Sophia b Demark. Vol: 9 Page: 014

ROBERTSON Everett B of Hopkinton & PAGE Dorothy Gladys of Henniker m Nov 27, 1929 Contoocook. Groom: age 17, marr 1st time, b Hopkinton s/o ROBERTSON Milo B b Henniker & BLANCHETT Emma b Goffston. Bride: age 17, marr 1st time, b Hillsboro d/o PAGE Willie H b Henniker & HOWLEY Mary b Portland Me. Vol: 9 Page: 015

PATCH Guy J of Hopkinton & DANFORTH Emma M of Hopkinton m Dec 22, 1929 Contoocook. Groom: age 21, marr 1st time, b Hopkinton s/o PATCH

George E b Hopkinton & FRENCH Elsie b Deerfield. Bride: age 21, marr 1st time, b Hopkinton d/o DANFORTH Edmund G b Hopkinton & FOSS Lucy A b Hopkinton. Vol: 9 Page: 015

NOLAN James K of Bradford & CONNELLEY Bernie of Hopkinton m Dec 25, 1929 Hopkinton. Groom: age 20, marr 1st time, b Sutton s/o NOLAN James A b Sutton & GOODRICH Charlotte b Montpelier Vt. Bride: age 18, marr 1st time, b Nova Scotia d/o CONNELLY Rufus A b Nova Scotia & SMITH Susie L b Nova Scotia. Vol: 9 Page: 015

WALTERS Thomas G of Concord & DAVIS Audrey Olive of Contoocook m Dec 28, 1929 Contoocook. Groom: age 28, marr 1st time, b Lunenburg N S s/o WALTERS William F b Lunenburg N S & SMITH Mary E b Port Medway N S. Bride: age 26, marr 1st time, b Contoocook d/o DAVIS Horace J b Warner & CARROLL Jennie b So Sutton. Vol: 9 Page: 016

BLANCHETTE Philip J of Hopkinton & CLARK Evelyn M of Hopkinton m Jan 13, 1930 Contoocook. Groom: age 34, marr 2nd time, b Goffstown s/o BLANCHETTE Joseph b & BEAUGARD Mary b Goffstown. Bride: age 16, marr 2nd time, b Hopkinton d/o CLARK James F b Warner & DROWNER Lilla M b Warner. Vol: 9 Page: 017

GEORGE Charles Adna of Contoocook & SLACK Beulah May of Weare m Jan 18, 1930 No Weare. Groom: age 23, marr 1st time, b Franklin s/o GEORGE Charles H b Webster & GEORGE Clara O b Three Rivers Que. Bride: age 19, marr 1st time, b Manchester d/o SLACK George L b Athens Ontario & Edith L b Ontario. Vol: 9 Page: 017

CARR John Sheldon of Contoocook & CONNOR Elsie D of Henniker m Jun 15, 1930 Warner. Groom: age 25, marr 1st time, b Hopkinton s/o CARR John F b W Hopkinton & SYMONDS Edna b Hopkinton. Bride: age 23, marr 1st time, b Henniker d/o CONNOR F T b Henniker & Annabelle b Antrim. Vol: 9 Page: 017

WALTERS Thomas G of Concord & DAVIS Audrey Olive of Contoocook m Dec 28, 1929 Contoocook. Groom: age 28, marr 1st time, b Concord s/o WALTERS William T b Lunenburg N S & SMITH Mary C b Port Medway N S. Bride: age 26, marr 1st time, b Contoocook d/o DAVIS Horace J b Warner & CARROLL Jennie b So Sutton. Vol: 9 Page: 016

BOOTH George W of Manchester & MacGINNES Charlotte of Contoocook m Jun 21, 1930 Manchester. Groom: age 22, marr 1st time, b Manchester s/o BOOTH George W b New York & BURKE Esther b Manchester. Bride: age 16, marr 1st time, b Contoocook d/o MacGINNES Charles & SANBORN Sadie b Contoocook. Vol: 9 Page: 018

SANBORN E Russell of Hopkinton & HARRIS Mary B of Hopkinton m Jun 25, 1930 Hopkinton. Groom: age 51, marr 2nd time, b Weymouth Ma s/o SANBORN Walter F b Wilton Me & THAYER Bryanetha b Quincy Ma. Bride: age 44, marr 2nd time, b Glenwood Kansas d/o HARRIS Merlin C b Elmira Ny & BAILEY Ortha J b Columbus Ohio. Vol: 9 Page: 018

STACY Richard Henry of Springfield Ma & COLBY Blanche Carr of Hopkinton m Jun 28, 1930 Hopkinton. Groom: age 65, marr 2nd time, b Springfield Ma s/o STACY Edwin S b Monson Ma & POMEROY Martha J b Springfield Ma.

Bride: age 42, marr 2nd time, b Hopkinton d/o COLBY Forrest b Litchfield & BARNARD Abbie H b Dunbarton. Vol: 9 Page: 018

LEROUX Richard Malcolm of Grasmer & LAKEMAN Ruby Mildred of Grasmere m Jun 28, 1930 Manchester. Groom: age 22, marr 1st time, b Stockbridge Mass s/o LEROUX Donald William b Montreal & MARSTON Lila b Meredith Center. Bride: age 22, marr 1st time, b Dunbarton d/o LAKEMAN Lafayette b Pembroke & BEAN Julia F b Windham. Vol: 9 Page: 019

ROBINSON John C of Longmeadow Ma & HARDING Helen Walker of Longmeadow m Jul 29, 1930 Hopkinton. Groom: age 65, marr 2nd time, b Longmeadow s/o ROBINSON Josiah C b Granville Ma & MOSELY Flavia I b West Field Ma. Bride: age 63, marr 2nd time, b Diabekir Turkey d/o WALKER Augustus b Baltimore Md & HARDY Eliza b Waltham Ma. Vol: 9 Page: 019

SPIEGEL Charles C Jr of Roslindale Ma & BRUCKER Helen L of Jamaica Plains m Sep 1, 1930 Hopkinton. Groom: age 20, marr 1st time, b Roxbury Ma s/o SPIEGEL Charles C b Roxbury Ma & KILEY Marguerite V b Jamaica Plains Ma. Bride: age 18, marr 1st time, b Boston Ma d/o BRUCKER Louis b France & DEINER Emma b France. Vol: 9 Page: 019

BARLTETT Charles R of Hopkinton & HOYT Arneta L of Hopkinton m Apr 25, 1934 Warner. Groom: age 21, marr 1st time, b Warner s/o BARTLETT Luther b Warner & NUDD Nellie b Warner. Bride: age 20, marr 1st time, b Laconia d/o HOYT Harry b Hopkinton & JOHNSON Lillian b Hopkinton. Vol: 10 Page: 002

LANG Thomas of Hopkinton & FOLEY Elizabeth of Manchester m Sep 14, 1930 Auburn. Groom: age 64, marr 3rd time, b Canada s/o LANG Thomas b Canada & Mary b Canada. Bride: age 52, marr 3rd time, b Manchester d/o FOLEY Jerry b Ireland & Catherine b Ireland. Vol: 9 Page: 020

BROWN Harold C of Warner & HILLIARD Jessie L of Contoocook m Sep 21, 1930 Newbury. Groom: age 26, marr 1st time, b Dunbarton s/o BROWN Reuben B b Dunbarton & HEATH Ida M b Boscawen. Bride: age 21, marr 1st time, b Amherst Ma d/o HILLIARD Frank R b Epsom & TOWLE Bessie A b Chichester. Vol: 9 Page: 020

SWAIN Oramel Walker of Concord & MATHESON Sarah M of Hopkinton m Sep 6, 1930 Hopkinton. Groom: age 27, marr 1st time, b Concord s/o SWAIN Stephen H b Hebron & WALKER Mary b Hebron. Bride: age 25, marr 1st time, b Concord d/o MATHESON Frank b Concord & HOYT Mabel b Concord. Vol: 9 Page: 021

POTTER Sidney A of No Cambridge Ma & HOLLAND Mary L of No Cambridge Ma m Dec 13, 1930 Hopkinton. Groom: age 30, marr 2nd time, b Boston Ma s/o POTTER Albert L b Boston Ma & DODGE Ella T b Boston Ma. Bride: age 26, marr 2nd time, b No Cambridge Ma d/o HOLLAND John & ---- ---- b Cambridge Ma. Vol: 9 Page: 021

CONNELLY Harvey O of Cambridge Ma & ROSS Alice L of Hopkinton m Dec 17, 1930 Hopkinton. Groom: age 23, marr 1st time, b Halifax N S s/o CONNELLY Rufus b Nova Scotia & SMITH Susie b Nova Scotia. Bride: age 23, marr 1st time, b Stoughton Ma d/o ROSS Forest E b Stoughton Ma & BUTLER Florence b Lynn Ma. Vol: 9 Page: 021

Hopkinton, NH Marriages 1914

CURTIS Seth W of Cheshire Ma & VINER Kate of Cheshire Ma m May 16, 1931 Contoocook. Groom: age 66, marr 5th time, b Cheshire Ma s/o CURTIS Martimer b Cheshire Ma & NOBLE Lizzie b Springfield Ma. Bride: age 66, marr 5th time, b Cheshire Ma d/o NICKERSON Edwin b Lenox Ma & PIERCE Almedia b Windsor Ma. Vol: 9 Page: 023

MacCALLEY Reginald H of Lowell Ma & HARRIS Ruth Jackson of Lowell Ma m Jun 13, 1931 Contoocook. Groom: age 28, marr 1st time, b Lowell Ma s/o MacCALLEY Daniel C b Malone NY & HUTCHINSON Alice b Lowell Ma. Bride: age 22, marr 1st time, b Lowell Ma d/o HARRIS Emmonds b Salem Me & JACKSON Ida b Windham Nh. Vol: 9 Page: 023

HALEY Louis W of No Adams Ma & CURTIS Anna A of Hopkinton m Jul 6, 1931 Contoocook. Groom: age 31, marr 1st time, b No Adams Ma s/o HALEY John P b Pownal Vt & CARDEN Corrine. Bride: age 20, marr 1st time, b Cheshire Ma d/o CURTIS Mortimer b Cheshire Ma & HARRINGTON Ella b Berlin Ny. Vol: 9 Page: 024

CHAPIN Merrick W Jr of Nashua & PRESTON Dorothea of Contoocook m Jun 6, 1931 Hopkinton. Groom: age 26, marr 1st time, b Hartford Conn s/o CHAPIN Merrick W b Hartford Conn & CHAMBERLAIN Maud b So Hadley Ma. Bride: age 25, marr 1st time, b Contoocook d/o PRESTON Charles A b Henniker & DAVIS Mary b Contoocook. Vol: 9 Page: 024

LaFLEUR Donald M of Concord & STEVENS Gertrude W of Hopkinton m Jul 10, 1931 Concord. Groom: age 21, marr 1st time, b Albany Vt s/o LaFLEUR Daniel H b Albany Vt & STEVENS Gertrude J b Windsor Can. Bride: age 23, marr 1st time, b Hopkinton d/o STEVENS Arthur b Manchester & WATTS Ida May b Hopkinton. Vol: 9 Page: 025

SHURTLEFF Joseph S of Hopkinton & GRANT Janet Cadell of Concord m Jul 13, 1931 Hillsboro. Groom: age 24, marr 1st time, b Hopkinton s/o SHURTLEFF Charles A b Hopkinton & MORAN Katherine b Hopkinton. Bride: age 25, marr 1st time, b Scotland d/o GRANT David b Scotland & DEWART Grace b Scotland. Vol: 9 Page: 025

SANBORN Frank M of Sunapee & RIPLEY May of Contoocook m Aug 1, 1931 Derry. Groom: age 34, marr 2nd time, b Sunapee s/o SANBORN Will E b Croydon & HARDING Mary b Newport. Bride: age 30, marr 2nd time, b Contoocook d/o UNKNOWN (orphan). Vol: 9 Page: 025

CILLEY Elden G of Hopkinton & WHITEHOUSE Maud M of Hopkinton m Aug 15, 1931 Woodsville. Groom: age 62, marr 2nd time, b Weare s/o CILLEY Benjamin F b Weare & CUSHING Mary S b Mass. Bride: age 47, marr 2nd time, b Alton d/o WHITEHOUSE Charles W b Alton & KENISTON Georgie E b Concord. Vol: 9 Page: 026

LUND Kenneth C of Revere Ma & McLAUGHLIN Marion of Revere Ma m Aug 10, 1931 Hopkinton. Groom: age 24, marr 1st time, b Farmington s/o LUND Carol b Dover & DUNN Delia b Hudson Ma. Bride: age 24, marr 1st time, b Boston Ma d/o McLAUGHLIN Thomas b Meriden Conn & MAHONEY Katherine b Providence R I. Vol: 9 Page: 026

MacDONALD Donald D of Towanda Pa & GILBERT Rita A of Philadelphia Pa m Aug 18, 1931 Contoocook. Groom: age 31, marr 1st time, b Towanda Pa s/o MacDONALD Richard b Towand Pa & Emma b Towana Pa. Bride: age 32, marr 1st time, b Philadelphia Pa d/o GILBERT William T b Philadelphia Pa & Jennie B b Philadelphia Pa. Vol: 9 Page: 026

ROLLINS William H of Hopkinton & CHASE Mildred M of Warner m Aug 31, 1931 Warner. Groom: age 41, marr 1st time, b Hopkinton s/o ROLLINS William H b Hopkinton & ROBINSON Margaret b Hopkinton. Bride: age 20, marr 1st time, b Warner d/o CHASE Fred A b Lisbon & Emma M b Stanstead P C Can. Vol: 9 Page: 027

CHASE Edward of Hopkinton & HOOD Eva M of West Newton Ma m Sep 19, 1931 Concord. Groom: age 20, marr 1st time, b Hopkinton s/o CHASE Oscar N b Hopkinton & THORNTON Margaret b Hopkinton. Bride: age 24, marr 1st time, b Lowell Ma d/o HOOD Harry E b Lowell Ma & Matilda b Canada. Vol: 9 Page: 027

REYCROFT G Moulton of Boston Ma & SHEPARD Dorothy of Boston Ma m Oct 5, 1931 Hopkinton. Groom: age 33, marr 1st time, b Arlington Ma s/o REYCROFT Louis W b Cambridge Ma & GAGE Eliza b Roxbury Ma. Bride: age 26, marr 1st time, b Concord d/o SHEPARD George E b Concord & DEVEREUX Isabel b Boston Ma. Vol: 9 Page: 027

FRENCH Ervin R of Hopkinton & MARTIN Dorothy A of Hopkinton m Oct 18, 1931 Hopkinton. Groom: age 29, marr 1st time, b Henniker s/o FRENCH Ernest E b Nashua & ROBERTSON Mertie D b Henniker. Bride: age 19, marr 1st time, b Manchester d/o MARTIN Fred J b Hillsboro & SARGENT Achsah b Goffstown. Vol: 9 Page: 028

MESSER William Earl of Naugatuck Conn & CURRIER Marian Ella of Waterbury Conn m Oct 10, 1931 Hopkinton. Groom: age 29, marr 1st time, b Barre Vt s/o MESSER William H b Boston Ma & CUSHMAN Emily E b Randolph Vt. Bride: age 39, marr 1st time, b Concord d/o CURRIER John H b Bedford & COOK Susan A b Franklin. Vol: 9 Page: 028

ORSWELL Merrill C of Hopkinton & THOROGOOD Doris M of Hopkinton m Oct 18, 1931 Contoocook. Groom: age 37, marr 2nd time, b Fall River Ma s/o ORSWELL Israel b Iowa & BARLOW Annie Eva b Fall River Ma. Bride: age 18, marr 2nd time, b Providence RI d/o THOROGOOD George b England & POOLE Louise M b Chelsea Ma. Vol: 9 Page: 028

BARTLETT Lewis of Hopkinton & GEORGE Helen M of Concord m Jan 10, 1932 Warner. Groom: age 24, marr 2nd time, b Warner s/o BARTLETT Luther b Warner & NUDD Nellie b Warner. Bride: age 24, marr 2nd time, b Concord d/o GEORGE Irving b Danville & MURPHY Julia b Roxbury Ma. Vol: 9 Page: 030

GRAZIANO Thomas A of Concord & NELSON Margary Lois of Contoocook m Jan 22, 1932 Concord. Groom: age 20, marr 1st time, b Concord s/o GRAZIANO Antonia b Italy & VARIN Odell b Suncook. Bride: age 19, marr 1st time, b Concord d/o NELSON Eddie & BOHANAN Etta L. Vol: 9 Page: 030

WILDER Albert Ransford of Hopkinton & WEBBER Florence Mae of Concord m Jan 30, 1932 Ossipee. Groom: age 25, marr 1st time, b Somerville Ma s/o WILDER Leland R b Bangor Me & TAYLOR Bessie J b Charlestown Ma. Bride: age 24, marr 1st time, b Westport N S d/o WEBBER Charles S b Nova Scotia & ELLIS Eva b Nova Scotia. Vol: 9 Page: 030

HALL George E of Hopkinton & BUNTEN Shirley of Hopkinton m Feb 24, 1932 Hopkinton. Groom: age 23, marr 1st time, b Hopkinton s/o HALL Frank E b Boscawen & WEEKS Annie M b Hopkinton. Bride: age 21, marr 1st time, b Hopkinton d/o BUNTEN Arthur b Manchester & FULLER Eva b Hopkinton. Vol: 9 Page: 031

HATHAWAY Melvin J of Hopkinton & NELSON Ruth E of Hopkinton m Mar 5, 1932 Hillsboro. Groom: age 30, marr 1st time, b NY s/o HATHAWAY Charles H b Canada & MURPHY Margaret b New York City. Bride: age 24, marr 1st time, b Hopkinton d/o NELSON Lewis A b Hopkinton & CHASE Maud b Hopkinton. Vol: 9 Page: 031

RICE Theodore K of Concord & WEAST Elnora M of Hopkinton m Mar 31, 1932 Manchester. Groom: age 23, marr 1st time, b Concord s/o RICE W A b Nova Scotia & HILL Mary E b Concord. Bride: age 17, marr 1st time, b Schenectady Ny d/o WEAST James A b Schenectady Ny & BARLOW Bessie M b Esperance Ny. Vol: 9 Page: 031

SEVERANCE Archie W of Hopkinton & GAGNON Odena I of Pembroke m Apr 30, 1932 Concord. Groom: age 29, marr 2nd time, b Hopkinton s/o SEVERANCE William J b Bradford & FOWLE Florence E b Washinton. Bride: age 29, marr 2nd time, b Pembroke d/o GAGNON Honore b Canada & PRIRE Rose b Canada. Vol: 9 Page: 032

FULLER Charles C of Hopkinton & FRENCH Esther A of Franklin m May 5, 1932 Hopkinton. Groom: age 59, marr 2nd time, b Littleton s/o FULLER Charles b Littleton & CLOUGH Melissia b Littleton. Bride: age 58, marr 2nd time, b Scotland d/o AYERS Samuel b Scotland & BELL Elizabeth b Ireland. Vol: 9 Page: 032

TONKIN Albert of Hopkinton & PERRIN Hazel V of Hopkinton m Jun 17, 1932 Concord. Groom: age 35, marr 1st time, b Concord s/o TONKIN George E b England & PROWSE Nannie b England. Bride: age 18, marr 1st time, b Concord d/o PERRIN William G b Maine & LYNA Addie b Concord. Vol: 9 Page: 032

ROBERTSON John P of Hopkinton & SANBORN Florence M of Newport m Jul 29, 1932 Keene. Groom: age 45, marr 2nd time, b Warner s/o ROBERTSON Charles D b Warner & BARTLETT Hattie M b Warner. Bride: age 34, marr 2nd time, b Wilmot d/o SHACKETT Peter b Ellensburg NY & HAY Julia M b Wilmot. Vol: 9 Page: 033

FLYNN Albert W of Providence RI & HAROLD Elizabeth A of Providence RI m Aug 27, 1932 Hopkinton. Groom: age 21, marr 1st time, b Providence RI s/o FLYNN Orlando b Providence RI & CROWLEY Emma F b Ireland. Bride: age 21, marr 1st time, b Providence RI d/o HAROLD Patrick b Boston Ma & CRONIN Catherine b Providence RI. Vol: 9 Page: 033

SANBORN John C of Hopkinton & CHAPMAN L Doris of Newbury Vt m Sep 1, 1932 Contoocook. Groom: age 56, marr 1st time, b Reading Ma s/o SANBORN Charles F b Boscawen & COLBY Jane b Salisbury. Bride: age 42, marr 1st time, b Hopkinton d/o BUSWELL Loren b Hopkinton & CARPENTER Mary b Hopkinton. Vol: 9 Page: 033

WUNDERLICK Frank H of Hopkinton & ROBERTSON Evelyn of Hopkinton m Sep 7, 1932 Concord. Groom: age 19, marr 1st time, b Hopkinton s/o

Hopkinton, NH Marriages 1914

WUNDERLICK Charles b Worcester Ma & CLARK Alice K b Warner. Bride: age 20, marr 1st time, b Hopkinton d/o ROBERTSON John T b Warner & NUDD Alice M b Warner. Vol: 9 Page: 034

KIMBALL Bernard A of Hopkinton & SANBORN Doris P of Amesbury Ma m Mar 6, 1932 Amesbury Ma. Groom: age 23, marr 1st time, b Hopkinton s/o KIMBALL Arthur C b Hopkinton & BOHANA Elsie b Weare. Bride: age 24, marr 1st time, b Webster Me d/o SANBORN William b Webster Me & SANBRON Ethel Jones b Brunswick Me. Vol: 9 Page: 034

GEORGE Earl E of Concord & BARTLETT Alice J of Hopkinton m Sep 8, 1932 Warner. Groom: age 21, marr 1st time, b Concord s/o GEORGE Erving b Danville & MURPHY Julia b Roxbury Ma. Bride: age 18, marr 1st time, b Hopkinton d/o BARTLETT Luther b Warner & NUDD Nellie b Warner. Vol: 9 Page: 034

CALL Eugene V of Hopkinton & SHERMAN Rosetta P of Hopkinton m Oct 2, 1932 Hopkinton. Groom: age 20, marr 1st time, b Cabool Mo s/o CALL Will H b Norward NY & PENNINGTON Mabel b Cabool Mo. Bride: age 18, marr 1st time, b Concord d/o SHERMAN Almer W b Hyannis Ma & FLANDERS Bernice b Harriman Tenn. Vol: 9 Page: 035

MORGAN Albert L of Hopkinton & HURLBUTT Ruth M of Hopkinton m Oct 8, 1932 Contoocook. Groom: age 24, marr 1st time, b Warner s/o MORGAN John W b Warner & AUSTIN Georgianna b Concord. Bride: age 16, marr 1st time, b Groveton d/o HURLBUTT Clarence b Groveton & ROSEBROOK Elsie b Lancaster. Vol: 9 Page: 035

STEVENS Charles A of Hopkinton & SHAW Bertha M of Hopkinton m Nov 7, 1932 Hopkinton. Groom: age 21, marr 1st time, b Hopkinton s/o STEVENS Arthur b Manchester & WATTS Ida b Hopkinton. Bride: age 15, marr 1st time, b Salisbury d/o SHAW Plumer S b Franklin & YOUNG Grace b Concord. Vol: 9 Page: 035

HUTCHINSON Lester W of Hopkinton & KIMBALL Hazel D of Hopkinton m Nov 2, 1932 Wilton. Groom: age 32, marr 2nd time, b Wilton s/o HUTCHIN-SON George W b Wilton & FAGAN Mary b Liverpool England. Bride: age 33, marr 2nd time, b Hopkinton d/o DERRY Joseph E b Concord & ELVIRA C b Dunbarton. Vol: 9 Page: 036

CHASE Edward O of Hopkinton & HOUDE Eva M of West Newton Ma m Sep 19, 1932 Concord. Groom: age 20, marr 1st time, b Hopkinton s/o CHASE Oscar N b Hopkinton & THORNTON Margaret b Manchester England. Bride: age 24, marr 1st time, b Lowell Ma d/o HOUDE Harry E b Lowell Ma & Matilda b Canada. Vol: 9 Page: 036

BLANCHARD Francis of Hopkinton & GILLINGHAM Ruth J of Hopkinton m Aug 3, 1932 Berwick Me. Groom: age 23, marr 1st time, b New Boston s/o BLANCHARD Bert G b Greenfield & BOHANAN Edna F b Hopkinton. Bride: age 21, marr 1st time, b Newbury d/o GILLINGHAM Forest L b Newbury & BROCKWAY Bertha b Newbury. Vol: 9 Page: 036

WALKER Ralph C of Dunbarton & SAWYER Reba Mudgett of Hopkinton m May 1, 1932 New London. Groom: age 35, marr 1st time, b Dunbarton s/o WALKER Walter C b Danbury & BRAYTON Belle M b Fall River Ma. Bride:

age 35, marr 1st time, b Pepperell Ma d/o SAWYER Elmer E b Sutton & MUDGETT Lillan C b Weare. Vol: 9 Page: 037

CRESSY William A of Hopkinton & HALL Olive M of Hopkinton m Apr 11, 1933 Contoocook. Groom: age 22, marr 1st time, b Bradford s/o CRESSY Byron A b Bradford & HEATH Gertrude b Deering. Bride: age 22, marr 1st time, b Hopkinton d/o HALL Frank E b Boscawen & WEEKS Annie M b Hopkinton. Vol: 9 Page: 038

STEVENS Howard A of Hopkinton & INESON Mary E of Weare m Apr 11, 1933 Concord. Groom: age 28, marr 1st time, b Hopkinton s/o STEVENS Arthur W b Manchester & WATTS Ida M b Hopkinton. Bride: age 20, marr 1st time, b Weare d/o INESON John H b England & PHILBROOK Edith E b Concord. Vol: 9 Page: 038

CRAWFORD Ralph Edwin of Hopkinton & BLETCHER Lena of Hopkinton m Apr 19, 1933 Hopkinton. Groom: age 30, marr 1st time, b Enfield Ma s/o CRAWFORD Charles & ANDERSON Edna. Bride: age 29, marr 1st time, b Dover d/o BLETCHER George b Lancashire England & HANSON Harriott b Yorshire England. Vol: 9 Page: 038

JONES Carl L of Hopkinton & JONES Alice G of Hopkinton m Jun 10, 1933 Contoocook. Groom: age 63, marr 2nd time, b Danvers Ma s/o JONES William R b Windham & Francis b Hudson. Bride: age 40, marr 2nd time, b Nashua d/o FORSIE Phillip b Nashua & Aura b Amesbury Ma. Vol: 9 Page: 039

TYLER Edwin N of Hopkinton & HOFFER Helen E of Piermont Ny m Jun 12, 1933 Hillsboro. Groom: age 21, marr 1st time, b Waterbury Conn s/o TYLER Newton H b Thomaston Conn & ALFRED Winfred A b Dunnellen Fla. Bride: age 18, marr 1st time, b Piermont Ny d/o HOFFER J S b Piermont NY & ESSEX Ella b Piermont NY. Vol: 9 Page: 039

MORAN Reginald of Hopkinton & BUNNELL Eleanor of Hopkinton m Jun 23, 1933 Contoocook. Groom: age 24, marr 1st time, b Hopkinton s/o MORAN Reginald b Concord & STRAW Blanche b Hopkinton. Bride: age 22, marr 1st time, b Hopkinton d/o BUNNELL Alva S b Henniker & MURRAY Ethel B b Nova Scotia. Vol: 9 Page: 039

LEONE Charles R of Sunapee & ADAMS Jennie C of Contoocook m Aug 15, 1933 Conway. Groom: age 28, marr 1st time, b Wayland Ma s/o LEONE Huston b Perry Me & McKENZIE Mable b Florence Ma. Bride: age 37, marr 1st time, b Sunapee d/o HARDING Frank M b Newport & PROWER Medora E. Vol: 9 Page: 040

GILLINGHAM Forrest L of Hopkinton & QUIMBY Dorothy M of Epsom m Jul 12, 1933 Portsmouth. Groom: age 58, marr 2nd time, b Newbury s/o GILLINGHAM Joel b Newbury & DODGE Ellen M b Newbury. Bride: age 32, marr 2nd time, b Northwood d/o QUIMBY Frank b Deerfield & BICKFORD Edna b Candia. Vol: 9 Page: 040

MARTIN Harold M of Hopkinton & FARMER Vivian M of Weare m Oct 11, 1933 Weare. Groom: age 25, marr 1st time, b Hillsboro s/o MARTIN Fred J b Hillsboro & SARGENT Achsah b Goffstown. Bride: age 25, marr 1st time, b Weare d/o FARMER Albert S b Weare & STUMPF Theresa A b New York. Vol: 9 Page: 040

Hopkinton, NH Marriages 1914

KEMP Harold Clifton of Contoocook & DUVAL Evelyn Miriam of Concord m Sep 3, 1933 Woodsville. Groom: age 43, marr 1st time, b Contoocook s/o KEMP Franklin b & EASTMAN Jennie S b Stoneham Ma. Bride: age 38, marr 1st time, b Plattsbury Ny d/o DUVAL Daniel b France & OBER Mathilda b Plattsburg Ny. Vol: 9 Page: 041

BABB Horace Owen of N Hadley Ma & RICE Dorothy Ella of Northampton Ma m Nov 11, 1933 Contoocook. Groom: age 26, marr 1st time, b N Hadley Ma s/o BABB David b Somerstshire Eng & OWEN Florence b Milverton Eng. Bride: age 27, marr 1st time, b Everett Wa d/o RICE Albert C b Northampton Ma & DUNNING Kitty Mae b Florence Ma. Vol: 9 Page: 041

MELCHER Lyle Walton of Hopkinton & JOHNSON Margaret V of Concord m Oct 7, 1933 Concord. Groom: age 25, marr 1st time, b Hopkinton s/o MELCHER Maurice b Hopkinton & LIBBY Alice b Hopkinton. Bride: age 21, marr 1st time, b Concord d/o JOHNSON Elmer b Karlskrona Sweden & WIK Esther b Jonkoping Sweden. Vol: 9 Page: 041

MORSE Arnold A of Henniker & CORLISS Doris Alma of Hopkinton m Nov 30, 1933 Hillsboro. Groom: age 27, marr 1st time, b Deering s/o MORSE Forristal b Henniker & EATON Abbie b Hillsboro. Bride: age 21, marr 1st time, b Pembroke Ma d/o CORLISS James A b Hudson & STONE Grace b Claremont. Vol: 9 Page: 042

JOHNSON Thomas H of Hopkinton & DOWNES Isabella of Warner m Dec 11, 1933 Warner. Groom: age 20, marr 1st time, b Mt Holly Vt s/o JOHNSON Danno V b Pittsburg & MARY A b Pittsburg. Bride: age 20, marr 1st time, b Concord d/o DOWNES Walldo V b Andover & KIRK Ruth M b St Johnsbury Vt. Vol: 9 Page: 042

BAILEY Ralph G of West Hopkinton & CLARK Nellie V of Weare m Sep 2, 1933 Goffstown. Groom: age 23, marr 1st time, b Contoocook s/o BAILEY George W b Warner & CHASE Gertrude M b Contoocook. Bride: age 20, marr 1st time, b Weare d/o CLARK Grace R b Weare. Vol: 9 Page: 042

BROWN Robert D of Hopkinton & SHURTLEFF Alice E of Warner m Sep 3, 1927 Contoocook. Groom: age 22, marr 1st time, b Concord s/o BROWN Lamson b Thornton & FLEMING Melissia b Canada. Bride: age 21, marr 1st time, b Warner d/o SHURTLEFF John J b Lebanon & ELLENWOOD Louisie B b Manchester. Vol: 9 Page: 004

HOYT Arnold E of West Hopkinton & NUDD Marguerite C of West Hopkinton m Sep 30, 1929 West Hopkinton. Groom: age 21, marr 1st time, b Contoocook s/o HOYT Harry L b Webster & JOHNSON Lillian M b Canada. Bride: age 18, marr 1st time, b West Hopkinton d/o NUDD Archie H b Webster & BLANCHETTE Clara b Boston Ma. Vol: 9 Page: 013

RICE Earl J of Hopkinton & MELCHER Evelyn of Hopkinton m Sep 5, 1930 Hopkinton. Groom: age 27, marr 1st time, b Hopkinton s/o RICE James G b Henniker & BOHANAN Bernice M b Hopkinton. Bride: age 24, marr 1st time, b Hopkinton d/o MELCHER Maurice C b Thornton & LIBBY Alice H b Hopkinton. Vol: 9 Page: 020

HOWLEY James Thomas of Hopkinton & BERGSTROM Audrey T of Hopkinton m Jan 29, 1934 Hillsboro. Groom: age 26, marr 1st time, b Hopkinton s/o HOWLEY James b Maine & COCKERSON Mary b New York. Bride: age 21, marr 1st time, b Chelses Ma d/o BERGSTROM Oscar b Maynard Ma & OSLUND Clara M b Providence RI. Vol: 10 Page: 001

COURCHENE Anatole of Concord & ALDRICH Doris of Hopkinton m Jan 22, 1934 Concord. Groom: age 21, marr 1st time, b Leominster Ma s/o COURCHENE Albert b Rhode Island & ADAMS Blanche b Three Rivers Pq. Bride: age 19, marr 1st time, b Concord d/o ALDRICH George b Fitchburg Ma & HENDERSON Reana b Francestown. Vol: 10 Page: 001

ROTHMAN Joseph of New York City & BURNS Eleanor M of Hopkinton m Apr 28, 1934 Hopkinton. Groom: age 34, marr 1st time, b Poland s/o ROTHMAN Michael b Poland & ROSENFIELD Anna b Poland. Bride: age 22, marr 1st time, b Cambridge Ma d/o BURNS Timothy F b Cambrige Ma & O'LEARY Catherine b Haverhill Ma. Vol: 10 Page: 002

BERGSTROM Ernest A of Hopkinton & PRENTISS Florence M of Concord m Apr 22, 1934 Hopkinton. Groom: age 18, marr 1st time, b Sangus Ma s/o BERGSTROM Sexton b Salem Ma & DALRYMPLE Edna M b Revere Ma. Bride: age 17, marr 1st time, b Concord d/o PRENTISS Lewis E b Concord & HENNEBERRY Elizabeh b Manchester. Vol: 10 Page: 002

HUNTOON Grovenar Ariel of Hopkinton & STONE Emma Louise of Wakefeild Ma m Jun 5, 1934 Wakefield Ma. Groom: age 30, marr 1st time, b Contoocook s/o HUNTOON Arthur C b Unity & EASTMAN Ethleyn b Warner. Bride: age 27, marr 1st time, b Wakefield Ma d/o STONE Fred I b Wakefield Ma & STETSON Amy b Hanover Ma. Vol: 10 Page: 003

GEORGE Murray R of Hopkinton & WALLING Irene E of Georgiaville RI m Aug 25, 1934 Georgiaville RI. Groom: age 25, marr time, b Manchester s/o GEORGE Charles b Manchester & DeMOUPIED Clare D b Canada. Bride: age 26, marr 1st time, b Georgiaville RI d/o WALLING Walter A b Georgiaville RI & SYKES Mary b England. Vol: 10 Page: 003

CUMMINGS Orville D of Hopkinton & EATON Jennie Kimball of Hopkinton m Sep 2, 1934 Contoocook. Groom: age 72, marr 2nd time, b Wentworth s/o CUMMINGS D K b Groton & BRADBURY M J E b Wentworth. Bride: age 64, marr 2nd time, b No Berwick Me d/o KIMBALL Clarion H b Hopkinton & CHALLEN Lucy A b Rickland Ill. Vol: 10 Page: 003

DANE Nelson of Concord & PIERCE Clar Louise of Hopkinton m Aug 27, 1934 Hopkinton. Groom: age 33, marr 1st time, b Ireland s/o DANE Gerald b England & GRAHAM Selina b England. Bride: age 22, marr 1st time, b Plymouth d/o PIERCE Charles & POTTER Harriet F. Vol: 10 Page: 004

LAWSON Clarence of Hopkinton & FLEWELLIN G Bertha of Gardner Ma m Sep 13, 1934 Rochester. Groom: age 22, marr 1st time, b Cambridge Ma s/o LAWSON Arthur V b Gatenburg Sweden & OLSON Anna b Leksand Sweden. Bride: age 18, marr 1st time, b Conville Me d/o FLEWELLING Byron & Adeline. Vol: 10 Page: 004

LAWSON Arthur O of Hopkinton & PROVENCHER Mary K of Hopkinton m Oct 6, 1934 Contoocook. Groom: age 20, marr 1st time, b Hopkinton s/o LAWSON Arthur V b Sweden & OLSON Anna b Sweden. Bride: age 20, marr 1st time, b Warner d/o PROVENCHER Albert J b Bay City Mich & BEAN Florence b Johnstown Ny. Vol: 10 Page: 005

BROWER Ernest Edwin of Hopkinton & DELANEY Anne Louise of Hillsboro m Sep 1, 1934 Hopkinton. Groom: age 25, marr 1st time, b New Jersey s/o BROWER George b New Jersey & SERVISS Catherine b New Jersey. Bride: age 23, marr 1st time, b No Walpole d/o DELANEY William b Colebrook & BASLEY Hannah b Athens Vt. Vol: 10 Page: 005

PLOURDE Elsworth F of Manchester & REARDON Helen F of Hopkinton m Nov 10, 1934 Hillsboro. Groom: age 26, marr 1st time, b Manchester s/o PLOURDE Adelon J b New York & BAMFORD Mabel b Manchester. Bride: age 20, marr 1st time, b New York d/o REARDON Thomas J b New York & NOONING Delia b Penna. Vol: 10 Page: 005

PAGE Harold E of Hopkinton & FREESE Eleanor M of Manchester m Nov 24, 1934 Contoocook. Groom: age 31, marr 2nd time, b Dover s/o PAGE Forest I b Keene & DOPHNY Sadie b New Durham. Bride: age 24, marr 2nd time, b Manchester d/o FREESE Henry C b Germany & TRASK Deidania b Deerfield Ma. Vol: 10 Page: 006

BROWN John Daniel of Hopkinton & SARGENT Evelyn D of Hopkinton m Dec 12, 1934 Contoocook. Groom: age 20, marr 1st time, b Hopkinton s/o BROWN John T b Thornton & HEMPHILL Laura M b Henniker. Bride: age 18, marr 1st time, b Roxbury Ma d/o SARGENT Arthur H b Boston Ma & PAGE Lillian M b Manchester. Vol: 10 Page: 006

BEAN William Arthur of Hopkinton & BRYANT Helen Wicks of New Bedford Ma m May 1, 1935 Hopkinton. Groom: age 25, marr 1st time, b New Bedford Ma s/o BEAN Edmund E b Concord & MacKENZIE Anna b Nova Scotia. Bride: age 25, marr 1st time, b New Bedford Ma d/o BRYANT John H b New Bedford Ma & WICKS Lillian b New Bedford Ma. Vol: 10 Page: 007

DREW Leon R of Sanbornville & GROSMITH Martha of Contoocook m Jul 10, 1935 Sanbornville. Groom: age 27, marr 1st time, b Madison s/o DREW Robert F b Madison & FROST Cora b Cambridge Ma. Bride: age 21, marr 1st time, b England d/o GROSMITH Charles b England & BLAIR Kate b London England. Vol: 10 Page: 007

KIMBALL Frank Moses of Hopkinton & HOLMES Dorothy E of Concord m Jun 21, 1935 Concord. Groom: age 27, marr 1st time, b Hopkinton s/o KIMBALL Herbert Moses b Hopkinton & COLBY Mary Abby b Bow. Bride: age 21, marr 1st time, b Concord d/o HOLMES Perley Ernest b Thornton & SHANNON Irene A b Lynn Ma. Vol: 10 Page: 007

JOHNSON Oliver Danna of Avon Me & WELLS Margaret E of Franklin m Aug 8, 1935 Contoocook. Groom: age 25, marr 1st time, b Acton Me s/o JOHNSON Danno D b Pittsburg & Mary A b Pittsburg. Bride: age 19, marr 1st time, b Franklin d/o WELLS Ralph B b Franklin & SANBORN Sadie b Hopkinton. Vol: 10 Page: 008

GEER Earl A of Hopkinton & MOODY Charlotte E of Henniker m Aug 31, 1935 Newport. Groom: age 21, marr 1st time, b Hopkinton s/o GEER Bert L b Canada & BRYANT Candice E b Moria Ny. Bride: age 18, marr 1st time, b Henniker d/o MOODY Henry L b Sutton & DOWLIN Alice M b Henniker. Vol: 10 Page: 008

HOWLEY Robert William of Contoocook & JORDAN Shirley J of Concord m Aug 9, 1935 Concord. Groom: age 25, marr 1st time, b Contoocook s/o HOWLEY

James b Maine & CORCORAN Mary b New York NY. Bride: age 25, marr 1st time, b Ireland d/o JORDAN Christopher b Ireland & BOHAN Julia b Ireland. Vol: 10 Page: 008

MONTGOMERY John Alvaro of Providence RI & MARSHALL Marjorie E of Hopkinton m Sep 28, 1935 Contoocook. Groom: age 34, marr 1st time, b Manchester s/o MONTGOMERY Scott b Hopkinton & CLOUGH Mary b Hopkinton. Bride: age 32, marr 1st time, b Contoocook d/o MARSHALL Harry W b Webster & CRESSY Nettie b Bradford. Vol: 10 Page: 009

WESCOTT Benjamin C of Concord & BOHANAN Josephine A of Concord m Mar 11, 1935 Pembroke. Groom: age 60, marr 3rd time, b Bristol s/o WESCOTT Charles H b & NUDD Mary R b Loudon. Bride: age 39, marr 3rd time, b Hopkinton d/o BOHANAN John W b Sutton & JEWELL Delia A b Weare. Vol: 10 Page: 009

HOUSTON Tyrus C of Hopkinton & PROVENCHER Evelyn M of Hopkinton m Apr 12, 1936 Concord. Groom: age 25, marr 1st time, b Pembroke s/o HOUSTON William E b Pr Ed Island & HOOPER Florence b Pr Ed Island. Bride: age 19, marr 1st time, b Hopkinton d/o PROVENCHER Albert J b Bay City Mich & BEAN Florence b Johnstown N Y. Vol: 10 Page: 012

OLKONEN Taivo Arthur of Concord & CARNEY Hazel Maude of Hopkinton m Nov 21, 1935 Concord. Groom: age 25, marr 1st time, b Finland s/o OLKONEN Arthur b Finland & PARKEOLA Gustave b Finland. Bride: age 19, marr 1st time, b Washington d/o CARNEY Hessel b P E Island & CLARK Louise b Weare. Vol: 10 Page: 009

ROBERTS William P of Hopkinton & SORNBERGER Viola R of Hopkinton m May 3, 1936 Hopkinton. Groom: age 21, marr 1st time, b Warner s/o ROBERTS Fred W b Canada & PARKER Angie b Newport. Bride: age 19, marr 1st time, b Hopkinton d/o SORNBERGER Eddie M b St Armand Pq Canada & McCAUBREY Mary J b Valcartier Pq Canada. Vol: 10 Page: 012

BARTON Harold Emery of Hopkinton & CLEARY Ave Marie of Bennington m May 10, 1936 Hillsboro. Groom: age 42, marr 1st time, b Concord s/o BARTON Robert W b Hopkinton & THOMPSON Mabel b Springfield. Bride: age 32, marr 1st time, b Bennington d/o CLEARY Andrew b Turners Falls Ma & CASHIAN Margaret b Greenfield. Vol: 10 Page: 012

CALL Robert L of Hopkinton & HOYT Clara B of West Hopkinton m May 25, 1936 Hopkinton. Groom: age 21, marr 1st time, b Cabool Mo s/o CALL Will H b Norwood Ny & PENNINGTON Mabel. Bride: age 18, marr 1st time, b West Hopkinton d/o HOYT Jesse J b East Washington & GRACE Etta M b Washington. Vol: 10 Page: 013

CORNACK Stanley of Concord & COLBURN Lorn H of Hopkinton m Jun 24, 1936 Chichester. Groom: age 23, marr 1st time, b Gloucester Eng s/o CORNACK William b Gloucester Eng & KEELING Ethel b Gloucester Eng. Bride: age 21, marr 1st time, b Warner d/o COLBURN Milo b Warner & FORSAITH Bernice b Webster. Vol: 10 Page: 013

SCHUYLER Philip H of Hopkinton & BANGS Dorothy L of Lisbon m Jun 21, 1936 Lisbon. Groom: age 24, marr 1st time, b Minneapolis Min s/o SCHUYLER H Philip b Albany Ny & Cherrell b Fort Wayne Ind. Bride: age 25, marr 1st time, b Lisbon d/o BANGS Fred W b Pack Isl Que & Lillian b Lancaster. Vol: 10 Page: 013

SWEATT Justin L of Hopkinton & GOODRICH Florence M of Concord m Jun 27, 1936 Concord. Groom: age 20, marr 1st time, b Concord s/o SWEATT Jessie J b Errol & LORD Mabel b Hopkinton. Bride: age 19, marr 1st time, b Hopkinton d/o GOODRICK John P b Hopkinton & WRIGHT Pauline b Thornton. Vol: 10 Page: 014

ASHFORD Ernest H of Antrim & SAWYER Sylvia I of Hopkinton m Jul 5, 1936 Antrim. Groom: age 25, marr 1st time, b Dublin s/o ASHFORD Duncan b New Brunswick & FRENCH Alice H b Henniker. Bride: age 22, marr 1st time, b Thetford Vt d/o SAWYER Charles F b Thetford Vt & CLOUGH Florence M b Thetford Vt. Vol: 10 Page: 014

HAMMOND Joy H of Contoocook & GODWIN Helen J of Brockton Ma m Nov 11, 1935 Brockton Ma. Groom: age 34, marr 1st time, b Akron In s/o HAMMOND Clement Haratio b Beaver Dam In & COOK Mary Jane b Hillsgrove Oh. Bride: age 21, marr 1st time, b Bridgewater d/o GOODWIN Merrit Allen b Brockton Ma & TUTTLE Frances T b Bridgewwater. Vol: 10 Page: 015

BESSE Harlan F of Concord & RUSS Alice E of Hopkinton m Aug 5, 1936 Hopkinton. Groom: age 41, marr 2nd time, b Concord s/o BESSE Frederick L b New Bedford Ma & PENTLAND Elizabeth b Swanzey. Bride: age 36, marr 2nd time, b Hopkinton d/o RUSS William b Lowell Ma & COLBY Nora b Seekonk Ma. Vol: 10 Page: 015

TILTON Robert E of Concord & MOUNT Anona of Hopkinton m Jun 10, 1936 Hopkinton. Groom: age 28, marr 1st time, b Concord s/o TILTON George A b Concord & BENNETT Ethlyn b Manchester. Bride: age 23, marr 1st time, b Brockton Ma d/o MOUNT Harold A b Somersworth & WAITE Cora E b Dover. Vol: 10 Page: 015

KIMBALL Raymond S of Hopkinton & MOSES Grace J of Franklin m Sep 9, 1936 Concord. Groom: age 25, marr 1st time, b Hopkinton s/o KIMBALL Nelson D b Hopkinton & PATCH Adelaide M b New Field Me. Bride: age 23, marr 1st time, b Meredith d/o MOSES Stephen D b Groton & CAMPBELL Laura b Lake Village. Vol: 10 Page: 016

SARGENT Arthur of Hopkinton & HURD Gertrude W of Hopkinton m Sep 7, 1936 Hopkinton. Groom: age 21, marr 1st time, b Roxbury Ma s/o SARGENT Arthur F b Boston Ma & PAGE Lillian b Manchester. Bride: age 15, marr 1st time, b Hopkinton d/o HURD Walter b England & NUTTALL Annie T b St John N B. Vol: 10 Page: 016

FOOTE William N of Hopkinton & BROWN Marion J of Concord m Sep 21, 1936 Hill. Groom: age 36, marr 1st time, b Hopkinton s/o FOOTE William b Skowhegan Me & WATTS Helen b Hopkinton. Bride: age 34, marr 1st time, b Concord d/o BROWN George W b Wolfboro & CLARK Mabel J b Concord. Vol: 10 Page: 016

FORD Richard L of Contoocook & BEAN Clara B Hook of Contoocook m Dec 28, 1935 Pepperell Ma. Groom: age 55, marr 1st time, b Pembroke Ma s/o FORD Edward H b Pembroke Ma & YOUNG Susan b Wolfboro. Bride: age 67, marr

1st time, b Hopkinton d/o HOOK James b Concord & LONG Mary b Hopkinton. Vol: 10 Page: 017

McCOY Philip J of Hopkinton & PATT Vilona M of Hopkinton m Feb 26, 1936 New York City. Groom: age 56, marr 1st time, b Hopkinton s/o McCOY James N b Thornton & EDMUNDS Alice b Hopkinton. Bride: age 59, marr 1st time, b Hillsboro d/o MURDOUGH Frank b Hillsboro & SMITH Emma b Washington. Vol: 10 Page: 017

CLARK Leonard Fayette of Holyoke Ma & PAGE Greta Lydia of Holyoke m Oct 24, 1936 Contoocook. Groom: age 29, marr 1st time, b Springfield Ma s/o CLARK Leonard Samuel b Springfield & SEAVER Kate Isabel b S Hadley Falls Ma. Bride: age 34, marr 1st time, d/o PAGE John Fife b Holyoke Ma & ROBINSON Fannie M b Plattsburg Ny. Vol: 10 Page: 017

SORNBERG Arville W of Hopkinton & BOISNNETT Margaret of Warner m Oct 26, 1936 Concord. Groom: age 23, marr 1st time, b Hopkinton s/o SORNBERGER Eddie M b Canada & McONBRY Mary J b Canada. Bride: age 20, marr 1st time, b Warner d/o BOISVERT Joseph A b Manchester & BODEN Beatrice b Albrighton England. Vol: 10 Page: 018

BARTON Clayton E of Hopkinton & BENNETT Edith of Barre Vt m Dec 5, 1936 Hopkinton. Groom: age 47, marr time, b West Concord s/o BARTON Elroy b Hopkinton & CURRIER Mary b Hopkinton. Bride: age 44, marr 1st time, b Derby Line d/o BENNETT Howard b Holland Vt & BLISS Mary b Beebe Vt. Vol: 10 Page: 018

BASTIAN Arthur T of Concord & STRAW Barbara of Concord m Oct 4, 1936 North Weare. Groom: age 21, marr 1st time, b Amesbury Ma s/o BASTIAN Arthur E b Norwood Ma & WHEELAN Alice G b Cambridge Ma. Bride: age 20, marr 1st time, b Manchester d/o STRAW Ernest G b Hopkinton & SYMONDS Mildred b Hopkinton. Vol: 10 Page: 018

DEXTER Stanley A of Concord & COOPER Lena B of Hopkinton m Dec 5, 1936 Concord. Groom: age 18, marr 1st time, b Concord s/o DEXTER Carl L b Whitefield & MOORE Myrtle M b Barre Ma. Bride: age 20, marr 1st time, b Hopkinton d/o COOPER Clarence b Concord & CROCKETT Lena B b Laconia. Vol: 10 Page: 019

PERKINS Norman E of Sunapee & DAMON Elizabeth R of Contoocook m Nov 30, 1935 Claremont. Groom: age 24, marr 1st time, b Sunapee s/o PERKINS Edward S b Fitchburg Ma & MERRILL Pearl b Sunapee. Bride: age 29, marr 1st time, b Scituate Ma d/o REDDY Albert S b Taunton Ma & WOOD Cora b Woodstock Vt. Vol: 10 Page: 010

PAGE Lester of Henniker & KRAZYZENIECK Helen of Contoocook m Jan 25, 1936 Contoocook. Groom: age 20, marr time, b Hopkinton s/o PAGE Willie H b Henniker & HOWLEY Mary b Portland Me. Bride: age 20, marr 1st time, b Hopkinton d/o KYZYZANIACK John T b Poland & CARTER Grace E b East Concord. Vol: 10 Page: 011

PAGE Horace G of Hopkinton & PETERSON Lillian C of Manchester m Jan 17, 1936 Salem. Groom: age 36, marr time, b Warner s/o PAGE Will b Henniker & DWINNELLS Jennie b Manchester. Bride: age 20, marr 1st time, b Manchester d/o PETERSON Oliver A b Sweden & EDITH C b Hooksett. Vol: 10 Page: 011

Hopkinton, NH Marriages 1914

SHAW Benjamin H of Hopkinton & RICHARDSON Jeananett of Warner m Mar 31, 1936 Hooksett. Groom: age 26, marr 1st time, b Henniker s/o SHAW Edward J b Franklin & PATTERN Nellie E b Henniker. Bride: age 18, marr 1st time, b Waterville Me d/o RICHARDSON Geo H b Roxbury Ma & GREEN Katherine E b Gorham. Vol: 10 Page: 011

CHANDLER Alfred N of Hopkinton & FLAD Barbara of Hopkinton m May 15, 1937 Hopkinton. Groom: age 21, marr 1st time, b Hopkinton s/o CHANDLER Arthur O b Fairlee Vt & MILLS Jean b Dundee Scotland. Bride: age 19, marr 1st time, b Warner d/o FLAD Philip J b Philadelphia Pa & HODGKINSON Ethel b England. Vol: 10 Page: 020

NORTHUP R?? of Hopkinton & DARRES Alice D of No Weare m 1937 Northup R??. Groom: age 36, marr 2nd time, b Lisbon s/o NORTHUP George M b Lisbon & WEAVER Alice b Lisbon. Bride: age 18, marr 2nd time, b Vt d/o DARRES Dilvert b Bear River N S & WILLEY Delma b No Woodstock Vt. Vol: 10 Page: 020

MOUNT Harold A of Hopkinton & PETERSON Della Pluff of Brockton Ma m Jul 26, 1937 Manchester. Groom: age 53, marr 2nd time, b Somersworth s/o MOUNT Francis A b Berwick Me & LESLIE Eleanor b Concord. Bride: age 50, marr 2nd time, b Marlboro d/o PLUFF Henry b Marlboro & BERGERON Adeline b Port Henry Ny. Vol: 10 Page: 021

RUSSELL George of Boscawen & WIGGIN Catherine A of Hopkinton m Sep 12, 1937 Hopkinton. Groom: age 22, marr 1st time, b Penacook s/o RUSSELL Thomas E b Boscawen & HANNIFORD Alice b Providence RI. Bride: age 23, marr 1st time, b Brookfield d/o WIGGIN Frank b Brookfield & PIKE Mable b Harrison Me. Vol: 10 Page: 021

BOHANAN Clifton Ralph of Contoocook & DUNHAM Florenece S of N.bennington Vt m Jun 30, 1936 Shaftsbury Vt. Groom: age 21, marr 1st time, b Hopkinton s/o BOHANAN Percy R b Hopkinton & FOWLER Alice N b Newbury. Bride: age 20, marr 1st time, b Shaftsbury Vt d/o DUNHAM Jesse L b Shaftsbury Vt & RACKWOOD Hazel L b Bennington Vt. Vol: 10 Page: 021

STONE Charles Alby of Hooksett & WEAST Florence Iola of Contoocook m Sep 11, 1937 Contoocook. Groom: age 33, marr 2nd time, b Pembroke s/o STONE Clarence E b Pembroke & GARLAND Ruth b Hopkinton. Bride: age 30, marr 2nd time, b Mariaville Ny d/o WEAST James A b Schenectady Ny & BARLOU Bessie b Mariaville Ny. Vol: 10 Page: 022

BROWN Fred S of Hopkinton & LAVIOLETTE Bertha S of Woodstock Vt m Oct 9, 1937 Henniker. Groom: age 60, marr 1st time, b Walpole s/o BROWN Lester b Bethel Vt & WATTS Stella E b Acworth. Bride: age 60, marr 1st time, b Calais Me d/o SLAYTON Herman b Calais Me & TEBBETTS Anna E b Bradford Vt. Vol: 10 Page: 022

METRO Thomas of Hopkinton & STAVRO Pandora of Franklin m Oct 17, 1937 Hopkinton. Groom: age 30, marr 1st time, b Albania s/o METRO Costa b Albania & Pina b Albania. Bride: age 25, marr 1st time, b Albania d/o STAVRO Alex b Albania & Katherine b Albania. Vol: 10 Page: 022

NICHOLS Robert A of So Portland Me & DUSTIN Adelaid of Hopkinton m Oct 30, 1937 Hopkinton. Groom: age 25, marr 1st time, b Kennebunk Me s/o NICHOLS Roger W b West Epping & CHASE Martha H b Bedford Ma. Bride:

age 20, marr 1st time, b Hopkinton d/o DUSTIN Daniel H b Hopkinton & ASHBY Sylvia E b Concord. Vol: 10 Page: 023

CHANDLER Warren G of Hopkinton & GRAVES Edith C of Hopkinton m Nov 14, 1937 Hopkinton. Groom: age 25, marr 1st time, b Hopkinton s/o CHANDLER Arthur O b Fairlee Vt & MILLER Jean C b Scotland. Bride: age 20, marr 1st time, b Sheldon Vt d/o GRAVES Buel H b Sheldon Vt & TENNY Harriett I b So Royalton Vt. Vol: 10 Page: 023

DEVOID Maxwell I of Hopkinton & ASHBLEY Katherine I of Concord m Nov 4, 1937 Henniker. Groom: age 21, marr 1st time, b Belmont s/o DEVOID Frank b Gardner Ma & LaFRANCE Gladys L b Franklin. Bride: age 18, marr 1st time, b Concord d/o ASHLEY George b Canaan & HUMPHREY Alice b Nova Scotia. Vol: 10 Page: 023

CONVERSE Albert E of Hopkinton & COLE Bertha M of Newbury m Nov 24, 1937 Contoocook. Groom: age 52, marr 2nd time, b Bradford s/o CONVERSE Edward F b Woburn Ma & HUSSEY Nettie M b Goshen. Bride: age 50, marr 2nd time, b Marlow d/o MASON Addison b Swanton Vt & RICHARDS Nellie H b Fondalac City Wis. Vol: 10 Page: 024

HAZELTON Maurice of Hopkinton & ASH Ruth of Concord m Nov 27, 1937 Hopkinton. Groom: age 23, marr 1st time, b Hopkinton s/o HAZELTON Homer H b Hopkinton & CARTER Susie b Concord. Bride: age 21, marr 1st time, b Concord d/o ASH Edgar E b Concord & HILLSGROVE Blanche b Concord. Vol: 10 Page: 024

MOULTON William L of Hopkinton & CHASE Charlotte C of Hopkinton m Dec 11, 1937 Hopkinton. Groom: age 75, marr 2nd time, b Chelsea Ma s/o MOULTON William H b Meredith & STRAW Susan Z b Hopkinton. Bride: age 64, marr 2nd time, b Winchester Ma d/o MORSE Fitz Henry b Sturbridge Ma & METCALF Catherine b Cambridge Ma. Vol: 10 Page: 024

BUTTRICK Ervin Warren of Concord & DOWNES Madeline F of Contoocook m Nov 25, 1937 Contoocook. Groom: age 21, marr 1st time, b East Andover s/o BUTTRICK Karl F b Alexander & LIBBY Helen Belle b East Andover. Bride: age 20, marr 1st time, b Greenfield Ma d/o DOWNS Daniel b Wilmot & SARGENT Alice b Warner. Vol: 10 Page: 025

FULLER Robert Reade of Hopkinton & COLBY Madelene P of Warner m Sep 15, 1934 Warner. Groom: age 20, marr 1st time, b Hopkinton s/o FULLER George I b Hopkinton & READE Blanche M b Marlboro. Bride: age 18, marr 1st time, b Warner d/o COLBY Addison B b Sutton & MORTON Elsie b Hanover Ma. Vol: 10 Page: 004

FREDERICK Edward W of Revere Ma & STONE Eleanor of Revere Ma m Jun 29, 1936 Hopkinton. Groom: age 23, marr 1st time, b Reverve Ma s/o FREDERICK Charles b Revere Ma & PLUCKETT Marcella b Boston Ma. Bride: age 19, marr 1st time, b Roxbury Ma d/o STONE George J b Boston Ma & GRANT Edith b Lowell Ma. Vol: 10 Page: 014

STEVENS Lee E of Concord & BLANCHARD Beatrice E of Hopkinton m Aug 1, 1937 Hopkinton. Groom: age 33, marr 1st time, b Concord s/o STEVENS Leon E & MOFFATT Harriett F b Plattsburg NY. Bride: age 24, marr 1st time, b Hopkinton d/o BLANCHARD Bert G b Greenfield & BOHANAN Edna F b Hopkinton. Vol: 10 Page: 020

Hopkinton, NH Deaths 1914-1937

Note: This chapter includes some deaths from 1856, 1892, 1899, 1900 and 1908.

PERLEY Charles W d Warner 1914-04-06 age 66yrs 2mos 7dys b Dunbarton 1848-01-29 Vol: 7 Page: 004

CHASE Lydia d New Haven Conn 1915 May age 64yrs 8mos 7dys b Providence RI child of HOPKINS Henry S & Phoebe Vol: 7 Page: 19

ROLLINS Alfred A d Bedford 1914-01-05 age 93yrs 8mos 17dys b Antrim 1820-04-18 child of ROLLINS Benjamin of Salem Vol: 7 Page: 001

CARR Morris Frank d Concord 1913-12-25 age 11mos 12dys b Concord Vol: 7 Page: 005

FLANDERS Edward F d Hopkinton 1914-02-22 age 67yrs 1mos 21dys b Wilmont 1847-01-01 child of FLANDERS Hiram C of Bradford & BROWN Louisa of Wilmont Vol: 7 Page: 002

HOWARD Susan M d Arlington Mass 1914-02-23 age 79yrs 20dys b Contoocook 1914-02-23 child of PATTERSON David of Henniker & WOODS Maria of Henniker Vol: 7 Page: 002

BROCKWAY John G d Hopkinton 1914-03-09 age 79yrs 9mos 2dys b Wilmot 1834-06-07 child of BROCKWAY John of Wilmot & EATON Mary Vol: 7 Page: 002

WALKER Mary A d Hopkinton 1914-03-17 age 47yrs 5mos 20dys b Hopkinton 1866-10-27 child of ELLIOTT John E of Webster & SANBORN Angelin A of Danville Vol: 7 Page: 003

ELLIOTT Eddie Elma d Hopkinton 1914-03-18 age 16yrs 11mos 15dys b Hopkinton 1897-04-03 child of ELLIOTT Edson E of Webster & COLBY Nettie of Deering Vol: 7 Page: 003

BURNHAM George W d Concord 1914-03-29 age 75yrs 7mos 28dys b Hillsboro 1838-07-31 child of BURNHAM Albert of Hillsboro & SYMONDS Fannie of Hillsboro Vol: 7 Page: 003

MARCY Margarite J d Hopkinton 1919-03-28 age 84yrs 5dys b Boston Mass 1835-03-23 Vol: 8 Page: 003

CAMPBELL Sarah Chandler d Dedham Mass 1915-06-10 age 85yrs 3mos 4dys Vol: 7 Page: 19

FELLOWS Charles d Boston Mass 1915-05-26 age 47yrs Vol: 7 Page: 19

SPOFFORD Frank L d West Concord 1914-01-11 age 8yrs 4mos 23dys b Hopkinton 1905-08-01 child of SPOFFORD Arthur F of Hopkinton & DODGE Maude E Vol: 7 Page: 001

TUTTLE Charles d Hopkinton 1914-01-04 age 95yrs 3mos 31dys b Franconia 1818-09-05 child of Tuttle of Arkworth[??] Mass & SARGENT Sarah of Campton Vol: 7 Page: 001

EASTMAN Wesley E d Hopkinton 1919-01-02 age 29yrs 6mos 4dys b Franklin 1889-06-28 child of EASTMAN Geo E of Andover & SAWYER Bessie of Andover Vol: 8 Page: 001

MARTIN Mable d Hopkinton 1919-01-03 age 19yrs 7mos 12dys b Henniker 1899-05-21 child of MARTIN Chas. W of So Reding Mass & TURNER Annah M of Antim Vol: 8 Page: 001

HOOK Mary A d Chichester 1919-01-15 age 87yrs 3mos 27dys b Danville P Q 1840-09-18 child of DOYING Wallace W of Danville P Q & BROWN Mary Ann of Danville P Q Vol: 8 Page: 001

WEEKS N Cogswell d Concord 1919-01-23 age 80yrs 5mos 27dys b Hopkinton 1838-07-26 child of WEEKS Thomas J of Hopkinton & SMITH Hannah of Ipsich Mass Vol: 8 Page: 002

CILLEY Lavinia d Hartford Conn 1919-04-25 age 77yrs 7mos 24dys b 1841-09-01 Vol: 8 Page: 003

DANFORTH Charles H d Hopkinton 1914-07-15 age 77yrs 3mos 15dys b Weare 1837-03-31 child of DANFORTH Gilman C of Haverhill Mass & FELCH Ruth of Weare Vol: 7 Page: 007

BENTON Levi Powers d Hopkinton 1914-07-19 age 17yrs 4mos 9dys b Derby Line Vt 1897-03-10 child of BENTON Herbert E of Vinton Iowa & POWERS Martha of Bethel Me Vol: 7 Page: 007

COLBY Abraham P d Henniker 1914-07-17 age 78yrs 2mos 24dys b Londonderry 1836-04-23 child of COLBY Abram of Londonderry & KIMBALL Adlin of Londonderry Vol: 7 Page: 007

TUTTLE Mary E d Hopkinton 1914-07-13 age 84yrs 5mos 13dys b Warner 1830-01-30 child of ROGERS John of Newburyport Mass & RAY Lucinda of Henniker Vol: 7 Page: 008

QUIMBY Mary A d Hopkinton 1914-04-09 age 91yrs 11mos 1dys b Hopkinton 1822-05-05 child of QUIMBY John of Hopkinton & BICKFORD Hannah of Hopkinton Vol: 7 Page: 004

STRAW Amanda M d Hopkinton 1914-04-21 age 81yrs 2mos 15dys b Hopkinton 1833-02-06 child of WEEKS Charles of Hopkinton & HEMPHILL Phoebe of Bow Vol: 7 Page: 004

LUTHER Charles H d Hopkinton 1914-04-25 age 66yrs 9mos 22dys b Charlestown Mass 1847-07-03 child of BLAISDELL Mary L Vol: 7 Page: 005

CROWELL Mary J d Hopkinton 1914-05-07 age 72yrs 10mos 12dys b Concord 1841-06-25 child of TIBBETTS John & ARLIN Arma A of Vol: 7 Page: 005

HIBBARD Sara J d Hopkinton 1914-06-05 age 78yrs 2mos 7dys b Loudon 1836-03-29 child of CHASE William & Haynes Vol: 7 Page: 006

SMITH Charles W d Hopkinton 1914-06-23 age 80yrs 1mos 4dys b   1834-05-19 child of CHASE Ruben Vol: 7 Page: 006

LAMPREY Daniel d Hopkinton 1914-07-16 age 78yrs 9mos 15dys b Concord 1835-10-01 child of LAMPREY Daniel Vol: 7 Page: 006

KIMBALL Mary F d Hopkinton 1915-04-10 age 95yrs b Hopkinton 1820-03-01 child of SMITH Josiah of Hopkinton & BAILEY Sarah Vol: 7 Page: 015 Note: ck original for dates

DWINNELLS James d Hopkinton 1915-04-10 age 82yrs 20dys b Hopkinton 1833-03-20 child of DWINNELLS James Vol: 7 Page: 016

LOVERING Dora C d Concord 1915-04-10 age 53yrs 9mos 16dys b   1861-06-24 child of CHANDLER Horatio J of Hopkinton & CURRIER Susan of Hopkinton Vol: 7 Page: 016

MILTON Mary A d Hopkinton 1915-04-14 age 86yrs 7mos b Nova Scotia 1829 Sep Oo child of CUMMINGS David of Nova Scotia & ---- ---- of Scotland Vol: 7 Page: 016

LIBBY George A d Hopkinton 1914-07-27 age 70yrs 5mos 27dys b Hopkinton 1844-01-30 child of LIBBY William T of Hopkinton & SMART Ellen of Hopkinton Vol: 7 Page: 008

STORY Harriett D d Hopkinton 1914-08-10 age 82yrs 4dys b Warner 1832-08-06 child of STORY Sewell of Warner & BARTLETT Mary of Warner Vol: 7 Page: 008

CHASE Martha Roberts d Hopkinton 1914-08-19 age 80yrs 1mos 10dys b Freedom 1834-07-09 child of BENNETT Charles of Lincoln & BRACKETT Olive E of Lincoln Vol: 7 Page: 009

DIMICK Eugene B d Concord 1914-08-23 age 42yrs 9mos b New Market 1871 Nov child of VERRELL Hiram & DIMICK Parmelia Vol: 7 Page: 009

TYLER Lucius d Hopkinton 1914-08-24 age 96yrs 9mos 5dys b 1817-11-19 child of TYLER Simeon of Hopkinton & ROWELL Hannah of Hopkinton Vol: 7 Page: 009

STONE Anna Frances d Hopkinton 1914-09-03 age 79yrs 7mos 23dys b Providence RI 1835-01-10 child of DARLING Welcome & ONLEY Sarah L Vol: 7 Page: 010

HAZELTON Homer N d Hopkinton 1914-09-15 age 27yrs 3mos 8dys b Hopkinton 1887-06-01 child of HAZELTON Hermana R of Hopkinton & DWINNELL Nellie of Hopkinton Vol: 7 Page: 010

BURNHAM Abbie J d Concord 1914-09-23 age 61yrs 8mos 11dys b Hopkinton 1853-01-12 child of KIMBALL Moses W & Judith Vol: 7 Page: 010

TIRRELL Georgianna d Hill 1914-10-11 age 64yrs 2mos 20dys b Warner 1850-07-22 child of CLARK Charles E & STICKNEY Mary A of Hookset Vol: 7 Page: 011

HUNTOON Ora M d Hopkinton 1914-11-01 age 75yrs 6mos b Unity 1839-05-01 child of HUNTOON Harvey of Unity & MOORE Myra of Newport Vol: 7 Page: 011

STORY Sarah J d Laconia 1914-10-19 age 79yrs 4mos 27dys b Salem Mass 1836-05-22 child of FRENCH Benjamin of Bow & STEVENS Eliza of Henniker Vol: 7 Page: 011

BAKER Effie V d Hopkinton 1914-11-20 age 49yrs 9mos 7dys b Hopkinton child of PALMER Anna of Hopkinton Vol: 7 Page: 012

NICHOLS Elwin B d Hopkinton 1914-12-17 b Weare 1862-05-25 child of NICHOLS Joshua of Weare & COLLINS Mary Vol: 7 Page: 012

MOULTON Susan Z d Hopkinton 1915-02-11 age 86yrs 4mos 18dys b Hopkinton 1828-09-24 child of STRAW Levi & CARLTON Harriet of Vol: 7 Page: 014

DWINNELLS Warren P d Sutton 1915-01-06 age 72yrs 10mos 28dys b Concord 1842-02-08 Vol: 7 Page: 014

FLANDERS Matthew H d Hopkinton 1915-03-15 age 66yrs 2mos 28dys b Manchester 1848-12-17 child of FLANDERS Daniel of Hopkinton & LERNED Mary E of Hopkinton Vol: 7 Page: 014

Hopkinton, NH Deaths 1914

FULTON Cordelia d Hopkinton 1915-01-03 age 82yrs 2mos 10dys b Fletcher Vt 1832-10-24 child of TAYLOR Elisha of Fairfield Vt & ---- ---- of Conn Vol: 7 Page: 013

COLBY John G d Hopkinton 1915-01-04 age 72yrs 5mos 25dys b Hopkinton 1842-07-10 child of COLBY James Vol: 7 Page: 013

DAVIS Alice M d Benton 1915-02-10 age 20yrs 8mos 27dys b Hopkinton 1894-05-13 child of DAVIS Henry B of Hopkinton & COOK Elizabeth J of Middleton Mass Vol: 7 Page: 013

CLEMONS Mary L d Salem Mass 1915-02-16 age 67yrs 11mos 11dys Vol: 7 Page: 015

SANBORN Triston d Hopkinton 1915-03-18 age 67yrs 9mos 9dys b Webster 1847-06-09 child of SANBORN J D of Webster & BATCHELDER Arnilla of Loudon Vol: 7 Page: 015

HOWE Jason C d Hopkinton 1918-04-16 age 67yrs 1mos 16dys b Bradford 1851-03-03 child of HOWE Lyman & HEMPHILL Sophronia Vol: 7 Page: 054

FELCH Franklin L d Hopkinton 1918-04-18 age 79yrs 21dys b Weare 1839-03-28 child of FELCH Harrison M & WILLEY Eunice Vol: 7 Page: 054

GUILD Royal E d Penacook 1918-04-20 age 82yrs 3mos 2dys Vol: 7 Page: 054

STANWOOD Louisa P d Concord 1918-04-26 age 75yrs Vol: 7 Page: 055

STORY David B d Laconia 1918-06-08 age 82yrs 4mos 19dys Vol: 7 Page: 055

SISCO Stephen F d Hopkinton 1915-04-19 age 84yrs 1mos 13dys b Fairlee Vt 1831-03-06 child of SISCO William & FOX Ruth Vol: 7 Page: 017

GOUGH William Everett d Hopkinton 1915-04-25 age 4mos 17dys b Hopkinton 1914-12-08 child of GOUGH Edward T of Benton Iowa & ROBBINS Edna M of Munster Iowa Vol: 7 Page: 017

VARNEY Anna M d Hopkinton 1915-04-30 age 77yrs 8mos 20dys b Andover 1837-08-10 child of MITCHELL Daniel of Andover & PARKINSON Betsy of Canterbury Vol: 7 Page: 017

ROLLINS Isabelle d Danvers Mass 1915-04-16 age 58yrs 9mos Vol: 7 Page: 018

BROCKWAY Amanda M d Hopkinton 1915-05-05 age 82yrs 9mos 2dys b Croydon 1832-08-03 child of CARROLL J P of Croydon & POWERS Rachell of Croydon Vol: 7 Page: 018

COOK Bridget E d Hopkinton 1915-05-09 age 47yrs b Ireland 1868 child of KEYS James F of Ireland & SALMOND Ellen of Ireland Vol: 7 Page: 018

WADE Annie R d Hopkinton 1915-06-23 age 71yrs 3mos 16dys b Hopkinton 1844-03-07 child of EMERSON James N of Hopkinton & FLANDERS Judith of Hopkinton Vol: 7 Page: 020

ASHLEY Ruamah N d Hopkinton 1915-06-25 age 65yrs 7mos 4dys b Lyman Maine 1849-11-21 child of CLOUGH Trow of Scotland & WADDIO Clarsia of Lyman Maine Vol: 7 Page: 020

SORNRBERGER Clifford W d Hopkinton 1915-06-28 age 6mos 9dys b Hopkinton 1914-12-19 child of SORNBERGER Eddie S of Canada & McCORBY May J of Canada Vol: 7 Page: 020

EDMUNDS Ellen G d Hopkinton 1915-07-25 age 77yrs 21dys b Hopkinton 1838-07-04 child of EDMUNDS Horace of Weare & CILLEY Bridget of Weare Vol: 7 Page: 021

RAND Johnathan d Hopkinton 1915-07-31 age 71yrs 5mos 24dys b Hopkinton 1844-02-07 child of RAND Mathew P of Hopkinton & HOLMES Sarah of Hopkinton Vol: 7 Page: 021

CHASE Alden M d Salisbury 1915-08-19 age 44yrs 11mos 10dys b Hopkinton 1870-09-29 child of CHASE David M of Hopkinton & DAMON Clara of Hopkinton Vol: 7 Page: 021

SEAVEY David d Hopkinton 1915-08-29 age 82yrs 10mos 6dys b Concord 1832-10-23 child of SEAVEY Andrew of Stewartstown & FISK Betsey of Concord Vol: 7 Page: 022

BENTON Rosaline d Hopkinton 1915-08-30 age 4dys b Hopkinton 1915-08-26 child of BENTON Joseph S of Newton Mass & BURNHAM Dorothy of Lowell Mass Vol: 7 Page: 022

KIMBALL John H d West Concord 1915-09-17 age 71yrs 1mos 13dys b Weare 1844-08-04 child of KIMBALL Charles N of Weare & HOLMES Martha of Hopkinton Vol: 7 Page: 022

FAGAN John C d Hopkinton 1915-09-04 age 7yrs 4mos 27dys b Boston Mass 1908-04-07 child of FAGAN John H of Hopkinton & BRENNAN Julia I of Nova Scotia Vol: 7 Page: 023

LANG Eliza P d Hopkinton 1915-10-03 age 76yrs 7mos 8dys b Hopkinton 1839-02-25 child of STORY Luther of Hopkinton & CROWELL Mary of Boscawen Vol: 7 Page: 023

PATSFIELD Shirley A d Concord 1915-10-20 age 29dys b Concord 1915-09-21 child of PATSFIELD John M of Halifax N S & BROWN Olive A of Warner Vol: 7 Page: 023

EASTMAN Timothy B d Hopkinton 1915-10-06 age 83yrs 9mos 20dys b Warner 1832-01-17 child of EASTMAN Timothy of Hopkinton & SIBLEY Polly of Hopkinton Vol: 7 Page: 024

HUTCHINS Teresa E d Hopkinton 1915-11-23 age 84yrs 10mos 22dys b Falmouth N S 1831-01-01 child of MARTIN Joseph of Nova Scotia & DAVISON Abigail of Nova Scotia Vol: 7 Page: 024

SPILLER Robert O d Hopkinton 1915-12-08 age 2mos 16dys b Hopkinton 1915-08-23 child of SPILLER Robert & FIFIELD Alice of Hopkinton Vol: 7 Page: 024

KAY Dorris May d Hopkinton 1915-12-10 age 1mos 13dys b Hopkinton 1915-10-27 child of KAY James of Fall River Mass & CLARK Lillian L of Warner Vol: 7 Page: 025

MORGAN Evaline L d Franport Phil 1916-03-03 age 75yrs Vol: 7 Page: 029

GUERIN George d Hopkinton 1916-01-01 age 32yrs 11mos 15dys b Manchester 1884-01-16 child of GUERIN Edward Vol: 7 Page: 027

HATHORN Sarah K d Hopkinton 1916-01-23 age 62yrs 4mos 4dys b Hopkinton 1853-09-19 child of EMERSON James of Hopkinton & Diamond of Hopkinton Vol: 7 Page: 027

MORSE Kate E d Hopkinton 1916-02-06 age 82yrs 7mos 26dys b Cambridge Mass 1833-06-10 child of METCALF Charles of Mass & CUSTMAN Nancy of Attleboro Mass Vol: 7 Page: 027

Hopkinton, NH Deaths 1914

SNOW Abigail J d Hopkinton 1916-02-14 age 71yrs 8mos 14dys b Smiths Cor N S 1844-05-30 child of HARDY Benj of Nova Scotia & MARSHALL Hannah of Nova Scotia Vol: 7 Page: 028

DANFORTH Jennette W d Hopkinton 1916-02-20 age 76yrs 3mos 1dys b Hopkinton 1839-11-19 child of PATTERSON David N Vol: 7 Page: 028

BROWN Melissa d Hopkinton 1916-02-24 age 38yrs 4mos 12dys b Ivanhoe Ont 1877-10-12 child of FLEMIMING Robert of Ontairao & ---- ---- of Ontairao Vol: 7 Page: 028

BROWN ---- d Hopkinton 1916-02-24 b Hopkinton 1916-02-24 child of BROWN Lanson O of Thornton & FLEMIMING Melissa of Ivanhow Ont Vol: 7 Page: 029

FLANDERS Angeline L d Warner 1916-02-25 age 81yrs 0mos 11dys child of EMERSON James of Hopkinton & FLANDERS Judith of Hopkinton Vol: 7 Page: 029

FRENCH Sarah Alice d Hopkinton 1916-03-16 age 68yrs 11mos b Hopkinton 1847-04-16 child of HARDY Albert of Dunbarton & LANCASTER Lydia Vol: 7 Page: 030

FRENCH Edward D d Concord 1916-03-18 age 79yrs 6mos 19dys b Hopkinton 1836-08-30 child of FRENCH Rueben E Vol: 7 Page: 030

NOYES Frank L d Warner 1916-03-14 age 63yrs 6mos 15dys b Cambridge Mass 1852-08-27 child of NOYES David of Warner & FISH Mary J of Hopkinton Vol: 7 Page: 030

BOUTWELL Lilly A d Concord 1916-04-02 age 40yrs 1mos 5dys b Cambridge Mass 1876-02-28 child of WARD Samuel of Cambridge Mass & HARRIS Lilly B of Boston Mass Vol: 7 Page: 031

PATTEE Esther Davis d Hopkinton 1916-04-04 age 80yrs 4mos 8dys b Aleander Me 1835-11-27 child of BABCOCK Grodin & Nodding Vol: 7 Page: 031

WHITE Mary E d Hopkinton 1916-05-01 age 48yrs b Waverly Mass 1868 child of BOWDOIN Capt Oliver of York Maine & ---- ---- of Elliott Maine Vol: 7 Page: 031

GRIFFIN Alfred E d Hopkinton 1916-05-12 age 63yrs 27dys b Bow 1853-04-15 child of GRIFFIN Joshua & CURRIER Emily Vol: 7 Page: 032

TILTON Willard John d Hopkinton 1916-05-17 age 2yrs 5mos 5dys b Hopkinton 1913-11-12 child of TILTON Joseph N of Hopkinton & ROLLINS M Alice of Hopkinton Vol: 7 Page: 032

DUSTIN Louise D d Hopkinton 1916-05-31 age 67yrs 4dys b 1849-05-27 child of EACOTT William of England & NORRIS Eliza of England Vol: 7 Page: 032

CURRIER Mary I Kilburn d Concord 1916-06-04 age 50yrs 9mos b Webster 1865-09-05 child of KILBURN John of Webster Vol: 7 Page: 033

HYNDS Mary A d Hopkinton 1916-07-05 age 90yrs 11mos 7dys b 1825-07-08 child of TEN Eyek Parrent C ?? & SMITH Joanna Vol: 7 Page: 033

WINCHESTER Sarah B d Grafton Mass 1916-03-25 age 87yrs 7mos Vol: 7 Page: 033

BECKWITH Elizabeth H d Hopkinton 1916-07-19 age 68yrs 7mos 22dys b Duber Ontario 1847-12-27 child of BLAIKLOOK George & BIRD Hannah Vol: 7 Page: 034

310

Hopkinton, NH Deaths 1914

AGER Walter C d Hopkinton 1916-08-19 age 77yrs 10mos 8dys b Warner 1838-10-11 child of AGER Mriah & SMITH Margaret Vol: 7 Page: 034

SWEATT William B d Hopkinton 1916-08-24 age 67yrs 5mos 12dys b Webster 1849-03-12 child of SWEATT Willaim M of Webster & DOWNER Sarah of Webster Vol: 7 Page: 034

HATHAWAY Warren Thomas d Hopkinton 1916-08-30 age 1mos 3dys b Hopkinton 1916-07-27 child of HATHAWAY Charles N of Canada & MURPHY Margaret of NY Vol: 7 Page: 035

NUTTING Helen L d Hopkinton 1916-08-30 age 7yrs 7mos 7dys b Worcester Mass 1909-01-23 child of NUTTING Charles A of Fitchbury Mass & NUKERSON Callie S of Yarmouth N S Vol: 7 Page: 035

CONNOR Sophia C d Manchester 1916-09-12 age 75yrs 8mos 24dys b Concord 1840-12-18 child of FLANDERS Charles C & FERRIN Clara Vol: 7 Page: 035

PERKINS John d Boscawen 1916-09-16 age 75yrs Vol: 7 Page: 036

STANLEY Mary E d Hopkinton 1916 age 57yrs 20dys b Hopkinton 1858-12-10 child of CLOUGH Charles F of Hopkinton & HARDY Mary of Hopkinton Vol: 7 Page: 036

BUSWELL Deborah D d Bow 1916-10-22 age 80yrs 5mos 12dys b Machias Me 1836-05-10 child of ELDER Charles E of Machias Me & LOWNEY Mary E of Machias Me Vol: 7 Page: 036

BUTNAM George d Hopkinton 1916-11-17 age 79yrs 10mos 7dys b Beverly Mass 1837-01-10 child of BUTNAM John G of Beverly Mass & ---- ---- of Beverly Mass Vol: 7 Page: 037

TILTON Clara J d Haverhill Mass 1916-11-23 age 64yrs 1mos 14dys Vol: 7 Page: 037

COLBY Abel M d Hopkinton 1916-12-08 age 69yrs 8mos 21dys b 1847-03-17 child of COLBY Abraham of Londonderry & KIMBALL Adeline of Londonderry Vol: 7 Page: 037

DAY Lily B d Hopkinton 1916-11-02 age 63yrs 4mos 30dys b Boston Mass 1853-06-04 child of HANES Chas of Nova Scotia & RINNESS Jane?? of Boston Mass Vol: 7 Page: 038

SYMONDS Emma J d Hopkinton 1916-12-13 age 60yrs 5mos 10dys b 1856-06-03 child of PARTER John of Vermont & WILBURN Lydia P of Augusta Me Vol: 7 Page: 038

GALE Sarah S d Newton 1916-12-13 age 96yrs 6mos 11dys b 1820-06-02 child of STORY William of Hopkinton & KNOWLTON Lydia of Hopkinton Vol: 7 Page: 038

LUND Julia A d Hopkinton 1916-12-26 age 60yrs 11mos 26dys b Hopkinton 1855-12-30 child of KEZER Moses of Hopkinton & Ordway of Hopkinton Vol: 7 Page: 039

BLAKE Ella Francis d Newport 1917-01-01 b Weare 1850-12-20 child of FOSTER Henry of Warner & COLBY Asenath of Henniker Vol: 7 Page: 040

GREENE Willard T d Hopkinton 1917-01-01 age 59yrs 6mos 22dys b Hopkinton 1855-06-07 child of GREENE Herman W of Hopkinton & WILLARD Fannie of Hopkinton Vol: 7 Page: 040

ROACH John d Hopkinton 1917-01-06 age 89yrs 6mos 7dys b Ireland 1827-06-29 child of ROACH John of Ireland & ROUNEY Ann of Ireland Vol: 7 Page: 040

Hopkinton, NH Deaths 1914

HOOK J Frank d Hopkinton 1917-01-10 age 64yrs 11mos 20dys b Concord 1852-01-20 child of HOOK Enos & HARRIETT N Vol: 7 Page: 041

LEAVETT Ralph J d Windsor Vt 1917-01-11 Vol: 7 Page: 041

CARLTON Brooks Louis Jr d Hopkinton 1917-01-21 age 2mos 29dys b Hopkinton 1916-10-22 child of BROOKS Carlton L of Antrim & MAXWELL Sarah of Antrim Vol: 7 Page: 041

SAWTELLE John N d Hopkinton 1917-01-31 age 67yrs 4mos 12dys b Warren 1849-09-18 child of SAWTELLE Isaiah & Brown Vol: 7 Page: 042

EASTMAN Helen C d Hopkinton 1917-02-04 age 79yrs 10mos 21dys b Hopkinton 1836-03-13 child of CHASE Ambrose of Hopkinton & Gould of Hopkinton Vol: 7 Page: 042

HARDY Emeline M d Hopkinton 1917-02-05 age 101yrs 8mos 4dys b Rummney 1815-05-01 child of WEBSTER David of Rummney & HUTCHINS Lucy of Rummney Vol: 7 Page: 042

GUERIN Dora d Manchester 1917-02-20 age 9yrs 2mos 16dys b Hopkinton 1906-12-04 child of GUERIN George of Canada & Sarah of Canada Vol: 7 Page: 043

CLOUGH Moses T d Rosell Park N J 1917-02-16 age 78yrs 11mos 24dys b Hopkinton 1838-03-22 child of CLOUGH Willard of Hopkinton & DUSTIN Charlotte of Hopkinton Vol: 7 Page: 043

BLAISDELL Geo C d Hopkinton 1917-03-04 age 72yrs 4mos 11dys b Goffstwown 1844-11-23 child of BLAISDELL Stephen & MARSHALL Omanda of E Weare Vol: 7 Page: 043

FISK Daniel Frank d Hopkinton 1917-03-14 age 57yrs 4mos 19dys b Hopkinton 1859-10-22 child of FISK D F of Hopkinton & CONNOR Lydia of Hopkinton Vol: 7 Page: 044

HOWE Eva M d Hopkinton 1917-03-16 age 30yrs 6mos 5dys b Warner 1886-09-10 child of HOWE Jason C of Bradford & KEMPHILL Hannah J of Warner Vol: 7 Page: 044

DANFORTH Charles H d Somerville Mass 1917-03-24 age 57yrs 7mos 24dys Vol: 7 Page: 044

CLOUGH Joseph S d Hopkinton 1917-03-31 age 63yrs 3mos 28dys b Hopkinton 1853-12-03 child of CLOUGH Charles F of Hopkinton & HARDY Mary of Hopkinton Vol: 7 Page: 045

CHASE Ellen Mariam d Baltimore Md 1917-04-18 age 74yrs Vol: 7 Page: 045

DEARBORN Infant Dau d New York NY 1913 Sep child of DEARBORN F M (Dr) Vol: 7 Page: 045

STRAW Mary Ann d Hopkinton 1917-05-05 age 94yrs 6mos 20dys b Weare 1822-10-15 child of FLANDERS James of Topsham Vt & PEASLEE Mary of Weare Vol: 7 Page: 046

JOHNSON Julia M d Hopkinton 1917-05-09 age 78yrs 11mos 2dys b Lowell Mass 1838-06-07 child of JOHNSON Joshua M of Deering & PATTERSON Clara A of Henniker Vol: 7 Page: 046

OSBORN Grace S d Hopkinton 1917-06-13 age 86yrs 7mos 8dys b Keene 1830-11-04 child of EVANS Nathaniel of Peterborough & WIGGIN Harriet of Concord Vol: 7 Page: 046

Hopkinton, NH Deaths 1914

BARTLETT Clifton R d Warner 1917-09-04 age 2yrs 11mos 18dys b Hopkinton 1914-04-17 child of BARTLETT J C of Hopkinton & CHASE Lida of Hopkinton Vol: 7 Page: 047

PIERCE George H d Hopkinton 1917-06-06 age 58yrs 4mos 13dys b Hopkinton 1859-01-24 child of PIERCE George W of Warner & COX Myra T of Hopkinton Vol: 7 Page: 047

GOODWIN Charles P d Hopkinton 1917-07-17 age 68yrs 11mos 29dys b Concord 1848-07-17 child of GOODRICH Alpheus & Nichols Vol: 7 Page: 048

PIERCE Luella d Concord 1917-07-15 age 70yrs b 1847 child of STRAW Wm of Hopkinton & FLANDERS Mary of Weare Vol: 7 Page: 048

FENTON Leander d Concord 1917-08-03 age 54yrs 5dys b Tiuro N S 1863-07-02 child of FENTON Jacob Vol: 7 Page: 048

KNUCKEY John T d Hopkinton 1917-08-21 age 29yrs 5mos 5dys b Canaan 1888-03-16 child of KNUCKEY John T of England & TRENONETH Annie of England Vol: 7 Page: 049

STORY Charles M d Hopkinton 1917-08-28 age 60yrs 1mos 1dys b Hopkinton 1857-07-27 child of STORY Moses of Hopkinton & Harriet of Warner Vol: 7 Page: 049

CARR Mary A B d Hopkinton 1917-09-19 age 73yrs 22dys b Hopkinton 1844-08-28 child of ---- ---- of Maine & STRAW Anna of Hopkinton Vol: 7 Page: 049

WILSON Eliza W d Manchester 1917-11-24 age 78yrs 11mos 6dys b Hopkinton 1838-12-18 Vol: 7 Page: 050

MONTGOMERY Scott d Hopkinton 1917-10-06 age 60yrs 10mos 18dys b Hopkinton child of MONTGOMERY Wm & Savory Vol: 7 Page: 050

PAGE Edson d Hopkinton 1918-01-13 age 72yrs 9mos 16dys b Dunbarton 1845-03-28 child of PAGE John of Kingston & COLBY Clymena of Bow Vol: 7 Page: 051

SHAMPNEY Francis M d Hopkinton 1918-01-14 age 2mos 23dys b Concord 1917-10-22 child of SHAMPNEY Lewis F of Sharon Vt & MORE Laura of Loudon Vol: 7 Page: 051

FELLOWS Harriet Ellen d Hopkinton 1918-01-16 age 73yrs 3mos 14dys b Hopkinton 1844-10-02 child of FELLOWS Ignatius W of Hopkinton & COPPS Sarah J of Plaistow Vol: 7 Page: 051

HATHAWAY Chas H d W Hopkinton 1918-01-28 b W Hopkinton child of HATHAWAY Chas H & MURPHY Margaret Vol: 7 Page: 052

ROWELL Charls S d Hopkinton 1918-02-01 age 60yrs 7mos 6dys b Hopkinton 1857-06-26 child of ROWELL Isaac of Hopkinton & ADAMS Harriett of Henniker Vol: 7 Page: 52

RAYMONS Marieann E d Hopkinton 1918-02-10 age 64yrs 5mos 21dys b Henniker 1853-08-19 child of PHILLIP Martin E of Henniker & EMERSON Mary Jane of Hopkinton Vol: 7 Page: 052

GEER Edmund D d Hopkinton 1918-03-04 age 79yrs 5mos 4dys b 1838-09-30 child of GEER Wells of P Q & MAGOP Sabrina of P Q Vol: 7 Page: 053

FLANDERS Louise M d Boscawen 1918-03-12 age 76yrs b Hopkinton Vol: 7 Page: 053

Hopkinton, NH Deaths 1914

WATSON Alma S d Hopkinton 1918-03-21 age 74yrs 11mos 16dys b Salisbury 1843-04-05 child of WATSON Nicodemus of Salisbury & WILKINS Eliza of Carlisle Mass Vol: 7 Page: 053

SYMONDS Helen K d Concord 1918-06-15 age 4mos 4dys Vol: 7 Page: 056

HALE John D d Northwood 1918-06-15 age 34yrs 3mos 15dys Vol: 7 Page: 056

MONTGOMERY Earl R d N Charleston Sc 1918-06-18 age 30yrs child of MONT-GOMERY Jerome & Eliza Vol: 7 Page: 056

FOSS Ida F d Hopkinton 1918-07-08 age 65yrs 5mos 6dys b Hopkinton 1853-02-03 child of HOLMES Willard of Hopkinton & KIMBALL Eliza of Hopkinton Vol: 7 Page: 057

GUIMOND Lawrence E d Hopkinton 1918-07-11 age 2mos 29dys b Hopkinton 1918-04-13 child of GUIMOND Fred of Manchester & CURRIER Doma F of Warner Vol: 7 Page: 057

GOMES Emma C d Hopkinton 1918-08-27 age 52yrs 9mos 5dys b Sweden 1865-11-22 child of ANDERSON John A of Sweden & ---- ---- of Sweden Vol: 7 Page: 057

CHASE Emma M d Portsmouth 1918-09-18 age 26yrs 5mos 5dys b Webster 1892-04-12 child of SHURTLEFF John J of Lebanon & ELLINWOOD Fannie B of Manchester Vol: 7 Page: 058

CONANT George Elmer d Hanover 1918-09-22 age 17yrs b Hopkinton child of CONANT Dwight E & KEMP Blanche L Vol: 7 Page: 058

MARSH George W d Concord 1918-09-27 age 63yrs 11dys b Boscawenn 1855-09-16 child of MARSH Hiram J of Grantham & GIBSON Nancy of Maine Vol: 7 Page: 058

TILTON Clarence L d Hopkinton 1918-10-03 age 28yrs 5mos 9dys b Webster 1890-04-24 child of TILTON L O of Alexandria & Sanborn of Manchester Vol: 7 Page: 059

FENTON Birge L d Concord 1918-10-06 age 29yrs 7dys b West Thornton 1889-09-28 child of FENTON Leander of Nova Scotia & ELKINS Rosa of W Thornton Vol: 7 Page: 059

MONTGOMERY ---- ---- d Hopkinton 1918-10-06 b Hopkinton child of MONT-GOMERY W L of Hopkinton & OMAN Agnes Vol: 7 Page: 059

WHITE Mildred L d Hopkinton 1918-10-08 age 20yrs 7mos 1dys b Franklin Mass 1898-03-07 child of JORDEN Oliver of Franklin Mass & LINTON Hellen of New Brunswick Vol: 7 Page: 060

MAGNAN Jane d Hopkinton 1918-10-15 age 86yrs 3mos 9dys b Hillsboro 1832-07-06 child of CARTER Samuel of Henniker & RAY Mary of Henniker Vol: 7 Page: 060

SPOFFORD Herman S d Concord 1918-10-15 age 35yrs 2mos 25dys b Hopkinton 1883-07-20 child of SPOFFORD Luther of Hopkinton & CHANDLER Dora of Hopkinton Vol: 7 Page: 060

ADAMS Howard D d Hopkinton 1918-10-13 age 23yrs 6mos 3dys b Hopkinton 1895-04-10 child of ADAMS Wm of Sutton & BROWN Laura of Thornton Vol: 7 Page: 061

NELSON Etta L d Hopkinton 1918-10-18 age 34yrs 4mos b Hopkinton 1884-06-18 child of BOHANAN John W of Sutton & JEWELL Delia of Weare Vol: 7 Page: 061

PHILLIPS Ira Clark d Concord 1918-11-03 age 71yrs 11mos 6dys b Henniker 1846-11-27 child of PHILLIPS Martin of Henniker & EMERSON Mary J Vol: 7 Page: 061

TALLANT Eugene A d Hopkinton 1918-11-04 age 33yrs 7mos 28dys b Pelham 1885-03-19 child of TALLANT Andrew K of Meredith & ROBEY Angie of Lawrence Mass Vol: 7 Page: 062

BOYNTON Charles J d Dunbarton 1918-11-28 age 6yrs 1mos 16dys Vol: 7 Page: 062

KIMBALL Elbridge G d Hopkinton 1918-12-09 age 87yrs 5mos 3dys b Hopkinton 1831-07-03 child of KIMBALL Daniel of Hopkinton & HERRICK Asenath of Hopkinton Vol: 7 Page: 0062

BARTON Philinda d Hopkinton 1918-12-13 age 79yrs 10mos 5dys b Goshen 1839-02-08 child of CUTTS Samuel Vol: 7 Page: 063

WATSON James E d Hopkinton 1918-12-18 age 69yrs 10mos 8dys b Boston Mass 1849-02-10 child of WATSON Geo & CANTERBURY Eliza Vol: 7 Page: 063

CONANT Dwight E d Hopkinton 1918-12-24 age 46yrs 8mos 3dys b Willimantic Conn 1872-04-21 child of CONANT Henry E of Mansfield Ct & SHATTELL Lina of Germany Vol: 7 Page: 063

BARNARD Maria G d Hopkinton 1918-12-31 age 87yrs 8mos 16dys b Canterbury 1831-04-15 child of GERRISH Abiel F of Boscawen & DODGE Eliza of Webster Vol: 7 Page: 064

EASTMAN Wesley E d Hopkinton 1919-01-02 age 29yrs 6mos 4dys b Franklin 1889-06-28 child of EASTMAN Geo E of Andover & SAWYER Bessie E of Andover Vol: 7 Page: 065

MARTIN Mable C d Hopkinton 1919-01-03 age 19yrs 7mos 12dys b Henniker 1899-05-21 child of MARTIN Chas W of So Reding Mass & TURNER Annah M of Antrim Vol: 7 Page: 065

HOOK Mary A d Chichester 1919-01-15 age 87yrs 3mos 27dys b Conwell Eng 1840-09-18 child of DOYING Wallace W of Danville P Q & BROWN Mary Ann of Danville P Q Vol: 7 Page: 065

WEEKS N Cogswell d Concord 1919-01-23 age 80yrs 5mos 27dys Vol: 7 Page: 066

ADAMS Anna Bell d Hopkinton 1919-05-13 age 52yrs 4mos 23dys b Canaan 1866-12-10 Vol: 8 Page: 003

BARRETT Thoms d Hopkinton 1919-01-30 age 64yrs 8mos 14dys b Cornwall England 1854-05-16 child of BARRETT Thomas of Cornwall England & JAMES Jane of Cornwall England Vol: 7 Page: 066

HOLMES ---- ---- d Hopkinton 1918-06-25 b Hopkinton 1918-06-25 child of HOLMES Myron of Hopkinton & FLANDERS Lucy J of Warner Vol: 7 Page: 055

BARRETT Thomas d Hopkinton 1919-01-30 age 64yrs 8mos 14dys b Cornwall England 1854-05-16 child of BARRETT Thomas of Cornwall Eng & JONES Jane of Cornwall Eng Vol: 8 Page: 002

PAIGE Maude E d Concord 1919-03-10 age 41yrs 7mos 24dys b Hopkinton 1877-07-16 child of PAIGE Frank W of Hopkinton & CURRIER Kate E of Hopkinton Vol: 8 Page: 002

BOUTWELL Frank E d Dunbarton 1919-06-03 age 50yrs 8mos 19dys b Salem 1868-09-22 child of BOUTWELL Elmer W of & WOODBURY Julia Vol: 8 Page: 004

GRAY Sarah L d Hopkinton 1919-06-15 age 74yrs 11mos 1dys b Bow 1844-07-14 child of GARDNER A L of Bedford & Colby of Bow Vol: 8 Page: 004

DAVIS Esther d Concord 1919-05-11 age 1dys b Concord 1919-05-11 child of DAVIS Willie N of Warner & EMERSON Florence of Webster Vol: 8 Page: 004

DAVIS Florence E d Concord 1919-05-15 age 36yrs 5mos 22dys b Webster child of EMERSON Fred H of Hopkinton & KIMBALL Nellie F of Maine Vol: 8 Page: 005

FULLER John A d Hopkinton 1919-08-23 age 71yrs 15dys b Bridgewater 1848-08-08 child of FULLER Abram George of Hopkinton & FELLOWS Adline of Hopkinton Vol: 8 Page: 005

SCRIBNER Elisha B d Hopkinton 1919-08-25 age 66yrs 11mos 30dys b West Salisbury 1852-08-26 child of SCRIBNER Hiram C of West Salisbury & BATCHELDER Harriet of Danville Vol: 8 Page: 005

SYMONDS Benjamin D d Hopkinton 1919-09-16 age 75yrs 10mos 11dys b Hillsborough 1843-11-05 child of SYMONDS Tilton of Hillsborough & DUTTON Catherine of Hillsborough Vol: 8 Page: 006

HARRINGTON Thomas O d Concord 1919-09-19 age 68yrs 9mos 3dys b Concord 1850-12-16 child of HARRINGTON Moses of New York & CURRIER Rebecca of Concord Vol: 8 Page: 006

LIBBEY L Dora d Hopkinton 1919-09-27 age 50yrs 3mos 3dys b Sweden 1869-06-22 child of NICHOLS Chas of Sweden Vol: 8 Page: 006

DANFORTH Maria E d Manchester 1919-10-01 age 77yrs 3mos 1dys b Canada 1842-05-30 child of SWEAT Moses & MITCHELL Caroline Vol: 8 Page: 007

SON William d Hopkinton 1919-10-23 age 75yrs b Canada Vol: 8 Page: 007

CHASE Hollis M d Hopkinton 1919-11-01 age 55yrs 3mos 14dys b Henniker 1864-07-18 child of CHASE Harvey of Henniker & Paige of Henniker Vol: 8 Page: 007

TAYLOR Clara d Lynn Mass 1919-09-16 age 83yrs 1mos 1dys b Warner 1836-08-15 child of UPTON Joseph of Reading Mass & MERRILL Carcinda of NH Vol: 8 Page: 008

STRAW Weldon Herbert d Hopkinton 1856-04-07 age 1yrs 4mos b Hopkinton 1855-03-12 Vol: 8 Page: 008

CLOUGH Adelaide d Worcester Mass 1919-12-02 age 63yrs 4mos 2dys b Fall River Mass child of BASSETT Davis T of Maine & SHERMAN Hannah of Tiverton RI Vol: 8 Page: 008

EMERTON John d Hopkinton 1919-12-21 age 76yrs 14dys b Wentworth 1843-12-07 child of EMERTON Ira of Colebrook & KIDDER Susan of Amherst Vol: 8 Page: 009

CHANDLER Alfred N d Concord 1920-01-02 age 91yrs 11mos 14dys b Hopkinton 1828-01-16 child of ANDREW Stephen & RIPLEY Mary Vol: 8 Page: 010

CHANDLER Helen M d Concord 1920-01-14 age 86yrs 3mos 12dys b Hopkinton 1833-10-02 child of Hammon of England & TEAGUE Lydia of Salem Mass Vol: 8 Page: 010

Hopkinton, NH Deaths 1914

HOWARD Daniel Edson d Arlington Mass 1920-01-18 age 84yrs 6mos 26dys b Grantham 1835-06-12 child of HOWARD Lewis of Bridgewater Mass & STOWELL Sally Vol: 8 Page: 010

CHASE Orrin d Concord 1920-01-21 age 76yrs 10mos 29dys b Hopkinton 1843-03-22 child of CHASE Rubin of Hopkinton & RYANS Betsy Vol: 8 Page: 011

CURRIER Carrie V d Hopkinton 1920-01-31 age 64yrs 4mos 2dys b Salisbury 1855-09-28 child of PETTINGILL A C of Salisbury & SHAW E A of Salisbury Vol: 8 Page: 011

CHENEY Herbert M d Hopkinton 1920-03-13 age 64yrs 7mos 21dys b Wilmont 1855-07-20 Vol: 8 Page: 011

PALMER Maria H d Hopkinton 1920-03-14 age 75yrs 3mos 14dys b Hopkinton 1844-12-01 child of PALMER William of Bradford Mass & CHASE Ann E of Methuen Mass Vol: 8 Page: 012

YOUNG Alice d Gerrish 1920-03-23 age 67yrs b Hopkinton Vol: 8 Page: 012

WILSON Elizabeth d Hopkinton 1920-04-14 age 52yrs 8mos 17dys b Deering 1867-07-27 child of GILMORE Benjamin F of Warner & CRESSEY Mary of Bradford Vol: 8 Page: 012

DANFORTH Lidia A d Hopkinton 1920-04-22 age 89yrs 2mos 2dys b Henniker 1830-02-20 child of CONNOR J A of Henniker & KIMBALL Lidia of Hopkinton Vol: 8 Page: 013

BARTLETT Raimond A d Warner 1920-04-15 age 2yrs 8mos 12dys b Warner 1917-09-20 child of BARTLETT Clifton J of Warner & Chase of Hopkinton Vol: 8 Page: 013

COLBY Ellen H d Concord 1920-04-26 age 66yrs 4dys b Hopkinton 1854-04-22 child of COLBY Melvin of Hopkinton & EDMUNDS Hannah of Hopkinton Vol: 8 Page: 013

NUDD John K d Hopkinton 1920-05-02 age 66yrs 15mos 17dys b Canterbury 1853-11-15 child of NUDD Ben J of Loudon & PERKINS Rebecca of Loudon Vol: 8 Page: 014

BURGESS Martha J d Hopkinton 1920-05-03 age 75yrs 7mos 13dys b Caribou Me 1844-09-18 Vol: 8 Page: 014

DOCKHAM ---- d Hopkinton 1920-05-11 b Hopkinton child of DOCKHAM Forrest of Gilford & BLETCHER Vera of Dover Vol: 8 Page: 014

HALL Rose E d Hopkinton 1920-05-15 age 39yrs 7mos 29dys b Wisconsin 1880-09-16 child of HALL Daniel of Plymouth Vt & STEVENS Adelins of Wisconsin Vol: 8 Page: 015

RILEY Harriet d Hopkinton 1920-06-08 age 63yrs b England Vol: 8 Page: 015

CHASE Wesley John d Hopkinton 1920-05-28 age 68yrs 4mos 5dys b Hopkinton 1852-01-23 child of CHASE Wyman of Hopkinton & ---- ---- of Hopkinton Vol: 8 Page: 015

TUCKER Mary Elizabeth d Hopkinton 1920-06-11 age 97yrs 8mos 2dys b Hopkinton 1822-10-09 child of STRAW Levi of Hopkinton & CARLTON Harriet of Fairlee Vt Vol: 8 Page: 016

DUNBAR George d Belmont 1920-05-24 age 52yrs 7mos 20dys b Hopkinton 1867-10-04 child of DUNBAR Elmer of Grantham & WEBER Ann of Hopkinton Vol: 8 Page: 016

Hopkinton, NH Deaths 1914

ATWATER Harriet Chase d Los Angeles Cal 1920-10-06 age 73yrs 9mos 15dys b Pennsylvania 1845-12-21 child of CHASE Benjamin of Mass & WIGGIN Ann of Pa Vol: 8 Page: 016

MILLS Charles A d Hopkinton 1920-06-15 age 18yrs 7mos 11dys b Hopkinton 1901-11-04 child of MILLS Charles A of Hopkinton & CLARK Effie M of East Weare Vol: 8 Page: 017

SARGENT Mary W d Newport 1920-06-17 age 97yrs 10mos 15dys b Hopkinton 1822-07-02 child of CHASE Jacob & BARKER Hannah Vol: 8 Page: 017

MANN Jennie D d Bristol 1920-05-07 age 71yrs 5mos 2dys b Webster 1848-12-05 child of DOW Lorenzo & STORY Mary Vol: 8 Page: 017

ROBEY Cloey (Mrs) d Hopkinton 1920-09-06 age 61yrs 9mos 1dys b Lyme 1858-12-05 child of INGERSON Hiram & Worthey Vol: 8 Page: 020

DAVIS Thomas E d Hopkinton 1920-09-08 age 33yrs 4mos 7dys b Hopkinton 1887-04-30 child of DAVIS Henry B of Hopkinton & COOK Eliza Vol: 8 Page: 020

JOHNSON Ellen Tuttle d Hopkinton 1920-09-09 age 76yrs 8mos 28dys b Hartford Conn 1843-12-11 child of TUTTLE Samuel I of Hartford Conn & Ellen of Hartford Conn Vol: 8 Page: 020

BARRETT Laura M d Manchester 1920-09-28 age 91yrs b Hopkinton 1829-09-28 child of NOYES Leonard & Julia Vol: 8 Page: 021

MERRILL Abbie Cross d Westboro Mass 1920-10-06 age 65yrs 9mos 23dys b Portland Me 1854-12-14 child of BIBBIS Joel of Maine & Martha of Portland Maine Vol: 8 Page: 021

COULTER ---- d Concord 1920-10-08 b Concord child of COULTER Macwell of Warren & BUCK Frances of Burlington Vt Vol: 8 Page: 021

GREENWOOD Herbert d Boston Mass 1920-10-17 age 66yrs 27dys Vol: 8 Page: 022

GREENE Austis I d Hopkinton 1920-11-07 age 80yrs 3mos 29dys b Canaan 1840-07-09 child of CLARKE Daniel W & COCHRAN Ruhannah Vol: 8 Page: 022

CLARK George Addison d Manchester 1920-11-10 age 33yrs 6mos 18dys b East Weare 1887-04-22 child of CLARK Addison M of Manchester & BROWN Ida M of Montpelier Vt Vol: 8 Page: 022

LIBBY John S d Hopkinton 1920-11-10 age 70yrs 5mos b Newport Vt child of LIBBY Joseph P of Gilmanton & MAGOON Cynthia of Newport Vol: 8 Page: 023

SORNBERGER Cyril W d Hopkinton 1920-11-14 age 3mos 21dys b Hopkinton 1920-10-22 child of SORNBERGER Eddie of Canada & COUBREY Mary of Canada Vol: 8 Page: 023

COLBY Christina A d Hopkinton 1920-12-01 age 79yrs 4mos 22dys b New Boston 1841-07-09 child of BARTLETT Richard of Goffstown & GREGG Jane Vol: 8 Page: 023

LIBBY Horace d Hopkinton 1920-12-14 age 13yrs 11mos 13dys b Hopkinton 1906-12-31 child of LIBBY Frank of Hopkinton & McINTIRE Dora Vol: 8 Page: 024

BURPEE ---- d Hopkinton 1920-12-23 b Hopkinton child of BURPEE Elijah of Canada & NORRIS Annie B of Weare Vol: 8 Page: 034

HAWTHORNE Frances P d Boston Mass 1921-01-05 age 88yrs 6mos 17dys Vol: 8 Page: 025

HOYT Deborah E d Hopkinton 1921-01-23 age 72yrs 2mos 12dys b Wareham Mass 1848-11-11 child of BOYD Henry of Ireland & ROBINSON H of Bridgewater Mass Vol: 8 Page: 025

HOPKINS Willie B d Hopkinton 1921-02-21 age 45yrs 3mos 19dys b Barnstead Canada 1875-11-02 child of HOPKINS John C of Troul Mass & GRUSBY Sarah of Westboro Canada Vol: 8 Page: 025

WUNDERLICH Ruth May d Hopkinton 1921-02-22 age 1yrs 2mos 1dys b Hopkinton 1919-12-20 child of WUNDERLICH Chas. & CLARK Alice Vol: 8 Page: 026

KNOWLES Nettie d Hopkinton 1921-02-23 age 62yrs 5mos 23dys b Charlestown Vt 1857-09-23 child of LIBBY Joseph of Charlestown Vt & MAGOON Cynthia of Vt Vol: 8 Page: 026

WADE Mary Anna d Malden Mass 1921-04-03 age 66yrs 1mos 1dys Vol: 8 Page: 027

BOHANAN ---- d Hopkinton 1921-03-22 age 5dys b Hopkinton 1921-03-17 child of BOHANAN J Harry of Hopkinton & MARCY Esther G of Cambridge Mass Vol: 8 Page: 027

HOLMES Mary E d Hookset 1921-04-09 age 84yrs 11mos 4dys b Plymouth 1836-05-09 child of SANBORN David & TUFTS Lydia of Somerville Mass Vol: 8 Page: 027

MARTELL John d Hopkinton 1921-04-12 age 77yrs 9mos 3dys b St Croix P Q 1844-07-09 Vol: 8 Page: 028

BROWN Laura A Elkins d Hopkinton 1921-04-24 age 84yrs 8mos 28dys b Thorton 1836-07-26 child of ELKINS Eben of Ellsworth & HALL Mary of Gilmanton Vol: 8 Page: 028

CUMMINGS Francis Jinnon d Barre Vt 1921-05-09 age 6mos 8dys b Hopkinton Vol: 8 Page: 028

CHASE Margaret T d Hopkinton 1921-05-06 age 50yrs 8mos 13dys b Manchester Eng 1870-07-23 child of THORNTON Henry of England Vol: 8 Page: 029

EMERSON Laura A d Nashua 1921-05-13 age 70yrs 7mos 7dys b Hudson 1850-10-06 Vol: 8 Page: 029

ELLINWOOD Sarah J d Concord 1921-05-21 age 79yrs 7mos 17dys b Claremont 1841-10-04 child of MILTON John of Woburn Mass & SEVERANCE Mary of Claremont Vol: 8 Page: 029

PATTERSON Olive A d Hancock 1921-05-22 age 81yrs 2mos 25dys b Deering 1840-02-27 child of ALLEN Willard of Grantham & STONE Elvira of Cornish Vol: 8 Page: 030

ELLIOTT Eva E E d Hopkinton 1921-06-16 age 24dys b Hopkinton 1921-05-22 child of ELLIOTT Eden E of Michigan & GLASIER Anna of New York Vol: 8 Page: 030

GRANT Louis M d Atlantic N J 1921-01-26 age 56yrs b Hopkinton Vol: 8 Page: 030

STORY Harry O Jr d Hopkinton 1921-07-19 b Hopkinton child of STORY Harry O of Hopkinton & FOSTER Mertie E of Rumney Vol: 8 Page: 031

LOCK Etta M d Lowell Mass 1921-07-21 age 61yrs 2mos 1dys b Hopkinton Vol: 8 Page: 031

Hopkinton, NH Deaths 1914

BARTON Maurice W d Hopkinton 1921-08-15 age 7mos 13dys b Hopkinton 1921-01-02 child of BARTON Leslie C of Concord & SEVERANCE Isabelle D of Washington Vol: 8 Page: 031

SANBORN Sophia W d Springfield Mass 1921-08-17 age 81yrs 1mos 29dys Vol: 8 Page: 032

STORY Mary H d Hopkinton 1921-08-28 age 68yrs 7mos 14dys b Hopkinton 1853-01-14 child of CHANDLER Alfred of Hopkinton & HAMMOND Helen of Vol: 8 Page: 032

BURBANK Augusta J d Hopkinton 1921-08-31 age 60yrs 5mos 8dys b Hopkinton 1861-03-23 child of FRENCH George W of Hopkinton & Runnells of Salisbury Vol: 8 Page: 032

DAVIS Dustin W d Hopkinton 1921-09-02 age 86yrs 26dys b Sutton 1835-08-07 child of DAVIS Amos of Sutton & HUNT Unice of Warner Vol: 8 Page: 033

DORRY Mildred Louise d Hopkinton 1921-09-16 age 10mos 18dys b Hopkinton 1920-10-29 child of DORRY Howard of Victory N S & DEMERRIT Lela E of Nottingham Vol: 8 Page: 033

DALBY Charles E d Hopkinton 1921-09-26 age 48yrs 5mos 17dys b Chelsea Mass 1873-04-09 child of DALBY Henry C & Elen M Vol: 8 Page: 033

ORDWAY ---- d Bow 1921-10-03 b Bow child of ORDWAY Norman of Concord & LEWIS Ava E of Everett Mass Vol: 8 Page: 034

CLARK Mildred Alice d Windsor Vt 1921-09-22 age 5mos 17dys Vol: 8 Page: 034

HOYT Florence E d Hopkinton 1921-10-25 age 14dys b Hopkinton 1921-10-11 child of HOYT Charles S of Brandford & SEVERENCE Effie E of East Washinton Vol: 8 Page: 034

HOYT Flora d Hopkinton 1921-10-25 age 14dys b Hopkinton 1921-10-11 child of HOYT Charles S of Brandford & SEVERENCE Effie E of East Washinton Vol: 8 Page: 035

GOMES John A L d Hopkinton 1921-10-17 age 62yrs 9mos 20dys b Portugal 1858-12-26 child of COREAR John Vol: 8 Page: 035

CHASE Cyrus F d Hopkinton 1920-08-20 age 75yrs 6mos 24dys b Hopkinton 1845-01-27 child of CHASE Moses Vol: 8 Page: 018

WADSWORTH Mary E d Hopkinton 1921-10-31 age 77yrs 3mos 12dys b Davisvillle 1844-07-19 child of DAVIS Nathaniel of Warner & CLOUGH Mary of Webster Vol: 8 Page: 035

CLARK Addison N d Concord 1899-10-04 age 42yrs 19dys b Londonderry child of CLARK Edward E of Vermont & MORSE Hannah of Londonderry Vol: 8 Page: 036 Note: moved from Weare in Nov 1921

FELLOWS Maria Louise d Concord 1921-11-18 age 85yrs 2mos 17dys b Bath Me 1836-09-01 child of McDEWELL James of Scotland & INNIS Dorothy of Holderness Vol: 8 Page: 036

MUDGE Lilla E d Hopkinton 1921-11-21 age 63yrs 4mos 9dys b 1858-07-08 child of GOODHUE William & BELL Caroline Vol: 8 Page: 036

FLANDERS Frank H d Brookline Mass 1920-08-19 age 64yrs 9mos 19dys b Hopkinton 1855-09-19 child of FLANDERS Benj of Hopkinton & DOW Jane N of Henniker Vol: 8 Page: 018

Hopkinton, NH Deaths 1914

CROWELL Henry H d Hopkinton 1920-08-20 age 86yrs 1mos 11dys b Hopkinton 1834-07-09 child of CROWELL Albert of Hopkinton & HILDRETH Lydia of Hopkinton Vol: 8 Page: 018

LIBBY Frank d Hopkinton 1920-08-24 age 74yrs 16dys b Hopkinton 1846-08-08 child of LIBBY William of Hopkinton Vol: 8 Page: 019

FRENCH Jennie L d Hopkinton 1920-08-24 age 86yrs 5mos 6dys b Boston Mass 1834-03-18 child of STEVENS Ebeneza (Dr.) of Plaistow & Lena of Henniker Vol: 8 Page: 019

ROACH Ann d Hopkinton 1920-08-10 age 92yrs 1mos 14dys b Ireland 1828-06-27 child of ROONEY Patrick of Ireland & McBRIDE Anne of Ireland Vol: 8 Page: 019

DOCKHAM Alonzo d Hopkinton 1921-11-28 age 86yrs 9mos 16dys b Gilford 1835-02-12 child of DOCKHAM John of Gilford & BEANE Clara of Boston Mass Vol: 8 Page: 037

COVILLE Harriett B d Webster 1921-12-09 age 47yrs 1mos 25dys b New Bedford Mass 1874-10-14 child of STANTON John of New Bedford Mass & Gibbs of New Bedford Mass Vol: 8 Page: 037

BURBANK Moses W d Peterborough 1921-12-14 age 86yrs 10mos 24dys b Contoocook 1835-01-30 child of BURBANK Hiram of Contoocook & ORDWAY Hannah of Contoocook Vol: 8 Page: 037

IRVINE Jessie d Pembroke 1921-05-16 age 35yrs b Nova Scotia   child of MORRISON Roderick of Nova Scotia & DILLISON Josephine of Prince Edward Is Vol: 8 Page: 038

KIMBALL Francis R d Waltham Mass 1922-01-05 age 62yrs 10mos 25dys Vol: 8 Page: 039

CLEMENT Abbie H d Rochester 1922-01-20 age 85yrs b Hopkinton 1836 Vol: 8 Page: 039

MONTGOMERY Scott d Washington DC 1922-01-29 age 29yrs 5mos 5dys b Manchester 1892-08-20 child of MONTGOMERY Albert of Warner & RUSSELL Susan of Vermont Vol: 8 Page: 039

SHAMPNEY Caroline d Hopkinton 1922-02-23 b Hopkinton child of SHAMPNEY Roger of Boscawen & CLARK Hester of Hopkinton Vol: 8 Page: 040

BURBEE Dorothy A d Hopkinton 1922-02-26 age 2mos b Hopkinton 1922-01-02 child of BURBEE Eliza of Canada & NORRIS Annie B of Weare Vol: 8 Page: 040

RUSS William C d Hopkinton 1922-02-26 age 68yrs 1mos 26dys b Nashua 1853-12-31 child of RUSS Nathan Kendall of Lyme & BARRETT Clairass D of Windham Vol: 8 Page: 040

GOODWIN Isabella A d Hopkinton 1922-03-07 age 80yrs 28dys b Manchester 1842-01-09 child of DOTY Joseph of Maine Vol: 8 Page: 041

RAYMOND Wm H d Hopkinton 1922-03-09 age 77yrs 8mos 16dys b Hopkinton 1844-06-23 child of RAYMOND Joshua O of Hopkinton & SIMONS Margaret Vol: 8 Page: 041

HOYT Frank A d Concord 1922-03-10 age 42yrs 6mos 14dys b Wareham Mass 1880-09-26 child of HOYT Myron of Tauton Mass & BOYD Deborah of Tauton Mass Vol: 8 Page: 041

GREEN Alonzo d Hopkinton 1922-03-17 age 75yrs 3mos b Hopkinton 1846-12-17 child of GREEN Newman of Hopkinton Vol: 8 Page: 042

BACON Leola H d Hopkinton 1922-03-26 age 55yrs 6mos 6dys Hopkinton 1866-09-20 child of ADAMS Joseph of Hopkinton & SARGENT Judith of Sutton Vol: 8 Page: 042

BURNHAM Georgiana d Hopkinton 1922-03-29 age 82yrs 10mos 3dys b Hopkinton Vol: 8 Page: 042

GILMORE Benj d Hopkinton 1922-04-11 age 83yrs 3mos 29dys b Warner 1838-12-12 child of GILMORE John of Warner & PUTNEY Susan of Weare Vol: 8 Page: 043

EMERSON Albert L d Hopkinton 1922-03-21 age 73yrs 10mos 2dys b Hopkinton 1848-05-19 child of EMERSON Isaac of Bow & FARRINGTON Lucretia of Concord Vol: 8 Page: 044

DAVIS Francis Lincoln d Hopkinton 1922-02-18 age 2yrs 6mos 4dys b Taunton Mass 1919-08-13 child of DAVIS Henry R of Warner & LINCOLN Mildred of Taunton Mass Vol: 8 Page: 043

UPTON Sarah C d Hopkinton 1922-02-01 age 70yrs b Hopkinton Vol: 8 Page: 044

DAVIS Chas C d Hopkinton 1922-06-03 age 62yrs 1mos 20dys b Hopkinton 1860-04-13 child of DAVIS Amos of Hopkinton & Cressy of Bradford Vol: 8 Page: 044

MONTGOMERY Susan L d Goffstown 1922-06-15 age 73yrs 4mos 5dys b Brandon Vt 1849-02-20 child of RUSSELL Louis of Springfield Vt & WALKER Louise of Salem Mass Vol: 8 Page: 045

HOLMES Charles d Boscowen 1922-07-01 age 69yrs 11mos 27dys Vol: 8 Page: 045

KEITH Mont H d Hopkinton 1922-07-08 age 37yrs 1mos 14dys b Canterbury 1885-05-24 child of KEITH Milford of Havlock N B & COLPETTS Florence of Elgin N B Vol: 8 Page: 045

DODGE Martha Jane d Concord 1922-07-07 age 86yrs 8mos 24dys b New Hampton 1835-10-12 child of EDGERLY David of New Hampton & SANBORN Sarah of New Hampton Vol: 8 Page: 046

COULTER Gladys d Concord 1892-08-14 age 1yrs 2mos 1dys b Hopkinton Vol: 8 Page: 046

LITTLE Clifton Eugene d Webster 1922-07-13 age 3mos 11dys b Webster Vol: 8 Page: 046

BADGER Frances A d Hopkinton 1922-07-16 age 69yrs 7mos 20dys b Hopkinton 1852-11-25 child of BARBER Robert of Brooklyn & WALSTENHAM Zila Vol: 8 Page: 047

GOVE Winfield Holmes d Hopkinton 1922-08-02 age 23yrs 10mos 18dys b Hillsboro 1898-10-20 child of GOVE George Fred of Deering & HOLMES Minnie V of Antrim Vol: 8 Page: 047

SKILLLEN Laura J d Henniker 1922-08-10 age 75yrs 9mos 29dys b Hopkinton 1846-11-11 child of PALMER William & CHASE Ann Vol: 8 Page: 047

STEVENS Horace F d Hopkinton 1922-09-04 age 88yrs 1mos 15dys b Manchester 1834-07-16 Vol: 8 Page: 048

TILTON George Frank d Concord 1922-09-06 age 70yrs 8mos 11dys b Concord 1851-12-25 child of TILTON Ransom S & SMITH Mary A of Concord Vol: 8 Page: 048

HUSE Irene d Contoocook 1922-10-09 age 75yrs 10mos 8dys b Rockland Mass 1846-12-01 child of POOL Micah & HUNT Sally Vol: 8 Page: 049

COLBY Sarah J d Boscawen 1922-10-06 age 79yrs 6mos 12dys b Hopkinton Vol: 8 Page: 049

DUNBAR Annie S d Concord 1922-10-18 age 28yrs 11mos 14dys b Bay Roberts N F 1893-11-04 child of SPENCER William of Coleys Point N F & ADAMS Fannie of Burguss N F Vol: 8 Page: 049

MORRILL Joseph P d Concord 1922-10-24 age 79yrs 9mos 19dys b Hopkinton 1842-12-05 child of MORRILL Ebenezer of Byfield Mass & SWEATT Phoebe of Webster Vol: 8 Page: 050

HARDY Woodbury d Hopkinton 1922-11-11 age 89yrs 7mos 17dys b Warner 1833-03-25 child of HARDY Ozias of Hopkinton & BARDEN Lavina?? of Hopkinton Vol: 8 Page: 050

FRENCH Albert d Manchester 1922-11-23 age 6yrs 10mos 21dys b Warner 1916-10-02 child of FRENCH Albert of Hopkinton & BOUTWELL Helen of Hopkinton Vol: 8 Page: 050

WHITE Frank E d Hopkinton 1922-11-27 age 73yrs 9dys b Hopkinton 1849-11-18 child of WHITE Thomas E of Hopkinton & ROGERS Lois of Henniker Vol: 8 Page: 051

MONTGOMERY Albert d Manchester 1922-12-15 age 71yrs 4mos 4dys b Warner 1851-08-11 child of MONTGOMERY William of Salem NY & SOVONY Lucy N of Warner Vol: 8 Page: 051

DAVIS Emma C d Hopkinton 1922-12-20 age 71yrs 2mos 8dys b Cincinnati Ohio 1851-10-15 child of DAVIS Wm Munroe of Frederick MD & MURPHY Parthina of Cleveland Ohio Vol: 8 Page: 051

CLINE Sarah C d Hopkinton 1922-12-27 age 68yrs 9mos 15dys b Nova Scotia 1854-03-12 child of LONG Step Chas Vol: 8 Page: 052

CAMPBELL Francis J d Hopkinton 1922-12-30 age 85yrs 10mos 7dys b New London 1857-02-23 child of CAMPBELL Jonah & JONES E T Vol: 8 Page: 052

MATOTT Louis L d Hopkinton 1923-01-19 age 78yrs 4mos 7dys b Champlain NY 1844-09-14 child of MATOTT Andrew of Canada & ASHLINER ?? Dora Vol: 8 Page: 052

HUBBARD Caroline S d Concod 1923-01-18 age 76yrs 3mos 20dys b Hopkinton Vol: 8 Page: 053

FISHER Samuel d Hopkinton 1923-06-20 age 70yrs 5mos 16dys b West Fairlee Vt 1853-01-04 child of FISHER Gilbert of West Fairlee Vt & Lucinda of Orange Vt Vol: 8 Page: 053

BARNARD ---- d Hopkinton 1921-03-08 age 18dys b Hopkinton 1921-03-08 child of BARNARD Raymond J of Hopkinton & FARNHAM Ruth of Lancaster Vol: 8 Page: 026

FLANDERS Marietta E M d Hopkinton 1922-04-30 age 64yrs 10mos b Boston Mass 1858-06-30 Vol: 8 Page: 043

DYER William d Boston Mass 1922-10-19 age 74yrs 8mos 27dys Vol: 8 Page: 049

Hopkinton, NH Deaths 1914

TANDY Edith M d Hopkinton 1923-02-03 age 2yrs 8dys b Henniker 1920-06-03 child of TANDY Everett J of West Hopkinton & BAILEY Rose J of Bradford Vol: 8 Page: 054

EASTMAN Christina S d Hopkinton 1923-02-15 age 85yrs 4mos 2dys b New London 1837-10-13 child of MORRILL Isaac of Warner & BEAN Achsah of Warner Vol: 8 Page: 054

DENSMORE Sadie D d Hopkinton 1823-02-16 age 1mos 25dys b Hopkinton 1823-12-22 child of DENSMORE Edward of Hopkinton & LIBBY Caiptola of Hopkinton Vol: 8 Page: 055

DUSTIN Eben F d Hopkinton 1923-02-22 age 79yrs 2mos 25dys b Hopkinton 1842-11-26 child of DUSTIN Cyrus D of Hopkinton & FISK Edna P of Salisbury Vol: 8 Page: 055

STANTON Chas d Hopkinton 1923-02-23 age 72yrs 1mos 23dys b Stewartstown 1850-12-30 Vol: 8 Page: 055

HOYT Effie E d Hopkinton 1923-02-28 age 28yrs 22dys b Washington 1895-02-06 child of SEVERANCE Will J of Washinton & FOWLER Florence E of Washinton Vol: 8 Page: 056

SEVERANCE Howard C d Hopkinton 1923-03-06 age 27yrs 3mos 29dys b Washington 1896-11-07 child of SEVERANCE W J of Washington & FOWLER Florence of Washington Vol: 8 Page: 056

FLANDERS Hazel A d Hopkinton 1923-03-17 age 1yrs 2mos 17dys b Hopkinton 1921-12-30 child of FLANDERS Fred of Goshen & BURBANK Helen of Hopkinton Vol: 8 Page: 056

DAVIS Henry B d Hopkinton 1923-04-04 age 63yrs 7mos 22dys b Hopkinton 1859-09-12 child of DAVIS Amos of Hopkinton & Cressey of Bradford Vol: 8 Page: 057

GOVE Newton d Hopkinton 1923-04-15 age 87yrs 11mos b Hopkinton 1835-05-23 child of GOVE Jerry of Deering & SHEPPARD Clarissa of Boscawen Vol: 8 Page: 057

KIMBALL Kate Pearl d Concord 1923-02-16 age 67yrs 1mos 13dys b Hopkinton Vol: 8 Page: 057

TILTON John A d Haverhill Mass 1923-06-05 age 64yrs 0mos 11dys Vol: 8 Page: 058

HARTHORNE Arthur d Contoocook 1923-06-13 age 76yrs 7mos 29dys b Palermo Me 1846-10-14 child of HARTHORN John of Liberty Me & MURTAS Margarete of Liberty Me Vol: 8 Page: 058

DOCKHAM Vera Bletcher d Hopkinton 1923-07-07 age 23yrs b Dover 1899-07-13 child of BLETCHER George of Lancaster Eng & HANSON Harriett of Yorkshire Eng Vol: 8 Page: 058

BROWN Charles d Manchester 1923-06-29 age 68yrs 5mos 12dys b Hopkinton 1855-01-12 child of BROWN Jonathan & DUNBAR Mary of Grantham Vol: 8 Page: 059

KNOWLTON Geo H d Hopkinton 1923-08-28 age 69yrs 11mos 28dys b Nashua 1853-09-30 child of KNOWLTON Asa D of Holderness & STRAW Lydia P Vol: 8 Page: 059

Hopkinton, NH Deaths 1914

STEVENS Caroline C d Hopkinton 1923-09-12 age 71yrs 1mos 4dys b Canada 1852-08-08 child of ROGERS Juslin of Canada & ---- ---- of Canada Vol: 8 Page: 059

BAILEY Everett C d Hopkinton 1923-10-02 age 3mos 8dys b Hopkinton 1923-06-24 child of BAILEY George W of Warner & CHASE Gertrude of Hopkinton Vol: 8 Page: 060

SMART Leslie d Manchester 1923-10-13 age 3mos 21dys b Nashua 1923-06-23 child of SMART Harold of Warner & HOOD Ruth of Hopkinton Vol: 8 Page: 060

MARSH Etta P d Concord 1923-10-14 age 70yrs 2mos 10dys b Concord 1853-08-14 child of BUSWELL Samuel S of Concord & ELDER Mary of Machias Me Vol: 8 Page: 060

VADNEY Ellen O d Charlestown 1923-10-03 age 60yrs 7mos 10dys Vol: 8 Page: 061

EMERSON William C d Hopkinton 1923-10-18 age 62yrs 4mos 3dys b Hopkinton 1861-06-15 child of EMERSON James of Hopkinton & DIAMOND Julia of Hopkinton Vol: 8 Page: 061

DENY Jos d Hopkinton 1923-10-04 age 93yrs 1mos 5dys b Canada 1830-08-28 child of DENY Louis of Canada Vol: 8 Page: 061

CHANDLER Mary A d Hopkinton 1923-10-19 age 92yrs 5mos 19dys b Canada 1831-05-06 child of Costello Vol: 8 Page: 062

PUTNAM Joseph E d Hopkinton 1923-12-06 age 80yrs 2mos 4dys b Hopkinton 1843-10-02 child of PUTNAM R of Hopkinton & Bailey of Warner Vol: 8 Page: 062

TUTTLE J S d Hopkinton 1923-11-12 age 87yrs 10mos 9dys b Hopkinton 1836-01-03 child of TUTTLE Chas. of Hopkinton & Ripley Vol: 8 Page: 062

FULLER Phoebe d Concord 1923-12-15 age 71yrs 8mos 14dys b Wilmont 1852-04-01 child of ROWE Oliver of Wilmont & WALKER Ann of Andover Vol: 8 Page: 063

STORY Katherin D d Hopkinton 1923-12-30 age 90yrs 7mos 22dys b Hopkinton 1833-05-08 child of STORY Moses of Hopkinton & NORTON Mary of Nova Scotia Vol: 8 Page: 063

BLANCHARD Harry E d Hopkinton 1924-01-07 age 46yrs 3mos 22dys b Washington 1878-09-14 child of BLANCHARD Galen E & ROACH Nellie Vol: 8 Page: 064

PUTNAM Isabel d Hopkinton 1924-02-11 age 82yrs 6mos 7dys b Maine 1841-08-04 Vol: 8 Page: 064

DOW George d Hopkinton 1924-03-28 age 73yrs 9mos 28dys b Henniker 30 May 1850 child of DOW Perley of Concord & SWEAT Abbie of Andover Vol: 8 Page: 064

CLINTON Cora May d Laconia 1924-03-27 age 42yrs 6mos b Warner 1881-09-27 child of BARTLETT Joseph of Hopkinton & BAILEY Eva E of Hopkinton Vol: 8 Page: 065

STRAW Alice B d Hopkinton 1924-04-24 age 49yrs 1mos 26dys b Lynn Mass 1875-02-28 child of WILLIAMS Chas W of Lynn Mass & BEAN Nellie H of Andover Mass Vol: 8 Page: 065

CORLISS Charles d Webster 1924-05-08 Vol: 8 Page: 065

325

Hopkinton, NH Deaths 1914

MOORE Eliza B d Hopkinton 1924-05-24 age 86yrs 9mos 20dys b Mercer Me 1857-09-04 child of BLONDIN Wm & WORKS Olive Vol: 8 Page: 066

BOOTH Daniel B d Hopkinton 1924-05-29 age 79yrs 5mos 18dys b Peterboro 1844-12-10 child of BOOTH Amos Vol: 8 Page: 066

ROBIE Charles E d Concord 1924-06-02 age 65yrs 1mos 1dys b Colebrook 1858-04-26 child of ROBIE John Vol: 8 Page: 067

DUNBAR Ann S d Hopkinton 1924-06-01 age 66yrs 7mos 19dys b Contoocook 1857-10-12 child of DUNBAR Justin of Contoocook & MORRILL Mary of Concord Vol: 8 Page: 066

NICHOLS Sarah C d Hopkinton 1924-05-29 age 91yrs 0mos 21dys b Hopkinton 1833-05-08 child of PALMER William of Haverhill & Anne E of Methuen Mass Vol: 8 Page: 067

ADAMS Charles E d Hopkinton 1924-06-08 age 62yrs 9mos 15dys b Derry 1861-06-23 child of ADAMS George F of Derry & WHITING Elizabeth of Nashua Vol: 8 Page: 067

UPTON Barlow d Worcestr Mass 1924-06-11 age 77yrs 5mos 8dys Vol: 8 Page: 068

ANNIS Charles d Warner 1924-06-14 age 70yrs 2mos 11dys b 1854-04-03 child of ANNIS Herrick C of Hopkinton & HARDY Cynthia of Hopkinton Vol: 8 Page: 068

SAWYER Nellis M d Weare 1924-07-07 age 72yrs 1mos 19dys Vol: 8 Page: 068

EMERSON Fred H d Hopkinton 1924-07-15 age 66yrs 10mos 18dys b Hopkinton 1857-08-26 child of EMERSON James H of Hopkinton & DIAMOND Julia A Vol: 8 Page: 069

DWINNELLS Susan M d Hopkinton 1924-08-04 age 77yrs 5mos 8dys b Penacook 1847-02-26 child of HEATH Alfred & Mary B of Vol: 8 Page: 069

HALL Frederick A d Hopkinton 1924-08-12 age 59yrs 3mos 3dys b Norway 1865-05-08 child of HALL Andrew of Norway & Alolested of Norway Vol: 8 Page: 069

WITHAM Betsy J d Hopkinton 1924-08-28 age 84yrs 6mos 22dys b Middleton 1840-02-06 child of Burden of So Berwich Me & BIDALL Lois Vol: 8 Page: 070

COOPER Joseph A d Boscawen 1924-09-21 age 68yrs child of ---- ---- West Deerfield Vol: 8 Page: 070

HALL Carrie F d Concord 1924-09-24 age 26yrs 1dys b Hopkinton 1898-09-23 child of ELLIOT Edson E of Warner & COLBY Nettie of West Derrfield Vol: 8 Page: 070

PATTERSON Annette N d Arlington Mass 1924-10-03 age 84yrs 10mos 4dys b Hopkinton Vol: 8 Page: 071

TILTON Elizabeth Baker d Concord 1924-10-04 age 73yrs 11mos 19dys b Willlinton Eng 1850-10-15 child of FORD James W of England & BAKER Elizabeth of England Vol: 8 Page: 071

BOHONAN Delia d Hopkinton 1924-08-15 age 69yrs 6mos 14dys b Weare 1855-02-01 child of JEWELL Otis F & SARGENT Mary Vol: 8 Page: 071

REED Helen G d Hopkinton 1924-10-20 age 50yrs 4mos 7dys b Barnstead 1874-05-13 child of GEORGE Henry W of Barnstead & THOMPSON Elizabeth of Gilmanton Vol: 8 Page: 072

PUTNAM Almira d Hopkinton 1924-10-27 age 85yrs 3mos 11dys b Hopkinton 1839-07-08 child of EASTMANA John G of Hopkinton & KIMBALL Charolotte of Hopkinton Vol: 8 Page: 072

BARON Maria d Concord 1924-10-27 age 78yrs 6mos 3dys b Fisherville 1846-04-24 child of SANBORN George Frank & FOWLER Martha Vol: 8 Page: 072

COLBY Forest d Hopkinton 1924-10-29 age 74yrs 10mos 24dys b Litchfield 1849-12-05 child of COLBY Abram of Londonderry & KIMBALL Adaline Vol: 8 Page: 073

HOYT Etta N d Hopkinton 1924-11-11 age 23yrs 2mos 27dys b Bradford 1901-08-14 child of GOVE George & FOWLER Addie of Washington Vol: 8 Page: 073

CHASE Oscar M d Hopkinton 1924-12-09 age 68yrs 9mos 21dys b Hopkinton 1856-02-17 child of CHASE Crosby N of Hopkinton & CURRIER Nancy of Hopkinton Vol: 8 Page: 073

HILAND John M d Hopkinton 1924-12-18 age 50yrs 1mos 7dys b Hopkinton 1874-11-11 child of HILAND George B of Hopkinton & KIMBALL Priscilla of Hopkinton Vol: 8 Page: 074

HOOD Wallace R d Hopkinton 1924-12-21 age 17yrs 10mos 6dys b Hopkinton 1907-02-15 child of HOOD George G of Peterboro & FRONIE E of Goffstown Vol: 8 Page: 074

BERRY Edgar F d Hopkinton 1925-01-04 age 71yrs 11mos 15dys b Wales 1853-02-16 child of BERRY J F of Wales & WILLIAMS Elsie of Wales Vol: 8 Page: 075

KEMPTON Willard H d Reading Mass 1925-01-06 age 82yrs 11mos 1dys Vol: 8 Page: 075

ADAMS Eda Mary d Hopkinton 1925-01-12 age 40yrs 1mos 11dys b Lawrence Mass 1883-11-20 child of FLATHERS Sam K of Fall River Mass & ARNOLD Ann of Schnectaly NY Vol: 8 Page: 075

ROGERS Clara C d Hopkinton 1925-03-04 age 82yrs 2mos 11dys b Hopkinton 1842-12-27 child of STORY Moses of Hopkinton & CURRIER Mehitable of Warner Vol: 8 Page: 076

CLARK Ellihu d Hopkinton 1925-03-23 age 63yrs 10mos 10dys b England 1861-05-13 child of CLARK John of England & JENNINGS Elizebith of England Vol: 8 Page: 076

COLBY Annie J d Concord 1925-03-25 age 75yrs 11mos 6dys b Hopkinton 1849-04-19 child of WEBBER Isiah J & ALLY Sally A Vol: 8 Page: 076

WEEKS Lavenia P d Raymond 1925-03-25 age 88yrs 2mos 22dys b Vol: 8 Page: 077

ROLLINS John d Londonderry 1925-04-01 age 75yrs Vol: 8 Page: 077

HICKS Anna M d Hopkinton 1925-04-17 age 75yrs 3mos 16dys b Leeds P Q Canada 1850-01-01 child of MANN J of Canada Vol: 8 Page: 077

PRINCE Roscoe P d Hopkinton 1925-04-23 age 58yrs 2mos 19dys b Orange 1867-02-04 child of PRINCE David of Amherst & PEARSON Caroline of Tewksbury Mass Vol: 8 Page: 078

DURELL James M d Hopkinton 1925-04-22 age 68yrs 2mos b Chester Ny 1857-02-27 child of DURELL Myron of Chester Ny & COLLINS Elizabeth of Sunapee Vol: 8 Page: 078

Hopkinton, NH Deaths 1914

MORGAN William J d Concord 1925-04-23 age 55yrs 1mos 9dys b Scranton Pa 1870-03-13 child of Morgan & Ann Vol: 8 Page: 078

FROST Humphrey L d Weare 1925-05-10 age 77yrs 11mos 28dys Vol: 8 Page: 079

COLBY Richard d Boscawen 1925-05-14 age 66yrs b Hopkinton Vol: 8 Page: 079

DIXON Edward H d Argyle Ny 1925-05-18 age 77yrs Vol: 8 Page: 079

NORTHRUP Sarah G d Hopkinton 1925-05-26 age 83yrs 5mos 6dys b Lisbon Ny 1842-12-20 child of Williamson of Canton Ny & McCUEN E of Canton Ny Vol: 8 Page: 080

SWEATT Nettie F d Hopkinton 1925-05-27 age 72yrs 3mos 15dys b Hopkinton 1853-02-12 child of DOWNING Dan Vol: 8 Page: 080

WOOD Ziba S d Hopkinton 1925-06-03 age 80yrs 7mos 4dys b Deering 1844-10-27 child of WOODS Emerson & Richardson Vol: 8 Page: 081

AYER Maria C d Hopkinton 1925-06-18 age 83yrs 4mos 2dys b Hopkinton 1842-02-16 child of CLOUGH Willard of Hopkinton & DUSTIN Charlote of Hopkinton Vol: 8 Page: 081

BEAN Frank T d Hopkinton 1925-06-28 age 76yrs b Sutton 1849-06-27 child of Bean of Sutton & Fitch of Sutton Vol: 8 Page: 081

SHURTLIFF John J d Warner 1925-07-06 age 56yrs 2mos 18dys Vol: 8 Page: 082

WILDER Julia E K d Hopkinton 1925-08-18 age 84yrs 8mos 5dys b E Wallingford Vt 1901-04-14 child of KEEN Austin of Wallingford Vt & COOK Julia E of Mt Holly Vt Vol: 8 Page: 082

LORD Harold B d Hopkinton 1925-08-22 age 40yrs 2mos 5dys b Lynn Mass 1885-06-17 child of LORD Charles of Lynn Mass Vol: 8 Page: 083

RUNNELLS Edward G d Hopkinton 1925-09-29 age 81yrs 8mos 29dys b Webster 1843-12-06 child of RUNNELLS Farnum of Concord & WEBBER Jerusha of Boscawen Vol: 8 Page: 083

DOW Harry M d Concord 1925-10-03 age 71yrs 7mos 27dys b Hopkinton 1854-02-06 child of DOW Samuel of Concord & HOYT Sarah of Hopkinton Vol: 8 Page: 083

RION Dennis d Warner 1925-10-11 age 72yrs 8mos 14dys Vol: 8 Page: 084

SANBORN Charles F d Hopkinton 1925-10-10 age 85yrs 10mos 17dys b Webster 1839-11-10 child of SANBORN John of Webster & COFFIN Rebekah of Webster Vol: 8 Page: 084

JAMESON Daniel D d Lowell Mass 1925-12-17 age 72yrs 3mos 28dys Vol: 8 Page: 084

CONNELLY Olja d Hopkinton 1926-02-28 age 16yrs 11mos 18dys b Halifax N S 1909-03-10 child of CONNELLY Rufus of Halifax Ns & SMITH Susan of Halifax Ns Vol: 8 Page: 086

ELLIOTT Nettie L d Vermont 1926-03-11 age 64yrs 4mos 15dys Vol: 8 Page: 086

GREEN Kate E d Hopkinton 1926-03-23 age 65yrs 11mos 16dys b Landaff 1860-04-07 child of HUNT Wm L of Bath & BOWLES Elizabeth of Ladaff Vol: 8 Page: 086

DEARBORN Lewis H d Hopkinton 1926-01-22 age 83yrs 11mos 5dys b Epsom 1842-02-17 child of DEARBORN Edwin of Hampton & STANYON Letice C of Penacook Vol: 8 Page: 085

Hopkinton, NH Deaths 1914

TUTTLE Katie Maria C d Newbury Vt 1926-02-13 age 70yrs 3mos 9dys b Hopkinton 1855-11-04 child of CARPENTER Guy of Derby Vt & KIMBALL Mary of Hopkinton Vol: 8 Page: 085

POTTS James d Hopkinton 1926-02-19 age 76yrs 6mos 27dys b Fall River Mass 1849-07-22 child of POTTS Edward of Storkport Eng & RAYNOR Elen of Storkport Eng Vol: 8 Page: 085

STACY Arlene E d Webster 1926-03-24 age 1yrs 4mos 20dys Vol: 8 Page: 087

CURRIER Ernest C d Hopkinton 1926-03-16 age 70yrs 10mos 24dys b Warner 1855-04-19 child of CURRIER Jesse D of Salisbury & WATSON Emma of Salisbury Vol: 8 Page: 087

LOVE Mary Ellen d Hopkinton 1926-04-08 age 80yrs 23dys b Smithfield RI 1846-03-15 child of COBURN Ira & BUCKLIN Martha Vol: 8 Page: 087

SPOFFORD Arthur d West Concord 1926-04-21 age 55yrs 3mos 23dys b Hopkinton 1870-12-29 child of SPOFFORD Alfred of Hopkinton & PAIGE Abbie of Hopkinton Vol: 8 Page: 088

CHANDLER Margery S d Concord 1926-03-31 age 63yrs 9mos Vol: 8 Page: 088

NEWMAN Ellen A d Hopkinton 1926-05-16 age 81yrs 12dys b Henniker 1845-05-04 child of BALL Hiram of Antrim & FRENCH Mary of Hancock Vol: 8 Page: 088

PRINCE George d Concord 1926-01-22 age 18yrs 3mos 2dys b NH 1907-03-02 child of PRINCE Roscoe of N H & PEARSON Carrie of N H Vol: 8 Page: 089

MILLS Emma d Hopkinton 1926-06-07 age 73yrs 5mos 17dys b Concord 1852-12-21 child of BROWN Walter Vol: 8 Page: 089

CHASE Edward E d Hopkinton 1926-06-25 age 70yrs 7mos 19dys b Hopkinton 1855-12-06 child of CHASE Horace & DODGE Mary Ann Vol: 8 Page: 089

KRAPHOL William d Hopkinton 1926-07-03 age 65yrs b Germany Vol: 8 Page: 090

FLANDERS Lorenzo d Hopkinton 1926-07-05 age 76yrs 9mos 22dys b West Stewartstown 1849-09-13 child of FLANDERS Nehemiah of Warner & COLBY Sarah of Warner Vol: 8 Page: 090

EMERSON Ella Josephine d Providence RI 1926-06-06 age 71yrs 1mos 12dys b Providence RI 1855-04-25 child of STONE William of Providence RI & DARLING Anna of Providence RI Vol: 8 Page: 090

GOODRICH Charles S d Concord 1926-07-25 age 53yrs 10mos 16dys b Hopkinton 1872-09-09 child of GOODRICH George K of Springfield Vt & LORD Lydia of Newmarket Vol: 8 Page: 091

COLBY Frank H d Hopkinton 1926-08-22 age 68yrs 8mos 5dys b Bow 1857-12-17 child of COLBY Francis of Bow & WHEELER Pauline of Dunbarton Vol: 8 Page: 091

JONES Emma C B d Hopkinton 1926-09-08 age 57yrs 21dys b Canaan 1869-08-17 child of BUCKLIN Alonzo of Grafton & GOSS Caln'ta of Canaan Vol: 8 Page: 091

POWERS Hester E d Concord 1926-09-17 age 67yrs b Hopkinton 1857-09-17 child of CURRIER George N of Hopkinton & FLANDERS Hannah of Hopkinton Vol: 8 Page: 092

Hopkinton, NH Deaths 1914

EASTMAN Sydney d Concord 1926-09-19 age 72yrs 2mos 29dys b Hopkinton 1847-06-20 child of EASTMAN Jonathan of Henniker & ROWELL Elizabeth of Hopkinton Vol: 8 Page: 092

PUTNEY True B d Laconia 1926-09-25 age 13yrs 8mos 17dys b Keene 1913-01-08 child of PUTNEY Ira A of Hopkinton & BAKER Bessie of Dublin Vol: 8 Page: 092

DUSTIN Henry D d Hopkinton 1926-10-14 age 77yrs 7mos 18dys b Hopkinton 1849-02-25 child of DUSTIN Daniel P of Hopkinton & BARNARD Sarah of Hopkinton Vol: 8 Page: 093

DORRY Avis E d Hopkinton 1926-10-21 age 1mos 16dys b Hopkinton 1926-09-05 child of DORRY Howard of Nova Scotia & DEMETT Lala of Nottingham Vol: 8 Page: 093

CHANDLER Frank W d Concord 1926-11-05 age 70yrs 7mos 10dys b Hopkinton 1856-03-22 child of CHANDLER Isaac of Hopkinton & SHAW Caroline E of Hopkinton Vol: 8 Page: 093

TOWNES Lewis E d Hopkinton 1926-11-11 age 63yrs 5mos 8dys b New Boston 1843-06-03 child of TOWNES Jacob of & THOMPSON Elewina ? of Vol: 8 Page: 094

DAVIS Frank R d Hopkinton 1926-11-10 age 75yrs b Hopkinton 1851 Oct child of DAVIS Amos H & Cressey Vol: 8 Page: 094

STORY Raymond W d Webster 1926-11-17 age 2mos 3dys Vol: 8 Page: 094

EDMUNDS Horace d Hopkinton 1926-11-28 age 91yrs 9mos 1dys b Hopkinton 1835-02-27 child of EDMUNDS Horace of Weare & CILLEY Bridget of Weare Vol: 8 Page: 095

CORSER Mary Isabel d Manchester 1925-05-25 age 70yrs 1mos 5dys b Webster 1855-04-20 child of HOLMES Ezra & COLBY Mahala Vol: 9 Page:

BROWN Emily A d Hopkinton 1925-08-22 age 24yrs 4mos 8dys b Hopkinton 1901-04-14 child of CHASE Fred of Hopkinton & HARDY Emma A of Warner Vol: 8 Page: 082

DODGE Henry d Concord 1927-01-14 age 64yrs 12dys b Hopkinton 1863-01-02 child of DODGE Moses E of NH & WEEKS Abbie of NH Vol: 9 Page: 001

HOWE?? Hannah Jane d Bristol Conn 1927-02-03 age 75yrs 1mos 14dys b 1997-02-03 Vol: 9 Page: 001

FLANDERS Frank L d Hopkinton 1927-02-04 age 73yrs 1mos 28dys b Hopkinton 1853-12-06 child of FLANDERS Daniel of Hopkinton & LEMARD Mary of Hopkinton Vol: 9 Page: 001

ROBERTSON June C d Hopkinton 1927-02-15 age 1mos 10dys b Hopkinton 1927-01-10 child of ROBERTSON Moses P of Henniker & BRIEE Muriel Vol: 9 Page: 002

SWEATT George W d Hopkinton 1927-02-18 age 76yrs 10mos 16dys b Hopkinton 1850-04-02 child of SWEATT Moses & MITCHELL Mary Vol: 9 Page: 002

LIBBY Estella A d Hopkinton 1927-02-23 age 73yrs 5mos 22dys b 1853-08-31 child of KENESITON George of England & ATWOOD Anna Vol: 9 Page: 002

CONANT Lena S d Hopkinton 1927-02-27 age 83yrs 10mos 21dys b Germany child of SHATTLE Jasper of Germany & Madlin of Germany Vol: 9 Page: 003

STRAW Wealthy d Webster 1927-03-22 age 85yrs 5mos 20dys Vol: 9 Page: 003

GRIFFIN Helen J d Hopkinton 1927-04-14 age 74yrs b Lowell Mass 1853-01-25 child of MORRILL Ezra of Hopkinton & AMES Ruth of Hopkinton Mass Vol: 9 Page: 004

TANDY Ellen J d Concord 1927-04-15 age 82yrs b Andover 1844 child of CILLEY Philip & Sally Vol: 9 Page: 004

BUSWEL Mabel R d Boston Mass 1927-01-04 age 53yrs b Concord 1874-04-17 child of BUSWELL S S of Concord & ELDER Doborah D of Machais Me Vol: 9 Page: 004

HEATH Charles J d Newport 1927-04-04 age 66yrs 5mos 28dys b Bradford 1860-10-07 child of HEATH Charles of Grafton & AUSTIN Melissa of Hill Vol: 9 Page: 005

JEWELL Lucy d Contoocook 1927-05-26 age 70yrs 4mos 9dys b Weare 1857-01-17 child of JEWELL Otis F of Sandwich & SARGENT Mary Vol: 9 Page: 005

BARTLETT Effie V d Lawrence Mass 1927-05-24 age 42yrs b Warner child of BARTLETT Woodbury of Warner & DAVIS Clara B of Brattleboro Vt Vol: 9 Page: 005

CHASE Ella F d Hopkinton 1927-06-23 age 72yrs 2mos 22dys b Warner 1855-04-01 child of BARTLETT Jasper H of Warner & CLARK Lucinda of Warner Vol: 9 Page: 006

SAINT W H d Hopkinton 1927-07-01 age 15yrs 17dys b Cambridge Mass child of SAINT Alexander & PUDDESTER Bertha Vol: 9 Page: 006

COLBY Frances E d Allston Mass 1927-06-28 age 44yrs b Derry 1883-05-04 child of COLBY George O of Hopkinton & CHANDLER Delia of Hopkinton Vol: 9 Page: 006

KIMBALL Lucy Challen d Hopkinton 1927-07-02 age 81yrs 10mos 21dys b Richland Ill 1845-08-20 child of CHALLEN John (dr) of New York City & KAVANAUGH Mary of Lexington Ky Vol: 9 Page: 007

CONNOR Carrie J d Rockport Mass 1927-07-10 age 61yrs 3mos 25dys Vol: 9 Page: 007

LUSCOMB Laura E d Henniker 1927-07-02 age 73yrs 3mos b Hope Maine 1854-04-02 child of ARTHEM J of Maine Vol: 9 Page: 007

SYMONDS Lucy A d Hopkinton 1927-07-30 age 79yrs b Vernon Conn 1848-01-23 child of WEBSTER Jame & CHAPIN Camelia Vol: 9 Page: 008

MILTON Carrie?? d Hopkinton 1927-07-01 age 65yrs 7mos 6dys b Otis Me 1861-12-25 child of THOMPSON Geo of Nashua & BLANDING Eliza of Maine Vol: 9 Page: 008 Note: ck town report

MYERS Ora L d Hopkinton 1927-08-18 age 63yrs 7mos 29dys b Pelham 1863-12-19 child of MYERS Thomas of New York & TITCOMB Mary of Pelham Vol: 9 Page: 008

SMITH Sarah G d Contoocook 1927-08-26 age 70yrs 10mos 4dys b No Hampton 1856-10-22 child of TAYLOR Richard of No Hampton & LAND Sarah of No Hampton Vol: 9 Page: 009

BROWN Lean L d Hopkinton 1927-08-28 age 39yrs 6mos 11dys b Concord 1888-02-17 child of BROWN Lester of Stockbridge Vt & WATTS Stella E of Alstead Vol: 9 Page: 009

EMERY William Stanley d Hopkinton 1927-08-29 age 69yrs 3mos 23dys b Portsmouth RI 1858-05-06 child of EMERY Chase of Springfield Mass & HILTON Susan of Northwood Vol: 9 Page: 009

MORGAN Gilman C d Norristown Pa 1927-08-28 age 96yrs Vol: 9 Page: 010

CURRIER Myrtle d Sunapee 1927-09-29 age 51yrs 1mos 3dys b Dunbarton 1876-08-26 child of FELCH Ira of Weare & CURRIER Addie A of Hookset Vol: 9 Page: 010

KEITH Edward Richard d Hopkinton 1927-10-06 age 12yrs 8mos 6dys b Canterbury child of KEITH Mout L of Canterbury & RICHARDS Isabel of Newark N J Vol: 9 Page: 010

BARTLETT Irving ??? d Newport 1892-11-04 age 3mos 29dys Vol: 9 Page: 011

PAGE Minnie B d Hopkinton 1927-10-12 age 61yrs 5mos 22dys b Hopkinton 1866-04-19 child of STRAW Gilman of Hopkinton & HOYT Wealtha of Hopkinton Vol: 9 Page: 011

MONTGOMERY Jean d Dunbarton 1927-10-23 age 4mos 12dys b Dunbarton 1927-06-11 child of MONTGOMERY Henry B of Manchester & DUNCAN Florence of Boston Mass Vol: 9 Page: 011

FRAZIER William C d Hopkinton 1927-10-27 age 65yrs 6mos 2dys b Sutton 1862-04-24 child of FRAZER Caleb of Sutton & COLBURN Sarah of Sutton Vol: 9 Page: 012

THOMPSON Josephine E d Hopkinton 1927-11-04 age 62yrs 3mos 5dys b Webster 1865-07-26 child of ELLIOTT Thomas of Webster & DUSTIN Sarah of Hopkinton Vol: 9 Page: 012

HASE Freeman V d Hopkinton 1927-11-23 age 64yrs 4mos 8dys b Farnham Canada 1863-07-15 child of HASE John of Canada & SCOTT Fannie Vol: 9 Page: 012

PUTNAM Grace d Contoocook 1927-10-27 age 59yrs 18dys b Hopkinton 1868-10-13 child of PUTNAM Charles of Hopkinton & Almyra of Hopkinton Vol: 9 Page: 013

GOODWIN William E d Hopkinton 1927-12-06 age 65yrs 10mos 4dys b Manchester 1862-02-02 child of GOODWIN Joseph of Manchester & DOTY Isabel of Maine Vol: 9 Page: 013

GOODWIN Hattie J d Medford Mass 1927-12-24 age 61yrs 14dys Vol: 9 Page: 013

BOYNTON ---- d Concord 1928-01-03 age 6dys b Concord 1927-12-29 child of BOYNTON Gordon of Hopkinton & PEASLEE Grace of Hopkinton Vol: 9 Page: 014

BRADBURY Charles H d Concord 1928-01-16 age 80yrs 5mos 28dys b Hopkinton 1847-07-18 child of BRADBURY Samuel of Concord & MELAND Martha of Wolfeboro Vol: 9 Page: 014

ELA William E d 1928-02-05 age 69yrs 8mos 2dys Vol: 9 Page: 014

BLAKE William E d Hopkinton 1928-02-04 age 72yrs 8mos 3dys b Thornton 1855-01-01 child of BLAKE Homer of Thornton & BLAISDELL Mary Vol: 9 Page: 015

ADAMS Ralph E d Hopkinton 1928-02-09 age 34yrs 2mos 2dys b Franklin 1893-12-08 child of ADAMS Eugene Vol: 9 Page: 015

PARTRIDGE Mary C d Hopkinton 1928-05-06 age 93yrs 5mos 12dys b Warner 1835-11-23 child of HARDY Joseph of Warner & CHASE Eliza of Warner Vol: 9 Page: 015

Hopkinton, NH Deaths 1914

BAILEY Frank W d Hopkinton 1928-03-06 age 69yrs 8mos 17dys b Henniker 1858-06-17 child of BAILEY Chester of Milwaukee Wis & CHASE Ellen C of Vermont Vol: 9 Page: 016

TUCKER Eva C d Hillsboro 1928-04-16 age 77yrs 7mos 1dys b Hopkinton 1850-09-15 child of PERRY William of Hopkinton & MORGAN Elizabeth of Hopkinton Vol: 9 Page: 016

STEPHEN Alpheus J d Amherst 1928-05-15 age 78yrs 5dys Vol: 9 Page: 016

OYSTON Arhtur Ford d Concord 1928-03-18 age 51yrs 5mos 24dys Vol: 9 Page: 017

RAHM Martin d Concord 1928-06-06 age 63yrs 2mos 7dys b Sweden Vol: 9 Page: 017

ROWELL Charles d Boscawen 1928-04-04 age 74yrs b Concord Vol: 9 Page: 017

MERRILL Stephen Atlin d Saugus Mass 1928-06-14 age 82yrs 5mos 4dys Vol: 9 Page: 018

BARRY Annie M d Hudson Ny 1928-07-07 age 70yrs 1mos 17dys Vol: 9 Page: 018

GOODSPEED Frederick d Tennessee 1928-07-29 age 28yrs b Phil Pa 1899-12-14 child of GOODSPEED Arthur W of Hopkinton & BAILEY Annie H of Frederickton N B Vol: 9 Page: 018

BARTLETT Nellie A d Contoocook 1928-08-05 age 58yrs 4mos 20dys b Newbury 1870-03-15 child of EMORY Samuel A of Suncook & FELLOWS Minerva of Newbury Vol: 9 Page: 019

FENIO ?? David F d Hopkinton 1928-09-10 age 82yrs 5dys b New York 1846-09-04 child of FENIO James?? of NY & WRIGHT Mary of NY Vol: 9 Page: 019

BLAISDELL Lenora A d Hopkinton 1928-10-12 age 84yrs 6mos 12dys b Lempster 1844-03-31 child of CURTICE Samuel & SWEATT Lenora Vol: 9 Page: 019

BROWN Lester d Hopkinton 1928-10-27 age 80yrs 1mos 21dys b Gayville Vt 1848-09-06 child of BROWN Isaac of Vermont & BLISS Sarah of Vermont Vol: 9 Page: 020

MORTON Mary A d 1927-08-19 age 75yrs 7mos 27dys b Hopkinton Vol: 9 Page: 020

MORRILL Harriott F d Hopkinton 1928-10-29 age 78yrs 10mos 19dys b Piermont 1849-12-05 child of STEVENS Grove A of Haverhill & WILSON Lydia J of Franklin Vol: 9 Page: 020

SANBORN Clara d Salisbury 1928-12-01 age 84yrs Vol: 9 Page: 021

CHANDLER Charles H d East Weare 1928-12-02 age 83yrs 10mos 1dys b Nashua Vol: 9 Page: 021

CROWELL Oliver William d Concord 1928-12-08 age 70yrs 5mos 8dys b Hopkinton 1858-06-30 child of CROWELL Albert of Hopkinton & KIMBALL Lydia L of Hopkinton Vol: 9 Page: 021

DENSMORE Eleanor J d Warner 1928-12-13 age 75yrs 7mos 8dys b Hopkinton 1853-05-19 child of LIBBY W T of Epsom & SMART Elinor of Hopkinton Vol: 9 Page: 022

EATON Ellen L d Hopkinton 1928-12-23 age 89yrs b Haverhill Mass 1839 child of EATON Ichobod of Hopkinton & JONES Louisa Vol: 9 Page: 022

TUCKER Henry W d Hopkinton 1928-12-26 age 79yrs 10mos 20dys b Goffstown 1848-04-06 child of TUCKER Joseph Vol: 9 Page: 022

333

Hopkinton, NH Deaths 1914

BATES Hannah E d Hopkinton 1929-01-29 age 99yrs 5mos 1dys b Brighton England 1829-08-18 child of BATES Edward of Brighton England & WHITING Mary of Brighton England Vol: 9 Page: 023

CILLEY Florence d Hopkinton 1929-01-26 age 53yrs 9mos 9dys b Hopkinton 1875-04-17 child of WIGHT Oscar & CURRIER Abbie Vol: 9 Page: 023

HOYT Elen A d Hopkinton 1929-01-29 age 91yrs 7mos 1dys b Sutton 1838-06-08 child of WHITTER Ora Vol: 9 Page: 023

GOLDWAITE Clara E d Hopkinton 1929-01-04 age 70yrs 10mos 23dys b Warner 1859-02-11 child of DAVIS Pain of Warner & PATTEN Esther of Alexander Vol: 9 Page: 024

PUTNAM Flora d Hopkinton 1929-02-01 age 67yrs 7mos 1dys b Hopkinton 1861-06-23 child of CLOUGH Charles E of Hopkinton & HARDY Mary of Hopkinton Vol: 9 Page: 024

HUNTOON Mary Vilona d Hopkinton 1929-02-08 age 80yrs 8mos 13dys b Windsor 1848-05-25 child of CURTICE Samuel of Windsor & SWEATT Lenora of Windsor Vol: 9 Page: 024

BROWN Stella E d Hopkinton 1929-02-17 age 79yrs 14dys b So Acworth 1850-02-03 child of WATTS Samuel Vol: 9 Page: 025

DUCLOS ---- d Hopkinton 1929-03-30 b Hopkinton 1929-03-30 child of DUCLOS Francis of Lewis NY & ROBAR Laura of Chesterfield NY Vol: 9 Page: 025

DUSTIN Cyrus F d Hopkinton 1929-03-31 age 76yrs 2mos 16dys b Hopkinton 1853-01-15 child of DUSTIN Daniel of Hopkinton & BARNARD Sarah of Hopkinton Vol: 9 Page: 025

SANBORN Emma J d Hopkinton 1929-04-09 age 70yrs 11mos 22dys b Hopkinton 1858-04-11 child of FLANDERS Benj of Hopkinton & DOW Melissa J of Henniker Vol: 9 Page: 026

CALL Arthur Clarence d Hopkinton 1929-04-15 age 71yrs 3mos 23dys b Webster 1857-12-22 child of CALL Frank of Webster & STONE Eliza of Webster Vol: 9 Page: 026

HICKEY Jeremiah d Concord 1929-03-20 age 61yrs 1mos 5dys b Dorchester Mass 1868-02-15 Vol: 9 Page: 026

DERRY Mary T d Hopkinton 1929-04-07 age 7yrs 7mos 12dys b Hopkinton 1921-08-26 child of DERRY Angus P of Hopkinton & LEET Mary of Novia Scotia Vol: 9 Page: 027

SCRIBNER Carrie J d Concord 1929-05-05 age 77yrs 2mos 24dys b West Salisbury 1852-02-24 child of HUNTOON John F of Salisbury & PUTNEY Effie K of Hopkinton Vol: 9 Page: 027

SMITH Harold R d New London 1929-05-21 age 25yrs 11mos 7dys b Contoocook 1903-06-14 child of SMITH Robert of Webster & BOYCE Ardelle L of Penacook Vol: 9 Page: 027

WILLAIMS Harry O d Hopkinton 1929-05-22 age 70yrs 8mos 14dys b West Concord 1858-09-08 child of WILLIAMS Augustus O of Lowell Mass & LOWGEE Thersea of Sanbornton Vol: 9 Page: 028

LESLIE Nellie B d Hopkinton 1929-05-30 age 73yrs 4mos 16dys b Stockport Eng 1856-01-14 child of DUNN William of England & UPOLOHUSE Elizabeth of England Vol: 9 Page: 028

CONWAY Raymond A d Concord 1929-06-06 age 35yrs 7mos 14dys b New York City 1893-10-22 child of CONWAY P J of England & KENNEDY Ella of N Y Vol: 9 Page: 028

SULLIVAN John d Concord 1929-06-08 age 4yrs b Hopkinton child of SULLIVAN John & Marion Vol: 9 Page: 029

BARTON Elmer Ray d Contoocook 1929-06-06 age 38yrs 6mos 8dys b Hopkinton 1890-09-27 child of BARTON E C of Hopkinton & CURRIER M E of Hopkinton Vol: 9 Page: 029

PRINCE Mary Elsie d Hopkinton 1929-06-25 age 23yrs 3mos 1dys b Salisbury 1906-03-06 child of PRINCE Roscoe P of Orange & PEARSON Carrie G of Salisbury Vol: 9 Page: 029

TAYLOR Georgia A d Hopkinton 1929-07-03 age 81yrs 4mos 15dys b Concord child of DOW Samuel H of Concord & HOYT Sarah of Hopkinton Vol: 9 Page: 030

NORRIS Ida E d Hopkinton 1929-06-29 age 73yrs 2mos 15dys b Landaff 1856-04-13 child of HALL Hiram of Stewartstown & SMITH Mary of Newbury Vt Vol: 9 Page: 030

MATOTT Sarah O d Hopkinton 1929-07-06 age 87yrs 10mos 5dys b Lake Champlain Ny 1841-08-01 child of MAHEW Francis A of France & Miner of France Vol: 9 Page: 030

KIMBALL Sarah U d Hopkinton 1929-07-11 age 82yrs b So Boston Mass 1847-07-11 child of KIMBALL Perkins of Pembroke & WILDER Lydia Reed Vol: 9 Page: 031

STEVENS Albertine A d Hopkinton 1929-07-11 age 75yrs 3mos 24dys b Hopkinton 1854-03-17 child of CURRIER Lozaro of Hopkinton & ANDERSON Anana of Sweden Vol: 9 Page: 031

DUNBAR Mary Ellen d Hopkinton 1929-07-18 age 73yrs 7mos 30dys b New York Ny 1856-11-19 child of FRAZIER Francis of New York Ny & Mcmanus of New York N Y Vol: 9 Page: 031

BEAN Mary Jane d Warner 1929-07-16 age 62yrs 4mos 19dys b Johnstown Ny 1867-01-25 child of MORISON Thomas of Ireland & CONCUNNOES Mary of Ireland Vol: 9 Page: 032

WEST Martha A d Hopkinton 1929-08-05 age 86yrs 2mos 21dys b Hopkinton 1843-05-01 child of HOYT French of Hopkinton & FLANDERS Mahala of Hopkinton Vol: 9 Page: 032

SLADER Rohoda A d Hopkinton 1929-09-04 age 78yrs 6mos 14dys b Randolph Mass 1851-01-20 child of BROAD Joseph of Randolph Mass & ---- ---- of Randolph Mass Vol: 9 Page: 032

ROLLINS Harry d Hopkinton 1929-09-15 age 54yrs 7mos 23dys b Lakeport 1875-01-22 child of ROLLINS G W T of Manchester & SMITH Mary F of Boston Mass Vol: 9 Page: 033

MUDGETT J Frank d Hopkinton 1929-10-11 age 86yrs 10mos 10dys b Weare 1842-12-01 child of MUDGETT Moser of Weare & BOYNTON Armanda of Weare Vol: 9 Page: 033

MUNRO Frank d Hopkinton 1929-11-11 age 67yrs 9mos 8dys b Kingston N S 1862-02-03 child of MUNRO Albert D of Kingston N S & NEWCOMB Mary A of Nova Scotia Vol: 9 Page: 033

NELSON John H d Hopkinton 1929-11-24 age 78yrs b Hopkinton child of NELSON Joseph L of Hopkinton & HUBBARD Esther Vol: 9 Page: 034

SHIRLAND Alice M d Hopkinton 1929-11-28 age 40yrs 1mos b East Washington 1889-10-28 child of PEASLEY C A of Newbury & BROWN Uenetta of Washington Vol: 9 Page: 034

RICE ---- d Hopkinton 1929-12-08 b Concord 1929-12-08 child of RICE Neal J of Hopkinton & HAVEN Eunice of Boscawen Vol: 9 Page: 034

RAND Clara F d Contoocook 1929-12-15 age 80yrs 15dys b Boscawen 1849-11-30 child of BURPEE Wm Vol: 9 Page: 035

PERRY Editheen E d Contoocook 1929-12-26 age 69yrs 10mos 15dys b Hopkinton 1860-02-11 child of KELLEY Frederick of Hopkinton & HOLLAND Harriet of Wilmot Vol: 9 Page: 035

STRAW James O d Hopkinton 1929-12-26 age 76yrs 4mos 20dys b Hopkinton child of STRAW Willam S & FLANDERS Mary A Vol: 9 Page: 035

DUNBAR Henry P d Fitchbury Mass 1929-12-25 age 71yrs 7mos 29dys b Hopkinton 1858-04-26 child of DUNBAR Elmer B of Grantham & WEBBER Ann T of Hopkinton Vol: 9 Page: 036

STRAW Mildred G d St Johnsbury Vt 1929-09-16 age 42yrs 6dys b NH 1887-09-10 child of SIMONS Samuel T of NH & JOHNSON Annie M of NH Vol: 9 Page: 036

SARGENT Frank B d Contoocook 1930-01-13 age 83yrs 8mos 5dys b New London 1846-04-08 child of SARGENT Edwin of New London & WOODWARD Eliza of New London Vol: 9 Page: 037

KIMBALL Mary Grace d Concord 1930-01-15 age 76yrs 3mos 6dys b Boston Mass 1853-10-09 child of KIMBALL John S of Pembroke & STEVENS Mary E of Goffstown Vol: 9 Page: 037

BALCH T Edward d Hopkinton 1930-01-20 age 59yrs 4mos 7dys b Thetford Vt 1870-09-13 child of BALCH J Freeman of Lyme & SANBORN Sarah of Webster Vol: 9 Page: 037

GLANVILLE Chas F d Hopkinton 1930-01-22 age 73yrs 8mos 12dys b Dorchester Eng 1856-05-10 child of GLANVILLE Francis of England & CORBIN Susan of England Vol: 9 Page: 038

TILTON Joseph N d Concord 1930-01-24 age 52yrs 11mos 25dys b Hopkinton 1877-01-30 child of TILTON George F of Concord & NADEAU Minnie of Minnesota Vol: 9 Page: 038

ELLIOTT Charles E d Hooksett 1930-01-06 age 69yrs 1mos 11dys b Hopkinton 1860-11-26 child of ELLIOTT Thomas of Webster & SANBORN Angeline P of Webster Vol: 9 Page: 038

PAGE Mary Ella d Hopkinton 1930-01-30 age 72yrs 10mos 6dys b Henniker 1857-03-24 child of DOW Jonathan P of Henniker & PEASLEE Anna P of Weare Vol: 9 Page: 039

RUNNELLS M Jennie d Hopkinton 1930-02-12 age 81yrs 9mos 2dys b Concord 1848-05-10 child of BOYNTON Lyman D of Concord & WEBSTER Rebecca of Danville Vol: 9 Page: 039

SYMONDS George d Concord 1930-02-13 age 91yrs 4mos 20dys b Concord 1838-09-23 child of SYMONDS David of Hillsboro & FLANDERS Nancy of Pembroke Vol: 9 Page: 39

Hopkinton, NH Deaths 1914

KEYOU Charles E d Hinsdale 1930-02-17 age 72yrs 11mos 26dys b New Ipswich child of KEYOU George P & HODGMAN Matilda Vol: 9 Page: 040

CILLEY Raymond G d St Petersbury FL 1930-02-28 age 24yrs 6mos 9dys b Hopkinton 1905-08-09 child of CILLEY Elden G of Weare & WIGHT Florence of Hopkinton Vol: 9 Page: 040

MORRISON Royal R d Hopkinton 1930-03-07 age 78yrs 11mos b New London 1851-04-07 child of MORRISON Iddo K of New London & RICHARDSON Mary of Goffstown Vol: 9 Page: 040

HARDEN Martha (Miss) d Hopkinton 1930-03-18 age 88yrs 6mos 11dys b Mansfield Mass 1841-09-06 child of HARDDON Nathan of Mansfield Mass & HODGES Sally of N H Vol: 9 Page: 041

FELCH James B d Hopkinton 1930-03-20 age 74yrs 3mos b Weare 1855-12-20 child of FELCH Squire of Weare & SILVER Mary Ann of Pembroke Vol: 9 Page: 041

HOYT Geneva P d West Hopkinton 1930-04-10 age 4mos 15dys b Hopkinton child of HOYT Edward of Bradford & BLANCHETTE Delia of Goffstown Vol: 9 Page: 041

SMITH John C d Contoocook 1930-05-01 age 67yrs b Hopkinton 1862-05-30 child of SMITH Chas of Hopkinton & Nancy of Maine Vol: 9 Page: 042

ELLIOTT Anna Gertrude d Hooksett 1930-04-29 age 62yrs 9mos 29dys b Boston Mass 1867-07-30 child of HOWE Edward W of Mass & JOHNSON Anna of Deering Vol: 9 Page: 042

DAVIS Lucretia A d Hopkinton 1930-05-02 age 88yrs b Davisville/Warner 1842-01-25 child of DAVIS Nathaniel A of Warner & CLOUGH Mary of Webster Vol: 9 Page: 042

FULLER Orrin F d Hopkinton 1930-05-20 age 75yrs 9mos 9dys b Bristol 1854-08-11 child of FULLER G Abram & ADELINE C of Hopkinton Vol: 9 Page: 043

SMITH Robert d Hopkinton 1930-07-06 age 57yrs 11mos 12dys b Webster 1872-07-25 child of HEATH Chas of Webster Vol: 9 Page: 043

HILL Charles d Goffstown 1930-07-07 age 72yrs 8mos 21dys b Oakama Mass 1857-11-05 child of HILL Clark of Fairfax Vt & MARY Anne of Mass Vol: 9 Page: 043

BLANCHARD Nellie d Goffstown 1930-07-23 age 84yrs 1mos 3dys b Hillsboro 1846-06-20 child of ROACH David of U S & Harriet of U S Vol: 9 Page: 044

EDGERLY J Frank d Concord 1930-08-12 age 77yrs 2mos 13dys b Sanbornton 1853-05-30 child of EDGERLY Timothy & PAGE Margaret Vol: 9 Page: 044

LIBBY Geo C d Hopkinton 1930-08-24 age 73yrs Vol: 9 Page: 044

MILLS Myra I d Hill 1930-08-22 age 62yrs 19dys b Contoocook 1868-08-03 child of BROWN Charles of Warner Vol: 9 Page: 045

CURRIER True P d Hopkinton 1930-09-07 age 58yrs 5mos 1dys b Hopkinton child of CURRIER John F of Hopkinton & PUTNEY Nellie of Hopkinton Vol: 9 Page: 045

SEABORN Priscilla May d Framingham Mass 1929-02-03 b Framingham Mass 1929-02-03 child of SEABORN Duane R of Franklin & WILBAR Grace L of Keene Vol: 9 Page: 045

Hopkinton, NH Deaths 1914

COLBY George O d Hopkinton 1930-09-23 age 85yrs 4mos 13dys b Hopkinton 1845-05-09 child of COLBY Isac of Warner & FLOYD Lucy A of Warner Vol: 9 Page: 046

MOULTON Augustus V d Webster 1930-09-13 age 54yrs 6mos 24dys Vol: 9 Page: 046

BEAN Herbert J d Manchester 1930-10-03 age 65yrs 9mos 25dys b Danville 1864-12-07 child of BEAN Amos of Danville & COLLINS Drucilla J of Danville Vol: 9 Page: 046

MILLS Ethel M d Franklin 1930-10-10 age 19yrs 4mos 8dys b Lakeport 1911-07-02 child of CHENEY Luke of Sutton & DOLE Edith M of Lowell Mass Vol: 9 Page: 047

HEALEY Florence N d Boston Mass 1930-10-06 age 47yrs b Contoocook child of CHASE Horace S of Contoocook & SPAULDING Florence of Contoocook Vol: 9 Page: 047

DAVIS Abbie D d Wilton 1930-09-16 age 87yrs 11mos b Pelham 1843-10-16 child of WOODBURY Hiram of Goffstown & WEBSTER Leafy of Pelham Vol: 9 Page: 047

POTTS Elaine Lore d Concord 1930-10-20 age 67yrs 27dys b Oran Algeria 1861-09-23 child of Destill of France & ---- ---- of France Vol: 9 Page: 048

CHASE Marl D d Concord 1930-10-26 age 57yrs 2mos 24dys b Warner 1873-08-01 child of CHASE Alonzo of NH & COLBY Katie F of NH Vol: 9 Page: 048

OSLUND Alfred d Hopkinton 1930-11-23 age 64yrs 5mos 14dys b Sweden 1866-06-09 Vol: 9 Page: 048

EATON Albert S d Hopkinton 1930-12-13 age 90yrs 4mos b Newbury 1840-08-13 child of EATON Eben & CROSS Hannah B Vol: 9 Page: 049

BURNHAM Eva F d Concord 1930-12-13 age 82yrs 7mos 21dys b Lawrence Mass1848-04-22 child of BURNHAM Charles of Antrim & HAM Elizabeth of Canterbury Vol: 9 Page: 049

BAKER Alma d Boston Mass 1930-11-06 age 72yrs 8mos 21dys b Salisbury 1858-02-10 child of WHITAKER Thomas of NH & ROBIE Abiah E of NH Vol: 9 Page: 050

PIERCE Elizabeth Ann d Contoocook 1931-01-03 age 94yrs 9mos 25dys b Hopkinton 1838-03-08 child of MILLS Joseph of Dunbarton & CLOUGH Celinda of Dunbarton Vol: 9 Page: 051

BLAKE Clara B d Contoocook 1931-01-05 age 66yrs 9mos 2dys b W. Thornton 1864-04-03 child of BROWN Daniel of Thornton & ELKINS Laura of Thornton Vol: 9 Page: 051

PAIGE Kate D d Concord 1931-01-11 age 75yrs 4mos 9dys b Hopkinton 1855-09-02 child of CURRIER George W of Hopkinton & FLANDERS Hannah of Hopkinton Vol: 9 Page: 051

PIERCE Frank J d Concord 1931-06-27 age 79yrs 1mos 16dys b Vershire Vt child of PIERCE John & WEED Melina Vol: 9 Page: 058

HOWE Dewitt d Hopkinton 1933-07-03 age 58yrs 9mos 265dys b Claremont 1872-10-01 child of HOWE Geo Vol: 9 Page: 060

CAMERON John Howard d Hopkinton 1931-01-26 age 66yrs 11mos 19dys b Watervale N S 1864-02-18 child of CAMERON James of Watervale N S & McGILVARY Annie of Watervale N S Vol: 9 Page: 052

RIPLEY Sara E d Hopkinton 1931-01-19 age 73yrs 8mos 20dys b Pittsfield 1857-04-29 child of MAY Allen & SNELL Nancy Vol: 9 Page: 052

JONES Fred Leon d Hopkinton 1931-01-21 age 48yrs 11mos 17dys b Nashua 1882-02-04 child of JONES N E of Londonderry & Mary E of Harvard Mass Vol: 9 Page: 053

CORSER Hamlet d Hopkinton 1931-02-26 age 87yrs 9mos 13dys b Webster 1844-05-13 child of CORSER Freeman of Webster & CROWELL Harriet of Webster Vol: 9 Page: 053

CHASE Samuel Myron d Hopkinton 1931-03-02 age 66yrs 7mos 18dys b Chicago 1864-07-14 child of CHASE Horace S of Hopkinton & SHERWIN Ellen M of Batavia NY Vol: 9 Page: 053

CHASE Harry G d Hopkinton 1931-03-05 age 59yrs b Newbury Mass 1871-09-10 Vol: 9 Page: 054

AHERN Joseph d Goffstown 1931-02-08 age 4mos b Manchester 1930-10-08 child of AHERN Ben of Penacook & TIERNERY Lucille of Belfast Me Vol: 9 Page: 054

FERGERSON Marlene C d Barre Vt 1931-03-05 b Hopkinton 1931-03-05 Vol: 9 Page: 054

DREW Marietta J d Contoocook 1931-03-21 age 71yrs 5mos 6dys b Henniker 1859-08-15 child of WHITCOMB Luther H of Henniker & WELCH Anna J of Canada Vol: 9 Page: 055

GILLINGHAM Bertha M d Contoocook 1931-03-28 age 59yrs 4mos 28dys b 1871-10-31 child of BROCKWAY Virgil C of Newbury & FOLSOM Sarah A of Newbury Vol: 9 Page: 055

MILLS Frank O d Hopkinton 1931-11-25 age 78yrs 3mos 15dys b Hopkinton 1852-12-06 child of MILLS Joseph of Dunbarton & CLOUGH Silva of Dunbarton Vol: 9 Page: 055

HAVEN Frank B d Hopkinton 1931-04-14 age 55yrs 11mos 5dys b Goshen 1875-05-07 child of HAVEN Henry H & LEAR Arvilla of Goshen Vol: 9 Page: 056

BEAN Emory C d Manchester 1931-03-04 age 70yrs 11mos 29dys Vol: 9 Page: 056

HASTINGS Sadie Belle d Concord 1931-04-28 age 52yrs 9mos 13dys b Hopkinton 1878-07-15 child of HASTING Alfred D of Hopkinton & PERRY Susan of Hopkinton Vol: 9 Page: 056

ARNOLD William d Contoocook 1931-05-18 age 75??yrs b Ny ?? Vol: 9 Page: 057

PENNELL Emma J d Hopkinton 1931-06-03 age 50yrs 6mos 13dys b Denby N S 1880-11-20 child of MUELLEN Walter of Weymouth N S & GRANT Maria of Weymouth N S Vol: 9 Page: 057

GREELEY Johanna d Hopkinton 1931-06-02 b Nova Scotia 1880 child of ---- ---- of Nova Scotia & ---- ---- of Nova Scotia Vol: 9 Page: 057

---- ---- d Hopkinton 1931 b Hopkinton Vol: 9 Page: 051

RIPLEY George Robert d Hopkinton 1931-06-20 age 9yrs 1mos 30dys b Grrenfield Mass 1922-04-29 child of RIPLEY Geo H of Hopkinton & MAY Danis Vol: 9 Page: 058

---- ---- d Hopkinton 1933 b Hopkinton Vol: 9 Page: 079

GOLDSTONE Sarah M d Hopkinton 1931-07-20 age 80yrs 17dys b Canada 1851-07-03 child of GOLDSTONE Geo of Canada Vol: 9 Page: 058

TUTTLE Jacob S d Hopkinton 1931-07-21 age 88yrs 1mos 23dys b Lincoln 1843-05-27 child of TUTTLE Chas N of Lincoln & BARNARD Mary of Hopkinton Vol: 9 Page: 059

DORRY Lila E d Hopkinton 1931-07-22 age 42yrs 1mos 6dys b Nottingham 1889-06-15 child of DIMERETTE Eddison of Nottingham & REEVES Anna of N S Vol: 9 Page: 059

HALL Florence L d Hopkinton 1931-07-28 age 67yrs 3mos 23dys b Chelsea Mass 1864-04-04 child of WADSWORTH Jesee of Keene & LEES Mary Lorraine of Scotland Vol: 9 Page: 059

BARNARD Geo M d Webster 1931-07-29 age 87yrs 9mos 28dys b 1843-09-30 Vol: 9 Page: 060

PAIGE Thomas W d Hopkinton 1931-08-02 age 77yrs 7mos 19dys b Lowell Mass 1853-12-13 child of PAIGE T E & Clark Vol: 9 Page: 060

EMERSON Arthur Stillman d Hopkinton 1931-09-23 age 50yrs 7mos 23dys b Hopkinton 1881-01-31 child of EMERSON Hanson David of Hopkinton & MILLS Mary Frances of Hopkinton Vol: 9 Page: 061

MOORE Charles D d Hopkinton 1931-09-25 age 92yrs 11mos 22dys b Princeton Mass 1838-10-04 child of MOORE Humphrey & SMITH Ann L Vol: 9 Page: 061

CONANT Frank E d Hopkinton 1931-10-10 age 66yrs 1mos 27dys b Mansfield Mass 1865-08-12 child of CONANT H E of Mansfield Mass & SHATTELL Lena of Germany Vol: 9 Page: 061

MANNING James C d Hopkinton 1931-10-12 age 75yrs 1mos 19dys b Chelsea Mass 1856-08-23 child of MANNING James of Mass & CORNELL Annie of Mass Vol: 9 Page: 062

HOOK Edward M d East Lempester 1931-10-21 age 54yrs 8mos 27dys b Quebec Canada 1877-01-24 child of HOOK James M of Concord & DAYING Mary A of Canada Vol: 9 Page: 062

BILLINGS ---- d Concord 1931-10-31 b Concord 1931-10-30 child of BILLINS H S of Manchester & WHITTERMORE E M of Penacook Vol: 9 Page: 062

SANDERS Edward M d Concord 1931-11-08 age 84yrs 2mos 13dys b Gardner Mass 1847-08-26 child of SANDERS Willard of Gardner Mass & COPEN Rosana of Stewartstown Vol: 9 Page: 063

WHEELER Sylvester Jr d Hopkinton 1931-11-01 age 86yrs 4mos 19dys b Barnston P Q 1845-06-12 child of WHEELER Sylvester of Randolph Vt & WEBSTER Martha of Randolph Vt Vol: 9 Page: 063

JOHNSON Ina E d Hopkinton 1931-11-28 age 64yrs 2mos 6dys b Weare 1867-09-22 child of COLBURN John of Weare & EMERY Mary of Weare Vol: 9 Page: 063

CHAPMAN William d Bradford 1931-12-31 age 86yrs 11mos 19dys b Hopkinton 1845-01-19 Vol: 9 Page: 065

KEMPTON Emma J d Concord 1931-11-27 age 83yrs 11mos 15dys b Contoocook 1847-12-12 child of HARDY Wm H of Hopkinton & MORGAN Priscilla of New Boston Vol: 9 Page: 064

HACKETT Edwin J d Franklin 1931-12-12 age 44yrs 11mos 4dys b Hopkinton 1887-01-08 child of HACKETT Walter of Sanbornton & CROWELL Nellie of Hopkinton Vol: 9 Page: 064

Hopkinton, NH Deaths 1914

RICHARDSON Perley E d Contoocook 1931-12-25 age 51yrs 4mos 22dys b Antrim 1880-08-03 child of RICHARDSON James B of Lempster & POTTER Emmeline of Lempster Vol: 9 Page: 064

HALL Robert R d Hopkinton 1932-01-16 age 57yrs 2mos b Bear Lake Mich 1874-11-16 child of HALL E L of Syracuse NY & Malinda of Syracuse NY Vol: 9 Page: 066

SANBORN George Frank d Georges Mills 1932-10-12 age 61yrs 7mos 16dys Vol: 9 Page: 074

DAVIS Henry Chase d Hopkinton 1932-02-02 age 81yrs 3mos 5dys b 1850-10-31 child of DAVIS Nathaniel of Warner & CLOUGH Mary of Webster Vol: 9 Page: 066

WATSON Mary D d Hopkinton 1932-02-06 age 82yrs 9mos 1dys b Ellington Ny 1850-09-01 child of FULLER W R of Bennington Vt & INGERSOL S M of New Haven Conn Vol: 9 Page: 066

SANBORN Herman d Hopkinton 1932-03-20 age 64yrs 2mos 28dys b Webster 1869-12-22 child of SANBORN Ezra of Webster & ELLIOTT Sarah of Webster Vol: 9 Page: 067

SHAMPNEY Annie d Concord 1932-10-12 age 46yrs 9mos 1dys b Mass 1885-01-11 child of WALLINGTON William of England & CONNORS Katherine of Ireland Vol: 9 Page: 067

HARDLEY Marie Louise d Hopkinton 1932-04-12 age 81yrs 3mos 4dys b NY City 1851-02-08 child of HARDLEY James of Isles Wright Eng & BENSON Maria of NY City Vol: 9 Page: 067

CUMMINGS Hannah M d W Hopkinton 1932-04-13 age 78yrs 11mos 5dys b Northfield 1853-05-06 child of FRENCH George of Mass & BUSWELL Nancy of Northfield Vol: 9 Page: 068

SWINDELHURST John R d Concord 1932-04-18 age 27yrs 4mos 20dys b Peterboro 1904-11-28 child of SWINDLEHURST Christophe of England & BAILEY Edith of Toronto Canada Vol: 9 Page: 068

CARTER Nelson N d Contoocook 1932-05-05 age 83yrs 9mos 16dys b East Dixfield Me 1847-07-19 child of CARTER Hiram of Bow & MAYHEW Hannah of Jay Maine Vol: 9 Page: 068

PALMER Mary J d Hopkinton 1932-07-05 age 83yrs 8mos 12dys b Warner 1848-10-22 child of MORGAN J O & FLANDERS Abigail Vol: 9 Page: 071

GRIFFIN Alfred W d Hopkinton 1932-07-10 age 65yrs b London England 1867-10-12 child of GRIFFIN James S of Plymouth England & OCKLAND Thirza of Plymouth England Vol: 9 Page: 071

HADLEY Mary A d Hopkinton 1932-07-26 age 69yrs 7mos 19dys b Weare 1862-11-07 child of COLBURN John of Henniker & EMERY Ann of Weare Vol: 9 Page: 071

EASTMAN Octavia d Concord 1932-05-31 age 81yrs 11mos 4dys b Salisbury 1850-06-27 child of GREELY S B of Salisbury & CORSER Louise of Webster Vol: 9 Page: 070

KELLEY Jennie M d Hopkinton 1932-07-01 age 74yrs 9mos 21dys b Hopkinton 1858-01-09 child of FISK Daniel of Hopkinton & CONNER Lydia of Hopkinton Vol: 9 Page: 070

KIMBALL Lydia A d Hopkinton 1932-07-07 age 88yrs 8mos 9dys b Exeter 1843 child of WALDRON George & LADD Huldah Vol: 9 Page: 070

DUSTIN Nellie S d Hopkinton 1932-08-07 age 72yrs 7mos 13dys b Manchester 1859-12-24 child of SPAULDING D A of Hudson & PUTNEY Simantha of Webster Vol: 9 Page: 072

CLARK Georgiana M d West Hopkinton 1932-08-14 age 17yrs 4mos 19dys b West Hopkinton 1915-03-25 child of CLARK James F of Warner & DROWN Lillie of Warner Vol: 9 Page: 072

BERGSTROM Oscar Robert d Concord 1932-08-22 age 45yrs 3mos 9dys b Maynard Mass 1887-05-04 child of BERGSTROM Gaston of Sweden & JOHNSON Annie of Sweden Vol: 9 Page: 073

RIPLEY George H d Concord 1932-08-29 age 58yrs 14dys b Hopkinton 1874-08-15 child of RIPLEY James & Keezer Vol: 9 Page: 073

HASTINGS George d Concord 1932-09-02 age 64yrs 7mos 2dys b Hopkinton 1868-01-30 child of HASTINGS Alfred S of Hopkinton & PERRY Susan E of Hopkinton Vol: 9 Page: 073

MEAD Freeman S d Belmont 1932-09-24 age 70yrs 10mos 7dys b Upper Bartlett 1861-10-07 child of MEAD Joseph of Bartlett & CUMMINGS Lucretia of Maddison Vol: 9 Page: 074

SANBORN Hubert S d Burlington Vt 1932-09-28 age 62yrs 1mos 29dys b Concord child of SANBORN Chas H of Concord & STORY Annette of Hopkinton Vol: 9 Page: 074

WHITE Lura F d Hopkinton 1932-10-25 age 55yrs 10mos 11dys b Hopkinton 1876-12-13 child of CHASE Cyrus of Hopkinton & BARTLETT Ella of Warner Vol: 9 Page: 075

SHURTLEFF Fannie Belle d Warner 1932-11-03 age 68yrs 2mos 19dys b Manchester 1864-08-24 child of ELLINWOOD John B of Deering & ALCOOK Lenora of Hillsboro Vol: 9 Page: 075

FRENCH Charles L d Concord 1932-11-02 age 72yrs 4mos 6dys b Hopkinton 1860-06-26 child of FRENCH Edward of Hopkinton & STEVENS Jane of So Boston Mass Vol: 9 Page: 075

CORSER Harriett Pauline d Hopkinton 1932-11-16 age 80yrs 6mos 9dys b Hopkinton 1852-05-07 child of HEATH James A of Webster/Salisbury & CLARK Harriett of Warner Vol: 9 Page: 076

BLAKE Grace E d Concord 1932-11-21 age 56yrs 7mos 20dys b Weare 1876-03-31 child of EMERSON Frank & Harriott Vol: 9 Page: 076

GRIFFIN Daniel A d Concord 1932-12-02 age 41yrs 9mos 12dys b Hopkinton 1891-03-19 child of GRIFFIN Alfred E of Bow & MORRILL Helen J of Lowell Mass Vol: 9 Page: 076

EARLE Fred d Hopkinton 1932-12-04 age 78yrs 5mos 18dys b Concord 1854-06-16 child of EARLE Horace A of Barre Vt & GRIFFIN Sarah E of Wht River Jct Vt Vol: 9 Page: 077

GUNN William E d Hopkinton 1932-12-11 age 50yrs 9mos 18dys b Penacook 1882-02-23 child of GUNN Bernard of Concord & FANEUFF Mary of St Albans Vt Vol: 9 Page: 077

HANSON George E d Boston Mass 1932-12-10 age 64yrs 6mos 5dys child of HANSON George of NH & FLANDERS Amelia of NH Vol: 9 Page: 077

Hopkinton, NH Deaths 1914

EMERSON Mary Frances d Hopkinton 1932-12-16 age 86yrs 22dys b Hopkinton 1846-11-24 child of MILLS Joseph & CLOUGH Selinda Vol: 9 Page: 078

HARDY ---- d Hopkinton 1932-12-29 b Hopkinton 1932-12-29 child of HARDY Ansel Francis of Wester & COOPER Ruth May of Hopkinton Vol: 9 Page: 0078

BARTLETT J Hazen d Concord 1933-02-04 age 53yrs b Warner 1879-08-17 child of BARTLETT Woodbury of Warner & DAVIS Clara Belle of Brattleboro Vt Vol: 9 Page: 080

NYBERG Thelma E d Concord 1933-02-09 age 4yrs 8mos 7dys b Manchester 1928-06-02 child of NYBERG Russell of Manchester & TIBBETTS Edna of Nashua Vol: 9 Page: 080

BURNHAM Frank Parker d Newton Mass 1933-02-13 age 63yrs 10mos 12dys b Contoocook child of BURNHAM Edward P of Contoocook & DAVIS Georgie P of Warner Vol: 9 Page: 080

FLANDERS Frank H (Mrs) d Miami Fla 1933-02-13 age 77yrs 1mos 7dys b Salem NY 1856-01-06 child of MONTGOMERY George of Salem NY & SNYDER Elizabeth of Fort Edward Ny Vol: 9 Page: 081

FRENCH Clara M d Concord 1933-02-26 age 56yrs b Hopkinton 1877 child of FRENCH Edward D of Hopkinton & STEVENS Jennie of Boston Mass Vol: 9 Page: 081

BILLINGS Beverly A d Contoocook 1933-03-03 age 6yrs 19dys b Contoocook 1927-02-12 child of BILLINGS Herbert S of Manchester & WHITTEMORE Emily M of Penacook Vol: 9 Page: 081

GEORGE Frank d Hopkinton 1933-03-09 age 77yrs 4mos b 1855 Oct Vol: 9 Page: 082

MURDO Frank d Hopkinton 1933-03-11 age 80yrs 23dys b Hillsboro 1853-02-18 child of MURDO Chas of Hillsboro & FARLEY Mary of Hollis Vol: 9 Page: 082

BARTLETT Kenneth H d Contoocook 1933-04-19 age 7mos 25dys b Concord 1932-08-24 child of BARTLETT Roy O of Contoocook & HANKS Esther B of Statford Vol: 9 Page: 082

SYMONDS Lilllah d Hopkinton 1933-06-23 age 70yrs 2mos 24dys b Smiths Cove N S 1863-03-29 child of HARDY Benjamin of Nova Scotia & MARSHALL Celia of Nova Scotia Vol: 9 Page: 083

MORRISON George A d Concord 1933-06-28 age 46yrs b Haverhill 1886-03-01 child of MORRISON Roy L of New London & TOWNE Ella of New Boston Vol: 9 Page: 083

STEVENS Baby d Concord 1933-07-06 age 3 wkdys b Concord child of STEVENS Howard Vol: 9 Page: 083

CLOUGH Mary Elsie d Bellow Falls Vt 1933-09-03 age 67yrs 9mos 28dys b Verginnes Vt 1865-11-10 child of Ballou Vol: 9 Page: 084

KILKENNEY M Caroline d Hopkinton 1933-09-01 age 6yrs 2mos 6dys b West Chazy NY 1865-06-26 child of LAWRENCE James K of West Chazy NY & ANDERSON Adeline of West Chazy NY Vol: 9 Page: 084

SHEPARD Isabelle D d Hopkinton 1933-09-11 age 63yrs 7mos 12dys b Boston Mass 1870-02-18 child of DEVEREUX Richard F of Pr Ed Islands & MIFFIRM Corinna of Boston Mass Vol: 9 Page: 085

DAVIS Amos d Newington Ct 1933-09-26 age 45yrs 1mos 18dys b   child of DAVIS Henry B of Hopkinton & Eliza Vol: 9 Page: 085

Hopkinton, NH Deaths 1914

PHILLIPS Angie M d Albany NY 1933-09-02 age 87yrs 8mos 22dys b Contoocook child of HARDY William of NH & MORGAN Purcella M of NH Vol: 9 Page: 085

PINEO William B d Concord 1933-10-05 age 75yrs 5mos b Nova Scotia 1858 Apr child of PINEO Isaac Benton of Canada & TUPPER Annie of Canada Vol: 9 Page: 086

FELLOWS Clara Maria d Concord 1933-10-28 age 84yrs 7mos 8dys b Hopkinton 1849-03-20 child of FELLOWS Ignatius of Hopkinton & COPP Sarah Jane of Haverhill Mass Vol: 9 Page: 086

SEVERANCE Herbert D d Hopkinton 1933-11-08 age 73yrs 7mos 23dys b Hopkinton 1860-03-10 child of SEVERANCE Joseph W of Marlow & PUTNEY Adaline of Bradford Vol: 9 Page: 086

MARSTON Rufus I d Concord 1933-11-26 age 94yrs 5mos 7dys b So Deerfield 1839-06-19 child of MARSTON Enas R of Pittsfield & BARTLETT Mary of So Deerfield Vol: 9 Page: 087

DEVEREUX Corinna E d Concord 1933-12-05 age 84yrs 7mos 19dys b Boston Mass 1849-04-16 child of MIFFIRN Edward of Philadelphia Pa & ---- ---- of England Vol: 9 Page: 087

BLAKE Frank H d Boscawen 1933-12-13 age 54yrs 2mos 14dys Vol: 9 Page: 087

BORDEN Lucie Elizabeth d Concord 1933-12-19 age 73yrs 6mos 9dys b Hopkinton 1860-06-10 child of PAGE Samuel S of Dunbarton & CUTTER Ellen M of Weston Mass Vol: 9 Page: 088

PHELPS Peter M d Contoocook 1933-12-21 age 85yrs 6mos b Jun 1848 6 Vol: 9 Page: 088

RIPLEY James W d Hopkinton 1933-12-16 age 78yrs 2mos 10dys b Londonderry 1852-10-05 child of RIPLEY William & MARSH Eliza M Vol: 9 Page: 049

CONNELLY Chas G d Hopkinton 1931-01-22 age 25yrs 6mos 17dys b Halifax N S 1905-07-15 child of CONNELLY Rufus A & SMITH Susie L Vol: 9 Page: 052

CLARK ---- d Hopkinton 1932-08-14 b West Hopkinton 1932-08-14 child of CLARK Georgiana M of West Hopkinton Vol: 9 Page: 072

ROBERTSON Hattie M d Hopkinton 1933-09-11 age 70yrs 2mos 26dys b Warner 1863-06-15 child of BARTLETT Chas & CHASE Melissa Vol: 9 Page: 084

HASELTON Nellie M d Hopkinton 1933-12-25 age 68yrs 6mos 11dys b Warner 1865-06-14 child of DWINNELLS Munroe & HEATH Susan Vol: 9 Page: 088

CLINTON Winfield M d Goffstown 1933-01-12 age 50yrs 11mos 29dys b Warren 1882-01-13 child of CLINTON John of Ireland & Sarah of Hopkinton Vol: 9 Page: 079

MILLS George W d Hopkinton 1933-01-11 age 94yrs 1mos 26dys b Hopkinton 1838-12-16 child of MILLS Joseph of Dunbarton & Clough of Bow Vol: 9 Page: 079

SANBORN Jennie E d Hopkinton 1933-01-18 age 85yrs 27dys b Salisbury 1847-12-22 child of COLBY J E of Salisbury & DUNLOP Eunice of Salisbury Vol: 9 Page: 079

ELLIOTT Edson E d Hopkinton 1932-05-08 age 76yrs 2mos 13dys b Webster 1856-02-25 child of ELLIOTT Joseph of Webster & SANBORN Angeline of Webster Vol: 9 Page: 069

BOUTWELL Baby d Dover 1932-02-20 Vol: 9 Page: 069

HILL Salina d Goffstown 1932-05-17 age 78yrs 5mos 28dys b Vermont 1853-11-19 child of BENNETT Peter of St Albans Vt & LITUCHE Viola of Manchester Vol: 9 Page: 069

DUSTIN Laura Sharpless d Wilmington Del 1934-02-12 age 76yrs 17dys b Union Pa 1858-01-26 child of SHARPLESS M Walter of Pa & HOLT Marcia of Pa Vol: 10 Page: 001

BAKER Frank E d Contoocook 1934-03-03 age 77yrs 6mos 14dys b Meriden 1856-08-19 child of BAKER Abel W of Bethleham & HADLEY Mary of Aetna Vol: 10 Page: 001

LOUD Charles W d Boscawen 1934-04-03 age 91yrs b Hopkinton Vol: 10 Page: 003

KIMBALL George N d Titusville Fla 1934-03-11 age 76yrs 7mos 3dys b Hopkinton Vol: 10 Page: 004 Note: See vol 10 pg 4 also

SMALL Laura A D d Hopkinton 1934-03-19 age 90yrs 1mos 17dys b Plainfield 1844-02-01 child of DAVIS Amasa of Hartland Vt & WHITE Hannah of Cornith Vol: 10 Page: 002

BURNHAM Emma d Contoocook 1934-03-23 age 98yrs 4mos 22dys b Deerfield 1835-11-29 child of MARSTON Enock R of Pittsfield & BARTLETT Mary of Deerfield Vol: 10 Page: 002

DUSTIN Sarah A d Hopkinton 1934-03-26 age 78yrs 1mos 16dys b Hopkinton 1856-02-09 child of RICHARDSON Daniel & DODGE Sarah Vol: 10 Page: 002

SAWYER Elmer E d Hopkinton 1934-03-27 age 71yrs 11mos 10dys b East Sutton 1862-04-17 child of SAWYER James B of Warner & RICHARDSON Lucy A of Sunapee Vol: 10 Page: 003

RICE Bernice d Hopkinton 1934-04-02 age 57yrs 0mos 17dys b Hopkinton 1877-03-15 child of BOHANAN John W of Sutton & JEWELL Delia of Weare Vol: 10 Page: 003

GUIMOND Zoel d Hopkinton 1934-04-30 age 75yrs 7mos 28dys b Canada 1858-09-02 child of GUIMOND Clement of Canada & JARVIS Rosalie of Canada Vol: 10 Page: 004

FRENCH Mary E d Concord 1934-01-22 age 75yrs 4mos 12dys Vol: 10 Page: 004

MIGNAULT Ethel d Concord 1934-05-13 age 56yrs b Mass 1878-05-13 child of BELCHER Warren of Boston Mass & HAMILTON Elizabeth of E Boston Mass Vol: 10 Page: 005

GRIFFIN Lu K d Hopkinton 1934-05-22 age 72yrs 5mos 22dys child of GRIFFIN Joseph & KELLEY Almira Vol: 10 Page: 005

FLANDERS Parker d Hopkinton 1934-04-05 age 71yrs 8mos 2dys b Hopkinton 1862-08-03 child of FLANDERS Parker M of Hopkinton & CONNOR Hannah of Henniker Vol: 10 Page: 005

NICHOLS G Arthur d Concord 1934-05-24 age 66yrs 1mos 12dys b Quincy Mass 1868-04-12 child of NICHOLS George H & DAVIS Lucy Vol: 10 Page: 006

BOLIVAR Ariel d Concord 1934-05-26 age 55yrs 8mos 26dys b Nova Scotia 1878-08-29 child of BOLIVAR James E of Nova Scotia & COLT Eliza A of Nova Scotia Vol: 10 Page: 006

PARRY Carrie Evelyn d Elberton Georgia 1934-01-08 age 66yrs 4mos 19dys Vol: 10 Page: 006

Hopkinton, NH Deaths 1914

CLOUGH Willard E d Mansfield Mass 1934-04-14 age 84yrs b Hopkinton Vol: 10 Page: 007

LINDQUIST Hilda d Hopkinton 1934-03-01 age 55yrs 1mos 11dys b Sweden 1879-01-20 child of ---- ---- of Sweden & ---- ---- of Sweden Vol: 10 Page: 007

BALCH Sarah S d Hopkinton 1934-06-17 age 92yrs 1mos 13dys b Webster 1842-05-04 child of SANBORN John W of Webster & COFFIN Rebecca of Boscawen Vol: 10 Page: 007

GIRARD William E d Hopkinton 1934-07-03 age 23yrs b Concord 1911-03-11 child of GIRARD Philias of Canada & TRUCHAN Exana of Canada Vol: 10 Page: 008

KENYON Frank F d Hopkinton 1934-07-06 age 76yrs 3mos 1dys b Pomfret Vt 1858-04-05 child of KENYON Albert Vol: 10 Page: 008

CURRIER Harlan d Sutton 1934-07-15 age 34yrs 18dys b Hopkinton 1900-06-28 child of CURRIER Willie A of Hopkinton & WEBSTER Gustie of Hopkinton Vol: 10 Page: 008

KIMBALL Nettie W d Manchester 1934-07-19 age 45yrs 3mos 14dys b Essex Jct Vt 1889-04-05 child of WAKEFIELD Chas C of Vermont & COLE Beatrice of Canada Vol: 10 Page: 009

BLOOD Nellie F d Hopkinton 1934-08-12 age 69yrs 5mos 16dys b Bristol 1865-02-26 child of MUDGETT Calvin & FISHER Julia Vol: 10 Page: 009

SHEPARD Geo Edward d Hopkinton 1934-08-22 age 64yrs 2mos 23dys b Concord 1870-05-30 child of SHEPARD Emory N of Worcester Mass & SIMONDS Caroline of Salem Mass Vol: 10 Page: 009

BLACK Elizabeth H d Hopkinton 1934-08-24 age 73yrs 3mos 5dys b Paris Kentucky 1861-05-09 child of HENILLE William of Germany & PETERS Maria of Germany Vol: 10 Page: 010

CARTER James S d Hopkinton 1934-09-02 age 83yrs 1mos 18dys b Warner 1851-07-14 child of CARTER E of Canada & SANBORN Betsey of Warner Vol: 10 Page: 010

CLOUGH Alta Moffat d Concord 1934-09-26 age 45yrs 10mos 7dys b Roxbury Mass 1888-11-19 child of MULLOGAN William of England & MOFFAT Mary of England Vol: 10 Page: 010

POWERS Joseph E d Rutland Mass 1934-10-10 age 31yrs 5mos 22dys b Roxbury Mass 1903-04-18 child of POWERS Harry E of Marlow & AHERN Katherine E of Boston Mass Vol: 10 Page: 011

ANDREWS Hattie d Hopkinton 1934-10-11 age 93yrs 1mos 7dys b Chester 1841-09-04 child of LANE David & FITTS Cynthia of Sandown Vol: 10 Page: 011

PAIGE Minnie d Boston Mass 1934-06-08 age 70yrs b Hopkinton Vol: 10 Page: 014

GOULD Mary Currier d Mt Dora Fla 1934-02-20 age 72yrs 1mos 26dys b Hopkinton 1861-12-14 child of CURRIER John F of Hopkinton & PUTNEY Hannah of Hopkinton Vol: 10 Page: 011

WOODWARD John W d Hopkinton 1934-11-01 age 75yrs 1mos 1dys b 1859-09-30 child of WOODWARD Sylvester & ATWOOD Hannah Vol: 10 Page: 012

BARNARD Lizzie M d Hopkinton 1934-11-15 age 69yrs 1mos 1dys b New Boston 1865-10-14 child of TUTTLE James B of Weare & ROWELL Mary A of Hopkinton Vol: 10 Page: 012

Hopkinton, NH Deaths 1914

RICHARDSON Edward S d Hopkinton 1934-11-26 age 88yrs 1mos 24dys b Charlestown Mass 1846-10-02 child of RICHARDSON Daniel of Hopkinton & DODGE Sarah Vol: 10 Page: 012

PALMER Willie O d Hopkinton 1934-12-07 age 80yrs 5mos 24dys b Hopkinton 1854-06-13 child of PALMER William & CHASE Ann E Vol: 10 Page: 013

DIMAN Lida Fisk d Concord 1934-12-06 age 46yrs 1mos 13dys b Contoocook 1888-10-23 child of FISK Daniel F of Hopkinton & CHANDLER Delta E of Hopkinton Vol: 10 Page: 013

PUTNEY John S Jr d Concord 1934-11-20 age 38yrs 6mos 9dys b Chicago Ill 1896-05-10 child of PUTNEY John S of Webster & MELTON Lucile of Norfolk Va Vol: 10 Page: 013

CURRIER Charles C d Concord 1935-01-11 age 69yrs 6mos 3dys b Hopkinton 1865-07-08 child of CURRIER John F of Hopkinton & PUTNEY Nellie H of Hopkinton Vol: 10 Page: 015

DUSTIN Helen M d Hopkinton 1935-01-28 age 82yrs 3mos 20dys b Hopkinton 1852-10-08 child of TUCKER David C of Henniker & STRAW Mary E of Hopkinton Vol: 10 Page: 015

FITTS Beverly d Peabody Mass 1935-02-09 age 9mos 29dys b Lynn Mass 1934-04-11 child of FITTS John S of Sandown & KIMBALL Mildred E of Hopkinton Vol: 10 Page: 015

PERRY Frank S d Hopkinton 1935-02-02 age 78yrs 6mos 28dys b Hopkinton 1856-05-10 child of PERRY Sylvestr W of Hopkinton & FLINT Bertha S of Damariscotta Me Vol: 10 Page: 016

EARLE Carrie B d Hopkinton 1935-02-02 age 66yrs 2mos 9dys b Concord 1868-11-13 child of EARLE Horace A of Bare Vt & GRIFFIN Sarah of Hardwick Vt Vol: 10 Page: 016

BLETCHER Geo d Hopkinton 1935-02-12 age 71yrs 1mos 17dys b Lancashire Eng 1863-12-26 child of BLETCHER Wm of England & JACKSON Mary of England Vol: 10 Page: 016

CLOUGH Levi Willard (Dr.) d Bellow Falls Vt 1935-02-15 age 71yrs 6mos 27dys b Hopkinton 1863-07-18 child of CLOUGH Moses T of Hopkinton & BEAN Mary of Candia Vol: 10 Page: 017

FOLLANSBEE Henry O d Weare 1935-02-24 age 69yrs 9mos 17dys b Dorchester child of FOLLANSBEE John & MUZZLY Seline Vol: 10 Page: 017

KIMBALL George A S d Concord 1935-03-23 age 75yrs 3mos 27dys b Boston Mass 1859-11-26 child of KIMBALL John Shakford of Boston Mass & STEVENS Mary E of Boston Mass Vol: 10 Page: 017

ST. HILAIRE Louis N d Hopkinton 1935-03-27 age 63yrs 10mos 12dys b Levis P Q 1871-05-15 child of ST. HILAIRE Louis N of Canada & THIBODEAU Marie of Canada Vol: 10 Page: 018

EDMUNDS Harvey d Plymouth 1935-03-26 age 93yrs 1mos 1dys b Hopkinton 1842-02-05 child of EDMUNDS Horace of Weare & CILLEY Bridget of Weare Vol: 10 Page: 018

BILLINGS Annie L d Hopkinton 1935-04-03 age 71yrs 8mos 12dys b Roxbury Mass 1863-07-21 child of FOX Edward & McDERMOT Mary of Mass Vol: 10 Page: 018

Hopkinton, NH Deaths 1914

HARDY Ida J d Concord 1935-04-02 age 75yrs 9mos 24dys b Contoocook 1859-06-08 child of HARDY Samuel A of Contoocook & PUTNEY Abbie Ann of Contoocook Vol: 10 Page: 019

ORDWAY Martha J d Hopkinton 1935-04-11 age 88yrs 4mos 10dys b Hopkinton 1841-12-01 child of CHASE Barrett of Hopkinton & MORRISON Lydia of Hopkinton Vol: 10 Page: 019

DEARBORN Alfred Howard d Concord 1935-04-17 age 59yrs 2mos 10dys b Hopkinton 1876-02-07 child of DEARBORN Lewis H of Epsom & FOLLANSBEE Elmira of Weare Vol: 10 Page: 019

SWEATT Edward C d Contoocook 1935-04-19 age 68yrs 7mos 29dys b Contoocook 1866-08-20 child of SWEATT John D & JONES May Vol: 10 Page: 020

STEVENS Nettie May d Hopkinton 1935-04-23 age 69yrs 9mos 18dys b Hopkinton 1865-07-05 child of RICHARDSON Thomas B of Deering & HARDY Eliza J of Michigian Vol: 10 Page: 020

ROBERTS Ellen Cuthbert d Hopkinton 1935-05-23 age 81yrs 6mos 0dys b Phil Pa 1853-11-23 child of ROBERTS Anthony C of Phil Pa & CHASE Ellen of Phil Pa Vol: 10 Page: 020

LOAN John M d Hopkinton 1935-05-26 age 74yrs 4mos 23dys b Waddington NY 1861-01-03 child of LOAN Wm. John of Ontario & McDONALD Eliza of Ontario Vol: 10 Page: 021

FELLOWS James Edward d Concord 1935-06-15 age 87yrs 6mos 1dys b Hopkinton 1858-01-14 child of FELLOWS Ignatius & COPPS Sarah Vol: 10 Page: 021

SULLIVAN Virginia May d Concord 1935-01-06 b Hopkinton 1935-01-06 child of SULLIVAN Homer A of Way Hills Canada & FRYE Dorie of Contoocook Vol: 10 Page: 021

WARREN Daniel d Hopkinton 1935-06-28 age 87yrs 19dys b East Fairfield Vt 1848-06-09 child of WARREN Joseph of East Fairfield Vt & LEWIS Sarah of East Fairfield Vt Vol: 10 Page: 022

GLEASBY Arthur d Manchester 1935-06-29 age 68yrs 4mos 28dys b Ipswich Mass 1867-02-01 child of GLEASBY Charles H of Haverhill Mass & BROWN Lillian M of Deerfield Vol: 10 Page: 022

FIFIELD Laura A d Hopkinton 1935-07-03 age 73yrs 11mos 25dys b Thornton 1861-07-07 child of BROWN Daniel of No Woodstock & ELKINS Laura of Thornton Vol: 10 Page: 022

DERRY Elvira Colby d Concord 1935-07-19 age 57yrs 9mos 22dys b Dunbarton 1877-09-27 child of PAGE Edson of Dunbarton & SIMONDS Mary of Goffstown Vol: 10 Page: 023

PUTNAM Almira * d Hopkinton 1924-10-27 b Hopkinton 1839-07-08 child of EASTMAN Jonathan of Hopkinton & KIMBALL Charlotte of Hopkinton Vol: 10 Page: 023 Note: correction in 1935

KIMBALL Theresa d Concord 1935-08-19 age 73yrs 6mos 29dys b Pittsfield 1862-01-21 child of GREENE Warren Vol: 10 Page: 023

MORGAN Wm Edgar d Hopkinton 1935-08-20 age 86yrs 1mos 18dys b Garndiffaith Eng 1849-07-02 child of MORGAN Soloman of Wales & DAVIES Jane of Wales Vol: 10 Page: 024

Hopkinton, NH Deaths 1914

BARRY William d Newton Mass 1935-09-01 age 5yrs 1mos 24dys b Hopkinton Vol: 10 Page: 024

CLARK Fred d Hopkinton 1935-09-06 age 80yrs 3mos 1dys b Hopkinton 1855-05-23 child of CLARK Benj of Hopkinton & KEEZER Mary A of Hopkinton Vol: 10 Page: 024

BROWN Reuben B d Waner 1935-08-31 age 58yrs 4mos 2dys b Dunbarton 1877-04-29 child of BROWN Elbridge C of Grafton & BARNARD Jennie L of Dunbarton Vol: 10 Page: 025

BOUTELLE Anna Kimber d Hopkinton 1935-09-11 age 54yrs 3mos 6dys b Winona Minn 1881-06-05 child of BOUTELLE Clarence M of Clinton & KIMBER Fannie of Barrytown NY Vol: 10 Page: 025

GRANT David Walter d Hopkinton 1935-11-08 age 73yrs 4mos 25dys b Somersworth 1862-06-14 child of GRANT Elizah of Somersworth & BURBANK Elizabeth of Maine Vol: 10 Page: 025

MELCHER Alice W d Contoocook 1935-11-25 age 49yrs 1mos 5dys b Hopkinton 1886-10-20 child of LIBBY Geo & KENISTON Estell Vol: 10 Page: 026

BAKER Philip d Concord 1935-11-12 age 52yrs 6mos 20dys b Newfoundland 1883-04-23 child of BAKER George of Newfoundland & WAY Martha of Newfoundland Vol: 10 Page: 026

ROBINSON Edward J d Hopkinton 1935-11-26 age 66yrs 9mos 4dys b Epping 1869-02-22 child of ROBINSON John of Haverhill Mass & ---- ---- of Haverhill Mass Vol: 10 Page: 026

MOUNT Francis A d Hopkinton 1935-12-07 age 81yrs 10mos 24dys b Berwick Me 1854-01-13 child of MOUNT Philip H of St Charles Canada & Henrietta M of Berwick Me Vol: 10 Page: 027

PAIGE Mary d Hopkinton 1935-12-12 age 58yrs 4mos 25dys b Portland Me 1877-06-17 child of HOWLEY Mathew of Ireland & LOW Sarah of Ireland Vol: 10 Page: 027

HOLMES Evangeline D d Warner 1935-12-17 age 82yrs 10mos 15dys b Hopkinton 1852-02-02 child of WEBBER Jewett of Hopkinton & ADAMS Sally Vol: 10 Page: 027

DALBY Peninnah Koon d Hopkinton 1936-01-13 age 53yrs 3mos 14dys b Auburn NY 1882-09-29 child of KOON Joseph of Felming NY & HOWELL Elizabeth of Auburn NY Vol: 10 Page: 029

DODGE Josephine d Hopkinton 1936-01-17 age 72yrs 10mos 10dys b Weareham Mass 1863-03-07 child of HOYT Benj of Henniker & REED Sarah C of Lakeville Mass Vol: 10 Page: 029

LOVEJOY Anna M d Hopkinton 1936-01-18 age 63yrs 11mos 6dys b So Royalton Vt 1872-02-12 child of LOVEJOY Arthur P of Littleton & COBURN Mary E of Smithfield RI Vol: 10 Page: 029

ELKINS Lydia Maria d Hopkinton 1936-01-19 age 69yrs 2mos 21dys b Canada 1866-10-28 child of ELKINS Mark L of Canada & HARDY Jane L of Canada Vol: 10 Page: 030

PARRY William W d Irvington NJ 1935-12-31 age 67yrs 8mos 8dys b Delta Penn 1868-04-23 child of PARRY William C of Wales & EVANS Catherine of Wales Vol: 10 Page: 030

Hopkinton, NH Deaths 1914

CURRIER Mabel N d Hopkinton 1936-01-26 age 67yrs 4mos 28dys b Hopkinton 1868-08-28 child of WHITEMORE William of Concord & RANDALL Nancy of Bradford Vol: 10 Page: 030

PAST Richard Taylor d Hopkinton 1936-01-31 age 63yrs 1mos 22dys b New York NY child of PAST Louis Richard of New York NY Vol: 10 Page: 031

BAILEY Ellen E d Hopkinton 1936-02-04 age 19dys b Hopkinton 1936-01-16 child of BAILEY Ralph G of Contoocook & CLARK Nellie V of Weare Vol: 10 Page: 031

CHASE Joseph Stanwood d Concord 1936-02-07 age 75yrs 10mos 7dys b Hopkinton 1860-03-12 child of CHASE Reginald H of Hopkinton & STANWOOD Susan of Hopkinton Vol: 10 Page: 031

SARGENT Walter Harriman d Hopkinton 1936-02-15 age 40yrs 8mos 21dys b Harriman Tenn 1895-05-24 child of SARGENT Frank H of Andover & COLBY Grace of Manchester Vol: 10 Page: 032

CURRIER Charles D d Concord 1936-02-20 age 75yrs 1mos 15dys b Manchester 1861-01-04 child of CURRIER Charles of Manchester Vol: 10 Page: 032

BLANCHETTE Harvey d Hopkinton 1936-02-26 age 1mos 17dys b Hopkinton 1936-01-09 child of BLANCHETTE Philip of Goffstown & CLARK Eveline of Hopkinton Vol: 10 Page: 032

SEVERANCE William d Concord 1936-02-27 age 5 hsdys b Concord 1936-02-27 child of SEVERANCE Archie of Hopkinton & GAGNE Adian of Suncook Vol: 10 Page: 033

PERRY James M d Contoocook 1936-04-03 age 81yrs 2mos 11dys b Hopkinton 1855-01-04 child of PERRY William P of Hopkinton & MORGAN Elizabeth of Salisbury Vol: 10 Page: 033

COOPER Herbert D d Hopkinton 1936-04-05 age 62yrs 10mos 4dys b Concord 1873-09-21 child of COOPER Joseph of Sunapee & POWELL Augusta of Concord Vol: 10 Page: 033

MILLS Fred Wilaim d Hopkinton 1936-04-13 age 73yrs 16dys b Boscawenn 1863-03-27 child of MILLS Joseph of Maine & GETCHEL Mary of Salisbury Vol: 10 Page: 034

KAY James d Boscawen 1936-04-10 age 57yrs Vol: 10 Page: 034

THOMPSON Baby d Concord 1936-04-26 b Concord 1936-04-26 child of THOMPSON Broownlow of Osceola Iowa & RICE Margaret of Everett Washington Vol: 10 Page: 035

CLIFFORD Mary Gertrude d Contoocook 1936-05-24 age 47yrs 8mos 13dys b Lowell Mass 1888-09-11 child of McCAFFREY John F of Ireland & FLYNN Margaret of New Haven Ct Vol: 10 Page: 035

COOPER Clarence d Boscawen 1936-05-25 age 22yrs Vol: 10 Page: 035

COLBY Mary E d Webster 1936-05-27 age 67yrs 4mos 14dys Vol: 10 Page: 036

MONTGOMERY Eliza J d Hopkinton 1936-05-28 age 79yrs 3mos 28dys b Warner 1857-02-01 child of DUNBAR J N & BRUCE Mary J Vol: 10 Page: 036

FANCY Eli d Concord 1936-06-08 age 72yrs 7mos 7dys b Chelsea NY 1863-10-31 child of FANCY Levi of New York & BOLAVAR Lucy of New York Vol: 10 Page: 036

DUVAL Matilda d Hopkinton 1936-06-13 age 76yrs 1mos 4dys b Canada 1860-05-09 child of OBIN Peter of Canada & GEBO Elizabeth of Plattsburg Vol: 10 Page: 037

UNDERWOOD Sanford Lewis d Pavilion NY 1936-04-01 age 34yrs 10mos 23dys Vol: 10 Page: 037

MURRAY Sarah d Contoocook 1936-07-14 age 77yrs 8mos 29dys b Nova Scotia 1858-10-15 child of ---- ---- of Nova Scotia & Jane of Nova Scotia Vol: 10 Page: 039

DEARBORN Elvira d Hopkinton 1936-06-24 age 86yrs 3mos 7dys b Weare 1850-03-07 child of FOLLANSBEE Jesse of Weare & MELVIN Mary of Weare Vol: 10 Page: 039

DUNBAR Jennie Stevens d Henniker 1936-07-23 age 85yrs 2mos 21dys b Stoneham Mass 1851-05-02 child of EASTMAN George of Warner & BUTMAN Mary of Stoneham Mass Vol: 10 Page: 039

COOPER George Edw d Concord 1936-06-24 age 29yrs 6mos 16dys b Hopkinton 1906-12-08 child of COOPER Clarence & CROCKETT Lena Vol: 10 Page: 038

JENKINS ---- d Concord 1936-06-25 b Concord 1936-06-25 child of JENKINS Carroll R of Warner & GARLAND Grace of Tilton Vol: 10 Page: 038

PAIGE Frank W d Concord 1936-07-04 age 83yrs 6mos 26dys b Hopkinton 1852-12-09 child of PAIGE John W of Dunbarton & BERRY Elizabeth of Concord Vol: 10 Page: 038

WELLMAN Marcus Burton d Concord 1936-09-09 age 59yrs 3mos 4dys b Manchester 1877-06-05 child of WELLMAN Marcus of Morrill Maine & BROWN Emma Louise Vol: 10 Page: 040

EMERSON Nellie F d Hopkinton 1936-09-14 age 74yrs 11mos 7dys b Turner Me 1861-10-07 child of KIMBALL B F & RICHARDSON Diantha Vol: 10 Page: 040

DUSTIN ---- d Laconia 1936-09-01 b Laconia 1936-09-01 child of DUSTIN E H of Contoocook & NICHOLS Rosampond of Kennibunkport Me Vol: 10 Page: 040

PEASELL Charles H d Hopkinton 1936-09-22 age 76yrs 11mos 19dys b Weare 1859-10-03 child of PEASELL Robert of Hopkinton & DODGE Persi of New Boston Vol: 10 Page: 041

KENNEY Benjamin Frankli d Concord 1936-09-27 age 77yrs 7mos 10dys b Braintree Vt 1859-02-07 child of KINNEY Andrew J of Mass & REED Sarah of Brookfield Vt Vol: 10 Page: 041

BURNHAM Walter N d Concord 1936-09-28 age 74yrs 11mos 5dys b Hopkinton 1861-10-23 child of BURNHAM J M of Hopkinton & MARSTON Emma F of So Deerfield Vol: 10 Page: 041

BOYCE Alice C d Franklin 1936-10-04 age 78yrs 6mos 18dys b Concord 1858-03-26 child of ORDWAY Jacob of Concord & MOSHER Judith Vol: 10 Page: 042

BALL Carrie B d Hopkinton 1936-10-15 age 77yrs 4mos 21dys b Antrim 1859-05-24 child of BROOKS Joseph of Maine & VENING Betsy of Maint Vol: 10 Page: 042

BALL Sumner N d Hopkinton 1936-10-18 age 82yrs 4mos 14dys b Washington 1854-06-04 child of BALL Dexter Vol: 10 Page: 042

PERRY William P d West Newton Mass 1936-10-27 age 75yrs 1mos 1dys Vol: 10 Page: 043

Hopkinton, NH Deaths 1914

PIERCE Charles d Cambridge Mass 1936-10-30 age 48yrs Vol: 10 Page: 043

BROWN ---- d Concord 1936-11-29 b Concord 1936-11-29 child of BROWN J Daniel of Contoocook & SARGENT Eveline of Roxbury Mass Vol: 10 Page: 043

MORTON Julia F d Hopkinton 1936-11-12 age 86yrs b Cambridge Mass child of KING Samuel A of Acworth & LANE Sarah A of Maine Vol: 10 Page: 044

COLBY Walter H d Worcester Mass 1936-11-05 age 88yrs child of COLBY Samuel of NH & FLANDERS Louise A of NH Vol: 10 Page: 044

EDDY Nellie A d Hopkinton 1936-12-06 age 60yrs 2mos 1dys b Oakham Mass 1876-10-05 child of CRAWFORD Henry & SIBLEY Ellen Vol: 10 Page: 044

DUNBAR Eugene E d Hopkinton 1936-12-05 age 72yrs 6mos 17dys b Hopkinton 1864-05-18 child of DUNBAR Elmer B of Grantham & WEBBER Ann of Mass Vol: 10 Page: 045

DOWNING Emma M d Lancaster Mass 1936-12-11 age 80yrs 22dys Vol: 10 Page: 045

CLOUGH Sylvia E d Hopkinton 1936-12-24 age 79yrs 23dys b Hopkinton 1857-12-01 child of CLOUGH Charles F of Hopkinton & HARDY Mary J of Warner Vol: 10 Page: 045

FLADD Philip d Hopkinton 1936-12-30 age 54yrs 7mos 29dys b Philadelphia Pa 1882-05-01 child of FLADD Philip J of Germany & HOELZLE Barbara of Germany Vol: 10 Page: 046

GUILD Fred J d Sandford Me 1936-12-21 age 66yrs 7mos 23dys b Hopkinton 1870-04-28 child of GUILD Royal E of Hartford Vt & STORY Abbie of Hopkinton Vol: 10 Page: 046

METRO Costa d Concord 1936-11-20 age 60yrs b Allbania 1876 child of METRO Spiro of Albania & JANAQ Evangeline of Albania Vol: 10 Page: 046

PERRIN Weston George d Concord 1936-12-28 age 17yrs 1mos 25dys b Concord 1919-11-03 child of PERRIN Wm G of Bucksport Me & LYNA Addie of Concord Vol: 10 Page: 047

BARTON Roy F d Hopkinton 1937-01-04 age 2mos 4dys b Hopkinton 1936-10-31 child of BARTON Leslie C of Concord & SEVERANCE Isabelle of East Washington Vol: 10 Page: 048

KIMBALL Mary E (Martha) d Hopkinton 1937-01-05 age 76yrs 4mos 28dys b Webster 1860-08-04 child of WEBBER Horatio & BURBANK Amanda of Webster Vol: 10 Page: 048

JAMESON Nellie M d Lowell Mass 1937-01-27 age 74yrs 4mos 8dys Vol: 10 Page: 048

CLARK Susie C d Hopkinton 1937-02-06 age 52yrs 5mos 13dys b Antrim 1884-08-21 child of CLARK Harry of Antrim & DAY Mary of Salem Vol: 10 Page: 049

DAVIS Willie N d Contoocook 1937-03-01 age 75yrs 9mos 13dys b Warner 1862-05-18 child of DAVIS Paine & BABOCK Esther Vol: 10 Page: 049

BRADOCK Florence D d Concord 1937-03-01 age 36yrs 3mos 29dys b Maine 1900-11-02 Vol: 10 Page: 049

FISK Delta E d Claremont 1937-02-27 age 72yrs 5mos 12dys b Contoocook 1864-09-15 child of CHANDLER Horatio of Hopkinton & CURRIER Susan V of Hopkinton Vol: 10 Page: 050

CONVERSE Alice Leota d Contoocook 1937-03-07 age 52yrs 7mos 5dys b Stillwater Me 1884-08-02 child of McKAY Roscoe of Stillwater Me & Evelyn of Amherst Me Vol: 10 Page: 050

DOHERTY Margaret d Contoocook 1937-03-13 age 65yrs 8mos b Ebbsfleet P E Q child of MOKLER Richard of Canada & RYAN Johann of Ireland Vol: 10 Page: 050

LOWE Edward E d Hopkinton 1937-03-13 age 80yrs 10mos 3dys b Windsor 1856-05-10 child of LOWE Fred M of Greefield & MESSINGER Anna H of Stoddard Vol: 10 Page: 051

PIERCE Alma Etta d Greenfield Mass 1937-03-24 age 83yrs 0mos 21dys b Hyde Park Vt child of SULLIVAN Jonas of Hyde Park Vt & MacKINISTRY Matilda of Glascow Scotland Vol: 10 Page: 051

MIGNAULT Albert M d Webster 1937-03-26 age 71yrs 1mos 11dys Vol: 10 Page: 051

UNDERWOOD Sanford Lewis d Pavilian NY 1936-04-01 age 34yrs 10mos 23dys b West Pittston Pa 1902-05-08 child of UNDERWOOD Sanford of Pittston Pa & LEWIS Virginia of Pa Vol: 10 Page: 052

HASELTON Fred Bailey d Hopkinton 1936-05-14 age 66yrs 1mos 25dys child of HASELTON William of Dunbarton & BAILEY Susan of Dunbarton Vol: 10 Page: 052

SPAULDING Anna Louise d Hopkinton 1936-06-04 age 61yrs 10mos 7dys b Concord 1874-07-28 child of LONG Moses Edivin & RUNNELLS Elmira of Concord Vol: 10 Page: 052

BAILEY Charles William d Hill 1937-05-12 age 54yrs 2mos 1dys b Warner 1885-03-11 child of BAILEY Eugene of Danville & BROWN Maria I of Contoocook Vol: 10 Page: 053

DOHERTY John J d Concord 1937-04-03 age 66yrs b Hopkinton Vol: 10 Page: 053

SMITH Harry d Sonora Calif 1937-02-11 age 82yrs Vol: 10 Page: 053

EARLE Clarence E d Hopkinton 1937-06-10 age 71yrs 4mos 14dys b Concord 1866-01-26 child of EARLE Harold of Windsor Vt Vol: 10 Page: 054

ROBARE Chas d Hopkinton 1937-07-04 age 80yrs 8mos 14dys b Keesville NY 1856-10-19 Vol: 10 Page: 054

WHITTAKER Olive M d Hopkinton 1937-07-04 age 81yrs 7mos 20dys b Salisbury 1855-11-11 child of WHITTAKER Thomas H of Atkinson & Roby of Bow Vol: 10 Page: 054

CATE Rodney Austin d Concord 1937 age 5mos 13dys b Hopkinton Vol: 10 Page: 055

CHASE Florence L d Hopkinton 1937-07-20 age 77yrs 4dys b Manchester 1860-07-17 child of SPAULDING Dustin G of Manchester & PUTNEY Samanthe of Webster Vol: 10 Page: 055

CURRIER Willie A d Hopkinton 1937-07-21 age 76yrs 7mos 16dys b Hopkinton 1860-12-05 child of CURRIER Lozaro of Hopkinton & ANDERSON Anna of Brgholm Sweden Vol: 10 Page: 055

BOYCE Harley A d Franklin 1937-07-24 age 48yrs 11mos 4dys b Hopkinton 1888-08-20 child of BOYCE Melzer D of Penacook & ORDWAY Alice C of Concord Vol: 10 Page: 056

Hopkinton, NH Deaths 1914

BURNHAM Mabel Rosalie d Hinsdale 1937-07-27 age 65yrs 7mos 27dys Vol: 10 Page: 056

ENGEL Fiesco d Contoocook 1937-08-02 age 76yrs 7mos 11dys b Lakeport 1860-11-22 child of ENGEL John of Germany & HARRINGTON Mary of Cork Ireland Vol: 10 Page: 056

GRIFFIN Alvah Clement d Hyannis Mass 1937-07-30 age 19yrs Vol: 10 Page: 057

YOUNG Harrie M d Contoocook 1937-08-20 age 70yrs 10mos 24dys b Manchester 1866-09-26 Vol: 10 Page: 057

CORSER David S d Contoocook 1937-08-27 age 90yrs 21dys b Webster 1847-08-06 child of CORSER Freeman & CROWELL Harriet Vol: 10 Page: 057

SYMONDS Grace H d Brentwood 1937-08-29 age 48yrs 4mos 18dys Vol: 10 Page: 058

CORBETT Peter Wilson d St Paul Minn 1900-08-31 age 34yrs 6mos 19dys b Edinburg Scotland 1866-01-12 child of John Vol: 10 Page: 058

DEVEREAUX Richard F d Boston Mass 1937-10-23 age 53yrs 4mos 20dys b Georgetown P E Q 1848-06-03 Vol: 10 Page: 058

FLANDERS Archie d Contoocook 1937-09-03 age 72yrs 27dys b Canada 1865-08-07 child of FLANDERS Thomas B of Warner & SPAULDING Rhoda of Warner Vol: 10 Page: 059

NORRIS Eula B d Concord 1937-09-03 age 52yrs 2mos 15dys b Derby Vt 1885-06-18 child of NORRIS George W of Derby Vt & HALL Ida E of Landaff Vt Vol: 10 Page: 059

SANBORN John C d Contoocook 1937-08-16 age 61yrs 10mos 13dys b Reading Mass 1875-10-03 child of SANBORN Charles F of Boscawen & COLBY Jennie E of Salisbury Vol: 10 Page: 059

COVILLE William H d Concord 1937-09-20 age 80yrs 9mos 8dys b Quincy Mass 1856-12-12 child of COVILLE William of Boston Mass & Mary of Boston Mass Vol: 10 Page: 060

MERRILL Frank d Plymouth 1937-09-25 age 85yrs 8mos 10dys b Warner 1852-01-15 child of MERRILL Steven A & HOLMES Miria Vol: 10 Page: 060

MARCY Mildred F Baker d Northfield Mass 1937-10-21 age 49yrs 2mos Vol: 10 Page: 061 Note: a correction in 1943

DEARBORN Sadie (Smith) d Grafton Mass 1937-10-20 age 83yrs 0mos 25dys b Hopkinton Vol: 10 Page: 061

HACKETT George A d Contoocook 1937-09-09 age 70yrs 8mos b Contoocook 1867-01-09 child of HACKETT Warren T of Henniker & SCRIBNER Ellen of Vt Vol: 10 Page: 061

HOLLAND Cornelia D d Concord 1908-06-14 b Hopkinton Vol: 10 Page: 062

PRESBY Myron d Hopkinton 1937-11-05 age 55yrs 4mos 1dys b Bradford 1882-07-04 child of PRESBY Henry F of New Boston & COLBY Lizzie of Bradford Vol: 10 Page: 062

HOYT James d Hopkinton 1937-11-07 age 78yrs 8mos 19dys b Wareham Mass 1859-02-15 child of HOYT Benjamin J of Hopkinton & REED Sarah of New Bedford Mass Vol: 10 Page: 062

MILLS Mary d Haverhill Mass 1937-11-29 age 64yrs 9mos 12dys Vol: 10 Page: 063

Hopkinton, NH Deaths 1914

BLANCHARD Sadie R d Hopkinton 1937-12-04 age 56yrs 3mos 6dys b Gloucester Mass 1881-08-28 child of RICHARDSON Edward Vol: 10 Page: 063

CHASE Ruth G d Hopkinton 1937-12-15 age 76yrs 1mos 11dys b Chicago Ill 1861-11-04 child of CHASE Samuel of Hopkinton & THOMPSON Emma of No Hampton Mass Vol: 10 Page: 063

SURNAME INDEX

BLAIR, 280 298
BLAISDELL, 14 148 306 312 332 333
BLAKE, 30 78 110 142 180 195 200 210
    211 220 230 270 276 278 311 332 338
    342 344
BLAKEY, 240
BLANCHARD, 11 28 60 74 79 146 188 194
    213 214 228 243 247 255 261 281 294
    303 325 337 355
BLANCHETT, 288
BLANCHETTE, 223 224 230 231 233 234
    236 238 240 242 254 257 258 259 261
    262 268 272 275 277 289 296 337 350
BLANDING, 102 331
BLANKHORN, 268
BLASDEL, 3
BLATCHER, 232
BLETCHER, 230 233 244 295 317 324 347
BLISS, 301 333
BLODGETT, 76
BLONDIN, 326
BLOOD, 180 185 200 210 247 346
BLUE, 276
BODEN, 301
BODWELL, 172 205 220
BODY, 164
BOHAN, 299
BOHANA, 294
BOHANAN, 138 216 222 223 228 229 231
    234 240 255 260 261 277 292 294 296
    299 302 303 314 319 345
BOHANON, 139 256
BOHMAN, 230
BOHONAN, 4 14 24 26 30 77 80 90 106
    110 112 130 133 134 135 139 140 142
    156 158 168 176 179 182 197 215 224
    235 246 248 251 253 258 326
BOHONANA, 216
BOISNNETT, 301
BOISVERT, 301
BOLAVAR, 350
BOLIVAR, 237 240 345
BOLIVER, 282 283
BOMAN, 230
BOMBARD, 221
BOMES, 229
BOND, 136
BOOTH, 289 326
BORDEN, 96 118
    214 344
BOSLIN?, 169
BOSSI, 199
BOSSIE, 199

BOUTELLE, 92 96 142 155 161 180 188
    204 349
BOUTILIER, 224
BOUTILL, 69
BOUTWELL, 22 30 89 103 104 123 126
    127 128 131 133 134 135 138 162 169
    170 175 176 187 194 195 197 199 204
    229 231 245 252 266 267 270 271 310
    316 323 344
BOWAN, 149
BOWDOIN, 310
BOWER, 186
BOWERS, 280
BOWLES, 328
BOWLEY, 283
BOWMAN, 87 179
BOYCE, 27 114 123 128 130 138 181 192
    198 212 216 246 248 253 254 273 334
    351 353
BOYD, 319 321
BOYNTON, 8 9 137 193 215 235 236 239
    250 253 255 261 267 271 280 315 332
    335 336
BRACKETT, 258 280 307
BRADBURY, 138 175 184 195 246 297 332
BRADOCK, 352
BRALEY, 227
BRANCH, 267
BRASSAU, 236 245
BRAYTON, 294
BREAD, 7
BREEN, 211
BRENNAN, 309
BRENNELL, 280
BRICKET, 27
BRIDGMAN, 106
BRIEE, 330
BRIGGS, 189 248
BRILL, 236
BROAD, 335
BROCKWAY, 20 30 73 79 148 170 181 294
    305 308 339
BROOKS, 223 265 285 312 351
BROUGHTON, 159
BROWELL, 27
BROWER, 298
BROWN, 2 4 5 7 10 14 16 17 20 21 22 25
    27 30 31 60 61 62 65 72 78 81 88 91 92
    93 100 101 104 105 110 114 115 116
    120 121 123 126 127 129 132 133 134
    137 138 139 146 149 151 153 155 156
    158 159 160 161 163 167 168 169 174
    175 179 180 182 183 185 187 188 191

DEINER, 290
DELANEY, 12 298
DELIA, 139
DELINO, 100 287
DELL, 117
DEMARS, 282
DEMERIT, 232
DEMERITT, 237
DEMERRIT, 320
DEMERRITT, 236
DEMETT, 330
DEMICK, 149
DEMMICK, 62
DEMOUPIED, 297
DEMSMORE, 224
DENEY, 234
DENNETT, 288
DENNIS, 268 273
DENOVAN, 280
DENSMORE, 109 121 145 192 196 215 220
    221 224 231 233 234 241 253 270 277
    324 333
DENY, 325
DERBY, 275
DERRICK, 61
DERRING, 270
DERRY, 37 84 97 135 140 209 229 230 231
    235 237 238 276 294 334 348
DESMOND, 60
DETTE, 215
DEVEREAUX, 354
DEVEREUX, 292 343 344
DEVINE, 235 239 280
DEVOID, 303
DEWART, 291
DEWOLFE, 202
DEXTER, 232 285 301
DIAMOND, 5 37 99 106
    160 325 326
DICKEY, 142
DILLISON, 321
DIMAN, 347
DIMERETTE, 340
DIMICK, 307
DIMIN, 251
DIMOND, 211
DINMAN, 278
DINSMORE, 201
DISCONOFF, 242
DIXON, 328
DOCKHAM, 230 233
    317 321 324
DOCKMAN, 232

DODGE, 2 8 37 67 79 89 95 115 135 137
    141 143 149 150 151 154 160 167 170
    177 179 180 183 195 200 203 209 248
    282 290 295 305 315 322 329 330 345
    347 349 351
DOHERTY, 277 353
DOLE, 105 151 338
DOLLOF, 279
DOLLOFF, 157 193
DONALDSON, 180
DONELL, 113
DONNELLY, 273
DONOVAN, 232
DONY, 232
DOOLEY, 275
DOPHNY, 298
DORA, 115
DORION, 137
DORR, 79
DORREY, 231 237
DORRY, 234 236 320 330 340
DOTY, 186 321 332
DOUSE, 123
DOW, 1 4 7 10 14 15 16 19 20 22 27 37 57
    59 64 72 73 75 82 83 88 89 91 92 94 95
    99 101 102 103 109 110 112 116 117
    130 139 142 143 144 146 149 165 166
    167 168 171 177 178 179 180 181 194
    196 198 199 204 205 209 212 213 216
    218 219 251 273 318 320 325 328 334
    335 336
DOWLIN, 298
DOWN, 70
DOWNER, 147 202 311
DOWNES, 37 104 195 222 235 243 244 257
    260 296 303
DOWNEY, 269
DOWNING, 2 22 37 83 87 96 121 124 126
    145 160 179 183 194 328 352
DOWNS, 15 37 79 93 200 219 255 257 284
    303
DOYEN, 201 217
DOYING, 105 110 173 221 266 306 315
DRAKE, 101 160 199
DRAPER, 274
DREW, 37 230 298 339
DRISCALL, 287
DROINCE, 286
DROUIN, 245
DROWN, 69 201 229 240 253 254 255 256
    257 342
DROWNER, 289
DROWNS, 233

DRUMIN, 198
DUCAT, 266
DUCHARME, 110
DUCLOS, 236 237 239 334
DUGAN, 288
DUKE, 163
DUNBAR, 1 11 18 20 21 27 37 38 58 66 87
    95 98 102 103 104 121 123 124 127 128
    130 131 135 147 149 162 169 170 187
    189 191 200 207 221 223 271 273 283
    317 323 324 326 335 336 350 351 352
DUNCAN, 332
DUNHAM, 240 302
DUNLAP, 241
DUNLOP, 344
DUNN, 134 228 231 291 334
DUNNING, 296
DURELL, 327
DURGIN, 17 19 57 121 129 140
DURIAN, 212
DURNIN, 136 138 211 248
DURRELL, 6
DUSTIN, 5 6 7 19 23 59 63 64 75 87 89 109
    112 116 124 127 130 132 138 142 143
    144 145 151 164 165 172 180 181 192
    194 196 201 204 206 218 219 221 224
    230 251 254 260 272 302 303 310 312
    324 328 330 332 334 342 345 347 351
DUSTIN??, 177
DUSTON, 100 125 128 138 161 170 193
    272 278
DUTTON, 116 118 166 217 316
DUVAL, 296 351
DWINELLS, 38 92 95 105 112 123 139 146
    155 158 159 169 203 234
DWINELS, 230
DWININ, 179
DWINNELL, 250 307
DWINNELLS, 4 5 14 38 65 69 85 87 89 113
    114 117 118 132 134 135 137 155 174
    180 182 185 189 210 219 222 227 229
    235 241 242 245 247 249 267 269 270
    277 301 306 307 326 344
DYER, 201 323
EACOTT, 310
EAGLE, 258
EAGLES, 258
EARLE, 342 347 353
EASTMAN, 1 10 12 23-4 28 38 79 96 99
    104-5 121 125 129 133 145 146 151 155
    158 167 170 176 178 181 187 192 201
    206 209 210 246 276 279 280 296 297
    305 309 312 315 324 330 341 348 351

EASTMANA, 327
EATON, 3 18 20 38 64 69 73 84 94 106 141
    145 148 149 156 160 167 168 176 177
    198 199 204 216 230 261 266 296 297
    305 333 338
EDDY, 174 242 243 244 352
EDGERLY, 209 322 337
EDITH, 301
EDLER, 273
EDMMUNDS, 75
EDMUNDS, 21 38 75 80 81 106 170 188
    206 222 301 308 317 330 347
EDWARDS, 28
ELA, 94 152 332
ELAE, 152
ELAET, 152
ELAETC, 152
ELDER, 219 311 325 331
ELIE, 222
ELIOTT, 16
ELKINS, 3 104 138 156 160 187 193 195
    196 203 211 212 215 246 247 252 257
    274 314 319 338 348 349
ELLENWOOD, 296
ELLINWOOD, 199 223 314 319 342
ELLIOT, 3 38 79 80 326
ELLIOTT, 17 22 25 38 39 80 87 98 103 113
    119 128 131 134 135 145 146 147 157
    161 163 169 178 185 186 191 194 200
    201 205 206 212 214 216 217 219 221
    231 246 247 249 250 253 255 256 258
    260 263 268 274 275 276 279 283 286
    305 319 328 332 336 337 341 344
ELLIS, 104 214 282 292
ELLSWORTH, 102 192
ELSWORTH, 201
ELVIRA, 294
ELWOOD, 100
EMERSON, 8 12 39 62 67 72 76 89 92 99
    106 111 114 118 131 140 150 158 160
    182 190 192 194 202 204 206 210 214
    228 229 230 234 235 238 242 249 260
    265 268 269 272 275 278 280 281 308
    309 310 313 315 316 319 322 325 326
    329 340 342 343 351
EMERTON, 316
EMERY, 185 240 274 332 340 341
EMMERSON, 149
EMMONS, 274
EMORY, 333
ENCOTT, 19
ENGEL, 242 354
ERICSON, 170

ESKRIDGE, 279
ESSEX, 295
ESTEY, 242 245
ESTOW, 24
ESTY, 245
ETCHELLS, 282
EVANS, 1 11 17 18 39 74 81 133 174 182 184 204 253 312 349
EVENS, 11
EVERETT, 6 68
EVERETTE, 74
EYMAN, 247
FABIAN, 282
FACKENTHAL, 135
FADESO??, 111
FAGAN, 39 81 84 122 147 151 162 189 194 204 294 309
FAIRBANKS, 8
FAIRFIELD, 171
FANCY, 350
FANEUFF, 342
FANNIE, 257
FARLEY, 177 183 343
FARMER, 244 295
FARNHAM, 231 234 237 242 272 281 323
FARNSWORTH, 66
FARNUM, 57 148 163 172 230 232 260
FARRAR, 242 244
FARRILL, 114 116
FARRINGTON, 72 179 192 322
FAVOR, 215
FEELY, 210
FELCH, 2 3 15 23 25 84 110 112 146 158 184 267 306 308 332 337
FELLOWS, 26 39 62 89 147 166 187 198 204 205 206 239 286 305 313 316 320 333 344 348
FELMING, 182 260
FELTIS, 238 278
FELTON, 155 171
FEMINGTON, 3
FENIO??, 333
FENNER, 114
FENTON, 187 193 247 313 314
FERGERSON, 339
FERGUSON, 269
FERNALD, 192
FERRIN, 39 60 110 311
FERRINGTON, 58
FERRON, 10
FEST, 280 282
FIELD, 129 239 281
FIELDS, 230

FIFIELD, 75 102 129 181 201 215 259 309 348
FINLEY, 89
FINNO, 274
FISH, 90 106 120 174 180 310
FISHER, 98 99 163 190 210 323 346
FISK, 4 20 26 27 39 63 71 72 89 92 102 132 133 134 142 163 176 180 188 190 196 214 245 249 272 278 309 312 324 341 347 352
FISKE, 117 122 147 179 201 205 222 288
FITCH, 75 94 143 154 194
FITTS, 127 131 133 134 162 195 235 245 250 252 253 270 278 346 347
FITZ, 11
FLAD, 302
FLADD, 352
FLAGG, 255 267
FLAKE, 279
FLAMAND, 237
FLAMMAND, 238
FLANDER, 201
FLANDERS, 1 4 7 9 10 16 19 24 27 39 40 62 64 65 67 75 76 78 82 83 88 89 90 94 97 99 101 102 104 113 114 115 118 121 130 133 136 137 141 142 147 149 152 154 160 162 164 165 171 172 173 175 179 180 181 182 187 188 190 191 192 196 197 199 200 201 202 203 205 206 210 212 217 227 228 229 230 232 237 238 246 248 250 258 260 268 280 281 282 285 286 294 305 307 308 310 311 312 313 315 320 323 324 329 330 334 335 336 338 341 342 343 345 352 354
FLANDES, 104
FLANIGAN, 12
FLATHER, 216
FLATHERS, 216 250 327
FLEMIMING, 310
FLEMING, 132 137 200 211 253 255 258 296
FLEMMING, 138 277
FLETCHER, 172 193 235 236 282
FLEWELLIN, 297
FLEWELLING, 297
FLINT, 19 103 154 176 218 347
FLOID, 177
FLOYD, 242 244 338
FLYNN, 293 350
FOGG, 64 77 182 214 233
FOGGS, 40
FOLANSBEE, 284
FOLEY, 236 283 290

FOLLANSBEE, 16 104 192 203 347 348 351
FOLSMON, 167
FOLSOM, 172 180 339
FOOT, 143
FOOTE, 105 130 132 134 136 138 176 184 192 249 288 300
FORD, 94 213 279 286 300 326
FORSAITH, 299
FORSIE, 295
FORSYTH, 280
FOSS, 6 12 18 40 63 87 90 109 139 146 173 192 193 209 251 289 314
FOSTER, 63 77 88 93 178 179 210 211 231 262 280 283 286 288 311 319
FOWLE, 293
FOWLER, 70 101 167 191 192 223 224 228 229 235 246 248 249 250 258 260 270 272 277 280 284 302 324 327
FOX, 308 347
FRANKLYLN, 192
FRANKLYN, 217
FRAZER, 83 332
FRAZIER, 9 92 134 143 145 149 151 163 216 332 335
FREDERICK, 303
FREESE, 298
FRENCH, 7 8 18 20 21 23 26 27 40 41 66 68 70 71 73 77 80 83 87 89 90 96 97 99 102 105 109 110 114 119 122 126 131 142 143 144 147 148 149 150 151 155 156 163 170 176 179 183 189 197 199 213 216 223 241 247 250 251 267 272 273 282 283 289 292 293 300 307 310 320 321 323 329 341 342 343 345
FRONIE, 327
FROST, 23 41 57 58 199 240 298 328
FRY, 166 283
FRYE, 71 76 80 143 206 216 235 254 283 348
FULER, 3
FULLER, 2 3 6 20 26 41 71 83 109 112 118 121 136 138 152 156 161 179 192 200 206 207 211 215 217 218 244 246 249 252 253 257 258 269 270 293 303 316 325 337 341
FULTON, 287 308
GAGE, 41 59 74 81 95 123 143 156 157 160 161 162 170 190 223 276 292
GAGNE, 244 350
GAGNON, 222 241 242 293
GALE, 41 71 88 155 210 311
GANDWELL, 279

GARDNER, 167 184 221 316
GARLAND, 218 221 245 302 351
GARRABAUDT, 143
GARVIN, 133
GATES, 57
GATLEY, 11
GAUDET, 288
GAULT, 261
GAUTHIER, 137
GEBO, 351
GEER, 214 231 233 236 247 254 257 288 298 313
GEORGE, 2 20 41 73 83 117 160 166 187 194 198 214 218 241 243 245 246 281 286 289 292 294 297 326 343
GEORGETTE, 275
GERISH, 3 152
GERRISH, 30 80 99 147 183 187 190 207 315
GETCHEL, 106 116 156 210 211 350
GETCHELL, 16 136 154
GETCHILL, 99
GIBBONS, 282
GIBSON, 10 172 314
GIDDINGS, 250
GIENTY, 171
GIGUERE, 237 238
GILBERT, 57 74 115 245 291 292
GILCHRIST, 25 217 250
GILE, 3 41 133 183 274
GILES, 272
GILL, 57 287
GILLINGHAM, 238 243 261 278 286 294 295 339
GILLINGHAMA, 261
GILLIS, 219
GILMAN, 7 9 15 53 78 128 164 206 243 252
GILMORE, 169 206 277 317 322
GILNES, 101
GINN, 161
GIRARD, 346
GIRDLY, 18
GITCHEL, 151
GLANVILLE, 235 239 280 336
GLASIER, 231 258 260 263 319
GLAWSON, 28
GLAYDIA, 280
GLAZIER, 253 255
GLEASBY, 348
GLEASON, 112 119 211
GLIDDEN, 187 193 195 203 211
GLINES, 101 113

GLOVER, 9 286
GLYNN, 277
GODWIN, 300
GOLD, 202
GOLDSTONE, 339
GOLDWAITE, 334
GOMES, 229 231 269 314 320
GOOD, 274
GOODHUE, 70 74 98 100 154 228 266 320
GOODNOW, 6
GOODRICH, 1 2 5 11 13 26 41 42 61 64 95
    109 141 173 182 232 260 269 271 289
    300 313 329
GOODRICK, 109 300
GOODSPEED, 1 42 77 106 184 196 333
GOODWIN, 24 42 90 102 105 127 128 130
    132 142 174 175 177 183 218 230 232
    235 243 246 261 267 300 313 321 332
GOOLY??, 287
GOORICH, 269
GORDEN, 75 203
GORDON, 174 265 277
GORMAN, 92 139 189
GOSS, 3 190 329
GOUGH, 258 308
GOUL, 138
GOULD, 16 42 61 77 84 105 110 122 142
    158 177 178 179 201 239 240 346
GOVE, 22 28 133 134 139 142 144 149 161
    322 324 327
GRACE, 228 229 232 266 299
GRAHAM, 185 222 240 297
GRAHAMA, 221
GRANT, 261 291 303 319 339 349
GRAVES, 235 237 303
GRAY, 76 137 173 180 183 213 237 243
    316
GRAZIANO, 243 244 292
GRAZINO, 240
GREELEY, 7 14 24 149 339
GREELEY??, 287
GREELY, 151 341
GREEN, 4 5 42 64 72 88 91 99 109 111 119
    205 214 232 302 322 328
GREEN??, 202
GREENE, 27 42 61 77 88 91 109 111 119
    120 151 156 161 172 206 265 311 318
    348
GREENEY, 136
GREENLAND, 132
GREENLEAF, 82 191 202 222 267
GREENLIE, 5
GREENLY, 230 233

GREENOUGH, 74
GREENWOOD, 174 318
GREER, 92 265
GREGG, 106 115 186 318
GRIFFIN, 42 112 114 116 119 123 209 212
    223 228 266 281 310 331 341 342 345
    347 354
GRIFFORD, 130
GROSMITH, 298
GRUSBY, 319
GUERIN, 193 217 227 229 247 251 252 253
    254 257 259 262 266 309 312
GUERNEY, 178
GUEST, 286
GUILBAULT, 252
GUILD, 15 202 203 213 223 308 352
GUILDBAULT, 247
GUILE, 113
GUILFORD, 7
GUILLETTE, 250
GUIMOND, 134 222 228 246 259 261 314
    345
GUIRIN, 217
GUNN, 124 254 342
GUNNERSON, 141
GUNNISON, 189
GURNEY, 218
GUYOL, 245
HACKET, 255
HACKETT, 2 42 101 102 118 129 200 202
    213 223 229 231 269 271 277 340 354
HADLEY, 42 90 141 166 341 345
HADLOCK, 151
HAGER, 169 202
HAIGH, 255
HAINES, 225
HAINTY, 197
HALE, 200 314
HALEY, 240 241 291
HALL, 18 25 72 95 99 106 145 154 162 196
    215 221 236 242 243 251 253 256 271
    274 275 284 293 295 317 319 326 335
    340 341 354
HALLIDAY, 130
HAM, 98 154 164 194 212 338
HAMBLET, 1
HAMILTON, 238 345
HAMMOND, 6 111 212 243 300 320
HANANAFORD, 137
HANES, 103 311
HANKS, 234 236 237 239 240 282 343
HANNAFORD, 137 183 212 262
HANNAH, 122

HANNIFORD, 302
HANSON, 10 22 188 288 295 324 342
HAPGOOD, 274
HARDDON, 337
HARDEN, 337
HARDING, 230 233 290 291 295
HARDLEY, 341
HARDON, 195 224
HARDY, 2 6 7 11 12 14 20 24 42 43 59 64
    66 69 70 71 73 75 78 79 80 92 94 100
    102 105 106 110 121 127 135 136 137
    137 138 143 144 146 148 152 153 155
    156 158 159 162 163 165 172 175 177
    179 184 186 187 188 190 193 194 199
    201 204 205 207 209 210 211 217 221
    227 231 234 235 238 239 241 243 244
    249 251 252 255 266 267 268 270 273
    275 277 278 281 290 310 311 312 323
    326 330 332 334 340 343 344 348 349
    352
HAROLD, 293
HARRIAM, 43
HARRIET, 10 241
HARRIETT, 312
HARRIMAN, 11 103 173 178 197 258 279
    286
HARRINGTON, 24 43 62 73 77 81 110 118
    136 144 190 198 210 288 291 316 354
HARRIS, 7 10 196 231 233 234 236 237
    239 270 271 272 289 291 310
HART, 185
HARTHORN, 99 105 324
HARTHORNE, 324
HARTSHORN, 192
HARTWELL, 186
HARTZ, 275 276
HARVEY, 6 8 27 59 67 70 87 112 143 146
    158 191 236
HARWOOD, 207
HASE, 332
HASELTON, 27 221 222 258 274 277 278
    281 344 353
HASKELL, 22
HASKINS, 246
HASTING, 339
HASTINGS, 13 43 70 73 84 102 115 127
    132 137 144 145 159 174 176 197 200
    202 205 210 234 238 241 245 274 277
    278 284 339 342
HATCH, 191
HATHAWAY, 228 235 238 260 262 274
    286 293 311 313
HATHORN, 105 309

HATHRON, 99
HAVEN, 235 238 277 336 339
HAWLEY, 279
HAWTHORN, 142
HAWTHORNE, 2 146 189 318
HAY, 293
HAYDEN, 148 286
HAYES, 146 221 223 259 262 284
HAYFORD, 230 275
HAYNES, 272
HAZARD, 247 255
HAZELTIN, 210
HAZELTINE, 182 224 282
HAZELTON, 27 43 89 102 119 123 136 138
    139 147 199 210 268 303 307
HEALEY, 228 259 338
HEAPS, 255
HEATH, 9 10 13 14 43 63 65 75 87 91 93
    98 110 111 114 122 130 133 146 147
    173 174 179 183 184 185 188 200 269
    290 295 326 331 337 342 344
HEDDING, 284
HEILBRON, 215
HEINEKEN, 283
HELEN, 212
HEMPHILL, 96 97 111 136 157 179 184
    212 257 298 306 308
HENDERSON, 90 297
HENILLE, 346
HENINEKEN, 283
HENNEBERRY, 297
HENRY, 43
HENSE, 66
HERBERT, 10
HERICK, 147
HERRICH, 190
HERRICK, 11 58 67 74 142 209 315
HERSEY, 10 142 172 177
HESLEY, 268
HEZELTON, 139
HIBBARD, 224 306
HICKEY, 334
HICKS, 222 327
HIGGINS, 248 265 284
HILAN, 43
HILAND, 137 150 168 172 177 184 202 209
    211 213 287 327
HILDREATH, 84
HILDRETH, 144 321
HILL, 13 16 22 25 88 174 177 186 190 293
    337 345
HILLDRETH, 205
HILLIARD, 290

HILLS, 77
HILLSGROVE, 303
HILTER, 82
HILTON, 192 332
HOAR, 223
HODGDON, 5 102 107 123 124 127 173 177 182 185 195 224 270
HODGE, 240
HODGEDON, 43 44
HODGES, 195 337
HODGKINSON, 302
HODGMAN, 124 137 337
HOELZLE, 352
HOFFER, 295
HOFFMAN, 44
HOGG, 172
HOIT, 14 17 22 259
HOLBROOK, 164 174
HOLDEN, 104 150
HOLLAND, 1 88 194 197 217 290 336 354
HOLMES, 2 4 5 16 18 19 25 44 60 66 70 75 76 78 82 87 95 96 101 102 107 113 115 116 117 118 120 122 124 137 139 141 146 149 151 156 161 162 167 168 173 175 177 180 182 183 185 186 188 189 196 198 201 203 206 210 211 217 222 228 229 238 240 249 285 298 309 314 315 319 322 330 349 354
HOLT, 19 141 171 272 345
HOOD, 44 192 227 236 246 250 276 279 292 325 327
HOOK, 44 93 95 105 109 110 114 115 117 150 155 160 173 177 192 201 202 217 221 227 250 254 255 257 266 301 306 312 315 340
HOOPER, 134 299
HOPKINS, 9 109 171 218 229 305 319
HOPKINSON, 154 278
HOTIAN, 242
HOUDE, 240 294
HOUGH, 217
HOUGHTON, 279
HOULE, 243
HOUSE, 44
HOUSTIER, 280
HOUSTON, 232 261 275 299
HOW, 44 202 281
HOWARD, 5 6 13 27 44 45 59 82 91 98 99 122 131 153 162 163 164 165 168 203 273 276 279 305 317

HOWE, 3 5 22 23 45 69 96 103 110 122 123 128 132 135 137 163 165 166 177 187 195 196 209 218 246 247 250 272 274 275 308 312 337 338
HOWE??, 330
HOWELL, 349
HOWLET, 257
HOWLETT, 12 14 23 24 45 77 152 223
HOWLEY, 134 137 227 229 243 244 247 249 250 251 252 256 258 259 288 296 298 301 349
HOWTHORN, 68
HOYT, 2 3 6 20 22 27 45 58 59 60 68 73 75 79 81 91 94 95 96 101 103 109 111 113 115 126 137 139 143 145 146 152 153 156 157 163 166 170 175 179 193 194 198 201 209 216 218 228 229 230 231 232 233 234 236 238 240 251 253 266 267 277 284 285 290 296 299 319 320 321 324 327 328 332 334 335 337 349 354
HUBBARD, 1 8 57 63 107 158 160 195 197 200 211 323 336
HUBLEND, 178
HUCHINS, 98 137 212
HUDDLESTON, 102
HUGHES, 45 69 193
HULL, 195
HUMPHREY, 303
HUNISTON, 233
HUNT, 20 93 120 143 158 187 188 192 204 216 218 266 320 323 328
HUNTINGTON, 277
HUNTOON, 26 45 57 59 60 105 111 128 133 143 155 175 214 246 247 251 254 262 297 307 334
HURD, 102 230 234 239 300
HURLBUTT, 243 245 294
HUSE, 11 24 74 80 141 146 155 167 183 195 323
HUSSEY, 303
HUTCHINS, 61 102 171 309 312
HUTCHINSON, 45 92 132 135 223 291 294
HUTCHINSOSN, 137
HUUNTOON, 214
HYDE, 201 256 271
HYNDS, 310
IDA, 118
ILLSLEY, 213 255
INESON, 238 242 295
INGALLS, 148 167
INGERSOL, 341
INGERSON, 214 318

370

INGRAM, 268 275
INNIS, 320
IRVINE, 321
JACKMAN, 10 59 106 142 145 155 177 178
    188 189 199 201 217
JACKMMAN, 135
JACKSON, 291 347
JACOBS, 272
JAMES, 315
JAMESON, 22 160 175 186 241 328 352
JANAQ, 352
JARDINE, 103 129
JARVIS, 345
JEFFERS, 45 101 152 176 197 276
JEFFERSON, 97
JEFFUS, 97
JENKINS, 168 245 351
JENNESS, 13
JENNIE, 140
JENNINGS, 327
JEPSON, 104 129 213
JEROLD, 224
JEWELL, 8 24 26 30 68 106 112 130 133
    139 140 169 181 182 191 215 216 222
    223 224 270 299 314 326 331 345
JEWETT, 57 60 144 147
JOHNSON, 3 4 21 22 27 63 93 96 102 105
    112 127 128 130 132 143 148 150 156
    163 166 173 176 179 182 184 201 202
    213 215 217 222 237 238 243 244 251
    253 259 265 267 269 288 290 296 298
    312 318 336 337 340 342
JONES, 11 23 45 62 65 66 71 81 83 96 97
    100 140 143 144 148 149 150 151 161
    189 191 199 201 202 204 214 271 282
    295 315 323 329 333 339 348
JORDAN, 243 244 259 283 298 299
JORDEN, 314
JOSLIN, 101 209
JOY, 215
JUDD, 234
KARPAHL, 285
KAST, 79
KAVANAUGH, 331
KAY, 200 227 229 256 257 258 259 309
    350
KEATON, 239 242 287
KEAZER, 168 215
KEELING, 299
KEEN, 328
KEEZER, 13 349
KEITH, 322 332
KEIZER, 151 160 161 163

KELLEY, 11 12 17 45 46 58 69 70 78 88 89
    113 124 138 143 153 169 184 186 187
    188 191 197 198 201 202 203 214 217
    248 277 278 336 341 345
KELLLEY, 202
KELLY, 8 46 167 181 250
KEMP, 104 105 121 130 131 134 136 146
    275 276 284 285 286 296 314
KEMPHILL, 312
KEMPT, 146
KEMPTON, 7 10 11 20 46 91 98 117 152
    153 156 163 196 203 205 210 220 275
    278 327 340
KENDALL, 151 180
KENESITON, 330
KENISTIN, 131
KENISTON, 92 191 200 222 291 349
KENNEDY, 269 335
KENNETT, 136
KENNEY, 105 252 351
KENNINSTON, 215
KENNISTON, 211 213 214 216 269
KENT, 65
KENYON, 275 278 346
KETCHUM, 25 87 186 196 277
KEYES, 91
KEYOU, 337
KEYS, 308
KEZER, 4 46 159 182 189 196 206 260 311
KEZIA, 5
KIBBALL, 74
KIDDER, 182 316
KILBORN, 4 103 128 278
KILBURN, 19 310
KILEY, 290
KILKENNEY, 343
KILLAM, 101
KIMBALL, 6 7 9 11 14 17 18 20 24 27 28
    46 58 60 61 62 63 69 72 74 75 78 81 82
    83 84 87 88 89 91 92 95 96 97 99 101
    105 110 111 113 116 122 124 125 127
    129 131 134 135 137 140 141 142 143
    145 146 148 150 151 152 154 159 164
    167 171 172 174 175 181 182 183 184
    185 186 187 190 192 193 195 196 198
    199 202 203 204 205 207 209 211 212
    214 215 216 217 220 224 227 235 236
    237 241 246 247 248 249 250 251 254
    265 266 267 268 271 272 273 274 275
    276 278 280 281 283 286 294 297 298
    300 306 307 309 311 314 315 316 317
    321 324 327 329 331 333 335 336 342
    345 346 347 348 351 352

KIMBER, 349
KING, 125 221 234 244 245 270 352
KINGSTON, 267
KINNE, 283
KINNEY, 351
KINSMAN, 12
KIRBY, 183
KIRK, 296
KITTRIDGE, 166
KNAPP, 46
KNIGHT, 10 180 215
KNOWLES, 319
KNOWLTON, 68 74 79 85 87 144 148 163
    167 175 178 186 190 311 324
KNOX, 22
KNUCKEY, 313
KOON, 279 349
KRAPAHL, 285
KRAPHOL, 329
KRAZYZENIECK, 301
KRZYANIAK, 245
KRZYZAMIAK, 257 259
KRZYZANIAK, 243
KRZYZINICH, 223
KYZYZANIACK, 301
LABONTEE, 252
LABONTY, 288
LACLAIR, 137
LADD, 113 160 165 200 205 209 231 241
    242 244 250 274 342
LAFAGE, 255
LAFLEUR, 291
LAFRANCE, 303
LAKE, 6
LAKEMAN, 290
LAKIN, 205
LAMONTE, 207
LAMPREY, 98 101 120 150 278 306
LAMPRON, 244
LAMPSON??, 137
LAMSLEY, 284
LANCASTER, 11 20 148 190 203 310
LAND, 331
LANDERS, 14
LANDRY, 210
LANE, 276 346 352
LANG, 46 290 309
LANGDON, 23
LANGLEV, 232
LANGLEY, 270 286
LAPORRITON, 121
LAROS, 71
LARSEN, 10

LAUGHTON, 14
LAURISTON, 21
LAVIOLETTE, 302
LAW, 5 64 153 191 210 211 250 287
LAWRENCE, 13 23 343
LAWSON, 244 258 260 297
LEACH, 22 23
LEAR, 339
LEARD, 218
LEARNARD, 79 188
LEAVETT, 149 312
LEAVITT, 220 244 262 280
LEBARON, 187
LECLAIR, 92 283
LEE, 79 178
LEES, 340
LEET, 89 229 230 231 234 238 334
LEHAY, 103
LEMARD, 330
LEONARD, 13
LEONE, 295
LEPAGE, 254
LERNED, 71 104 162 171 307
LERNERD, 166
LEROUX, 283 290
LEROY, 183
LESLIE, 6 216 253 302 334
LESSARD, 239 241 243 244 273 275 287
LEWIS, 46 190 210 320 348 353
LIBBEY, 46 110 134 255 316
LIBBIE, 92 109 112 116 117 149 168 185
LIBBY, 46 47 84 88 94 109 114 117 118
    119 120 121 122 123 125 126 131 132
    135 136 139 153 154 155 163 164 167
    169 173 176 182 185 191 192 196 200
    211 213 214 215 216 217 220 221 224
    231 232 233 234 237 241 245 249 250
    251 253 260 265 266 269 270 277 282
    296 303 307 318 319 321 324 330 333
    337 349
LIBERTY, 268 273
LIBLEY, 110 113
LILLA, 117
LILLIEFORD, 135
LILLIFORD, 135
LINCOLN, 124 127 192 221 251 322
LINDERSTROM, 269
LINDQUEST, 251
LINDQUIST, 229 249 256 346
LINTON, 314
LITTLE, 9 27 61 76 116 122 125 142 162
    172 173 175 191 197 203 206 224 232
    236 237 241 259 272 281 322

372

LITTLEFIELD, 248
LITUCHE, 345
LIVINGSTON, 89 256
LOAN, 348
LOCK, 2 26 101 194 319
LOCKE, 47 67 69 73 101 111 114 148 149
    155 184 195 198 201 215 217 250 260
LOCKE??, 216
LONG, 24 26 47 61 62 74 151 154 157 174
    190 200 301 323 353
LORD, 13 18 79 106 107 123 124 127 131
    149 161 173 178 193 197 224 228 231
    233 234 235 269 300 328 329
LORING, 219
LOTHROP, 105 223 229 257 263
LOTHROPE, 261
LOUD, 345
LOUISE, 258
LOUNSBURY, 12
LOUYD, 87
LOVE, 329
LOVEJOY, 47 117 153 163 199 349
LOVEREA, 163
LOVEREN, 145 185
LOVERING, 15 97 121 151 180 306
LOW, 96 167 175 271 349
LOWE, 238 273 285 353
LOWGEE, 334
LOWNEY, 311
LOWYD, 87
LOWYD-LOUYD, 87
LUFKIN, 122
LULL, 17 214 252
LUND, 224 291 311
LUSCOMB, 331
LUTHER, 306
LYDIA, 115
LYFORD, 194
LYMAN, 145
LYNA, 293 352
LYNCH, 141 238 239
LYON, 233 276
MACDONALD, 243 291
MACDOUGAL, 192 251
MACDOUGALL, 192
MACGINNES, 289
MACHINO, 238 278
MACKENZIE, 298
MACKINISTRY, 353
MACPHER, 257
MADOX, 93
MAGNAN, 269 314
MAGNUSON, 221 270

MAGOON, 318 319
MAGOP, 313
MAHEW, 335
MAHON, 96 117
MAHONEY, 157 291
MAJERSON, 285
MAKEPEACE, 25 83 133 164 227 268
MALIAN, 286
MALLARD, 195
MALONEY, 211
MALONY, 211
MANN, 179 318 327
MANNING, 232 237 260 269 340
MANSFIELD, 78 168
MANSUR, 239 240 242 244
MARA, 103
MARCEY, 234
MARCIE, 262
MARCY, 222 228 229 230 231 240 256 258
    261 267 305 319 354
MARDEN, 161
MARSH, 109 111 113 117 136 138 177 178
    180 192 218 251 314 325 344
MARSHALL, 217 246 287 299 310 312 343
MARSTON, 175 181 274 283 290 344 345
    351
MARTEL, 227
MARTELL, 135 319
MARTIN, 13 117 149 164 165 204 207 215
    230 242 244 251 269 276 279 292 295
    306 309 315
MARY, 217 283 296 337
MASCHINO, 235
MASON, 77 165 185 219 303
MASTER, 178
MATHERSON, 241
MATHESON, 137 290
MATHEUS, 178
MATOTT, 323 335
MATTIE, 224
MAXFIELD, 116 139 195
MAXFILED, 139
MAXWELL, 312
MAY, 339
MAYHEW, 341
MAYLAN, 243
MAYNARD, 21 173
MAYO, 250
MCALMIRA, 102
MCALPINE, 6 7 15 17 47 106 142 176 180
    189 215
MCALPPINE, 47
MCBRIDE, 321

MCCAFFREY, 235 350
MCCALLEY, 291
MCCANTISH, 144
MCCARTHY, 224 242
MCCAUBREY, 299
MCCAW, 281
MCCLELLEN, 282
MCCLENNER, 79
MCCOFFEY, 233
MCCONNELL, 281
MCCONOR, 221
MCCORBY, 308
MCCOUBREY, 231 235 256 258 261
MCCOY, 47 133 301
MCCUEN, 328
MCCULLIS, 138
MCCUTCHUN, 260
MCDERMOT, 347
MCDEVITT, 218
MCDEWELL, 320
MCDIARMID, 266
MCDOLE, 284
MCDONALD, 221 249 256 274 288 348
MCEWEN, 115 271
MCFEELERS, 137
MCFLARITY, 195
MCFOSTER, 282
MCGILVARY, 338
MCGINNIS, 258
MCGOWAN, 279
MCGUIRE, 275
MCINTIER, 180
MCINTIRE, 132 211 245 318
MCKAY, 353
MCKENNA, 245
MCKENZIE, 47 60 184 295
MCKINLEY, 280
MCLANE, 248
MCLAREN, 240
MCLAUGHLIN, 291
MCLEAN, 263
MCLEOD, 249 287
MCMALON, 228
MCMANARA, 288
MCMANN, 222
MCMASTER, 220
MCNEIL, 149
MCONBRY, 301
MCPHERSON, 265
MCVEY, 270
MEAD, 265 274 342
MEALEY, 17
MEATLY, 231

MECCOY, 21
MELAND, 332
MELANSO, 283
MELCHER, 104 214 218 227 240 249 251
    252 253 257 296 349
MELOON, 15
MELTON, 347
MELVIN, 78 144 161 175 186 206 351
MERCER, 285
MERKLE, 285
MERRILL, 2 5 18 20 47 59 61 69 75 76 83
    84 87 89 105 125 126 127 133 142 143
    148 152 155 158 160 166 167 172 173
    184 186 189 195 203 230 246 254 255
    267 277 281 301 316 318 333 354
MESSER, 78 80 182 245 248 292
MESSIER, 287
MESSINGER, 353
METCALF, 303 309
METRO, 302 352
MIDDLEN, 280
MIFFIRM, 343
MIFFIRN, 344
MIGNAULT, 121 140 184 233 245 345 353
MILAN, 156
MILAND, 90
MILL, 99
MILLER, 129 239 241 243 247 248 253 260
    262 279 280 288 303
MILLS, 3 10 13 15 16 22 47 48 72 80 99
    104 106 111 113 114 115 118 120 122
    131 133 134 135 136 138 142 146 154
    155 162 165 178 179 209 212 213 220
    222 243 257 259 267 269 272 281 286
    302 318 329 337 338 339 340 343 344
    350 354
MILNER, 283
MILTON, 48 52 67 70 97 100 101 102 109
    129 132 156 166 224 231 266 268 275
    287 307 319 331
MINER, 171 197 200 255 256 277
MINIUTTE, 288
MINNIE, 277
MITCHEL, 211
MITCHELE, 190
MITCHELL, 11 48 190 235 236 249 259
    265 266 282 284 285 308 316 330
MITHCELL, 190
MIXER, 177
MMMAHON, 231
MOFFAT, 346
MOFFATT, 303
MOFFETT, 224

MOKLER, 353

MONGOMERY, 153

MONTGOMERY, 15 24 48 60 73 87 88 91
95 96 103 104 112 114 115 117 123 124
126 127 135 153 166 170 173 174 176
177 181 190 193 197 198 204 206 212
221 228 230 232 233 236 247 249 251
253 256 257 266 267 276 284 299 313
314 321 322 323 332 343 350

MONTOGOMERY, 48

MOODY, 147 288 298

MOOERS, 66

MOORE, 73 88 102 129 132 167 174 228
244 266 269 287 301 307 326 340

MORAM, 234

MORAN, 48 81 96 97 117 120 125 129 140
172 194 204 219 224 227 250 252 253
255 262 286 291 295

MORAND, 233

MORE, 313

MORGAN, 4 6 10 20 48 49 68 75 76 88 89
97 100 110 123 134 141 143 148 149
154 156 164 183 188 199 204 206 243
245 294 309 328 332 333 340 341 344
348 350

MORIN, 169

MORISON, 335

MORRILL, 3 13 17 26 27 49 57 60 61 68 69
73 76 82 91 93 100 103 105 111 112
114 123 124 136 138 141 143 144 145
149 155 164 165 166 170 173 178 180
183 184 185 186 187 188 189 191 197
199 200 207 211 214 217 223 247 248
249 250 251 252 257 262 266 270 323
324 326 331 333 342

MORRISON, 9 10 84 85 206 218 223 260
321 337 343 348

MORSE, 1 19 49 73 93 148 151 162 169
178 190 215 279 288 296 303 309 320

MORTON, 242 303 333 352

MOSELY, 290

MOSES, 276 300

MOSHER, 218 351

MOTTS, 111

MOULD, 232 236 237 259

MOULTON, 6 63 65 76 113 120 136 145
161 194 204 233 266 287 303 307 338

MOUNT, 241 242 245 300 302 349

MUDGE, 25 140 229 233 320

MUDGETT, 8 9 22 49 63 69 98 99 102 112
133 163 174 185 189 193 199 202 210
219 247 267 284 295 335 346

MUELLEN, 339

MULLOGAN, 346

MUNRO, 335

MUNROE, 2 104

MURDER, 95 212

MURDO, 343

MURDOUGH, 199 301

MURPHY, 104 228 260 262 274 277 281
286 292 293 294 311 313 323

MURRAY, 254 295 351

MURTAS, 324

MUSTARD, 106

MUSY, 146

MUTTART, 218

MUZZEY, 95 170 187

MUZZLY, 347

MUZZY, 104 197 212 256

MYERS, 331

NADEAU, 17 166 215 336

NAY, 284

NEAL, 201

NEALY, 49 59

NEASKERN, 276

NEDEAU, 237

NELSON, 62 63 89 112 126 165 171 198
201 211 214 215 216 232 240 243 244
246 249 251 252 253 256 259 277 287
292 293 314 336

NEVINS, 157

NEWCOMB, 335

NEWELL, 267 276

NEWMAN, 157 262 329

NEWMANS, 203

NICHOL, 98 187

NICHOLS, 14 49 65 100 144 147 157 175
201 205 224 249 272 277 302 307 316
326 345 351

NICHOLSON, 261

NICKELSON, 211

NICKERSON, 291

NILAN, 17

NILE, 118

NILES, 153

NILSON, 229

NOBLE, 291

NOLAN, 239 289

NOONING, 298

NORCROSS, 213

NOREEN, 228 259

NORRIS, 231 232 310 318 321 335 354

NORRISS, 213

NORTHRUP, 234 284 328

NORTHUP, 241

NORTHUP??, 302

PENNELL, 339
PENNIMAN, 28
PENNINGTON, 294 299
PENTLAND, 300
PEPLER, 228
PERKINS, 23 71 79 93 124 130 160 163
    166 175 177 181 194 197 198 202 203
    216 256 279 301 311 317
PERLEY, 183 305
PERNELLO, 270
PERO, 139
PERRIN, 293 352
PERRY, 5 6 13 16 23 49 60 62 63 72 88 102
    103 112 113 119 120 124 136 138 145
    154 163 176 179 181 191 197 200 203
    209 210 211 214 234 236 247 248 250
    267 277 278 333 336 339 342 347 350
    351
PETERS, 15 61 219 346
PETERSON, 301 302
PETTEY, 8
PETTINGILL, 152 317
PHALEN, 130
PHELPS, 24 27 78 95 102 109 139 146 169
    218 344
PHILBRICK, 8 22 78 88 111 113 139 146
    161 166 171 288
PHILBROOK, 295
PHILLIP, 143 187 313
PHILLIPS, 77 81 101 143 315 344
PICKERING, 247
PIERCE, 49 50 59 61 93 101 135 141 187
    204 221 230 233 240 242 259 282 285
    291 297 313 338 352 353
PIERSON, 174
PIKE, 18 96 150 302
PILBRICK, 26
PILLSBURY, 18 26 188 196 261
PINARD, 221 224
PINEO, 344
PINIO, 180
PINKHAM, 8
PINNEY, 137
PIPER, 14 18 22 101 149 156 182 215 222
    276
PIZBYLSKI, 261
PLOURDE, 243 298
PLOYER, 269
PLUCKETT, 303
PLUFF, 302
PLUMA, 29
PLUMER, 16
PLUMMER, 67 140 265

PLUMNER, 268
POLAND, 50 133 268
POLFREY, 71
POLLARD, 153 161
POMEROY, 289
POOL, 323
POOLE, 292
POOR, 114 188 214 279
POPE, 266
PORTER, 109 122 143 236 269
POTHOFF, 104 220
POTTER, 90 290 297 341
POTTS, 329 338
POWELL, 26 50 154 215 218 271 350
POWELLL, 109
POWERS, 91 110 113 127 158 169 196 306
    308 329 346
PRAY, 117
PRENTISS, 245 297
PRESBY, 9 214 354
PRESCOTT, 5 26 105 143 164 235 281
PRESSEY, 101 166 200 209
PRESTON, 170 219 248 291
PRICE, 163 172 210
PRICHARD, 186 242 244
PRIEST, 90
PRIM, 250
PRINCE, 109 176 195 253 254 285 327 329
    335
PRIRE, 293
PROCTOR, 106 204 279
PROVENCHER, 227 229 244 261 297 299
PROVENCHIER, 232
PROVINACHA, 201
PROWER, 295
PROWSE, 273 293
PRUNE, 252
PRZYBYLSKA, 244
PUDDESTER, 331
PUFFER, 161
PUNTENNEYE, 203
PURINGTON, 202 276
PURLINGTON, 260
PURMONT, 217
PUTAUM, 18
PUTNAM, 2 3 4 7 17 20 27 28 50 61 97 100
    143 150 155 165 166 171 185 190 200
    203 204 209 212 214 247 278 325 327
    332 334 348
PUTNEY, 1 2 50 83 88 91 95 105 111 118
    143 144 146 153 154 155 156 161 175
    181 185 187 197 198 201 203 207 210
    219 221 227 229 232 256 261 275 322

PUTNEY (continued)
330 334 337 342 344 346 347 348 353
QUIGLEY, 288
QUIMBY, 8 27 65 79 146 147 167 180 188
247 295 306
QUINN, 151
RACKWOOD, 302
RAHM, 333
RAMSDELL, 196
RAND, 4 12 16 18 23 50 60 68 123 136 159
161 180 185 190 196 206 215 276 309
336
RANDALL, 74 76 90 124 159 163 171 350
RAWSON, 144
RAY, 88 214 215 247 269 281 306 314
RAYMOND, 50 65 66 67 74 153 161 170
172 256 321
RAYMONS, 313
RAYNO, 169 227 251
RAYNOR, 329
REA, 210
READ, 269 279
READE, 215 249 258 303
REARDON, 243 298
REDDEY, 286
REDDINGTON, 242
REDDY, 238 261 284 286 301
REDINGTON, 135 237 285
REED, 7 50 77 92 94 185 192 237 241 246
286 326 349 351 354
REEVES, 340
REID, 105 139 144 189 211 280
REILEY, 178
REILY, 90
RELATION, 50 57
RENDER, 267
RENNIE, 268
RENO, 119 163
RESTIEAUX, 26 58 152
RESTIEUX, 17
RETA, 266
REYCROFT, 292
REYNO, 116 117 121 122 153 154 163 164
REYNOLDS, 268
REYNOLDS?, 283
REYSEN, 6
RICE, 106 135 138 171 197
215 235 238 239 240
246 253 277 279 293
296 336 345 350
RICHARDS, 8 13 23 50
205 219 249 260 303
332

RICHARDSON, 6 17 50 72 82 89 90 99 100
112 116 131 136 158 159 166 177 180
184 195 199 200 206 219 238 274 302
337 341 345 347 348 351 355
RICHMOND, 21
RICKETTS, 222
RIDER, 204
RILEY, 97 317
RIMMER, 165
RING, 285 286
RINIS, 183
RINMER, 165
RINNESS, 311
RION, 50 66 109 139 172 195 328
RIPLES, 7
RIPLEY, 14 50 78 151 185 199 204 227 230
237 291 316 339 342 344
RIVERS, 273 275 287
ROACH, 50 51 73 75 210 213 311 321 325
337
ROBAR, 236 237 239 334
ROBARE, 353
ROBB, 218
ROBBINS, 93 258 308
ROBERSON, 258
ROBERST, 210
ROBERSTON, 262
ROBERTIE, 114
ROBERTS, 4 58 62 93 138 199 219 265 272
299 348
ROBERTSON, 188 236 240 244 255 259
261 288 292 293 294 330 344
ROBERTSONS, 222
ROBEY, 224 315 318
ROBIE, 214 248 275 326 338
ROBINSON, 11 15 99 106 122 169 198 243
262 267 281 290 292 301 319 349
ROBY, 1 51 90 115 154 234 259 265 273
283 287
ROCHON, 269
ROCKWELL, 202
RODERS, 91
ROGER, 220
ROGERS, 1 26 51 62 76 82 88 89 101 113
117 120 125 129 131 149 164 181 187
190 193 204 206 220 265 282 306 323
325 327
ROLLINS, 2 7 51 92 96 111 116 122 125
128 145 149 150 152 156 157 165 185
187 195 197 215 217 218 228 232 236
239 240 250 251 252 254 257 262 268
270 275 292 305 308 310 327 335
ROLLOFF, 230

ROMAN, 154
RONAN, 75
ROONEY, 321
ROONY, 210
ROSEBROOK, 238 241 294
ROSENFIELD, 297
ROSS, 158 197 218 262 290
ROTHMAN, 297
ROUNEY, 311
ROUSE, 202 228 256 259
ROWAN, 82
ROWE, 3 95 102 104 130 135 159 173 177
     325
ROWELL, 4 7 8 12 22 23 24 51 67 75 77 80
     94 110 113 133 134 138 139 144 150
     152 155 158 165 166 177 182 186 206
     214 307 313 330 333 346
ROY, 157
RUGG, 9
RUNNELLS, 3 13 15 51 74 97 155 163 213
     328 336 353
RUNNELS, 193
RUSS, 102 129 132 136 271 300 321
RUSSELL, 11 51 79 102 104 126 143 168
     180 302 321 322
RUSSELLL, 284
RUSSELLS, 143
RUTHERFORD, 125 205
RYAN, 258 270 271 353
RYANS, 317
RYDER, 189
RYON, 105
SADLOW, 280
SAFFORD, 143 176 178 182
SAGE, 184
SAINT, 331
SAINTHILAIRE, 347
SALMOND, 308
SALTMARSH, 94 262
SANBORN, 3 6 9 11 12 22 23 32 51 72 87
     89 94 100 102 112 120 123 127 128 131
     132 135 139 146 151 153 157 161 171
     172 177 178 179 186 189 193 195 202
     203 213 216 219 223 233 254 258 283
     289 291 293 294 298 305 308 319 320
     322 327 328 333 334 336 341 342 344
     346 354
SANBRON, 294
SANDERS, 92 148 162 190 209 268 340
SANDERSON, 133 198
SANFERN, 266
SANVILLE, 199
SARAH, 213

SARGENT, 5 8 10 11 20 51 58 59 68 84 91
     93 104 111 116 117 150 152 154 160
     163 164 173 175 177 178 187 190 199
     200 203 204 210 213 215 216 217 218
     222 229 231 233 235 236 239 240 244
     245 247 257 267 271 273 286 292 295
     298 300 303 305 318 322 326 331 336
     350 352
SARTELLE, 124 126
SAUNDERS, 161
SAVAGE, 214
SAVORY, 1 51 71 87 103 177 197 212
SAWTELLE, 96 259 312
SAWYER, 6 8 74 88 94 157 160 165 166
     192 209 236 239 241 247 250 284 294
     295 300 305 315 326 345
SCALES, 8 79
SCHMITT, 282
SCHONLTON, 220
SCHRIBER, 281
SCHUYLER, 299
SCHWARTS, 51
SCHWARTZ, 51
SCOTT, 51 102 129 166 224 332
SCRIBNER, 2 6 7 76 98 104 131 164 171
     173 180 185 187 196 198 316 334 354
SCRIGGINS, 219 220
SCRUTON, 203
SEABERG, 231 239
SEABERRY, 237
SEABORN, 187 337
SEABURY, 236
SEALEY, 234
SEALY, 233
SEAVER, 279 301
SEAVEY, 3 4 9 25 51 60 89 106 112 126
     142 144 156 162 166 169 201 210 214
     275 309
SEGALL, 233
SELKISH, 279
SENTER, 145
SERGEANT, 286
SERGENT, 59
SERVISS, 298
SEVERANCE, 2 94 156 192 195 219 235
     242 244 245 246 248 249 250 253 258
     259 260 261 270 280 284 293 319 320
     324 344 350 352
SEVERENCE, 82 111 182 227 228 229 230
     232 235 238 239 241 261 272 320
SEWELL, 151
SHACKETT, 293
SHALLIES, 212

SHALLLIES, 212
SHAMPANY, 234
SHAMPNEY, 280 313 321 341
SHANNON, 298
SHARP, 281
SHARPE, 272
SHARPLESS, 272 345
SHATTELL, 315 340
SHATTLE, 105 190 330
SHATTUCK, 17 185 209
SHAW, 10 26 87 101 166 181 190 191 196
   238 241 243 245 294 302 317 330
SHEFFIELD, 110
SHEPARD, 51 182 275 292 343 346
SHEPHERD, 95
SHEPPARD, 51 190 324
SHERBURN, 85
SHERDEN, 177
SHERMAN, 118 224 294 316
SHERWIN, 213 339
SHIRLAND, 336
SHORT, 195 224 227 246 250 254
SHREVE, 259
SHREWE, 221
SHUBURNE, 169
SHURTLEFF, 100 109 150 223 224 250 261
   262 291 296 314 342
SHURTLETT, 223 250
SHURTLIFF, 52 161 328
SHUTE, 52
SIBLEY, 73 201 309 352
SIGRIST, 288
SILL, 276
SILLEY, 155
SILVER, 14 102 190 203 267 337
SIMEON, 132
SIMINO, 276
SIMMONS, 161 278
SIMON, 127 128
SIMONDS, 52 209 346 348
SIMONS, 321 336
SIMPSON, 200
SINCLAIR, 13
SISCO, 308
SITARH??, 98
SJORN, 271
SKILLEN, 52 203
SKILLLEN, 322
SLACK, 273 289
SLADER, 335
SLATH, 164
SLAYTON, 302
SLEEPER, 84 145 247 262

SLOCOMB, 105
SMALL, 106 115 345
SMART, 1 9 24 25 52 67 69 82 99 120 122
   132 159 165 167 168 171 173 174 175
   179 202 211 220 236 238 242 279 286
   307 325 333
SMILEY, 8 52
SMITH, 3 6 7 12 19 21 26 52 71 78 79 81
   85 89 96 97 100 103 122 134 138 140
   145 147 169 171 172 176 177 178 183
   187 189 192 193 195 196 197 199 201
   202 204 205 207 212 221 224 227 229
   230 232 234 238 239 241 243 244 246
   248 250 256 257 259 261 265 267 268
   273 278 287 289 290 301 306 310 311
   323 328 331 334 335 337 340 344 353
SNALLOW??, 270
SNELL, 339
SNOW, 166 310
SNYDER, 87 88 176 278 343
SOMBERGER, 261
SOMBORGER, 256
SON, 52 104 193 316
SONERBERGER, 235
SONNA, 20
SONS, 151
SORNBERG, 301
SORNBERGER, 231 299 301 308 318
SORNRBERGER, 308
SOUNBERGER, 258
SOUTHWICK, 111 114 203
SOVONY, 323
SPAULDING, 87 88 90 113
   124 127 130 165 172 198
   201 206 338 342 353 354
SPEED, 183
SPEERS, 233
SPENCER, 271 272 273 323
SPIEGEL, 290
SPIERS, 246
SPILLER, 259 309
SPOFFORD, 16 17 24 25 26 52 53 58 68 78
   81 93 94 115 118 119 135 136 137 142
   143 154 155 160 178 184 194 205 209
   213 248 305 314 329
SPRINGER, 68
SPRONL[??], 192
SPROWL, 216 218
SPURLIN, 240
STACKPOLE, 118
STACY, 284 289 329
STAMIELS, 228
STANIELS, 259

TEAGUE, 316
TEAKLES, 230
TEBBETTS, 239 302
TEMPLE, 83
TEN, 310
TENNEY, 5 12 235 237
TENNY, 303
TERRILL, 77 115 218
TERRY, 15 143 182 206
TEWKSBURY, 2 57 68 81 82 181
TEWSBURY, 9
TEWSKSBURY, 78
THATCHER, 275
THAYER, 84 99 122 127 166 266 289
THERRON, 136
THIBODEAU, 347
THOMAS, 184 189 192 217
THOMPSON, 25 59 63 81 85 96 101 117
    132 136 137 159 161 162 207 212 233
    246 254 260 268 270 276 281 299 326
    330 331 332 350 355
THOPMSON, 85
THORNDIKE, 154 157 173 178
THORNTON, 102 103 130 196 235 255 279
    292 294 319
THOROGOOD, 292
THORTON, 267
THURSTON, 22
TIBBETTS, 4 242 306 343
TIBBITTS, 4
TIERNERY, 339
TIERNEY, 287
TILTON, 3 15 16 17 54 66 70 82 145 166
    167 168 179 181 186 195 197 215 228
    241 250 251 252 254 257 300 310 311
    314 323 324 326 336
TINKHAM, 285
TIRRELL, 141 218 262 307
TIRRILL, 60
TITCHEL?, 203
TITCOMB, 331
TOBYNE, 127 276
TONKIN, 273 293
TOWLE, 290
TOWNE, 134 205 212 230 343
TOWNES, 222 223 238 242 270 286 330
TOWNS, 3 104 113 154 178 270
TOWNSEND, 179
TRASK, 298
TRASKER, 19
TREEN, 263
TRENONETH, 313
TRIP, 202

TROWBRIDGE, 71
TRUCHAN, 346
TRUE, 96 144 175
TRUEHART, 157
TRUMBALL, 165 177
TRUSSELL, 68 85 187 189 202
TUCK, 9
TUCKER, 19 54 72 78 79 98 119 124 143
    152 154 165 172 175 179 184 186 190
    211 237 239 280 317 333 347
TUFTS, 200 255 319
TUPPER, 344
TURCOTT, 94
TURGEON, 238 241
TURNER, 306 315
TUTTLE, 8 14 58 69 80 94 126 160 168 173
    176 300 305 306 318 325 329 340 346
TYLER, 5 18 54 67 68 70 80 85 94 99 100
    123 126 141 143 159 162 174 204 243
    272 275 295 307
TYRELL, 23
TYRILL, 15
UNDERHILL, 4 146 254 265
UNDERWOOD, 351 353
UNKNOWN, 291
UPHAM, 16
UPOLOHUSE, 334
UPTON, 6 9 16 54 87
    104 109 134 147
    160 173 189 218
    316 322 326
VADNEY, 325
VARIN, 292
VARNEY, 308
VEINO, 286
VENING, 351
VERRELL, 307
VINCENT, 267
VINER, 291
VINTON, 142
VINTON??, 142
VITTY, 209
VONHAAS, 279
WADDIO, 308
WADE, 63 308 319
WADLEIGH, 21 163 189 190
WADLEY, 154
WADSWORTH, 153 320 340
WAHLGREW, 189
WAITE, 300
WAKEFIELD, 273 346
WALACE, 96
WALDRON, 12 162 179 209 342

WALKER, 10 14 17 27 54 62 80 81 98 119 132 135 138 149 166 177 178 182 184 188 191 194 210 215 246 269 282 283 286 290 294 305 322 325
WALL, 258
WALLING, 297
WALLINGFORD, 219
WALLINGTON, 341
WALSH, 227
WALSTENHAM, 322
WALTERS, 186 289
WALTON, 98
WANZEL, 287
WARD, 2 102 103 117 128 133 216 247 255 259 267 271 276 283 310
WARNER, 9
WARREN, 245 348
WASHBURN, 274
WATERBURY, 116 119
WATERS, 286
WATERSON, 164
WATKINS, 8 25 54 142 273
WATSON, 2 8 10 91 180 187 279 314 315 329 341
WATTERSON, 119 167 172 192
WATTS, 54 105 109 118 125 129 130 132 136 138 139 148 176 199 227 248 249 251 254 258 270 271 288 291 294 295 300 302 331 334
WAY, 60 67 161 349
WAYNE, 110 180 183 201
WEAST, 228 293 302
WEAVER, 302
WEBB, 156
WEBBER, 21 25 54 55 84 88 94 95 97 101 102 103 111 113 126 133 144 146 154 155 157 173 175 176 178 179 180 184 185 186 191 196 197 199 205 207 223 224 272 292 327 328 336 349 352
WEBER, 147 317
WEBSTER, 7 9 55 96 100 101 111 124 126 130 133 135 141 152 174 194 210 213 219 221 222 265 287 312 331 336 338 340 346
WEBSTR, 181
WEED, 271 338
WEEKS, 2 22 23 55 64 73 80 84 90 95 96 109 147 159 161 162 164 179 181 184 195 199 200 204 215 219 231 234 251 253 268 278 293 295 306 315 327 330
WEINZEIRL, 280
WEISBECKER, 281

WELCH, 91 128 130 133 137 138 164 256 259 268 283 339
WELCOME, 217 227 251 252 253 254 257 259
WELFRYS, 269
WELGARECKA, 223
WELLMAN, 21 274 351
WELLS, 15 55 145 148 155 156 165 197 215 237 298
WELSH, 266
WESCOTT, 103 213 222 228 260 299
WESSMAN, 265
WEST, 55 118 148 153 154 169 273 335
WETHERBEE, 219
WHEDEN, 219
WHEELAN, 301
WHEELER, 17 55 201 209 219 270 272 288 329 340
WHIPPLE, 106 125 217 218 220
WHITAKER, 6 217 338
WHITCHER, 135
WHITCOMB, 185 205 339
WHITE, 55 68 70 71 75 88 91 101 102 141 146 149 157 159 167 168 171 176 183 184 189 197 199 200 207 216 218 276 278 310 314 323 342 345
WHITEHOUSE, 291
WHITEMAN, 5
WHITEMORE, 350
WHITFORD, 253
WHITING, 326 334
WHITMAN, 26 61 202
WHITMARSH, 102
WHITNEY, 25 146 151 191 217 241 258 268
WHITTAKER, 353
WHITTEMORE, 55 90 99 128 189 233 236 240 261 343
WHITTENDER, 218
WHITTER, 334
WHITTERMORE, 340
WHITTIER, 2 10 16 61 64 88 98 132 168 172 184 195 197 205 219 221 223 232 265 268 270
WHITTIMORE, 112 116 170 171 204
WHYLOCK, 138
WHYTOCK, 126 128 132 182
WHYTUCK, 170
WICKS, 298
WICKSTROM, 261
WIGGIN, 11 14 17 81 146 167 174 182 206 275 302 312 318
WIGGINS, 18 81 159 189 266

WIGHT, 19 55 130 141 158 159 178 199 211 248 334 337
WIK, 296
WIKSTROM, 269
WILBAR, 337
WILBURN, 311
WILCOX, 224 262
WILDER, 292 328 335
WILKINS, 268 314
WILKINSON, 213 219
WILLAIMS, 334
WILLARD, 77 101 106 152 236 284 311
WILLETT, 199
WILLEY, 55 285 302 308
WILLIAM, 213
WILLIAMS, 6 55 60 63 125 158 179 199 205 325 327 334
WILLIAMSON, 284
WILLOUGHBY, 14
WILSON, 11 18 24 147 155 167 172 176 185 187 195 201 224 230 233 258 259 267 313 317 333
WINCH, 135 138
WINCHESTER, 21 310
WING, 182 212 245 248
WINIAS??, 156
WINSLOW, 253
WISE, 11
WITHAM, 326
WITHEY, 93
WITHINGTON, 15 58

WODLEY, 12
WOLCOTT, 98
WOLFREYS, 261
WOLFSON, 175
WOLSTENHOLM, 221
WOLSTENTHOLMS, 220
WONDERLICK, 194 254
WOOBURN, 11
WOOD, 71 78 98 112 130 138 147 177 284 301 328
WOODBURN, 11
WOODBURY, 24 72 76 103 104 110 118 158 166 169 194 198 210 220 227 270 316 338
WOODMAN, 106 123
WOODRIDGE, 231
WOODS, 7 55 77 103 172 196 305 328
WOODWARD, 216 246 271 274 336 346
WORKS, 326
WRIGHT, 9 26 47 55 68 77 83 111 114 138 164 167 171 176 182 187 195 198 206 215 216 232 260 266 269 300 333
WUNDERLICH, 230 240 243 252 257 259 261 319
WUNDERLICK, 254 293 294
WYMAN, 75 83 103 110 123 132 137 153 159 160 172 174 184 187 210 213 220
YARLAND, 275
YEATON, 193
YORK, 198
YOUNG, 19 95 99 110 149 162 231 238 240 268 276 283 285 294 300 317 354

Made in the USA
Las Vegas, NV
02 August 2022

52580037R00223